Designing Concurrent, Distributed, and Real-Time Applications with UML

The Addison-Wesley Object Technology Series

Grady Booch, Ivar Jacobson, and James Rumbaugh, Series Editors
For more information check out the series web site [http://www.awl.com /cseng/otseries/] as well as the pages
on each book [http://www.awl.com/cseng/I-S-B-N/] (I-S-B-N represents the actual ISBN, including dashes).

Frank Armour and Granville Miller, *Advanced Use Case Modeling, Volume 1*, ISBN 0-201-61592-4

David Bellin and Susan Suchman Simone, *The CRC Card Book*, ISBN 0-201-89535-8

Robert V. Binder, *Testing Object-Oriented Systems: Models, Patterns, and Tools*, ISBN 0-201-80938-9

Bob Blakley, *CORBA Security: An Introduction to Safe Computing with Objects*, ISBN 0-201-32565-9

Grady Booch, *Object Solutions: Managing the Object-Oriented Project*, ISBN 0-8053-0594-7

Grady Booch, *Object-Oriented Analysis and Design with Applications, Second Edition*, ISBN 0-8053-5340-2

Grady Booch, James Rumbaugh, and Ivar Jacobson, *The Unified Modeling Language User Guide*, ISBN 0-201-57168-4

Don Box, *Essential COM*, ISBN 0-201-63446-5

Don Box, Keith Brown, Tim Ewald, and Chris Sells, *Effective COM: 50 Ways to Improve Your COM and MTS-based Applications*, ISBN 0-201-37968-6

Alistair Cockburn, *Surviving Object-Oriented Projects: A Manager's Guide*, ISBN 0-201-49834-0

Dave Collins, *Designing Object-Oriented User Interfaces*, ISBN 0-8053-5350-X

Jim Conallen, *Building Web Applications with UML*, ISBN 0-201-61577-0

Desmond Frances D'Souza and Alan Cameron Wills, *Objects, Components, and Frameworks with UML: The Catalysis Approach*, ISBN 0-201-31012-0

Bruce Powel Douglass, *Doing Hard Time: Developing Real-Time Systems with UML, Objects, Frameworks, and Patterns*, ISBN 0-201-49837-5

Bruce Powel Douglass, *Real-Time UML, Second Edition: Developing Efficient Objects for Embedded Systems*, ISBN 0-201-65784-8

Martin Fowler, *Analysis Patterns: Reusable Object Models*, ISBN 0-201-89542-0

Martin Fowler, Kent Beck, John Brant, William Opdyke, and Don Roberts, *Refactoring: Improving the Design of Existing Code*, ISBN 0-201-48567-2

Martin Fowler with Kendall Scott, *UML Distilled, Second Edition: A Brief Guide to the Standard Object Modeling Language*, ISBN 0-201-65783-X

Hassan Gomaa, *Designing Concurrent, Distributed, and Real-Time Applications with UML*, ISBN 0-201-39859-1

Ian Gorton, *Enterprise Transaction Processing Systems: Putting the CORBA OTS, Encina++ and Orbix OTM to Work*, ISBN 0-201-39859-1

Peter Heinckiens, *Building Scalable Database Applications: Object-Oriented Design, Architectures, and Implementations*, ISBN 0-201-31013-9

Christine Hofmeister, Robert Nord, and Soni Dilip, *Applied Software Architecture*, ISBN 0-201-32571-3

Ivar Jacobson, Grady Booch, and James Rumbaugh, *The Unified Software Development Process*, ISBN 0-201-57169-2

Ivar Jacobson, Magnus Christerson, Patrik Jonsson, and Gunnar Overgaard, *Object-Oriented Software Engineering: A Use Case Driven Approach*, ISBN 0-201-54435-0

Ivar Jacobson, Maria Ericsson, and Agneta Jacobson, *The Object Advantage: Business Process Reengineering with Object Technology*, ISBN 0-201-42289-1

Ivar Jacobson, Martin Griss, and Patrik Jonsson, *Software Reuse: Architecture, Process and Organization for Business Success*, ISBN 0-201-92476-5

David Jordan, *C++ Object Databases: Programming with the ODMG Standard*, ISBN 0-201-63488-0

Philippe Kruchten, *The Rational Unified Process, An Introduction, Second Edition*, ISBN 0-201-70710-1

Wilf LaLonde, *Discovering Smalltalk*, ISBN 0-8053-2720-7

Dean Leffingwell and Don Widrig, *Managing Software Requirements: A Unified Approach*, ISBN 0-201-61593-2

Lockheed Martin Advanced Concepts Center and Rational Software Corporation, *Succeeding with the Booch and OMT Methods: A Practical Approach*, ISBN 0-8053-2279-5

Chris Marshall, *Enterprise Modeling with UML: Designing Successful Software through Business Analysis*, ISBN 0-201-43313-3

Thomas J. Mowbray and William A. Ruh, *Inside CORBA: Distributed Object Standards and Applications*, ISBN 0-201-89540-4

Bernd Oestereich, *Developing Software with UML: Object-Oriented Analysis and Design in Practice*, ISBN 0-201-39826-5

Meilir Page-Jones, *Fundamentals of Object-Oriented Design in UML*, ISBN 0-201-69946-X

Ira Pohl, *Object-Oriented Programming Using C++, Second Edition*, ISBN 0-201-89550-1

Rob Pooley and Perdita Stevens, *Using UML: Software Engineering with Objects and Components*, ISBN 0-201-36067-5

Terry Quatrani, *Visual Modeling with Rational Rose 2000 and UML*, ISBN 0-201-69961-3

Brent Rector and Chris Sells, *ATL Internals*, ISBN 0-201-69589-8

Paul R. Reed, Jr., *Developing Applications with Visual Basic and UML*, ISBN 0-201-61579-7

Doug Rosenberg with Kendall Scott, *Use Case Driven Object Modeling with UML: A Practical Approach*, ISBN 0-201-43289-7

Walker Royce, *Software Project Management: A Unified Framework*, ISBN 0-201-30958-0

William Ruh, Thomas Herron, and Paul Klinker, *IIOP Complete: Understanding CORBA and Middleware Interoperability*, ISBN 0-201-37925-2

James Rumbaugh, Ivar Jacobson, and Grady Booch, *The Unified Modeling Language Reference Manual*, ISBN 0-201-30998-X

Geri Schneider and Jason P. Winters, *Applying Use Cases: A Practical Guide*, ISBN 0-201-30981-5

Yen-Ping Shan and Ralph H. Earle, *Enterprise Computing with Objects: From Client/Server Environments to the Internet*, ISBN 0-201-32566-7

David N. Smith, *IBM Smalltalk: The Language*, ISBN 0-8053-0908-X

Jos Warmer and Anneke Kleppe, *The Object Constraint Language: Precise Modeling with UML*, ISBN 0-201-37940-6

Brian White, *Software Configuration Management Strategies and Rational ClearCase: A Practical Introduction*, ISBN 0-201-60478-7

Designing Concurrent, Distributed, and Real-Time Applications with UML

Hassan Gomaa

George Mason University

ADDISON–WESLEY

Boston • San Francisco • New York • Toronto • Montreal
London • Munich • Paris • Madrid
Capetown • Sydney • Tokyo • Singapore • Mexico City

Many of the designations used by manufacturers and sellers to distinguish their products are claimed as trademarks. Where those designations appear in this book, and we were aware of a trademark claim, the designations have been printed with initial capital letters or in all capitals.

The author and publisher have taken care in the preparation of this book, but make no expressed or implied warranty of any kind and assume no responsibility for errors or omissions. No liability is assumed for incidental or consequential damages in connection with or arising out of the use of the information or programs contained herein.

The publisher offers discounts on this book when ordered in quantity for special sales. For more information, please contact:

Pearson Education Corporate Sales Division
One Lake Street
Upper Saddle River, NJ 07458
(800) 382-3419
corpsales@pearsontechgroup.com

Visit AW on the Web: www.awl.com/cseng/

Library of Congress Cataloging-in-Publication Data
Gomaa, Hassan.
    Designing concurrent, distributed, and real-time applications with UML / Hassan Gomaa.
        p. cm. — (The Addison-Wesley object technology series)
    Includes bibliographical references and index.
    ISBN 0-201-65793-7
    1. Application software—Development. 2. UML (Computer science) I. Title. II. Series.

    QA76.76.A65 G65 2000
    005.1'17—dc21   00-038613

ISBN 0-201-65793-7
Text printed on recycled paper
1 2 3 4 5 6 7 8 9 10—CRW—0403020100
First printing, July 2000

To Gill, William, Alexander, Amanda,
Edward, and my mother Johanna

Contents

Foreword
by Peter Freeman

The recent and rapid advances in hardware and communications have led to an explosion of concurrent, real-time, and distributed applications. This, in turn, is changing forever the nature of the demands on practical software development. The widespread advent of object-oriented approaches and now the use of UML are changing practice, but as usual, at a pace that lags behind the needs.

One reason for this lag has been the absence of good, authoritative, practical guides to the object-oriented analysis and design of concurrent applications, especially those that are distributed and/or real-time. This book goes a long way toward fulfilling that need.

I cannot think of a better person to write a definitive text on this topic than Hassan Gomaa. For more than 20 years, Hassan has contributed to a deeper understanding of concurrent, distributed, and real-time applications through his work in industry as a designer, his research into new real-time design methods, and his teaching as a university professor. This book shows the results of his experience.

It is superbly organized and illustrated, as only an experienced teacher could have done. It shows the depth of understanding of the technology that comes from long and deep research focused on the subject matter. It has the illustrations and practical knowledge that come from long and direct contact with practical software design.

I hope that you enjoy this book as much as I did, and that you will be able to use it for many years to come.

Peter A. Freeman
John P. Imlay, Jr., Dean and Professor
Georgia Institute of Technology
May 2000

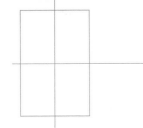

Foreword
by Bran Selic

Errors using inadequate data are much less than those using no data at all.
—Charles Babbage

A recent search of a popular bookseller's Web site revealed a total of 1,188 titles (and growing daily) that are classified as dealing with "software engineering." Despite this apparent glut, there is precious little engineering in most of them and, correspondingly, little or no engineering in much of the software being developed these days. This book aims to change that.

Traditional engineering disciplines invariably involved the use of science and mathematics to ensure that a design would meet its objectives at an acceptable cost. Thus, one could proceed with high confidence to construct a bridge based on predictions made from a mathematical model of the design. In the case of software, however, design is primarily an informal process too often devoid of formal predictive models or techniques. From this perspective, it is highly instructive to contrast how software and hardware have evolved over the last several decades. Whereas hardware has become smaller, faster, cheaper, and more reliable, software has become larger, slower, more expensive, and less reliable over the same period. Significantly, modern hardware design relies heavily on constructing predictive models.

The absence of engineering fundamentals from software practice can be attributed in part to the fickle, almost chaotic, nature of software, which makes it notoriously difficult to model mathematically. Despite this inherent difficulty, however, a number of very useful analytical techniques have been developed. In particular, such techniques have evolved in the embedded real-time domain, where it is often critical to predict the temporal properties of software with a high degree of certainty because human lives may depend on it. Yet, regardless of their proven effectiveness, these methods are not used very often. In fact, many real-time developers are not even aware of their existence.

The issue here is one of culture, or, more appropriately, the lack of one. Writing software is primarily an intellectual exercise, unhampered by physical limitations such as the need to cut and shape material or to expend large amounts of energy. Seduced by this apparent lack of resistance and the common perception that when all is said and done, only the code matters, far too many practitioners still equate software design with the process of writing software. Strangely enough, the same individuals have no trouble understanding the difference between designing a jumbo jet and assembling it.

Another incidental hurdle to the introduction of these techniques into software practice is that for historical reasons, some of them are defined in the context of the traditional procedural programming model. Although the techniques are not fundamentally dependent on that model, there remains the problem of mapping them to the newer object-oriented programming model for those who want to exploit the many advantages of that paradigm.

Hassan Gomaa's book is the first one I have seen that addresses these issues in a systematic and comprehensive manner. Much more than a mere compilation of unconnected "patterns" and point techniques, it explains clearly and in detail a way of reconciling specific traditional engineering techniques with the industry-standard Unified Modeling Language. Furthermore, it shows how such techniques fit into a fully defined development process, one that is specifically oriented toward developing concurrent, distributed, real-time systems. (Experienced software developers recognize fundamentally hard problems behind each of these terms individually—systems that combine all three typically belong to the category of the most challenging engineering problems.)

Based on the well-known dictum that we learn best by doing, fully worked-out, non-trivial examples take up a major portion of this book. The reader will benefit greatly from working through one or more of these examples to gain an intuitive feel for the approach, and, on a higher plane, for what software engineering should ultimately look like.

Bran Selic
May 2000

Preface

The UML Notation and Software Design Methods

This book describes the object-oriented analysis and design of concurrent applications, in particular distributed and real-time applications. Object-oriented concepts are crucial in software analysis and design because they address fundamental issues of adaptation and evolution. With the proliferation of notations and methods for the object-oriented analysis and design of software systems, the Unified Modeling Language (UML) has emerged to provide a standardized notation for describing object-oriented models. However, for the UML notation to be effectively applied, it needs to be used in conjunction with an object-oriented analysis and design method.

Most books on object-oriented analysis and design only address the design of sequential systems or omit the important design issues that need to be addressed when designing distributed and real-time applications. Blending object-oriented concepts with the concepts of concurrent processing is essential to the successful designing of these applications. Because the UML is now the standardized notation for describing object-oriented models, this book uses the UML notation throughout.

The COMET Concurrent Object Modeling and Architectural Design Method

COMET is a Concurrent Object Modeling and Architectural Design Method for the development of concurrent applications—in particular, distributed and real-time applications. The COMET Object-Oriented Software Life Cycle is a highly iterative software life cycle, based around the use case concept. The Requirements Modeling phase views the system as a black box. A use case model is developed, which defines the functional requirements of the system in terms of actors and use cases.

In the Analysis Modeling phase, static and dynamic models of the system are developed. The static model defines the structural relationships among problem domain classes. Object structuring criteria are used to determine the objects to be considered for the analysis model. A dynamic model is then developed, in which the use cases from the requirements model are refined to show the objects that participate in each use case and their interactions with each other. In the dynamic model, state-dependent objects are defined by using statecharts.

In the Design Modeling phase, the software architecture of the system is designed, in which the analysis model is mapped to an operational environment. The analysis model, with its emphasis on the problem domain, is mapped to the design model, with its emphasis on the solution domain. Subsystem structuring criteria are provided to structure the system into subsystems. For distributed applications, the emphasis is on the division of responsibility between clients and servers, including issues concerning the centralization versus distribution of data and control. In addition, the design of message communication interfaces is considered, including synchronous, asynchronous, brokered, and group communication. Each subsystem is then designed. For the design of concurrent applications, including real-time applications, the emphasis is on object-oriented and concurrent tasking concepts. Task communication and synchronization interfaces are designed. The performance of the real-time design is analyzed by using the Software Engineering Institute's rate monotonic analysis approach.

What This Book Provides

Several textbooks on the market describe object-oriented concepts and methods, intended for all kinds of applications. However, distributed and real-time applications have special needs, which are treated only superficially in most of these books. This book provides a comprehensive treatment of the application of fundamental object-oriented concepts to the analysis and design of distributed (including client/server) and real-time applications. In addition to the object-oriented concepts of information hiding, classes, and inheritance, this book also describes the concepts of finite state machines, concurrent tasks, distributed object technology, and real-time scheduling. It then describes in considerable detail the COMET method, which is a UML based object-oriented analysis and design method for concurrent, distributed and real-time applications. To show how COMET is applied in practice, this book also describes several comprehensive case studies, presented by application area: real-time software design, client/server software design, and distributed application design.

The following are distinguishing features of this book:

- Emphasis on structuring criteria to assist the designer at various stages of the analysis and design process: subsystems, objects, and concurrent tasks

- Emphasis on dynamic modeling, in the form of both object interaction modeling and finite state machine modeling, describing in detail how object collaborations and statecharts work together

- Emphasis on concurrency, describing the characteristics of active and passive objects

- Emphasis on distributed application design and the ways in which distributed components can communicate with each other

- Emphasis on performance analysis of real-time designs, using real-time scheduling

- Comprehensive case studies of various applications to illustrate in detail the application of concepts and methods

Organization of Book

The book is divided into three parts. Part I of the book provides a broad overview by describing concepts, technology, life cycles and methods for designing concurrent, distributed, and real-time applications. Chapter 1 starts with a brief description of the difference between a method and a notation, followed by a discussion of the characteristics of real-time and distributed applications. Chapter 2 presents a brief overview of the aspects of the UML notation used by the COMET method. Next, there is a description of the important design concepts (Chapter 3) and necessary technology support (Chapter 4) for concurrent and distributed systems. This is followed in Chapter 5 by a brief survey of software life cycles and design methods.

Part II of the book describes the COMET method (Concurrent Object Modeling and architectural design mEThod). In Chapter 6, there is an overview of the object-oriented software life cycle used by COMET. Chapter 7 describes the requirements modeling phase of COMET, in particular, use case modeling, and

Chapters 8 through 11 describe the analysis modeling phases of COMET. Chapters 12–16 describe the design modeling phase of COMET. Chapter 17 describes the performance analysis of real-time designs using real-time scheduling—in particular, rate monotonic analysis.

Finally, in Part III, the COMET method is illustrated through five detailed case studies of concurrent application design: two real-time design case studies, one client/server case study, and two distributed application case studies. The real-time Elevator Control System case study is described in Chapter 18, with both non-distributed and distributed solutions presented. The client/server Banking System case study is described in Chapter 19. The real-time Cruise Control System case study is described in Chapter 20. The distributed Factory Automation case study is described in Chapter 21, and the distributed Electronic Commerce case study is described in Chapter 22.

Ways to Read This Book

This book may be read in various ways. Reading it in the order it is presented, Chapters 1–5 provide introductory concepts and technology, Chapter 6 provides an overview of COMET, Chapters 7–17 provide an in-depth treatment of designing applications with COMET, and Chapters 18–22 provide detailed case studies.

Part I is introductory and may be skipped by experienced readers, who will want to proceed directly to the description of COMET in Part II. Readers familiar with the UML may skip Chapter 2. Readers familiar with software design concepts may skip Chapter 3. Readers familiar with concurrent and distributed system technology may skip Chapter 4. Readers familiar with software life cycles and methods may skip the survey in Chapter 5. Readers particularly interested in COMET may proceed directly to Parts II and III. Readers particularly interested in distributed application design should read Chapters 4, 12, and 13, the additional information on concurrent subsystem design in Chapters 14–16, as well as the distributed application case studies in Chapters 18, 19, 21, and 22. Readers particularly interested in real-time design and scheduling should read Chapters 4, 14–17, and the hard real-time design case studies in Chapters 18 and 20.

Experienced designers may also use this book as a reference, referring to various chapters as their projects reach that stage of the analysis or design process. Each chapter is relatively self-contained. For example, at different times, you might refer to Chapter 7 for a concise description of use cases, Chapter 10 when designing statecharts, Chapter 11 for developing the dynamic model, Chapter 13 for distributed component design, Chapter 14 when designing concurrent tasks, or Chapter 17 for real-time scheduling. You can also understand how to use the COMET method by reading the case studies, because each case study explains the decisions made at each step of the design process.

Acknowledgments

The author gratefully acknowledges the reviewers of earlier drafts of the manuscript. Of the reviewers, he is particularly grateful to Jeff Magee, Larry McAlister, Kevin Mills, Robert G. Pettit IV, and Maria Ericsson for their insightful reviews. I would also like to thank Anhtuan Q. Dinh, Ghulam Ahmad Farrukh, Johan Galle, Kelli Houston, Jishnu Mukerji, Leslee Probasco, Sanjeev Setia, and Duminda Wijesekera for their helpful reviews.

Additional thanks are due to Kevin Mills for his contributions on the use of stereotypes in COMET, Shigeru Otsuki for his assistance with the section on design patterns, Roger Alexander for his help with one of the examples in Chapter 15, and Larry McAlister, who contributed Figure 21.1. Particular thanks are due to Tyrrell Albaugh for her hard work coordinating the lengthy production process, to Kristin Erickson who coordinated the editorial process, and to Malinda McCain for her meticulous copyediting of the manuscript.

The author is also grateful to his students in his Software Design and Software Project Lab courses at George Mason University for their enthusiasm, dedication, and valuable feedback. The author gratefully acknowledges the Software Engineering Institute (SEI) for the material provided on real-time scheduling, on which parts of Chapter 17 are based. The author also gratefully acknowledges the Software Productivity Consortium's sponsorship of the development of an earlier version of the material described in Chapters 9–11 of this book. He also thanks Arman Anwar, Hua Lin, and Michael Shin for their hard work producing earlier versions of the figures.

Last, but not least, I would like to thank my wife, Gill, for her encouragement, understanding, and support.

part

UML Notation, Design Concepts, Technology, Life Cycles, and Methods

Introduction

With the massive reduction in the cost of microprocessor and semiconductor chips and the large increase in microprocessor performance over the past few years, real-time and distributed microcomputer based systems are a cost-effective solution to many problems. Nowadays, more and more commercial, industrial, military, medical, and consumer products are microcomputer based and either are software controlled or have a crucial software component to them. These systems range from microwave ovens to video cassette recorders, from telephones to television sets, from automobiles to aircraft, from submarines that explore the depths of the oceans to spacecraft that explore the far reaches of space, from automated vending machines to automated teller machines, from patient monitoring systems to factory monitoring systems, from robot controllers to elevator controllers, from city traffic control to air traffic control, from electronic mail to electronic commerce, from "smart" transportation highways to "smart" information highways—the list is continually growing. These systems are concurrent. Many of them are also real-time or distributed.

Object-oriented concepts are crucial in software analysis and design because they address fundamental issues of adaptation and evolution. More recently, the Unified Modeling Language (UML) has emerged to provide a standardized notation for describing object-oriented models [Booch, Rumbaugh, Jacobson 1998; Eriksson and Penker 1998; Fowler and Scott 1999; Jacobson, Booch, and Rumbaugh 1999; Rumbaugh, Booch, and Jacobson 1999]. However, most books on object-oriented analysis and design address the design of only sequential applications or omit the important design issues that need to be addressed when designing concurrent, distributed, and real-time applications. Blending object-oriented concepts with concurrency concepts is essential to successfully designing distributed and real-time applications. Because the UML is now the standardized notation for describing object-oriented models, this book uses the UML notation throughout. It places emphasis on dynamic modeling, of particular importance for distributed and real-time applications.

This book describes object-oriented analysis and design of concurrent applications, using the Unified Modeling Language (UML) notation. In particular, it describes two important categories of concurrent applications: distributed and real-time applications. This book is intended for those who want to design, evaluate, or understand the software for concurrent, real-time, and distributed applications.

This chapter introduces object-oriented concepts and discusses the characteristics of concurrent, distributed, and real-time applications.

1.1 Object-Oriented Methods and the Unified Modeling Language

Object-oriented methods are based on the concepts of information hiding, classes, and inheritance [Wegner 1990]. Information hiding [Parnas 1972, Parnas 1979] can lead to more self-contained and hence modifiable and maintainable systems. Inheritance [Meyer 1987, Meyer 1997, Wegner 1990] provides an approach for adapting a class in a systematic way.

With the proliferation of notations and methods for the object-oriented analysis and design of software applications [Booch 1994; Coad and Yourdon 1991; Jacobson 1992; Rumbaugh et al. 1991; Shlaer and Mellor 1988; Wirfs-Brock, Wilkerson, and Wiener 1990; and others], the Unified Modeling Language (UML) is an industry standard providing a standardized notation for describing object-oriented models. However, for the UML notation to be effectively applied, it needs to be used in conjunction with an object-oriented analysis and design method.

The COMET method (Concurrent Object Modeling and architectural design mEThod) described in this book uses a combination of use cases [Jacobson 1992], static modeling [Rumbaugh et al. 1991, Booch 1994], statecharts [Harel 1988, Harel and Politi 1998, Coleman et al. 1994, Rumbaugh et al. 1991], and event sequence diagrams used by several methods [Booch 1994, Gomaa 1993, Jacobson 1992, Rumbaugh et al. 1991]. The notation used is based on the Unified Modeling Language (UML) [Booch, Rumbaugh, and Jacobson 1998; Eriksson and Penker 1998; Fowler and Scott 1999; Jacobson, Booch, and Rumbaugh 1999; Rumbaugh, Booch, and Jacobson 1999]. In **use case modeling**, the functional requirements of the system are defined in terms of use cases and actors. **Static modeling** provides a static view of the information aspects of the system. Classes are defined in terms of their attributes and their relationship with other classes. **Dynamic modeling** provides a dynamic view of the system. The use cases are refined to show the interaction among the objects participating in each use case. Collaboration diagrams and sequence diagrams are developed to show how objects collaborate with each other to execute the use case. The state-dependent aspects of the system are defined by using statecharts. In particular, each state-dependent object is defined in terms of its constituent statechart.

In the analysis model, the emphasis is on understanding the problem; hence, the emphasis is on identifying the problem domain objects and the information passed between them. Problem domain objects and classes are categorized based on the object structuring criteria. Issues such as whether the object is active or passive, whether the message sent is asynchronous or synchronous, and what operation is invoked at the receiving object are deferred until design time.

During design, the objects are further analyzed to determine the active objects (referred to as tasks) and the passive objects (referred to as objects). Tasks are determined by using task structuring criteria. Task interfaces are also designed. The operations of each passive class are also determined.

1.2   Method and Notation

A design method has different goals than a design notation. A **software design notation** is a means of describing a software design. A design notation suggests a particular approach for performing a design; however, it does not provide a systematic approach for producing a design. A **software design method** is a systematic approach that describes the steps for creating a design.

A **software design notation** describes a software design graphically or textually. For example, class diagrams are a graphical design notation and Pseudocode is a textual design notation.

A **software design concept** is a fundamental idea that can be applied to designing a system. For example, information hiding is a software design concept.

A **software design strategy** is an overall plan and direction for performing a design. For example, object-oriented decomposition is a software design strategy.

Software structuring criteria are heuristics or guidelines used to help a designer in structuring a software system into its components. For example, object structuring criteria provide guidelines for decomposing the system into objects.

A **software design method** describes a sequence of steps for a designer or design team to follow when creating a design, given the software requirements of the application. It helps identify the design decisions to be made, the order in which to make them, and the criteria to use in making them. A design method is based on a set of design concepts, employs one or more design strategies, and documents the resulting design using a design notation. During a given design step, the method might provide a set of structuring criteria to help the designer in decomposing the system into its components.

The COMET method uses the UML notation to describe the design. It is based on the design concepts of information hiding, classes, inheritance, and concurrent tasks. It uses a design strategy of concurrent object design, which addresses structuring a software system into active and passive objects and defining the interfaces between them. It provides structuring criteria to help structure the system into objects during analysis, and further criteria to determine the subsystems and concurrent tasks during design.

1.3 Concurrent Applications

In the early days of computing, most computer applications were batch programs. Each program was sequential and ran offline. Today, with the proliferation of interactive applications and the tendency toward distributed microcomputer systems, many applications are concurrent in nature.

A growing number of applications, including real-time and distributed applications, exhibit substantial concurrency. A characteristic of a concurrent application is that it typically has many activities occurring in parallel. In these applications, the order of incoming events is often not predictable and might be overlapping.

1.3.1 Sequential and Concurrent Problems

In sequential problems, activities take place in strict sequence. For example, with a conventional compiler, several compilation phases are executed in sequence before the compiled program is produced. With a batch payroll application, payroll records for each employee are processed in sequence and paychecks are produced.

In concurrent problems, many activities are happening in parallel. In a multiuser interactive system, several users are interacting with the system in parallel. There is no way of predicting which user will provide the next input. In an air traffic control system, the system is monitoring several aircraft, so many activities are occurring in parallel. Changes in weather conditions can lead to unexpected loads and unpredictable patterns of behavior in the system.

Dijkstra [1968] recognized that some applications were concurrent in nature, in which several activities were logically occurring in parallel. Mapping these concurrent activities to one sequential program leads to a more complex design. It is often much simpler to design each activity as a separate task (also referred to as a process). The tasks execute concurrently—that is, in parallel. Frequently, these tasks need to cooperate with each other; thus they need to communicate information or synchronize their operations [Gomaa 1993].

1.3.2   Sequential and Concurrent Applications

A sequential application is a sequential program that consists of **passive objects** and has only one thread of control. When an object invokes an operation in another object, control is passed from the calling operation to the called operation. When the called operation finishes executing, control is passed back to the calling operation. In a sequential application, only synchronous message communication (procedure call or method invocation) is supported.

In a concurrent application, there are typically several **active objects**, each with its own thread of control. Asynchronous message communication is supported, so an active source object can send an asynchronous message to an active destination object and then continue executing, regardless of when the destination object receives the message. If the destination object is busy when the message arrives, the message is buffered for the object.

1.3.3   Concurrent Tasks

The concept of **concurrent tasks**, also frequently referred to as **concurrent processes**, is fundamental in the design of concurrent applications. A concurrent application consists of many tasks that execute in parallel. The design concepts for concurrent applications are generally applicable to real-time and distributed applications.

The concurrent tasking concept has been applied extensively in the design of operating systems, database systems, real-time systems, interactive systems, and distributed systems [Bacon 1997]. Key issues for developing concurrent applications include providing a capability for structuring the application into concurrent tasks and providing a capability for tasks to communicate and synchronize their operations with each other. For real-time and distributed applications, additional considerations are necessary, as outlined in the next two sections.

1.4   Real-Time Systems and Applications

Real-time systems (Figure 1.1) are concurrent systems with timing constraints. They have widespread use in industrial, commercial, and military applications. The term "real-time system" usually refers to the whole system, including the real-time application, real-time operating system, and the real-time I/O subsystem, with special-purpose device drivers to interface to the various sensors and actuators. Because the emphasis in this book is on designing real-time applications, we use the term "real-time application" and not real-time system. However, this section describes real-time applications in the broader context of real-time systems.

Real-time systems are often complex because they have to deal with multiple independent streams of input events and produce multiple outputs. These events have arrival rates that are often unpredictable, although they must be responded to subject to timing constraints specified in the software requirements. Frequently, the order of incoming events is not predictable. Furthermore, the input load might vary significantly and unpredictably with time.

Real-time systems are frequently classified as hard real-time systems or soft real-time systems. A hard real-time system has time-critical deadlines that must be met to prevent a catastrophic system failure. In a soft real-time system, missing deadlines occasionally is considered undesirable but not catastrophic.

Real-time software systems have several characteristics that distinguish them from other software systems:

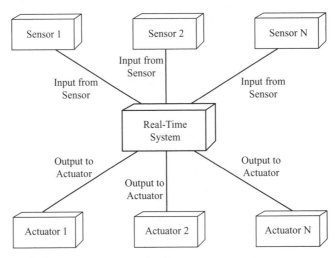

Figure 1.1   *Real-time system*

- **Embedded systems.** A real-time system is often an embedded system; in other words, the real-time software system is a component of a larger hardware/software system. An example of this is a robot controller that is a component of a robot system consisting of one or more mechanical arms, servomechanisms controlling axis motion, and sensors and actuators for interfacing to the external environment. A computerized automobile cruise control system is embedded in the automobile.

  A real-time software system usually consists of the real-time application, the real-time operating system, and possibly some additional system software such as communications software, middleware, or special-purpose device drivers.

- **Interaction with external environment.** A real-time system typically interacts with an external environment that is to a large extent nonhuman. For example, the real-time system might be controlling machines or manufacturing processes, or it might be monitoring chemical processes and reporting alarm conditions. This often necessitates sensors for receiving data from the external environment and actuators for outputting data to and controlling the external environment (see Figure 1.1).

- **Timing constraints.** Real-time systems have timing constraints; in particular, they must process events within a given time frame. Whereas in an interactive system, a human might be inconvenienced if the system response is delayed, a delay in a real-time system might be catastrophic. For example, inadequate response in an air traffic control system could result in a mid-air collision of two aircraft. The required response time will vary by application, ranging from milliseconds in some cases to seconds or even minutes in others.

- **Real-time control.** A real-time system often involves real-time control. That is, the real-time system makes control decisions based on input data, without any human intervention. An automobile cruise control system has to adjust the throttle based on measurements of current speed to ensure that the desired speed is maintained.

  A real-time software system might also have non-real-time components. For example, real-time data collection necessitates gathering the data under real-time constraints; otherwise, the data could be lost. However, once collected, the data can be stored for subsequent non-real-time analysis.

- **Reactive systems.** Many real-time systems are reactive systems [Harel and Politi 1998]. They are event driven and must respond to external stimuli. It is usually the case in reactive systems that the response made by the system to an input stimulus is state-dependent; that is, the response depends not only on the stimulus itself but also on what has previously happened in the system.

1.5   Distributed Systems and Applications

A distributed application is a concurrent application that executes in an environment consisting of multiple nodes that are in geographically different locations (Figure 1.2). Each node is a separate computer system; the nodes are connected to each other by means of a local or wide area network. Because the system software required to support distributed applications is so complex, the term "distributed system" is often used to refer to distributed operating systems, distributed file systems, and distributed databases. Because the emphasis in this book is on designing applications that use these services, the term "distributed application" is used and not distributed system.

The advantages of distributed processing are

- **Improved availability.** Operation is feasible in a reduced configuration in cases where some nodes are temporarily unavailable. There is also no single point of failure.

- **More flexible configuration.** A given application can be configured in different ways by selecting the appropriate number of nodes for a given instance of the application.

- **More localized control and management.** A distributed subsystem, executing on its own node, can be designed to be autonomous, so it can to a large extent execute independently relative to other subsystems on other nodes.

- **Incremental system expansion.** If the system gets overloaded, the system can be expanded by adding more nodes.

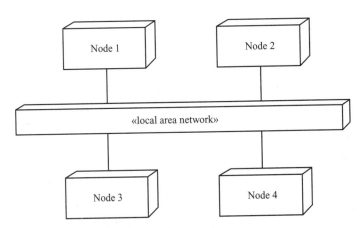

Figure 1.2   *Distributed processing environment*

- **Reduced cost.** Frequently a distributed solution is cheaper than a centralized solution. With the rapidly declining costs and rapidly increasing performance of microcomputers, a distributed solution can be significantly more cost-effective than an equivalent centralized solution.

- **Load balancing.** In some applications, the overall system load can be shared among several nodes.

- **Improved response time.** Local users on local systems can have their requests processed in a more timely fashion.

1.6 Summary

This chapter has described the characteristics of concurrent applications and two important categories of concurrent applications, namely real-time and distributed applications. It has described the difference between a method and a notation, and hence described how the COMET method relates to the Unified Modeling Language notation. Chapter 2 describes the aspects of the UML notation that are used by COMET. Chapter 3 provides more information on the fundamental concepts, first introduced in this chapter, upon which concurrent object-oriented design is based. It describes the concurrent tasking concept in more detail—in particular, task communication and synchronization. In addition, providing support for concurrent tasks in the operating system and/or programming language is necessary, as described in Chapter 4.

Overview of UML Notation

The notation used for the COMET method is the Unified Modeling Language (UML). The UML notation primarily combines the notations of Booch [1994], Jacobson [1992], Rumbaugh et al. [1991], and Harel [1988, 1998]. This section provides a brief overview of the UML notation. The UML notation is described in more detail in introductory references, in particular, *The Unified Modeling Language User Guide* [Booch, Rumbaugh, and Jacobson 1998] and *UML Distilled* [Fowler 1999], and in more detail in *The Unified Modeling Language Reference Manual* [Rumbaugh, Booch, and Jacobson 1999]. These three books conform to UML 1.3, as does this book. Several other books also describe the UML notation at various levels of detail, such as Eriksson [1998]; Jacobson, Booch, and Rumbaugh [1999]; and Pooley [1999].

The UML notation has grown substantially over the years, with many diagrams supported. The approach taken in this book is the same as Fowler's [1999], which is to use only those aspects of the UML notation that provide a distinct benefit. This chapter describes the main features of the UML notation that are particularly suited to the COMET method. The purpose of this chapter is not to be a full exposition of the UML, because several detailed books exist on this topic, but rather to provide a brief review. The main features of each of the UML diagrams used in this book are briefly described, but lesser-used features are omitted.

2.1 UML Diagrams

The UML notation supports nine diagrams:

1. Use case diagram, briefly described in Section 2.2.
2. Class diagram, briefly described in Section 2.4.

3. The object diagram, an instance version of the class diagram, is not used by COMET. In its place, a consolidated collaboration diagram is used, as described in Chapter 12.

4. Collaboration diagram, briefly described in Section 2.5.

5. Sequence diagram, briefly described in Section 2.5.

6. Statechart diagram, briefly described in Section 2.6.

7. The activity diagram is not used in COMET.

8. The component diagram is not used in COMET. The term "component" is used in this book to describe a distributed component, as used in component technology and described in Chapters 4 and 13, and not a component in the UML.

9. Deployment diagram, briefly described in Section 2.9.

How these UML diagrams are used by the COMET method is described in subsequent chapters of this book.

2.2 Use Case Diagrams

An **actor** initiates a use case. A **use case** defines a sequence of interactions between the **actor** and the system. An actor is depicted as a stick figure on a use case diagram. The system is depicted as a box. A use case is depicted as an ellipse inside the box. Communication associations connect actors with the use cases in which they participate. Relationships among use cases are defined by means of *include* and *extend* relationships. The notation is depicted in Figure 2.1.

2.3 UML Notation for Classes and Objects

Classes and objects are shown as boxes in the UML notation, as shown in Figure 2.2. The class box always holds the class name. Optionally, the attributes and operations of a class may also be depicted. When depicting all three, the top compartment of the box depicting the class holds the class name, the middle compartment holds the attributes, and the bottom compartment holds the class operations.

To distinguish between a class (the type) and an object (an instance of the type), an object is shown underlined. An object may be depicted as <u>anObject</u>, <u>anotherObject:Class</u>, or <u>:Class</u>. Classes and objects are depicted on various UML diagrams, as described next.

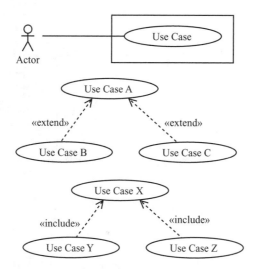

Figure 2.1 *UML notation for use case diagram*

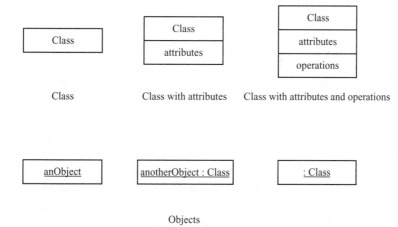

Figure 2.2 *UML notation for objects and classes*

2.4 Class Diagrams

In a **class diagram**, classes are depicted as boxes and the static (i.e., permanent) relationships between them are depicted as arcs. The following three main types of relationships between classes are supported, as shown in Figure 2.3.

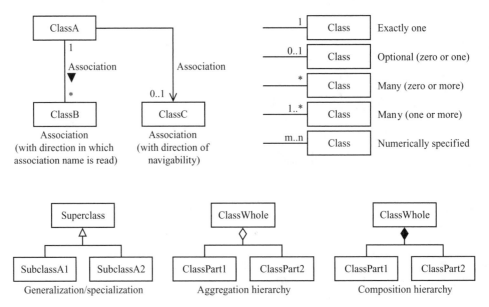

Figure 2.3 *UML notation for relationships on class diagrams*

1. **Associations.** An association between two classes, which is referred to as a binary association, is depicted as a line joining the two class boxes. An association has a name and optionally a small arrowhead to depict the direction in which the association name should be read. On each end of the association line joining the classes is the multiplicity of the association, which indicates how many instances of one class are related to an instance of the other class. Optionally, a stick arrow may also be used to depict the direction of navigability.

   The multiplicity of an association can be exactly one (1), optional (0..1), zero or more (*), one or more (1..*), or numerically specified (n..m), where n and m have numeric values.

2. **Aggregation and composition hierarchies.** These are *whole/part* relationships. The composition relationship (shown by a black diamond) is a stronger form of whole/part relationship than the aggregation relationship (shown by a hollow diamond). The diamond touches the aggregate/composite (Class Whole) class box.

3. **Generalization/specialization hierarchy.** This is an *is-a* relationship. A generalization is depicted as an arrow joining the subclass (child) to the superclass (parent), with the arrowhead touching the superclass box.

   A fourth relationship, the dependency relationship, is often used to show relationships between packages, as described in Section 2.7.

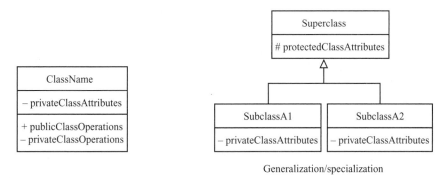

Generalization/specialization

Figure 2.4 *UML notation for visibility on class diagram*

Visibility refers to whether an element of the class is visible from outside the class, as depicted in Figure 2.4. Depicting visibility is optional on a class diagram. Public visibility, denoted with a + symbol, means that the element is visible from outside the class. Private visibility, denoted with a – symbol, means that the element is visible only from within the class that defines it and is thus hidden from other classes. Protected visibility, denoted with a # symbol, means that the element is visible from within the class that defines it and within all subclasses of the class.

2.5 Interaction Diagrams

UML has two kinds of interaction diagrams, which depict how objects interact with each other: the **collaboration diagram** and the **sequence diagram.** Collaboration diagrams and sequence diagrams are semantically equivalent to each other. The main features of these diagrams are described next.

2.5.1 Collaboration Diagrams

A **collaboration diagram** shows how cooperating objects dynamically interact with each other by sending and receiving messages. The diagram depicts the structural organization of the objects that interact with each other. Objects are shown as boxes, and arcs joining boxes represent object interconnection. Labeled arrows adjacent to the arcs indicate the name and direction of message transmission between objects. The sequence of messages passed between the objects is numbered. The notation for collaboration diagrams is illustrated in Figure 2.5. An optional iteration is indicated by an *, which means a message is sent more than once. An optional condition means the message is sent only if the condition is true.

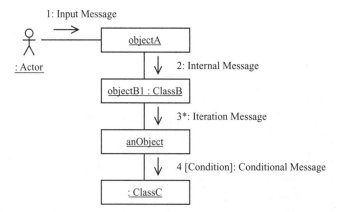

Figure 2.5 *UML notation for collaboration diagram*

2.5.2 Sequence Diagrams

A different way of showing the interaction among objects is to show them on a sequence diagram, which shows object interaction arranged in time sequence, as shown in Figure 2.6. A **sequence diagram** is a two-dimensional diagram in which the objects participating in the interaction are depicted horizontally and the vertical dimension represents time. Starting at each object box is a vertical dashed line, referred

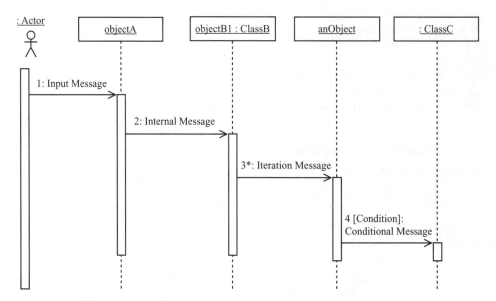

Figure 2.6 *UML notation for sequence diagram*

to as a lifeline. An activation depicts a period when the object is executing (e.g., an operation is executed), for which the lifeline is shown by a double solid line.

The actor is usually shown at the extreme left of the page. Labeled horizontal arrows represent messages. Only the source and destination of the arrow are relevant. The message is sent from the source object to the destination object. Time increases from the top of the page to the bottom. The spacing between messages is not relevant.

2.6 Statechart Diagrams

In the UML notation, a state transition diagram is referred to as a **statechart diagram**. In this book, the shorter-term **statechart** is generally used. Using the UML notation, states are represented by rounded boxes and transitions are represented by arcs that connect the rounded boxes (as shown in Figure 2.7). The initial state of the statechart is depicted by an arc originating from a small black circle. Optionally, a final state may be depicted by a small black circle inside a larger white circle, sometimes referred to as a bull's eye. A statechart may be hierarchically decomposed such that a **superstate** is decomposed into **substates.**

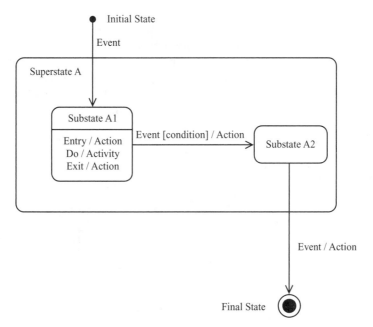

Figure 2.7 *UML notation for statechart: superstate with sequential substates*

On the arc representing the state transition, the notation **event [condition] / action** is used. The **event** causes the state transition. The optional Boolean **condition** must be true, when the event occurs, for the transition to take place. The optional **action** is performed as a result of the transition. Optionally, associated with a state, there may be

- An **entry action.** Performed when the state is entered
- An **activity.** Performed for the duration of the state
- An **exit action.** Performed on exit from the state

Figure 2.7 depicts a superstate A, decomposed into sequential substates A1 and A2. In this case, the statechart is in only one substate at a time. Thus, first substate A1 is entered and then substate A2. Figure 2.8 depicts a superstate B, decomposed into concurrent substates BC and BD. In this case, the statechart is in each of the concurrent substates BC and BD at the same time. Each concurrent substate is further decomposed into sequential substates. Thus, when the superstate B is initially entered, each of the substates B1 and B3 is also entered.

2.7 Packages

In UML, a **package** is a grouping of model elements, for example, to represent a system or subsystem. It is depicted by a folder icon, a large rectangle with a small rectangle attached on one corner, as shown in Figure 2.9. Packages may also be nested within other packages. Possible relationships between packages are the dependency (shown in Figure 2.9) and generalization/specialization relationships. Packages may be used to contain classes, objects, or use cases.

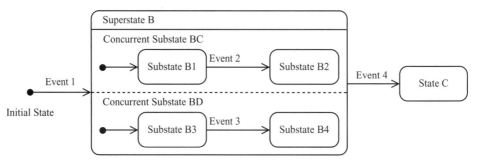

Figure 2.8 *UML notation for statechart: superstate with concurrent substates*

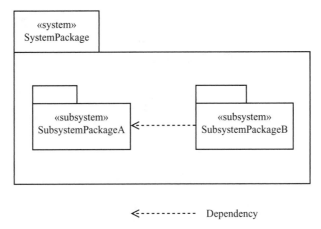

Figure 2.9 *UML notation for packages*

2.8 Concurrent Collaboration Diagrams

In the UML notation, an active object or task is depicted by using a thick outline for the object box. An active object has its own thread of control and executes concurrently with other objects. This is in contrast to a passive object, which does not have a thread of control.

A passive object executes only when another object (active or passive) invokes one of its operations. In this book, we refer to an active object as a task and a passive object as an object. Tasks are depicted on **concurrent collaboration diagrams**, which depict the concurrency aspects of the system [Douglass 1999b]. On a concurrent collaboration diagram, a task is depicted as a box with thick black lines and a passive object is depicted as a box with thin black lines. An example is given in Figure 2.10, which also shows the notation for multiobjects, used when more than one object is instantiated from the same class.

2.8.1 Message Communication on Concurrent Collaboration Diagrams

Message interfaces between tasks on concurrent collaboration diagrams are either **loosely coupled** (asynchronous) or **tightly coupled** (synchronous). With tightly coupled message communication, the producer sends a message to the consumer and then immediately waits for a response. For tightly coupled message communication, two possibilities exist: **tightly coupled message**

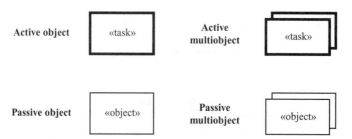

Figure 2.10 *UML notation for active and passive objects*

communication with reply and **tightly coupled message communication without reply.**

The UML notation for message communication is summarized in Figure 2.11. Figure 2.12 depicts a concurrent collaboration diagram, a version of the collaboration diagram that shows active objects (concurrent tasks or processes) and the various kinds of message communication between them.

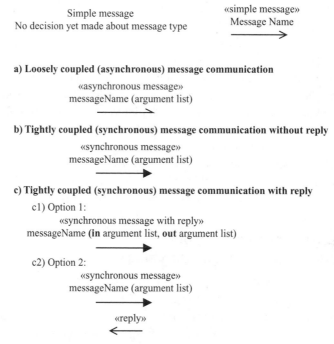

Figure 2.11 *UML notation for messages*

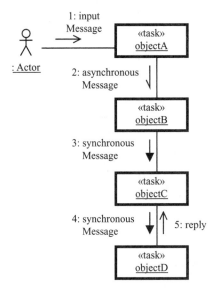

Figure 2.12   *UML notation for concurrent collaboration diagram*

2.9   Deployment Diagrams

A deployment diagram shows the physical configuration of the system in terms of physical nodes and physical connections between the nodes, such as network connections. A node is shown as a cube and the connection is shown as an arc joining the nodes. A deployment diagram is essentially a class diagram that focuses on the system's nodes [Booch, Rumbaugh, and Jacobson 1998].

In this book, nodes usually represent a computer node, with a constraint (see Section 2.10) describing how many instances of this node may exist. The physical connection has a stereotype (see Section 2.10) to indicate the type of connection, such as «local area network» or «wide area network». Figure 2.13 shows two node types: an ATM Client, of which there is one node for each ATM, connected to a Bank Server, for which there is one node. Optionally, the objects that reside at the node may be depicted in the node cube. In the second example, where several client and server nodes are connected via a local area network, the network is shown as a node. This form of the notation is used when more than two computer nodes are connected by a network.

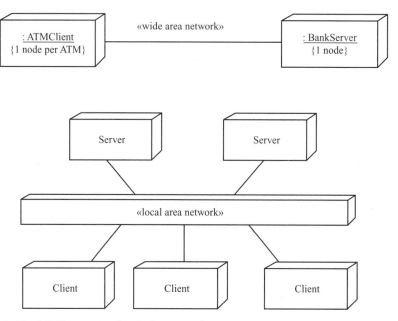

Figure 2.13 *UML notation for deployment diagram*

2.10   UML Extension Mechanisms

UML provides three mechanisms to allow the language to be extended [Booch, Rumbaugh, and Jacobson 1998; Rumbaugh, Booch, and Jacobson 1999]. These are

1. **Stereotypes.** A stereotype defines a new building block that is derived from an existing UML modeling element but tailored to the modeler's problem [Booch, Rumbaugh, and Jacobson 1998]. This book makes extensive use of stereotypes. Several standard stereotypes are defined in the UML. In addition, a modeler may define new stereotypes. This chapter includes several examples of stereotypes, both standard and COMET-specific. Stereotypes are depicted by using guillemets « ». In Figure 2.1, two specific kinds of dependency between use cases are depicted by using the stereotype notation, «include» and «extend». Figure 2.9 shows the stereotypes of «system» and «subsystem» to distinguish between two different kinds of packages. Figure 2.10 uses stereotypes to distinguish between active and passive objects: an active object is depicted with the stereotype «task» and a passive object is depicted with the stereotype «object». Figure 2.11 uses stereotypes to distinguish between different kinds of messages.

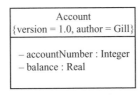

{balance ≥ 0}

Figure 2.14 *UML notation for tagged values and constraints*

2. **Tagged values.** A tagged value extends the properties of a UML building block [Booch, Rumbaugh, and Jacobson 1998], thereby adding new information. A tagged value is enclosed in braces in the form {tag = value}. Commas separate additional tagged values. For example, a class may be depicted with the tagged values {version = 1.0, author = Gill}, as depicted in Figure 2.14.

3. **Constraints.** A constraint specifies a condition that must be true. In UML, a constraint is an extension of the semantics of a UML element to allow addition of new rules or modifications to existing rules [Booch, Rumbaugh, and Jacobson 1998]. For example, for the `Account` class depicted in Figure 2.14, the constraint on the attribute `balance` is that the balance can never be negative, depicted as {`balance` ≥ 0}. Optionally, UML provides the Object Constraint Language [Warmer 1999] for expressing constraints.

2.11 The UML as a Standard

This section briefly reviews the evolution of the UML into a standard. The history of UML's evolution is described in detail by Cobryn [1999]. UML 0.9 unified the modeling notations of Booch, Jacobson, and Rumbaugh. This formed the basis of a standardization effort, with the additional involvement of a diverse mix of vendors and system integrators. This effort culminated in the submission of the initial UML 1.0 proposal to the Object Management Group (OMG) in January 1997. After some revisions, the final UML 1.1 proposal was submitted later that year and adopted as an object modeling standard in November 1997. Since then, there have been some minor revisions. At the time of writing, the current version of the standard is UML 1.3. *The Unified Modeling Language User Guide*, by Booch, Rumbaugh, and Jacobson [1998], *UML Distilled*, by Fowler [1999], and *The Unified Modeling Language Reference Manual*, by

Rumbaugh, Booch, and Jacobson [1999], all conform to UML 1.3, as does this book. There have been various proposals for evolving the UML standard, with a major revision, UML 2.0, planned for 2001.

2.12 Summary

This chapter has briefly described the main features of the UML notation and the main characteristics of the UML diagrams used in this book. The use case diagram depicts the actors and use cases. How it is used by COMET is described in Chapter 7. The class diagram depicts classes and their relationships; how class diagrams are used by COMET is described in Chapter 8 for the analysis phase and Chapter 15 for the design phase. The statechart describes how a class can be modeled by using a hierarchical finite state machine. Chapter 10 describes how COMET uses statecharts. There are two kinds of interaction diagrams, the collaboration diagram and the sequence diagram, which depict the dynamic sequence of message interactions between objects. Chapter 11 compares the two approaches, which are semantically equivalent, and describes how they are used in COMET. Packages can be used to depict subsystems, as described in Chapter 9. Deployment diagrams are used to show the physical configuration of the system, which is particularly useful in modeling distributed applications, as described in Chapter 13. Concurrent collaboration diagrams are used to depict the architecture of distributed application, as described in Chapter 13, and of task architectures, as described in Chapter 14. Of the extensibility mechanisms provided by the UML, COMET uses stereotypes the most, in particular for depicting the object, subsystem, and task structuring criteria, as described in Chapters 9, 12, and 14, respectively.

For further reading on the UML notation at a tutorial level, Fowler [1999] provides an overview, and more detail can be found in Booch, Rumbaugh, and Jacobson [1998]. A comprehensive and detailed reference to the UML is Rumbaugh, Booch, and Jacobson [1999].

3 chapter

Software Design and Architecture Concepts

This chapter describes key concepts in the software design of concurrent object-oriented systems as well as important concepts for developing the architecture of these systems. First, object-oriented concepts are introduced, with the description of objects and classes, as well as a discussion of the role of information hiding in object-oriented design and an introduction to the concept of inheritance. Next, the concurrent processing concept is introduced and the issues of communication and synchronization between concurrent tasks are described.

These design concepts are building blocks in designing the architecture of a system: the overall structure of the system, its decomposition into components, and the interfaces between these components.

3.1 Object-Oriented Concepts

The term **object-oriented** was first introduced in connection to object-oriented programming and Smalltalk [Goldberg and Robson 1983], although the object-oriented concepts of information hiding and inheritance have earlier origins. Information hiding and its use in software design date back to Parnas [1972], who advocated using information hiding as a way to design modules that were more self-contained and hence could be changed with little or no impact on other modules. The concepts of classes and inheritance were first used in Simula 67 [Dahl and Hoare 1972] but only started gaining widespread acceptance with the introduction of Smalltalk.

This section describes object-oriented concepts at the problem (analysis) level and the solution (design) level.

3.1.1 Basic Concepts

An **object** is a real-world physical or conceptual entity that provides an understanding of the real world and hence forms the basis for a software solution. A real-world object can have physical properties (they can be seen or touched); examples are a door, motor, or lamp. A conceptual object is a more abstract concept, such as an account or transaction.

Object-oriented applications consist of objects. From a design perspective, an object packages both data and procedures that operate on the data. The procedures are usually called operations or methods. Some approaches, including the UML notation, refer to the operation as the specification of a function performed by an object and the method as the implementation of the function [Rumbaugh, Booch, and Jacobson 1999]. In this book, we will use the term **operation** to refer to both the specification and the implementation, in common with Gamma 1995, Meyer 1997, and others.

The *signature* of an operation specifies the operation's name, the operation's parameters, and the operation's return value. An object's **interface** is the set of operations it provides, as defined by the signatures of the operations. An object's type is defined by its interface. An object's implementation is defined by its class. Thus, Meyer refers to a class as an implementation of an **abstract data type** [Meyer 1997].

3.1.2 Objects and Classes

An **object** (also referred to as an object instance) is a single "thing"; for example, John's car or Mary's account. A **class** (also referred to as an object class) is a collection of objects with the same characteristics; for example, account, employee, car, customer. Figure 3.1 depicts a class Customer and two objects, a Customer and

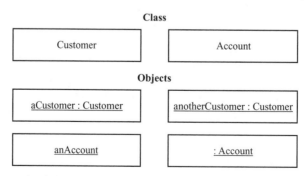

Figure 3.1 *Example of classes and objects*

another Customer, which are instances of the class Customer. The objects an Account and : Account are instances of the class Account.

An *attribute* is a data value held by an object in a class. Each object has a specific value of an attribute. Figure 3.2 shows a class with attributes. The class Account has two attributes, namely account Number and balance. Two objects of the Account class are shown, namely an Account and another Account. Each account has specific values of the attributes. For example, the account Number of the object an Account is 1234 and the account Number of the object another Account is 5678. The balance of the former object is $525.36 and the balance of the latter is $1,897.44. An attribute name is unique within a class, although different classes may have the same attribute name; for example, both the Customer and Employee classes have attributes name and address.

An **operation** is the specification of a function performed by an object. An object has one or more operations. The operations manipulate the values of the attributes maintained by the object. Operations may have input and output parameters. All objects in the same class have the same operations. For example, the class Account has the operations read Balance, credit, debit, open, and close. Figure 3.3 shows the Account class with its operations.

An object is an instance of a class. Whereas in a language such as Pascal, a record type can be defined from which actual record instances can be created

Figure 3.2 *Example of class with attributes*

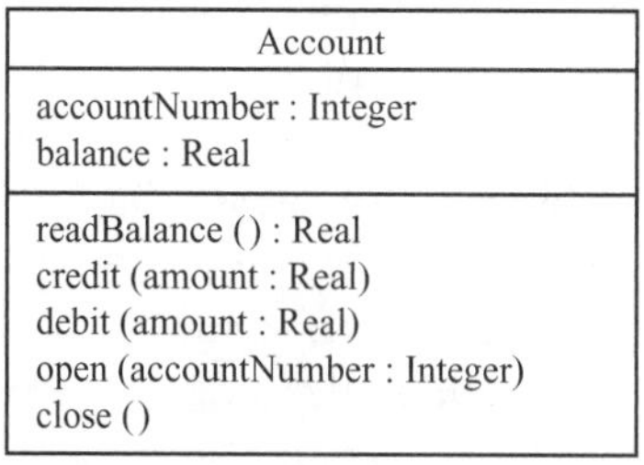

Account
accountNumber : Integer balance : Real
readBalance ( ) : Real credit (amount : Real) debit (amount : Real) open (accountNumber : Integer) close ( )

Figure 3.3   *Class with attributes and operations*

(instantiated), a class-based language extends the concept to support object types consisting of encapsulated data and operations on that data. Individual objects, which are instances of the class, are instantiated as required at execution time.

Each object has a unique identity, which is the characteristic that distinguishes it from other objects. In some cases, this may be an attribute (e.g., an account number or a customer name), but it does not need to be. Consider two blue balls—they are identical in every respect; however, they have different identities.

3.2   Information Hiding

Information hiding is a fundamental software design concept relevant to the design of all software systems. Early systems were frequently error-prone and difficult to modify because they made widespread use of global data. Parnas [1972, 1979] showed that by using information hiding, software systems could be designed to be substantially more modifiable by greatly reducing or—ideally—eliminating global data. Parnas advocated information hiding as a criterion for decomposing a software system into modules. Each information hiding module should hide a design decision that is considered likely to change. Each changeable decision is called the secret of the module. By using this approach, the goal of **design for change** could be achieved.

3.2.1   Information Hiding in Object-Oriented Design

Information hiding is a basic concept of object-oriented design. Information hiding is used in designing the object, in particular when deciding what information should be visible and what information should be hidden. Those aspects of an object that need not be visible to other objects are hidden. Hence, if the internals of the object change, only this object is impacted. The term **encapsulation** is also used to describe hiding information by an object.

With information hiding, the information that could potentially change is encapsulated (i.e., hidden) inside an object. External access to the information can only be made indirectly by invoking operations—access procedures or functions—that are also part of the object. Only these operations can access the information directly. Thus the hidden information and the operations that access it are bound together to form an **information hiding object**. The specification of the operations (i.e., the name and the parameters of the operations) is called the interface of the object. The object's interface is also referred to as the abstract interface, virtual interface, or external interface of the object. The interface represents the visible part of the object, that is, the part that is revealed to users of the object. Other objects access the hidden information indirectly by calling the operations provided by the object.

Two examples of applying information hiding in software design are given next and compared with the functional approach, which does not use information hiding. The first example is information hiding applied to the design of internal data structures, and the second is information hiding applied to the design of interfaces to I/O devices. This is followed by some guidelines on designing objects.

3.2.2 Information Hiding Applied to Internal Data Structures

A potential problem in application software development is that an important data structure, one that is accessed by several objects, might need to be changed. Without information hiding, any change to the data structure is likely to require changes to all the objects that access the data structure. Information hiding can be used to hide the design decision concerning the data structure, its internal linkage, and the details of the operations that manipulate it. The information hiding solution is to encapsulate the data structure in an object. The data structure is only accessed directly by the operations provided by the object.

Other objects may only indirectly access the encapsulated data structure by calling the operations of the object. Thus if the data structure changes, the only object impacted is the one containing the data structure. The external interface supported by the object does not change; hence, the objects that indirectly access the data structure are not impacted by the change. This form of information hiding is called **data abstraction**.

To illustrate the benefits of information hiding in data structure design, consider the functional and information hiding solutions to the following problem. A stack is accessed by several modules; the modules are procedures or functions in the functional solution and objects in the information hiding solution. In the functional solution, the stack is a global data structure. With this approach, each module accesses the stack directly, so each module needs to know the representation of the table (array or linked list) in order to manipulate it (Figure 3.4).

The information hiding solution is to hide the representation of the stack from the objects needing to access it. An information hiding object—the stack object—is designed as follows (see Figure 3.5):

- **A set of operations is defined to manipulate the data structure.** In the case of the stack, typical operations are push, pop, full, and empty.

- **The data structure is defined.** In the case of the stack, for example, a one-dimensional array is defined. A variable is defined to reference the top of the stack; and another variable has the value of the size of the array.

- **Other objects are not permitted to access the data structure directly.** They can only access the data structure indirectly by calling the object's operations.

Now assume a change is made to the design of the stack from an array to a linked list. Consider its impact on the functional and information hiding solutions. In both cases, the data structure for the stack has to change. However, in the functional solution, the stack is implemented as a global data structure, so every

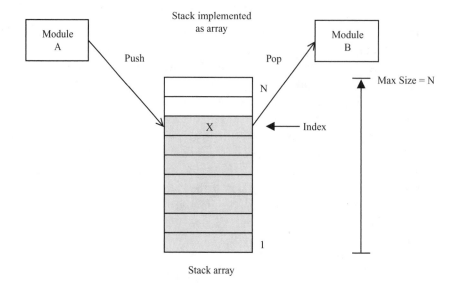

NB (*nota bene*, take careful note): This diagram does not use the UML notation.

Figure 3.4   *Example of global access to stack array*

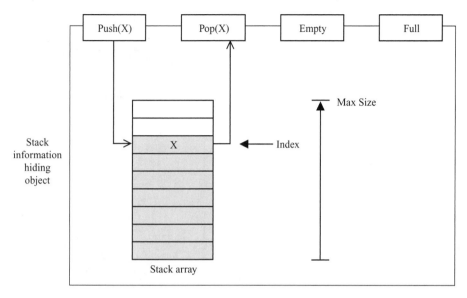

NB: This diagram does not use the UML notation.

Figure 3.5 *Example of stack information hiding object implemented as array*

module that accesses the stack also has to change because it operates directly on the data structure. Instead of manipulating array indexes, the module has to manipulate the pointers of the linked list (Figure 3.6).

In the information hiding solution, the internals of the information hiding object's operations have to change because they now access a linked list instead of an array (Figure 3.7). However, the external interface of the object, which is what is visible to the other objects, does not change. Thus the objects that use the stack are not impacted by the change; they continue to call the object's operations without even needing to be aware of the change.

The same concepts can be applied to designing a stack class, which is a template for creating stack objects. A stack class is defined containing the data structure to be used for the stack and the operations that manipulate it. Individual stack objects are instantiated as required by the application. Each stack object has its own identity. It also has its own local copy of the stack data structure, as well as a local copy of any other instance variables required by the stack's operations.

3.2.3 Information Hiding Applied to Interfacing to I/O Devices

Information hiding can be used to hide the design decision of how to interface to a specific I/O device. The solution is to provide a virtual interface to the device

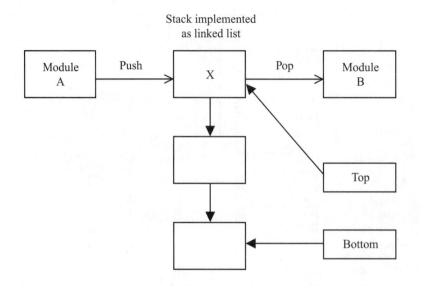

NB: This diagram does not use the UML notation.

Figure 3.6   *Example of global access to a stack linked list*

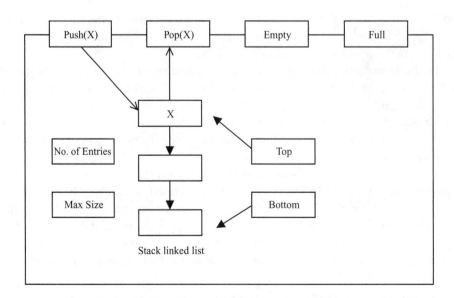

NB: This diagram does not use the UML notation.

Figure 3.7   *Example of stack information hiding object implemented as linked list*

that hides the device-specific details. If the designer decides to replace the device with a different one having the same overall functionality, the internals of the object will need to change. In particular, the internals of the object's operations need to change because they must deal with the precise details of how to interface to the real device. However, the virtual interface, represented by the specification of the operations, remains unchanged, as shown in Figure 3.8; hence, the objects that use the device interface will not need to change.

As an example of information hiding applied to I/O devices, consider an output display used on an automobile to display the average speed and fuel consumption. A virtual device can be designed that hides the details of how to format data for and how to interface to the mileage display.

The operations supported are

```
displayAverageSpeed (speed)
displayAverageMPG (fuelConsumption)
```

Details of how to position the data on the screen, special control characters to be used, and other device-specific information are hidden from the users of the object. If we replace this device by a different device with the same general functionality, the internals of the operations need to change, but the virtual interface remains unchanged. Thus, users of the object are not impacted by the change to the device.

3.2.4 Designing Information Hiding Objects

The main purpose of the previous two examples is to illustrate the benefits of information hiding. It is important to realize that encapsulation raises the level of abstraction by abstracting away the internal complexity of the object. This

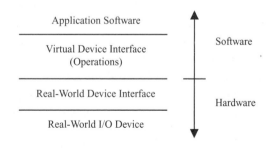

NB: This diagram does not use the UML notation.

Figure 3.8 *Information hiding applied to I/O device interface*

increases the size of granularity. It is only necessary to consider the interface, not the internal complexity; thus, in the stack example, we do not need to initially consider the internal details of the stack. In fact, we should start the design of an information hiding object by considering what interface the object should provide. For the design of the stack, for example, the important aspects of the interface are the push, pop, empty, and full operations. For a message queue, there should be operations to enqueue and dequeue a message; the actual data structure for the queue can be decided later. In applying information hiding to the design of the I/O device interface, the crucial issue is the specification of the operations that constitute the virtual device interface, and not the details of how to interface to the real-world device.

Thus, the design of an object (or class) is a two-step process, first to design the interface, which is the external view, and then to design the internals. The first step is part of the high-level design, and the second step is part of the detailed design. This is likely to be an iterative process because there are usually tradeoffs to consider in deciding what should be externally visible and what should not. It is generally not a good idea to reveal all the variables encapsulated in an object—for example, through get and set operations—because that means that little information is hidden.

3.3 Inheritance

Inheritance is a useful abstraction mechanism in analysis and design. Inheritance naturally models objects that are similar in some but not all respects, thus having some common properties but other unique properties that distinguish them. Inheritance is a classification mechanism that has been widely used in other fields. An example is the taxonomy of the animal kingdom, where animals are classified as mammals, fish, reptiles, and so on. Cats and dogs have common properties that are generalized into the properties of mammals. However, they also have unique properties: a dog barks and a cat mews.

Inheritance is a mechanism for sharing and reusing code between classes. A child class inherits the properties (encapsulated data and operations) of a parent class. It can then adapt the structure (i.e., encapsulated data) and behavior (i.e., operations) of its parent class. The parent class is referred to as a *superclass* or base class. The child class is referred to as a *subclass* or derived class. The adaptation of a parent class to form a child class is referred to as specialization. Child classes may be further specialized, allowing the creation of class hierarchies, also referred to as **generalization/specialization** hierarchies.

Class inheritance is a mechanism for extending an application's functionality by reusing the functionality specified in parent classes. Thus, a new class can be incrementally defined in terms of an existing class. A child class can adapt the encapsulated data (referred to as instance variables) and operations of its parent class. It adapts the encapsulated data by adding new instance variables. It adapts the operations by adding new operations or by redefining existing operations. It is also possible for a child class to suppress an operation of the parent; however, this is not recommended because the subclass no longer shares the interface of the superclass.

The concept of inheritance has been applied very effectively in object-oriented programming. Inheritance is used as a code-sharing and adaptation mechanism, where a new class is based on the definition of an existing class without having to manually copy the actual code. Used in this way, the biggest benefit is in detailed design and coding, where substantial gains can be obtained from code sharing [Meyer 1997]. The use of inheritance in design is described in more detail in Chapter 15.

3.4 Active and Passive Objects

An object may be *active* or *passive*. Whereas objects are often passive—they wait for a message to invoke an operation and never initiate any actions—some object-oriented methods and languages, such as Ada and Java, support active objects. An active object is an autonomous object that executes independently of other active objects.

Active objects are concurrent tasks [Wegner 1990; Booch, Rumbaugh, and Jacobson 1998; Douglass 1999b]. A **task** has its own thread of control (sometimes referred to as its own "life") and can initiate actions that impact other objects. Passive objects have operations that are invoked by active objects. **Passive objects** can invoke operations in other passive objects. A passive object has no thread of control; thus, passive objects are instances of passive classes. An operation of a passive object, once invoked by an active object (task), executes within the thread of control of the active object.

In many versions of object-oriented design and programming, objects conceptually communicate by means of messages. For each kind of message sent to an object, there is an operation to process the message. The name of the message corresponds to the name of the operation, and the parameters of the message correspond to the parameters of the operation. In many object-oriented languages, this form of message-passing is very restrictive, being synchronous (tightly coupled), and actually corresponds to a procedure call. With this approach, objects are passive and always inactive when a message is received. On the other hand, an active object can be busy when a message arrives. It accepts the message when it has completed processing the previous one.

In Java, it is possible for an object to encapsulate a thread but also to have operations (methods in Java) that may be invoked by other threads. These operations do not necessarily need to be synchronized with the internal thread. In this case, the object has both active and passive characteristics. In this book, however, we will preserve a distinction between active and passive objects. Thus, an object is defined to be active or passive, but not both.

3.5 Concurrent Processing

A **task** represents the execution of a sequential program or a sequential component in a concurrent program. Each task deals with one sequential thread of execution; thus, no concurrency is allowed within a task. However, overall system concurrency is obtained by having multiple tasks executing in parallel. The tasks often execute asynchronously (i.e., at different speeds) and are relatively independent of each other for significant periods of time. From time to time, the tasks need to communicate and synchronize their operations with each other.

The body of knowledge on cooperating concurrent tasks has grown substantially since Dijkstra's seminal work [1968]. Among the significant early contributions were Brinch Hansen 1973, who developed an operating system based on concurrent tasks that incorporated semaphores and message communication, and Hoare 1974, who developed the monitor concept that applies information hiding to task synchronization. Several algorithms were developed for concurrent task communication and synchronization, such as the multiple readers and writers algorithm, the sleeping barber algorithm, the dining philosophers algorithm, and the banker's algorithm for deadlock prevention. Many of the original papers are out of print. Because concurrent processing is such a fundamental concept, it has been described in textbooks for over three decades. The best source of information on concurrency is books on operating systems—e.g., Silberschatz and Galvin [1998], Tanenbaum [1992]—or books on concurrent programming languages such as Java [Lea 1999] or Ada [Barnes 1995]. Two excellent recent references are Bacon [1997], which describes concurrent systems, both centralized and distributed, and Magee and Kramer [1999], which describes concurrent programming with Java.

3.5.1 Advantages of Concurrent Tasking

The advantages of using concurrent tasking in software design are

- Concurrent tasking is a natural model for many real-world applications because it reflects the natural parallelism that exists in the problem domain, where several activities are often happening simultaneously. For these applications, the target system is best designed with concurrency explicitly defined at the outset. A design emphasizing concurrent tasks is clearer and easier to understand because it is a more realistic model of the problem domain than a sequential program.

- Structuring a concurrent system into tasks results in a separation of concerns about *what* each task does from *when* it does it. This usually makes the system easier to understand, manage, and construct.

- A system structured into concurrent tasks can result in an overall reduction in system execution time. On a single processor, concurrent tasking results in improved performance by allowing I/O operations to be executed in parallel with computational operations. With the use of multiple processors, improved performance is obtained by having different tasks actually execute in parallel on different processors.

- Structuring the system into concurrent tasks allows greater scheduling flexibility because time-critical tasks with hard deadlines can be given a higher priority than less critical tasks.

- Identifying the concurrent tasks early in the design can allow an early performance analysis to be made of the system. Many of these tools and techniques, (for example, Petri Net modeling and real-time scheduling) use concurrent tasks as a fundamental component in their analysis.

However, it should be pointed out that whereas concurrent tasking is recommended for many real-world applications, having too many tasks in a system can unnecessarily increase complexity and overhead because of the additional inter-task communication and synchronization. How to resolve these issues is described in Chapter 14 of this text.

3.5.2 Heavyweight and Lightweight Processes

The term "process" is used in operating systems as a unit of resource allocation for the processor (CPU) and memory. The traditional operating system process has a single thread of control and thus has no internal concurrency. Some modern operating systems allow a process, referred to as a **heavyweight process**, to have multiple **threads** of control, thereby allowing internal concurrency within a process. The heavyweight process has its own memory. Each thread of control, also referred to as a **lightweight process,** shares the same memory with the heavyweight process. Thus the multiple threads of a heavyweight process can access shared data in the process's memory, although this access must be synchronized.

The terms "heavyweight" and "lightweight" refer to the context switching overhead. When the operating system switches from one heavyweight process to another, the context switching overhead is relatively high, requiring CPU and memory allocation. With the lightweight process, context switching overhead is low, involving only CPU allocation.

The terminology varies considerably in different operating systems, although the most common is to refer to the heavyweight process as a process (or task) and the lightweight process as a thread. For example, the Java virtual machine usually executes as an operating system process supporting multiple threads of control [Magee and Kramer 1999]. However, some operating systems do not recognize that a heavyweight process actually has internal threads and only schedule the heavyweight process to the CPU. The process then has to do its own internal thread scheduling.

Bacon uses the term **process** to refer to a dynamic entity that executes on a processor and has its own thread of control, whether it is a single threaded heavyweight process or a thread within a heavyweight process [Bacon 1997]. This book uses instead the term **task** to refer to such a dynamic entity. The task corresponds to a thread within a heavyweight process (i.e., one that executes within a process) or to a single threaded heavyweight process. Many of the issues of concerning task interaction apply whether the threads are in the same heavyweight process or in different heavyweight processes. Task scheduling and context switching are described in more detail in the next chapter.

3.6 Cooperation between Concurrent Tasks

In the design of concurrent systems, several problems need to be considered that do not arise when designing sequential systems. In most concurrent applications, it is necessary for concurrent tasks to cooperate with each other in order to perform the services required by the application. The following three problems commonly arise when tasks cooperate with each other:

1. **The mutual exclusion problem.** This occurs when tasks need to have exclusive access to a resource, such as shared data or a physical device. A variation on this problem, where the mutual exclusion constraint can be relaxed in certain situations, is the multiple readers and writers problem.

2. **Task synchronization problem.** Two tasks need to synchronize their operations with each other.

3. **The producer/consumer problem.** This occurs when tasks need to communicate with each other in order to pass data from one task to another. Communication between tasks is often referred to as inter-process communication (IPC).

These problems and their solutions are described next.

3.6.1 Mutual Exclusion Problem

Mutual exclusion arises when it is necessary for a shared resource to be accessed by only one task at a time. With concurrent systems, more than one task might simultaneously wish to access the same resource. Consider the following situations:

- If two or more tasks are allowed to write to a printer simultaneously, output from the tasks will be randomly interleaved and a garbled report will be produced.

- If two or more tasks are allowed to write to a data repository simultaneously, inconsistent and/or incorrect data will be written to the data repository.

To solve this problem, it is necessary to provide a synchronization mechanism to ensure that access to a critical resource by concurrent tasks is mutually exclusive. A task must first acquire the resource, that is, get permission to access the resource, use the resource, and then release the resource. When task A releases the resource, another task B may now acquire the resource. If the resource is in use by A when task B wishes to acquire it, B must wait until A releases the resource.

The classical solution to the mutual exclusion problem was first proposed by Dijkstra [1968], using binary semaphores. A binary semaphore is a Boolean variable that is accessed only by means of two atomic (i.e., indivisible) operations, **acquire (semaphore)** and **release (semaphore)**. Dijkstra originally called these the P (for acquire) and V (for release) operations.

The indivisible acquire (semaphore) operation is executed by a task when it wishes to acquire a resource. The semaphore is initially set to 1, meaning that the resource is free. As a result of executing the acquire operation, the semaphore is decremented by 1 to 0 and the task is allocated the resource. If the semaphore is already set to 0 when the acquire operation is executed by task A, this means that another task, say B, already has the resource. In this case, task A is suspended until task B releases the resource by executing a release (semaphore) operation. As a result, task A is allocated the resource. It should be noted that the task executing the acquire operation is suspended only if the resource has already been acquired by another task. The code executed by a task while it has access to the mutually exclusive resource is referred to as the **critical section** or **critical region**.

3.6.2 Example of Mutual Exclusion

An example of mutual exclusion is a shared sensor data repository, which contains the current values of several sensors. Some tasks read from the data repository in order to process or display the sensor values, and other tasks poll the external environment and update the data repository with the latest values of the sensors. To ensure mutual exclusion in the sensor data repository example, a sensor Data Repository Semaphore is used. Each task must execute an *acquire* operation before it starts accessing the data repository and execute a *release* operation after it has finished accessing the data repository. The Pseudocode for acquiring the sensor Data Repository Semaphore to enter the critical section and releasing the semaphore is as follows:

```
acquire (sensorDataRepositorySemaphore)
Access sensor data repository [This is the critical section.]
release (sensorDataRepositorySemaphore)
```

The solution assumes that during initialization, the initial values of the sensors are stored before any reading takes place.

In some concurrent applications, it might be too restrictive to only allow mutually exclusive access to a shared resource. Thus, in the sensor data repository example just described, for a writer task to have mutually exclusive access to the data repository is essential. However, it is permissible to have more than one reader task concurrently reading from the data repository, providing there is no writer task writing to the data repository at the same time. This is referred to as the multiple readers and writers problem [Bacon 1997; Silberschatz and Galvin 1998; Tanenbaum 1992]. This problem may also be solved by using semaphores and is described further in Chapter 16.

3.6.3 Task Synchronization Problem

Event synchronization is used when two tasks need to synchronize their operations without communicating data between the tasks. The source task executes a *signal (event)* operation, which signals that an event has taken place. Event synchronization is asynchronous. In the UML, the two tasks are depicted as active objects with an asynchronous event signal sent from the sender task to the receiver task (Figure 3.9).

The destination task executes a *wait (event)* operation, which suspends the task until the source task has signaled the event. If the event has already been signaled, the destination task is not suspended.

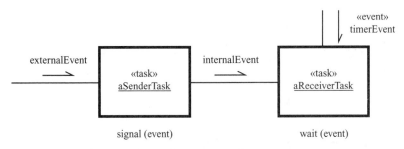

Figure 3.9 *Task synchronization with event signals*

3.6.4 Example of Task Synchronization

Consider an example of event synchronization from concurrent robot systems. Each robot system is designed as a concurrent task and controls a moving robot arm. A pick-and-place robot brings a part to the work location so that a drilling robot can drill four holes in the part. On completion of the drilling operation, the pick-and-place robot moves the part away.

Several synchronization problems need to be solved. First, there is a collision zone where the pick-and-place and drilling robot arms could potentially collide. Second, the pick-and-place robot must deposit the part before the drilling robot can start drilling the holes. Third, the drilling robot must finish drilling before the pick-and-place robot can remove the part. The solution is to use event synchronization, as described next.

The pick-and-place robot moves the part to the work location, moves out of the collision zone, and then signals the event `partReady`. This awakens the drilling robot, which moves to the work location and drills the holes. After completing the drilling operation, it moves out of the collision zone and then signals a second event, `partCompleted`, which the pick-and-place robot is waiting to receive. After being awakened, the pick-and-place robot removes the part. Each robot task executes a loop, because the robots repetitively perform their operations. The solution is as follows (Figure 3.10):

```
pick & Place Robot:

while workAvailable do
    Pick up part
    Move part to work location
    Release part
    Move to safe position
```

Figure 3.10   *Example of task synchronization with two event signals*

```
    signal (partReady)
    wait (partCompleted)
    Pick up part
    Remove from work location
    Place part
end while;

drilling Robot:

while workAvailable do
    wait (partReady)
    Move to work location
    Drill four holes
    Move to safe position
    signal (partCompleted)
end while;
```

Next, consider the case where a giver robot hands over a part to a receiver robot. Once again, there is the potential problem of the two robot arms colliding with each other. However, this time we cannot prevent both robots from being in the collision zone at the same time because, during the hand-over, there is a time when both robots are holding the same part.

The solution we adopt is to allow only one robot to move within the collision zone at any given time. First, one robot moves into the collision zone. It then signals to the other robot that it has reached the exchange position. The second robot now moves into the collision zone. An event signal collision Zone Safe is used for this purpose. The giver robot signals a second event, part Ready, to notify the receiver robot that it is ready for the hand-over. Two more event signals are used during the hand-over, part Grasped and part Released. The part hand-over has to be as precise as a baton hand-over in a relay race. The solution is illustrated in Figure 3.11 and described as follows:

```
Giver robot (robot A):

while workAvailable do
    Pick up Part
    Move to edge of collision zone
```

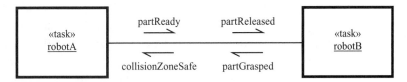

Figure 3.11   *Example of task synchronization with four event signals*

```
   wait (collisionZoneSafe)
   Move to exchange position
   signal (partReady)
   wait (partGrasped)
   Open Gripper to release part
   signal (partReleased)
   wait (collisionZoneSafe)
   Leave collision zone
end while;

Receiver robot (robot B):

while workAvailable do
   Move to exchange position
   signal (collisionZoneSafe)
   wait (partReady)
   Close Gripper to grasp part
   signal (partGrasped)
   wait (partReleased)
   Leave collision zone
   signal (collisionZoneSafe)
   Place part
end while;
```

Task synchronization may also be achieved by means of message communication as described next.

3.6.5   Producer/Consumer Problem

A common problem in concurrent systems is that of producer and consumer tasks. The producer task produces information, which is then consumed by the consumer task. For this to happen, data needs to be passed from the producer to the consumer. In a sequential program, a calling operation (procedure) also passes data to a called operation. However, control passes from the calling operation to the called operation at the same time as the data.

In a concurrent system, each task has its own thread of control and the tasks execute asynchronously. It is therefore necessary for the tasks to synchronize their operations when they wish to exchange data. Thus, the producer must produce the data before the consumer can consume it. If the consumer is ready to receive the data but the producer has not yet produced it, then the consumer must wait for the producer. If the producer has produced the data before the consumer is ready to receive it, then either the producer has to be held up or the data needs to be buffered for the consumer, thereby allowing the producer to continue.

A common solution to this problem is to use message communication between the producer and consumer tasks. Message communication between tasks serves two purposes:

1. Transfer of data from a producer (source) task to a consumer (destination) task.

2. Synchronization between producer and consumer. If no message is available, the consumer has to wait for the message to arrive from the producer. In some cases, the producer waits for a reply from the consumer.

Message communication between tasks may be loosely coupled or tightly coupled. The tasks may reside on the same node or be distributed over several nodes in a distributed application.

With loosely coupled message communication, the producer sends a message to the consumer and continues without waiting for a response. Loosely coupled message communication is also referred to as asynchronous message communication.

With tightly coupled message communication, the producer sends a message to the consumer and then immediately waits for a response. Tightly coupled message communication is also referred to as synchronous message communication and in Ada as a rendezvous.

3.6.6   Loosely Coupled Message Communication

With **loosely coupled message communication**, also referred to as **asynchronous message communication**, the producer sends a message to the consumer and either does not need a response or has other functions to perform before receiving a response. Thus the producer sends a message and continues without waiting for a response. The consumer receives the message. As the producer and consumer tasks proceed at different speeds, a first-in-first-out (FIFO) message queue can build up between producer and consumer. If there is no message available when the consumer requests one, the consumer is suspended.

An example of **loosely coupled message communication** is given in Figure 3.12. The producer task sends messages to the consumer task. A FIFO message

Figure 3.12 *Loosely coupled (asynchronous) message communication*

queue can exist between the producer and the consumer. The message is labeled with the stereotype «asynchronous message». Parameters of the message are depicted in parentheses, that is, `message (parameter1, parameter2)`.

3.6.7 Tightly Coupled Message Communication with Reply

In the case of **tightly coupled message communication with reply**, also referred to as **synchronous message communication with reply,** the producer sends a message to the consumer and then waits for a reply. When the message arrives, the consumer accepts the message, processes it, generates a reply, and then sends the reply. The producer and consumer then both continue. The consumer is suspended if no message is available. For a given producer/consumer pair, no message queue develops between the producer and the consumer.

An example of **tightly coupled message communication with reply** is given in Figure 3.13. The producer sends a message to the consumer. After receiving the message, the consumer sends a reply to the producer. The message is labeled with the stereotype «synchronous message with reply». Parameters of the message are depicted in parentheses, that is, `message (parameter1, parameter2)`. The reply is actually depicted by a separate simple message with the arrowhead pointing in the reverse direction of the original message.

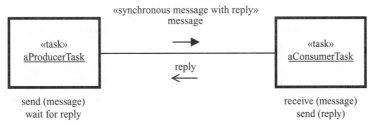

Figure 3.13 *Tightly coupled (synchronous) message communication with reply*

3.6.8   Tightly Coupled Message Communication without Reply

In the case of **tightly coupled message communication without reply**, also referred to as **synchronous message communication without reply,** the producer sends a message to the consumer and then waits for acceptance of the message by the consumer. When the message arrives, the consumer accepts the message, thereby releasing the producer. The producer and consumer then both continue. The consumer is suspended if no message is available. For a given producer/consumer pair, no message queue develops between the producer and the consumer.

An example of **tightly coupled message communication without reply** is shown in Figure 3.14. The producer sends a message to the consumer and then waits for its acceptance. The message is labeled with the stereotype «synchronous message without reply». Parameters of the message are depicted in parentheses, that is, message (parameter1, parameter2).

3.6.9   Example of Producer/Consumer Message Communication

As an example of **tightly coupled message communication with reply**, consider the case where a vision system has to inform a robot system of the type of part coming down a conveyor, for example, whether the car body frame is a sedan or station wagon. The robot has a different welding program for each car body type. In addition, the vision system has to send the robot information about the location and orientation of a part on a conveyor. Usually this information is sent as an offset (i.e., relative position) from a point known to both systems. The vision system sends the robot a tightly coupled message, the car ID Message, which contains the car Model ID and car Body Offset, and then waits for a reply from the robot. The robot indicates that it has completed the welding operation by sending the done Reply.

In addition, the following event synchronization is needed. Initially, a sensor signals the external event car Arrived to notify the vision system. Finally, the vision system signals the actuator move Car, which results in the taking away of the car by the conveyor. The solution is illustrated in Figure 3.15 and described next.

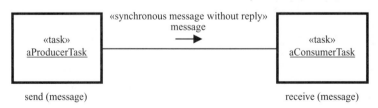

Figure 3.14   *Tightly coupled (synchronous) message communication without reply*

Figure 3.15 *Example of message communication*

```
Vision System:

while workAvailable do
    wait (carArrived)
    Take image of car body
    Identify the model of car
    Determine location and orientation of car body
    send carIDMessage (carModelID, carBodyOffset) to Robot System
    wait for reply
    signal (moveCar)
end while;

Robot System:

while workAvailable do
    wait for message from Vision System
    receive carIDMessage (carModelID, carBodyOffset)
    Select welding program for carModelID
    Execute welding program using carBodyOffset for car position
    send (doneReply) to Vision System
end while;
```

3.7 Information Hiding Applied to Access Synchronization

The solution to the mutual exclusion described previously is error-prone. It is possible for a coding error to be made in one of the tasks accessing the shared data, which would then lead to serious synchronization errors at execution time. Consider, for example, the mutual exclusion problem described in Section 3.6.2. If the acquire and release operations were reversed by mistake, the Pseudocode would be

```
release (sensorDataRepositorySemaphore)
Access sensor data repository [should be critical section]
acquire (sensorDataRepositorySemaphore)
```

As a result of this error, the task enters the critical section without first acquiring the semaphore. Hence, it is possible to have two tasks executing in the critical section, thereby violating the mutual exclusion principle. Instead, the following coding error might be made:

```
acquire (sensorDataRepositorySemaphore)
Access sensor data repository [should be critical section]
acquire (sensorDataRepositorySemaphore)
```

In this case, a task enters its critical section for the first time but is then not able to leave because it is trying to acquire a semaphore it already possesses. Furthermore, it prevents any other task from entering its critical section, thus provoking a **deadlock**, where no task is able to proceed.

In these examples, synchronization is a global problem that every task has to be concerned about, which makes these solutions error-prone. By using information hiding, the global synchronization problem can be reduced to a local synchronization problem, making the solution less error-prone. With this approach, only one information hiding object need be concerned about synchronization. An information hiding object that hides details of synchronizing concurrent access to data is also referred to as a **monitor** [Hoare 1974], as described in Section 3.8.

3.7.1 Information Hiding Classes and Objects

Information hiding classes are used for encapsulating data repositories, that is, hiding their contents and internal representation. A task accesses the data repository indirectly via operations (i.e., access procedures and/or functions) that manipulate the contents of the data repository. Where an information hiding class is accessed by more than one task, the operations must synchronize the access to the data.

An **information hiding object** is an instance of an information hiding class and is depicted on a collaboration diagram. An example of an information hiding object is shown in Figure 3.16 , where it is accessed by two tasks. A `writer Task` writes to the object, and a `reader Task` reads from the object. In both cases, the UML synchronous message communication notation is used, originating from the task to the object. However, it is important to note that, in this context, the mes-

Figure 3.16 *Task communication with information hiding object*

sage actually represents an operation call. The object provides two operations, read and write. The writer Task calls the write operation and the reader Task calls the read operation. In the case of invoking a read operation, the data returned to the calling task is depicted as an output parameter.

3.8 Monitors

A monitor combines the concepts of information hiding and synchronization. A **monitor** is a data object that encapsulates data and has operations that are executed mutually exclusively. The critical section of each task is replaced by a call to a monitor operation. An implicit semaphore is associated with each monitor, referred to as the *monitor lock*. Thus, only one task is active in a monitor at any one time. A call to a monitor operation results in the calling task acquiring the associated semaphore. However, if the lock is already taken, the task blocks until the monitor lock is acquired. An exit from the monitor operation results in a release of the semaphore, i.e., the monitor lock is released so that it can be acquired by a different task. The mutually exclusive operations of a monitor are also referred to as *guarded* operations or *synchronized* methods in Java.

3.8.1 Example of Monitor

An example of a monitor is given next. Consider the sensor data repository described above. The monitor solution is to encapsulate the data repository in an Analog Sensor Repository information hiding object, which supports read and update operations. These operations are called by any task wishing to access the data repository. The details of how to synchronize access to the data repository are hidden from the calling tasks.

The monitor provides for mutually exclusive access to an analog sensor repository. There are two mutually exclusive operations to read from and to update the contents of the analog repository. The two operations are

```
readAnalogSensor (in sensorID, out sensorValue, out upperLimit, out
lowerLimit, out alarmCondition)
```

This operation is called by reader tasks that wish to read from the sensor data repository. Given the sensor ID, this operation returns the current sensor value, upper limit, lower limit, and alarm condition to users who might wish to manipulate or display the data. The range between the lower limit and upper limit is the normal range within which the sensor value can vary without causing an alarm. If the value of the sensor is below the lower limit or above the upper limit, the alarm condition is equal to low or high, respectively.

```
updateAnalogSensor (in sensorID, in sensorValue)
```

This operation is called by writer tasks that wish to write to the sensor data repository. It is used to update the value of the sensor in the data repository with the latest reading obtained by monitoring the external environment. It checks whether the value of the sensor is below the lower limit or above the upper limit, and if so, sets the value of the alarm to low or high, respectively. If the sensor value is within the normal range, the alarm is set to normal.

The Pseudocode for the mutually exclusive operations is as follows:

```
monitor AnalogSensorRepository

readAnalogSensor (in sensorID, out sensorValue, out upperLimit,
out lowerLimit, out alarmCondition)
    sensorValue := sensorDataRepository (sensorID, value);
    upperLimit := sensorDataRepository (sensorID, upLim);
    lowerLimit := sensorDataRepository (sensorID, loLim);
    alarmCondition := sensorDataRepository (sensorID, alarm);
end readAnalogSensor;

updateAnalogSensor (in sensorID, in sensorValue)

    sensorDataRepository (sensorID, value) := sensorValue;
    if sensorValue ≥ sensorDataRepository (sensorID, upLim)
          then sensorDataRepository (sensorID, alarm) := high;
    else if sensorValue ≤ sensorDataRepository (sensorID, loLim)
        then sensorDataRepository (sensorID, alarm) := low;
        else sensorDataRepository (sensorID, alarm) := normal;
    end if;
end updateAnalogSensor;
end AnalogSensorRepository;
```

3.8.2 Condition Synchronization

In addition to providing synchronized operations, monitors support *condition synchronization*. This allows a task executing the monitor's mutually exclusive operation to block, by executing a *wait* operation until a particular condition is true, for example, waiting for a buffer to become full or empty. When a task in a monitor blocks, it releases the monitor lock, allowing a different task to acquire the monitor lock. A task that blocks in a monitor is awakened by some other task executing a *signal* operation (referred to as *notify* in Java). For example, if a reader task needs to read an item from a buffer and the buffer is empty, it executes a wait operation. The reader remains blocked until a writer task places an item in the buffer and executes a signal operation.

If semaphore support is unavailable, mutually exclusive access to a resource may be provided by means of a monitor with condition synchronization, as described next. The Boolean variable busy is encapsulated by the monitor to represent the state of the resource. A task that wishes to acquire the resource calls the acquire operation. The task is suspended on the wait operation if the resource is busy. On exiting from the wait, the task will set busy equal to true, thereby taking possession of the resource. When the task finishes with the resource, it calls the release operation, which sets busy to false and calls the signal operation to awaken a waiting task.

The following is the monitor design for mutually exclusive access to a resource:

```
monitor Semaphore

-- Declare Boolean variable called busy, initialized to false.
private busy : Boolean = false;
-- acquire is called to take possession of the resource
-- the calling task is suspended if the resource is busy
public acquire ()
    while busy = true do wait;
    busy := true;
    end acquire;

-- release is called to relinquish possession of the resource
-- if a task is waiting for the resource, it will be awakened
public release ()
    busy := false;
    signal;
end release;
end Semaphore;
```

Additional examples of monitors and condition synchronization are given in Chapter 16.

3.9 Design Patterns

A **design pattern** describes a recurring design problem to be solved, a solution to the problem, and the context in which that solution works [Buschmann et al. 1996, Gamma et al. 1995]. The description is in terms of communicating objects and classes customized to solve a general design problem in a particular context. A design pattern is a larger-grained form of reuse than a class, because it involves more than one class and the interconnection among objects from different classes. A design pattern is sometimes referred to as a micro-architecture.

A design pattern typically describes

- Pattern name.
- Alias.
- Context. When the pattern should be used.
- Problem. Brief description of the problem.
- Summary of solution.
- Strengths of solution.
- Weaknesses of solution.
- Applicability. When you can use the pattern.
- Related patterns.

The producer/consumer problems described in Section 3.6 are examples of recurring design problems that can be documented as design patterns. For example, the loosely coupled message communication design pattern is documented as follows:

- **Pattern name:** Loosely coupled message communication.
- **Alias:** Asynchronous Communication.
- **Context:** Concurrent systems.
- **Problem:** Concurrent application with concurrent tasks that need to communicate with each other. Producer does not need to wait for consumer. Producer does not need reply.
- **Summary of solution:** Use message queue between producer task and consumer task. Producer sends message to Consumer and continues. Consumer receives message. Messages may be queued FIFO (first-in-first-out) if Consumer is busy. Consumer is suspended if no message is available.
- **Strengths:** Consumer does not hold up Producer.
- **Weaknesses:** If Producer produces messages more quickly than Consumer can consume them, the message queue will eventually overflow.
- **Applicability:** Centralized and distributed environments: Real-time systems, client/server and distribution applications.
- **Related patterns:** Tightly coupled message communication with/without reply.

3.10   Software Architecture and Component-Based Systems

A software architecture [Shaw and Garlan 1996; Bass, Clements, and Kazman 1998] separates the overall structure of the system, in terms of components and their interconnections, from the internal details of the individual components. The emphasis on components and their interconnections is sometimes referred to as "programming-in-the-large," and detailed design of individual components is referred to as "programming-in-the-small."

3.10.1   Components and Connectors

To fully specify a **component**, it is necessary to define it in terms of the operations it *provides* and the operations it *requires* [Magee, Dulay, and Kramer 1994; Shaw and Garlan 1996]. This is in contrast to conventional object-oriented approaches, which describe an object only in terms of the operations it *provides*. However, if a preexisting component is to be integrated into a component-based system, it is just as important to understand—and to therefore explicitly represent—the operations the component *requires* as well as those it *provides*.

In addition to defining the components, a software architecture must define the connectors that join the components together. A **connector** encapsulates the interconnection protocol between two or more components. Several different kinds of message communication between tasks were described in Section 3.6, including loosely coupled and tightly coupled message communication. The interaction protocols for each of these types of communication could be encapsulated in a connector. Although logically the same, loosely coupled message communication between tasks on the same node could be handled by a different connector (e.g., a shared memory buffer) than is used for tasks on separate nodes, where the connector would involve sending messages over a network. Connectors for distributed applications are described in Chapter 13. The design of connectors using monitors and condition synchronization is described in Chapter 16.

3.10.2   Component-Based Systems

In component-based systems, an infrastructure is provided that is specifically intended to accommodate preexisting components. Previously developed components are integrated with other components. For this to be possible, components must conform to a particular software architecture standard.

Object broker approaches such as CORBA [Mowbray and Ruh 1997] are designed to allow communication between objects on heterogeneous platforms.

Server objects provide services that can be invoked from client objects by means of the Object Request Broker (ORB). The infrastructure to support component-based systems is discussed in more detail in the next chapter.

3.11 Summary

This chapter has described key concepts in the software design of concurrent object-oriented systems as well as important concepts for developing the architecture of these systems. The object-oriented concepts introduced here form the basis of several of the forthcoming chapters. From an analysis perspective, the static structural aspects of classes are described in more detail in Chapter 8 on Static Modeling and Chapter 9 on Object and Class Structuring. The dynamic aspects of object interaction are described in Chapter 11 on Dynamic Modeling. From a design perspective, class design is described in Chapter 15. Concurrent tasking and inter-task communication aspects are addressed in more detail from two perspectives. A large-grained perspective is given in Chapter 13 on the software architecture of distributed applications. A smaller-grained perspective on task design is described in Chapters 14 and 16. Issues relating to synchronization of access to information hiding-classes are addressed in more detail in Chapter 16. Software architecture is described in more detail in chapters 12 and 13. Finally, the infrastructure for supporting concurrent and distributed applications is described in the next chapter, Chapter 4.

chapter

Concurrent and Distributed System Technology

This chapter provides an overview of the infrastructure, that is, the concurrent and distributed processing technology required for real-time and distributed applications. The infrastructure is provided by the operating system, communication networks, and middleware. The operating system support for multiprogramming and symmetric multiprocessing environments is described first, with further information provided on task scheduling and device input/output. The technology for distributed processing environments is then described. This includes an overview of client/server technology and the technology of the World Wide Web. The ISO and TCP/IP layered network protocols are introduced. Distributed operating system services are reviewed, followed by a description of middleware technology, including RPC, RMI, CORBA, and Java Beans. Finally, an overview of transaction processing systems is given.

4.1 Environments for Concurrent Processing

The main environments for concurrent systems can be broadly categorized as: multiprogramming environments, symmetric multiprocessing environments, and **distributed processing environments**.

4.1.1 Multiprogramming Environment

In the multiprogramming (also referred to as multitasking) environment, multiple tasks share one processor. Virtual concurrency is achieved by having the operating system control the allocation of the processor to the individual tasks, so that it appears as if each task has a dedicated processor. An example of a multiprogramming environment is illustrated in Figure 4.1. The figure shows a processor (CPU) board and a memory board (there may be more than one), where the code and data for each task are stored, as well as the operating system software. The boards are connected to each other via the system bus. In this example, the system interfaces to two I/O devices, a display device and a sensor input device, via the device interface boards. There is a device controller on each device interface board.

4.1.2 Symmetric Multiprocessing Environment

In the symmetric multiprocessing environment, there are two or more processors with shared memory. One physical address space is common to all the processors, and all the processes reside in the shared memory. In a multiprocessing environment, real concurrency is supported because the processors are executing concurrently. The tasks executing on different processors can communicate with each other via the shared memory. The multiprocessing environment is illustrated in Figure 4.2.

4.1.3 Distributed Processing Environment

A typical distributed processing environment is shown in Figure 4.3, where several nodes are interconnected by means of a communications network. Each node consists of a computer with its own local memory, typically consisting of a multi-

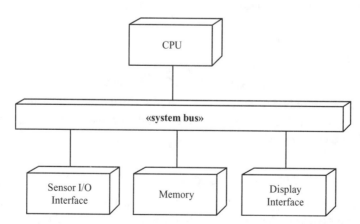

Figure 4.1 *Multiprogramming (single CPU) environment*

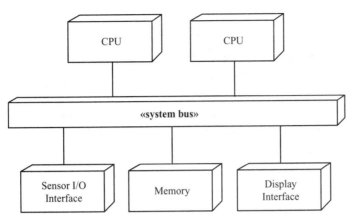

Figure 4.2 *Symmetric multiprocessing environment*

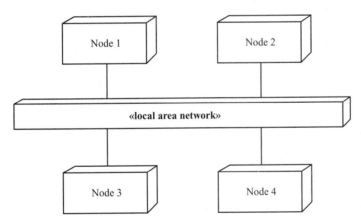

Figure 4.3 *Distributed processing environment*

programming system (as shown in Figure 4.1) or a shared memory multiprocessing system (as shown in Figure 4.2). In addition, each node needs to have a network interface board. An important characteristic of a distributed processing environment is that there is no shared memory between the nodes. Thus, a distributed application consists of concurrent processes, where processes are allocated to different nodes. Each process can consist of multiple threads that all execute on the same node. Because there is no shared memory, processes on different nodes must communicate with each other by means of messages sent over the network.

4.2   Runtime Support for Multiprogramming and Multiprocessing Environments

Runtime support for concurrent processing may be provided by

- **Kernel of an operating system.** This has the functionality to provide services for concurrent processing. In some modern operating systems, a micro-kernel provides minimal functionality to support concurrent processing, with most services provided by system level tasks.

- **Runtime support system** for a concurrent language.

- **Threads package.** Provides services for managing threads (lightweight processes) within heavyweight processes.

With sequential programming languages, such as C, C++, Pascal, and Fortran, there is no support for concurrent tasks. To develop a concurrent multitasked application using a sequential programming language, it is therefore necessary to use a kernel or threads package.

With concurrent programming languages, such as Ada and Java, the language supports constructs for task communication and synchronization. In this case, the language's runtime system handles task scheduling and provides the services and underlying mechanisms to support inter-task communication and synchronization.

4.2.1   Operating System Services

Following are typical services provided by an operating system kernel:

- **Priority preemption scheduling.** The highest priority task executes as soon as it is ready; for example, after being activated by an I/O interrupt.

- **Inter-task communication using messages.**

- **Mutual exclusion using semaphores**.

- **Event synchronization using signals.** Alternatively, messages may be used for synchronization purposes.

- **Interrupt handling and basic I/O services.**

- **Memory management.** This handles the mapping of each task's virtual memory onto physical memory.

Examples of widely used operating systems with kernels that support concurrent processing are several versions of Unix (including Linux, Solaris, and AIX), MS Windows 98, MS Windows NT, and MS Windows 2000.

With an operating system kernel, the *send message* and *receive message* operations for message communication and the *wait* and *signal* operations for event synchronization are direct calls to the kernel. Mutually exclusive access to critical sections is ensured by using the *acquire* and *release* semaphore operations, which are also provided by the kernel.

4.2.2 The POSIX Operating System Standard

POSIX (Portable Operating System Interface Standard) is an operating system software standard produced by the IEEE Computer Society, which is referred to as POSIX 1003. POSIX is based on the Unix operating system, the most widely used portable operating system. POSIX 1003.1 defines the basic operating system services. POSIX 1003.1b defines real-time extensions to the base operating system. POSIX 1003.1c defines parallel processing extensions.

POSIX 1003.1 defines a set of library procedures that every POSIX-compliant UNIX system must supply. Typical procedures are open, read, and fork. POSIX 1003.1b defines a standard interface in the form of real-time operating system services. It defines the system calls, parameter lists, and status information returned for each service.

The services provided by the POSIX 1003.1b standard are

1. Concurrent task management services

   The following three services provide a means for tasks to communicate with each other and to synchronize their operations.

   a. Binary semaphores

   b. Real-time signals

   c. Message passing

   The following service allows the highest priority task to execute as soon it is ready to use the CPU, hence assuring fast response to the most time-critical tasks.

   d. Priority preemption scheduling

2. Timing services

   The following service is important to provide accurate timer events and measurements in time-critical real-time systems:

   a. Real-time clocks and timers

3. Memory management services

   a. Task memory locking (see next section)

   b. Memory mapped files and shared memory

4. I/O services

   a. Synchronous I/O

   b. Asynchronous I/O. This service is important to allow overlap of CPU execution and I/O.

POSIX 1003.1c provides a parallel thread extension to the POSIX standard. Parallel threads allow a program to spawn several copies of a subroutine as separate parallel threads (tasks) of execution. A program in execution is a heavyweight process; that is, it has its own address space. A thread is a lightweight process.

In POSIX terminology, heavyweight processes are called "processes" and lightweight processes are called "threads." Thus, all threads of a given process execute in that process's address space.

4.2.3 Real-Time Operating Systems

Much of the operating system technology for concurrent systems is also required for real-time systems. Most real-time operating systems support a kernel or micro-kernel, as described previously. However, real-time systems have special needs, many of which relate to having predictable behavior. It is more useful to consider the requirements of a real-time operating system than to provide an extensive survey of available real-time operating systems, because the list changes on a regular basis. Thus, a real-time operating system must

- Support multitasking.
- Support priority preemption scheduling. This means each task needs to have its own priority.
- Provide task synchronization and communication mechanisms.
- Provide a memory-locking capability for tasks. In hard real-time systems, it is usually the case that all concurrent tasks are memory resident. This is to eliminate the uncertainty and variation in response time introduced by paging overhead. This memory-locking capability allows all time-critical tasks with hard deadlines to be locked in main memory so they are never paged out.
- Provide a mechanism for priority inheritance. When a task, task A, enters a critical section, its priority must be raised (see Chapter 17). Otherwise, task A is liable to get preempted by a higher priority task, which is then unable to enter its critical section because of task A; hence, the higher priority task blocks indefinitely.
- Have a predictable behavior (for example, for task context switching, task synchronization, and interrupt handling). Thus, there should be a predictable maximum response time under all anticipated system loads.

A recent study of Windows NT 4.0 determined that it does not meet the requirements of a real-time operating system [Timmerman 1998b] and that Windows CE 2.0 is most appropriate for small embedded applications [Timmerman 1998a]. However, many special-purpose real-time operating systems exist, including pSOS, VRTX, and iRMX. There are also a growing number of real-time operating systems that conform to the POSIX standard, including LynxOS, QNX, and HP-RT. In addition, some real-time operating systems have extended Windows NT to introduce real-time features; these include RTX, INTime, and Hyperkernel [Timmerman 1998b].

4.3   Task Scheduling

On a single processor (CPU) system, the operating system kernel has to schedule concurrent tasks for the CPU. The kernel maintains a Ready List of all tasks that are ready to use the CPU. Various task scheduling algorithms have been designed to provide alternative strategies for allocating tasks to the CPU, such as round-robin scheduling and priority preemption scheduling.

4.3.1   Task Scheduling Algorithms

The goal of the round-robin scheduling algorithm is to provide a fair allocation of resources. Tasks are queued on a first-in-first-out (FIFO) basis. The top task on the Ready List is allocated the CPU and given a fixed unit of time called a "time slice." If the time slice expires before the task has blocked (for example, to wait for I/O or wait for a message), the task is suspended by the kernel and placed on the end of the Ready List. The CPU is then allocated to the task at the top of the Ready List.

However, in real-time systems, round-robin scheduling is not satisfactory. A fair allocation of resources is not a prime concern, and tasks need to be assigned priorities according to the importance of the operations they are executing. Thus, time-critical tasks need to be certain of executing before their deadlines elapse. A more satisfactory scheduling algorithm for real-time systems is priority preemption scheduling. Each task is assigned a priority and the Ready List is ordered by priority. The task with the highest priority is assigned the CPU. The task will then execute until it blocks or is preempted by a higher priority task (which has just become unblocked). Tasks with the same priority are assigned the CPU on a FIFO basis. It should be noted that priority preemption scheduling does not use time slicing.

4.3.2   Task States

Consider the various states a task goes through from creation to termination, as depicted on the statechart in Figure 4.4. These states are maintained by a multi-tasking kernel that uses a priority preemption scheduling algorithm.

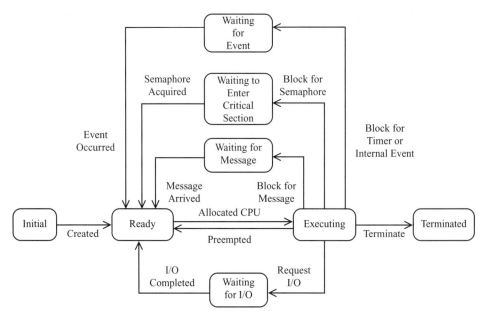

Figure 4.4 *Statechart for concurrent task*

When a task is first created, it is placed in Ready state, during which time it is on the Ready List. When it reaches the top of the Ready List, it is assigned the CPU, at which time it transitions into Executing state. The task might later be pre-empted by another task and re-enter Ready state, at which time the kernel places it on the Ready List in a position determined by its priority.

Alternatively, while in Executing state, the task may block, in which case it enters the appropriate blocked state. A task can block while waiting for I/O, while waiting for a message from another task, while waiting for a timer event or an event signaled by another task, or while waiting to enter a critical section. A blocked task re-enters Ready state when the reason for blocking is removed—in other words, when the I/O completes, the message arrives, the event occurs, or the task gets permission to enter its critical section.

4.3.3 Task Context Switching

When a task is suspended because of either blocking or preemption, its current context or processor state must be saved. This includes saving the contents of the hardware registers, the task's program counter (which points to the next instruction to be executed), and other relevant information. When a task is assigned the

CPU, its context must be restored so it can resume executing. This whole process is referred to as "context switching."

In a shared memory multiprocessing environment, an instance of the kernel usually executes on each processor. Each processor selects the task at the top of the Ready List to execute. Mutually exclusive access to the Ready List is achieved by means of a hardware semaphore typically implemented by means of a *Test and Set Lock* instruction. Thus, the same task can execute on different processors at different times. In some multiprocessing environments, threads of the same multithreaded process can concurrently execute on different processors. More information on task scheduling is given in books on operating systems, such as those by Nutt [1991], Silberschatz and Galvin [1998], and Tanenbaum [1992], and on distributed systems [Bacon 1997].

4.4   Operating System Input/Output Considerations

This section provides an overview of how input/output devices are handled by the operating system. There are two general mechanisms for performing input/output: interrupt driven I/O and polled I/O. The purpose of this section is to introduce the reader to how concurrent tasks interact with external I/O devices. More information on input/output handling in general is given in Bacon [1997] and Tanenbaum [1992], and specifically for real-time systems in Burns and Wellings [1996].

4.4.1   Device Controllers

I/O devices interface with the system via I/O device controllers, which reside on the I/O device interface boards shown in Figures 4.1 and 4.2. The CPU interfaces with the device controller rather than the I/O device itself. A controller has some registers that are used for communicating with the CPU. On some computers, there are separate instructions for accessing the controller's registers. With memory-mapped I/O, the controller's registers are part of the regular memory address space.

An example of a simple I/O device controller for an I/O device is given in Figure 4.5. There is an input buffer, which buffers a single input character, and an output buffer, which buffers a single output character. There are also control and status registers. After placing a character in the input buffer, the device controller sets a bit in the status register to indicate that the input buffer is full. For output, a different bit is used in the status register to indicate that the output buffer is full. After outputting a character, the device controller clears this bit. These status bits

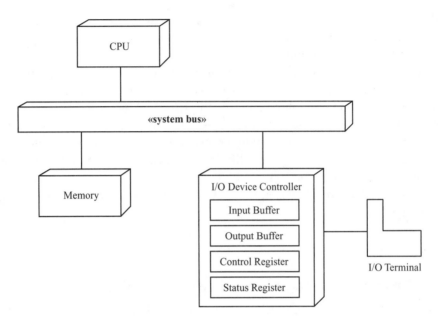

Figure 4.5 *Organization of I/O device controller*

are used to control the transfer of data between the processor and the device, as described in the next two sections.

The control register has a bit to indicate whether interrupts are enabled or disabled. If interrupts are enabled, the device controller generates interrupts as described below. If interrupts are disabled, the processor must poll the device by testing the status bits.

Device drivers execute on the CPU and are responsible for communicating with the I/O devices via the device controllers. Usually there is one device driver for each device type. The kernel supports the device drivers for standard I/O devices such as keyboards, displays, disks, and line printers. However, the device drivers for special-purpose I/O devices, frequently necessary in real-time systems, are usually developed as part of the application software.

4.4.2   Interrupt Handling

With interrupt-driven I/O, an interrupt is generated when input arrives or after an output operation completes. Many different approaches are available for interrupt-driven I/O. Two widely used approaches are interrupt-driven program-controlled I/O and interrupt-driven program-initiated I/O. In the former case, an interrupt is usually generated after each character has been read or written. In the latter case, a direct memory access (DMA) device is placed between the I/O device and main memory. The DMA device controls the transfer of a block of data between the I/O device and main memory. When the transfer has completed, the DMA device generates an interrupt.

Arrival of the interrupt results in the CPU suspending the executing task, saving its context, and invoking an interrupt handler (assuming the interrupt handler has a higher priority than the task) to process the interrupt. After the interrupt has been serviced, the interrupted task's context is restored so it can resume execution.

In the I/O subsystem of the kernel, interrupt handlers (also referred to as interrupt service routines) are low-level routines. The job of the interrupt handler is to determine which task should be activated when the interrupt occurs and then to activate it by using one of the task synchronization mechanisms supported by the kernel, such as event synchronization. With this approach, the device driver can be implemented as a concurrent task. The device driver has to know the specific details of how to interface to the device controller of the I/O device.

Consider the communication between the task and device controller via the controller's registers in the example described earlier. In the case of input, the input device driver sends the device controller a command to read the character and then suspends itself, waiting to be activated by the interrupt handler. The device controller reads the character from the external device, places it in the input buffer, sets the status register to input buffer full, and generates an interrupt. The interrupt handler receives the interrupt and awakens the device driver task. The device driver task then reads the character from the input buffer and sets the status register bit to indicate that the input buffer is free.

In the case of output, the output device driver writes the character to the output buffer, sets the output buffer status bit to busy, and sends the device controller a command to output the character. The device driver task then suspends itself. The device controller outputs the character from the output buffer to the external device, sets the status to output buffer free in the status register, and generates an interrupt. The interrupt handler receives the interrupt and awakens the device driver task, which can then output the next character.

In some systems, the arrival of the interrupt results in direct activation of the device driver task without the intervention of the low-level interrupt handler. In this case, the device driver task does its own interrupt handling.

4.4.3 Polled I/O

With polled I/O, interrupts are not used. Hence, the system must periodically sample an input device to determine whether any input has arrived and periodically sample an output device to determine whether an output operation has completed.

In the case of polled input, the device driver task must poll the input device—that is, it must periodically test the input buffer full flag to determine if there is new input. The device controller will set the input buffer full flag when new input is available. When it detects that the flag is set, the device driver reads the input character and then resets the flag to input buffer free.

On output, the device driver will initiate the output and then periodically test the output buffer free flag to determine when the output operation has completed. When it detects that the flag has been set, the device driver can start outputting the next character.

4.5   Client/Server and Distributed System Technology

Distributed applications execute on geographically distributed nodes supported by a local or wide area network. Typical applications are client/server applications, distributed real-time data collection applications, and distributed real-time control applications. The rest of the chapter provides an overview of the underlying technology that supports client/server and distributed applications.

4.5.1   Client/Server and Distributed System Configurations

A **client/server system** consists of two logical components, a **client** that requests services and a **server** that provides services. A **server** is a provider of services whereas the **client** is a consumer of services. A **client/server system** is a distributed application where the clients and server(s) are geographically distributed (Figure 4.6). The computer network that connects the clients and servers may be a Local Area Network (LAN) or a Wide Area Network (WAN). The client sends a request to the server over the network. The server processes the request and then returns the results to the client.

Clients and servers typically run on different computer systems. They may use different platforms, different operating systems, and different networks. The client is typically a desktop PC or workstation. It often supports a graphical user interface (GUI). The server typically has increased memory, disk storage, and CPU power and greater reliability. It provides the application services, in addition to data management and storage. The simplest client/server system has one server and many clients. A typical example of a client/server system with one server is an ATM application for a single bank, in which ATMs are distributed around the state that communicate with the bank's central server.

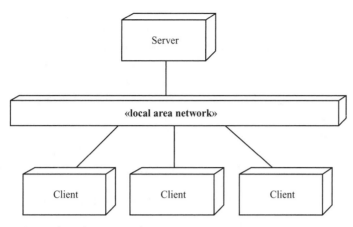

Figure 4.6 *Basic client/server configuration*

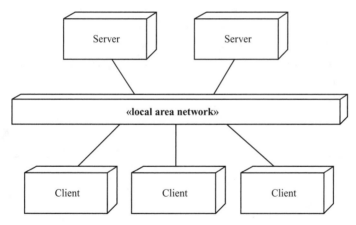

Figure 4.7 *Distributed processing configuration*

A more complex client/server system might have multiple servers. A client might communicate with several servers and servers might communicate with each other (see Figure 4.7). Following on from the ATM application in the previous paragraph, an example of a multi-server application is a federated banking application in which any ATM can communicate with any federation member's bank server. In multi-tier client/server systems, a server can itself be a client of another server.

In a distributed application, there is usually a significant amount of peer-to-peer communication using asynchronous message communication in addition to client/server communication. The distributed factory automation system described in Chapter 21 is an example of a distributed application.

Several hardware trends have encouraged the growth of client/server and distributed computing. These include the increase in CPU power in desktop machines, the reduction in cost of mass-produced chips, and the increase in memory size, both main memory and disk capacity. In addition, there are trends in network communications technology toward higher-speed networks coupled with the enormous growth of the Internet.

Software trends include the spread of relational databases providing distributed access to data, the proliferation of graphical user interfaces, the growth of multitasking software with Windows, and the emergence of middleware technology. Middleware technology makes it easier to interconnect distributed heterogeneous systems, as described in Section 4.8.

One possible client/server configuration is shown in Figure 4.8. On the client node is the client application, which uses a GUI interface. There is a standard operating system, such as Windows 98, and network communications software, such as TCP/IP. There is a layer of software called **middleware** that sits above the operating system and the network communications software. On the server node, there is the server application software, which makes use of the middleware services that reside on top of the operating system (for example, Unix or Windows

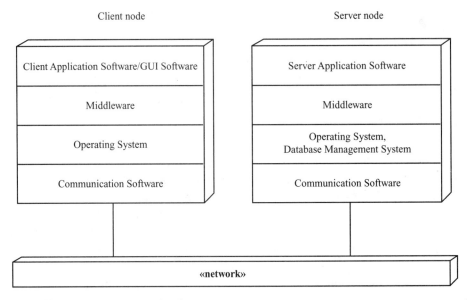

Figure 4.8 *Client/server technologies*

NT), and the network communications software. A file or database management system, usually relational, is used for long-term information storage.

4.5.2 Communication Network Protocols

The most widely referenced network protocol is the layered architecture of the International Standards Organization Open Systems Interconnection (ISO OSI) Reference Model, a standard for networked communication between open systems (see Figure 4.9). The ISO model is a seven-layer architecture, where each layer deals with one specific aspect of network communications and provides an interface, as a set of operations, to the layer above it [Tanenbaum 1996]. For each layer on the sender node, there is an equivalent layer on the receiver node.

The ISO model does not have a layer for Internet protocols. TCP/IP is the most widely used protocol on the Internet [Comer 1999]. It is organized into five conceptual layers, as shown in Figure 4.10. Layers 1 and 2, the physical and network interface layers, correspond to the ISO reference model. The physical layer corresponds to the basic network hardware. The network interface layer specifies how data is organized into frames and how frames are transmitted over the network. Layer 3, the Internet layer (IP) specifies the format of packets sent over the Internet and the mechanisms for forwarding packets through one or more routers

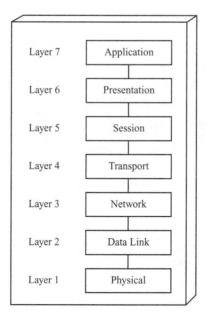

Figure 4.9 *Seven layers of International Standards Organization (ISO) reference model*

from a source to a destination (see Figure 4.11). The router node in Figure 4.11 is a gateway that interconnects a local area network to a wide area network.

The transport layer assembles packets into messages in the order they were originally sent. TCP is the Transmission Control Protocol and is the transport

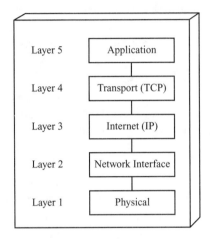

Figure 4.10 *Five layers of Internet (TCP/IP) reference model*

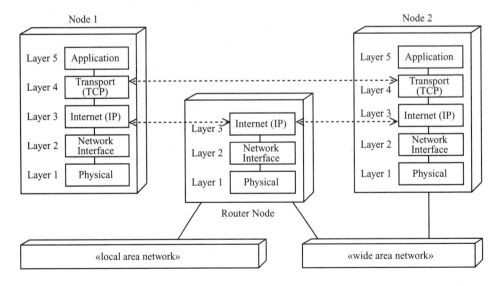

NB: The dashed arrows are shown for illustrative purposes only and do not conform to the UML notation.

Figure 4.11 *Internet communication with TCP/IP*

layer protocol for IP network protocol. The IP layer uses the inherently unreliable datagram service. TCP has to compensate for this and provide a reliable delivery service. It provides a virtual connection from an application on one node to an application on a remote node, hence providing what is termed an end-to-end protocol (see Figure 4.11). TCP uses IP to carry the messages. Layer 5 is the application level, which supports various network applications such as file transfer (FTP), electronic mail, and the World Wide Web.

4.6 World Wide Web Technology

The great popularity of the *World Wide Web (WWW)*, which was invented by Berners-Lee [Berners-Lee et al. 1994] at CERN, Geneva, has resulted in a huge growth in use of the Internet. A user's view into the WWW is through a web browser, such as Netscape or Internet Explorer, which executes on the user's node. World Wide Web pages are maintained on web servers. Each web page typically contains text, images, and links to other web pages.

A web page can be created by using a markup language such as the widely used *hypertext markup language (HTML)* and, more recently, the *extensible markup language (XML)*. Each web page is identified by means of a *universal resource locator (URL)*, which is used as part of any link to the page. Whenever the web page is selected by the user, the Web Browser gets the name of the Web Server from the URL and contacts the Web Server, requesting it to download the page (Figure 4.12). The browser then displays the downloaded page to the user. The Web Browser and Web Server communicate with each other using the *hypertext transfer*

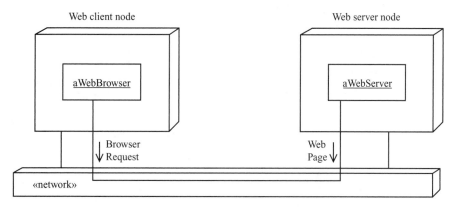

Figure 4.12 *Web Browser and Web Server in World Wide Web application*

protocol (HTTP). The Web Server receives web page requests concurrently from many web browser clients.

A *plug-in* is a software executable that is inserted into the browser and extends its capabilities, for example, for processing audio and video data sent by a server. A plug-in can be packaged with a browser or downloaded from a server.

4.6.1   Java and the World Wide Web

With the introduction of the World Wide Web and web browsers in the early nineties, the browser has become a widely used user interface for distributed applications. The growth in popularity of the WWW has also led to the growing popularity of the Java programming language, which is widely used in WWW applications for developing Java applets.

A *Java applet* is a Java program downloaded from a server to a client in intermediate code. The applet is used in conjunction with a web browser, which interprets the Java applet. The web browser is Java-enabled; that is, it is capable of receiving and interpreting Java applets. The Java interpreter at the client interprets the intermediate code and generates object code that executes at the client. The Java applet is thus an object downloaded from the web server, which executes at the client (see Figure 4.13). Java applets are frequently used to animate web pages at the client. The Java client object can also interact with a server object, which resides on the node from which the applet was downloaded. Communication between distributed Java objects is usually by means of **remote method invocation (RMI)**, as described in Section 4.8.

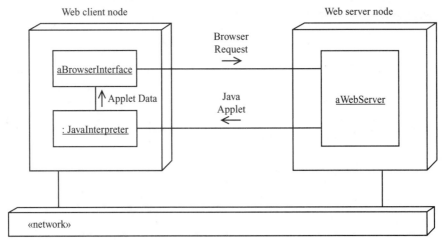

Figure 4.13   *Java applet downloaded from Web Server in World Wide Web application*

Java programs may also be run on the Web Server, where they are referred to as *servlets*. Servlets, like applets, are often tightly integrated with the Web Server environment to satisfy security and performance requirements. With a definite trend toward connecting many nontraditional devices to the Internet, such as telephones and automated teller machines, there is also an emerging trend of ultra-thin clients. With this approach, the client consists of the browser only. User interface presentation layer objects remain on the server, in addition to the business objects, running as servlets.

4.7 Distributed Operating System Services

A distributed system consists of computers connected by a communications medium such as a local area network [Bacon 1997]. This section describes some basic services provided by a distributed operating system, which is an operating system that provides network communication services in addition to the operating system services previously described.

4.7.1 Name Service

In a distributed environment, it is desirable to have location transparency; that is, a component that wishes to send a message to another component does not need to know where that component resides. For a component A to explicitly refer to another component B by its location is inflexible. If component B is moved, then component A will need to be updated. Thus, it is desirable to have a global naming service with location-independent names.

With a global naming service, a name server maintains the names of all global services. It is assumed that the location of the name server is well known. Servers register the symbolic name and location of the service with the name server. When a client wishes to access a service, it requests the service information from the name server.

An example of a name service is the Domain Name System (DNS) used on the Internet [Comer 1999]. Nodes on the Internet are given a unique ID called the IP address, as well as a unique symbolic name. The IP address is a 32-bit number that uniquely identifies the computer node on the Internet. It is depicted by using a dotted decimal notation, in which each 8-bit section is depicted as a decimal value, with a period to separate the sections—for example, 128.174.40.15. Each node is also assigned a symbolic name—for example, ise.gmu.edu. Internet name servers maintain name tables, which contain the mapping of symbolic names (referred to as domain names) to IP addresses. Because the number of Internet users is so large, the Internet name service is distributed over several name servers.

4.7.2   Binding between Clients and Servers

The term *binding* refers to the association between client and server. *Static binding* is the conventional binding between client and server and is done at compile time; in other words, all calls from client to server are hard coded.

Dynamic binding refers to binding being done at run time. It is more flexible than static binding but is less efficient. *Dynamic binding* needs a name server that maintains a directory of names and addresses of servers. The server object registers its service and location with the name server, in particular, some symbolic name by which it is known and a remote reference to allow it to be located. The client object queries the name server, passing to it the name of the object, and obtains a remote reference to the server object. The client uses the remote reference to access the server object.

4.7.3   Distributed Message Communication Services

Transparent message communication between distributed tasks can be handled by means of a distributed kernel of a distributed operating system. Figure 4.14 shows an example of task communication using a distributed kernel. There is one

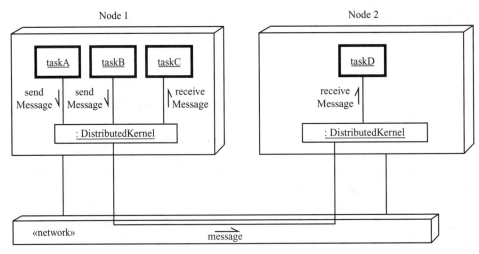

Figure 4.14   *Location transparency in distributed applications*

instance of the distributed kernel at each node. The name server maintains the master copy of the name table. In distributed applications where the number of tasks is relatively stable, each instance of the distributed kernel can maintain its own copy of the name table. At system startup, the distributed kernel sends a request to the name server, asking it to download the name table.

When a source task sends a message to a destination task, the local kernel looks up the name table to determine where the destination task resides. If the destination task resides on the same node as the source task, the local kernel routes the message directly to the destination task. For example, in Figure 4.14, a message from task B is routed directly to task C because both tasks reside on Node 1. If, on the other hand, the destination task resides on a remote node, the local kernel sends the message to its counterpart kernel on the remote node. On receiving the message, the remote kernel routes the message to the destination task on that node. This is illustrated in Figure 4.14 with task A, which resides on Node 1, sending a message to task D, which resides on Node 2. The message request from task A is handled by the local kernel on Node 1, which sends it to the remote kernel on Node 2, from where it is routed to task D.

4.7.4 Socket Services

Sockets are an application programming interface (API) provided by many operating systems. Sockets define a set of operations an application can call when it communicates with another application over a network (for example, between a client and a server), using a specific protocol such as TCP/IP. Sockets are a very low-level mechanism for client/server communication. Consequently, interfaces that are more abstract have been developed that offload much of the low-level details from the application. These include RPC and the various middleware technologies.

4.7.5 Message Communication Using Ports

In some distributed systems, message communication between remote nodes is made even more loosely coupled by supporting ports. A component (process or thread) on one node does not send a message to an explicit destination component by name. Instead, it sends the message to an output port. A destination component receives messages at its input ports. During system configuration, the output port of one component is connected to the input port of another component (referred to as "binding"). This provides greater flexibility and greater potential for reuse because at design time, a component does not have to explicitly know to whom it will be connected. Such decisions are made later, and instances of the same component type can execute in different environments in different applications. Several distributed operating systems provide message communication via ports, including V, Mach, CHORUS, and Amoeba [Bacon 1997]. Examples of distributed programming environments providing ports and flexible configuration are Conic [Kramer 1985; Magee, Kramer, and Sloman 1989] and Regis [Magee, Dulay, and Kramer 1994].

4.7.6 Error Recovery

It is assumed that as long as the network is operational, the message will arrive at the remote node. For example, if there is a parity error, the network communication software—assumed here to be part of the distributed operating system software— will retransmit the message. However, if the remote node does not respond within a given timeframe, either because the network connection to the remote node is down or because the remote node itself is down, then the transmission will time out. In this case, the local kernel will receive a negative acknowledgment from the network communication software, indicating that the remote node did not receive the message. The local kernel will then return the negative acknowledgment to the source task. If the message does not arrive at the remote node, it is the responsibility of the source task to decide what to do, because the decision is application-dependent. More information on distributed operating systems is given in Bacon [1997] and Tanenbaum [1992].

4.8 Middleware

Distributed systems often need to operate in a heterogeneous environment, where different nodes consist of different hardware and operating systems—for example, a PC Windows client interacting with a Unix server. **Middleware** is a layer of software that sits above the heterogeneous operating system to provide a uniform platform above which distributed applications can run [Bacon 1997]. An early form of middleware was the remote procedure call (RPC). Other examples of middleware technology [Orfali, Harkey, and Edwards 1999] are DCE (Distributed Computing Environment), which uses RPC technology, Java remote method invocation (RMI), COM, and CORBA.

By providing a uniform way of interconnecting and reusing objects, middleware technologies such as CORBA, COM, and Java Beans promote component reuse, and hence are also referred to as component technologies [Szyperski 1997].

4.8.1 Platforms for Distributed Computing

Early platforms for distributed processing were based on the client/server model. More recently, the object model has gained in popularity [Bacon 1997]. Communication in the client/server model is often based on the remote procedure call. With this approach, procedures are located in the address space of the servers and are invoked by remote procedure calls from clients. The server receives a request from a client, invokes the appropriate procedure, and returns a reply to the client.

With the object model, objects are named globally and may be invoked directly at the server. There are two approaches to distributed computing, using either the distributed object model or the mobile code model [Bacon 1997]. In the first approach, objects are located at the server and are invoked remotely, as is the case with Java RMI and CORBA. In the second case, invoked objects migrate from the server to the client, as is the case with Java applets.

4.8.2 Remote Procedure Calls

Some distributed systems support remote procedure calls (RPC). A client subsystem on one node makes a remote procedure call to a server subsystem on another node [Bacon 1997; Orfali, Harkey, and Edwards 1999]. A remote procedure call is similar to a local procedure call, so the fact that the server is on a remote node is hidden from the client. The procedure called by the client, sometimes referred to as a "client stub," takes the request and any parameters, packs them into a message (this process is often referred to as "marshaling"), and sends the message to the server node.

At the server node, a counterpart server stub unpacks the message (referred to as "unmarshaling"), and calls the appropriate server procedure (which represents the remote procedure), passing it any parameters. When the server procedure finishes processing the request, it returns any results to the server stub. The server stub packs the results into a response message, which it sends to the client stub. The client stub extracts the results from the message and returns them as output parameters to the client.

Thus the role of the client and server stubs is to make the remote procedure call appear like a local procedure call to both the client and server, as illustrated in Figure 4.15. Figure 4.15a depicts one object making a local procedure call to another object. Figure 4.15b depicts a distributed solution to the same problem, with an object on the client node making a remote procedure call to an object on the server node. The local procedure call is to the client stub, which *marshals* the procedure name and parameters into the message, which the network interface sends over the

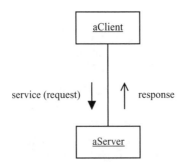

Figure 4.15a *Local procedure call*

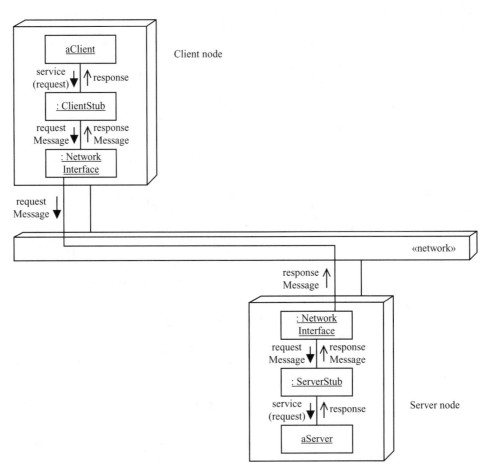

Figure 4.15b *Remote procedure call*

network. The network interface on the remote node receives the message and passes it on to the server stub (also referred to as a server skeleton), which *unmarshals* the message and calls the remote procedure of the server object. For the response, the server stub *marshals* the response and sends it over the network. The client stub *unmarshals* the response and passes it back to the client object.

4.8.3   Java Remote Method Invocation

The Java programming environment, referred to as the Java Development Kit (JDK), supports a middleware technology called Java remote method invocation (RMI) to allow distributed Java objects to communicate with each other [Orfali and Harkey 1998]. With RMI, instead of sending a message to a specific procedure (as with RPC), the client object sends the message to a specific object and invokes the object's method (procedure or function).

A client proxy at the client side performs the role of the client stub in the RPC (see Figure 4.16). The client proxy provides the same interface to the client object as the server object and hides all the details of the communication from the client. On the server side, a server proxy performs the role of the server stub, hiding all the details of the communication from the server object. The server proxy invokes the server object's method. If the server object is not present, the server proxy instantiates the server object.

Different server objects may provide the same interface and hence be capable of servicing a given client request. The choice of which server object should service the request can be made at runtime.

4.9   Common Object Request Broker Architecture (CORBA)

CORBA is an open systems standard developed by the Object Management Group, which allows communication between objects on heterogeneous platforms [Mowbray and Ruh 1997; Orfali, Harkey, and Edwards 1996]. The Object Request Broker (ORB) middleware allows client/server relationships between distributed objects. Server objects provide services that can be invoked from client objects by means of the ORB. In general, clients and servers are roles played by objects. Thus, an object might act as a client in a relationship with one object and act as a server in a relationship with a different object. Using an ORB, a client object can invoke an operation on a server object without having to know where the object is located, what platform (hardware/OS) it is running on, what communications protocol is required to reach it, or what programming language it is implemented in.

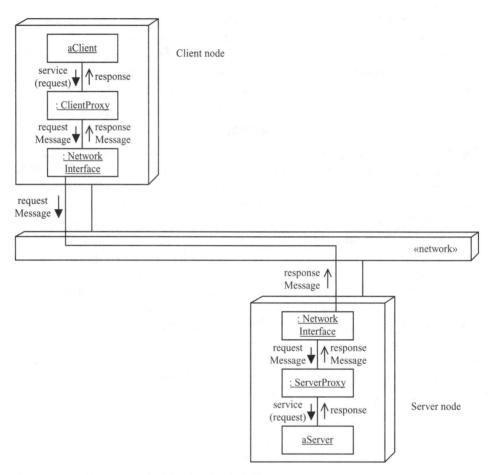

Figure 4.16 *Remote method invocation (RMI)*

4.9.1   Object Request Broker

A client with an object reference can invoke any service (interface operation) supported by the server object via the ORB. The ORB provides the following [Bacon 1997]:

- **Location transparency.** The ORB locates the server object from the object reference.

- **Implementation transparency.** The client does not need to know how the server object is implemented, in what language or on what hardware it is running, or under what operating system.

- **Object execution state transparency.** If the server object is inactive, the ORB activates it before delivering the request to it.
- **Communication mechanism transparency.** The client is unaware of the underlying protocol used by the ORB.

4.9.2 CORBA Interface Definition Language

The server object's interface is written in an Interface Definition Language (IDL), which is programming language independent. The interface is defined separately from the implementation. The object's IDL specification is then translated into the target object's implementation language. The object's implementation is written directly in the target object's implementation language. OMG provides standard language mappings from IDL to the target language. Programming languages supported include C, C++, Ada 95, and Java. OMG IDL compilers generate client-side stubs and server-side skeletons, which are similar to the client and server proxies described earlier in the section on remote method invocation. The client-side stub creates the request and sends it on behalf of the client. The server-side skeleton receives the request and delivers it to the CORBA object implementation. The CORBA stub and skeleton functionality are similar to RPC stubs and skeletons.

The stub program provides marshaling of parameter information, using an approach similar to that used for remote procedure calls. High-level language data types sent over a network have to be packed into a data structure that can be sent over the network, for example, a byte stream. The receiving skeleton has to unpack the incoming message and invoke the operation on the server object.

4.9.3 Static and Dynamic Binding

With static invocation, the stubs and skeletons are prelinked with their executables. The static interfaces are defined by IDL definitions written by the developer. The IDL definitions are then compiled into stubs, skeletons, and header files as defined by the specific language mapping. This is relatively simple and efficient, but inflexible. This approach is shown in Figure 4.17.

A more flexible approach is dynamic invocation. With this approach, a client object can decide at runtime to which server object it should communicate. A server registers the IDL definitions in an interface repository, which can be queried dynamically at runtime.

The client uses the Dynamic Invocation Interface (see Figure 4.17), which is a generic stub provided by the ORB that is independent of the IDL interface of the object being invoked. This approach allows a client to invoke an object at runtime without compile-time knowledge of its interface.

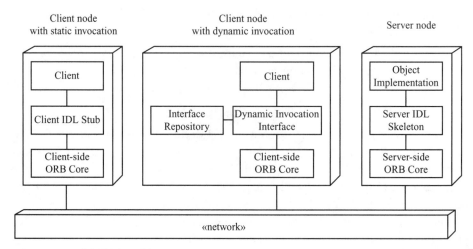

Figure 4.17   *CORBA architecture*

CORBA also supports a Dynamic Skeleton Interface at the server side, which provides a runtime binding mechanism for servers that need to handle incoming service calls for objects that do not have IDL-based compiled skeletons. This is useful for communicating with external objects such as gateways or browsers [Mowbray and Ruh 1997].

4.9.4   CORBA Services

The ORB allows a client to transparently invoke an operation on a server object. It provides a naming service. When a CORBA object is created, the object is given an object reference, which is a unique identifier. An object's reference may be obtained by means of a directory lookup. For example, the CORBA naming service will provide the object reference for a named object. The client may then invoke the operation on the object. The naming service provides a directory service similar to the telephone white pages directory.

Another CORBA service is the trader service. This service allows object references to be retrieved based on matching characteristics associated with the object (such as type of service) to characteristics sent by the client. The trader service provides a directory service similar to the telephone yellow pages directory.

4.9.5   Integrating Legacy Applications into a Distributed Object Framework

Many legacy applications cannot be easily integrated into a distributed object framework. One approach to doing this is to develop wrapper objects. A **wrapper object** is a distributed application object that handles the communication and management of client requests to legacy applications [Mowbray and Ruh 1997]. A wrapper registers its service with the naming service so it can receive client service requests.

Most legacy applications were developed as standalone applications. In some cases, the legacy code is modified so the wrapper object can access it. However, this is often impractical because there is often little or no documentation and the original developers are no longer present. Consequently, wrapper objects often interface to legacy code through crude mechanisms such as files, which might be purely sequential or indexed sequential files. The wrapper object would read or update files maintained by the legacy application. If the legacy application uses a database, the database could be accessed directly by using database wrapper objects that would hide the details of how to access the database. For example, with a relational database, the database wrapper would use SQL statements to access the database. Other options include making wrapper inputs appear as if they came from the keyboard and redirecting screen or printer outputs to the wrapper, a technique sometimes referred to as "screen scraping."

4.10 Other Component Technologies

Besides CORBA, there are other distributed component technologies, including ActiveX and COM from Microsoft and JavaBeans and Jini connection technology from Sun.

4.10.1 COM

DCOM is a Microsoft distributed object technology that builds on the **COM** (Component Object Model) architecture [Box 1998]. COM provides a framework for application interoperation in a Windows environment. DCOM allows a client to communicate with a component on a remote node. DCOM intercepts the client call and forwards it to the server. Although both COM and CORBA provide an IDL, CORBA is intended as a standard, whereas COM is proprietary and Windows-specific.

An ActiveX component is a software executable that conforms to the Microsoft COM standard and runs on Windows platforms [Shan and Earle 1998]. It can be loaded and executed by COM-compatible containers. Microsoft's Internet Explorer Web browser is enabled to handle ActiveX components.

4.10.2 JavaBeans

JavaBeans are a Java-based component technology intended for domain-specific applications [Orfali and Harkey 1998, Szyperski 1997]. JavaBeans are user interface client components, whereas Enterprise JavaBeans are server-side components. A bean is a component that consists of a set of classes and resources.

Beans can be assembled into applications by means of an assembly builder tool. During assembly, a bean's behavior can be inspected (referred to as "introspection") and can be customized. Beans can trigger events and handle incoming events. An assembly builder tool can determine the events a bean triggers and the events it receives. The assembly tool can then connect event source beans to event receiver beans. Customized and connected beans can be saved for later use.

4.10.3   Jini Connection Technology

Jini (Java Intelligent Network Infrastructure) is a connection technology for embedded systems and network-based computing applications whose objective is to make it easy to interconnect computers and devices. Jini is intended for digital devices such as cellular phones, digital cameras, televisions, and videocassette recorders. The Jini technology uses Java technology, and devices in a network are connected by using Java RMI.

Jini provides a lookup service, which performs a brokering role between service providers and clients. Jini also provides protocols for discovery, join, and lookup. A provider of a service—for example, a digital videocassette recorder—registers with the Jini lookup service. Thus, a new provider must first dynamically locate the lookup service (referred to as "discovery") and then register itself with the lookup service (referred to as "join"). For each service it wishes to provide, the provider must upload a Java object that provides the interface for that service.

A Jini client—for example, a digital camera—locates the Jini lookup service by using the discovery protocol. The client then uses the lookup service to locate an appropriate service—for example, a recording service provided by the videocassette recorder (VCR). The client then downloads a Java object from the lookup service, which allows the client to interact directly with the device. Thus, the digital camera would use the Jini lookup service to locate the VCR recording service, download the VCR recording Java object, and then communicate directly with the VCR.

4.11   Transaction Processing Systems

Transaction processing (TP) applications are mission-critical or business-critical applications [Bacon 1997; Orfali, Harkey, and Edwards 1999]. They include order entry, inventory, airline reservation systems, and point-of-sale systems. TP applications involve the updating of information maintained in a database. The transaction load in a TP application is usually predictable, with a high proportion of database updates, known peak demands, and predictable access patterns to the database. Some TP applications have to run continuously, but in others, brief interruptions can be tolerated.

4.11.1 Characteristics of Transactions

A **transaction** is a request from a client to a server, consisting of two or more operations that perform a single logical function and which must be completed in its entirety or not at all. Transactions are generated at the client and sent to the server for processing. In a basic client/server configuration, the processing is done entirely at the server. In a distributed application, the server may delegate one or more operations to be processed at other servers.

A transaction must be completed in its entirety or not at all. Consider an interbank electronic funds transfer. For a transaction to be considered complete, all its operations must be performed successfully. If any operation of the transaction cannot be performed, the transaction must be aborted. This means individual operations that have been completed need to be undone so the effect of an aborted transaction is as if it never occurred.

Transactions have the following properties, sometimes referred to as ACID properties:

- **Atomicity (A).** A transaction is an indivisible unit of work. It is either entirely completed (committed) or aborted (rolled back).

- **Consistency (C).** After the transaction executes, the system must be in a consistent state.

- **Isolation (I).** A transaction's behavior must not be affected by other transactions.

- **Durability (D).** Changes are permanent after a transaction completes. These changes must survive system failures. This is also referred to as "persistence."

4.11.2 Transaction Processing Monitors

A transaction processing monitor (TP monitor) coordinates the flow of information between user clients, who initiate the transaction requests, and the transaction processing application that responds to the requests. TP monitors have existed for many years in the mainframe environment. The best known is IBM's CICS, which operates with IBM operating systems and database management systems.

In heterogeneous client/server environments, TP monitors perform the following:

- Send and receive messages between clients and servers
- Manage the flow of transactions and distribute the workload among the servers
- Support global transactions that impact multiple distributed databases, including backup and recovery of global transactions
- Interface to resource managers such as operating systems and database management systems
- Provide a system administration capability

Modern TP monitors such as Tuxedo and Encina [Orfali, Harkey, and Edwards 1999] support a three-tier client/server architecture as follows:

1. **Client functionality.** Presentation of information and user interaction. For example, the client software is PC-based.

2. **Application server functionality, supporting the business application.** The client communicates with the application server by means of messages.

3. **Data management.** For example, an Oracle relational database could be distributed over several database server nodes.

Separating client functionality from the application server supports separation of concerns, where design and development of the business application can proceed independently of the user interface.

4.12 Summary

This chapter has given an overview of the concurrent and distributed processing technology required for concurrent, real-time, and distributed applications. The infrastructure is provided by the operating system, networks, and middleware. The operating system support for multiprogramming and symmetric multiprocessing environments was described, with more detail provided on task scheduling and device input/output. More information on these topics can be found in Bacon [1997], Silberschatz and Galvin [1998], and Tanenbaum [1992]. The design of concurrent tasks, which make use of this technology, is described in Chapter 14. The issue of what priorities to assign to concurrent tasks with hard deadlines is described in more detail in Chapter 17 on real-time scheduling.

The technology for distributed processing environments was then described. This includes an overview of client/server technology and the technology of the

World Wide Web. The ISO and TCP/IP network protocols were described. Distributed operating system services were reviewed, followed by a description of middleware technology (including RPC, RMI, and CORBA) and transaction processing systems. More information on distributed systems is given in Coulouris, Dollimore, and Kindberg [1994]; on communication networks in Comer [1999] and Tanenbaum [1996]; and on distributed operating systems in Bacon [1997], Silberschatz and Galvin [1998], and Tanenbaum [1994]. More information on client/server systems and transaction processing systems can be found in Orfali, Harkey, and Edwards [1999]; on distributed object technologies in Orfali, Harkey, and Edwards [1996], Shan and Earle [1998], and Szyperski [1997]; on CORBA in Mowbray and Ruth [1997] and Orfali and Harkey [1998]; and on COM in Box [1998]. The design of distributed applications, which make use of this technology, is described in Chapter 13.

chapter

Software Life Cycles and Methods

This chapter takes a software life cycle perspective on software development. Different software life cycle models (also referred to as software process models), including the spiral model and the Unified Software Development Process, are briefly described and compared. The roles of design verification and validation and of software testing are discussed. The chapter then briefly describes the evolution of software design methods, object-oriented analysis and design methods, and concurrent and real-time design methods.

5.1 Software Life Cycle Approaches

As with any software system, concurrent and real-time systems should be developed using a software life cycle. The "Waterfall" model [Boehm 1976, Fairley 1985] is the most widely used software life cycle model. This section gives an overview of the waterfall model. Alternative software life cycle models are then outlined that have been developed to overcome some of the waterfall model's limitations. These are the Throwaway Prototyping life cycle model [Agresti 1986, Gomaa 1981b], the Incremental Development life cycle model (also referred to as evolutionary prototyping) [Basili and Turner 1975, Gomaa 1986a], and the spiral model [Boehm 1988].

5.1.1 "Waterfall" Life Cycle Model

In the past thirty years, the cost of developing software has grown steadily while the cost of developing and purchasing hardware has rapidly decreased. Furthermore, software now typically costs 80% of a total project, whereas only 30 years ago the hardware was by far the largest project cost [Boehm 1976, Boehm 1981].

Thirty years ago, the problems of developing software were not clearly understood. In the late sixties, it was realized that a software crisis existed. The term "software engineering" was coined to refer to the management and technical methods, procedures, and tools required to effectively develop a large-scale software system. With the application of software engineering concepts, many large-scale software systems have been developed using a software life cycle, which is a phased approach to developing software. The most widely used software life cycle model, often referred to as the waterfall model, is shown in Figure 5.1. It is generally considered the conventional or "classical" software life cycle. The waterfall model is an idealized process model in which each phase is completed before the next phase is started, and a project moves from one phase to the next without iteration or overlap.

5.1.2 Limitations of the Waterfall Model

The waterfall model is a major improvement over the undisciplined approach used on many early software projects and has been successfully used on many projects. In practice, however, some overlap is often necessary between successive phases of the life cycle, as well as some iteration between phases when errors are

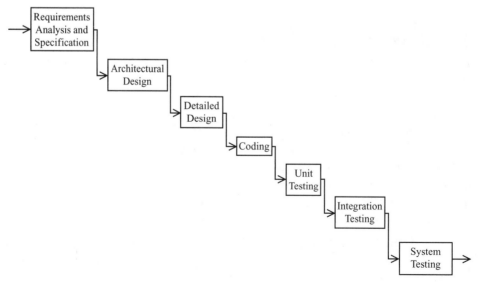

Figure 5.1 *Waterfall model*

detected. Moreover, for some software development projects, the waterfall model presents the following significant problems:

- Software requirements, a key factor in any software development project, are not properly tested until a working system is available to demonstrate to the end-users. In fact, several studies [Boehm 1976] have shown that errors in the requirements specification are usually the last to be detected (often not until system or acceptance testing) and the most costly to correct.

- A working system becomes available only late in the life cycle. Thus a major design or performance problem might go undetected until the system is almost operational, at which time it is usually too late to take effective action.

For software development projects with a significant risk factor—for example, due to requirements that are not clearly understood or are expected to change—variations or alternatives to the waterfall model have been proposed.

Two different software prototyping approaches have been used to overcome some of the limitations of the waterfall model: throwaway prototypes and evolutionary prototypes. Throwaway prototypes can help resolve the first problem of the waterfall model outlined above, and evolutionary prototypes can help resolve the second problem.

5.1.3 Throwaway Prototyping

Throwaway prototypes can be used to help clarify user requirements [Agresti 1986, Gomaa 1981b]. This approach is particularly useful for getting feedback on the user interface and can be used for systems that have a complex user interface.

A throwaway prototype may be developed after a preliminary requirements specification (see Figure 5.2). By giving users the capability of exercising the prototype, much valuable feedback can be obtained that is otherwise frequently difficult to get. Based on this feedback, a revised requirements specification can be prepared. Subsequent development proceeds, following the conventional software life cycle.

Throwaway prototyping, particularly of the user interface, has been shown to be an effective solution to the problem of specifying requirements for interactive information systems. Gomaa [1981b] described how a throwaway prototype was used to help clarify the requirements of a highly interactive manufacturing application. The biggest problem it helped overcome was the communications barrier that existed between the users and the developers.

Throwaway prototypes can also be used for experimental prototyping of the design (see Figure 5.3). This can be used to determine if certain algorithms are logically correct or to determine if they meet their performance goals.

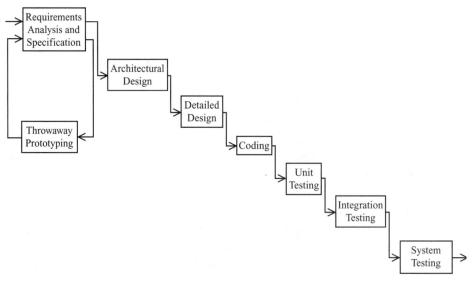

Figure 5.2   *Throwaway prototyping of software requirements*

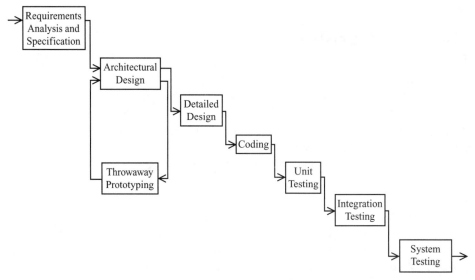

Figure 5.3   *Throwaway prototyping of architectural design*

5.1.4   Evolutionary Prototyping by Incremental Development

The evolutionary prototyping approach is a form of incremental development in which the prototype evolves through several intermediate operational systems (see

Figure 5.4) into the delivered system [McCracken 1982, Gomaa 1986a]. This approach can help in determining whether the system meets its performance goals and for testing critical components of the design. It also reduces development risk by spreading the implementation over a longer time frame. Event sequence diagrams may be used to assist in selecting system subsets for each increment [Gomaa 1986b].

One objective of the evolutionary prototyping approach is to have a subset of the system working early, which is then gradually built on. It is advantageous if the first incremental version of the system tests a complete path through the system from external input to external output.

An example of evolutionary prototyping by means of incremental development is described in Gomaa [1986a]. Using this approach on a real-time robot controller system [Gomaa 1986b] resulted in availability of an early operational version of the system, providing a big morale boost for both the development team and management. It also had the important benefits of verifying the system design, establishing whether certain key algorithms met their performance goals, and spreading system integration over time.

5.1.5 Combining Throwaway Prototyping and Incremental Development

With the Incremental Development life cycle model approach, a working system in the form of an evolutionary prototype is available significantly earlier than with the conventional waterfall life cycle. Nevertheless, much greater care needs to be taken

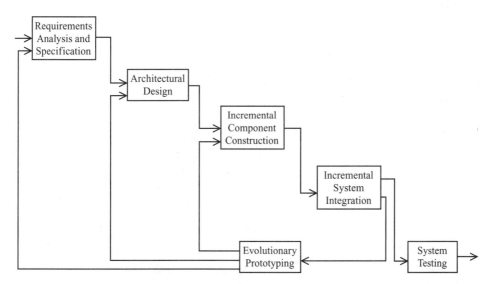

Figure 5.4 *Incremental development software life cycle*

in developing this kind of prototype than with a throwaway prototype because it forms the basis of the finished product and thus software quality has to be built into the system from the start and cannot be added as an afterthought. In particular, the software architecture needs to be carefully designed and all interfaces specified.

The conventional waterfall life cycle is impacted significantly by the introduction of throwaway prototyping or incremental development. It is also possible to combine the two approaches, as shown in Figure 5.5. A throwaway prototyping exercise is carried out to clarify the requirements. After the requirements are understood and a specification is developed, an incremental development life cycle is pursued. After subsequent increments, further changes in requirements might be necessary due to changes in the user environment.

5.1.6 Spiral Model

The spiral model is a risk-driven process model originally developed by Boehm [1988] to address known problems with earlier process models of the software life cycle, in particular the waterfall model. In the spiral model (see Figure 5.6), the radial coordinate represents cost and the angular coordinate represents progress in completion of a cycle of the model. Each cycle involves traversing through four quadrants. The first quadrant is to determine objectives, alternatives, and constraints for the cycle. The second quadrant is a risk analysis and evaluation of

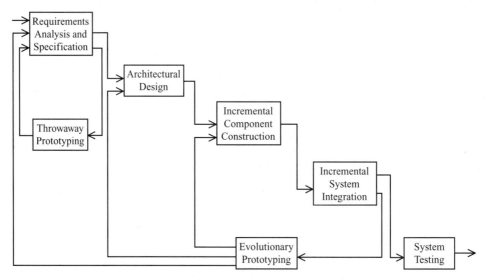

Figure 5.5 *Combined throwaway prototyping/incremental development software life cycle model*

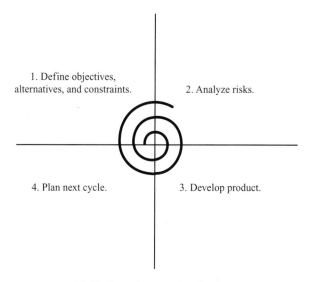

NB: This diagram does not use the UML notation.

Figure 5.6 *The spiral process model*

alternatives for the cycle. The third quadrant is to develop and verify the next-level product. The fourth quadrant involves planning for the next phases.

The spiral model is intended to encompass other life cycle models, such as the waterfall model, the incremental development model, and the throwaway prototyping model. During risk analysis, the key characteristics of the project are determined, referred to as "process drivers." The process drivers are used to determine which process model is most appropriate for the project. In this way, the spiral model can be considered a process model generator [Boehm 1989].

The spiral model consists of the following four quadrants, as shown in Figure 5.6:

- Define Objectives, Alternatives, and Constraints
- Analyze Risks
- Develop Product
- Plan Next Cycle

Each cycle of the spiral model iterates through these four quadrants. The number of cycles is project-specific, so the descriptions of the activities in each quadrant are intended to be general enough that they can be included in any cycle.

The goal of the spiral model is to be risk-driven, so the risks in a given cycle are determined during the Analyze Risks quadrant. To manage these risks, certain additional project-specific activities may be planned to address the risks, such as

Requirements Prototyping, if the risk analysis indicates that the software requirements are not clearly understood. These project-specific risks are termed "process drivers." For any process driver, one or more project-specific activity needs to be performed to manage the risk.

5.1.7 The Unified Software Development Process

The Unified Software Development Process (USDP), as described in Jacobson, Booch, and Rumbaugh [1999] is a use case–driven software process that uses the UML notation. The USDP consists of five core workflows and four phases and is iterative. Each cycle goes through all four phases and addresses the development of a core workflow. The workflows and products of each workflow are as follows:

1. **Requirements.** The product of the Requirements workflow is the Use Case model.

2. **Analysis.** The product of the Analysis workflow is the Analysis model.

3. **Design.** The products of the Design workflow are the Design model and the Deployment model.

4. **Implementation.** The product of the Implementation workflow is the Implementation model.

5. **Test.** The product of the Test workflow is the Test model.

Like the Spiral model, the USDP is a risk-driven process. The life cycle phases of the USDP are

1. Inception

2. Elaboration

3. Construction

4. Transition

5.2 Design Verification and Validation

Boehm [1981] differentiates between *software validation* and *software verification*. The goal of *software validation* is to ensure that the software development team "builds the right system," that is, to ensure that the system conforms to the user's needs. The goal of *software verification* is to ensure that the software development team "builds the system right," that is, to ensure that each phase of the software system is built according to the specification defined in the previous phase.

Topics discussed briefly in this section are software quality assurance and performance analysis of software designs. Another important activity is testing the fully integrated system against the software requirements, which is carried out during system testing, as described in Section 5.3 on software testing.

5.2.1   Software Quality Assurance

Software quality assurance is a name given to a set of activities whose goal is to ensure the quality of the software product. Software verification and validation are important goals of software quality assurance.

Throwaway prototyping can be used for validation of the system (before it is developed) against the user requirements, to help ensure that the team "builds the right system," that is, a system that actually conforms to the user's requirements. Throwaway prototypes can also be used for experimental prototyping of the design.

Software technical reviews can help considerably with software verification and validation. In software verification, ensuring that the design conforms to the software requirements specification is important. Requirements tracing and technical reviews [Fagan 1976] of the software design, help with this activity.

5.2.2   Performance Analysis of Software Designs

For real-time applications, analyzing the performance of the real-time design before implementation is also necessary to estimate whether the design will meet its performance goals. If potential performance problems can be detected early in the life cycle, steps can be taken to overcome them. An approach described in Chapter 17 of this book is to analyze the performance of real-time designs by using real-time scheduling theory.

Other approaches for evaluating software designs use queuing models [Kleinrock 1975, Menascé, Almeida, and Dowdy 1994, Menascé and Almeida 1998, Menascé, Gomaa, and Kerschberg 1995, Menascé and Gomaa 1998] and simulation models [Smith 1990]. For concurrent systems, Petri nets [Peterson 1981, David 1994, Jensen 1997, Pettit and Gomaa 1996, Stansifer 1994] can be used for modeling and analyzing concurrent designs. Timed Petri nets [Coolahan 1983, Elmstrom 1993] can be used for analyzing concurrent designs with timing constraints.

5.3   Software Testing

Some aspects of testing concurrent and real-time systems are no different than for testing other systems. Most of the differences occur either because the software system consists of several concurrent tasks or because the system interfaces to several external devices. A considerable amount has been written about software testing in general (for example, Beizer [1990] and Myers [1979]).

A major problem in testing concurrent systems is that execution of such systems is nondeterministic; that is, the response of the system to its inputs varies in a way that is difficult to predict. An approach for the deterministic testing of concurrent systems is described in Tai 1991.

Because of the difficulty of detecting errors and then locating and correcting the detected errors, software systems are usually tested in several stages. Unit and integration testing are "white box" testing approaches, requiring knowledge of the internals of the software; system testing is a "black box" testing approach based on the software requirements specification.

5.3.1   Unit Testing

In unit testing, an individual component is tested before it is combined with other components [Beizer 1990, Myers 1979]. Unit testing approaches use test-coverage criteria. Frequently used test coverage criteria are *statement coverage* and *branch coverage*. *Statement coverage* requires that each statement should be executed at least once. *Branch coverage* requires that every possible outcome of each branch should be tested at least once.

Since unit testing usually deals with testing components that are smaller than a concurrent task, this topic is not discussed any further here.

5.3.2   Integration Testing

Integration testing involves combining tested components into progressively more complex groupings of components and then testing these groupings until the whole software system has been put together and the interfaces tested.

A distinguishing feature of integration testing for concurrent systems is that concurrent task interfaces need to be tested. A systematic method for the integration testing of concurrent tasks is described by Gomaa [1986b].

5.3.3   System Testing

System testing is the process of testing an integrated hardware and software system to verify that the system meets its specified requirements [IEEE 1990]. The whole system or major subsystems are tested to determine conformance with the requirements specification. To achieve greater objectivity, it is preferable to have system testing performed by an independent test team.

Statistical usage testing [Cobb 1990], in which "black-box" test scenarios are developed by an independent test team based on the expected usage profile of the system, has been advocated for both integration and system testing.

During system testing, several aspects of either a concurrent or real-time system need to be tested [Beizer 1995]. These include

- **Functional testing.** To determine that the system performs the functions described in the requirements specification.
- **Load (stress) testing.** To determine whether the system can handle the large and varied workload it is expected to handle when operational.
- **Performance testing.** To test that the system meets its response time requirements.

System testing of real-time systems can be greatly assisted by the construction of environment simulators [Gomaa 1986b], which simulate the behavior of the external environment. By this means, the software can be tested in a controlled reproducible environment.

5.3.4 Acceptance Testing

The user organization or its representative usually carries out acceptance testing, typically at the user installation, prior to acceptance of the system. Most of the issues relating to system testing also apply to acceptance testing.

5.4 Evolution of Software Design Methods

In the 1960s, programs were often implemented with little or no systematic requirements analysis and design. Graphical notations—in particular, flowcharts— were often used, either as a documentation tool or as a design tool for planning a detailed design prior to coding. Subroutines were originally created as a means of allowing a block of code to be shared by calling it from different parts of a program. They were soon recognized as a means of constructing modular systems and were adopted as a project management tool. A program could be divided up into modules, where each module could be developed by a separate person and implemented as a subroutine or function.

With the growth of structured programming in the early seventies, the ideas of top-down design and stepwise refinement [Dahl 1972, Wirth 1974] gained prominence as program design methods, with the goal of providing a systematic approach for structured program design. Dijkstra developed one of the first software design methods with the design of the T.H.E. operating system [Dijkstra 1968], which used a hierarchical architecture. This was the first design method to address the design of a concurrent system, namely, an operating system.

In the mid to late 1970s, two different software design strategies gained prominence, data flow oriented design and data structured design. The data flow oriented design approach as used in Structured Design [Yourdon 1979, Page-Jones 1988] was one of the first comprehensive and well-documented design methods to emerge. The view was that a better understanding of the functions of the system could be obtained by considering the flow of data through the system. It provided a systematic approach for developing data flow diagrams for a system and then mapping them to structure charts. Structured Design introduced the coupling and cohesion criteria for evaluating the quality of a design. This approach emphasized functional decomposition into modules and the definition of module interfaces. The first part of Structured Design, based on data flow diagram development, was refined and extended to become a comprehensive analysis method, namely Structured Analysis [DeMarco 1978, Gane 1979].

An alternative software design approach was that of data structured design. This view was that a full understanding of the problem structure is best obtained from consideration of the data structures. Thus the emphasis is on first designing the data structures and then designing the program structures based on the data structures. The two principal design methods to use this strategy were Jackson Structured Programming [Jackson 1975] and the Warnier/Orr method [Orr 1977].

In the database world, the concept of separating logical data and physical data was a key concept in the development of database management systems. Various approaches were advocated for the logical design of databases, including the introduction of entity-relationship modeling by Chen [1976].

Parnas [1972] made a great contribution to software design with his advocacy of information hiding. A major problem with early systems, even in many of those designed to be modular, resulted from the widespread use of global data. This made these systems error-prone and difficult to change. Information hiding provided an approach for greatly reducing, if not eliminating, global data.

For the design of concurrent and real-time systems, a major contribution came in the late seventies with the introduction of the MASCOT notation [Simpson 1979] and later the MASCOT design method [Simpson 1986]. Based on a data flow approach, MASCOT formalized the way tasks communicate with each other, via either channels for message communication or pools (information hiding modules that encapsulate shared data structures). The data maintained by a channel or pool is accessed by a task only indirectly by calling access procedures provided by the channel or pool. The access procedures also synchronize access to the data, typically using semaphores, so that all synchronization issues are hidden from the calling task.

The 1980s saw a general maturation of software design methods, and several system design methods were introduced. Parnas's work with the Naval Research

Lab in which he explored the use of information hiding in large-scale software design led to the development of the Naval Research Lab (NRL) Software Cost Reduction Method [Parnas, Clements, and Weiss 1984]. Work on applying Structured Analysis and Structured Design to concurrent and real-time systems led to the development of Real-Time Structured Analysis and Design (RTSAD) [Ward 1985, Hatley 1988] and the Design Approach for Real-Time Systems (DARTS) [Gomaa 1984] methods.

Another software development method to emerge in the early 1980s was Jackson System Development (JSD) [Jackson 1983]. JSD views a design as being a simulation of the real world and emphasizes modeling entities in the problem domain by using concurrent tasks. JSD was one of the first methods to advocate that the design should model reality first and, in this respect, predated the object-oriented analysis methods. The system is considered a simulation of the real world and is designed as a network of concurrent tasks, where each real-world entity is modeled by means of a concurrent task. JSD also defied the then conventional thinking of top-down design by advocating a middle-out behavioral approach to software design. This approach was a precursor of object interaction modeling, an essential aspect of modern object-oriented development.

5.5 Evolution of Object-Oriented Analysis and Design Methods

In the mid to late 1980s, the popularity and success of object-oriented programming led to the emerging of several object-oriented design methods, including Booch [1986, 1991], Wirfs-Brock, Wilkerson, and Wiener [1990], Rumbaugh et al. [1991], Shlaer and Mellor [1988, 1992], and Coad and Yourdon [1991, 1992]. The emphasis in these methods was on modeling the problem domain, information hiding, and inheritance.

Parnas advocated using information hiding as a way to design modules that were more self-contained and hence could be changed with little or no impact on other modules. Booch introduced object-oriented concepts into design [Booch 1986], initially with information hiding, in the **object-based design** of Ada-based systems and later extended this to using information hiding, classes, and inheritance in **object-oriented design** [Booch 1991, Booch 1994]. Shlaer and Mellor [1988], Coad, and others introduced object-oriented concepts into analysis. The object-oriented approach is generally considered to provide a smoother transition from analysis to design than the functional approach.

Object-oriented analysis methods apply object-oriented concepts to the analysis phase of the software life cycle. The emphasis is on identifying real-world objects in the problem domain and mapping them to software objects. The initial attempt at object modeling was a static modeling approach that had its origins in information modeling, in particular, entity-relationship (E-R) modeling [Chen 1976], or more generally semantic data modeling [Peckham 1988] as used in logical database design. Entities in E-R modeling are information intensive objects in the problem domain. The entities, the attributes of each entity, and relationships among the entities, are determined and depicted on E-R diagrams; the emphasis is entirely on data modeling. During design, the E-R model is mapped to a database, usually relational. In object-oriented analysis, objects in the problem domain are identified and modeled as software classes, and the attributes of each class are determined as well as the relationships among classes [Booch 1994, Coad 1991, Rumbaugh et al. 1991, Shlaer and Mellor 1988].

The main difference between *classes* in static object-oriented modeling and *entity types* in entity-relationship modeling is that classes have operations but entity types do not have operations. In addition, whereas information modeling only models persistent entities that are to be stored in a database, other problem domain classes are also modeled in static object modeling [Booch 1994]. The advanced information modeling concepts of aggregation and generalization/specialization are also used. The most widely used notation for static object modeling before the UML was the Object Modeling Technique (OMT) [Rumbaugh et al. 1991].

Static object modeling was also referred to as *class modeling* and *object modeling* because it involves determining the classes to which objects belong and depicting classes and their relationships on class diagrams. The term *domain modeling* is also used to refer to static modeling of the problem domain [Shlaer and Mellor 1992, Rosenberg and Scott 1999].

The early object-oriented analysis and design methods emphasized the structural aspects of software development through information hiding and inheritance but neglected the dynamic aspects. A major contribution by the Object Modeling Technique [Rumbaugh et al. 1991] was to clearly demonstrate that dynamic modeling was equally important. In addition to introducing the static modeling notation for the object diagrams, OMT showed how dynamic modeling could be performed with statecharts for showing the state-dependent behavior of active objects and with sequence diagrams to show the sequence of interactions between objects. Rumbaugh et al. [1991] used statecharts, which are hierarchical state transition diagrams originally conceived by Harel [1988, 1998], for modeling active objects. Shlaer and Mellor [1992] also used state transition diagrams for modeling active objects. Booch initially used object diagrams to show the instance-level interactions among objects [1991] and later sequentially numbered the interactions [1994] to more clearly depict the collaboration among objects.

Jacobson [1992] introduced the use case concept for modeling the system's functional requirements. Jacobson also used the sequence diagram to describe the sequence of interactions between the objects that participate in a use case. The use case concept was fundamental to all phases of Jacobson's object-oriented software engineering life cycle. The use case concept, which can be applied to non-object-oriented systems as well as object-oriented systems, has had a profound impact on modern object-oriented software development.

Prior to UML, there were earlier attempts to unify the various object-oriented methods and notations, including Fusion [Coleman et al. 1993] and the work of Texel and Williams [1997]. The Unified Modeling Language notation was originally developed by Booch, Jacobson, and Rumbaugh to integrate the notations for use case modeling, static modeling, and dynamic modeling (using statecharts and object interaction modeling), as described in Chapter 2. Other methodologists also contributed to the development of UML. An interesting discussion of how UML has evolved and how it is likely to evolve in the future is given in Cobryn [1999] and Selic [1999].

5.6 Survey of Concurrent and Real-Time Design Methods

The CODARTS (Concurrent Design Approach for Real-Time Systems) method [Gomaa 1993] builds on the strengths of earlier concurrent design, real-time design, and early object-oriented design methods. These included Parnas's Naval Research Laboratory Software Cost Reduction Method (NRL) [Parnas, Clements, and Weiss 1984], early Booch Object-Oriented Design [Booch 1991], Jackson System Development [Jackson 1983], and the DARTS (Design Approach for Real-Time Systems) method [Gomaa 1984, Gomaa 1986b] by emphasizing both information hiding module structuring and task structuring.

In CODARTS, concurrency and timing issues are considered during task design, and information hiding issues are considered during module design. Thus, tasks are considered as active objects and information hiding modules as passive objects. The real-time system is viewed from the dynamic and static perspectives. The dynamic view is provided by the concurrent tasks, which are determined by using the task structuring criteria. The static view is provided by the information hiding modules, which are determined by using the module structuring criteria. Guidelines are then provided for integrating the task and module views.

Octopus [Awad, Kuusela, and Ziegler 1996] is a real-time design method based on use cases, static modeling, object interactions, and statecharts. By combining concepts from Jacobson's use cases with Rumbaugh's static modeling and statecharts, Octopus anticipated the merging of the notations that is now the UML. For real-time design, Octopus places particular emphasis on interfacing to external devices and on concurrent task structuring.

ROOM [Selic, Gullekson, and Ward 1994] is a real-time design method that is closely tied in with a **CASE** (Computer Assisted Software Engineering) tool called ObjecTime. ROOM is based around actors, which are active objects that are modeled using a variation on statecharts called ROOMcharts. A ROOMchart defines the states of an actor, the signals that initiate transitions between states, and the actions performed at transitions. Actors are connected to each other via ports. A protocol specifies the direction-dependent messages that may be exchanged between actors. A ROOM model, which has been specified in sufficient detail, may be executed. Thus, a ROOM model is operational and may be used as an early prototype of the system.

Buhr [1996] introduced an interesting concept called the use case map (based on the use case concept) to address the issue of dynamic modeling of large-scale systems. Use case maps consider the sequence of interactions between objects (or aggregate objects in the form of subsystems) at a larger grained level of detail than do collaboration diagrams.

For UML-based real-time software development, Douglass [1999b, 1999a] has provided a comprehensive description of how UML can be applied to real-time systems. The first book describes applying the UML notation to the development of real-time systems. The second book is a detailed compendium covering a wide range of topics in real-time system development, including safety-critical systems, interaction with real-time operating systems, real-time scheduling, behavioral patterns, real-time frameworks, debugging, and testing.

5.7 Summary

This chapter has taken a software life cycle perspective on software development. Various software life cycle models, also referred to as software process models (including the spiral model and the Unified Software Development Process) were briefly described and compared. The roles of design verification and validation and of software testing were discussed. This chapter then briefly described the evolution of software design methods, object-oriented analysis and design methods, and real-time design methods. Chapter 6 describes the object-oriented software life cycle for the COMET method.

part II

COMET: Concurrent Object
Modeling and Architectural
Design with UML

chapter

Overview of COMET

C OMET (Concurrent Object Modeling and architectural design mEThod) is a design method for concurrent applications—in particular, distributed and real-time applications. This chapter considers the COMET method from a software life cycle perspective. The development process for the COMET method is an object-oriented software process, which is compatible with the Unified Software Development Process (USDP) [Jacobson, Booch, and Rumbaugh 1999] and the spiral model [Boehm 1988]. This chapter presents the COMET object-oriented software life cycle and describes how the COMET method may be used with the Unified Software Development Process or the spiral model. It then outlines the main activities of the COMET method and concludes with a description of the steps in using COMET.

6.1 COMET Object-Oriented Software Life Cycle

The COMET object-oriented software life cycle model is a highly iterative software development process based around the **use case** concept. The functional requirements of the system are defined in terms of actors and use cases. Each use case defines a sequence of interactions between one or more actors and the system.

A use case can be viewed at various levels of detail. In a requirements model, the functional requirements of the system are defined in terms of actors and use cases. In an analysis model, the use case is refined to describe the objects that participate in the use case, and their interactions. In the design model, the software architecture is developed, addressing issues of distribution, concurrency, and information hiding. The full COMET object-oriented software life cycle model is illustrated in Figure 6.1 and described next.

6.1.1 Requirements Modeling

During the **Requirements Modeling** phase, a requirements model is developed in which the functional requirements of the system are defined in terms of actors and use cases. A narrative description of each use case is developed. User inputs and active participation are essential to this effort. If the requirements are not well understood, a *throwaway prototype* can be developed to help clarify the requirements, as described in Chapter 5.

6.1.2 Analysis Modeling

In the **Analysis Modeling** phase, static and dynamic models of the system are developed. The static model defines the structural relationships among problem

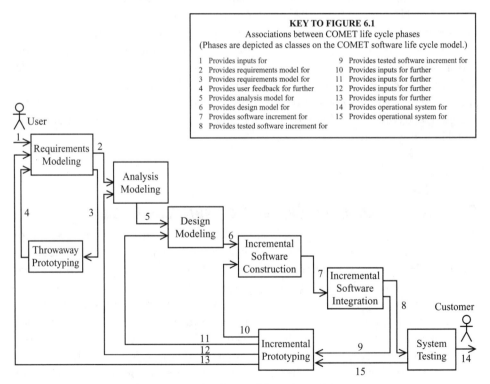

KEY TO FIGURE 6.1
Associations between COMET life cycle phases
(Phases are depicted as classes on the COMET software life cycle model.)

1 Provides inputs for
2 Provides requirements model for
3 Provides requirements model for
4 Provides user feedback for further
5 Provides analysis model for
6 Provides design model for
7 Provides software increment for
8 Provides tested software increment for
9 Provides tested software increment for
10 Provides inputs for further
11 Provides inputs for further
12 Provides inputs for further
13 Provides inputs for further
14 Provides operational system for
15 Provides operational system for

Figure 6.1 *COMET object-oriented software life cycle model*

domain classes. The classes and their relationships are depicted on class diagrams. Object structuring criteria are used to determine the objects to be considered for the analysis model. A dynamic model is then developed in which the use cases from the requirements model are refined to show the objects that participate in each use case and how they interact with each other. Objects and their interactions are depicted on either collaboration diagrams or sequence diagrams. In the dynamic model, state-dependent objects are defined using statecharts.

6.1.3   Design Modeling

In the **Design Modeling** phase, the software architecture of the system is designed, in which the analysis model is mapped to an operational environment. The analysis model, with its emphasis on the problem domain, is mapped to the design model, with its emphasis on the solution domain. Subsystem structuring criteria are provided to structure the system into subsystems, which are considered as aggregate or composite objects. Special consideration is given to designing distributed subsystems as configurable components that communicate with each other using messages. Each subsystem is then designed. For sequential systems, the emphasis is on the object-oriented concepts of information hiding, classes, and inheritance. For the design of concurrent systems, such as real-time, client/server, and distributed applications, it is necessary to consider concurrent tasking concepts in addition to object-oriented concepts.

6.1.4   Incremental Software Construction

After completion of the software architectural design, an *incremental software construction* approach is taken. This approach is based on selecting a subset of the system to be constructed for each increment. The subset is determined by choosing the use cases to be included in this increment and the objects that participate in these use cases. Incremental software construction consists of the detailed design, coding, and unit testing of the classes in the subset. This is a phased approach by which the software is gradually constructed and integrated until the whole system is built.

6.1.5   Incremental Software Integration

During *incremental software integration*, the integration testing of each software increment is performed. The integration test for the increment is based on the use cases selected for the increment. Integration test cases are developed for each use case. Integration testing is a form of white box testing, in which the interfaces between the objects that participate in each use case are tested.

Each software increment forms an *incremental prototype*. After the software increment is judged to be satisfactory, the next increment is constructed and integrated by iterating through the Incremental Software Construction and Incremental Software Integration phases. However, if significant problems are detected in the software increment, iteration through the Requirements Modeling, Analysis Modeling, and Design Modeling phases might be necessary.

6.1.6   System Testing

System Testing includes the functional testing of the system—namely, testing the system against its functional requirements. This testing is black box testing and is based on the black box use cases. Thus, functional test cases are built for each black box use case. Any software increment released to the customer needs to go through the System Testing phase.

6.2   Comparison of the COMET Life Cycle with Other Software Processes

This section briefly compares the COMET life cycle with the Unified Software Development Process (USDP) and the spiral model. The COMET method can be used in conjunction with either the USDP or the spiral model.

6.2.1   Comparison of the COMET Life Cycle with Unified Software Development Process

The USDP, as described in Jacobson, Booch, and Rumbaugh [1999] and briefly surveyed in Chapter 5, emphasizes process and—to a lesser extent—method. The USDP provides considerable detail about the life cycle aspects and some detail about the method to be used. The COMET method is compatible with USDP. The workflows of the USDP are the Requirements, Analysis, Design, Implementation, and Test workflows.

Each phase of the COMET life cycle corresponds to a workflow of the USDP. The first three phases of COMET have the same names as the first three workflows of the USDP—not surprising because the COMET life cycle was strongly influenced by Jacobson's earlier work [Jacobson 1992]. The COMET Incremental Software Construction activity corresponds to the USDP Implementation workflow. The Incremental Software Integration and System Test phases of COMET map to the Test workflow of USDP. COMET separates these activities because integration testing is viewed as a development team activity, whereas a separate test team should carry out system testing.

6.2.2   Comparison of the COMET Life Cycle with the Spiral Model

The COMET method can also be used with the spiral model [Boehm 1988]. During the project planning for a given cycle of the spiral model, the project manager decides what specific technical activity should be performed in the third quadrant, which is the Product Development quadrant. The selected technical activity, such as Requirements Modeling, Analysis Modeling, or Design Modeling, is then performed in the third quadrant. The Risk Analysis activity, performed in the second quadrant, and Cycle Planning, performed in the fourth quadrant, determine how many iterations are required through each of the technical activities.

6.3   Requirements, Analysis, and Design Models

The UML notation supports Requirements, Analysis, and Design concepts. The COMET method described in this book separates requirements activities, analysis activities, and design activities.

Requirements modeling addresses defining the functional requirements of the system. COMET differentiates analysis from design as follows: *analysis* is breaking down or decomposing the problem so it is understood better; *design* is synthesizing or composing (putting together) the solution. These activities are described in more detail in the next sections.

6.3.1   Activities in Requirements Modeling

In the requirements model, the system is considered as a black box. The use case model is developed.

- **Use Case Modeling.** Define actors and black box use cases. The functional requirements of the system are defined in terms of use cases and actors. The use case descriptions are a behavioral view; the relationships among the use cases give a structural view. Use case modeling is described in Chapter 7.

6.3.2   Activities in Analysis Modeling

In the analysis model, the emphasis is on understanding the problem; hence, the emphasis is on identifying the problem domain objects and the information passed between them. Issues such as whether the object is active or passive, whether the message sent is asynchronous or synchronous, and what operation is invoked at the receiving object are deferred until design time.

In the analysis model, the analysis of the problem domain is considered. The activities are

- **Static modeling.** Define problem-specific static model. This is a structural view of the information aspects of the system. Classes are defined in terms of their attributes, as well as their relationship with other classes. Operations are defined in the design model. For information intensive systems, this view is of great importance. The emphasis is on the information modeling of real-world classes in the problem domain. Static modeling is described in Chapter 8.

- **Object structuring.** Determine the objects that participate in each use case. Object structuring criteria are provided to help determine the objects, which can be entity objects, interface objects, control objects, and application logic objects. Object structuring is described in Chapter 9. After the objects have been determined, the dynamic relationships between objects are depicted in the dynamic model.

- **Finite State Machine Modeling.** The state-dependent aspects of the system are defined using hierarchical statecharts. Each state-dependent object is defined in terms of its constituent statechart. Finite state machines are described in Chapter 10.

- **Dynamic Modeling.** The use cases are refined to show the interaction among the objects participating in each use case. Collaboration diagrams or sequence diagrams are developed to show how objects collaborate with each other to execute the use case. Chapter 11 describes dynamic modeling, including the dynamic analysis approach, which is used to help determine how objects interact with each other to support the use cases. For state-dependent use cases, the interaction among the state-dependent control objects and the statecharts they execute needs to be explicitly modeled.

6.3.3   Activities in Design Modeling

In the design model, the solution domain is considered. During this phase, the analysis model is mapped to a concurrent design model. For concurrent applications, such as distributed and real-time applications, the following activities are performed:

- Consolidate the object collaboration model. Develop consolidated object collaboration diagram(s). This is described in Chapter 12.

- Make decisions about subsystem structure and interfaces. Develop the overall software architecture. Structure the application into subsystems. This is described in Chapter 12.

- Make decisions about how to structure the distributed application into distributed subsystems, in which subsystems are designed as configurable components.

    For a distributed application, design the distributed software architecture by decomposing the system into distributed subsystems and defining the message communication interfaces between the subsystems. This is described in Chapter 13.

- Make decisions about the characteristics of objects, in particular, whether they are active or passive. For each subsystem, structure the system into concurrent tasks (active objects). During task structuring, tasks are structured using the task structuring criteria, and task interfaces are defined. This is described in Chapter 14.

- Make decisions about the characteristics of messages, in particular, whether they are asynchronous or synchronous (with or without reply). This is also described in Chapter 14.

- Make decisions about class interfaces. For each subsystem, design the information hiding classes (passive classes). Design the operations of each class and the parameters of each operation. This is described in Chapter 15.

- Develop the detailed software design, addressing detailed issues concerning task synchronization and communication, and the internal design of concurrent tasks. This is described in Chapter 16.

In particular, COMET emphasizes the use of structuring criteria at certain stages in the analysis and design process. Object structuring criteria are used to help determine the objects in the system; subsystem structuring criteria are used to help determine the subsystems; and concurrent task structuring criteria are used to help determine the tasks (active objects) in the system. UML stereotypes are used throughout to clearly show the use of the structuring criteria.

6.4 The COMET in a Nutshell

Following the convention of Rosenberg [1999], who summarized his approach in a "nutshell," this section provides an overview of the COMET method in a nutshell. The steps in using COMET are briefly described. Outputs of each phase consist of various models depicted by using the UML notation as outlined in Chapter 2 and supplemented with additional documentation summarized in this section.

6.4.1 Develop Requirements Model

The steps in the **Requirements Modeling** phase are as follows:

1: Develop use case model. This consists of

1.1: Develop use case diagrams to depict the actors and use cases. Define the relationships between use cases. Use cases may be packaged to group large functional areas.

1.2: Document each use case in a use case description, which provides a narrative description of each use case.

6.4.2 Develop Analysis Model

The steps in the **Analysis Modeling** phase are as follows:

2: Develop Analysis Model

2.1: Develop static model of problem domain (real-world). Analyze static viewpoint of the system in the static model, in terms of the classes, relationships, and attributes. This consists of

2.1.1: Develop static model of the problem domain by using class diagrams, which show the relationships between the physical classes in the problem domain.

2.1.2: Develop a system context model by using a class diagram, which shows how the external classes interface to the system. This is derived from the above static physical model of the problem domain (step 2.1.1). This step is necessary for any system that interfaces to a variety of external I/O devices, such as sensors and actuators, and external systems.

2.1.3: Develop a static model of the entity classes in the problem domain, which shows the relationship between the data intensive classes in the problem domain, that is, classes whose primary role is to store data. This step is necessary for any system that has a significant number of entity classes.

2.1.4: Define all classes in the class dictionary, which describes the classes and attributes.

2.2: Structure the system into classes and objects. Apply the object structuring criteria to determine the objects and classes in the system. Determine high-level subsystems, for example, client/server. Add these classes to the class dictionary. Alternatively, this step may be performed iteratively as part of step 2.3.1.

2.3: Develop dynamic model. For each use case, perform the following:

2.3.1: Determine the objects that participate in the use case.

2.3.2: Develop an object interaction diagram (collaboration or sequence) showing the sequence of interactions between the objects that participate in the use case. Analyze the sequence of interactions between the objects. Analyze the information passed between the objects.

2.3.3: Develop a statechart for each state-dependent object in a state-dependent collaboration. Determine that the events and actions of the statechart are consistent with the input and output messages of the state-dependent object that executes the statechart.

2.3.4: Develop message sequence descriptions for each interaction diagram, which describe the sequence of interactions.

6.4.3 Develop Design Model

The steps in the **Design Modeling** phase are as follows:

3: Develop Design Model

3.1: Synthesize artifacts of the analysis model to produce initial software architecture. This step represents a transition from analysis to design and corresponds to the robustness analysis step described in Rosenberg [1999]. If any problems are detected during the synthesis step, iterate back to Analysis Modeling. This synthesis consists of

3.1.1: Synthesize statecharts. Synthesize the statechart for each state-dependent object from the partial use case-based statecharts for that object. This is necessary for any state-dependent object (and hence statechart) that participates in more than one use case. Alternatively, this step can be carried out as the final part of step 2.3.3.

3.1.2: Synthesize a collaboration model. Consolidate all the collaboration diagrams into an overall collaboration model for the system. For large systems, it is necessary to develop a subsystem collaboration model. Iteration is required between this step and step 3.2.

3.1.3: Synthesize a static model. Determine all the classes and their relationships. The refined static model is a refinement of the problem domain static model, or if the latter is too conceptual, the synthesized static model is determined from the consolidated collaboration model. A combination of the two approaches is possible.

3.2: Design overall software architecture. Structure the applications into subsystems. Define the subsystem interfaces. Apply the subsystem structuring criteria to determine the subsystems. Develop collaboration diagrams for each subsystem and a high-level collaboration diagram for the whole system.

3.3: Design distributed component-based software architecture. For distributed applications, determine the distributed component subsystems by using the distributed configuration criteria. Define the message communication interfaces between the component subsystems. This step is only required for distributed application design.

3.4: Design the concurrent task architecture for each subsystem. This consists of

3.4.1: Structure subsystems into concurrent tasks by applying the task structuring criteria.

3.4.2: Define the tasks and their interfaces.

3.4.3: Develop concurrent collaboration diagrams for each subsystem, depicting the tasks and their interfaces.

3.4.4: Document the design of each task in a task behavior specification.

3.5: Analyze the performance of the design. Apply real-time scheduling to determine if the concurrent real-time design will meet performance goals. Iterate through steps 3.3 and 3.4, if necessary. This step is only required for real-time application design.

3.6: Design the classes in each subsystem. Design the class interfaces, including all operations. Develop inheritance hierarchies. For applications needing a database, design the database and develop database wrapper classes (these topics are covered only briefly in this book). For each class, develop the class interface specification.

3.7: Develop the detailed software design for each subsystem. This consists of

3.7.1: Design the internals of composite tasks, which contain nested passive objects.

3.7.2: Design the details of task synchronization mechanisms for objects that are accessed by multiple tasks.

3.7.3: Design the connector classes that encapsulate the details of inter-task communication.

3.7.4: Design and document each task's internal event sequencing logic.

3.8: Analyze the performance of the real-time design in greater detail for each subsystem. If necessary, iterate through steps 3.4–3.7. This step is only required for real-time application design.

6.5 Summary

This chapter has described the COMET object-oriented software life cycle for the development of concurrent applications, in particular, distributed and real-time applications. It compared the COMET life cycle with the Unified Software Development Process and the spiral model, and described how the COMET method can be used with either the USDP or the spiral model. The chapter then described the main activities of the COMET method and concluded with a description of the steps in using COMET.

chapter

Use Case Modeling

The functional requirements of the system—also referred to as its external requirements—define what the system will do for the user. When defining the external requirements of the system, the system should be viewed as a black box, so that only the external characteristics of the system are considered.

This chapter describes the use case approach to defining the functional requirements of the system. It describes the concepts of **actors** and **use cases**. It also describes use case relationships, in particular, the *extend* and *include* relationships. Several examples are given.

7.1 Use Cases

With the use case approach, functional requirements are defined in terms of **actors**, who are users of the system, and **use cases**. An actor participates in a use case. A **use case** defines a sequence of interactions between one or more **actors** and the system. In the requirements phase, the use case model considers the system as a black box and describes the interactions between the actor(s) and the system in a narrative form consisting of user inputs and system responses. The **use case model** describes the functional requirements of the system in terms of the actors and use cases. The use cases in the use case model define the external requirements of the system. Each use case defines the behavior of some aspect of the system without revealing its internal structure. During subsequent analysis modeling, the objects that participate in each use case are determined.

Consider a simple banking example in which an Automated Teller Machine (ATM) allows customers to withdraw cash from their bank accounts. There is one actor, the ATM Customer, and one use case, Withdraw Funds. This is shown in Figure 7.1. The Withdraw Funds use case describes the sequence of interactions between the customer and the system, starting when the customer inserts an ATM card into the card reader and eventually receives the cash dispensed by the ATM machine.

7.2 Actors

An **actor** characterizes an outside user or related set of users who interact with the system [Rumbaugh, Booch, and Jacobson 1999]. In the use case model, **actors** are the only external entities that interact with the system.

There are several variations on how actors are modeled [Fowler and Scott 1999]. An actor is very often a human user. In many information systems, humans are the only actors. It is also possible in information systems for an actor to be an external system. In real-time and distributed applications, an actor can also be an external I/O device or a timer. External I/O devices and timer actors are particularly prevalent in real-time embedded systems, where the system interacts with the external environment through sensors and actuators.

A **primary actor** initiates a use case. Thus, a primary actor takes a proactive role and initiates actions in the system. Other actors, referred to as **secondary actors**, may also participate in the use case by receiving outputs and providing inputs. At least one of the actors must gain value from the use case. Usually, this is the primary actor. However, in real-time embedded systems, where the primary actor can be an

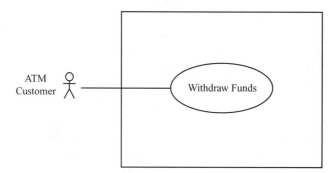

Figure 7.1 *Example of actor and use case*

external I/O device or timer, the primary beneficiary of the use case can be a secondary human actor, who receives some information from the system.

A human actor may use various I/O devices to physically interact with the system. A human actor may interact with the system via standard I/O devices, such as a keyboard, display, or mouse. A human actor may also interact with the system via non-standard I/O devices, such as various sensors. In all these cases, the human is the actor and the I/O devices are not actors.

Consider some examples of human actors. In a banking system, an example of an actor is a human teller who interacts with the system via standard I/O devices, such as keyboard, display, or mouse. Another example of an actor is a human customer who interacts with the system via an automated teller machine. In this case, the customer interacts with the system by using several I/O devices, including a card reader, cash dispenser, and receipt printer, in addition to a keyboard and display.

In some cases, however, an actor can be an I/O device. This can happen when a use case does not involve a human, as often happens in real-time applications. Typically, the I/O actor interacts with the system via a sensor. An example of an actor that is an input device is the Arrival Sensor in the Elevator Control System (see Figure 7.2). This sensor identifies that the elevator is approaching a floor at which it might need to stop. It thus initiates the Stop Elevator at Floor use case. The other actor in the Elevator Control System is the human passenger who interacts with the system via floor buttons and elevator buttons. The actor's inputs are actually detected via floor button sensors and elevator button sensors, respectively.

An actor can also be a timer that periodically sends timer events to the system. Periodic use cases are needed when certain information needs to be output by the system on a regular basis. This is particularly important in real-time systems, but can also be useful in information systems. Although some methodologists consider timers to be internal to the system, it is more useful in real-time

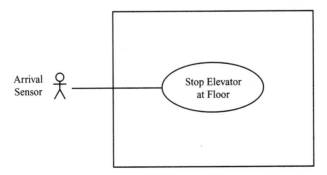

Figure 7.2 *Example of input device actor*

application design to consider timers as logically external to the system and to treat them as primary actors that initiate actions in the system. For example, in the Cruise Control and Monitoring System, several use cases are initiated by a timer actor. An example is given in Figure 7.3. The Timer actor initiates the Calculate Trip Speed use case, which periodically computes the average speed over a trip and displays this value to the Driver. In this case, the timer is the primary actor and the driver is the secondary actor.

An actor can also be an external system that either initiates (as primary actor) or participates (as secondary actor) in the use case. An example of an external system actor is the Factory Robot in the Factory Automation System. The Factory Robot initiates the Generate Alarm and Notify use case, as shown in Figure 7.4. The robot generates alarm conditions that are sent to interested factory operators who have subscribed to receive alarms. In this use case, the Factory Robot is the primary actor that initiates the use case, and the Factory Operator is a secondary actor who receives the alarms.

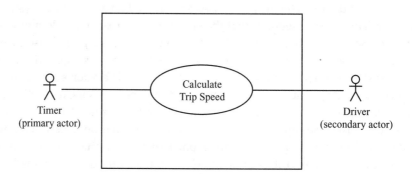

Figure 7.3 *Example of timer actor*

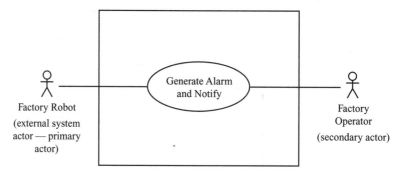

Figure 7.4 *Example of external system actor*

7.3   Actors, Roles, and Users

An actor represents a role played in the application domain, typically by a user. A user is an individual, whereas an actor represents the role played by all users of the same type. For example, in a Factory Automation System, there are three human actors: the `Factory Operator`, `Process Engineer`, and `Production Manager`. If it is possible for a human user to play two or more independent roles, this is represented by a different actor for each role. For example, the same user might play, at different times, both a `Production Manager` role and a `Factory Operator` role and thus be modeled by two actors.

It is also possible to have multiple users playing the same role; for example, there may be several operators in the Factory Automation System. Thus an actor models a user type, and individual users are instances of the actor.

7.4   Identifying Use Cases

A use case starts with input from an actor. The use case is a complete sequence of events initiated by an actor, specifying the interaction between the actor and the system. Simple use cases might involve only one interaction with an actor, and more complicated use cases involve several interactions with the actor. More complex use cases might also involve more than one actor.

To determine the use cases in the system, it is useful to start by considering the actors and the actions they initiate in the system. Each use case describes a sequence of interactions between the actor and the system. A use case should provide some value to an actor.

Thus, the functional requirements of the system are defined in terms of the use cases, which constitute an external specification of a system. However, when developing use cases, it is important to avoid a functional decomposition in which several small use cases describe individual functions of the system rather than describing a sequence of events that provides a useful result to the actor.

Let us consider the banking example again. In addition to withdrawing cash from the ATM, the `ATM Customer` actor is also allowed to query an account or transfer funds between two accounts. Because these are distinct functions initiated by the customer with different useful results, the query and transfer functions should be modeled as separate use cases, rather than being part of the original use case. Thus, the customer can initiate three use cases as shown in Figure 7.5: `Withdraw Funds`, `Query Account`, and `Transfer Funds`.

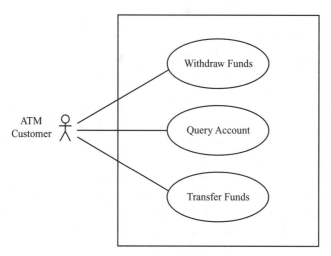

Figure 7.5 *Banking System actor and use cases*

The main sequence of the use case describes the most common sequence of interactions between the actor and the system. There may also be branches off the main sequence of the use case, which address less frequent interactions between the actor and the system. These deviations from the main sequence are executed only under certain circumstances—for example, if the actor makes an incorrect input to the system. Depending on the application requirements, these alternative branches through the use case sometimes join up later with the main sequence. The alternative branches are also described in the use case.

In the Withdraw Funds use case, the main sequence is the sequence of steps for successfully achieving a withdrawal. Alternative branches are used to address various error cases, such as when the customer enters the wrong PIN and must be re-prompted, when an ATM card is not recognized or has been reported stolen, and so on.

7.5 Documenting Use Cases in the Use Case Model

Use cases are documented in the use case model as follows:

- **Use Case Name.** Each use case is given a name.

- **Summary.** A brief description of the use case, typically one or two sentences.

- **Dependency.** This optional section describes whether the use case depends on other use cases, that is, whether it includes or extends another use case.

- **Actors.** This section names the actors in the use case. There is always a primary actor who initiates the use case. In addition, there may be secondary actors who also participate in the use case. For example in the `Withdraw Funds` use case, the `ATM Customer` is the actor.

- **Preconditions.** One or more conditions that must be true at the start of use case; for example, the ATM machine is idle, displaying a Welcome message.

- **Description.** The bulk of the use case is a narrative description of the main sequence of the use case, which is the most usual sequence of interactions between the actor and the system. The description is in the form of the input from the actor, followed by the response of the system. The system is treated as a black box, that is, dealing with what the system does in response to the actor's inputs, not the internals of how it does it.

- **Alternatives.** Narrative description of alternative branches off the main sequence. There may be several alternative branches from the main sequence. For example, if the customer's account has insufficient funds, display apology and eject card.

- **Postcondition.** Condition that is always true at the end of the use case if the main sequence has been followed; for example, customer's funds have been withdrawn.

- **Outstanding questions.** Questions about the use case are documented for discussions with users.

7.6   Examples of Use Cases

Examples of use cases are given in this section for a Banking System (these are part of the Banking System case study described in Chapter 19). Figure 7.5 shows an initial attempt at a use case diagram for the Banking System. There is one actor—namely, the `ATM Customer`—and three use cases that are the major functions initiated by the actor—`Withdraw Funds`, `Query Account`, and `Transfer Funds`.

The customer interacts with the system via the ATM card reader and the keyboard. It is the customer who is the actor, not the card reader and keyboard; these input devices provide the means for the customer to initiate the use case and respond to prompts from the system. The printer and cash dispenser are output devices; they are not actors, because it is the customer who benefits from the use cases.

Because there are three types of transactions, we start by considering three use cases, `Withdraw Funds`, `Query Account`, and `Transfer Funds`—one for each transaction type. Consider the `Withdraw Funds` use case. In this use case, the main sequence assumes a successful cash withdrawal by the customer. This involves reading the ATM card, validating the customer's PIN, checking that the customer has enough funds in the requested account, and then—providing the validation is successful—dispensing cash, printing a receipt, and ejecting the card.

The alternative branches deal with all the possible error conditions. These include if the customer enters the wrong PIN and must be re-prompted, if an ATM card is not recognized or has been reported stolen, and so on. Because these can be described quite simply, splitting them off into separate use cases is not necessary.

The use cases are described in detail in the next three subsections.

7.6.1   Withdraw Funds Use Case

Use Case Name: Withdraw Funds

Summary: Customer withdraws a specific amount of funds from a valid bank account.

Actor: ATM Customer

Precondition: ATM is idle, displaying a Welcome message.

Description:

1. Customer inserts the ATM Card into the Card Reader.

2. If the system recognizes the card, it reads the card number.

3. System prompts customer for PIN number.

4. Customer enters PIN.

5. System checks the expiration date and whether the card is lost or stolen.

6. If card is valid, the system then checks whether the user-entered PIN matches the card PIN maintained by the system.

7. If PIN numbers match, the system checks what accounts are accessible with the ATM Card.

8. System displays customer accounts and prompts customer for transaction type: Withdrawal, Query, or Transfer.

9. Customer selects Withdrawal, enters the amount, and selects the account number.

10. System checks whether customer has enough funds in the account and whether daily limit has been exceeded.

11. If all checks are successful, system authorizes dispensing of cash.

12. System dispenses the cash amount.

13. System prints a receipt showing transaction number, transaction type, amount withdrawn, and account balance.

14. System ejects card.

15. System displays Welcome message.

Alternatives:

- If the system does not recognize the card, the card is ejected.

- If the system determines that the card date has expired, the card is confiscated.

- If the system determines that the card has been reported lost or stolen, the card is confiscated.

- If the customer entered PIN does not match the PIN number for this card, the system re-prompts for the PIN.

- If the customer enters the incorrect PIN three times, the system confiscates the card.

- If the system determines the account number is invalid, then it displays an error message and ejects the card.

- If the system determines there are insufficient funds in the customer's account, then it displays an apology and ejects the card.

- If the system determines the maximum allowable daily withdrawal amount has been exceeded, it displays an apology and ejects the card.

- If the ATM is out of funds, the system displays an apology, ejects the card, and shuts down the ATM.

- If the customer enters Cancel, the system cancels the transaction and ejects the card.

Postcondition: Customer funds have been withdrawn.

7.6.2 Query Account Use Case

Use Case Name: Query Account
Summary: Customer receives the balance of a valid bank account.
Actor: ATM Customer
Precondition: ATM is idle, displaying a Welcome message.
Description:

1. Customer inserts the ATM Card into the Card Reader.

2. If the system recognizes the card, it reads the card number.

3. System prompts customer for PIN number.

4. Customer enters PIN.

5. System checks the expiration date and whether the card is lost or stolen.

6. If card is valid, the system then checks whether the user-entered PIN matches the card PIN maintained by the system.

7. If PIN numbers match, the system checks what accounts are accessible with the ATM Card.

8. System displays customer accounts and prompts customer for transaction type: Withdrawal, Query, or Transfer.

9. Customer selects Query, enters account number.

10. System reads account balance.

11. System prints a receipt showing transaction number, transaction type and account balance.

12. System ejects card.

13. System displays Welcome message.

Alternatives:

- If the system does not recognize the card, the card is ejected.
- If the system determines that the card date has expired, the card is confiscated.
- If the system determines that the card has been reported lost or stolen, the card is confiscated.
- If the customer-entered PIN does not match the PIN number for this card, the system re-prompts for the PIN.
- If the customer enters the incorrect PIN three times, the system confiscates the card.
- If the system determines the account number is invalid, it displays an error message and ejects the card.
- If the customer enters Cancel, the system cancels the transaction and ejects the card.

Postcondition: Customer account has been queried.

7.6.3 Transfer Funds Use Case

Use Case Name: Transfer Funds
Summary: Customer transfers funds from one valid bank account to another.
Actor: ATM Customer
Precondition: ATM is idle, displaying a Welcome message.
Description:

1. Customer inserts the ATM Card into the Card Reader.

2. If the system recognizes the card, it reads the card number.

3. System prompts customer for PIN number.

4. Customer enters PIN.

5. System checks the expiration date and whether the card is lost or stolen.

6. If card is valid, the system then checks whether the user-entered PIN matches the card PIN maintained by the system.

7. If PIN numbers match, the system checks what accounts are accessible with the ATM Card.

8. System displays customer accounts and prompts customer for transaction type: Withdrawal, Query, or Transfer.

9. Customer selects Transfer, enters `amount`, `from account`, and `to account`.

10. If the system determines that the customer has enough funds in the `from account`, it performs the transfer.

11. System prints a receipt showing transaction number, transaction type, amount transferred, and account balance.

12. System ejects card.

13. System displays Welcome message.

Alternatives:

- If the system does not recognize the card, the card is ejected.
- If the system determines the card date has expired, the card is confiscated.
- If the system determines the card has been reported lost or stolen, the card is confiscated.
- If the customer-entered PIN does not match the PIN number for this card, the system re-prompts for the PIN.
- If the customer enters the incorrect PIN three times, the system confiscates the card.
- If the system determines that the `from account` number is invalid, it displays an error message and ejects the card.
- If the system determines that the `to account` number is invalid, it displays an error message and ejects the card.
- If the system determines there are insufficient funds in the customer's `from account`, it displays an apology and ejects the card.
- If the customer enters Cancel, the system cancels the transaction and ejects the card.

Postcondition: Customer funds have been transferred.

7.7 Use Case Relationships

When use cases get too complex, dependencies between use cases can be defined by using the *include* and *extend* relationships. The objective is to maximize extensibility and reuse of use cases. *Abstract use cases* are determined to identify common patterns in several use cases, which can then be extracted and reused.

Another use case relationship provided by the UML is the use case generalization. *Use case generalization* is similar to the extend relationship because it is also used for addressing variations. However, users often find the concept of use case generalization confusing, so in the COMET method, the concept of generalization is confined to classes. Use case variations can be adequately handled by the extend relationship.

7.7.1 The Extend Relationship

In certain situations, a use case can get very complex, with many alternative branches. The extend relationship is used to model alternative paths that a basic use case might take. A use case can become too complex if it has too many alternative, optional, and exceptional sequences of events. A solution to this problem is to split off an alternative or optional sequence of events into a separate use case. The purpose of this new use case is to *extend* the old use case, if the appropriate conditions hold. The use case that is extended is referred to as the "base use case," and the use case that does the extending is referred to as the "extension use case."

For example, under certain conditions, a base use case B can be extended by a description given in the extension use case E. A base use case can be extended in different ways, depending on whether certain conditions are true. The extend relationship can be used as follows:

- To show a conditional part of the base use case, which is only executed under certain circumstances.
- To model complex or alternative paths.

It is important to note that the base use case does not depend on the extension use case and can function independently of it. On the other hand, the extension use case only executes if the condition in the base use case that causes it to execute is true. The extension use case cannot function without the presence of a base use case. Although an extension use case usually extends only one base use case, it is possible for it to extend more than one.

It is possible to declare extension points to specify precisely the locations in the base use case at which extensions can be added. The extension use case may only extend the base use case at those extension points [Fowler and Scott 1999; Rumbaugh, Booch, and Jacobson 1999].

An example of the extend relationship is from the Factory Automation System case study. A process engineer defines several manufacturing operations and then defines a process plan describing a sequence of operations to manufacture a part. This could be modeled as one use case. However, more flexibility results from having an extension use case, as shown in Figure 7.6. `Create/Update Operation` is a base use case, which is executed once for each operation created. The `Create/Update Process Plan` use case extends the `Create/Update Operation` use case. Thus a process engineer can create several operations with the `Create/Update Operation` use case and then optionally follow this by creating a process plan with the `Create/Update Process Plan` use case. The alternative section of the `Create/Update Operation` use case description would state that the process engineer may choose to create a process plan defining a sequence of operations that have previously been created.

Figure 7.6 also shows a way to reduce the number of use cases. Several use cases are of the form `Create/Read/Update`. One approach is to have separate use cases for each function, for example, `Create Operation`, `Update Operation`, and `Read Operation`. However, a more concise approach is to combine these three functions into one use case called `Create/Update Operation`. For the same reason, there is one use case for `Create/Update Process Plan`. In these examples, a choice exists between making create, read, or update the main sequence. One approach is to choose the create function for the main sequence, because it involves more interactions, and use the update and read functions as

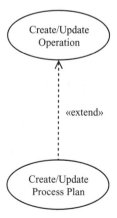

Figure 7.6 *Example of extend relationship*

alternative sequences. Another approach is to cover both create and update in the main sequence, with one line of the use case as follows:

```
If this is a new operation, prompt the operator for the name of the
operation.
```

You may insert simple options such as this into the description of the overall sequence, because one-line decisions do not impact the overall sequence. Placing if-then-else statements into the description is not recommended, however, because this would look too much like Pseudocode.

7.7.2 The Include Relationship

After the use cases for an application are initially developed, common sequences of interactions between the actor and the system can sometimes be determined that span several use cases. These common patterns reflect functionality that is common to more than one use case. A common pattern can be extracted from several of the original use cases and made into a new use case, which is called an *inclusion use case*. An inclusion use case is abstract, that is, it cannot be executed on its own. An abstract use case must be executed as part of a concrete, that is, executable, use case.

When this common functionality is separated out into an inclusion use case, this abstract use case can now be reused by several other use cases. It is then possible to define a more concise version of the old use case, with the common pattern removed. This concise version of the old use case is referred to as a *concrete use case* (also referred to as base use case), which *includes* the abstract use case.

Abstract use cases always reflect functionality that is common to more than one use case. When this common functionality is separated out into an abstract use case, the abstract use case can be reused by several concrete (executable) use cases. Abstract use cases can usually be developed only after an initial iteration in which several use cases have been developed. Only then can repeated sequences of interactions be observed that form the basis for the abstract use cases.

An abstract use case is never executed alone. It is executed in conjunction with a concrete use case, which includes, and hence executes, the abstract use case. To give a programming analogy, an abstract use case is analogous to a library routine, and a concrete use case is analogous to a program that calls the library routine.

An abstract use case might not have a specific actor. The actor is in fact the actor of the concrete use case that includes the abstract use case. Because different concrete use cases use the abstract use case, it is possible for the abstract use case to be used by different actors.

As an example of an abstract use case, consider the `Withdraw Funds`, `Query Account`, and `Transfer Funds` use cases described earlier. After analyzing these use cases, it can be determined that the first part of each use case—namely, validating the customer's Personal Identification Number (PIN)—is identical. There is no advantage to repeating the PIN validation process in each use case. Instead, the PIN validation sequence is split off into a separate abstract use case called `Validate PIN`, which is used by the (revised) `Withdraw Funds`, `Query Account`, and `Transfer Funds` use cases. The use case diagram is shown in Figure 7.7. The abstract use case for `Validate PIN` and the concrete `Withdraw Funds` use case are described in detail in the Banking System case study (Chapter 19). The relationship between the two use cases is an *include* relationship; the `Withdraw Funds`, `Query Account`, and `Transfer Funds` use cases *include* the `PIN Validation` use case.

7.7.3   Some Guidelines

Careful application of use case relationships can help with the overall organization of the use case model; however, they should be used judiciously. It should be noted that small abstract use cases corresponding to individual functions (such as dispense cash, print receipt, and eject card) should not be considered. These functions are too small, and making them separate use cases would result in a functional decomposition with fragmented use cases in which the use case descriptions would only be a sentence each and not a description of a sequence of events. This would result in a use case model that is overly complex and difficult to understand; in other words, a problem of not being able to see the forest (the overall sequence of events) for the trees (the individual functions)!

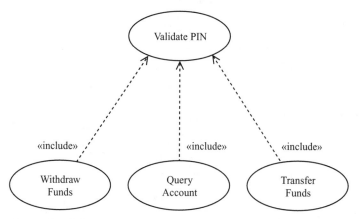

Figure 7.7   *Example of abstract use case and include relationship*

7.8   Use Case Packages

For large systems, having to deal with a large number of use cases in the use case model often gets unwieldy. A good way to handle this scale-up issue is to introduce a **use case package** that encompasses a related group of use cases. In this way, use case packages can represent high-level requirements that address major subsets of the functionality of the system. Because actors often initiate and participate in related use cases, use cases may also be grouped into packages based on the major actors who use them.

For example, in the Factory Automation System, the major actors of the system are the process engineer, factory operator, and production manager, each of whom initiates and participates in several use cases. Use case packages can be defined for each of these major actors: Process Engineer Use Cases, Factory Operator Use Cases, and Production Manager Use Cases. Figure 7.8 shows an example of a use case package for the Factory Automation System, namely the Factory Operator Use Case Package, encompassing four use cases. The Factory Operator is the primary actor of the View Alarms and View Workstation Status use cases and a secondary actor of the other use cases. The Factory Robot is the primary actor of the Generate Alarm and Notify and Generate Workstation Status and Notify use cases.

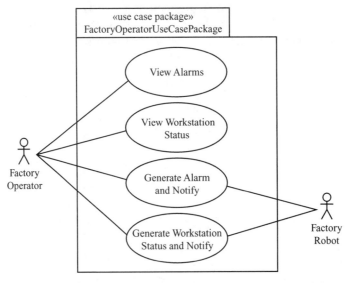

Figure 7.8   *Example of use case package*

7.9   Summary

This chapter has described the use case approach to defining the functional requirements of the system. It has described the concepts of actor and use cases. It has also described use case relationships, in particular the extend and include relationships.

The use case model has a strong influence on subsequent software development. Thus, use cases are refined in the analysis model during dynamic modeling, as described in Chapter 11. For each use case, the objects that participate in the use case are determined by using the object structuring criteria described in Chapter 9, and the sequence of interactions between the objects is defined. Software can be incrementally developed by selecting the use cases to be developed in each phase of the project, as described in Chapter 5. Integration and system test cases should also be based on use cases.

Static Modeling

The **static model** addresses the static structural aspects of a problem by modeling classes in the real world. A static model describes the static structure of the system being modeled, which is considered less likely to change than the functions of the system. In this chapter, we use the term **static modeling** for the modeling process and the UML **class diagram** notation to depict the static model.

A static model defines the classes of objects in the system, the attributes of the classes, the relationships between classes, and the operations of each class. The concepts of objects and classes are described in Chapter 3. This chapter describes the relationships between classes. Three types of relationship are described: **associations**, **composition** and **aggregation** relationships, and **generalization/specialization** relationships. In addition, this chapter addresses special considerations in static modeling of the problem domain, including static modeling of the system context and static modeling of entity classes. Design of class operations is deferred to the design phase. It is addressed during class design, as described in Chapter 15.

Static models are depicted on class diagrams, as described in Chapter 2. In addition, a class is depicted with a stereotype. Many of the examples given in this chapter are of entity classes, which are data-intensive classes and are depicted with the stereotype «entity».

8.1 Associations between Classes

An **association** defines a relationship between two or more classes, denoting a static, structural relationship between classes. For example, Employee <u>Works in</u> Department, where Employee and Department are classes and <u>Works in</u> is an association.

A *link* is a connection between object instances and represents an instance of an association between classes. For example, Jane Works in Manufacturing, where Jane is an instance of Employee and Manufacturing is an instance of Department. A link can exist between two objects if, and only if, there is an association between their corresponding classes.

In class diagrams, association names usually read from left to right and top to bottom. Associations are inherently bidirectional. The name of the association is in the forward direction: Employee Works in Department. There is also an opposite direction of the association: Department Has Employee. Associations are most often binary, that is, representing a relationship between two classes. However, they can also be unary (self-associations), ternary, or higher order.

8.1.1 Depicting Associations on Class Diagrams

On class diagrams, an association is shown as an arc joining the two class boxes, with the name of the association next to the arc. An example is given in Figure 8.1 of the association Company Has President. On a large class diagram with many classes, classes are usually in different positions relative to each other. To avoid ambiguity when reading class diagrams, the following conventions may be used:

- When reading the association from top (Company) to bottom (President), the name of the association (Has) is shown on the right side of the arc (see Figure 8.1).
- When reading the association from bottom to top, the name of the association is shown on the left side of the arc.
- When reading the association from left to right, the name of the association is shown above the arc.
- When reading the association from right to left, the name of the association is shown below the arc.

However, to avoid confusion, a small arrowhead may be used to point in the direction in which the association name should be read, as shown in Figure 8.1. Seeing the direction of the association name illustrated is usually easier to understand than remembering the conventions described in the previous list. Consequently, the UML arrowhead notation is used by COMET to depict the direction of associations in static modeling of the problem domain.

8.1.2 Multiplicity of Associations

The *multiplicity* of an association specifies how many instances of one class may relate to a single instance of another class. The multiplicity of an association may be:

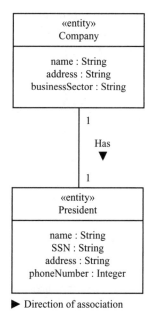

Figure 8.1   *Example of one-to-one association*

- A **one-to-one association**. In a one-to-one association between two classes, the association is one-to-one in both directions. Thus, an object of one class has a link to only one object of the other class. For example, in the association Company Has President, a particular company has only one president, and a president is president of only one company. An example is the company Microsoft with its president Steve Ballmer. The static modeling notation for a one-to-one association is illustrated in Figure 8.1.

- A **one-to-many association**. In a one-to-many association, there is a one-to-many association in one direction between the two classes and a one-to-one association between them in the opposite direction. For example, in the association, Bank Manages Account, a bank manages many accounts, but an account is managed by only one bank. The static modeling notation for a one-to-many association is illustrated in Figure 8.2.

- **Numerically specified association.** A numerically specified association is an association that refers to a specific number. For example, in the association Car Has Door, one car has two doors or four doors (depicted as 2,4) but never one, three, or five doors. The association in the opposite direction is still one-to-one, that is, a door belongs to only one car. Note that a particular car manufacturer makes the decision of how many doors a car can have; another manufacturer might make a different decision. A numerically specified association is illustrated in Figure 8.3.

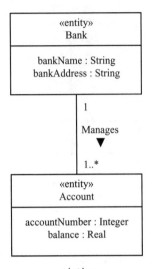

Figure 8.2 *Example of one-to-many association*

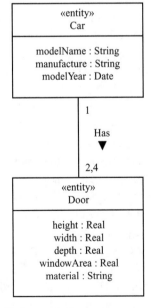

Figure 8.3 *Numerically specified association*

- An **optional association**. In an optional association, there might not always be a link from an object in one class to an object in the other class. For example, in the association Customer <u>Owns</u> Debit Card, customers may choose whether or not they have a debit card. The optional (zero or one) association is shown in Figure 8.4. It is also possible to have a zero, one, or more association. For example, in the association Customer <u>Owns</u> Credit Card, a customer may have no credit cards, one credit card, or many credit cards, as shown in Figure 8.5.

- **Many-to-many association.** A many-to-many association is an association between two classes with a one-to-many association in each direction. For example, in the association Course <u>Has</u> Student, Student <u>Attends</u> Course, there is a one-to-many association between a course and the students who attend it, because a course has many students. There is also a one-to-many association in the opposite direction, because a student may attend many courses. This is illustrated in Figure 8.6, which shows the association in each direction.

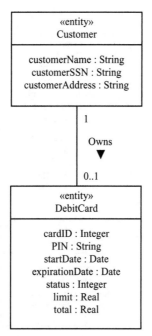

Figure 8.4   *Optional (zero or one) association*

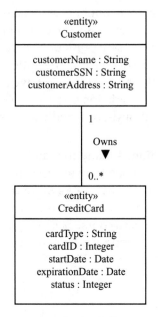

Figure 8.5 *Optional (zero, one, or many) association*

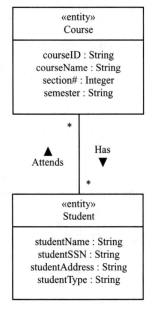

Figure 8.6 *Many-to-many association*

8.1.3 Other Associations

A ternary association is a three-way association among classes. An example of a ternary association is among the classes `Buyer`, `Seller`, and `Agent`. The association is that the `Buyer` negotiates a price with the `Seller` through an `Agent`. This is illustrated in Figure 8.7. The ternary association is shown as a diamond joining the three classes. A higher-order association, which is an association among more than three classes, is quite rare.

A unary association, also referred to as a self-association, is an association between an object of one class and another object in the same class. Examples are `Person` `is-child-of` `Person`, `Person` `is-married-to` `Person`, and `Employee` `is-boss-of` `Employee`.

8.1.4 Link Attributes

In a complex association between two or more classes, it is possible for a link to have attributes. This happens most often in many-to-many associations, where an attribute does not belong to any of the classes but belongs to the association. For example, in the many-to-many association between `Project` and `Employee` classes:

```
Project Has Employee
Employee Works on project
```

A project has many employees, and an employee may work on many projects.

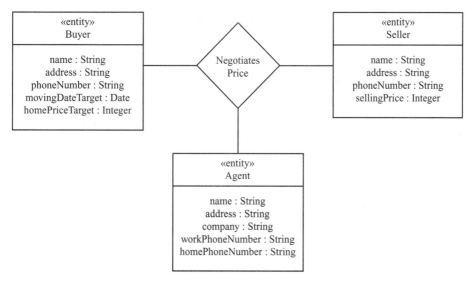

Figure 8.7 *Example of ternary association*

The attribute `hours Worked` is not an attribute of either the `Employee` or `Project` classes. It is an attribute of the association between `Employee` and `Project` because it represents the hours worked by a specific employee (of which there are many) on a specific project (an employee works on many projects). This is illustrated in Figure 8.8.

8.1.5 Association Classes

Instead of using link attributes, an alternative is to use an *association class*. An association class is a class that models an association between two or more classes. It is most useful in many-to-many associations. The attributes of the association class are the attributes of the association. An association class is usually preferable to link attributes because the association class promotes a complex association, which has its own attributes, to the level of a class. Furthermore, in most database management systems, an association class would need to be modeled separately; thus it is modeled as a relation in a relational database.

In the earlier example, instead of using link attributes, we could use an association class so that the attributes of the link become attributes of the association class. Thus in the many-to-many association between `Project` and `Employee` classes:

```
Project Has Employee
Employee Works on project
```

Figure 8.9 illustrates an association class called `Hours`, whose attribute is `hours Worked`.

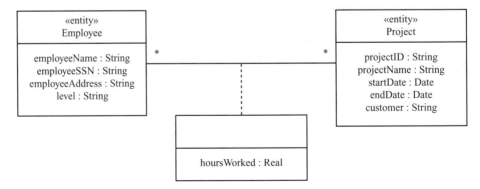

Figure 8.8 *Example of link attribute*

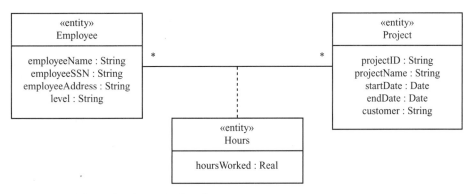

Figure 8.9 *Example of association class*

8.2 Composition and Aggregation Hierarchies

Both composition and aggregation hierarchies address a class that is made up of other classes. Composition and aggregations are special forms of relationship in which the classes are tightly bound by the whole/part relationship. In both cases, the relationship between the parts and the whole is an IS PART OF relationship.

Composition is a stronger form of aggregation, and an aggregation is stronger than an association. In particular, the composition relationship demonstrates a stronger relationship between the parts and the whole than does the aggregation relationship. A composition is also a relationship among instances. Thus, the part objects are created, live, and die together with the whole. The part object can only belong to one whole.

A composite class often involves a physical relationship between the whole and the parts. Thus, in the static modeling examples, both the elevator and the automated teller machine are composite classes. The elevator door, elevator motor, elevator buttons, and elevator lamps can be modeled as objects that are part of an elevator composite object. Thus, the Elevator composite class is composed of four parts: the Elevator Button, Elevator Lamp, Motor, and Door classes (as shown in Figure 8.10). Each Elevator composite object is composed of one Motor object, one Door object, n Elevator Button objects, and n Elevator Lamp objects. Thus, in Figure 8.10, the Elevator composite class has one-to-one associations with the Motor and Door classes, and one-to-many associations with the Elevator Button and Elevator Lamp classes.

The aggregation hierarchy is a weaker form of whole/part relationship. In an aggregation, part instances can be added to and removed from the aggregate

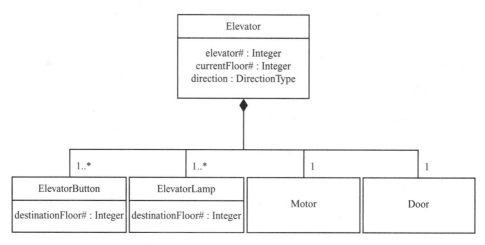

Figure 8.10 *Example of composition hierarchy*

whole. For this reason, aggregations are likely to be used to model conceptual classes rather than physical classes. In addition, a part may belong to more than one aggregation. An example of an aggregation hierarchy is a College in a university (see Figure 8.11), whose parts are an Administration Office, several

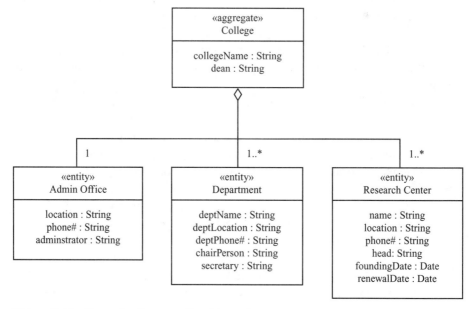

Figure 8.11 *Example of aggregation hierarchy*

Departments and several Research Centers. New departments can be created, and old departments are occasionally removed or merged with other departments. Research centers can also be created, removed, or merged.

In both composition and aggregation, attributes are propagated from the whole to the part. Thus, the elevator # also identifies the specific motor and door, which are part of the elevator composite class. However, for an elevator button or elevator lamp, an additional attribute, the destination Floor # is also needed to identify a specific button or lamp.

8.3   Generalization/Specialization Hierarchy

Some classes are similar but not identical. They have some attributes in common and others that are different. In a **generalization/specialization hierarchy,** common attributes are abstracted into a generalized class, which is referred to as a *superclass*. The different attributes are properties of the specialized class, which is referred to as a *subclass*. There is an IS A relationship between the subclass and the superclass. The superclass is also referred to as a parent class or ancestor class. The subclass is also referred to as a child class or descendent class.

Each subclass inherits the properties of the superclass but then extends these properties in different ways. The properties of a class are its attributes or operations. Inheritance allows the adaptation of the superclass to form the subclass. The subclass inherits the attributes and the operations from the superclass. The subclass may then add attributes, add operations, or redefine operations. Each subclass may also be a superclass, which is specialized further to develop other subclasses.

Consider the example of bank accounts given in Figure 8.12. Checking accounts and savings accounts have some attributes in common and others that are different. The attributes that are common to all accounts—namely account Number and balance—are made the attributes of an Account superclass. Attributes specific to a savings account, such as the interest accumulated (in this bank, checking accounts do not accumulate any interest), are made the attributes of the subclass Savings Account. Attributes specific to a checking account, such as the last Deposit Amount, are made the attributes of the subclass Checking Account.

```
Savings Account IS A Account
Checking Account IS A Account
```

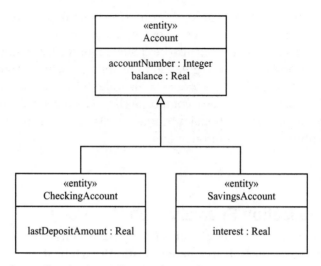

Figure 8.12   *Generalization/specialization hierarchy*

A *discriminator* is an attribute that indicates which property of the object is being abstracted by the generalization relationship. For example, the *discriminator* in the Account generalization just given, account Type, discriminates between Checking Account and Savings Account, as shown in Figure 8.13.

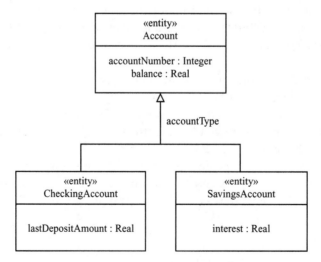

Figure 8.13   *Discriminator in generalization/specialization*

8.4 Constraints

A *constraint* specifies a condition or restriction that must be true [Rumbaugh, Booch, and Jacobson 1999]. A constraint is expressed in any textual language. The UML also provides a constraint language, the Object Constraint Language (OCL) [Warmer and Kleppe 1999], which may optionally be used.

One kind of constraint is a constraint on an attribute. Consider the following: in the banking example, it may be stipulated that accounts are not allowed to have a negative balance. This can be expressed as a constraint on the attribute `balance` of the `Account` class, {balance ≥ 0}. On a class diagram, the constraint on the attribute is shown next to the class to which it applies, as illustrated in Figure 8.14.

Another kind of constraint is a constraint on an association link. Usually objects on the "many" side of an association have no order. However, in some cases, objects in the problem domain might have an explicit order that is desirable to model. Consider, for example, the following one-to-many association:

```
Account Modified by ATM Transaction
```

In this association, ATM transactions are ordered by time and hence the constraint can be expressed as {ordered by time}. This constraint can be depicted on a class diagram as shown in Figure 8.15.

8.5 Static Modeling and the UML

Although class diagrams are standard in the UML, there is less agreement on how static modeling should be applied, that is, what method to use to develop the class diagrams. Some methodologists suggest that static modeling should be used

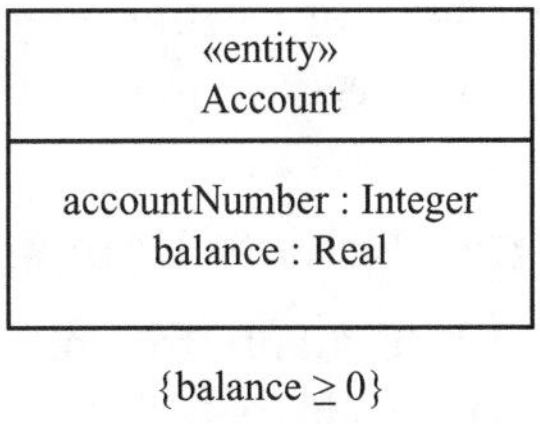

Figure 8.14 *Example of constraints on objects*

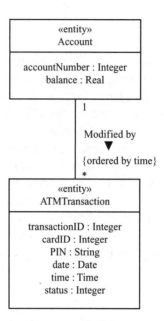

Figure 8.15   *Example of ordering in an association*

to model all classes [Booch 1994]. Other methodologists suggest that static model-ing should be used only for modeling entity classes [Rosenberg and Scott 1999], which are data-intensive classes that are usually persistent and mapped to a data-base. Still others recommend different levels of static modeling, starting with con-ceptual static modeling in the analysis phase and more detailed static modeling in the design phase [Fowler and Scott 1999].

The approach used in COMET is to have a conceptual static model early in the analysis phase that is used to model and help understand the problem domain. The goal is to focus on those aspects of the problem domain that benefit most from static modeling, in particular the physical classes and the data-intensive classes, which are called entity classes. This section describes the initial conceptual static modeling carried out during analysis; the more detailed static modeling carried out during design is described in Chapters 12 and 15.

8.5.1   Static Modeling of the Problem Domain

In static modeling of the problem domain, the initial emphasis in COMET is on modeling physical classes and entity classes. Physical classes are those classes that have physical characteristics, that is, they can be seen and touched. These include

physical devices (which are often part of the problem domain in embedded applications), users, external systems, and timers. Entity classes are conceptual data-
intensive classes that are often persistent, that is, long-living. Entity classes are
particularly prevalent in information systems; in the banking application, there
are debit cards, accounts, and transactions.

In embedded systems, where there are several sensors and actuators, class
diagrams help with modeling these real-world devices. For example, in the Elevator Control System, it is useful to model real-world devices (such as elevator
motors, door, buttons, and lamps), their associations, and the multiplicity of the
associations. Composite classes are often used to show how a real-world class is
composed of other classes. Thus, the elevator is a composite class that consists of a
motor, a door, and several buttons and lamps, as depicted in Figure 8.10.

Consider the static model of the problem domain for the Banking System. A bank
has several ATMs, as shown on Figure 8.16. Each ATM is a composite class consisting
of a Card Reader, a Cash Dispenser, a Receipt Printer, and a user, the ATM
Customer, who interacts with the system by using a keyboard/display. The Card
Reader reads an ATM Card, which is a plastic card and hence a physical entity. The
Cash Dispenser dispenses ATM Cash, which is also a physical entity in terms of
paper money of given denominations. The Receipt Printer prints a Receipt,
which is a paper physical entity. The physical entities represent classes in the problem
domain, for which there will need to be a conceptual representation in the software

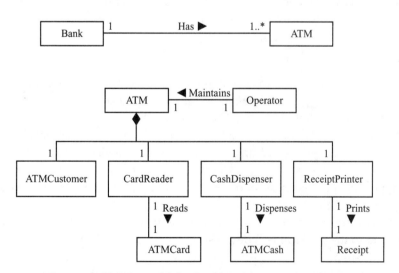

Figure 8.16 *Conceptual static model for Banking System*

system. In most cases, there will need to be software entity classes to represent these physical entities. These decisions are made during object and class structuring, as described in Chapter 9. In addition, the Operator is also a user whose job is to maintain the ATM. As with the ATM Customer, the Operator interacts with the system via a keyboard/display.

8.6   Static Modeling of the System Context

Understanding the interface between the system and the external environment is important. This is referred to as the *system context*. In Structured Analysis, the system context is shown on a *system context diagram*. The UML notation does not explicitly support a system context diagram; however, the system context can be depicted by using either a static model or a collaboration model [Douglass 1999b]. When modeling the problem domain, it is instructive to understand the boundary of the system by developing a **system context class diagram**. This is a more detailed view of the system boundary than that provided by a use case diagram.

The system context class diagram can be determined by static modeling of the external classes that connect to the system. In particular, the physical classes described in the previous section are often I/O devices that are external classes to the system. Alternatively, the system context class diagram can be determined from the use cases by considering the actors and what devices they use to interface to the system. Both approaches are described in this section.

8.6.1   External Classes

Using the UML notation for the static model, the system context is depicted showing the system as an aggregate class with the stereotype «system», and the external environment is depicted as external classes to which the system has to interface.

External classes are categorized by using stereotypes. An external class can be an «external input device», an «external output device», an «external I/O device», an «external user», an «external system», or an «external timer». Using stereotypes for the classification of external classes is described in more detail in Chapter 9.

For a real-time system, it is desirable to identify low-level external classes that correspond to the physical I/O devices to which the system must interface. These external classes are depicted with the stereotype «external I/O device». Examples are the Shaft external input device in the Cruise Control and Monitoring System and the Motor external output device in the Elevator Control System.

A human user often interacts with the system by means of standard I/O devices such as a keyboard/display and mouse. The characteristics of these standard I/O devices are of no interest because they are handled by the operating system. The interface to the user is of much greater interest in terms of what information is being output to the user and what information is being input from the user. For this reason, an external user interacting with the system via standard I/O devices is depicted as an «external user».

A general guideline is that a human user should be represented as an external user class only if the user interacts with the system via standard I/O devices. On the other hand, if the user interacts with the system via application-specific I/O devices, these I/O devices should be represented as external device I/O classes.

An «external timer» class is used if the application needs to keep track of time and/or if it needs external timer events to initiate certain actions in the system. External timer classes are most frequently needed in real-time systems. An example from the Cruise Control and Monitoring System is the Digital Clock. It is needed because the system needs to keep track of elapsed time to compute the speed of the vehicle and needs external timer events to initiate various periodic activities. Sometimes the need for periodic activities only becomes apparent during design.

An «external system» class is needed when the system interfaces to other systems, to either send data or receive data. Thus, in the Factory Automation System, the system interfaces to two external systems: the Pick & Place Robot and the Assembly Robot.

The associations between the system aggregate class and the external classes are depicted on the system context class diagram, showing in particular the multiplicity of the associations. The standard association names on system context class diagrams are Inputs to, Outputs to, Interfaces to, Interacts with, and Awakens. These associations are used as follows:

«external input device» Inputs to «system»
«system» Outputs to «external output device»
«external user» Interacts with «system»
«external system» Interfaces to «system»
«external timer» Awakens «system»

8.6.2 Example of Developing a System Context Class Diagram from External Classes

An example of a system context class diagram is shown in Figure 8.17, which shows the external classes to which the Banking System has to interface. The external classes are determined directly from the static model of the problem domain described previously.

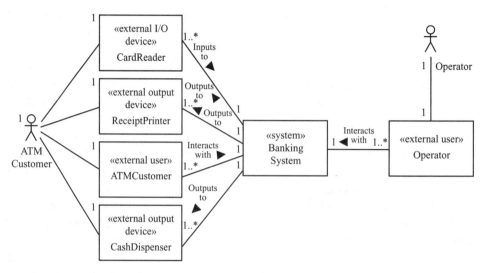

Figure 8.17 *Banking System context class diagram*

From the total system perspective—that is, both hardware and software—the ATM customer is external to the system, whereas the I/O devices, which include the card reader, cash dispenser, and receipt printer, are part of the system. From a software perspective, the I/O devices are external to the software system and hence are modeled as external classes.

The example includes three external device classes: the Card Reader, the Receipt Printer, and the Cash Dispenser. It also includes two external user classes, the ATM Customer and the Operator, who both interact with the system via a keyboard and display. There is one instance of each of these external classes for each ATM.

8.6.3 Actors and External Classes

Consider next how to derive the system context class diagram by analyzing the actors who interact with the system. Actors are a more abstract concept than external classes. The relationship between actors and external classes is as follows:

- An **I/O device actor** is equivalent to an external I/O device class. This means the I/O device actor interfaces to the system via an external I/O device class.

- An **external system actor** is equivalent to an external system class.

- A **timer actor** interfaces to the system via an external timer class, which provides timer events to the system.

- A **human user actor** has the most flexibility. In the simplest case, the user actor interfaces to the system via a standard user I/O device. The external class is given the name of its user actor because what is of interest is the logical information coming from the user. However, in more complex use cases, it is possible for a human actor to interface with the system through a variety of external classes. An example of this is the customer actor in the Banking System. Thus, the actor may interface with the system via several external I/O devices, as illustrated by the following example.

8.6.4   Example of Developing a System Context Class Diagram from Actors

In order to determine the external classes from the actors, it is necessary to understand the characteristics of each actor and how each actor interacts with the system, as described in the use cases. Consider a situation where all the actors are human users. In the Banking System, there are two actors, both of whom are human users: the ATM Customer and the Operator.

Figure 8.17 shows the system context class diagram for the Banking System, with the Banking System as one aggregate class and external classes that interface to it. The operator interfaces to the system via a standard user I/O device and so is depicted as an «external user», because in this case the user's characteristics are more important than those of the I/O devices. However, the customer actor actually interfaces to the system via one standard user I/O device representing the keyboard/display and three application-specific I/O devices. The application-specific I/O devices are an «external input/output device», the Card Reader, and two «external output devices», the Receipt Printer and the Cash Dispenser. Similarly, the operator interfaces to the system via standard I/O devices; hence, the operator is depicted as an «external user». These five external classes all have one-to-many associations with the Banking System. The actors are depicted in Figure 8.17 to show how they relate to the external classes. However, depicting actors on system context class diagrams is optional.

8.7   Static Modeling of Entity Classes

Entity classes are conceptual data-intensive classes. They store persistent (that is, long lasting) data that is accessed by several use cases. Entity classes are particularly prevalent in information systems; however, many real-time and distribution applications have significant data-intensive aspects. Entity classes are often mapped to a database in the design phase, as described in Chapter 15.

During static modeling of the problem domain, the emphasis is on determining the entity classes that are defined in the problem, their attributes, and their relationships. For example, in the Banking System, there are banks, accounts, customers, debit cards, and transactions all mentioned in the problem description. Each of these real-world conceptual entities is modeled as an entity class and depicted with the stereotype «entity». The attributes of each entity class are determined and the relationships among entity classes are defined.

An example of a conceptual static model for the entity classes in the Banking System is shown in Figure 8.18 and described in the case study in Chapter 19. Figure 8.18 shows the Bank entity class, which has a one-to-many relationship with the Customer class and the Debit Card class. Customer has a many-to-many relationship with Account, which in turn is specialized into Checking Account and Savings Account. Association classes might also be needed in cases where the attributes are of the association rather than of the classes connected by the association. For example, in the many-to-many association between Debit Card

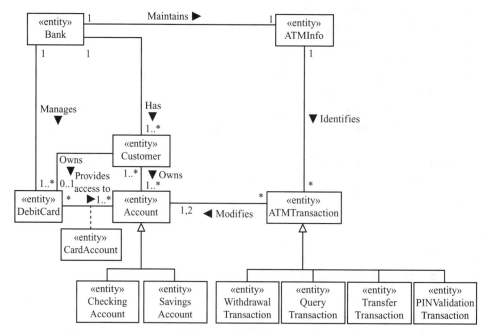

Figure 8.18 *Conceptual static model for Banking System: entity classes*

and `Account`, the individual accounts that can be accessed by a given debit card are attributes of the `Card Account` association class and not of either `Debit Card` or `Account`. Another entity class is the `ATM Transaction`, which is specialized to depict the various types of transactions. This class diagram is described in more detail in Chapter 19, which also describes the attributes of each of the classes.

8.8 Summary

This chapter has described some of the basic aspects of static modeling, including the relationships between classes. Three types of relationships have been described: **associations**, **composition/aggregation** relationships, and **generalization/specialization** relationships. In addition, this chapter has described how static modeling is used to model the structural aspects of the problem domain. This consists of static modeling of the system context, which depicts the classes external to the system, and static modeling of the entity classes, which are conceptual data-intensive classes.

Static modeling of the solution domain is deferred to the design phase. Although static modeling also includes defining the operations of each class, it is easier to determine the operations of a class after dynamic modeling. Because of this, determining the operations of a class is deferred to class design, as described in Chapter 15. Issues concerning the navigability between classes are also deferred to the design phase and are described further in Chapter 12.

chapter

9

Object and Class Structuring

Afternoon defining the use cases and developing a static model of the problem domain, a first attempt is made to determine the software objects in the system. At this stage, the emphasis is on software objects that model real-world objects in the problem domain.

Software objects are usually determined from the use cases and from the static model of the problem domain. This chapter provides guidelines on how to determine the objects in the system. Object structuring criteria are provided, and the objects are categorized by using stereotypes. The emphasis is on problem domain objects to be found in the real world and not on solution domain objects, which are determined at design time.

The static modeling described in the previous chapter was used to determine the external classes, which were then depicted on a system context class diagram. These external classes are used to help determine the software interface classes, which are the software classes that interface to the external environment. The entity classes and their relationships were also determined during static modeling. In this chapter, the objects and classes needed in the software system are determined and categorized. In particular, we focus on the additional objects and classes that were not determined during the static modeling of the problem domain.

The static relationship between classes is considered in the **static model**, as described in the previous chapter, and the dynamic relationship between the objects is considered in the **dynamic model**, as described in the next two chapters.

9.1   Object Structuring Criteria

There is no one unique way to decompose a system into objects. The decomposition of a problem into objects is based on the judgment of the analyst and the characteristics of the problem. Whether objects are in the same class or in a different class depends on the nature of the problem. For example, in an automobile catalog, cars, vans, and trucks might all be objects of the same class. However, for a vehicle manufacturer, cars, vans, and trucks might all be objects of different classes.

Object structuring criteria are provided to assist the designer in structuring a system into objects. The approach used for identifying objects is to look for real-world objects in the problem domain and then design corresponding software objects that model the real world. After the objects have been identified, the interactions among object instances (usually referred to as objects) are depicted in the dynamic model on **collaboration diagrams** or **sequence diagrams,** as described in Chapter 11. During dynamic modeling, the message interaction among objects is determined.

Several object-based and object-oriented analysis methods provide criteria for determining objects in the problem domain [Booch 1994; Coad and Yourdon 1991; Gomaa 1993; Jacobson 1992; Parnas, Clements, and Weiss 1984; Shlaer and Mellor 1988]. The object structuring criteria described in this chapter build on these methods.

9.2   Categorization of Application Classes

The traditional definition of "category" is *a specifically defined division in a system of classification*. In object structuring, we categorize objects in order to group together objects with similar characteristics. Whereas classification based on inheritance is an objective of object-oriented modeling, it is essentially tactical in nature. Thus, we decide that classifying the Account class into a Checking Account and a Savings Account is a good idea because Checking Account and Savings Account have some attributes and operations in common and others that differ. Categorization, however, is a strategic classification—a decision to organize classes into certain groups because most software systems have these kinds of classes and categorizing classes in this way helps us understand the system we are to develop. Of course, different types of systems will have a preponderance of classes in one or another category. Thus, information intensive systems will have a preponderance of entity classes, which is why static modeling is so vital for these systems. On the other hand, real-time systems will have many device interface classes to interface to the various sensors and actuators. They will also have complex state-dependent control classes because these systems are highly state-dependent.

Figure 9.1 shows the categorization of application classes. Stereotypes are used to distinguish among the various kinds of application classes. A **stereotype** is a subclass of an existing modeling element, in this case an application class, which is used to represent a usage distinction, in this case the kind of class. A stereotype is depicted in guillemets, like this: «interface».

In Figure 9.1, each box represents a different category of application class, and the relationships between them are inheritance relationships. Thus, an application class is classified as an «entity» class, an «interface» class, a «control» class, or an «application logic» class. The three latter stereotypes are classified further, as shown in Figure 9.1 and described below. An instance of a stereotype class is a stereotype object, which can also be shown in guillemets, like this: the stereotype «entity» object.

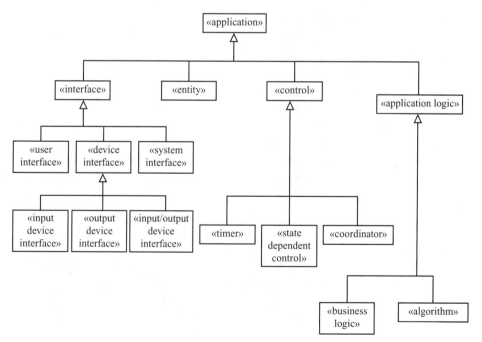

Figure 9.1 *Classification of application classes using stereotypes*

9.3 Object Structuring Categories

Objects are categorized based on the role they play in the application. There are four main object structuring categories, as shown in Figure 9.1. Most applications will have objects from each of the four categories. The object structuring categories are as follows:

1. **Interface object.** Object that interfaces to the external environment. Sometimes also referred to as *boundary* object. Interface objects can be further categorized as:

   - **Device interface object.** Interfaces to a hardware I/O device.
   - **User interface object.** Provides an interface to a human user.
   - **System interface object.** Interfaces to an external system or subsystem.

2. **Entity object.** Long-living object that stores information. These are the classes that would typically be modeled as entities in entity-relationship models.

3. **Control object.** Provides the overall coordination for a collection of objects in a use case. Control objects may be **coordinator objects**, **state-dependent control objects**, or **timer objects**. Because control objects coordinate the interaction among several objects, they are usually considered only at the time of developing the dynamic model and not the initial conceptual static model.

4. **Application logic object.** Contains the details of the application logic. Needed when it is desirable to hide the application logic separately from the data being manipulated because it is considered likely that the application logic could change independent of the data. For information systems, application logic objects are usually **business logic objects**, whereas for real-time, scientific, or engineering applications, they are usually **algorithm objects**. As with control objects, application logic objects are more likely to be considered at the time of developing the dynamic model and not the initial conceptual static model.

In most cases, what category an object fits into is usually obvious. However, in some cases, it is possible for an object to satisfy more than one of the above criteria. For example, an object can be both an entity object, in that it encapsulates some data, and an algorithm object, in that it executes a significant algorithm. In such cases, allocate the object to the category it seems best to fit. Note that it is more important to determine all the objects in the system than to be unduly concerned about how to categorize a few borderline cases.

9.4   External Classes and Interface Classes

External classes are classes that are external to the system and that interface to the system. Interface classes are classes internal to the system that interface to the external classes. To help determine the interface classes in the system, it is useful to consider the external classes to which they interface.

9.4.1   Categorization of External Classes

External classes that interface to the system can also be categorized by using stereotypes. As depicted in Figure 9.2, an external class is classified as an «external user», an «external device», an «external system», or an «external timer». An external user interfaces to the system via standard user I/O devices, such as a keyboard, display, and mouse, which are typically handled by the operating system. An external device is one that is not handled by the operating system and needs to have a device interface object; external devices are used particularly in real-time systems. An external device is further classified as one of the following:

- **External input device.** A device that only provides input to the system, for example, a sensor.
- **External output device.** A device that only receives output from the system, for example, an actuator.
- **External input/output device.** A device that both provides input to the system and receives output from the system, for example, an ATM card reader.

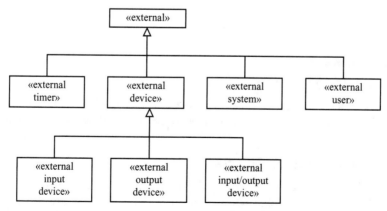

Figure 9.2 *Classification of external classes using stereotypes*

Chapter 8 discusses how a system context class diagram can be developed, depicting the interfaces between the external classes and the system.

9.4.2   Identifying Interface Classes

Identifying the external classes that interface to the system helps identify some of the classes in the system itself, namely, the interface classes. Each of the external classes interfaces to an interface class in the system. There is a one-to-one association between the external class (assuming it has been identified correctly) and the internal interface class to which it interfaces. External classes interface to internal interface classes as follows:

- An **external system class** interfaces to a **system interface class**. In this case, the external system class is equivalent to the external system actor.
- An **external device class** interfaces to a **device interface class**. Continuing with this classification:
  - An **external input device class** interfaces to an input device interface class.
  - An **external output device class** interfaces to an output device interface class.
  - An **external input/output device class** interfaces to an input/output device interface class.
- An **external user class** interfaces to a **user interface class**.
- An **external timer class** interfaces to an internal **timer class**.

An external device class represents an I/O device type. An external I/O device object represents a specific I/O device, that is, an instance of the device type. In the next section, we consider the internal interface objects that interface to the external objects.

9.5   Interface Objects

This section describes the characteristics of the three different kinds of interface objects: device interface objects, user interface objects, and system interface objects.

9.5.1   Device Interface Objects

A **device interface object** provides the software interface to a hardware I/O device. Device interface objects are needed for nonstandard application-specific I/O devices, which are more prevalent in real-time systems although often needed in other systems as well.

A physical object, also referred to as a concrete object, in the application domain is a real-world object that has some physical characteristics—for example, it can be seen and touched. For every real-world physical object that is relevant to the problem, there should be a corresponding software object in the system. For example, in the elevator control system, elevator motors, elevator doors, elevator and floor lamps, elevator and floor buttons are all relevant real-world physical objects, because they impact the elevator control system. On the other hand, the elevator shaft and elevator cabin are not relevant real-world objects, because they do not impact the elevator control system. In the software system, the relevant real-world physical objects are modeled by means of elevator motor, elevator door, elevator and floor lamp, and elevator and floor button software objects, respectively.

Real-world physical objects usually interface to the system via sensors and actuators. These real-world objects provide inputs to the system via sensors or are controlled by (receive outputs from) the system via actuators. Thus to the software system, the real-world objects are actually I/O devices that provide inputs to and receive outputs from the system. Because the real-world objects correspond to I/O devices, the software objects that interface to them are referred to as device interface objects [Parnas, Clements, and Weiss 1984].

For example, in the elevator control system, the elevator button, floor button, and floor arrival indicator are all real-world objects that have sensors (input devices) that provide inputs to the system. The motor and door are real-world objects that are controlled by means of actuators (output devices) that receive outputs from the system.

Figure 9.3 shows an example of an input device interface object on a collaboration diagram. An input device interface object, a `Temperature Sensor Interface` object, receives temperature sensor input from an external real-world hardware object, a `Real-World Temperature Sensor` input device. Figure 9.3 also shows the hardware/software boundary, as well as the stereotypes for the hardware «external input device» and the software «input device interface» objects. Thus, the device interface object provides the software system interface to the external hardware input device.

It should be pointed out that Figure 9.3 represents a logical model of the problem, in which the input is sent from the real-world hardware input device to the software device interface object. At design time, the decision is made as to whether the device is *active* and sends the input to the software object, or *passive*, in which case it needs to be polled by the software object. These design issues are described in Chapter 14.

Figure 9.4 shows an example of an output device interface object, `Red Light Interface`, which provides outputs to an external real-world object, the `Red Light Actuator` external output device. The `Red Light Interface` software object

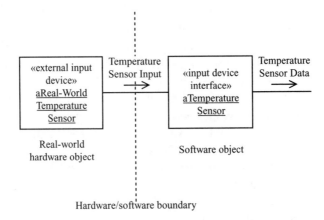

Figure 9.3 *Example of input device interface object*

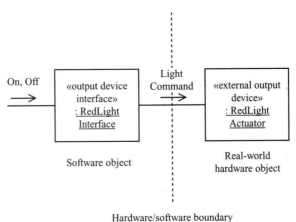

NB: The dashed line for the hardware/software boundary is for illustrative purposes only and does not conform to the UML notation.

Figure 9.4 *Example of output device interface object*

receives On and Off requests, which it sends as Light commands to the hardware Red Light Actuator. Figure 9.4 also shows the hardware/software boundary.

A hardware I/O device can also be both an input and an output device. The corresponding software object is an I/O device interface object. This is the case with the ATM Card Reader Interface object, which receives ATM card input from the external card reader, the ATM Card Reader external I/O device. In addition, it receives Eject and Confiscate commands, which it sends as Card Reader Output to the card reader (see Figure 9.5).

Each software object should hide the details of the interface to the real-world object from which it receives input or to which it provides output. However, a software object should model the events experienced by the real-world object to which it corresponds. The events experienced by the real-world object are inputs to the system, in particular, to the software object that interfaces to it. In this way, the software object can simulate the behavior of the real-world object. In the case of a real-world object that is controlled by the system, the software object outputs an event that determines the behavior of the real-world object.

In some applications, there are many real-world objects of the same type. These are modeled by means of one device interface object for each real-world object, where all the objects are instances of the same class. For example, the Elevator Control System has many elevator buttons of the same type and many elevator lamps of the same type. These are modeled as one Elevator Lamp Interface class and one Elevator Button Interface class, each of which can be instantiated several times.

9.5.2 User Interface Objects

A **user interface object** provides an interface to a human user via standard I/O devices such as the keyboard, visual display, and mouse. Standard I/O devices

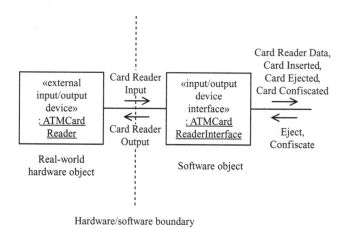

NB: The dashed line for the hardware/software boundary is for illustrative purposes only and does not conform to the UML notation.

Figure 9.5 *Example of I/O device interface object*

are typically handled by the operating system and so do not need special-purpose device interface objects developed as part of the application. Depending on the user interface technology, the user interface could be very simple (such as a command line interface) or it could be more complex (such as a graphical user interface [GUI] object). A user interface object may be a composite object composed of several simpler user interface objects. This means that the actor interacts with the system via several user interface objects, either sequentially or concurrently. Such objects are depicted with the «user interface» stereotype.

An example of a simple user interface object is the `Operator Interface` object (see Figure 9.6), which accepts operator commands; requests sensor data from an entity object, `Sensor Data Repository`; and displays the data it receives to the operator. More complex user interface objects are also possible. For example, the `Operator Interface` object could be a composite user interface object composed of several simpler user interface objects. This would allow the operator to receive dynamic updates of workstation status in one window, receive dynamic updates of alarm status in another window, and interact with the system by using a third window. Each window is composed of several GUI widgets, such as menus, buttons, and simpler windows. Note that only the composite object is depicted in the analysis model. The design of the internal GUI objects is deferred to class design as described in Chapter 15.

9.5.3   System Interface Objects

A **system interface object** interfaces to an external system, which communicates with the system under development. The system interface object hides the details of "how" to communicate with the external system.

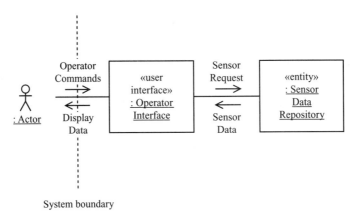

System boundary

NB: The dashed line for the system boundary is for illustrative purposes only and does not conform to the UML notation.

Figure 9.6   *Example of user interface object*

An example of a system interface object is a `Pick & Place Robot Inter-face` object in a Factory Automation System (see Figure 9.7), which interfaces to the `External Pick & Place Robot`. The `Pick & Place Robot Interface` object receives `Pick` and `Place` requests, which it sends as robot commands to the `External Pick & Place Robot`. The real-world robot responds to the commands, which the system interface object sends to the original requestor.

Each system interface object hides the details of how to interface to the particular external system. A system interface object is more likely to communicate by means of messages to an external, computer-controlled system, rather than through sensors and actuators as is the case with device interface objects. However, these issues are not addressed until the design phase.

9.5.4   Depicting External Classes and Interface Classes

In Chapter 8, we discussed how to determine the boundary of the system and how to develop a **system context class diagram**, which shows all the external classes that interface to the system. It is useful to refine this diagram to show the interface classes that interface to the external classes. The interface classes are classes inside the system, which are at the boundary between the system and the external environment. The system is shown as a package, and the interface classes, which are part of the system, are shown inside the system package. Each external class, which is external to the system, has a one-to-one association with an interface class, as described in Section 9.4.2. Thus, starting with the external classes, as depicted on the system context class diagram, helps determine the interface classes.

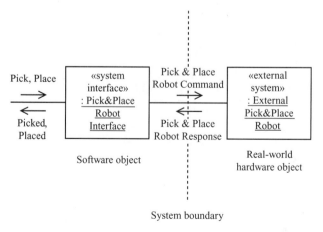

NB: The dashed line for the system boundary is for illustrative purposes only and does not conform to the UML notation.

Figure 9.7   *Example of system interface object*

Starting with the system context class diagram for the Banking System, we determine that each external class interfaces to an interface class (see Figure 9.8). The system is depicted as a package, which contains the interface classes that interface to the external classes. In this application, there are three device interface classes and two user interface classes. The device interface classes are the `Card Reader Interface`, through which ATM cards are read, the `Cash Dispenser Interface`, which dispenses cash, and the `Receipt Printer Interface`, which prints receipts. The `Customer Interface` is a user interface class, which displays textual messages and prompts to the customer and receives the customer's inputs. The `Operator Interface` class provides the user interface to the ATM operator, who replenishes the ATM machine with cash. There is one instance of each of these interface classes for each ATM.

9.6 Entity Objects

An **entity object** is a long-living object that stores information. An entity object is typically accessed by many use cases. The information maintained by an entity object persists over access by several use cases. Entity objects are instances of

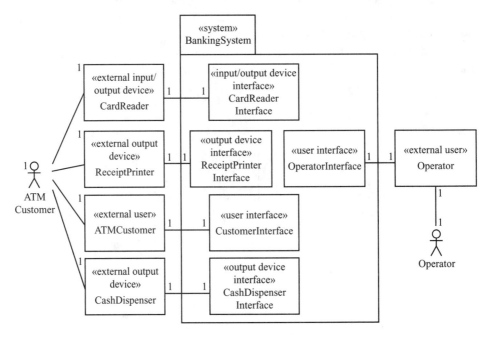

Figure 9.8 *Banking System external classes and interface classes*

entity classes, whose attributes and relationships with other entity classes are determined during static modeling, as described in Chapter 8.

Entity objects store data and provide limited access to that data via operations they provide. In some cases, an entity object might need to access other entity objects in order to update the information it encapsulates.

In real-time systems, entity objects are often stored in main memory. In many information system applications, the information encapsulated by entity objects is stored in a database. These issues are addressed during the design phase, as described in Chapter 15.

An example of an entity class from the banking application is the Account class (see Figure 9.9). The stereotype «entity» is shown to clearly identify what kind of class it is. Instances of the Account class are entity objects (as shown in Figure 9.9), which are also identified by the stereotype «entity». The attributes of Account are account Number and balance. In Figure 9.9, which shows a fragment of a collaboration diagram, an object an Account receives messages Open, Close, Credit, Debit, and Read, and responds with the account Balance and Status information. The object an Account is a persistent (long-living) object that is accessed by several use cases. These use cases include customer use cases for account withdrawals, inquiries, and transfers at various ATM machines, as well as human teller use cases to open and close the account and to credit and debit the account. The account is also accessed by a use case that prepares and prints monthly statements for customers.

An example of an entity class from a real-time sensor monitoring example is the Sensor Data class (see Figure 9.10). This class stores information about analog sensors. The attributes are sensor Name, sensor Value, upper Limit, lower Limit, and alarm Status. An example of an instance of this class is the temperature Sensor Data object, which receives Read and Update messages. It responds with Current Sensor Data. As shown in Figure 9.10, an object that needs to obtain the status of the sensor sends a Read message. An object that has read the latest value of the real-world sensor and wishes to update the temperature Sensor Data object sends the Update message.

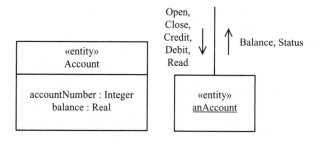

Figure 9.9 *Example of entity class and object*

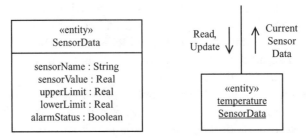

Figure 9.10 *Example of entity class and object*

9.7 Control Objects

A **control object** provides the overall coordination for execution of a use case. Simple use cases do not need control objects. However, in a more complex use case, a control object is usually needed. A control object can be thought of as the conductor of an orchestra, who orchestrates (controls) the behavior of the other objects that participate in the use case, notifying each object when and what it should perform. Depending on the characteristics of the use case, the control object may be state-dependent. There are several kinds of control objects, as described next.

9.7.1 Coordinator Objects

A **coordinator object** is an overall decision-making object that determines the overall sequencing for a collection of related objects. A coordinator object is often required to provide the overall sequencing for execution of a use case. It makes the overall decisions and decides when, and in what order, other objects participate in the use case. A coordinator object makes its decision based on the input it receives and is not state-dependent. Thus an action initiated by a coordinator object depends only on the information contained in the incoming message and not on what previously happened in the system.

An example of a coordinator object is the `Bank Coordinator`, which receives a client transaction from a client ATM. Depending on the transaction type, the `Bank Coordinator` sends the transaction to the appropriate object to execute the transaction. In the Banking System, these are a `Withdrawal Transaction Manager` object, a `Transfer Transaction Manager` object, a `Query Transaction Manager` object, or a `PIN Validation Transaction Manager` object (see Figure 9.11).

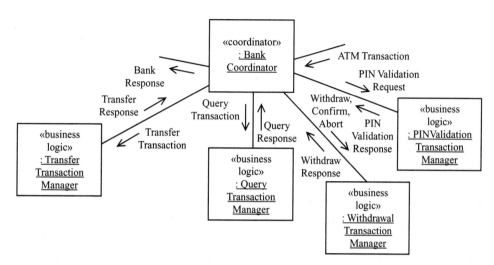

Figure 9.11 *Example of coordinator and business logic objects*

9.7.2 State-Dependent Control Objects

A **state-dependent control** object is a control object whose behavior varies in each of its states. A finite state machine is used to define a state-dependent control object and is depicted by using a statechart. Statecharts, which were originally conceived by Harel [1988, 1998], can be either flat (not hierarchical) or hierarchical, as described in Chapter 10. This section only gives a brief overview of state-dependent control objects, which are described in much more detail in Chapter 11.

A state-dependent control object receives incoming events that cause state transitions and generates output events that control other objects. The output event generated by a state-dependent control object depends not only on the input received by the object but also on the current state of the object. An example of a state-dependent control object is the ATM Control object (see Figure 9.12), which is defined by means of the ATM Control statechart. In the example, ATM Control is shown controlling two other device interface objects, Receipt Printer Interface and Cash Dispenser Interface.

In a real-time control system, there are usually one or more state-dependent control objects. It is also possible to have multiple state-dependent control objects of the same type. Each object executes an instance of the same finite state machine (depicted as a statechart), although each object is likely to be in a different state. An example of this is the Banking System, which has several ATMs, where each ATM has an instance of the state-dependent control class, ATM Control. Each ATM Control object executes its own instance of the ATM Control statechart. Another example is from the

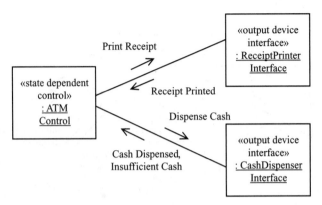

Figure 9.12 *Example of state-dependent control object*

Elevator Control System, where the control aspects of each elevator are modeled by means of a state-dependent control object, Elevator Control, and defined by means of a statechart. Consequently, each elevator has an elevator control object. More information about state-dependent control objects is given in Chapter 11.

9.7.3 Timer Objects

A timer object is a control object that is activated by an external timer, for example, a real-time clock or operating system clock. The timer object either performs some action itself or activates another object to perform the desired action.

An example of a timer object is given in Figure 9.13. The timer object, Distance Timer, is activated by a timer event from an external timer, the Digital

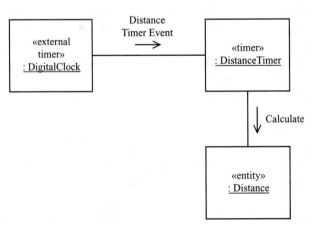

Figure 9.13 *Example of a timer object*

`Clock`. The timer object then sends a `Calculate` message to the `Distance` object to determine the cumulative distance traveled by the car.

9.8   Application Logic Objects

This section describes the two kinds of application logic objects, namely, business logic objects and algorithm objects.

9.8.1   Business Logic Objects

A **business logic object** defines the business-specific application logic for processing a client request. The goal is to encapsulate (hide) business rules that could change independently of each other into separate business logic objects. Usually a business logic object accesses various entity objects during its execution.

Business logic objects are only needed in certain situations. Sometimes, there is a choice between encapsulating the business logic in a separate business logic object or, if the business logic is sufficiently simple, having it as an operation of an entity object. The guideline is that if the business rule can be executed only by accessing two or more entity objects, there should be a separate business logic object. On the other hand, if accessing one entity object is sufficient to execute the business rule, it should be provided by an operation of that object.

An example of a business logic object is the `Withdrawal Transaction Manager` object shown in Figure 9.11, which services withdrawal requests from ATM customers. It encapsulates the business rules for processing an ATM withdrawal request. For example, the first business rule is that the customer must have a minimum balance of $50 after the withdrawal takes place; the second business rule is that the customer is not allowed to withdraw more than $250 per day with a debit card. The `Withdrawal Transaction Manager` object accesses an `Account` object to determine if the first business rule will be satisfied. It accesses the `Debit Card` object, which maintains a running total of the amount withdrawn by an ATM customer on this day, to determine if the second business rule will be satisfied. If either business rule is not satisfied, the withdrawal request is rejected.

A business logic object usually has to interact with entity objects in order to execute its business rules. In this way, it resembles a coordinator object. However, unlike a coordinator object, whose main responsibility is to supervise other objects, the prime responsibility of a business logic object is to encapsulate and execute the business rules.

9.8.2 Algorithm Objects

An **algorithm object** encapsulates an algorithm used in the problem domain. This kind of object is more prevalent in real-time, scientific, and engineering domains. Algorithm objects are used when there is a substantial algorithm used in the problem domain that can change independently of the other aspects of the domain. Simple algorithms are usually operations of an entity object, which operate on the data encapsulated in the entity. In many scientific and engineering domains, algorithms are refined iteratively because they are improved independently of the data they manipulate, for example, for improved performance or accuracy.

For example, in a Cruise Control System, an algorithm object, `Cruiser`, calculates what the adjustments to the throttle should be by comparing the current vehicle speed with the desired cruising speed (see Figure 9.14). The algorithm is complex because it must provide gradual accelerations or decelerations of the car when they are needed, so as to have minimal effect on the passengers.

An algorithm object frequently encapsulates data it needs for computing its algorithm. This data may be initialization data, intermediate result data, or threshold data, such as maximum or minimum values.

An algorithm object frequently has to interact with other objects in order to execute its algorithm, for example, `Cruiser`. In this way, it resembles a coordinator object. However, unlike a coordinator object, whose main responsibility is to supervise other objects, the prime responsibility of an algorithm object is to encapsulate and execute the algorithm.

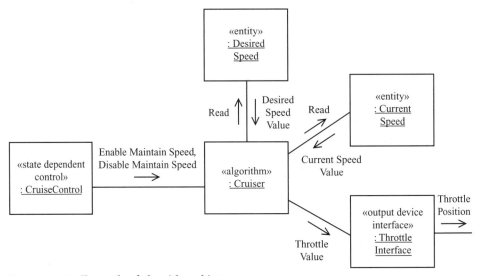

Figure 9.14 *Example of algorithm object*

9.9 Subsystems

A system is structured into **subsystems**, which contain objects that are functionally dependent on each other. The goal is for objects with high coupling among each other to be in the same subsystem, and objects that are weakly coupled to be in different subsystems. A subsystem can be considered a composite or aggregate object that contains the simple objects that compose that subsystem. There can be many subsystems of the same type. In this section, packages will be used to depict the whole system and to show the organization of the system into **subsystems**.

9.9.1 Using Packages to Depict Subsystems

Packages can be used to represent subsystems. Thus, one package representing the whole system may be decomposed into subsystems, where the subsystems are shown as nested packages within the system package. An example of this is given in Figure 9.15 for the Banking System, shown as one package, which consists of two subsystems, the ATM Client Subsystem and the Bank Server Subsystem. The two subsystems are shown as packages nested within the system package.

It is also possible to show relationships between the packages. One option is to depict dependencies in order to show that one package depends on another package. In a package diagram, dependencies among packages are shown by a dashed line.

For example, in the Banking System example, the ATM Client Subsystem depends on the Bank Server Subsystem. Although it would seem logical to show other relationships such as aggregation, generalization/specialization, and

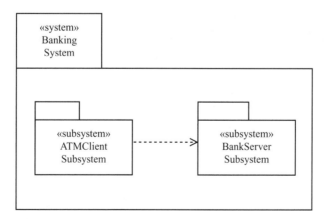

Figure 9.15 *Banking System: major subsystems depicted as packages*

other associations, only the dependency and generalization/specialization relationships are allowed between packages in the UML. Therefore, to model other relationships between subsystems, class diagrams need to be used as shown in the following example.

Figure 9.16 shows the decomposition of the banking system into subsystems, where the subsystems are depicted as aggregate classes. There is a one-to-many association between the Bank Server Subsystem and the ATM Client Subsystem. Each of the external classes actually interfaces to the ATM Client Subsystem and has a one-to-one association with the client subsystem

9.9.2 Issues in Subsystem Structuring

In some applications, such as client/server systems, the subsystems are easily identifiable. Thus in the Banking Application shown in Figure 9.15, there is a client subsystem called ATM Client located at each ATM machine and a central server subsystem called the Bank Server Subsystem. This is an example of

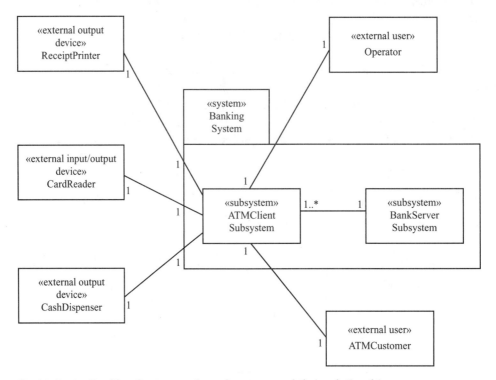

Figure 9.16 *Banking System: major subsystems and their relationships*

geographical subsystem structuring, where the geographical distribution of the system is given in the problem description.

In other applications, it might not be so obvious how to structure the system into subsystems. Because one of the goals of subsystem structuring is to have objects that are functionally related and highly coupled in the same subsystem, a good place to start is with the use cases. Objects that participate in the same use case are candidates to be in the same subsystem. Because of this, subsystem structuring is often done after the interaction among the constituent objects of each use case has been determined during dynamic modeling. In particular, it is carried out early in the design phase, as described in Chapter 12.

9.10 Summary

This chapter has described how to determine the software objects in the system. Object structuring criteria were provided, and the objects were categorized by using stereotypes. The emphasis is on problem domain objects to be found in the real world and not on solution domain objects, which are determined at design time. The object structuring criteria are usually applied to each use case in turn during dynamic modeling, as described in Chapter 11, to determine the objects that participate in each use case. The sequence of interaction among the objects is then determined. Subsystem structuring criteria are described in Chapter 12. Issues about whether an object is active or passive are addressed during the design phases, as described in Chapters 14–16. The design of the operations provided by each class is described in Chapter 15.

chapter 10

Finite State Machines and Statecharts

F inite state machines are used for modeling the dynamic aspects of a system. Many systems, in particular real-time systems, are highly state-dependent. That is, their actions depend not only on their inputs but also on what has previously happened in the system.

Notations used to define finite state machines are the state transition diagram and the state transition table. A **state transition diagram** is a graphical representation of a finite state machine in which the nodes represent states and the arcs represent state transitions. A **state transition table** is a tabular representation of a finite state machine.

In highly state-dependent systems, state transition diagrams or tables can help substantially by providing a means of understanding the complexity of these systems. A finite state machine specification is typically more precise and understandable than a verbal description.

In the UML notation, a state transition diagram is referred to as a **statechart diagram**. The UML statechart diagram notation is based on Harel's statechart notation [Harel 1988, Harel 1998]. In this section, the terms **statechart** and **statechart diagram** are used interchangeably. We refer to a traditional state transition diagram, which is not hierarchical, as a *flat statechart* and use the term *hierarchical statechart* to refer to the concept of hierarchical state decomposition. To show the benefits of hierarchical statecharts, we start with the simplest form of flat statechart and gradually show how it can be improved upon to achieve the full modeling power of hierarchical statecharts.

This chapter starts by considering the characteristics of flat statecharts and then describes hierarchical statecharts. Guidelines for developing statecharts are given. The process of developing statecharts from use cases is then described in detail. Several examples are given throughout the chapter from two case studies, the Automated Teller Machine and Cruise Control finite state machines.

10.1   Finite State Machines

A **finite state machine** is a conceptual machine with a finite number of states. It can be in only one of the states at any specific time. A **state transition** is a change in state that is caused by an input event. In response to an input event, the finite state machine might transition to a different state. Alternatively, the event has no effect and the finite state machine remains in the same state. The next state depends on the current state as well as on the input event. Optionally, an output action may result from the state transition.

10.2   Events and States

We now introduce the basic concepts of events and states before giving some examples of statecharts.

10.2.1   Events

An **event** is an occurrence at a point in time; it is also known as a discrete signal or stimulus. An event is an atomic occurrence (not interruptible) and conceptually has zero duration. Examples of events are ATM Card Inserted, Pin # Entered, Brake Pressed, and Elevator Departed.

Events can depend on each other. For example, the event ATM Card Inserted always precedes Pin # Entered for a given sequence of events. On the other hand, events can be completely independent of each other. For example, the event ATM Card Inserted at Vienna ATM is independent of the event ATM Card Inserted at Richmond ATM.

A **timer event** is a special event, specified by the keyword **after**, which indicates that an event occurs after an elapsed time identified by an expression in parentheses, such as **after** (10 seconds) or **after** (elapsed time). On a statechart, the timer event causes a transition out of a given state. The elapsed time is measured from the time of entry into that state until exit from the state, which is caused by the timer event.

10.2.2   States

A **state** represents a recognizable situation that exists over an interval of time. Whereas an **event** occurs at a point in time, a finite state machine is in a given **state** over some interval of time. The arrival of an event at the finite state machine usually causes a transition from one state to another. Alternatively, an event can have a null effect, in which case the finite state machine remains in the same state. In theory, a state transition is meant to take zero time to occur. In practice, the time for a state transition to occur is negligible compared to the time spent in the state.

The initial state of a statechart is the state that is entered when the statechart is activated.

10.3   Finite State Machines and Objects

Although a whole system can be modeled by means of a finite state machine, in object-oriented analysis and design, a finite state machine is encapsulated inside one object. In other words, the object is state-dependent and is always in one of the states of the finite state machine. The object's finite state machine is depicted by using a statechart. In an object-oriented model, the state dependent aspects of a system are defined by means of one or more finite state machines, where each finite state machine is encapsulated inside its own object. If the finite state machines need to communicate with each other, they do so indirectly: the objects that contain them send messages to each other, as described in Chapter 11.

10.4   Examples of Statecharts

The use of flat statecharts is illustrated by means of three examples, an account statechart, an ATM statechart, and a Cruise Control statechart.

10.4.1   Example of Account Statechart

The first example shows a simple statechart consisting of two states, with the initial and final states (see Figure 10.1). When an account is opened with a positive balance, the `Account Opened` event causes a transition to the initial state `Account in Good Standing`. Subsequent `Deposit` and `Regular Withdrawal` events, which keep the account with a positive balance, do not result in a change of state. However, the `Authorized Withdrawal` event, which results in a negative account balance, causes

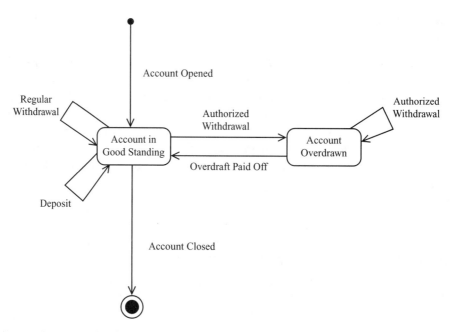

Figure 10.1 *Example of Account statechart*

a transition to the state Account Overdrawn. In this state, other Authorized Withdrawal events may occur. A subsequent event, Overdraft Paid Off, causes the account to transition back to the Account in Good Standing state. Finally, when the account is closed, a transition is made to the final state, depicted by a bull's eye.

10.4.2   Example of ATM Statechart

Consider an example, shown in Figure 10.2, of a statechart for an automated teller machine. The initial state of the ATM statechart is Idle. When the Card Inserted event is received, the ATM transitions from the Idle state to the Waiting for PIN state, during which time the ATM is waiting for the customer to input the PIN. When the PIN Entered event occurs, the ATM transitions to the Validating PIN state. In this state the bank system determines whether the customer-entered PIN matches the stored PIN for this card. There are four possible state transitions out of the Validating PIN state. If the two PIN numbers match, the Valid PIN transition is taken to the Waiting for Customer Choice state. If the PIN numbers do not match, the Invalid PIN transition is taken to re-enter the Waiting for PIN state and the customer is prompted to enter a different PIN number. If the customer-entered PIN is invalid after the third attempt, the Third

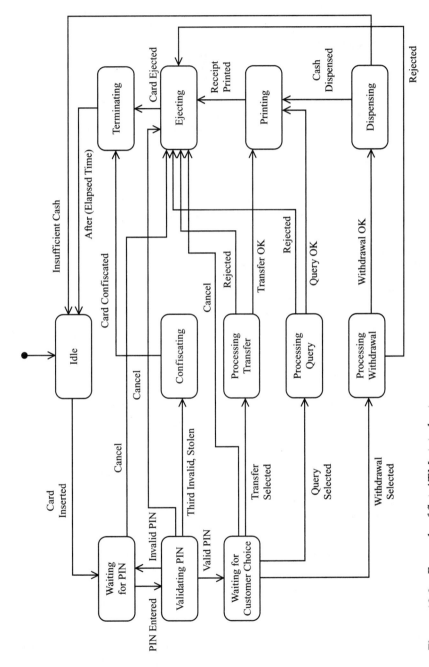

Figure 10.2 *Example of flat ATM statechart*

Invalid transition is taken to the Confiscating state. The same transition is also taken if the ATM card has been reported lost or stolen. In addition, the customer may decide to enter Cancel, which results in the ATM card being ejected and the transaction terminated.

From the Waiting for Customer Choice state, the customer enters a selection—for example, for withdrawal. The statechart receives a Withdrawal Selected event, upon which the Processing Withdrawal state is entered. If the withdrawal is approved, the statechart goes into the Dispensing state, where the cash is dispensed. After the Cash Dispensed event has taken place, the ATM transitions to the Printing state to print the receipt. When the receipt is printed, the Ejecting state is entered. When the card has been ejected, as indicated by the Card Ejected event, the Terminating state is entered.

From the Terminating state, a timer event causes a transition back to the Idle state. The timer event is depicted by **after** (Elapsed Time), where Elapsed Time is the time spent in the Terminating state (from entry into the state until exit from the state caused by the timer event).

10.4.3   Example of Cruise Control Statechart

Figure 10.3 shows a simplified statechart for a Cruise Control object. Initially the statechart is in Idle state. When the driver switches the ignition switch on, the Engine On event occurs and the Cruise Control statechart transitions to Initial state. When the driver engages the cruise control lever in the ACCEL position, the Accel event occurs and the statechart transitions to Accelerating state. While in Accelerating state, when the driver releases the cruise control lever, the Cruise event occurs, and the statechart transitions to Cruising state. If the driver places his/her foot on the brake, the Brake Pressed event occurs, and the statechart transitions to Cruising Off state.

The statechart in Figure 10.3 allows the object to transition from Initial state to Accelerating state even if the driver has pressed the brake. Clearly, this is undesirable, because pressing the brake should deactivate cruise control. One way to avoid this situation is to distinguish between the states of Initial Not Braking and Initial Braking, as shown in Figure 10.4. Transition to Accelerating state is only allowed from Initial Not Braking state and is prohibited from Initial Braking state. Thus the Accel event has no impact on the statechart if it is in Initial Braking state, but causes the statechart to transition to Accelerating state if it is in Initial Not Braking state. The Brake Pressed event causes the statechart to transition from Initial Not Braking state to Initial Braking state, and the Brake Released event causes the statechart to transition from Initial Braking state to Initial Not Braking state.

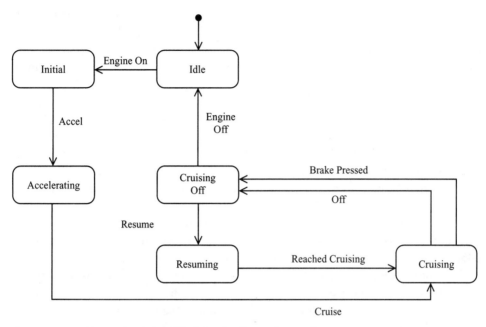

Figure 10.3 *Example of simplified Cruise Control statechart*

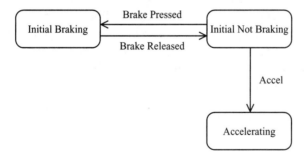

Figure 10.4 *Partial statechart*

10.5 Events and Conditions

Although the case just described prevents one problem, it introduces another problem. If there is always a need to distinguish between braking and not braking, the number of states could potentially be doubled. An alternative approach is to allow conditions as well as events. A **condition** defines some aspect of the system that can be true or false for some finite interval of time. It thus represents the value of a Boolean variable. For example, a condition could be defined for the brake, whose value is either `Brake On` or `Brake Off`. It is possible for a condition to represent the state of some other aspect of the system, in this case, the brake. A condition is sometimes referred to as a state variable.

Figure 10.5 shows the relationship between events and conditions. Initially the brake condition is `Brake Off`. When the `Brake Pressed` event occurs, representing the moment the driver's foot is placed on the brake, the brake condition changes from `Brake Off` to `Brake On`. When the `Brake Released` event occurs, representing the moment the driver's foot is taken off the brake, the brake condition changes from `Brake On` back to `Brake Off`. An event takes negligible time, but a condition is true or false for a finite interval of time.

Events and conditions may be combined in defining a state transition. The notation used is that of **event [condition]**. Thus an event is allowed to cause a state transition, providing the condition given in brackets is *true*.

In some cases, an event occurs that does not cause an immediate state transition, but whose effect needs to be remembered because it will affect some future state transition. The fact that an event has occurred can be stored as a condition that can be checked later.

Figure 10.6 shows how the brake condition is used. The states `Initial Not Braking` and `Initial Braking` are merged into one state called `Initial`. When the `Accel` event occurs, the `Brake` condition is tested. If the condition [`Brake Off`] is true, meaning that the driver does not have his/her foot on the brake, the transition to `Accelerating` state is allowed. If the condition [`Brake Off`] is false, meaning that the driver does have his/her foot on the brake, the transition to `Accelerating` state is prohibited and so the statechart remains in `Initial` state.

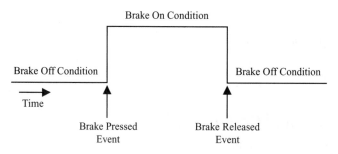

NB: This diagram does not use the UML notation.

Figure 10.5 *Relationship between events and conditions*

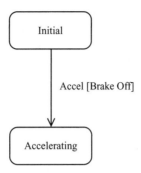

Figure 10.6 *Use of events and conditions in statechart*

Another example of using a condition is given in Figure 10.7, illustrating the situation when the ATM machine is to be closed down for maintenance. If a customer is currently using the ATM, the requirement is to allow this customer to finish the transaction before closing down the ATM. This can be achieved by setting the Boolean condition Closedown Was Requested to true at the time the maintenance is requested. If the ATM is idle when the Closedown event occurs, the ATM will transition immediately to Down state. On the other hand, if the ATM is in a different state, the Closedown event has no immediate impact and the condition Closedown Was Requested is set to true.

The Closedown Was Requested condition is checked when the customer's transaction has terminated. The condition [Closedown Was Requested] is used in conjunction with the timer event after (Elapsed Time). When the event

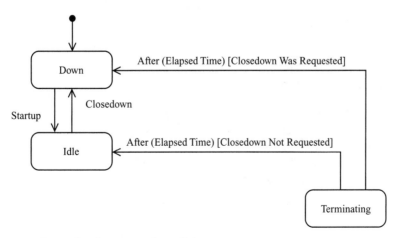

Figure 10.7 *Example of events and conditions*

after (Elapsed Time) occurs while the ATM is in Terminating state, the condition Closedown Was Requested is checked. If the condition is true, the ATM will transition to Down state. If the condition is false, indicated by Closedown Not Requested, the ATM will transition to Idle state, ready for the next transaction.

10.6 Actions

Associated with a state transition is an optional output **action**. An action is a computation that executes as a result of a state transition. An action is triggered at a state transition. It executes and then terminates itself. The action executes instantaneously at the state transition and thus conceptually an action is of zero duration. In practice, the duration of an action is very small compared to the duration of a state.

An action is shown on a statechart by labeling the transition **event [condition] / action**. For example, when the ATM transitions from Waiting for PIN state to Validating PIN state as a result of the PIN Entered input event, the action Validate PIN is executed. This state transition is labeled PIN Entered / Validate PIN. This example is shown in Figure 10.8, which shows the partial

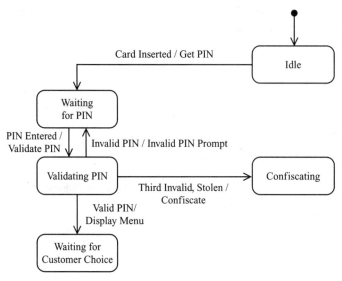

Figure 10.8 *Example of actions*

statechart for the ATM (shown in Figure 10.2) with the actions added. There may be more than one action associated with a transition. The actions all execute simultaneously; consequently, there must not be any interdependencies between the actions. For example, it is not correct to have two simultaneous actions such as Compute Change and Display Change. Because there is a sequential dependency between the two actions, the change cannot be displayed before it has been computed. To avoid this problem, introduce an intermediate state called Computing Change. The Compute Change action is executed on entry to this state and the Display Change action is executed on exit from this state.

As another example, Figure 10.9 shows the original statechart for the Cruise Control object (shown in Figure 10.3), with the conditions and actions added. This example shows the complete statechart for the Cruise Control object, with several additional state transitions.

10.6.1 Activities

In addition to actions, it is also possible to have an **activity** executed as a result of a state transition. An **activity** is a computation that executes for the duration of a state. Thus, unlike an action, an activity executes for a finite amount of time. An activity is enabled on entry into the state and disabled on exit from the state. Enable and disable actions always come in pairs. The cause of the state change, which results in disabling the activity, is usually due to some input event from a source that is not related to the activity. However, in some cases, the activity itself generates the event that causes the state change.

One way to depict an activity on the statechart is by labeling the transition into the state in which the activity executes **event / enable activity** and labeling the transition out of the state **event / disable activity**. However, it is more concise not to show the **enable** and **disable** actions on the transitions and instead to show the **activity** as being associated with the state. This is achieved by showing the activity in the state box and having a dividing line between the state name and the activity name. The activity is shown as **do / activity**, where "do" is a reserved word. This means the **activity** is enabled on entry into the state and disabled on exit from the state.

As an example of an activity, consider the transition from Initial state into Accelerating state on the Cruise Control statechart, as shown in Figure 10.9. An activity—namely, Increase Speed—is enabled on entry into Accelerating state. This activity executes for the duration of this state and is disabled on exit from this state.

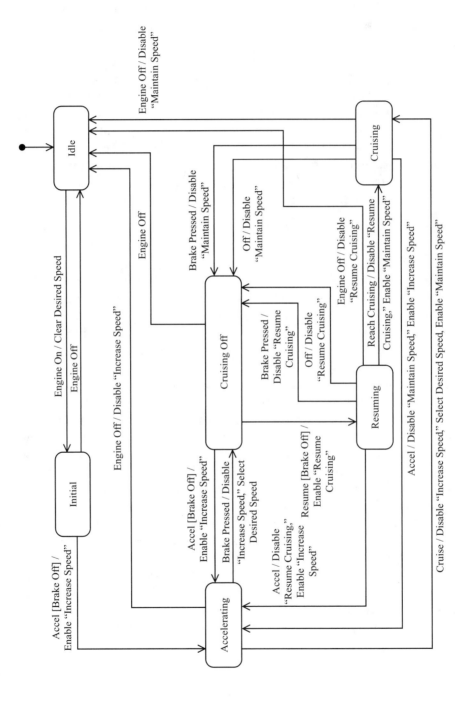

Figure 10.9 *Detailed Cruise Control statechart with actions and conditions*

If a transition from one state to another has a combination of actions, enabled activities, and disabled activities, there are specific rules about the order in which these occur:

1. First, the activity in the state being exited is disabled.
2. Second, the action(s) is executed.
3. Third, the activity in the state being entered is enabled.

For example, consider the Cruise event that causes a transition from Accelerating state to Cruising state. First, the activity Increase Speed is disabled, and then the activity Maintain Speed is enabled and remains active throughout Cruising state. The Select Desired Speed action is also performed. The semantics of this state transition are:

- Increase Speed is disabled on exit from Accelerating state.
- The Select Desired Speed action is executed at the transition from Accelerating state to Cruising state.
- Maintain Speed is enabled on entry into Cruising state.

A more concise way of depicting these activities is shown in Figure 10.10. Instead of depicting the activities as being enabled on the transitions into the state and disabled on the transitions out of the state, the **do / activity** notation is shown. This is shown for the three activities Increase Speed, Maintain Speed, and Resume Cruising. Comparing Figures 10.9 and 10.10, it can be seen that using the **do / activity** notation instead of the **enable** and **disable** actions is more concise and less cluttered.

10.6.2 Entry and Exit Actions

Certain actions may also be depicted more concisely as being associated with the state rather than with the transition into or out of the state. These are *entry* and *exit* actions, for which there are the reserved words "entry" and "exit." An **entry action** is depicted as **entry / action** and is an instantaneous action that is performed on entry to the state. An **exit action** is depicted as **exit / action** and is an instantaneous action that is performed on exit from the state.

It is not usually necessary to use entry and exit actions; instead, the actions can be labeled on the transitions into and out of the state, respectively. The best time to use an **entry action** is when

- There is more than one transition coming into a state.
- The same action needs to be performed on each transition
- The action is associated with entering this state and not with leaving the previous state.

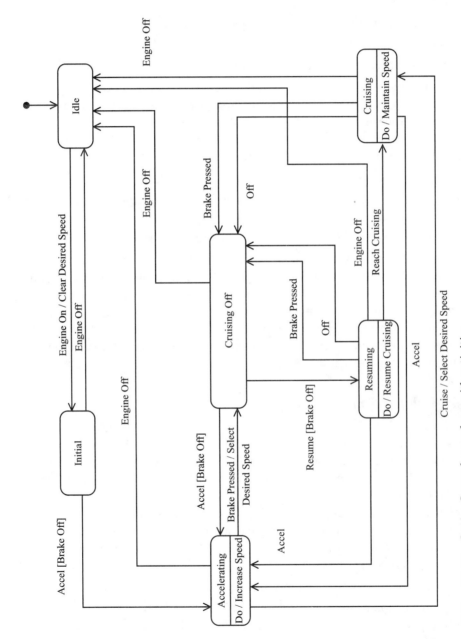

Figure 10.10 *Cruise Control statechart with activities*

In this situation, the action is only depicted once in the state box, instead of on each transition into the state.

The best time to use an exit action is when

- There is more than one transition leaving a state.
- An action needs to be performed on each transition.
- The action is associated with leaving this state and not with entering the next state.

In this situation, the action is only depicted once in the state box, instead of on each transition out of the state.

An example of an entry action is given in Figure 10.11. In Figure 10.11a, actions are shown on the state transitions. It can be seen that the action Display System Down is generated on all three transitions into Down state, and the action Display Welcome is generated on both transitions into Idle state. The alternative approach of using the entry action is shown in Figure 10.11b, where on entry into Down state the instantaneous action Display System Down is executed, and on entry into Idle state, the instantaneous action Display Welcome is executed. It should be noted that the Eject action is shown as an action on the state transition from Terminating Transaction state into Down state. This is because it is executed only on that particular transition into Down state and not on the other transitions.

As an example of an **exit action**, consider the action Select Desired Speed shown in Figure 10.12a. This action should be executed after the speed has been increased in Accelerating state through the activity Increase Speed. Thus, it

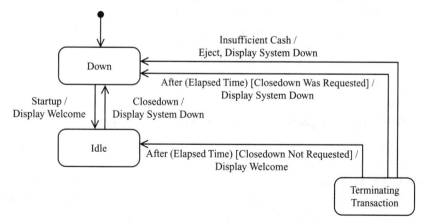

Figure 10.11a *Actions on state transitions*

Figure 10.11 *Example of entry actions*

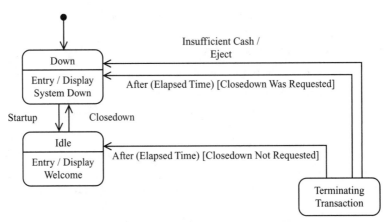

Figure 10.11b   *Entry actions*

Figure 10.11   *Example of entry actions (continued)*

is shown in Figure 10.12a as an action on the two transitions out of `Accelerating` state. It can instead be shown more concisely as an exit action in `Accelerating` state, as in Figure 10.12b. The activity `Increase Speed` is executed throughout `Accelerating` state. On exit from the state, the sequence of actions is that first the activity is deactivated and then the exit action is executed.

It is also possible for an activity, which executes for the duration of a state, to itself generate the event that causes the next state change. An example of this is the activity `Resume Cruising`, which executes in `Resuming` state (see Figure 10.10). This activity generates the event `Reached Cruising`, which causes the statechart to transition into `Cruising` state. It is also possible for a different event to cause the statechart to transition out of `Resuming` state—for example, if the `Brake Pressed` event is received from the external environment.

10.7   Modeling Different Aspects of the System

Another way to simplify the modeling of complex systems is to use separate statecharts to model different aspects of the system. For example, the Cruise Control statechart in Figure 10.10 models the cruise control aspects of the problem. However, a different statechart could be used to model the brake, as shown in Figure 10.13. The Brake statechart has two possible states, `Brake On` and `Brake Off`. Initially the brake is in `Brake Off` state. The `Brake Pressed` event causes the brake to transition to `Brake On` state. The `Brake Released` event causes the brake to transition back to `Brake Off` state.

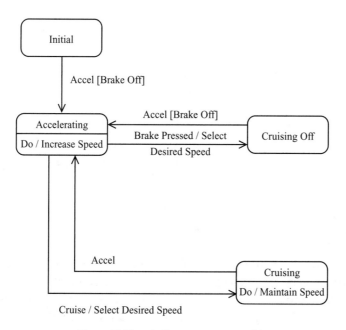

Figure 10.12a *Actions on state transitions*

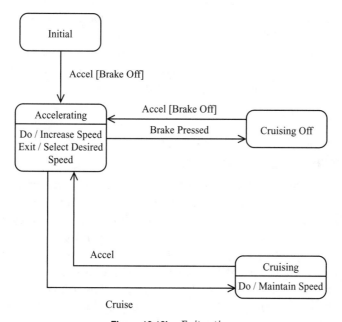

Figure 10.12b *Exit action*

Figure 10.12 *Example of exit action*

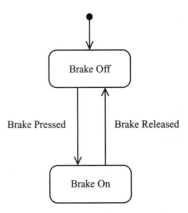

Figure 10.13   *Example of Brake statechart*

Depending on the characteristics of the problem, the Brake and Cruise Control statecharts may be related to each other or may be completely independent of each other. An example of related statecharts is one in which an output event on one statechart could correspond to an input event on the second statechart. In that case, the output event on the first statechart is the cause, and the input event on the second statechart is the effect. Modeling different objects in the system with separate statecharts means that any communication among the statecharts requires communication between the objects that contain the statecharts. This aspect of dynamic modeling is described in Chapter 11.

The hierarchical statechart notation, which is described next, and in particular the capability of modeling concurrent statecharts, provides a different approach for managing complexity than using separate statecharts.

10.8   Hierarchical Statecharts

One of the potential problems of flat statecharts is the proliferation of states and transitions, thereby making the statechart very cluttered and difficult to read. The use of conditions, entry and exit actions, and activities can help alleviate the clutter but is often not enough. A very important way of simplifying statecharts and increasing their modeling power is to introduce superstates and the hierarchical decomposition of statecharts. With this approach, a superstate at one level of a statechart is decomposed into several substates on a lower-level statechart.

The objective of hierarchical statecharts is to exploit the basic concepts and visual advantages of flat statecharts and state transition diagrams while overcoming many of their disadvantages. The main features of hierarchical statecharts are described next, with the examples of the automated teller machine and cruise control problems.

It should be pointed out that any hierarchical statechart can be mapped to a flat statechart, so for every hierarchical statechart there is a semantically equivalent flat statechart.

10.8.1 Hierarchical State Decomposition

Significant simplification of statecharts can often be achieved through the use of hierarchical decomposition of states, where a superstate is decomposed into two or more interconnected substates. This decomposition is sometimes referred to as the **or** decomposition, because being in the superstate means that the statechart is in one and only one of the substates. The notation also allows both the superstate and substates to be shown on the same diagram or, alternatively, on separate diagrams, depending on the complexity of the decomposition.

An example of hierarchical state decomposition is given in Figure 10.14, where the `Processing Customer Input` superstate consists of the `Waiting for PIN`, `Validating PIN`, and `Waiting for Customer Choice` substates. (On the hierarchical statechart, the superstate is shown as the outer rounded box, with the name of the superstate shown at the top left of the box. The substates are shown as inner rounded boxes). When the system is in `Processing Customer Input` superstate, it is in one (and only one) of the `Waiting for PIN`, `Validating PIN`, and `Waiting for Customer Choice` substates. Hence the term *"or decomposition."*

It should be noted that each transition into the superstate `Processing Customer Input` is, in fact, a transition into one (and only one) of the substates on the lower-level statechart. Each transition out of the superstate has to actually originate from one (and only one) of the substates on the lower-level statechart. Thus the input event `Card Inserted` causes a transition to the `Waiting for PIN` substate within the `Processing Customer Input` superstate.

10.8.2 Aggregation of State Transitions

The hierarchical statechart notation also allows a transition out of every one of the substates on a statechart to be aggregated into a transition out of the superstate. Careful use of this feature can significantly reduce the number of state transitions on a statechart.

Consider the following example where aggregation of state transitions would be useful. In the flat statechart shown in Figure 10.2, it is possible for the customer to press the Cancel button on the ATM machine in any of the three states `Waiting`

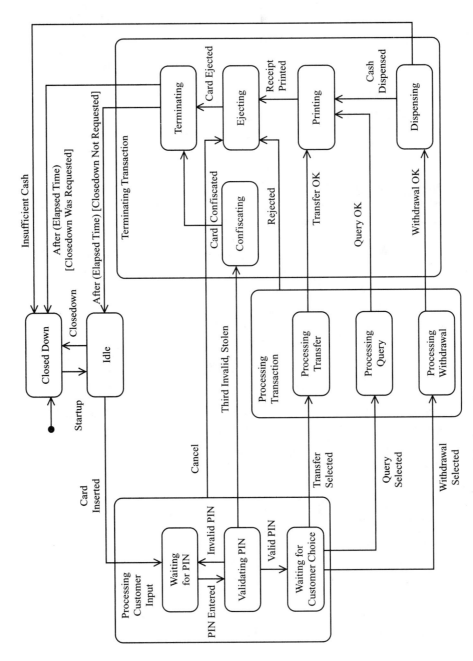

Figure 10.14 *Example of hierarchical statechart*

for PIN, Validating PIN, and Waiting for Customer Choice. In each case, the Cancel event transitions the ATM to Ejecting state. This is depicted by a Cancel arc leaving each of these states and entering the Ejecting state.

This can be expressed more concisely on a hierarchical statechart. From each of the three substates of the Processing Customer Input superstate, the input event Cancel causes a transition to the Ejecting state. Because the Cancel event can take place in any of the three Processing Customer Input substates, a Cancel transition could be shown leaving each substate. However, it is more concise to show one Cancel transition leaving the Processing Customer Input superstate, as shown in Figure 10.14. The transitions out of the substates are not shown. This kind of state transition, where the same event causes a transition out of several states to another state, usually results in a plethora of arcs on flat statecharts and state transition diagrams.

In contrast, because the Third Invalid event only occurs in Validating PIN state, it is shown leaving this state only and not from the superstate.

10.9 Concurrent Statecharts

Another kind of hierarchical state decomposition supported is the **and** decomposition. That is, a state on one statechart can be decomposed into two or more concurrent statecharts. The two concurrent statecharts are shown separated by a dashed line. Consider the case of a superstate on a statechart that is decomposed into two lower-level concurrent statecharts. When the higher-level statechart is in the superstate, it is simultaneously in one of the substates on the first lower-level concurrent statechart *and* in one of the substates on the second lower-level concurrent statechart.

Although the name concurrent statechart implies that there is concurrent activity within the object containing the statechart, the **and** decomposition can be used to show different aspects of the same object, which do not need to be concurrent. The term *orthogonal statechart* describes a concurrent statechart used to depict the states of different aspects of an object. In COMET, the term *concurrent statechart* is reserved for cases where true concurrent activity is depicted within the object. Designing objects with only one thread of control is simpler; to address concurrency, use multiple concurrent objects. You are therefore encouraged to use the concurrent statechart notation to depict orthogonal statecharts, which show different aspects of an object, but not to depict concurrency within an object. In the latter case, where true concurrency is required, use two separate objects and define each with its own statechart.

Using orthogonal statecharts to depict conditions may be used in the ATM example. This case is illustrated in Figure 10.15, where the statechart for the ATM Machine, ATM Control, is now decomposed into two orthogonal statecharts, one for ATM Processing and one for Closedown Request Condition. The two statecharts are depicted on a high-level statechart, with a dashed line separating them.

It should be noted that at any one time, the ATM Control superstate is in one of the substates of the ATM Processing statechart and one of the substates of the Closedown Request Condition statechart. Closedown Request Condition is a simple statechart with two states reflecting whether closedown has been requested or not, with Closedown Not Requested as the initial state. The Closedown event causes a transition to the state Closedown Was Requested, and the Startup event causes a transition back to Closedown Not Requested. The ATM Processing statechart (see Figure 10.14) depicts the states the ATM goes through while processing a customer request. The ATM Control statechart is the union of the Closedown Request Condition and the ATM Processing statecharts. Hence the term *"and decomposition."*

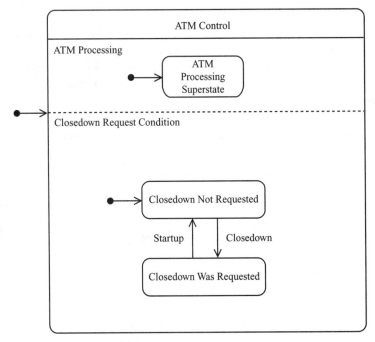

Figure 10.15 *Example of orthogonal statecharts in the ATM problem*

The `Closedown Was Requested` and `Closedown Not Requested` states of the `Closedown Request Condition` statechart (see Figure 10.15) are the conditions checked on the `ATM Processing` statechart, when the `after (Elapsed Time)` event is received in `Terminating` state (see Figure 10.14). Note that the `Closed Down` state is actually a state on the `ATM Processing` statechart.

10.10 Guidelines for Developing Statecharts

The following guidelines apply to developing either flat or hierarchical statecharts, unless otherwise explicitly stated:

- A state name must reflect an identifiable situation or an interval of time when something is *happening* in the system. Thus a state name is often an adjective (for example, `Initial`), a phrase with an adjective (for example, `Elevator Idle`), or a gerund (for example, `Elevator Moving`). The state name should not reflect an event or action such as `Elevator Moves` or `Move Elevator`.

- On a given statechart, each state must have a unique name. It is usually ambiguous to have two states with the same name. In theory, a substate within one superstate could have the same name as a substate of a different superstate; however, this is confusing and should therefore be avoided.

- It must be possible to exit from every state. It is often the case that a statechart does not have a terminating state.

- On a flat statechart, the statechart is in only one state at a time. Two states cannot be active simultaneously, for example, `Elevator Moving` and `Elevator at Floor`. One state must follow sequentially from the other.

- On a hierarchical statechart, the following guidelines apply:
  - On a hierarchical sequential statechart (**or** decomposition), when the statechart is in a superstate, it is in one and only one of the substates.
  - If a hierarchical concurrent statechart notation is used (**and** decomposition), when the statechart is in the superstate, it is in one substate on each of the lower-level concurrent statecharts.

- Do not confuse events and actions. An **event** is the *cause* of the state transition, and the **action** is the *effect* of the state transition.

- An **event** happens at a moment in time. The event name indicates that something has just happened, for example, `Up Request`, `Door Closed`.

- An **action** is a command—for example, `Stop`, `Close Door`, `Enable Maintain Speed`.

- An **action** executes instantaneously. An **activity** executes throughout a given state.

- You may have more than one **action** associated with a **state transition**. All of these actions conceptually execute simultaneously; hence, no assumptions can be made about the order in which the actions are executed. Consequently, no interdependencies must exist between the actions. If a dependency does exist, you need to introduce an intermediate state.

- A condition is a Boolean value. If a state transition is labeled **event [condition]**, a state transition takes place only if, at the moment the event happens, the condition is *true*. A condition is *true* for some interval of time. The state transition `Accel [Brake Off]` is designed to specifically preclude a state transition from taking place if the brake is pressed at the time the `Accel` event occurs.

- Actions, activities, and conditions are optional. Use them only when necessary.

10.11 Developing Statecharts from Use Cases

To develop a statechart from a use case, start with a typical scenario given by the use case, that is, one particular path through the use case. Ideally, this scenario should be the most typical path through the use case, involving the most usual sequence of interactions between the actor(s) and the system. Now consider the sequence of external events given in the scenario. In each case, an input event from the external environment causes a transition to a new state, which is given a name corresponding to what happens in that state. If an action is associated with the transition, the action occurs in the transition from one state to the other. If an activity is to be performed in that state, the activity is enabled on entry to the state and disabled on exit from the state. Actions and activities are determined by considering the response of the system to the input event, as given in the use case description.

Initially, a flat statechart is developed, which follows the event sequence given in the scenario. The states depicted on the statechart should all be externally visible states. That is, the actor should be aware of each of these states. In fact, the states represent consequences of actions taken by the actor, either directly or indirectly. This is illustrated in the detailed example given in the next section.

To complete the statechart, determine all the possible external events that could be input to the statechart. You do this by considering the description of alternative paths given in the use case. Several alternatives describe the reaction of the system to alternative inputs from the actor. Determine the effect of the arrival of these events on each state of the initial statechart; in many cases, an event could not occur in a given state or will have no impact. However, in other states, the arrival of an event will cause a transition to an existing state or some new state that needs to be added to the statechart. The actions resulting from each state transition also need to be considered, as given in the use case description of the system reaction to the alternative event.

10.12 Example of Developing a Statechart from a Use Case

To illustrate how to develop a statechart from a use case, consider the following Control Speed use case describing the sequence of interactions between the actor—in this case, the driver—and the system. This is followed by the derivation of the statechart.

10.12.1 Control Speed Use Case

Actor: Driver

Summary: This use case describes the automated cruise control of the car, given the driver inputs via the cruise control lever, brake, and engine external input devices.

Precondition: Driver has switched on the engine and is operating the car manually.

Description:

This use case is described in terms of a typical scenario consisting of the following sequence of external events:

1. Driver moves the cruise control lever to the ACCEL position and holds the lever in this position. The system initiates automated acceleration so that the car automatically accelerates.

2. Driver releases the cruise control lever in order to cruise at a constant speed. The system stops automatic acceleration and starts maintaining the speed of the car at the cruising speed. The cruising speed is stored for future reference.

3. Driver presses the brake to disable cruise control. The system disables cruise control so that the car is once more under manual operation.

4. Driver moves the cruise control lever to the RESUME position in order to resume cruising. The system initiates acceleration (or deceleration) toward the previously stored cruising speed.

5. When the system detects that the cruising speed has been reached, it stops automatic acceleration (or deceleration) and starts maintaining the speed of the car at the cruising speed.

6. Driver moves the cruise control lever to the OFF position. The system disables cruise control, so the car is once more under manual operation.

7. The driver stops the car and switches off the engine.

Alternatives:
The driver actor interacts with the system, using three external input devices: the cruise control lever, the brake, and the engine. Following are the complete set of input events initiated by the driver actor using these external devices, and the reaction of the system to them:

- The Accel, Cruise, Resume, and Off external events from the cruise control lever. The Accel event causes automated acceleration, providing the brake is not pressed. The Cruise event may only follow an Accel event. The Resume event may only occur after cruising has been disabled and the desired cruising speed has been stored. The Off event always disables cruise control.

- The Brake Pressed and Brake Released external events from the brake. The Brake Pressed event always disables cruise control. Automated vehicle control is not possible as long as the brake is pressed. After the brake is released, automated vehicle control may be enabled.

- The Engine On and Engine Off external events from the engine. The Engine Off event disables any activity in the system.

Postcondition: The car is stationary, with the engine switched off.

10.12.2 Developing the Statechart

Given the above use case, the following statechart may be constructed as illustrated in Figure 10.16, where the numbers describe the event sequence. The initial state of the statechart is Idle state. When the engine is switched on, the statechart transitions to Initial state. This represents the precondition of the use case. Now consider the sequence of events given in the scenario.

When the driver engages the lever in the ACCEL position, the Accel event occurs (event 1 in Figure 10.16) and, providing the brake is off, the system should automatically increase the speed of the car. We therefore name the next state into which the statechart transitions Accelerating state. During this state, the system needs to automatically increase the speed of the vehicle. Consequently, an activity called Increase Speed needs to be enabled on entry into Accelerating state, shown as event 2E (E for enable).

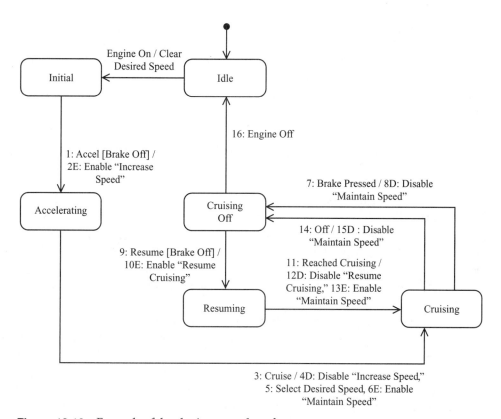

Figure 10.16 *Example of developing statechart from use case*

The next external event is when the driver releases the cruise control lever so the car will cruise at a constant speed. This is depicted by the `Cruise` input event (event 3), which causes the transition from `Accelerating` state into a state we call `Cruising`. The following actions result from the transition:

1. The system needs to stop automatic acceleration, so the `Increase Speed` activity is disabled on exit from `Accelerating` state, shown as event 4D (D for disable).

2. The cruising speed is stored for future reference, so the action `Select Desired Speed` (event 5) is triggered at the transition from `Accelerating` state. This is treated as an action and not an activity because selecting the desired speed is considered an instantaneous action and not an ongoing activity.

3. The system needs to start maintaining the speed of the car at the cruising speed, so the activity `Maintain Speed` is enabled on entry into the `Cruising` state (event 6E) and remains active throughout this state.

The next external event is the driver pressing the brake (event 7), which results in disabling of automated control of the car. Consequently, the next state is called `Cruising Off` and the `Brake Pressed` event causes the statechart to transition from `Cruising` state to `Cruising Off` state. The resulting action is to disable the `Maintain Speed` activity (event 8D), because within `Cruising Off` state, the car is once more under manual operation.

Following the scenario, the next external event is the driver engaging the cruise control lever in the RESUME position to resume cruise control. This `Resume` event (event 9) causes a transition to a state we call `Resuming`, and results in the enabling of the `Resume Cruising` activity (event 10E), where the system initiates acceleration (or deceleration) toward the previously stored cruising speed. When the `Resume Cruising` activity recognizes that the cruising speed has been reached, it generates the `Reached Cruising` event (event 11), which causes the statechart to transition back to `Cruising` state. The resulting actions are first to disable `Resume Cruising` on exit from the `Resuming` state (event 12D) and then to enable `Maintain Speed` on entry into the `Cruising` state (event 13E).

The next external event is the driver engaging the cruise control lever in the OFF position. This `Off` event (event 14) causes the transition to `Cruising Off` state (where the car is once more under manual operation) and disabling of the `Maintain Speed` activity (event 15D). Finally, the engine is switched off (event 16) and `Idle` state is entered.

In the above example, the states of the Cruise Control statechart are all externally visible; that is, the driver of the vehicle is aware of each of these states. In fact, the states represent consequences of actions taken by the driver, either directly or indirectly. All the state transitions, apart from one, result directly from actions taken by the driver. The only exception is the transition from `Resuming` state to `Cruising` state. This transition is a delayed reaction by the system to the driver's engaging the cruise control lever in the Resume position and occurs when the cruising speed has been reached.

10.12.3 Consider Alternative External Events

After the first version of the statechart is completed, further refinements can be made. First, a simplification can be made. In Figure 10.16, the three activities, `Increase Speed`, `Maintain Speed`, and `Resume Cruising`, are all enabled on entry into the state and disabled on exit from the state. The enables are depicted as actions that occur on the transitions into the state, and the disables are depicted as actions that occur on the transitions out of the state. It is more concise to express these as activities that are associated with the states in which they occur.

For example, the activity Increase Speed is active for the duration of the Accelerating state and is depicted inside the Accelerating state box (do /Increase Speed in Figure 10.17). When a transition occurs into the Accelerating state, the Increase Speed activity is enabled (shown as event 2E). When a transition occurs out of the Accelerating state, the Increase Speed activity is disabled (shown as event 4D).

To complete the statechart, it is necessary to consider the effect of each of the external events described in the **alternatives** section of the use case. Thus, the Accel event could also occur while the statechart shown in Figure 10.17 is in the Resuming, Cruising, or Cruising Off states. This event causes a transition to Accelerating state and the enabling of the Increase Speed activity. The brake could be pressed while in Accelerating, Cruising, or Resuming states, causing the disabling of the currently active automated control activity and a transition to Cruising Off state. The Off event could occur while in Resuming or Cruising states, and also results in the disabling of the enabled automated control activity. The

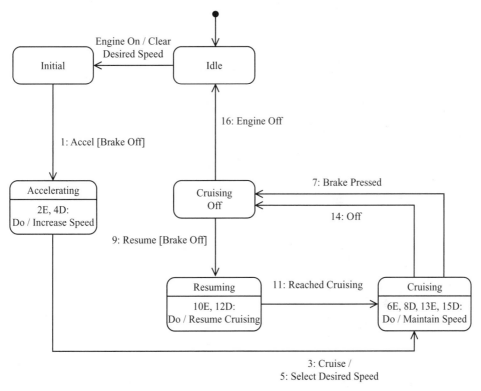

Figure 10.17 *Example of developing statechart from use case with activities*

Engine Off state could occur in any state except Idle state. It results in a transition to Idle state and the disabling of any enabled activity. The statechart in Figure 10.10 shows the result of adding the transitions caused by these events while in relevant states of the initial statechart (shown in Figure 10.17); however, no new states need to be added.

10.12.4 Develop Hierarchical Statechart

It is usually easier to initially develop a flat statechart. After enhancing the flat statechart by considering alternative events, look for ways to simplify the statechart by developing a hierarchical statechart. Look for states that can be aggregated because they constitute a natural superstate. In particular, look for situations where the aggregation of state transitions simplifies the statechart. Inspection of the flat statechart in Figure 10.10 reveals that the Accelerating, Cruising, and Resuming states can be considered substates of a superstate called Automatic Control, as depicted in Figure 10.18. These three substates

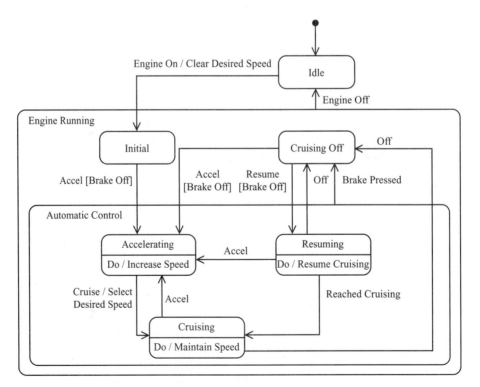

Figure 10.18 *Hierarchical Cruise Control statechart with activities*

have a common characteristic: in each substate, the speed of the car is controlled by the system. In addition, the Brake Off event, which causes a transition to Cruising Off state from each of the above substates, can be aggregated into an event out of the Automatic Control superstate, which has the same effect. Furthermore, all the states on the flat statechart (apart from Idle) can be aggregated into a superstate called Engine Running. Because there is an Engine Off transition out of every one of these substates, these transitions can be aggregated into one transition out of the Engine Running superstate into the Idle state.

Consider the hierarchical Cruise Control statechart depicted in Figure 10.18 in more detail. There is an Engine Running superstate, which consists of the Initial, Cruising Off, and Automatic Control substates. The Automatic Control substate is itself a superstate, which is decomposed into Accelerating, Cruising, and Resuming substates. Thus, when the system is in the Automatic Control superstate, it is in one (and only one) of the Accelerating, Cruising, or Resuming substates.

The advantage of aggregation of state transitions is clearly shown. Thus, from each of the substates of the Engine Running superstate, the event Engine Off causes a transition to the Idle state. This is depicted by one transition out of the Engine Running superstate, which is semantically equivalent to a transition out of each of the substates. The transitions out of the substates are not shown. Comparing this to the flat statechart, where each state has an Engine Off transition to Idle state, shows that the hierarchical notation is much more concise. The aggregation of events is also shown for transitioning out of the Automatic Control superstate, where the Brake Pressed event could occur from any of the substates.

A careful comparison of Figures 10.10 and 10.18 reveals a subtle difference. On Figure 10.10, the Brake Pressed transition out of Accelerating state has an action associated with it—Select Desired Speed—but the Brake Pressed transitions out of the Cruising and Resuming states do not have this action. To aggregate these state transitions on a hierarchical statechart, they must be identical. This can be achieved by making Select Desired Speed an **exit action** from Accelerating state instead of an action on the state transition, as shown in Figures 10.12 and 10.19.

10.12.5 Develop Orthogonal Statechart

In some cases, further refinement can be achieved by developing an orthogonal statechart to model a different aspect of the state-dependent object. Consider the orthogonal statechart in Figure 10.20, which is used to model a different aspect of the Cruise Control object, namely, the brake condition. The superstate Cruise

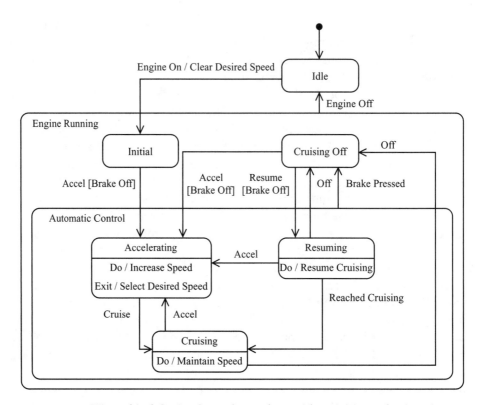

Figure 10.19 *Hierarchical Cruise Control statechart with activities and exit action*

`Control` is decomposed into two orthogonal statecharts for `Auto Cruise Control` and the `Brake Condition`. It should be noted that at any one time, the `Cruise Control` superstate is in one of the `Brake Condition` substates and one of the `Auto Cruise Control` substates. The `Cruise Control` statechart is the union of the `Brake Condition` and `Auto Cruise Control` statecharts.

The brake condition is depicted as two possible states, `Brake On` and `Brake Off`. The `Brake Pressed` event causes the brake condition to change from `Brake Off` to `Brake On`, and the `Brake Released` event causes the brake condition to change from `Brake On` to `Brake Off`.

10.13 Summary

This chapter has described the characteristics of flat statecharts, followed by hierarchical statecharts. Guidelines for developing statecharts were given. The pro-

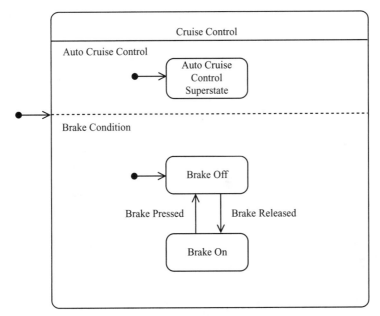

Figure 10.20 *Example of orthogonal statecharts in the Cruise Control problem*

cess of developing a statechart from a use case was then described in detail. It is also possible for a statechart to support several use cases, with each use case contributing to some subset of the statechart. Such cases are often easier to model by considering the statechart in conjunction with the object interaction model, in which a state-dependent object executes the statechart, as described in the next chapter. Several other examples of statecharts are given in the case studies.

chapter

Dynamic Modeling

D ynamic modeling addresses the dynamic (also referred to as behavioral) aspects of the system. The dynamic model is both *inter-object*, describing how objects interact with each other, and *intra-object*, describing how a state-dependent object is defined by means of a finite state machine and depicted as a statechart. The intra-object aspect of dynamic modeling involving finite state machines and statecharts is described in Chapter 10. This chapter describes object interaction modeling for inter-object collaboration, although for state-dependent objects, it describes how statecharts are also used to describe state-dependent object interactions.

Dynamic modeling is based on the use cases developed during use case modeling. For each use case, you need to determine the objects that participate in the use case and show how these objects interact with each other in order to satisfy the needs described in the use case. You depict the interaction between these objects on an **interaction diagram**. You should use one kind of interaction diagram, either the **collaboration diagram** or the **sequence diagram**. You should also provide a narrative description of the object interaction in a **message sequence description**. If the object interaction involves a state-dependent control object, you then need to develop the **statechart** it executes, and show the corresponding events on both the **statechart** and **interaction diagram**.

This chapter first describes object interaction modeling using collaboration diagrams and sequence diagrams before describing how they are used in dynamic modeling. It then describes the details of the **dynamic analysis** approach for determining how objects collaborate with each other. *State-dependent dynamic analysis* involves a state-dependent collaboration controlled by a statechart, but *non-state-dependent dynamic analysis* does not.

For large systems, a preliminary determination of the subsystems is usually necessary—for example, based on geographical distribution, as in the client/server systems described in Chapter 9. The analysis is then conducted to determine the object collaboration in each subsystem. Subsystem structuring is carried out in more depth during the design phase.

11.1 Object Interaction Modeling

Dynamic modeling relies heavily on messages and events. It is important to understand how messages relate to events. A **message** consists of an **event** together with the data that accompanies the event, referred to as the *attributes* of the message. For example, the event ATM Card Inserted has two attributes, which are the data items that accompany the event. These are Card ID and Expiration Date—the data items read off the magnetic strip on the card when the card is inserted into the ATM. The message is depicted as

> message = event (message attributes); for example:
> ATM Card Inserted (Card ID, Expiration Date)

It is possible for an event not to have any data associated with it; for example, the event Card Ejected does not have any attributes.

The message name corresponds to the name of the event. The message parameters correspond to the message attributes. Thus, for interaction diagrams we can use the terms "event sequence" and "message sequence" synonymously. To understand the sequence of interactions among objects, we often initially concentrate on the events; hence the term **event sequence analysis**.

11.1.1 Collaboration Diagrams

After the objects have been determined by using the object structuring criteria given in Chapter 9, the way objects dynamically cooperate with each other can be depicted on collaboration diagrams.

In the analysis model, messages represent the information passed between objects. Collaboration diagrams help in determining the operations of the objects, because the arrival of a message at an object usually invokes an operation. However, in COMET, the emphasis during analysis is on capturing the information passed between objects, rather than the operations invoked. During design, we might decide that two different messages arriving at an object invoke different operations—or alternatively, the same operation, with the message name being a parameter of the operation. However, these decisions should be postponed to the design phase. The kind of message passed between objects, synchronous or asynchronous, is a design decision that is also postponed to the design phase. At the analysis stage, all messages passed between objects are shown as simple messages.

A **collaboration diagram** is developed for each use case; only objects that participate in the use case are depicted. Some objects might only appear on a single collaboration diagram, while other objects might appear on several collaboration diagrams. On a collaboration diagram, the sequence in which the objects participate in each use case is described and depicted by using message sequence numbers. The message sequencing on the collaboration diagram should correspond to the sequence of interactions between the actor and the system already described in the use case. A collaboration diagram can be depicted with or without the message sequence numbers, although without the sequence numbers, the sequencing information is lost.

An example of a collaboration diagram from the Cruise Control System is given in Figure 11.1. Consider the interaction between the objects that participate in the Update Shaft Rotation Count use case, which addresses the arrival of a shaft input from the Shaft external input device (a hardware sensor). The shaft input is received by the Shaft Interface input device interface object (message number Sh1), which then updates the Shaft Rotation Count entity object (message number Sh1.1).

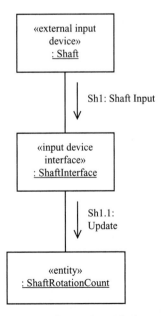

Figure 11.1 *Collaboration diagram for Update Shaft Rotation Count use case*

11.1.2 Sequence Diagrams

The interaction among objects can also be shown on a sequence diagram, which shows object interaction arranged in time sequence. A **sequence diagram** shows the objects participating in the interaction and the sequence in which messages are sent. Sequence diagrams and collaboration diagrams depict similar information, but do so in different ways. Usually, either collaboration diagrams or sequence diagrams are used to describe a system, but not both.

Because the sequence diagram shows the order of messages sent sequentially from the top to the bottom of the diagram, numbering the messages is not necessary. However, in the following example, the messages on the sequence diagram are numbered to show their correspondence to the collaboration diagram.

An example of a sequence diagram for the Update Shaft Rotation Count use case is shown in Figure 11.2. This sequence diagram conveys the same information as the collaboration diagram shown in Figure 11.1. The messages are numbered on this diagram to show the correspondence with the collaboration diagram. In fact, the message sequence description given in the previous section is applicable to both the sequence diagram and the collaboration diagram.

It should be noted that in the analysis phase, no decision is made about whether an object is active or passive, and so no assumptions should be made about object activation. Consequently, the object lifeline is always shown as a dashed line in the analysis model. On the other hand, the lifeline for the actor is always shown as an activation (double line), because it is assumed that the actor is active.

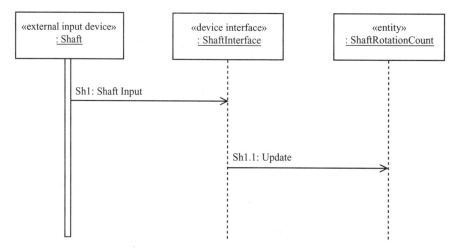

Figure 11.2 *Sequence diagram for Update Shaft Rotation Count use case*

11.1.3   Sequence Diagram versus Collaboration Diagram

Either a sequence diagram or a collaboration diagram can be used to depict the object interaction and sequence of messages passed among objects. The sequence diagram clearly shows the order in which messages are passed between objects, but seeing how the objects are connected to each other is difficult. The collaboration diagram shows the layout of the objects—in particular, how the objects are connected to each other. The message sequence is shown on both diagrams. Because the message sequence depicted on the collaboration diagram is less readily visible than on the sequence diagram, the message sequence is numbered. However, even with the message numbering on the collaboration diagram, it sometimes takes longer to see the sequence of messages. On the other hand, with a large number of objects involved in an interaction, a sequence diagram also becomes difficult to read. The diagram might have to be shrunk to fit on a page or the diagram might span several pages. Ways to address these problems are described later.

The COMET preference is to use collaboration diagrams rather than sequence diagrams, because an important step in the transition to design is the synthesis of the collaboration diagrams to create the software architecture of the system, as described in Chapter 12. This can be done much more readily with collaboration diagrams than with sequence diagrams. If you started with sequence diagrams, you would need to convert each sequence diagram to a collaboration diagram before the synthesis could be done. However, there are cases when the sequence diagram is very helpful—in particular, for very complex interactions and for timing diagrams, as described in Chapter 17.

11.1.4   Use Cases and Scenarios

A **scenario** is one specific path through a use case. Thus, a particular message sequence depicted on an interaction diagram actually depicts a scenario and not a use case. To show all the alternatives through a use case, development of more than one interaction diagram is often necessary.

By using conditions, it is possible to depict alternatives on an interaction diagram and hence to depict the whole use case on a single interaction diagram. However, this usually makes the interaction diagram more difficult to read. For this reason, in practice, depicting an individual scenario on an interaction diagram is usually clearer.

11.1.5   Generic and Instance Forms of Interaction Diagrams

The two forms of an interaction diagram are the *generic form* and the *instance form*. The instance form describes a specific scenario in detail, depicting one possible sequence of interactions. The generic form describes all possible interactions, and so can include loops, branches, and conditions. The generic form of an interaction diagram can be used to describe both the main sequence and the alternatives of a use case. The instance form is used to depict a specific scenario, which is one instance of the use case. Using the instance form might require several interaction diagrams to depict a given use case, depending on how many alternatives are described in the use case. Examples of instance and generic forms of collaboration diagrams are given in Section 11.7.

For all but the simplest use cases, an interaction diagram is usually much clearer when it depicts an instance rather than a generic form of interaction. It can rapidly get too complicated if several alternatives are depicted on the same diagram.

In the instance form of the sequence diagram, time moves down the page. In the generic form, with loops, branches, and conditions, this is no longer always the case. Thus, one of the main benefits of using sequence diagrams is lost.

11.2   Message Labels on Interaction Diagrams

A message label has the following syntax. Only those parts of the message label that are relevant in the analysis phase are described here.

Sequence expression, message name, argument list

where **sequence expression** consists of

message sequence number, recurrence

You can also have optional return values from the message sent. However, it is recommended that you use only simple messages during the analysis phase, in which case there are no return values.

- The **message sequence number** is described in the following subsection.

- The **recurrence** term is optional and represents conditional or iterative execution. This represents zero or more messages that are sent depending on the conditions being met. There are two choices:

  1. *[iteration-clause] to indicate an iteration. An iteration is indicated by an asterisk (*), meaning that more than one message is sent. The optional iteration clause is used to specify repeated execution, such as [j := 1,n]. An example of an iteration by putting an asterisk after the message sequence number is 3*.

  2. [condition-clause] to indicate a branch condition. The optional condition clause is used for specifying branches, for example, [x < n], meaning that

the message is sent only if the condition is true. Examples of conditional message passing by showing a condition after the message sequence number are 4[x < n] and 5[Normal]. In each case, the message is sent only if the condition is true.

- The **message name** is specified.
- The **argument list** of the message is optional and specifies any parameters sent as part of the message.

11.2.1 Message Sequence Numbering

Messages on a collaboration diagram are given message sequence numbers. Some guidelines for message sequence numbering on collaboration diagrams are now given. These guidelines follow the general UML conventions; however, they have been extended to better address concurrency, alternatives, and large message sequences. To illustrate the use of message sequence numbering, examples are given from a Validate PIN collaboration diagram (Figure 11.3).

On a collaboration diagram supporting a use case, the sequence in which the objects participate in each use case is described and depicted by using message sequence numbers. A message sequence number for a use case is of the form:

[first optional letter sequence] [numeric sequence] [second optional letter sequence]

An example is A1, where the *letter* A identifies the use case and the *number* identifies the message sequence within the collaboration diagram supporting the use case. The object sending the first message—A1—is the initiator of the use case-based collaboration. In a concrete use case, the initiator of the use case should be an actor; however, in an abstract use case, the initiator can be an object.

Details on the parts of the message sequence number **[first optional letter sequence] [numeric sequence] [second optional letter sequence]**, for example, Use1.1a, are given next.

The **[first optional letter sequence]** is an optional use case ID and identifies a specific concrete use case or abstract use case. The first letter is an uppercase letter. This might be followed by one or more upper- or lowercase letters if a more descriptive use case ID is desired.

[numeric sequence] The first message sequence number represents the event that initiates the message sequence depicted on the collaboration diagram. Typical message sequences are 1, 2, 3......; A1, A2, A3.....; Use1, Use2, Use3,......

A more elaborate message sequence can be depicted by using the Dewey classification system [Awad, Kuusela, and Ziegler 1996; Coleman et al. 1994], such

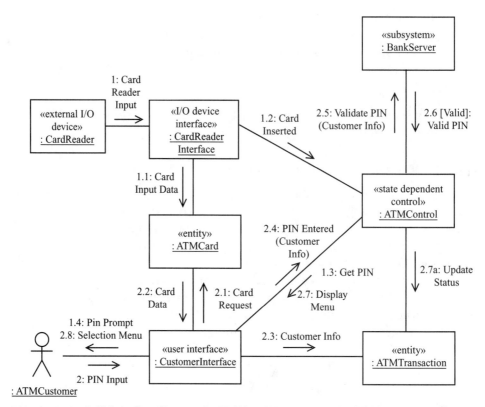

Figure 11.3 *Collaboration diagram for Validate PIN use case: Valid PIN*

that A1.1 precedes A1.1.1, which in turn precedes A1.2. Thus, the following would be a typical message numbering sequence: A1, A1.1, A1.1.1, and A1.2.

In an interactive system with several external inputs from the actor, it is often helpful to number the external events as whole numbers followed by decimal numbers for the ensuing internal events. For example, the actor's inputs are A1, A2, A3, and the full message sequence depicted on the collaboration diagram would be A1, A1.1, A1.2, A1.3, ..., A2, A2.1, A2.2......, A3, A3.1, A3.2, and so on.

As an example, consider the message sequence in Figure 11.3. The first external event from the customer actor (via the card reader) is `Card Reader Input`, message number 1, which is received by the `Card Reader Interface` object. The subsequent messages (for example, 1.2: `Card Inserted`) correspond to internal events that follow. The second external event from the actor is `PIN Input`, event number 2, which is followed by 2.1: `Card Request`, and so on.

The [second optional letter sequence] is used to depict special cases of branches in the message sequence numbering, either concurrent or alternative branches.

Concurrent message sequences may also be depicted on a collaboration diagram. A lowercase letter represents a concurrent sequence; in other words, A3 and A3a are concurrent sequences. For example, the arrival of message A2 at an object X might result in the sending of two messages from object X to two objects Y and Z, which then execute in parallel. This can be depicted by sending message A3 to object Y and message A3a to object Z. Subsequent messages in A3 sequence are A4, A5, A6... and subsequent messages in the independent A3a sequence are A3a.1, A3a.2, A3a.3. Because the sequence numbering is more cumbersome for the A3a sequence, you use A3 for the main message sequence and A3a and A3b for the supporting message sequences. An alternative way to show two concurrent sequences is to use the sequence numbers A3a and A3b; however, this can lead to a more cumbersome numbering scheme if A3a initiates another concurrent sequence, so the former approach is preferred.

An example of parallel message sequences is given in Figure 11.3. As a result of receiving message 2.6: Valid PIN, ATM Control sends out two messages, 2.7: Display Menu to Customer Interface and 2.7a: Update Status to ATM Transaction. These two actions are executed concurrently.

Alternative message sequences are depicted with the condition indicated after the message. An uppercase letter is used to name the alternative branch. For example, the main branch is labeled 1.4 [Normal], and the other, less frequently used branch is named 1.4A[Error]. The message sequence numbers for the normal branch are 1.4[Normal], 1.5, 1.6, and so on. The message sequence numbers for the alternative branch are 1.4A[Error], 1.4A.1, 1.4A.2, and so on.

11.2.2 Message Sequence Description

A **message sequence description** is developed as part of the analysis model and describes how the analysis model objects participate in each use case. The message sequence description is a narrative description, describing what happens when each message arrives at a destination object depicted on a collaboration diagram or sequence diagram. The message sequence description uses the message sequence numbers that appear on the collaboration diagram. It describes the sequence of messages sent from source objects to destination objects and describes what each destination object does with a message it receives. The message sequence description usually provides additional information that is not depicted on the object interaction diagram. For example, every time an entity object is accessed, the message sequence description can provide additional information, such as which attributes of the object are referenced.

11.3   Dynamic Analysis

An analyst develops a use case by identifying the sequence of interactions (external events) between the actor and the system. In the dynamic model, the use case is refined by considering the objects that participate in the use case and the sequence of internal events that are initiated by the arrival of each external event.

Dynamic analysis (also referred to as behavioral analysis) is a strategy to help determine how the analysis model objects interact with each other to support the use cases. Dynamic analysis is carried out for each use case. It starts with an external event arriving at an interface object and then follows with an analysis of the ensuing sequence of internal events and eventual system response. These internal events involve messages being sent among the objects that participate in the use case. A use case may support a sequence of external events, for example, several interactions with the actor. In each case, the sequence of internal events that follow each external event is defined. The sequence of events are numbered and shown on a collaboration diagram. A message consists of the event and the data associated with it.

The dynamic analysis approach is iterative. A first attempt is made to determine the objects that participate in a use case, using the object structuring criteria described in Chapter 9. An analysis is then carried out of how these objects collaborate with each other to execute the use case. This analysis might reveal a need for additional objects and/or additional interactions to be defined.

Dynamic analysis can be either state-dependent or non-state-dependent, depending on whether the use case is state-dependent. Non-state-dependent dynamic analysis is described in Section 11.4, and state-dependent dynamic analysis is described in Section 11.6. Examples of each are given in Sections 11.5 and 11.7, respectively.

In some cases, subsystem structuring is also carried out, in particular, when geographical distribution is appropriate—for example, in a client/server system.

11.4   Non-State-Dependent Dynamic Analysis

Starting with the use case, a first attempt is made at determining the objects that participate in the use case. There will need to be at least one interface object to receive inputs from the actor. Generally, there will need to be some entity objects, which store information that lasts longer than the execution of a given use case. Simple use cases might only consist of user interface and entity objects. For example, a simple client/server use case might only consist of a user interface client interacting with an entity server object. In more complex use cases involving several objects, there is usually also a need for a control object, which coordinates the interaction among several objects. For example, a control object could be used to coordinate the retrieval and manipulation of information from several entity objects before it is presented to the actor via a user interface object.

A non-state-dependent control object, such as a coordinator or timer object, is needed if some coordination and decision-making is required. An entity object is used if information needs to be stored or retrieved.

In the case of periodic activities—for example, reports that are generated periodically—it is necessary to consider timer objects that are activated by timer events, which trigger actions that lead to generation of system outputs. Each significant system output, such as a report, requires an object to produce the data and then typically send the data to an interface object, which outputs it to the external environment.

The non-state-dependent dynamic analysis strategy starts with the use case and considers each interaction between the primary actor and the system. The actor starts the interaction with the system through an external event. The sequence of external events generated by the actor is described in the use case. Simple use cases might involve only one interaction (external event), whereas complex use cases might involve several. Consider each interaction in sequence, as follows:

1. **Determine interface object(s).** Consider the actor (or actors) who participates in the use case; determine through which external objects (external to the system) the actor interfaces with the system, and which software internal objects receive the actor's inputs.

   Start by considering the events generated by the external objects that interface to the system and participate in the use case. For each external event, the software objects required to process the event are considered. An interface object is needed to receive the external event from the external environment. On receipt of the external input, the interface object does some processing and typically sends a message to an internal object.

2. **Determine internal objects.** Start with the main sequence of the use case. Using the object structuring criteria, a first attempt is made to determine the internal objects that participate in the use case.

3. **Determine object collaboration.** For each external event generated by an actor, consider the collaboration required between the interface object that receives the event and the subsequent objects—entity or control objects—that cooperate in processing this event. Draw a collaboration diagram or sequence diagram showing the objects participating in the use case and the sequence of messages passing between them. Repeat this process for each subsequent

interaction between the actor(s) and the system. This might result in additional object participation but will definitely require additional collaboration and the resulting message sequence numbering.

4. **Consider alternative sequences.** Consider the different alternatives, such as error handling, that the use case needs to address. Then consider what objects need to be involved in executing the alternative branches.

In the case of a periodic activity, a timer object is activated periodically. It triggers an entity object or algorithm object to perform the required activity. In a periodic use case, the external timer is the actor and the timer object is the control object.

11.5 Example of Non-State-Dependent Dynamic Analysis

As an example of non-state-dependent dynamic analysis, consider the `View Workstation Status` use case, briefly described as follows:

Use Case Name: View Workstation Status
Actor: Factory Operator
Summary: This use case describes the factory operator viewing the status of one or more factory workstations.
Precondition: The factory operator is logged in.
Description: The factory operator requests to view the status of one or more factory workstations. Operator requests may be made on demand. The operator may also subscribe to receive notification of changes in workstation status.
Alternatives: Factory workstation is down. Warning message is displayed to operator.
Postcondition: Workstation status has been displayed.

`View Workstation Status` is a client/server use case. Because this is a simple client/server use case, only two objects—a client object and a server object—participate in the use case. The collaboration diagram for this use case depicts the client object, the `Operator Interface`, making a request to the server object, the `Workstation Status Server` (see Figure 11.4). The message sequence description is as follows:

V1: The operator requests a workstation status service—for example, to view the status of a factory workstation.

V1.1: `Operator Interface` object sends a workstation status request to the `Workstation Status Server`.

V1.2: `Workstation Status Server` responds—for example, with the requested workstation status data.

V1.3: `Operator Interface` object displays the workstation status information to the operator.

11.6 State-Dependent Dynamic Analysis

State-dependent dynamic analysis addresses the interaction among objects that participate in state-dependent use cases. A state-dependent use case is a use case in which the outputs to the actor do not just depend on what the actor has input, but also on what has previously happened in the system. A state-dependent use case has a state-dependent control object, which executes a statechart providing the overall control and sequencing of the use case. In more complex use cases, it is possible to have more than one state-dependent control object participating in the use case. Each state-dependent control object is defined by a statechart. Deriving the statechart from the use case is described in Chapter 10.

This section gives a detailed description of state-dependent dynamic analysis and is followed by two examples of the approach. The first example, `Validate PIN`, has a simpler main sequence but several alternative sequences that are considered in detail. The second example, `Cruise Control`, has a more complex main sequence.

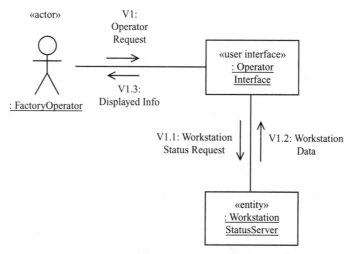

Figure 11.4 *Collaboration diagram for View Workstation Status use case*

11.6.1 Determine Objects and Interactions

In state-dependent dynamic analysis, the objective is to determine the interaction between the following objects:

- The state-dependent control object, which executes the statechart
- The objects, usually interface objects, that send the events to the control object that cause the state transitions
- The objects that provide the actions and activities, which are triggered by the control object as a result of the state transitions
- Any other objects that participate in the use case

The interaction among these objects is depicted on a collaboration diagram or sequence diagram. Because of this analysis, some changes to the statechart originally developed might be required.

As explained in Section 11.1, a message consists of an event and the data that accompanies the event. Consider the relationship between messages and events in the case of a state-dependent control object, which executes a statechart. When a message arrives at the control object on a collaboration diagram, the event part of the message causes the state transition on the statechart. The action on the statechart is the result of the state transition and corresponds to the output event depicted on the collaboration diagram. In general, we refer to *messages* on interaction diagrams (collaboration or sequence diagrams) and *events* on statecharts; however, when describing a state-dependent dynamic scenario, we use the term "event." A source object sends an event to the state-dependent control object. The arrival of this input event causes a state transition on the statechart. The effect of the state transition is one or more output events. The state-dependent control object sends each output event to a destination object. As described in Chapter 10, an output event is depicted on the statechart as an action (which can be a state transition action, an entry action, or an exit action), an enable activity, or a disable activity.

The main steps in the state-dependent dynamic analysis strategy are as follows:

1. **Determine the interface object(s).** These are determined by considering the objects that receive the inputs sent by the actor.
2. **Determine the state-dependent control object.** There is at least one control object, which executes the statechart. Others might also be required.
3. **Determine the other internal objects.** These are internal objects that interact with the control object or interface objects.
4. **Determine object collaboration.** This step needs to be carried out in conjunction with step 5 because the interaction between the control object and the statechart it executes needs to be determined in detail, as described in the next section.

5. **Determine the execution of the statechart.** This is described in the next section.

6. **Consider alternative sequences.** Perform the state-dependent dynamic analysis on the alternative sequences of the use case. This is described in the section after next.

11.6.2   Execute the Statechart

Execution of the statechart is considered in conjunction with the objects that interact directly with the state-dependent control object. It is often easier to initially consider a flat statechart, as described in Chapter 10.

The statechart represents the state-dependent aspects of the use case. The statechart, which is executed by the control object, provides the overall control and sequencing for the state-dependent use case. To avoid too much detail initially, considering only externally visible states (that is, visible to the actor) is advisable when developing the statechart. It is also necessary to consider the events that arrive directly or indirectly from the external environment to cause the control object to change state. When a state-dependent object receives an input event, the output event it generates depends not only on the input event but also on the current state of the statechart.

The statechart needs to be considered in conjunction with the collaboration diagram. In particular, it is necessary to consider the messages that are received and sent by the control object, which executes the statechart. An input event into the control object on the collaboration diagram must be consistent with the same event depicted on the statechart. The output event (which causes an action, an enable activity, or a disable activity) on the statechart must be consistent with the output event shown on the collaboration diagram.

An initial statechart might have already been developed to get a better understanding of the state-dependent aspects of the system. At this stage, the statechart needs further refinement. If the statechart was developed prior to the collaboration diagram, it needs to be reviewed to see if it is consistent with the collaboration diagram and, if necessary, adapted.

Developing the collaboration diagram and the statechart is usually iterative; each input event (to the control object and its statechart) and each output event (from the statechart and control object) need to be considered in sequence. They can actually be further broken down as follows:

1. The arrival of an event at the control object (often from an interface object) causes a state transition. For each state transition, determine all the actions and activities that result from this change in state. Remember that an action is executed instantaneously, whereas an activity executes for a finite amount of time—conceptually, an action is executed at a state transition and an activity

executes for the duration of the state. When triggered by a control object at a state transition, an action executes instantaneously and then terminates itself. An activity is enabled by the control object on entry into the state and disabled by the control object on exit from the state.

Determine all the objects that execute the identified actions and activities. An action is triggered and an activity is enabled. It is also necessary to determine if any activity should be disabled.

2. For each triggered or enabled object, determine what messages it generates and whether these messages are sent to another object or output to the external environment.

3. Show the external event and the subsequent internal events on both the statechart and the collaboration diagram. The events are numbered to show the sequence in which they are executed. The same event sequence numbers are used on the collaboration diagram and statechart, as well as on the message sequence description that describes the object interaction.

11.6.3 Consider Alternative Sequences

1. When the state-dependent dynamic analysis has been completed for the main sequence, the alternative sequences need to be considered. You analyze the alternative branches described in the use case to develop additional states and transitions on the statechart. For example, alternative branches are needed for error handling.

2. To complete the state-dependent dynamic analysis, it is necessary to walk through the object collaboration scenarios to ensure that

   - The statechart has been driven through every state and every state transition at least once.

   - Each action and activity has been performed at least once, so that each state-dependent action has been triggered and each state-dependent activity has been enabled and subsequently disabled.

11.7 Example of State-Dependent Dynamic Analysis: Banking System

As an example of state-dependent dynamic analysis, consider the following example from the Banking System, the Validate PIN abstract use case. The objects that participate in this use case are determined by using the object structuring criteria described in Chapter 9, as described next. First, the main sequence is considered, followed by the alternative sequences.

11.7.1 Determine Main Sequence

Consider the `Validate PIN` abstract use case. It describes the customer inserting the ATM card into the card reader, the system prompting for the PIN, and the system checking whether the customer-entered PIN matches the PIN maintained by the system for that ATM card number. The scenario for a valid ATM card and PIN is shown as a collaboration diagram in Figure 11.3 and as a sequence diagram in Figure 11.5.

From this use case, we first determine the need for the `Card Reader Interface` object to read the ATM card. The information read off the ATM card needs to be stored, so we identify the need for an entity object to store the `ATM Card` information. The `Customer Interface` object is used for interacting with the customer via the keyboard/display—in this case to prompt for the PIN. The information to be sent to the `Bank Server` subsystem for PIN validation is stored in an `ATM Transaction`. For PIN validation, the transaction information needs to contain the PIN number and the ATM card number. To control the sequence in which actions take place, we identify the need for a control object, `ATM Control`, which executes a statechart.

This use case starts when the customer inserts the ATM card into the card reader. The message sequence number starts at 1, which is the first external event initiated by the actor. Subsequent numbering in sequence, representing the objects in the system reacting to the actor, is 1.1, 1.2, 1.3, ending with 1.4, which is the system's response displayed to the actor. The next input from the actor is the external event numbered 2, and so on.

The following message sequence description describes the messages on the collaboration diagram (shown in Figure 11.3) and the messages on the sequence diagram (shown in Figure 11.5). A message arriving at the `ATM Control` object causes a state transition on the `ATM Control` statechart (shown in Figure 11.6). The message sequence description is as follows:

1: The `ATM Customer` actor inserts the ATM card into the `Card Reader`. The card input is read by the `Card Reader Interface` object.

1.1: The `Card Reader Interface` object sends the `Card Input Data`, containing Card ID and Expiration Date to the entity object `ATM Card`.

1.2: `Card Reader Interface` sends the `Card Inserted` event to `ATM Control`. This results in transition of the `ATM Control` statechart from `Idle` state (the initial state) to `Waiting for PIN` state. The action associated with

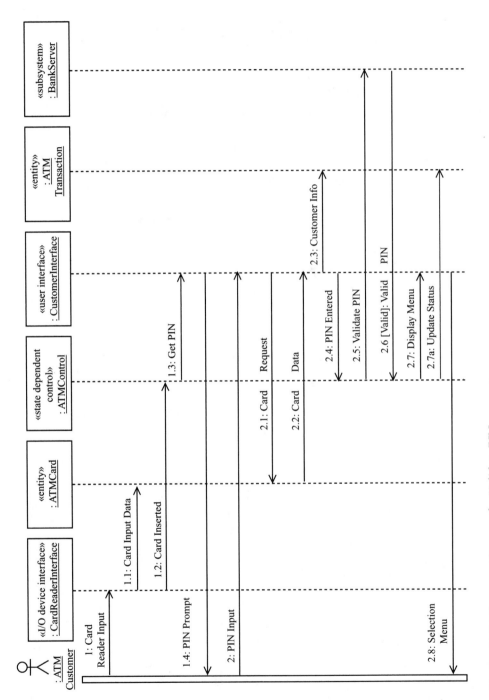

Figure 11.5 *Sequence diagram for Validate PIN use case*

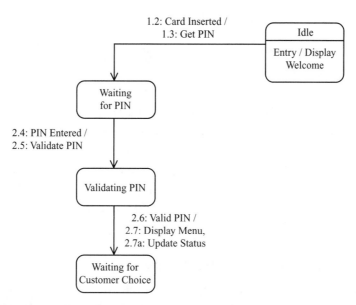

Figure 11.6 *Validate PIN statechart*

this transition is Get PIN. The action Get PIN on the statechart corresponds to the output event Get PIN on both the collaboration diagram and the sequence diagram.

1.3: ATM Control sends the Get PIN event to Customer Interface.

1.4: Customer Interface displays the Pin Prompt to the ATM Customer actor.

2: ATM Customer inputs the PIN number to the Customer Interface object.

2.1: Customer Interface requests Card Data from ATM Card.

2.2: ATM Card provides the Card Data to the Customer Interface.

2.3: Customer Interface sends the Customer Info, containing Card ID, PIN, and Expiration Date, to the ATM Transaction entity object.

2.4: Customer Interface sends the PIN Entered (Customer Info) event to ATM Control. This causes ATM Control to transition from Waiting for PIN state to Validating PIN state. The output event associated with this transition is Validate PIN.

2.5: ATM control sends a Validate PIN (Customer Info) request to the Bank Server.

2.6: Bank Server validates the PIN and sends a Valid PIN response to ATM Control. Because of this event, ATM Control transitions to Waiting for Customer Choice state. Two output events are associated with this transition, as described next.

2.7: ATM Control sends the Display Menu event to the Customer Interface.

2.7a: ATM Control sends an Update Status message to the ATM Transaction.

2.8: Customer Interface displays a menu showing the Withdraw, Query, and Transfer options to the ATM Customer actor.

A concurrent sequence is shown in Figure 11.3 with messages 2.7 and 2.7a. ATM Control sends these two messages at the same state transition so the two message sequences may execute concurrently, one to Customer Interface and the other to ATM Transaction.

11.7.2 Determine Alternative Sequences

Next, we consider the alternative sequences of the Validate PIN use case. The main sequence, as described in the previous message sequence description, assumes that the ATM card and PIN are valid.

Consider the various alternatives of the Validate PIN use case in dealing with invalid cards and incorrect PIN numbers. These can be determined from the *Alternatives* section of the use case (given in full in Chapter 19). Consider the Validate Pin message sent to the Bank Server (message 2.5). Several alternative responses are possible from the Bank Server. At the stage in the message sequencing where alternatives are possible, each alternative is shown with a different uppercase letter. Thus the alternatives to message sequence number 2.6 are message numbers 2.6A, 2.6B, 2.6C, as described next:

- A valid card and PIN were entered. This case, which corresponds to the main sequence, is given the condition [Valid]:

  2.6 [Valid]: Valid PIN
  In this case, the Bank Server sends the Valid Pin message.

- An incorrect PIN was entered. This alternative is given the condition [Invalid]:

  2.6A* [Invalid] : Invalid PIN
  In this case, the Bank Server sends the Invalid Pin message. The iteration of messages applies to the sequence 2.6A group of messages, namely, 2.6A.1 through 2.6A.8.

- An incorrect PIN was entered three times. This alternative is given the condition [Third Invalid].

2.6B [Third Invalid]: Third Invalid PIN
In this case, the Bank Server sends the Third Invalid PIN message.

- The card was stolen or the expiration data has expired.

2.6C [Stolen OR expired] : Card Stolen, Card Expired
In either the stolen or the expired case, the message sequence is the same, resulting in confiscation of the card.

Each of these alternative scenarios can be depicted on an interaction diagram. Figure 11.7 depicts on a collaboration diagram the case of an invalid PIN entered. In this case, the guard condition [Invalid] is true, indicating that message 2.6A: Invalid PIN is sent from the Bank Server. The use of the * indicates that the Invalid PIN message may be sent more than once (in this example, it may be sent twice). If an Invalid PIN message is sent, the sequence of messages from 2.6A through 2.6A.8 is executed. This whole sequence may be repeated a second time if a second incorrect PIN is entered.

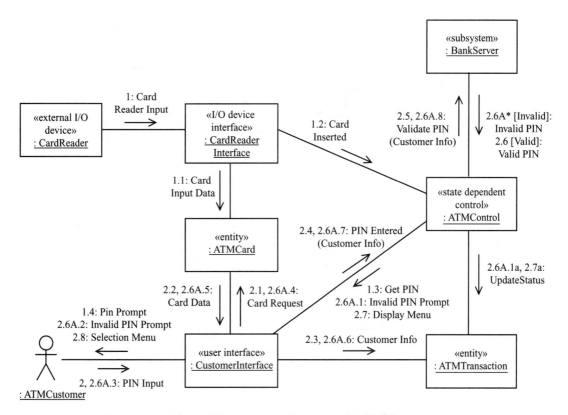

Figure 11.7 *Collaboration diagram for Validate PIN use case: Invalid PIN*

An alternative, shown in Figure 11.7, is for the user to enter the correct PIN number on the second or third attempt. In this case, the response from the Bank Server is Pin Valid and the guard condition [Valid] is true. The message sequence from 2.6 to 2.8 is the same as that shown in Figure 11.3.

Another alternative is for the customer to enter the incorrect PIN for the third time, the [Third Invalid] condition (as shown in Figure 11.8), in which case the card is confiscated (message sequence 2.6B–2.6B.2). Another alternative is depicted in Figure 11.9 when the ATM card has expired or been reported as stolen (message sequence 2.6C–2.6C.2). These two cases are handled in the same way, with confiscation of the ATM card.

It is possible to show all these alternatives on a generic collaboration diagram, as shown in Figure 11.10. This represents a generic collaboration diagram for the use case, which covers the main sequence as well as the alternative sequences. As can be seen, although all the alternatives can be shown, resulting in a compact

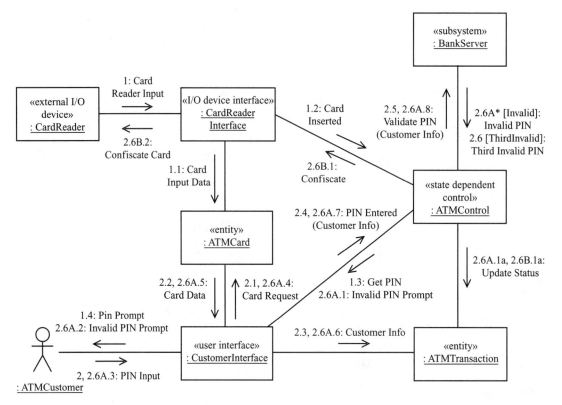

Figure 11.8 *Collaboration diagram: Validate PIN use case: Third Invalid PIN*

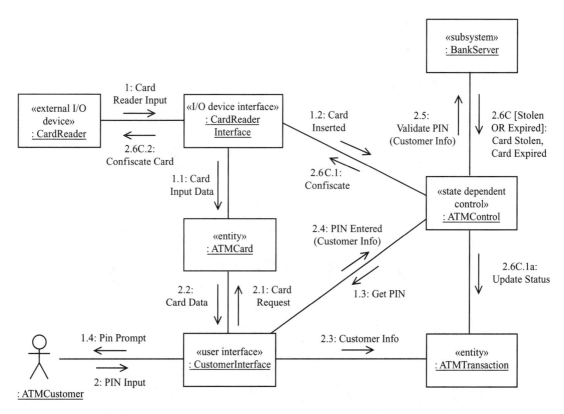

Figure 11.9 *Collaboration diagram: Validate PIN use case: stolen or expired card*

depiction of the object interactions, the diagram is more difficult to read than the previous ones. A generic collaboration diagram (depicting all the alternatives) should be used only if the alternatives can be clearly depicted. If the generic collaboration diagram is too cluttered, use separate collaboration diagrams or sequence diagrams for each alternative.

The control object ATM Control, shown in Figures 11.7–11.10, executes the statechart depicted in Figure 11.11. The statechart shows the various states during the execution of the Validate PIN use case, as well as the alternatives shown in Figure 11.10. Thus, when the PIN Entered event (event number 2.4) is received from Customer Interface, ATM Control transitions to Validating PIN state and sends the Validate PIN message to the Bank Server. The possible responses from the Bank Server are shown in Figure 11.10. The resulting states and actions are shown in Figure 11.11, and the resulting interactions with the controlled objects are shown in

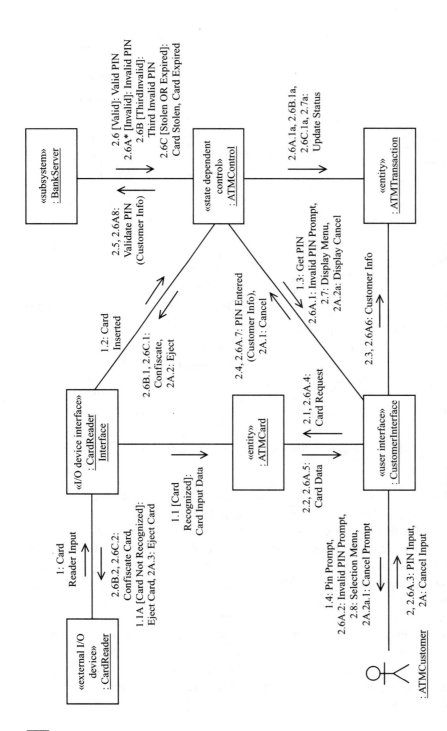

Figure 11.10 *Collaboration diagram: Validate PIN use case, generic form showing alternatives*

Figure 11.10. The Valid PIN response (event 2.6) results in a transition to Waiting for Customer Choice. The Invalid PIN response (event 2.6A) results in transitioning of the statechart to the Waiting for PIN state and triggering of the Invalid PIN prompt action (event 2.6A.1) in the Customer Interface. The Third Invalid PIN (2.6B) response results in transitioning of the statechart to the Confiscating state and triggering of the Confiscate action (event 2.6B.1) in the Card Reader Interface object. A Card Stolen response (event 2.6C) is treated in the same way. Finally, if the customer decides to Cancel (event 2A.1) instead of re-entering the PIN, the statechart transitions to Ejecting state and triggers the Eject action (event 2A.2) in the Card Reader Interface object. Because the customer can Cancel while ATM Control is in any of the substates Waiting for PIN, Validating PIN, or Waiting for Customer Choice, the state transition is shown out of the superstate Processing Customer Input (see Figure 11.11).

The statechart also initiates concurrent action sequences, which are triggered at the same state transition. Thus, all actions that occur at a given transition are

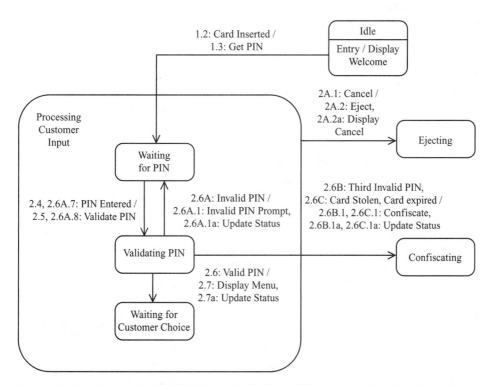

Figure 11.11 *Statechart for ATM Control: Validate PIN use case, showing alternatives*

executed in an unconstrained, non-deterministic order. For example, the actions 2.7: Display Menu and 2.7a: Update Status, which result from the Valid Pin state transition (Figure 11.11), execute concurrently, as also depicted in Figure 11.10. Concurrent action sequences are also associated with the Invalid PIN, Third Invalid PIN, and Cancel state transitions.

11.8 Example of State-Dependent Dynamic Analysis: Cruise Control System

As a second example of the state-dependent dynamic analysis strategy, consider the Control Speed use case described in the previous chapter. In particular, consider the scenario used to develop the statechart.

An initial attempt is made to determine the objects in the Control Speed use case. A state-dependent control object, Cruise Control, is required, which executes the Cruise Control statechart. The use case description identifies the need for device interface objects, in particular, the Cruise Control Lever Interface, Engine Interface, and Brake Interface objects. Inputs from these objects could potentially cause the Cruise Control object to change state. The Throttle Interface object is also needed because the whole purpose of this use case is to control the output to the throttle.

The scenario is now executed. By manually executing this scenario, we can determine the device interface objects that provide input events to the Cruise Control object and the state-dependent actions and activities, whose execution is controlled, that is, triggered, enabled, and disabled, by Cruise Control. The sequence of events is numbered and shown on a collaboration diagram. The relevant event sequence numbers are also shown on the statechart to show the correspondence between the events on the collaboration diagrams and the statechart. The cruise control statechart is the initial statechart described in Chapter 10, which is flat because at this stage the hierarchical aspects have not been factored in.

Consider the first external event, in which the driver engages the real-world cruise control lever in the Accel position. The input device interface object, Cruise Control Lever Interface, reads this input from the Cruise Control Lever external input device, which is shown as event C1 in Figure 11.12. The Cruise Control Lever Interface object sends the Accel event to the Cruise Control object (event C1.1 in Figure 11.12). The Cruise Control object conceptually executes the Cruise Control statechart. The Accel event into Cruise Control corresponds to the Accel event on the statechart, which causes a transition from Initial state to Accelerating state (see Figure 11.13).

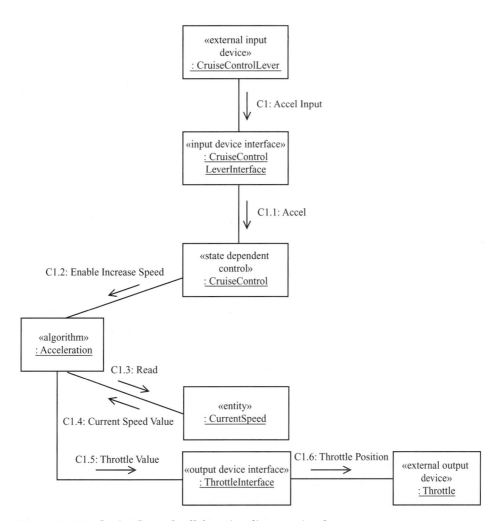

Figure 11.12 *Cruise Control collaboration diagram: Accel event*

Next, consider what actions result from this state transition. In `Initial` state, the car is under driver control. However, in `Accelerating` state, the car is under automatic control and should accelerate automatically throughout the state. Because of the transition, the state-dependent activity `Increase Speed` must be enabled. `Increase Speed` is an activity that should be continuously active while the vehicle is automatically accelerating. Its function is to periodically execute the algorithm that determines to what degree the throttle value should be adjusted so that the speed of the vehicle gradually increases.

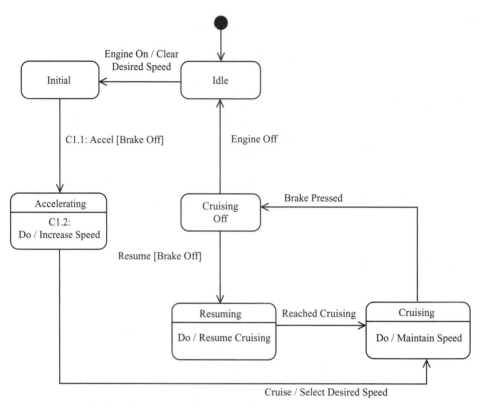

Figure 11.13   *Cruise Control statechart: Accel event*

Increase Speed should therefore be enabled when the statechart transitions from Initial to Accelerating state. This is shown as event C1.2 in Figures 11.12 and 11.13. The Increase Speed activity is executed by the Acceleration object, which is an algorithm object. Increase Speed has to read the Current Speed to ensure that a maximum allowable speed has not been exceeded (C1.3, C1.4) and then send the calculated throttle value (C1.5) to the Throttle Interface device interface object. The Throttle Interface object determines the finely tuned throttle position (C1.6) to output to the real-world Throttle output device.

The next external event results when the driver decides to release the cruise control lever. The Cruise Control Lever Interface object reads this external input (event C2 in Figure 11.14) and sends the Cruise event to the Cruise Control object (event C2.1 in Figure 11.14). This input event causes Cruise Control to transition into Cruising state. Because the Cruise event is the same event

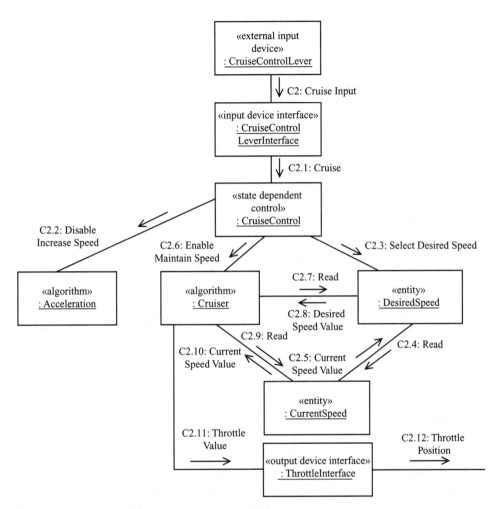

Figure 11.14 *Cruise Control collaboration diagram: Cruise event*

shown on two different diagrams, it is numbered as event C2.1 in both Figures 11.14 and 11.15. Consider the actions that now need to take place, as shown in Figures 11.14 and 11.15. The first action is to disable the Increase Speed activity (event C2.2) because the vehicle must no longer accelerate. The second action is to record the cruising speed; because this is a "one shot" action, this is achieved by triggering Select Desired Speed (event C2.3), which reads the Current Speed and stores this value as the Desired Speed. (The Select Desired Speed action is executed by the Desired Speed entity object.) The third action is to enable the Maintain

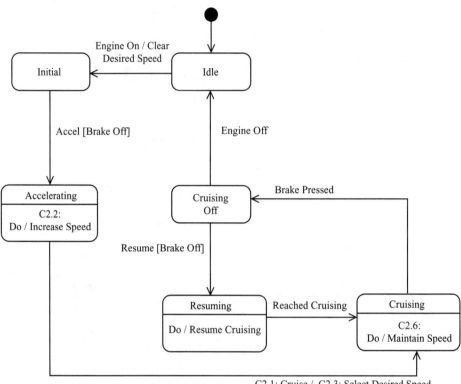

Figure 11.15 *Cruise Control statechart: Cruise event*

Speed activity (event C2.6), which periodically executes the algorithm that continuously reads Current Speed and Desired Speed and adjusts the throttle value to
maintain the cruising speed. The Maintain Speed activity automatically controls
the speed of the car by calculating the adjustments needed to the throttle on a regular basis.

It is important to note that the event sequence numbering reflects the
sequence in which the previous state-dependent actions are executed when the
Cruise transition occurs. The first action is to disable the Increase Speed
activity (event C2.2), the second action is the instantaneous action Select
Desired Speed (events C2.3–C2.5), and the third action is to enable the Maintain Speed activity (event C2.6). Maintain Speed reads the Desired Speed
(events C2.7, C2.8) and the Current Speed (events C2.9, C2.10), compares the
two values, and sends the Throttle Value (event C2.11) to the Throttle
Interface object, with the goal of maintaining a constant speed.

The next external event occurs when the driver presses the real-world brake because of some obstacle ahead. This needs a different device interface object, the `Brake Interface` object, to read the `Brake Input` (event C3 in Figure 11.16) from the `Brake` external input device and send a `Brake Pressed` event (event C3.1). This event causes the statechart to transition from `Cruising` to `Cruising Off` state (event C3.1 in Figure 11.17). The action associated with this transition is to disable the `Maintain Speed` activity (event C3.2 in Figures 11.16 and 11.17). A disable `Throttle Value` message also needs to be sent to the `Throttle Interface` object (event C3.3). The vehicle is now back under driver control.

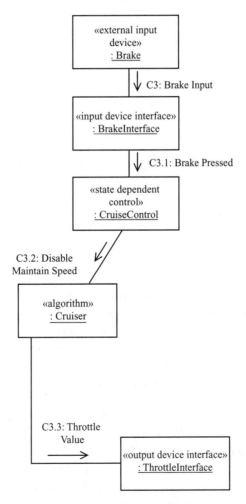

Figure 11.16   *Cruise Control collaboration diagram: Brake event*

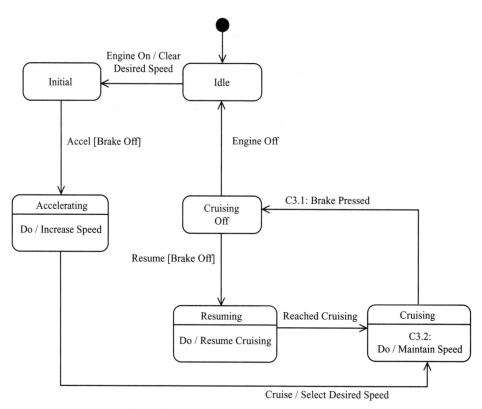

Figure 11.17   *Cruise Control statechart: Brake event*

Later, the driver wishes to resume cruising. The driver engages the cruise control lever in the Resume position (event C4 in Figure 11.18). The Cruise Control Lever Interface object sends the Resume event to Cruise Control (event C4.1 in Figure 11.18), which causes the statechart to transition from Cruising Off state to Resuming state (event 4.1 in Figure 11.19). The action associated with this transition is to enable the Resume Cruising activity (event C4.2 in Figures 11.18 and 11.19). Resume Cruising reads the Desired Speed (events C4.3, C4.4) and the Current Speed (events C4.5, 4.6) values, and periodically adjusts the Throttle Value (C4.7) so the speed of the vehicle increases or decreases to reach the cruising speed. The Resume Cruising activity is executed by the Resumption algorithm object. When the car reaches cruising speed, Resume Cruising sends the Reached Cruising event to Cruise Control (event C4.9 in Figure 11.18).

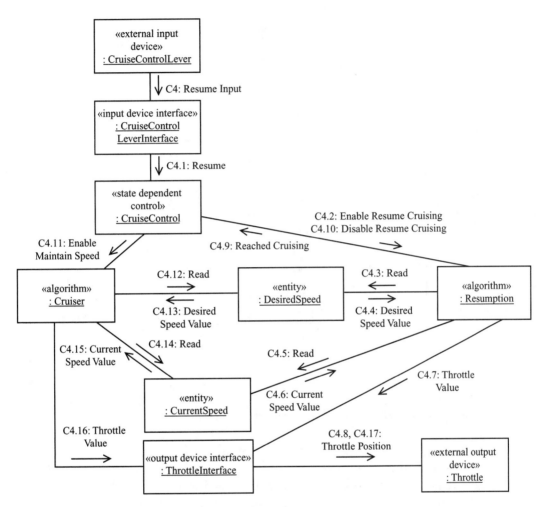

Figure 11.18   *Cruise Control collaboration diagram: Resume event*

The Reached Cruising event causes the statechart to transition from Resuming state back to Cruising state (event C4.9 in Figure 11.19) so the car can cruise at the desired speed. The resulting actions are to disable the Resume Cruising activity (event C4.10 in Figures 11.18 and 11.19) and to enable the Maintain Speed activity (event C4.11 in Figures 11.18 and 11.19).

Each of the collaboration diagrams shows the response of the system to an external event, except for one where the response is to an internal event. The

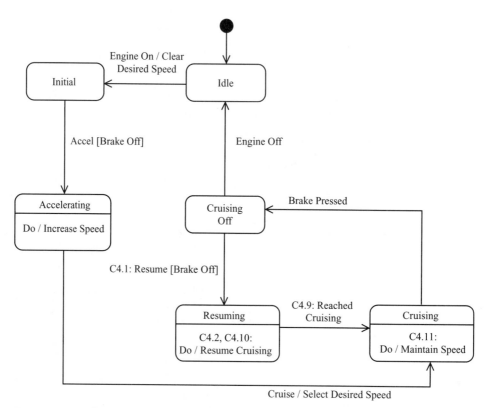

Figure 11.19   *Cruise Control statechart: Resume event*

internal event Reached Cruising results indirectly from the previous external event, when the driver engages the cruise control lever in the Resume position.

It is necessary to continue with the scenario to ensure that all states are entered and all state transitions are taken. Further analysis leads to the addition of the Engine Interface device interface object and the Clear Desired Speed action, which is also executed by the Desired Speed object. Identifying the additional state transitions is described in Chapter 10.

Based on this state-dependent dynamic analysis, the collaboration diagram showing all the objects that participated in the scenario is shown in Figure 11.20. The input device interface objects are Cruise Control Lever Interface, Brake Interface, and Engine Interface. The state-dependent control object is Cruise Control. The output device interface object is Throttle Interface. There are two entity objects, Current Speed and Desired Speed. Finally, there are three algorithm objects, the Acceleration, Cruiser, and Resumption objects. The statechart showing all the events and actions is shown in Figure 11.21.

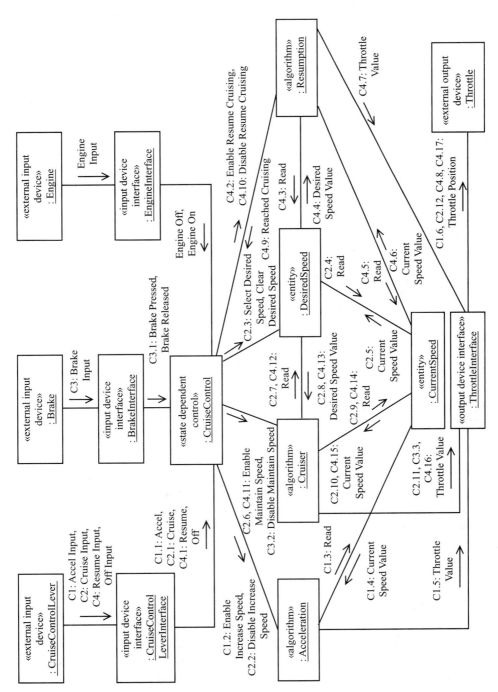

Figure 11.20 *Cruise Control collaboration diagram: Cruise Control scenario*

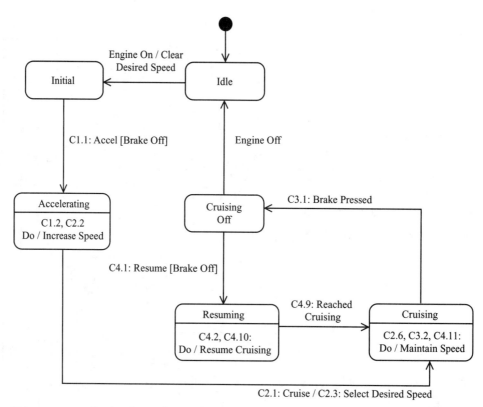

Figure 11.21   *Cruise Control statechart: Cruise Control scenario*

To complete the state-dependent dynamic analysis, it is necessary to consider all the alternative sequences of the Control Speed use case, as described in the *Alternatives* section in Chapter 10. Figure 11.22 shows a hierarchical statechart, which includes the events and actions corresponding to the main sequence and all the alternative sequences.

11.9 Summary

This chapter has described dynamic modeling, in which the objects that participate in each use case are determined, as well as the sequence of their interactions. This chapter first described **collaboration diagrams** and **sequence diagrams** before describing how they are used in dynamic modeling. It then described the

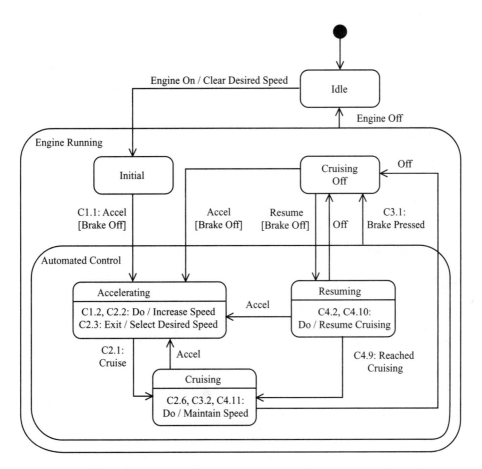

Figure 11.22 *Hierarchical Cruise Control statechart with all states and transitions*

details of the **dynamic analysis** approach for determining how objects collaborate with each other. **State-dependent dynamic analysis** involves a state-dependent collaboration controlled by a statechart, and **non-state-dependent dynamic analysis** does not.

During design, the collaboration diagrams corresponding to each use case are synthesized into a consolidated collaboration diagram, which represents the first step in developing the software architecture of the system, as described in Chapter 12. During analysis, all message interactions are depicted as simple messages, because no decision has yet been made about the characteristics of the messages. During design, the message interfaces are defined as described in Chapters 13 and 14.

chapter

Software Architecture
Design

To successfully manage the inherent complexity of a large-scale software system, it is necessary to provide an approach for decomposing the system into subsystems and developing the overall software architecture of the system. As described in Chapter 3, the software architecture separates the overall structure of the system, in terms of components and their interconnections, from the internal details of the individual components. Hence, this chapter describes an approach for decomposing the system into subsystems and for defining the interfaces between the subsystems. After performing this decomposition, each subsystem can then be designed independently.

A brief introduction to subsystem structuring was given in Chapter 9. This chapter provides detailed guidelines for developing the overall software architecture by describing different kinds of software architectures and providing a set of subsystem structuring criteria for determining the subsystems. Guidelines specific to the architectural design of distributed applications are described in Chapter 13.

12.1 Software Architectural Styles

Software architectural style refers to recurring architectures used in a variety of software applications [Shaw and Garlan 1996, Bass 1998]; they are also referred to as architecture patterns [Buschmann et al. 1996]. Shaw and Buschmann identify several styles or patterns of software architecture. This section describes the architectural styles most relevant to concurrent, real-time, and distributed applications.

12.1.1 Client/Server Architectural Style

A widely used architectural style in distributed applications is the **client/server architecture**, in which the **server** is a provider of services and the **client** is a consumer of services. The simplest client/server architecture has one server and many clients—for example, an ATM application for a single bank, in which ATMs distributed around the state communicate with the bank's central server. More complex client/server systems might have multiple servers. A client might communicate with several servers, and servers might communicate with each other. Thus, a banking consortium consisting of multiple interconnected banks is an example of a multiple-client/multiple-server system.

More complex client/server architectures might involve object brokers that register services provided by servers. Clients might then request these services via the broker. This provides location transparency and platform transparency, as described in Chapters 4 and 13. Sophisticated object brokers provide white pages (naming services) and yellow pages (trader services) to enable services to be more easily located by clients. Another variation on client/server architectures is the use of communicating software agents that act as intermediaries between clients and servers.

Most distributed applications are based either entirely or partially on a client/server architectural style. In this book, the Banking System is based entirely on a client/server architectural style (see Figure 12.1), and the Factory Automation System case study is partially based on a client/server architectural style. The agent-based Electronic Commerce System uses a variation on the theme with a client/agent/server architecture. Both the Factory Automation System and the Electronic Commerce System use object broker technology to enable communication between objects on heterogeneous platforms and use wrappers to enable access to legacy databases.

12.1.2 Layers of Abstraction Architectural Style

The layers of a hierarchy are sometimes referred to as levels or layers of abstraction. Operating systems, database management systems, and network communication software are examples of software systems often structured as hierarchies. One of the first hierarchically structured software systems was the T.H.E. operating system developed by Dijkstra and his team [Dijkstra 1968]. Dijkstra's goals were to provide a systematic approach for designing, coding, and testing a hierarchical system. The T.H.E system was structured into several layers, with modules at one layer providing services for modules at higher layers. Thus, a module can invoke a module in a lower layer but not one in a higher layer. Each layer provides a distinct class of service, such as Processor Management, Memory Management, and File Management.

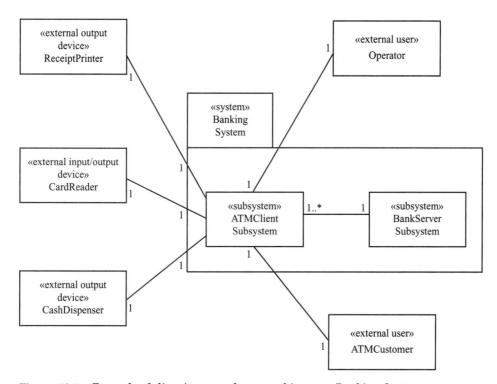

Figure 12.1 *Example of client/server software architecture: Banking System*

A layered architecture is also used in the International Standards Organization Open Systems Interconnection (ISO OSI) Reference Model, which is a standard for networked communication between open systems (see Figure 12.2). The ISO model has seven layers. Each layer deals with a specific aspect of network communications and provides an interface, as a set of operations, to the layer above it. For each layer on the sender node, there is an equivalent layer on the receiver node.

The subsystem design of the Cruise Control and Monitoring System is a hierarchy, with lower-level subsystems computing essential data values that are used by other subsystems of the system (see Figure 12.3). Each subsystem depends on subsystems at lower layers, but no subsystem depends on subsystems at layers above it.

12.1.3 Communicating Tasks Architectural Style

A third example of widely used software architectures is that of a network of concurrent tasks with a separate thread of control for each task. The two variations of this style are communicating tasks with shared memory and communicating tasks without shared memory. Concurrent tasks that share memory must reside

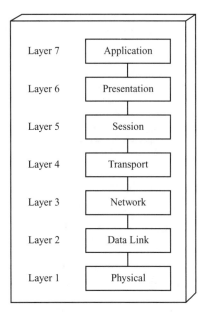

Figure 12.2 *Example of hierarchical layers of abstraction: ISO open systems interconnection reference model*

on the same computational node. Greater flexibility is achieved with concurrent tasks that have no shared memory, because tasks can then be allocated to different nodes in a distributed environment. Task communication occurs through discrete messages. If tasks have shared memory, they can also communicate and synchronize their operations by using monitors, as described in Chapter 3.

The communicating tasks architectural style is very common in real-time and distributed applications because concurrency is a characteristic of the problem domain. All the case studies in this book use networks of concurrent tasks, either in the concurrent shared memory style or in the concurrent distributed style. Two solutions are provided for the Elevator Control System case study in Chapter 18: a non-distributed architecture with shared memory and a distributed architecture without shared memory (see Figure 12.4).

12.1.4   Blending Architectural Styles

These architectural styles are not mutually exclusive. For example, it is possible for the layered architecture to have each of its layers implemented as a network of concurrent tasks. This approach is used in the Cruise Control and Monitoring System. It is also possible for a network of distributed tasks to have some cli-

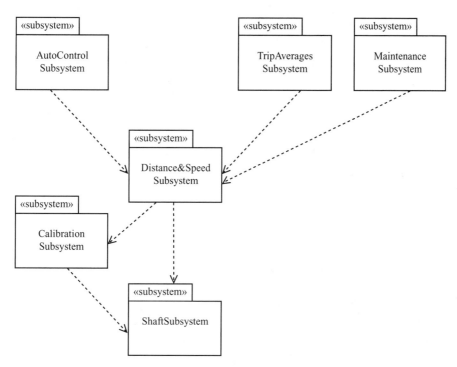

Figure 12.3   *Example of hierarchical architecture: Cruise Control and Monitoring System*

ent/server communication among a subset of the tasks. This approach is used in the distributed Factory Automation System.

12.2   System Decomposition Issues

A system is structured into subsystems, which contain objects that are functionally dependent on each other. A subsystem should be relatively independent of other subsystems and should therefore have low coupling with other subsystems. On the other hand, the coupling between the objects within a subsystem should be high. A subsystem can be considered a composite or aggregate object that contains the simple objects that compose that subsystem. There can be many subsystems of the same type.

In analyzing the problem domain and decomposing a system into subsystems, the emphasis is on separation of concerns. Each subsystem performs a

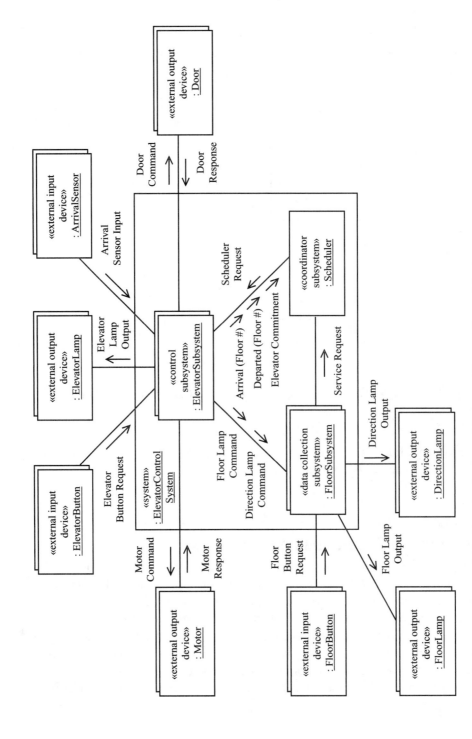

Figure 12.4   *Example of distributed software architecture: Elevator Control System*

major function, which is relatively independent of the functionality provided by other subsystems. A subsystem can be decomposed further into smaller subsystems, consisting of a subset of the functionality provided by the parent subsystem. After the interface between subsystems has been defined, subsystem design can proceed independently.

A subsystem provides a larger-grained information hiding solution than an object. To structure the system into subsystems, we start with the use cases. The object interaction model for a use case forms the basis of a subsystem because the objects in it are all related to each other. They have higher coupling because they communicate with each other and have lower (or no) coupling with objects in other use cases. An object that participates in more than one use case needs to be allocated to a single subsystem—usually the subsystem with which it is most highly coupled. In some cases, a subsystem might incorporate the objects from more than one use case. This is most likely to occur when the use cases share common objects because they are functionally related.

12.3   Guidelines for Determining Subsystems

In some applications, for example, client/server systems, the subsystems are easily identifiable. Thus, in the Banking System (Figure 12.1), there is a client subsystem called ATM Client, which is located at each ATM machine, and a central server subsystem called the Bank Server subsystem. This is an example of geographical subsystem structuring, where the geographical distribution of the system is given in the problem description. Geographical distribution is a very strong reason for subsystem structuring.

In other applications, what the subsystems should be might not be so obvious. Because one of the goals of subsystem structuring is to have objects that are functionally related with high coupling in the same subsystem, a good place to start is with the use cases. Objects that participate in the same use case (abstract or concrete) are candidates to be in the same subsystem, providing they are not geographically distributed. Because of this, subsystem structuring is often done after the use cases and their constituent objects, as depicted on object interaction diagrams, have been determined.

Whereas an object may participate in many use cases, an object may only be part of one subsystem. Thus, for objects that participate in more than one use case, a decision has to be made about which subsystem it should be in. The object is usually placed in the subsystem with which it has higher coupling.

12.4   Consolidated Collaboration Diagrams

To transition from analysis to design and to determine the subsystems, it is necessary to synthesize an initial software design from the analysis carried out so far. This is done by integrating the various parts of the analysis model. In the analysis model, a collaboration diagram is developed for each use case. The **consolidated collaboration diagram** is a synthesis of all the collaboration diagrams developed to support the use cases. It is a merger of the collaboration diagrams, usually without the message sequencing numbers because these would only add clutter.

The consolidation performed at this stage is analogous to the *robustness analysis* performed in other methods [Jacobson 1992, Rosenberg and Scott 1999]. Although these other methods use the static model for robustness analysis, COMET emphasizes the dynamic model because it addresses the message communication interfaces, which is crucial in the design of real-time and distributed applications.

Frequently, there is a precedence order in which use cases are executed. The order of the synthesis of the collaboration diagrams should correspond to the order in which the use cases are executed. From a visual perspective, the consolidation is done as follows: Start with the collaboration diagram for the first use case and superimpose the collaboration diagram for the second use case on top of the first to form a consolidated diagram. Next, superimpose the third diagram on top of the consolidated diagram of the first two, and so on. In each case, add new objects and new message interactions from each subsequent diagram onto the consolidated diagram, which gradually gets bigger as more objects and message interactions are added. Objects and message interactions that appear on more than one collaboration diagram are shown only once.

It is important to realize that the consolidated collaboration diagram must show all message communication. Collaboration diagrams often show the main sequence through a use case, but not all the alternative sequences. In the consolidated collaboration diagram, it is necessary to show the messages that are sent as a result of executing the alternative sequences in addition to the main sequence through each use case. An example was given in Chapter 11 of collaboration diagrams supporting several alternative sequences for the Banking System. All these additional messages need to appear on the consolidated collaboration diagram, which is thus intended to be a complete description of all message communication. Naturally, this adds much more information to the diagram. One way to reduce the amount of information is to aggregate the messages—that is, if one object sends several individual messages to another, instead of showing all these messages on the diagram, you use one aggregate message. For example, all incoming messages to the Cruise Control object can be aggregated into `Cruise Control Messages`. A message dictionary is then used to define the contents of `Cruise Control Messages`.

The **consolidated collaboration diagram** is thus a synthesis of several collaboration diagrams showing all objects and their interactions. On the consolidated collaboration diagram, objects and messages are shown, but the message sequence numbering is not shown. An example of a consolidated collaboration diagram for the ATM Client subsystem of the Banking System is given in Figure 12.5.

The consolidated collaboration diagram can get very large for a large system, and showing all the objects on one diagram might not be practical. One approach to reduce the amount of information on the diagram is to show the objects and their message interconnections but to label the interconnections with aggregate message names as described previously. Examples of aggregate message names in Figure 12.5 are ATM Transactions, Bank Responses, and Customer Events. Another approach is to develop consolidated collaboration diagrams for each subsystem and develop a higher-level subsystem collaboration diagram to show the interaction between the subsystems, as described next.

12.5 Subsystem Software Architecture

Subsystems can be depicted on collaboration diagrams or class diagrams. A *subsystem class diagram* shows the structural relationship between the subsystems. Figure 12.1 gives an example of a class diagram showing the relationship between the Bank Server and the ATM Clients for the Banking System.

The dynamic interactions between subsystems can be depicted on a **subsystem collaboration diagram**, which is a high-level consolidated collaboration diagram. The structure of an individual subsystem can be depicted on a consolidated collaboration diagram, which shows all the objects in the subsystem and their interconnections.

Figure 12.6 depicts an example of a subsystem collaboration diagram for the Banking System, which shows two subsystems: ATM Client, of which there are many instances, and Bank Server, of which there is one instance.

12.6 Separation of Concerns in Subsystem Design

To ensure high coupling within a subsystem and low coupling between subsystems, the following guidelines addressing *separation of concerns* should be observed in decomposing the system into subsystems.

Aggregate/composite object. Objects that are part of the same aggregate or composite object should be in the same subsystem and separate from objects that are

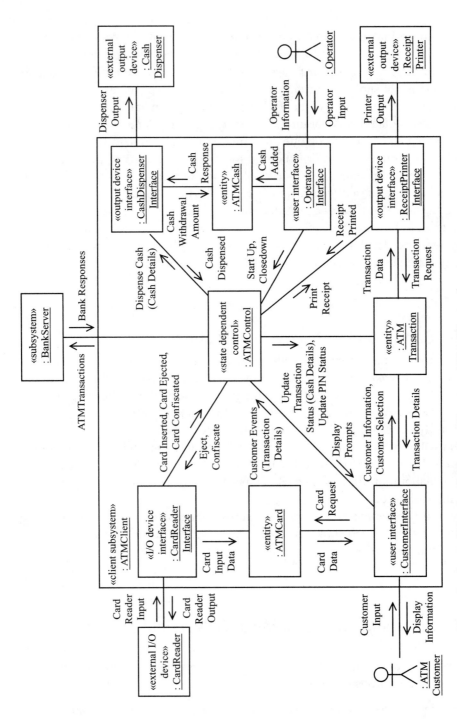

Figure 12.5 *Example of consolidated collaboration diagram: ATM Client subsystem*

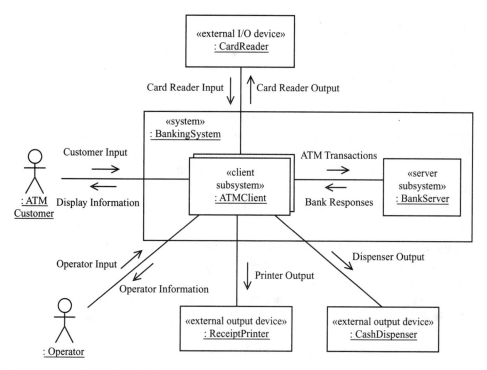

Figure 12.6 *Example of subsystem design: high-level collaboration diagram for Banking System*

not part of the same aggregate or composite object. As described in Chapter 8, both aggregation and composition are whole/part relationships; however, composition is a stronger form of aggregation. With composition, the composite object (the whole) and its constituent objects (the parts) are created together, live together, and die together. Thus, a subsystem consisting of a composite object and its constituent objects is more strongly coupled than one consisting of an aggregate object and its constituent objects.

A subsystem supports information hiding at a more abstract level than does an individual object. A software object can be used to model a real-world object in the problem domain. A composite object models a composite real-world object in the problem domain. A composite object is typically composed of a group of related objects that work together in a coordinated fashion. This is analogous to the assembly structure in manufacturing. It is often the case that multiple instances of a composite object (and hence multiple instances of each of its constituent objects) are needed in an application. The relationship between a composite class and its constituent classes is best depicted in the static model, because the class diagram depicts the multiplicity of the association between each constituent class and the composite class. It is possible for an aggregate subsystem to be a higher-level subsystem that contains composite subsystems, as described in more detail in Chapter 13.

An example of a composite class is the `Elevator` class (see Figure 12.7). Each `Elevator` composite object is composed of n `Elevator Button` objects, n `Elevator Lamp` objects, one `Motor` object, and one `Door` object. There are several instances of the `Elevator` composite class, one for each elevator. Another example of a composite class is the `Floor`. A `Floor` composite object consists of two `Floor Button` objects (for up and down requests), two `Floor Lamp` objects, and two `Direction Lamp` objects, except for the top and bottom floors, which have only one of each. There are several instances of the `Floor` composite class, one for each floor.

Geographical location. If two objects could potentially be physically separated in different locations, they should be in different subsystems. In a distributed environment, communication between distributed subsystems is only by means of messages that can be sent from one subsystem to another. In the Elevator Control System shown in Figure 12.4, each instance of the `Elevator` subsystem could physically reside on a separate microprocessor located in the real-world elevator. Each instance of the `Floor` subsystem could reside on a separate microprocessor located at the specific floor.

Clients and servers. Clients and servers must be in separate subsystems. This guideline can be viewed as a special case of the geographical location rule,

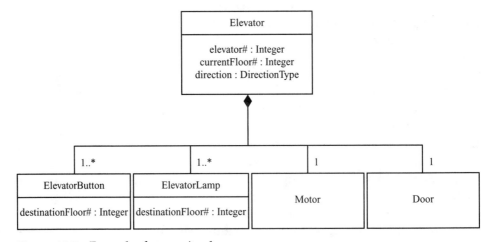

Figure 12.7   *Example of composite class*

because clients and servers are usually at different locations. For example, the Banking System shown in Figure 12.1 has many ATM Client subsystems of the same type, which reside at physical ATMs distributed around the country. The Bank Server is located at a centralized location, perhaps in New York City.

User Interface. Users often use their own PCs as part of a larger distributed configuration, so it is most flexible to keep user interface objects in separate subsystems. Because user interface objects are usually clients, this guideline can be viewed as a special case of the client/server guideline. Furthermore, as described in Chapter 9, a user interface object may be a composite graphical user interface object composed of several simpler user interface objects.

Interface to external objects. A subsystem deals with a subset of the actors shown in the use case model and a subset of the external real-world objects shown on the context diagram. An external real-world object should interface to only one subsystem. Examples are given for the Elevator and Floor subsystems in Figure 12.4.

Scope of control. A control object and all the entity and interface objects it directly controls should all be part of one subsystem and not split among subsystems.

Entity objects. An entity object has stronger cohesion with objects that update it than with objects that read from it. Thus, given a choice, an entity object should be in the same subsystem as the objects that update it.

12.7 Subsystem Structuring Criteria

Subsystems are likely to be application-dependent. The kinds of subsystems often needed in the application domain of concurrent, real-time, or distributed application domains are described next.

Control. A control subsystem controls a given aspect of the system. The subsystem receives its inputs from the external environment and generates outputs to the external environment, usually without any human intervention. A control subsystem is often state-dependent, in which case it includes at least one state-dependent control object. In some cases, some input data might be gathered by some other subsystem(s) and used by this subsystem. Alternatively, this subsystem might provide some data for use by other subsystems.

An example of a control subsystem is the Cruise Control subsystem in Figure 12.8). This subsystem receives its inputs from the cruise control lever, brake,

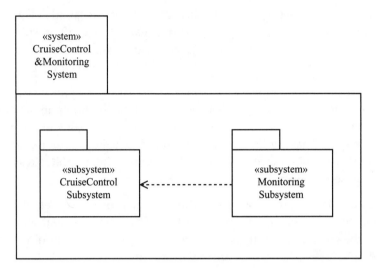

Figure 12.8 *Cruise Control and Monitoring System: major subsystems*

and engine. Its outputs control the throttle. Decisions about what adjustments should be made to the throttle are state-dependent and made without human intervention.

Coordinator. In cases with more than one control subsystem, it is sometimes necessary to have a coordinator subsystem that coordinates the control subsystems. If the multiple control subsystems are completely independent of each other, no coordination is required. Another possibility is for the control subsystems to coordinate activities among themselves. This is usually possible if the coordination is relatively simple, as between the workstation controllers in the Factory Automation System described in Chapter 21. However, if the coordination activity is relatively complex, it is usually more advantageous to have a separate coordinator subsystem. For example, the coordinator subsystem might decide what item of work a control subsystem should do next.

An example of a coordinator subsystem is the `Scheduler` subsystem in the Elevator Control System (see Figure 12.4). In this system, any service request made by a passenger in a given elevator has to be handled by that elevator. However, when a service request is made by a prospective passenger at a floor, a decision has to be made concerning which elevator should service that request. If an elevator is already on its way to this floor and moving in the desired direction, no special action is required. However, if this is not the case, an elevator needs to be dispatched to this floor. The decision made about this usually takes into account the proximity of the elevators to this floor and the direction in which they are heading. This decision can be handled by a `Scheduler` subsystem, as shown in Figure 12.4. When the `Scheduler` receives a `Service Request` from the `Floor Subsystem`, it has to decide whether an elevator should be dispatched to the floor; if so, it sends a `Scheduler Request` to the selected `Elevator Subsystem`.

Data collection. A data collection subsystem collects data from the external environment. In some cases, it stores the data, possibly after collecting, analyzing, and reducing the data. Depending on the application, the subsystem responds to requests for values of the data. Alternatively, the subsystem passes on the data in reduced form—for example, it might collect several raw sensor readings and pass on the average value, converted to engineering units. In other cases, it might output results directly to the external environment. Some combination of the above is also possible.

An example of a data collection subsystem is the `Sensor Data Collection` subsystem in Figure 12.9, which collects raw data from a variety of digital and analog sensors in real time. The frequency with which the data is collected depends on the characteristics of the sensors. Data collected from analog sensors is converted to engineering units. Processed sensor data is sent to consumer subsystems such as the `Sensor Data Analysis` subsystem.

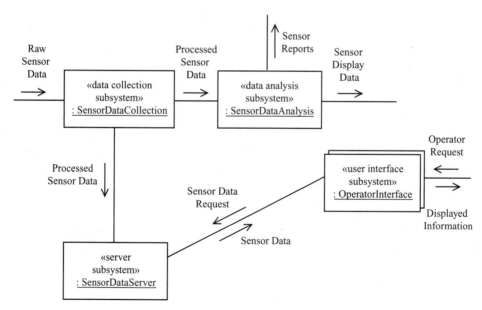

Figure 12.9 *Examples of subsystems*

Data analysis. A data analysis subsystem analyzes data and provides reports and/or displays for data collected by another subsystem. It is possible for a subsystem to provide both data collection and data analysis, as is the case with the Monitoring subsystem in Figure 12.8. In some cases, data collection is done in real time, whereas data analysis is a non-real-time activity.

An example of a data analysis subsystem is the Sensor Data Analysis subsystem shown in Figure 12.9, which receives sensor data from the Sensor Data Collection subsystem. The Sensor Data Analysis subsystem analyzes current and historical sensor data, performs statistical analysis (such as computing the means and standard deviations), produces trend reports, and generates alarms if disturbing trends are detected.

Server. A server subsystem provides a service for other subsystems. It responds to requests from client subsystems; however, it does not initiate any requests. A server object is any object that acts in a server capacity, servicing client requests. In the simplest case, a server object could consist of a single entity object. More complex server objects are composite objects composed of two or more objects. These include entity objects, coordinator objects that service client requests and determine what object should be assigned to handle them, and business logic objects that encapsulate application logic. Frequently, the server provides services that are associated with a data repository or set of related data repositories, or it might provide access to a database or to some relations in a database. Alternatively, the server might be associated with an I/O device or set of related I/O devices. Examples of servers are file servers and line printer servers.

An example of a data server is the Sensor Data Server shown in Figure 12.9, which stores current and historical sensor data. It receives new sensor data from the Sensor Data Collection subsystem. Sensor data is requested by other subsystems, such as the Operator Interface subsystem, which displays the data. Another example of a server subsystem is the Bank Server in the Banking System in Figures 12.1 and 12.6, which services ATM Client requests. Server subsystems are frequently used in distributed applications. The design of server subsystems is described in Chapter 13.

User interface. A user interface subsystem provides the user interface and acts as a client, providing user access to services provided by one or more servers. There may be more than one user interface subsystem, one for each category of user. A user interface subsystem is usually a composite object that is composed of several simpler user interface objects.

Figure 12.9 gives an example of a user interface subsystem, the Operator Interface subsystem, of which there are several instances. The Factory Automation System has one user interface subsystem for factory operators (Operator Interface) and a different user interface subsystem for factory supervisors (Production Manager Interface). The Operator Interface subsystem has one user interface object to display factory alarms and a different user interface object to display factory workstation status.

I/O subsystem. In some systems, grouping all the device interface classes into an I/O subsystem might be useful, because developing device interface classes is a specialized skill. Thus a relatively small number of developers would develop and maintain the I/O subsystem.

System services. Certain services are not problem domain-specific but provide system-level services, such as file management and network communications management. Although these subsystems are not usually developed as part of the application, it should be recognized that they exist. System-level services are provided by system services subsystems and are used by the application subsystems. The middleware services described in Chapter 4 are an example of system services.

12.8 Examples of Subsystem Decomposition

An example of client/server decomposition for the Banking System is given in Section 12.3 and illustrated in Figures 12.1 and 12.6. The Banking System is an example of a three-tier client/server application (see Figure 12.10). Because the third tier is provided by a database management system, it is not part of the application software and so is not explicitly depicted in the application-level diagrams.

In the Cruise Control and Monitoring System, an analysis of the problem indicates that there are two relatively independent and loosely coupled subsystems, namely the Cruise Control Subsystem and the Monitoring Subsystem (see Figure 12.8). The Cruise Control Subsystem is a control

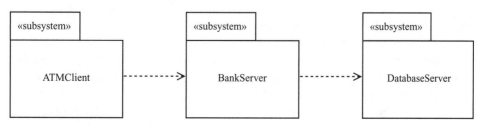

Figure 12.10 *Example of three-tier client/server software architecture: Banking System*

subsystem, and the Monitoring Subsystem provides data collection and analysis. By analyzing the problem further, the interface between the two subsystems can be determined. Thus, the only data item needed by both subsystems is Cumulative Distance, which is computed by the Cruise Control Subsystem and used by the Monitoring Subsystem.

As another example, consider the Elevator Control System. By analyzing the problem, it is determined that elevators and floors are separate composite objects, as described in Section 12.6. The number of floors is usually different from the number of elevators, but each Floor composite object has the same constituent objects and each Elevator composite object has the same constituent objects. Thus in the elevator system, the system is decomposed into a Floor Subsystem and an Elevator Subsystem, with one instance of the Floor Subsystem for each floor and one instance of the Elevator Subsystem for each elevator. With multiple elevators, it is necessary to coordinate the activities of the elevators—in particular, when a floor request is made, which has to be serviced by a specific elevator. A coordinator subsystem is therefore needed, the Scheduler, which schedules each floor request to a given elevator. The decomposition of the Elevator Control System into the three subsystems is shown in Figure 12.4.

12.9   Static Modeling at the Design Level

During static modeling in the analysis phase (Chapter 8), a conceptual static model is developed, which reflects the problem domain, and is depicted on a class diagram(s). In the design model, a more detailed static model is developed that reflects the solution domain. If the conceptual static model is sufficiently detailed, it can form the basis of the solution domain refined static model. However, if the conceptual static model is too abstract, an alternative approach is to develop the solution domain class diagram from the consolidated collaboration diagrams. Objects on the collaboration diagram are mapped to the classes from which they are instantiated. For each link between objects on the collaboration diagram, a corresponding relationship exists on the class diagram.

Because dynamic models have different objectives than static models, some of the relationships that appear on class diagrams do not have a corresponding view in the dynamic model. Thus, class inheritance hierarchies, which are shown on class diagrams, do not appear on collaboration diagrams.

At the design level, it is more appropriate to consider the direction of navigability in an association. This refers to the direction in which a traversal is made from an object of one class to an object or set of objects of the class attached to the end of the association [Rumbaugh, Booch, and Jacobson 1999]. The direction of navigability is determined by considering which class provides the operation and which class uses the operation. Thus, the direction of navigation is from the user class to the provider class. The design of class operations is described in Chapter 15, and this step can be deferred to class design.

As an example, consider the Banking System, which, as previously described, is structured as a client/server system as depicted in Figures 12.1 and 12.6. After the software architecture has been designed and the consolidated collaboration diagrams have been developed for the client and server subsystems, a more detailed static model at the design level can be developed. The conceptual static model (see Figure 12.11), which models the entity classes in the problem domain, does not explicitly differentiate between client classes and server classes. In fact, most of these entity classes reside at the server and hence can be depicted on the refined static model of the `Bank Server` (see Figure 12.12). To determine the additional classes at the `Bank Server`, it is necessary to consider the consolidated

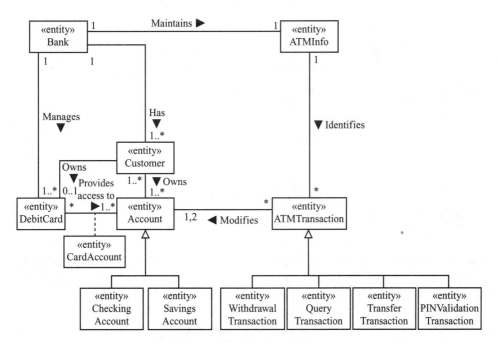

Figure 12.11 *Conceptual static model for Banking System*

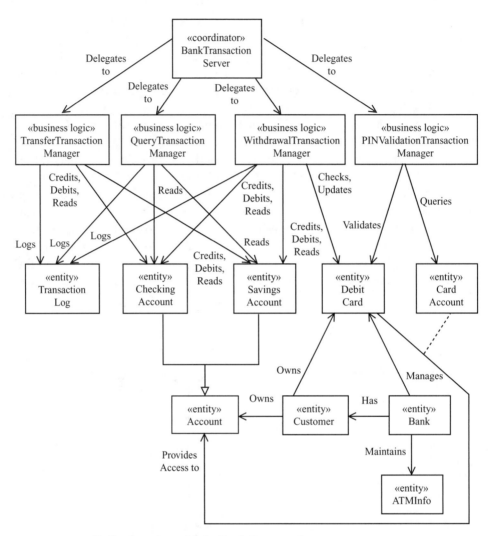

Figure 12.12 *Refined static model for Bank Server subsystem*

collaboration diagram for the Bank Server, which is depicted in Figure 12.13. From this, the coordinator class and business logic classes can be added to the refined static model. These classes are developed by considering the objects (instantiated from the classes depicted on the class diagram) depicted on the consolidated collaboration diagram and how these objects communicate with each other.

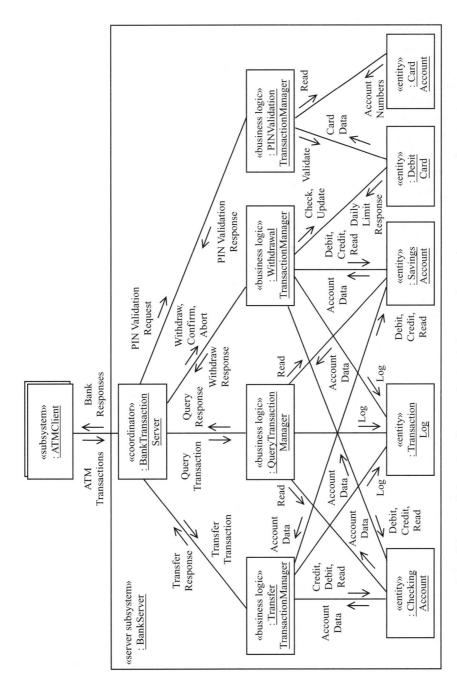

Figure 12.13 *Consolidated collaboration diagram for Bank Server subsystem*

12.10 Summary

To successfully manage the inherent complexity of a large-scale software system, it is necessary to provide an approach for decomposing the system into subsystems and developing the overall software architecture of the system by providing subsystem structuring criteria. After performing this decomposition and carefully defining the interfaces between the subsystems, each subsystem can be designed independently. By describing different kinds of software architectures and providing a set of structuring criteria for determining the subsystems, this chapter has provided detailed guidelines for developing the overall software architecture. Guidelines specific to the architectural design of distributed applications are described in Chapter 13. The design of individual subsystems is described in Chapters 14–16.

chapter

Architectural Design of Distributed Applications

This chapter describes how the COMET design method addresses the design of distributed concurrent and distributed real-time applications. These types of applications execute on geographically distributed nodes supported by a local or wide area network. Client/server applications, distributed real-time data collection applications, and distributed real-time control applications are all examples of distributed applications.

With COMET, a distributed application is structured into distributed subsystems, where a subsystem is designed as a configurable component and corresponds to a logical node. Thus, a subsystem component is defined as a collection of concurrent tasks executing on one logical node. However, because more than one subsystem component (logical node) may execute on the same physical node, the same application could be configured to have each subsystem component allocated to its own separate physical node or to have all or some of its subsystem components allocated to the same physical node. From now on in this chapter, the term "component" will be used to refer to a logical node and the term "node" will be used to refer to a physical node.

Chapter 4 provides an overview of distributed system technology. This chapter describes the steps in designing distributed applications that exploit this technology, distributed component configuration criteria, and the design of component subsystem interfaces. The message communication interfaces include asynchronous communication, synchronous communication, client/server communication, group communication, brokered communication, and negotiated communication. The two-phase commit protocol used in transaction processing systems is described next. The design of server subsystems, which are particularly relevant to distributed applications, is also described. Finally, issues in distributed system configuration are discussed. Three examples of distributed applications are used to illustrate the topics described in this chapter, all taken from the case studies described later—in particular, the distributed Banking System, the distributed Elevator Control System, and the distributed Factory Automation System.

With COMET, no assumptions are made about the availability of a distributed database. One of the objectives of COMET is to structure the distributed application into relatively independent and autonomous subsystems, where any one subsystem may use a local database if it needs to. Distributed access to the data is provided via server subsystems.

13.1   Configurable Architectures and Software Components

An important goal of software architecture for a distributed application is to provide a concurrent message-based design that is highly configurable. In other words, the objective is that the same software architecture should be capable of being mapped to many different system configurations. Thus, a given application could be configured to have each subsystem allocated to its own separate physical node, or alternatively to have all or some of its subsystems allocated to the same physical node. To achieve this flexibility, it is necessary to design the application in such a way that the decision about mapping subsystems to physical nodes is not made at design time, but is made later, at system configuration time. Consequently, communication between those tasks that are in separate subsystems must be restricted to message communication.

A component-based development approach, in which each subsystem is designed as a distributed self-contained component type, helps achieve the goal of a distributed, highly configurable, message-based design. A distributed **component** is an active object with a well-defined **interface**. A component is usually a composite object composed of other objects. A component type is self-contained and thus can be compiled separately, stored in a library, and then subsequently instantiated and linked into an application. A well-designed component type is capable of being reused in different applications from that for which it was originally developed.

13.2   Steps in Designing Distributed Applications

A distributed application consists of distributed subsystems that can be configured to execute on distributed physical nodes. The three main steps in designing a distributed application are

1. **System Decomposition.** Structure the distributed application into component subsystems that potentially could execute on separate nodes in a distributed environment. Because subsystems can reside on separate nodes, all communication between subsystems must be restricted to message communication. The interfaces between subsystems are defined. The subsystem structuring criteria, as described in the previous chapter, are used to initially determine the subsystems. However, to design a configurable distributed application, a set of distributed component configuration criteria are then used to ensure that the subsystems are designed as configurable components that can be effectively mapped to physical nodes.

2. **Subsystem Decomposition.** Structure subsystems into concurrent tasks and information hiding objects. Because, by definition, a subsystem can execute on only one node, each subsystem can be designed by using a design method for non-distributed concurrent systems.

3. **System Configuration.** After a distributed application has been designed, instances of it can be defined and configured. During this stage, the component instances of the target system are defined, interconnected, and mapped onto a hardware configuration consisting of distributed physical nodes.

13.3   System Decomposition

To successfully manage the inherent complexity of large-scale distributed applications, it is necessary to provide an approach for structuring the application into subsystems, where each subsystem can potentially execute on its own node. Communication between subsystems is by means of messages so subsystems can be mapped to different nodes. After this decomposition is performed and the interfaces between the subsystems are carefully defined, each subsystem can be designed independently.

13.3.1   Designing Distributed Subsystems

To determine subsystems, it is helpful to consider the use-case-based collaboration diagrams, which show the objects that communicate frequently with each other, as described in Chapter 12. This is generally a good basis for subsystem structuring, because objects that communicate frequently with each other are good candidates for being in the same subsystem. Although it is possible for an object to be depicted on several collaboration diagrams—one for each use case in which it participates—an object can only be part of one subsystem.

Some subsystems can be determined relatively easily because of geographical distribution or server responsibility. To give a simple example, if one object is located at a geographically remote location from another object, the two objects should be in different subsystems. One of the most common forms of geographical distribution involves clients and servers, which are always allocated to different subsystems: a client subsystem and a server subsystem. An example of this is the ATM Client and the Bank Server in the Banking System in Figure 13.1. It is also possible for peer subsystems (i.e., those that have a peer-to-peer relationship and not a client/server relationship) to be geographically distributed. For example, the Elevator and Floor subsystems in Figure 13.2 are peer subsystems that are geographically distributed.

13.3.2 Aggregate and Composite Subsystems in COMET

When designing distributed applications, we also differentiate between *aggregate* subsystems and *composite* subsystems. A composite subsystem is a component and adheres to the principle of geographical distribution. Thus, objects that are part of a composite subsystem must reside at the same location, but objects in different geographical locations are never in the same composite subsystem. On the other hand, an aggregate subsystem is a subsystem grouped by functional similarity, which might span geographical boundaries. The objects contained in an aggregate subsystem, which might be composite objects, are grouped together because they are functionally similar or because they interact with each other in the same use case(s). Aggregate subsystems can be used as a convenient higher-level abstraction than composite subsystems, particularly when there are many composite subsystems in a highly distributed application.

In COMET, an **aggregate subsystem** is a logical grouping of subsystems and/or objects. It can be depicted as a package in UML, although UML packages have limited usage. In particular, because packages are not used on collaboration diagrams, an aggregate subsystem is depicted instead as an aggregate object that contains other objects. However, an aggregate subsystem is only a logical container and is not intended to have a physical connotation. Thus, in Figure 13.3, the

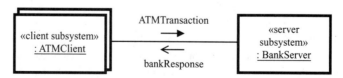

Figure 13.1 *Example of client/server Banking System*

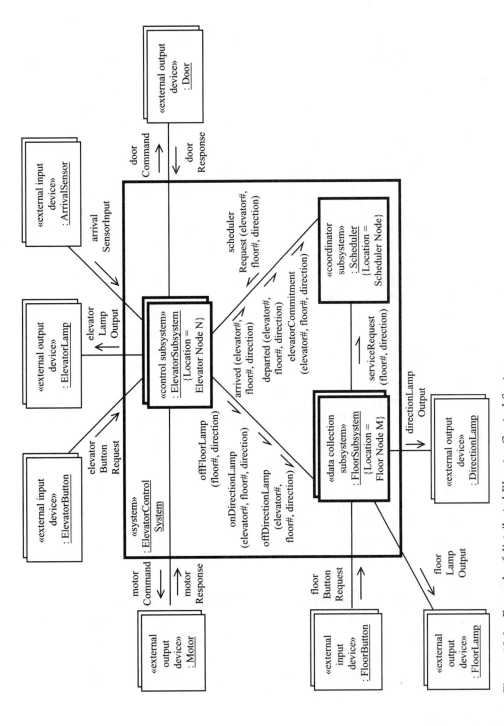

Figure 13.2 *Example of distributed Elevator Control System*

`Part Processing` aggregate subsystem is a useful higher-level grouping of four component subsystems.

In COMET, a **composite subsystem** is a component that encapsulates the objects it contains. The component is both a logical and a physical container; however, it adds no further functionality. Thus all functionality provided by a component is provided by the objects it contains. Incoming messages to a component are passed through to the appropriate internal destination task (active object), and outgoing messages from an internal task are passed through to the appropriate destination. The exact pass-through mechanisms are implementation-dependent. This is a view of whole/part relationships [Buschmann et al. 1996] that is shared by many component-based systems [Bass, Clements, and Kazman 1998; Magee, Kramer, and Sloman 1989; Magee, Dulay, and Kramer 1994, Selic, Gullekson, and Ward 1994; Shaw and Garlan 1996; Szyperski 1997].

Examples of applications with only composite subsystems are the Banking System and the Elevator Control System. An example of a distributed application with both aggregate and composite subsystems is the Factory Automation System (see Figure 13.3). In this distributed application, the `Part Processing` subsystem is an aggregate subsystem because it deals with a major functional area of the system—namely the manufacturing of parts on the factory floor—but it physically spans the whole factory. On the other hand, the `Receiving Workstation Controller`, `Line Workstation Controller`, and `Shipping Workstation Controller` are composite subsystems designed as software components. In any configuration of the Factory Automation System, there is one instance each of the `Receiving Workstation Controller` and the `Shipping Workstation Controller` and several instances of the `Line Workstation Controller` and `Workstation Status Server` subsystems. The exact number and location of the multiple-instance components are determined at system configuration time, as described later. Other examples of aggregate subsystems from the Factory Automation System are the `Process Planning` and `Production Management` subsystems, which are both aggregate client/server subsystems that consist of composite client and server subsystems.

13.3.3   Designing Configurable Distributed Subsystems

In decomposing a distributed application into subsystems, the subsystem structuring criteria described in Chapter 12 are applied. These criteria relate to application-specific characteristics. Additional criteria are needed to ensure that the subsystems determined during subsystem structuring are indeed capable of being designed as distributed components that can be mapped to distributed nodes.

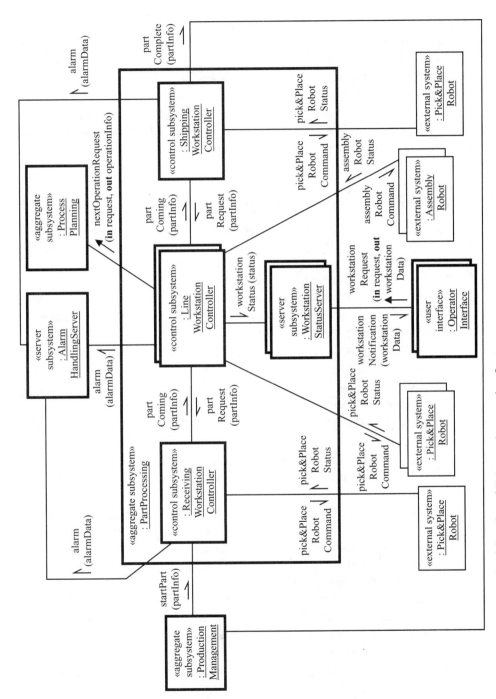

Figure 13.3 *Example of distributed Factory Automation System*

A distributed application needs to be designed with an understanding of the distributed environments in which it is likely to operate. The actual mapping of subsystems to physical nodes is done later when an individual target system is instantiated and configured. However, it is necessary to design the subsystems as configurable components so as to ensure that subsystem instances can later be effectively mapped to distributed physical nodes. Consequently, additional component configuration criteria are required to help ensure that the subsystems are designed as distributed components. These criteria consider the characteristics of distributed environments.

13.3.4   Distributed Component Configuration Criteria

In a real-time and/or distributed environment, a service provided by a subsystem might be associated with a particular physical location or constrained to execute on a given hardware resource. In such a case, a subsystem is constrained to execute on the node at that location or on the given hardware.

The distributed component configuration criteria are provided to help ensure that subsystems are designed effectively as configurable distributed components. A component can satisfy more than one of the criteria, which are as follows:

- **Proximity to the source of physical data.** In a distributed environment, the sources of data might be physically distant from each other. This criterion aims to provide proximity of the component to the source of physical data. This ensures fast access to the data and is particularly important if data access rates are high.

- **Localized autonomy.** With this criterion, the component controls a given aspect of the system. It might receive some high-level commands from another component giving it overall direction, after which it provides the lower-level control, sending status information to other nodes, either on an ongoing basis or on demand.

  With either proximity to the source of physical data or localized autonomy, the component is usually performing a specific site-related service. Often the same service is performed at multiple sites. Each instance of the component type resides on a separate node, thereby providing greater local autonomy. Assuming a component on a given node operates relatively independent of other nodes, it can be operational even if the other nodes are temporarily unavailable. Examples of components that satisfy both of these criteria are the ATM Client subsystem in Figure 13.1, the Elevator Subsystem in Figure 13.2, and the Line Workstation Controller subsystem in Figure 13.3.

- **Performance.** By providing a time-critical function within a node, better and more predictable component performance can often be achieved. In a given distributed application, a real-time component can perform a time-critical service at a given node, with non-real-time or less time-critical services performed elsewhere. Examples of components that satisfy this criterion are all three subsystems of the Elevator Control System shown in Figure 13.2 and the `Line Workstation Controller` subsystem in Figure 13.3.

- **Specialized hardware.** A component might need to reside on a particular node because it supports special-purpose hardware, such as a vector processor, or because it has to interface to special-purpose peripherals, sensors, or actuators that are connected to a specific node. Both the `Elevator` and `Floor` subsystems interface to sensors and actuators.

- **User Interface.** With the proliferation of graphical workstations and personal computers, a component providing a user interface might run on a separate node, interacting with components on other nodes. This kind of component can provide rapid response to simple requests supported completely by the node, and relatively slower responses to requests requiring the cooperation of other nodes. This kind of component usually needs to interface to specific user I/O devices, such as graphical displays and line printers. The `ATM Client` subsystem in Figure 13.1 and the `Operator Interface` subsystem in Figure 13.3 satisfy this criterion.

- **Server.** A server component provides a service for other components. It responds to requests from client components; however, it does not initiate any requests. Frequently, the server provides services that are associated with a data repository or set of related data repositories. Alternatively, the server might be associated with an I/O device or set of related I/O devices.

   A server component is often allocated its own node. A data server supports remote access to a centralized database or file store. An I/O server services requests for a physical resource that resides at that node. Examples of servers are the `Bank Server` in Figure 13.1 and the `Workstation Status Server` in Figure 13.3. The design of server subsystems is described later in this chapter.

13.4   Designing Subsystem Interfaces

Because component subsystems potentially reside on different nodes, all communication between component subsystems must be restricted to message communication. Tasks in different subsystems may communicate with each other using several different types of message communication, as described in this section. Refer to Section 3.6 for an introduction to this topic.

Loosely coupled (asynchronous) message communication is by means of either FIFO message queues or priority message queues. In distributed environments, loosely coupled message communication is used wherever possible for greater flexibility. Group communication, where the same message is sent from a source task to all destination tasks that are members of the group (referred to as multicast communication), is also supported.

Tightly coupled (synchronous) message communication is in the form of either single-client/server communication or multiple-client/server communication. In both cases, a client sends a message to the server and waits for a response; in the latter case, a queue might build up at the server. In a client/server architecture, it is also possible for a server to delegate the processing of a client's request to another server, which then responds directly to the original client.

Message communication between two tasks in the same or different subsystems is generally handled in the same way. The main difference is that there is a possibility of a failure in message transmission when sending a message to a remote task. Whereas Chapter 14 describes message communication between tasks in the same subsystem and hence on the same node, this chapter describes message communication between tasks in different subsystems and hence on different nodes.

13.4.1   Loosely Coupled (Asynchronous) Message Communication

With **loosely coupled message communication**, the producer task sends a message to the consumer task and does not wait for a reply, as described in Chapter 3. The two tasks proceed asynchronously, and a message queue might build up between them. In distributed environments, loosely coupled message communication is used wherever possible for greater flexibility. This approach can be used if the sender does not need a response from the receiver. Alternatively, if it does not need an immediate response, the sender can receive it later.

In a distributed environment, an additional requirement is that the producer needs to receive a positive or negative acknowledgment, indicating whether or not the message arrived at its destination. This is not an indication that the message has been received by the destination task—merely that it has safely arrived at the destination node. Thus some significant additional time might elapse before the message is actually received by the destination task.

A timeout is associated with sending a message so that a failure in message transmission will result in a negative acknowledgement being returned to the source task. It is up to the source task to decide how to handle this failure.

An example of loosely coupled message communication in a distributed environment is given in Figure 13.2, where all communication between the distributed subsystems is loosely coupled. Thus the `Elevator Subsystem` sends `arrived` and `departed` messages (indicating what floor it is at and what direction it is heading in) and `elevator Commitment` messages (indicating what floors it is planning to visit) to the `Scheduler` subsystem. The `Elevator Subsystem` also sends lamp command messages to the `Floor Subsystem` to switch on and off the floor and direction lamps. The `Floor Subsystem` sends `service Request` messages to the `Scheduler`, which are requests for an elevator to come to that floor. The `Scheduler` subsystem sends `scheduler Request` messages to the `Elevator Subsystem`, requesting it to visit specific floors.

13.4.2 Tightly Coupled (Synchronous) Message Communication

First consider **tightly coupled message communication with reply**. The producer task sends a message to the consumer task and then waits for a reply from the consumer. The response might be a negative acknowledgement, indicating that the destination node did not receive the message. This form of communication is typically between a client and a server and is supported by the **remote procedure call** or **remote method invocation** described in Chapter 4. If there is only one client and one server, the tightly coupled message communication with reply notation from Chapter 3 can be used. It is more often the case, however, that tightly coupled message communication involves multiple clients and one server.

If the client and server are to have a dialog that involves several messages and responses, a connection can be established between the client and the server. Messages are then sent and received over the connection.

It should be noted that in distributed message communication, supporting **tightly coupled message communication without reply** is usually not necessary. Communication between subsystems should be loosely coupled whenever possible; tightly coupled message communication should be used only when a response is required.

13.4.3 Multiple Client/Server Message Communication

In the typical client/server situation, several clients request services from a server by sending messages to it. In this case, a message queue can build up at the server. The client can use tightly coupled message communication and wait for a response from the server. Alternatively, the client can use loosely coupled message communication, in which case the client can wait for messages from other sources in addition to the response from the server.

Whether the client uses loosely coupled or tightly coupled message communication with the server is application-dependent and does not affect the design of the server. Indeed it is possible for a server to have some of its clients communicating with it via tightly coupled message communication and others via loosely coupled message communication. The design of server subsystems is described in more detail later in this chapter.

An example of multiple client/server message communication using tightly coupled communication is shown in Figure 13.1, where the server is the Bank Server, which responds to service requests from multiple clients. The Bank Server has a message queue of incoming requests from the multiple clients, together with a tightly coupled response. The server processes each incoming ATM Transaction message on a FIFO basis and then sends the bank Response to the client. Each ATM Client sends a message to the Bank Server and then waits for the response.

13.4.4 Subscription/Notification and Group Message Communication

The message communication described so far has involved one source and one destination task. A desirable property in some distributed applications is group communication. This is a form of one-to-many message communication in which a sender sends one message to many recipients. Two kinds of group message communication (sometimes referred to as groupcast communication) supported in distributed applications are broadcast and multicast communication.

With **broadcast communication**, an unsolicited message is sent to all recipients, perhaps informing them of a pending shutdown. Each recipient must then decide whether it wishes to process the message or discard it.

Multicast communication (also referred to as **subscription/notification**) provides a more selective form of group communication. Tasks subscribe to a group and receive messages destined for all members of the group. A task can subscribe to (request to join) or unsubscribe from (leave) a group and can be a member of more than one group. A sender, also referred to as a publisher, sends a message to the group without having to know who all the individual members are. The message is then sent to all members of the group. Sending the same message to all members of a group is referred to as multicast communication. A message sent to a subscriber is also referred to as an event notification. While on a subscription list, a member can receive several event notification messages. Subscription/notification communication is popular on the Internet.

An example of multicast communication is shown in Figure 13.4. First, three instances of the Operator Interface subsystem subscribe to the Alarm Handling Server to receive alarms of a certain type (messages S1, S2, and S3). Every time the Alarm Handling Server subsystem receives a new alarm message of this type—for example, from the Event Monitor (N1)—it multicasts the alarm Notification message to all subscriber Operator Interface subsystems (messages N2a, N2b, and N2c).

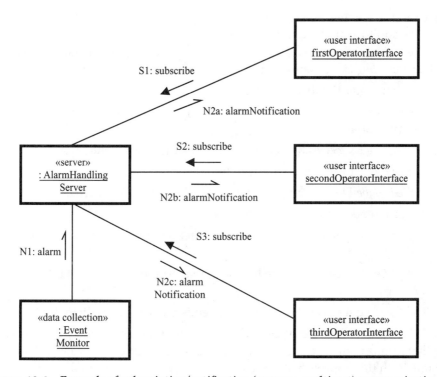

Figure 13.4 *Example of subscription/notification (message multicast) communication*

13.4.5 Brokered Communication

In a distributed object environment, clients and servers are designed as distributed objects. An **object broker** is an intermediary in interactions between clients and servers (see Chapter 4). It frees clients from having to maintain information about where a particular service is provided and how to obtain that service. It also provides *location transparency*, so that if the server object is moved to a different location, only the object broker need be notified.

Servers register the services they provide and the location of these services with the object broker. This type of object brokering service is referred to as a *name service*. Instead of a client having to know the location of services provided by servers, the client queries the object broker for services provided. A client sends a message identifying the service required, for example, to withdraw cash (service) from a given bank (server name). The object broker receives the client request, determines the location of the server (the node the server resides on), and forwards the message to the server at the specific location. The message arrives at the server and the requested service is invoked. The object broker receives the server response and forwards the response back to the client.

There is actually more than one way for the object broker to handle the request. In the *Forwarding Design* approach, the dialog is as follows (Figure 13.5):

1. `Client` sends a request to the `Broker`.

2. The `Broker` looks up the location of the server and forwards the request to the appropriate `Server`.

3. The `Server` services the request and sends the reply to the `Broker`.

4. The `Broker` forwards the reply to the `Client`.

In the *Handle-Driven Design* approach, the dialog is as follows (see Figure 13.6):

1. `Client` sends a request to the `Broker`.

2. The `Broker` looks up the location of the server and returns a service handle to the `Client`.

3. The `Client` uses the service handle to request the service from the appropriate `Server`.

4. The `Server` services the request and sends the reply directly to the `Client`.

This approach is more efficient if the client and server are likely to have a dialog that results in the exchange of several messages. CORBA uses a handle-driven design. With this approach, it is the responsibility of the client to discard the handle after the dialog is over. Using an old handle is liable to fail, as the `Server` might have moved in the interval. If the `Server` does move, it needs to inform the `Broker` so it can update the name table.

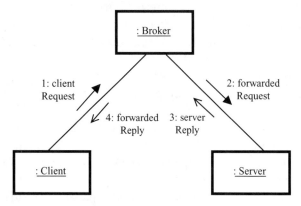

Figure 13.5 *Object broker architecture (white pages: forwarding design)*

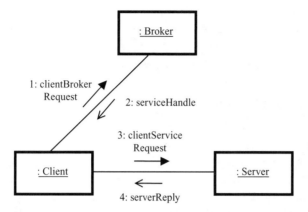

Figure 13.6 *Object broker architecture (white pages: handle-driven design)*

This mode of communication, in which the client knows the service required but not the location, is referred to as *white page* brokering, analogous to the white pages of the telephone directory. Another type of brokering is through *yellow page* brokering, analogous to the yellow pages of the telephone directory, in which the client knows the type of service required but not the specific server. This interaction is shown in Figure 13.7. The client sends a query request to the Object Broker, requesting all servers of a given type—for example, software travel agents (depicted as message 1 in Figure 13.7). The Object Broker responds with a list of all travel agent servers that match the client's request (message 2). The client,

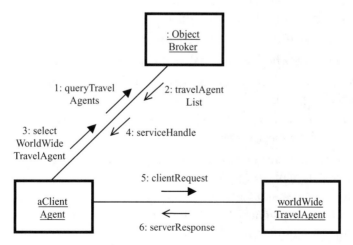

Figure 13.7 *Object broker architecture (yellow pages)*

typically after consultation with the user, selects a specific travel agent server (message 3). The `Object Broker` returns the service handle (message 4). The client then communicates with the server (messages 5 and 6) directly, using the service handle returned to it by the `Object Broker`.

13.4.6 Negotiated Communication

In multi-agent systems, it is necessary to allow software agents to negotiate with each other so they can cooperatively make decisions. In the negotiation paradigm, a client agent acts on behalf of the user and makes a proposal to a server agent. The server agent attempts to satisfy the client's proposal, which might involve communication with other servers. Having determined the available options, the server agent then offers the client agent one or more options that come closest to matching the original client agent proposal. The client agent may then request one of the options, propose further options, or reject the offer. If the server agent can satisfy the client agent request, it accepts the request; otherwise, it rejects the request.

To allow software agents to negotiate with each other, the following lists detail the communication services provided [Pitt, Anderton, and Cunningham 1996].

1. The client agent, who acts on behalf of the client, may do any of the following:

   - **Propose service.** The client agent proposes a service to the server agent. This proposed service is negotiable, meaning that the client agent is willing to consider counter offers.

   - **Request service.** The client agent requests a service from the server agent. This requested service is not negotiable, meaning that the client agent is not willing to consider counter offers.

   - **Reject server offer.** The client agent rejects an offer made by the server agent.

2. The server agent, who acts on behalf of the server, may do any of the following:

   - **Offer a service.** In response to client proposal, a server agent may offer a counter-proposal.

   - **Reject client request/proposal.** The server agent rejects the client agent's proposed or requested service.

   - **Accept client request/proposal.** The server agent accepts the client agent's proposed or requested service.

Consider the following example involving negotiation between a client agent and a software travel agent, which follows a scenario similar to that between a human client and a human travel agent. In this travel agency example, the client agent locates an appropriate server travel agent—for our purposes, the `World Wide Travel Agent`—via the object broker's yellow pages (see Figure 13.7). The client agent then initiates the negotiation on behalf of a user who wishes to take an airplane trip from Washington, D.C., to London, departing on 14 September and returning on 21 September, for a price of less than $700. The negotiation process is depicted on a collaboration diagram (see Figure 13.8) and described next:

1. The Client Agent uses the propose service to propose the trip to London with the stipulated constraints.

2. The World Wide Travel Agent determines that three airlines, Britannic Airways (BA), Unified Airlines (UA), and Virtual Atlantic (VA) service the Washington D.C.-to-London route. It sends a flight Query to the three respective servers—UA Server (2a), BA Server (2b), and VA Server (2c)—for flights on those dates. It receives responses from all three servers with the times and prices of the flights.

3. The World Wide Travel Agent sends an offer message to the Client Agent consisting of the available flights at the proposed price. If only more expensive flights are available, the World Wide Travel Agent offers the cheapest it can find. In this case, it determines that the two best offers for the proposed dates are from UA for $750 and BA for $775. There is no flight below $700, so it offers the two available flights that come closest to the proposed price. It sends the offer message to the Client Agent.

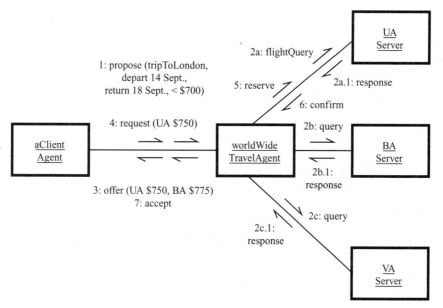

Figure 13.8 *Example of software agent negotiation*

4. The `Client Agent` displays the choice to the user. The `Client Agent` may then `request` a service, i.e., request one of the choices offered by the server agent. (Alternatively, the `Client Agent` may `reject` the server offer if the user does not like any of the options and `propose` a service on a different date.) In this case, the user selects the UA offer and the `Client Agent` sends the `request` UA flight message to the `World Wide Travel Agent`.

5. The `World Wide Travel Agent` makes a `reserve` request to the UA `Server`.

6. Assuming the flight is still available, the UA `Server` confirms the reservation.

7. The `World Wide Travel Agent` responds to the `Client Agent's` request with an `accept` message. If the flight were no longer available, the `World Wide Travel Agent` would send a `reject` message.

It should be noted that in this example, the `World Wide Travel Agent` plays a server role when communicating with the `Client Agent` and plays a client role when communicating with the airline servers.

13.5   Transaction Management

As described in Chapter 4, a **transaction** consists of two or more operations that perform a single logical function, and which must be completed in its entirety or not at all. Transactions are generated at the client and sent to the server for processing. For transactions that need to be atomic (i.e., indivisible), services are needed to begin the transaction, commit the transaction, or abort the transaction. This is typically used for updates to a distributed database that need to be atomic, for example, transferring funds from an account at one bank to an account at a different bank. Using this approach, updates to the distributed database are coordinated such that they are either all performed (commit) or all rolled back (abort).

13.5.1   Two-Phase Commit Protocol in Transaction Processing Systems

Consider two examples of banking transactions:

1. **Withdrawal transaction.** A withdrawal transaction can be handled in one operation. A semaphore is needed for synchronization to ensure that access to the customer account record is mutually exclusive. The transaction processing monitor locks the account record for this customer, performs the update, and then unlocks the record.

2. **Transfer transaction.** Consider a transfer transaction between two accounts—for example, from a savings account to a checking account—in which the accounts are maintained at two separate banks (servers). In this case, the transaction needs to debit the savings account and credit the checking account. Therefore, the transfer transaction consists of two operations that must be atomic: a debit operation and a credit operation, and the transfer transaction must be either

- **Committed.** Both credit and debit operations occur.

- **Aborted.** Neither the credit nor the debit operation occurs.

One way to achieve this result is to use the **two-phase commit protocol**, which is used to synchronize updates on different nodes in distributed applications. The result of the two-phase commit protocol is that either the transaction is committed, in which case all updates succeed, or the transaction is aborted, in which case all updates fail.

One server is designated the Commit Server. There is one participant server for each node. There are two participants in the bank transfer transaction, the first Bank Server, which maintains the from Account, and the second Bank Server, which maintains the to Account. In the first phase of the two-phase commit protocol, the Commit Server sends a prepare To Commit message (1a, 1b) to each participant server. Each participant server locks the record (1a.1, 1b.1), performs the update (1a.2, 1b.2), and then sends a ready To Commit message (1a.3, 1b.3) to the Commit Server, as shown in Fig 13.9. If a participant server is unable to perform the update, it sends a refuse To Commit message. The Commit Server waits to receive responses from all participants.

When all participant servers have responded, the Commit Server proceeds to the second phase of the two-phase commit protocol. If all participants have sent ready To Commit messages, the Commit Server sends the commit message (2a, 2b) to each participant server. Each participant server makes the update permanent (2a.1, 2b.1), unlocks the record (2a.2, 2b.2), and sends a commit Completed message (2a.3, 2b.3), to the Commit Server, as shown in Fig 13.10. The Commit Server waits for all commit Completed messages.

If a participant server responds to the prepare To Commit message with a ready To Commit message, it is committed to completing the transaction. The participant server must complete the transaction even if a delay occurs (for example, even if it goes down after it has sent the ready To Commit message). If on the other hand, any participant server responds to the prepare To Commit message with a refuse To Commit message, the Commit Server sends an abort message to all participants. The participants then roll back the update.

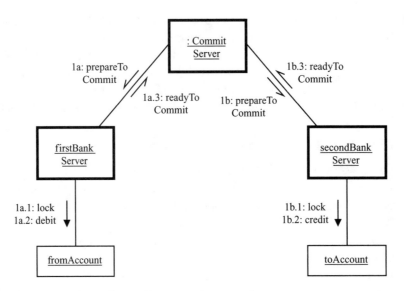

Figure 13.9   *First phase of two-phase commit protocol*

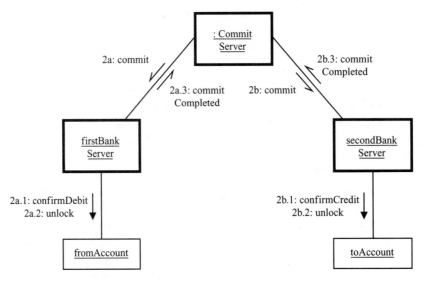

Figure 13.10   *Second phase of two-phase commit protocol*

13.5.2   Transaction Design Considerations

The previous transfer transaction is an example of a flat transaction, which has an "all-or-nothing" characteristic. A compound transaction might need only a partial rollback. For example, if a travel agent makes an airplane reservation, followed by a hotel reservation and a rental car reservation, it is more flexible to treat this reservation as consisting of three flat transactions. This allows part of a reservation to be changed or canceled without impacting the other parts of the reservation.

With transactions involving human interaction, it is undesirable to keep records locked while the human is considering various options. For example, in an airline reservation using a flat transaction, the record would be locked for the duration of the transaction. With human involvement in the transaction, the record could be locked for a long time. In this case, it is better to split the reservation process into two transactions. First, there is a `query` transaction to display the available seats. This is followed by a `reserve` transaction. With this approach, it is necessary to re-check seat availability before the update is made. A seat available at query time might no longer be available at reserve time because several agents might be querying the same flight at the same time. If only one seat is available, the first agent will get the seat but not the others. Note that this problem still applies even if the airline allows seat overbooking, although the upper limit would then be the number of actual seats on the aircraft plus the number of seats allowed to be overbooked on the flight. This approach is followed in the travel agent example depicted in Figure 13.8, where the travel agent first queries the airline servers (2a, 2b, and 2c) to determine available flights and then reserves a flight (5).

13.6   Design of Server Subsystems

Server subsystems play an important role in the design of distributed applications. A server subsystem provides a service for client subsystems. Typical server subsystems are file servers, database servers, and line printer servers.

In a non-distributed application, a data structure is encapsulated in a data abstraction object (as discussed in Chapter 15). Tasks that need to access the data maintained by the object invoke operations provided by the object. In a distributed application, tasks on separate nodes cannot directly access a passive data abstraction object. It is therefore necessary for the passive data abstraction object to be encapsulated in a server component. In this case, an active object (i.e., a thread provided by the distributed subsystem) accesses the passive object.

The server subsystem responds to client requests to read or update the data maintained by the passive object. It is also possible for a server subsystem to encapsulate a set of related passive data abstraction objects and provide services for all of them. A simple server subsystem does not initiate any requests for services from other subsystems. There are two kinds of server subsystems, the sequential server subsystem and the concurrent server subsystem.

13.6.1 Sequential Server Subsystem

A sequential server subsystem services client requests sequentially, that is, it completes one request before it starts servicing the next. A **sequential server** is designed as one task that provides one or more services and responds to requests from client tasks to access the service. For example, a simple sequential server subsystem responds to requests from client tasks to update or read data from a passive data abstraction object. When the server task receives a message from a client task, it invokes the appropriate service provided by the passive data abstraction object—for example, to credit or debit an account object in a Banking System.

The server task typically has a message queue of incoming service request messages. There is one message type for each service provided by the server. The server coordinator unpacks the client's message and, based on the message type, invokes the appropriate operation provided by a server object. The parameters of the message are used as the parameters of the operation. The server object services the client's request and returns the appropriate response to the server coordinator, which packs the response into a service response message and sends it to the client. The server coordinator is equivalent to the server stub used in remote procedure calls or the server proxy used in remote method invocations, as described in Chapter 4.

An example of a sequential server is given in Figure 13.11. The Bank Server sequentially services client Transactions requesting credits, debits, and queries. The Bank Transaction Server, which is a coordinator object, receives a client Transaction and invokes a credit, debit, or read operation provided by the Checking Account or Savings Account object, and then returns the bank Response to the client.

13.6.2 Concurrent Server Subsystem

If the client demand for services is high, so that the server subsystem could potentially be a bottleneck in the system, an alternative approach is for the services to be provided by a concurrent server subsystem and hence shared among several tasks. This assumes that improved throughput can be obtained by having concur-

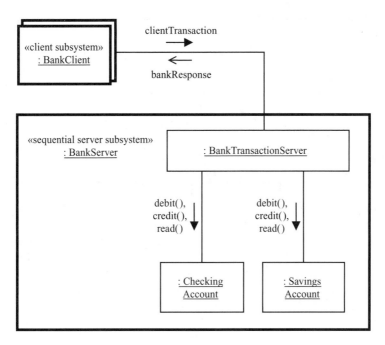

Figure 13.11   *Example of sequential server subsystem*

rent access to the data, for example, if the data is stored on secondary storage. In this case, while one task is blocked, waiting for some disk I/O operation to be completed, another task is allocated the CPU.

In a concurrent server subsystem, several tasks might wish to access the data repository at the same time, so access needs to be synchronized. The most appropriate synchronization algorithm to use is typically application-dependent. Possible algorithms include the **mutual exclusion** algorithm and the **multiple readers and writers** algorithm. In the latter case, multiple readers are allowed to access a shared data repository concurrently; however, only one writer is allowed to update the data repository at any one time and only after the readers have finished.

In the multiple readers and writers solution shown in Figure 13.12, each service is performed by one task. The Server Coordinator keeps track of all service requests—those currently being serviced and those waiting to be serviced. When it receives a request from a client, the Server Coordinator allocates the request to an appropriate reader or writer task to perform the service. For example, if the Coordinator receives a read request from a client, it instantiates a Reader task and increments its count of the number of readers. The Reader notifies the Coordinator when it finishes, so that the Coordinator can decrement the reader

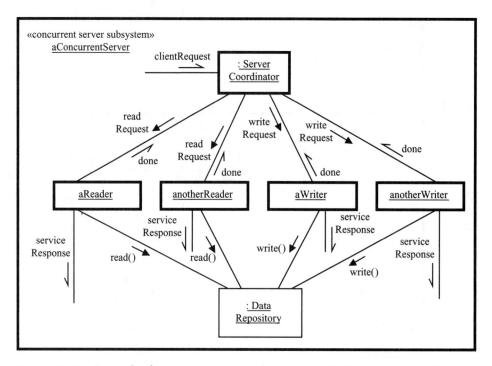

Figure 13.12 *Example of concurrent server subsystem: multiple readers and writers*

count. If a write request is received from a client, the `Coordinator` allocates the request to a `Writer` task only when all readers have finished. This ensures that writer tasks have mutually exclusive access to the data. The `Coordinator` does not allocate any new read requests until the `Writer` task has finished. If the overhead of instantiating new tasks is too high, the `Coordinator` can maintain a pool of `Reader` tasks and one `Writer` task, and allocate new requests to free tasks.

If new readers keep coming and are permitted to read, a writer could be indefinitely prevented from writing; this problem is referred to as "writer starvation." The `Coordinator` avoids writer starvation by holding up new reader requests after receiving a writer request. After the current readers have finished reading, the waiting writer is then allowed to write before any new readers are permitted to read.

In this example, the clients communicate with the server by using asynchronous communication. This means the clients do not wait and can do other things before receiving the server response. In this case, the server response can be handled as a **callback**. With the callback approach, the client sends an operation handle with the original request. The server uses the handle to remotely call the client operation (the callback) when it finishes servicing the client request. In this example, the `Server Coordinator` passes the client's callback handle to the reader (or writer). On completion, the `Reader` task remotely invokes the callback, which is depicted on Figure 13.12 as the `service Response` message sent to the client.

Another example of a concurrent server is shown in Figure 13.13. This server maintains an event archive and also provides a **subscription/notification** service to its clients. An example is given of a `Real-Time Event Monitor` task that monitors external events. The `Subscription Server` maintains a subscription list of clients that wish to be notified of these events. When an external event occurs, the `Real-Time Event Monitor` updates an event archive and informs the `Event Distributor` of the event arrival. The `Event Distributor` queries

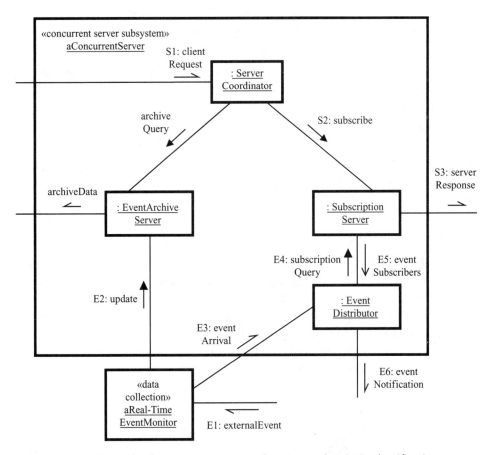

Figure 13.13 *Example of concurrent server subsystem: subscription/notification*

the `Subscription Server` to determine the clients who have subscribed to receive events of this type, and then notifies them of the new event.

The concurrent server is depicted on a concurrent collaboration diagram (see Figure 13.13), which shows two separate interactions: a client subscription use case and an event notification use case. First consider the client subscription use case:

S1: `Server Coordinator` receives a subscription request from a client.

S2: The `Server Coordinator` sends a `subscribe` message to the `Subscription Server`.

S3: The `Subscription Server` confirms the subscription by sending the `server Response` to the client.

Now consider the event notification use case:

E1: An external event arrives at the `Real-Time Event Monitor`.

E2: The `Real-Time Event Monitor` determines that this is a significant event and sends an update message to the `Event Archive Server`.

E3: The `Real-Time Event Monitor` sends an event `Arrival` message to the `Event Distributor` object.

E4, E5: The `Event Distributor` queries the `Subscription Server` to get the list of event subscribers (i.e., clients that have subscribed to receive events of this type).

E6: The `Event Distributor` multicasts an event `Notification` message to all clients that have subscribed for this event.

13.7   Distribution of Data

Both the sequential and concurrent server subsystems are single-server subsystems; thus, the data repositories they encapsulate are centralized. In distributed applications, the potential disadvantages of centralized servers are that the server could become a bottleneck and that it is liable to be a single point of failure. A solution to these problems is data distribution. Two approaches to data distribution are the distributed server and data replication.

13.7.1   Distributed Server

With the **distributed server**, data that is collected at several locations is stored at those locations. Each location has a local server, which responds to client requests for that location's data. This approach is used in the distributed Factory Automation System case study (see Figure 13.3), where manufacturing workstation status data is maintained at each location by a local `Workstation Status Server`, which responds to client requests from factory operators.

13.7.2   Data Replication

With **data replication**, the same data is duplicated in more than one location to speed up access to the data. Ensuring that procedures exist for updating the local copies of the replicated data is of course important so the data does not get out of date. This approach is used in the Distributed Elevator Control System case study in Figure 13.2. Each instance of the `Elevator Subsystem` (one per elevator) maintains its own `Local Status & Plan` data abstraction object to keep track of where the elevator is and what floors it is committed to visit. In order for the `Scheduler` to select an elevator when a floor request is made, it needs to have access to the status and plan data for all the elevators. To expedite this, the `Scheduler` maintains its own copy of each elevator's status and plan in an `Overall Status & Plan` data abstraction object. This data is updated by elevator status and commitment messages sent to the `Scheduler` by each instance of the `Elevator Subsystem`.

13.8   System Configuration

After a distributed application has been designed, instances of it can be defined and configured. During system configuration, an instance of the distributed application—referred to as a target system—is defined and mapped to a distributed configuration consisting of multiple geographically distributed physical nodes connected by a network.

13.8.1   System Configuration Issues

As described earlier, for greatest flexibility, subsystems need to be designed as configurable component types. During system configuration, a decision is made about what component instances are required. In addition, it is necessary to determine how the component instances should be interconnected and how the component instances should be allocated to nodes.

During *target system configuration*, the following activities need to be performed:

1. **Instances of the component types are defined.** For each component type that can have multiple instances, it is necessary to define the instances desired. For example, in the distributed Elevator Control System, it is necessary to define

the number of elevators and the numbers of floors required in the target system. It is also necessary to define one Elevator Subsystem instance for each elevator and one Floor Subsystem instance for each floor. Each Elevator Subsystem and Floor Subsystem instance must have a unique name so it can be uniquely identified.

For components that are parameterized, the parameters for each instance need to be defined. Examples of component parameters are instance name (such as elevator ID or floor ID), sensor names, sensor limits, and alarm names.

2. **Component instances are interconnected.** The target system architecture defines how subsystem components communicate with one another. At this stage, the component instances are connected together. For example, in the distributed Elevator Control System in Figure 13.2, each instance of the Floor Subsystem sends a service Request message to the Scheduler subsystem. The Scheduler sends scheduler Request messages to individual instances of the Elevator Subsystem, so it must identify to which elevator it is sending the message. Similarly, when an Elevator Subsystem instance sends a message to a Floor Subsystem instance, it must identify to which floor it is sending the message.

3. **The component instances, which are logical nodes, are mapped to physical nodes.** For example, two components could be configured such that they each could run on a separate physical node. Alternatively, they could both run on the same physical node.

13.8.2 Example of Target System Configuration

As an example of target system configuration, consider the distributed Elevator Control System. The deployment diagram is shown in Figure 13.14. Each component instance of the Elevator Subsystem (1 per elevator) is allocated to a node to achieve localized autonomy and adequate performance. Thus the failure of one elevator node will not impact other elevator nodes. Each instance of the Floor Subsystem (1 per floor) is allocated to a node because of proximity to the source of physical data. Loss of a floor node means that floor will not be serviced but service to other floors is not impacted. The Scheduler is allocated to a separate node for performance reasons, so it can rapidly respond to elevator requests. Loss of the scheduler node (preferably temporarily) means that no new floor requests will be assigned to elevators but current passengers on elevators will continue to be serviced until they arrive at their destinations.

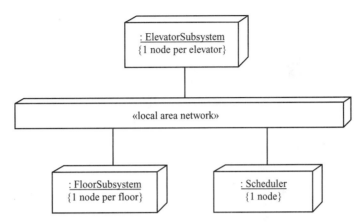

Figure 13.14 *Example of distributed system configuration*

13.9 Summary

This chapter has described how the COMET design method addresses the design of distributed concurrent and distributed real-time applications. These types of applications execute on geographically distributed nodes supported by local or wide area networks. Topics covered were the steps in designing distributed applications, distributed component configuration criteria, and the design of subsystem interfaces. For greater flexibility and potential reuse, distributed subsystems are designed as configurable components.

This chapter also described the message communication interfaces between subsystems, which include asynchronous communication, synchronous communication, client/server communication, group communication, brokered communication, and negotiated communication. The two-phase commit protocol used in transaction processing systems was then described. The design of server subsystems, which are particularly relevant to distributed applications, was also described. Finally, issues in distributed system configuration were described.

After determining the subsystems in the distributed application and defining the message interfaces between them, the next step is to design each subsystem. Each subsystem consists of one or more concurrent tasks. By definition, all tasks within a given subsystem always execute on the same node. Each subsystem is decomposed into tasks, as described in Chapter 14. Tasks within the same subsystem may, in addition to message communication, use event synchronization, and communication via passive information hiding objects, which reside in shared memory.

Task Structuring

During subsystem design, the application is decomposed into subsystems. The design of a subsystem consists of designing the concurrent tasks, as described in this chapter, and designing the information hiding classes from which passive objects are instantiated, as described in Chapter 15. Following this, Chapter 16 describes the detailed software design, in which tasks that contain nested passive objects are designed, detailed task synchronization issues are addressed, connector classes are designed that encapsulate the details of inter-task communication, and each task's internal event sequencing logic is defined.

An important objective in task and class structuring is *separation of concerns*. A task uses information hiding to address *concurrency concerns*, in particular details of timing, control, sequencing, and communication. A class uses information hiding to address *structural (static) concerns*, of which there are different kinds, such as hiding device information or data abstraction.

A task type is an active class and a **task** is an active object. A task has its own thread of control. A passive object is an instance of passive class. In the discussion of the design model, the term "object" will be used to refer to a passive object, and the term "task" will be used to refer to an active object.

During the task structuring phase, a **task architecture** is developed in which the system is structured into concurrent tasks and the task interfaces and inter-connections are defined. To help determine the concurrent tasks, task structuring criteria are provided to assist in mapping an object-oriented analysis model of the system to a concurrent tasking architecture. These criteria are a set of heuristics, also referred to as guidelines, which capture expert designer knowledge in the software design of concurrent and real-time systems.

Each task determined by using the task structuring criteria executes a sequence of operations. However, the information hiding objects that provide the operations are not designed until the class design phase, which is described in Chapter 15.

After introducing some general aspects of task structuring, the chapter describes the task structuring categories. This is followed by a detailed description, with the aid of examples, of the criteria within each category, namely **I/O task structuring criteria**, **internal task structuring criteria**, **task priority criteria**, **task clustering criteria,** and **task inversion** criteria. Following this are some guidelines on the order of applying the task structuring criteria. After this, there is a detailed description of defining task communication and synchronization interfaces.

14.1   Concurrent Task Structuring Issues

A **task** is an active object, also referred to as a process or thread. In this chapter, the term "task" is used to refer to an active object with one thread of control. In some systems, a task would be implemented as a single-threaded process; in other systems, it might be implemented as a thread (lightweight process) within a heavyweight process.

As described in Chapter 3, there are many advantages to having a concurrent tasking design; however, the designer must be careful in designing the task structure. Too many tasks in a system can unnecessarily increase complexity because of greater inter-task communication and synchronization, and can lead to increased overhead because of additional context switching (see Chapter 4). The system designer has, therefore, to make tradeoffs between, on the one hand, introducing tasks to simplify and clarify the design and, on the other hand, not introducing too many tasks, which could make the design too complex. The task structuring criteria are intended to help the designer make these tradeoffs. They also enable the designer to analyze alternative task architectures.

The concurrent structure of a system is best understood by considering the dynamic aspects of the system. In the analysis model, the system is represented as a collection of collaborating objects that communicate by means of messages. During the task structuring phase, the concurrent nature of the system is formalized by defining the concurrent tasks and the communication/synchronization interfaces between them.

The objects in the analysis model are analyzed to determine which of these may execute concurrently and which need to execute sequentially. Objects that execute concurrently are structured into separate tasks. A set of objects that is constrained to execute sequentially is grouped into the same task; thus, a task may encompass one or more objects. It is also possible for one task to execute one operation of an object and a different task to execute a different operation of the same object.

14.2   Task Structuring Categories

The task structuring criteria are grouped into categories based on how they are used to assist in the task structuring activity. Following are the five task structuring categories:

1. **I/O task structuring criteria.** Address how device interface objects are mapped to I/O tasks and when an I/O task is activated.

2. **Internal task structuring criteria.** Address how internal objects are mapped to internal tasks and when an internal task is activated.

3. **Task priority criteria.** Address the importance of executing a given task relative to others.

4. **Task clustering criteria.** Address whether and how objects should be grouped into concurrent tasks.

5. **Task inversion criteria.** Used for merging tasks to reduce task overhead either during initial task structuring or during design restructuring.

Tasks are activated either periodically or aperiodically (i.e., on demand). A task may exhibit more than one of the task structuring criteria.

The task structuring criteria are applied in two stages. In the first stage, the I/O task structuring criteria, the internal task structuring criteria, and the task priority criteria are applied. This results in a one-to-one mapping of objects in the analysis model to tasks in the design model. In the second stage, the task clustering criteria are applied, with the objective of reducing the number of physical tasks. For an experienced designer, these two stages can be merged. After the tasks have been determined, the task interfaces are defined.

Following the approach used in Chapter 9 for object structuring, stereotypes are used to depict the different kinds of tasks. Stereotypes are also used to depict the kinds of devices to which the tasks interface. During task structuring, if an object in the analysis model is determined to be active, it is categorized further to show its task characteristics. For example, an active «I/O device interface» object is considered a task and categorized as one of the following: an «asynchronous

I/O device interface» task, a «periodic I/O device interface» task, a «passive I/O device interface» task, or a «resource monitor» task. Similarly, an «external input device» is classified, depending on its characteristics, into an «asynchronous input device» or a «passive input device».

14.3 I/O Task Structuring Criteria

This section describes the various I/O task structuring criteria. An important factor in deciding on the characteristics of an I/O task is to determine the characteristics of the I/O device to which it has to interface.

14.3.1 Characteristics of I/O Devices

There is certain hardware-related information concerning I/O devices that is typically not provided with an analysis model. Nevertheless, this information is essential to determining the characteristics of tasks that interface to the devices. Before the I/O task structuring criteria can be applied, it is necessary to determine the hardware characteristics of the I/O devices that interface to the system. It is also necessary to determine the nature of the data being input to the system by these devices or being output by the system to these devices. I/O considerations were introduced in Chapter 4. In this section, the following I/O issues specific to task structuring are described:

- **Characteristics of I/O devices.** It is necessary to determine whether the I/O device is asynchronous (active) or passive. Three major classes of I/O devices are

  1. **Asynchronous I/O devices** (sometimes referred to as active I/O devices), which are interrupt-driven I/O devices. An asynchronous input device generates an interrupt when it has produced some input that requires processing by the system. An asynchronous output device generates an interrupt when it has finished processing an output operation and is ready to perform some new output.

  2. **Passive I/O devices.** A passive device does not generate an interrupt on completion of the input or output operation. Thus the input from a passive input device needs to be read either on a polled basis or on demand. Similarly, in the case of a passive output device, output needs to be provided on either a regular (i.e., periodic) basis or on demand.

  3. **Communications link.** Some microprocessor-driven I/O devices or external systems are connected to the system by means of a communication link. A communication protocol defines how the two systems communi-

cate with each other (for example, TCP/IP). At the application level, tasks in the various systems communicate by means of messages. The types of message communication for interfacing to external systems are described in Chapter 13.

- **Characteristics of data.** It is necessary to determine whether the I/O device provides discrete data or continuous data. **Discrete data** is either Boolean or has a finite number of values. **Analog data** is continuous data and can in principle have an infinite number of values. An I/O device that provides analog data will almost certainly have to be polled or accessed on demand. If an analog device generated an I/O interrupt every time its value changed, it would probably flood the system with interrupts.

- **Passive I/O device.** For a passive I/O device, it is necessary to determine whether

  - Sampling the device on demand is sufficient, in particular when some consumer needs the data.

  - The device needs to be polled on a periodic basis so that any change in value is sent to a consumer without being explicitly requested, or it is written to a data abstraction object with sufficient frequency so that the data does not get out of date.

- **Polling frequency.** If a passive I/O device is to be polled on a periodic basis, it is necessary to determine the polling frequency. The polling frequency depends on how critical the input is and how frequently it is expected to change.

  In the case of an output device, the polling frequency depends on how often the data should be output in order to prevent it from getting out of date.

14.3.2 Asynchronous I/O Device Interface Tasks

An asynchronous I/O device interface task is needed when there is an asynchronous I/O device to which the system has to interface. For each asynchronous I/O device, an asynchronous I/O device interface task is needed to interface to it. The asynchronous I/O device interface task is activated by an interrupt from the asynchronous device. During task structuring, each device interface object in the analysis model that interfaces to an asynchronous I/O device is mapped to an asynchronous I/O device interface task. Asynchronous I/O device interface tasks are also known as aperiodic I/O device interface tasks.

An asynchronous I/O device interface task is constrained to execute at the speed of the asynchronous I/O device with which it is interacting. Thus an input task might be suspended indefinitely awaiting an input. However, when activated by an interrupt, the input task often has to respond to a subsequent interrupt within a few milliseconds to avoid any loss of data. After the input data is read, the input task may send the data to be processed by another task. This frees the input task to respond to another interrupt that might closely follow the first.

The concept of one task for each asynchronous I/O device was originally proposed by Dijkstra [Dijkstra 1968] in his early work on cooperating sequential processes and was used by Brinch Hansen [Brinch Hansen 1973] in his work on operating system design based on concurrent processes.

An asynchronous I/O device interface task is a device driver task. It is typically activated by a low-level interrupt handler or—in some cases—directly by the hardware, as described in Chapter 4.

Another kind of asynchronous interface task is the *asynchronous system interface* task, which interfaces to an external system instead of an I/O device. An asynchronous system interface task usually interacts with an external system by using messages.

As an example of an asynchronous I/O device interface task, consider the `Cruise Control Lever Interface` device interface object shown on the analysis model collaboration diagram in Figure 14.1a. The `Cruise Control Lever Interface` object receives cruise control inputs from the real-world cruise control lever, which is depicted as an external input device. The `Cruise Control Lever Interface` object then converts the input to an internal format and sends the cruise control request to the `Cruise Control` object. For task structuring, it is given that the cruise control lever is an asynchronous input device, depicted on the design model concurrent collaboration diagram (see Figure 14.1b) with the stereotype «asynchronous input device», which generates an interrupt when a cruise control input is available. The `Cruise Control Lever Interface` object is mapped to an asynchronous input device interface task of the same name, depicted on the concurrent collaboration diagram with the stereotype «asynchronous input device interface». When the task is activated by the `Cruise Control Interrupt`, it reads the `Cruise Control Input`, converts the input to an internal format, and sends it as a `Cruise Control Request` message to the `Cruise Control` task.

14.3.3   Periodic I/O Device Interface Tasks

While an asynchronous I/O device interface task deals with an asynchronous I/O device, a periodic I/O device interface task deals with a passive I/O device, where the device is polled on a regular basis. In this situation, the activation of the task is periodic but its function is I/O-related. The periodic I/O device interface task is activated by a timer event, performs an I/O operation, and then waits for the next timer event. The task's period is the time between successive activations.

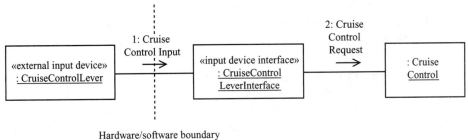

NB: The dashed line for the hardware/software boundary is for illustrative purposes only and does not conform to the UML notation.

Figure 14.1a   *Analysis model: collaboration diagram*

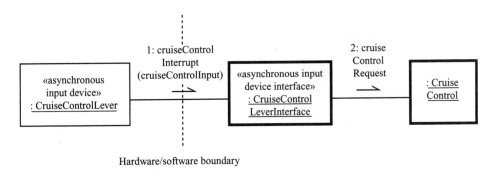

NB: The dashed line for the hardware/software boundary is for illustrative purposes only and does not conform to the UML notation.

Figure 14.1b   *Design model: concurrent collaboration diagram*

Figure 14.1   *Example of asynchronous I/O device interface task*

Periodic I/O tasks are often used for simple I/O devices that, unlike asynchronous I/O devices, do not generate interrupts when I/O is available. Thus, they are often used for passive sensor devices that need to be sampled periodically.

Sensor-Based Periodic I/O Device Interface Tasks

The concept of a periodic I/O task is used in many sensor-based industrial systems. Such systems often have a large number of digital and analog sensors. A periodic I/O task is activated on a regular basis, scans the sensors, and reads their values.

Consider a passive digital input device—for example, the engine sensor. This is handled by a **periodic input device interface task**. The task is activated by a timer event and then reads the status of the device. If the value of the digital sensor has changed since the previous time it was sampled, the task indicates the change in status. In the case of an analog sensor—a temperature sensor, for example—the device is sampled periodically and the current value of the sensor is read.

As an example of a periodic input device interface task, consider the Engine Interface object shown in Figure 14.2a. In the analysis model depicted on the

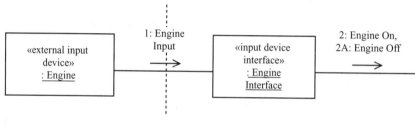

Hardware/software boundary

NB: The dashed line for the hardware/software boundary is for illustrative purposes only and does not conform to the UML notation.

Figure 14.2a   *Analysis model: collaboration diagram*

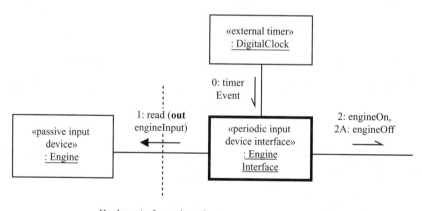

Hardware/software boundary

NB: The dashed line for the hardware/software boundary is for illustrative purposes only and does not conform to the UML notation.

Figure 14.2b   *Design model: concurrent collaboration diagram*

Figure 14.2   *Example of a periodic input device interface task*

collaboration diagram, the Engine Interface object is an «input device interface» object that receives engine inputs from the real-world Engine, depicted with the stereotype «external input device». Because the engine is a passive device, it is depicted on the concurrent collaboration diagram with the stereotype «passive input device» (see Figure 14.2b). Because a passive device does not generate an interrupt, an asynchronous input device interface task cannot be used. Instead, this case is handled by a periodic input device interface task, the Engine Interface task, which is activated periodically by a timer device to sample the value of the engine sensor. Thus the Engine Interface object is mapped to the Engine Interface «periodic input device interface» task, as depicted on the concurrent collaboration diagram. To activate the Engine Interface task periodically, it is necessary to add an «external timer» object, the Digital Clock, as depicted in Figure 14.2b. When activated, the Engine Interface task samples the engine sensor; if there is a change in status, it sends the appropriate message, engine On or engine Off, to the consumer task. It then waits for the next timer event.

Timing Considerations for Periodic I/O Tasks

The frequency with which a task samples a sensor depends on the frequency with which the sensor's value is expected to change. It also depends on the delay that can be tolerated in reporting this change. For example, ambient temperature varies slowly and so can be polled with a frequency in minutes. On the other hand, to provide a fast response to the pressing of the automobile brake, assuming the brake is a passive device, the brake sensor might need to be polled every 100 milliseconds.

Although digital input can be supported by means of an asynchronous input device, analog input is rarely supported by means of an asynchronous input device. If an analog input device generated an interrupt every time its value changed, it would very probably impose a heavy interrupt load on the system.

The higher the sampling rate of a given task, the greater the overhead that will be generated. For a digital input device, a periodic input task is likely to consume more overhead than the equivalent asynchronous input task. This is because there will probably be times when the periodic input task is activated and the value of the sensor being monitored will not have changed. If the sampling rate chosen is too high, significant unnecessary overhead could be generated. The sampling rate selected for a given task depends on the characteristics of the input device as well as the characteristics of the environment external to the application.

14.3.4   Passive I/O Device Interface Tasks

Passive I/O device interface tasks are used when dealing with passive I/O devices that do not need to be polled and hence do not need periodic I/O device interface tasks. In particular, they are used when it is considered desirable to overlap computation with I/O. A passive I/O device interface task is used in such a situation to interface to the passive I/O device. Note that the term "passive" refers to the device, not the object. The object is active because it is a task. Consider the following cases:

- In the case of input, overlap the input from the passive device with the computational task that receives and consumes the data. This is achieved by using a passive input device interface task to read the data from the input device when requested to do so.

  Separate passive input and computational tasks are only useful if the computational task has some computation to do while the input task is reading the input. If the computational task has to wait for the input, the input can be performed in the same thread of control.

- In the case of output, overlap the output to the device with the computational task that produces the data. This is achieved by using a passive output device interface task to output to the device when requested to do so, usually via a message.

Passive I/O device interface tasks are used more often with output devices than with input devices, because the output can be overlapped with the computation more often, as shown in the following example. Usually, if the I/O and computation are to be overlapped for a passive input device, a periodic input task is used.

Consider a passive output task that receives a message from a producer task. Overlapping computation and output is achieved as follows: the consumer task outputs the data contained in the message to the passive output device, the display, while the producer is preparing the next message. This case is shown in Figure 14.3. The Sensor Statistics Display Interface is a passive output device interface task. It accepts a message to display from the Sensor Statistics Algorithm task, and it displays the sensor statistics while the Sensor Statistics Algorithm task is computing the next set of values to display. Thus the computation is overlapped with the output. The Sensor Statistics Display Interface task is depicted on the concurrent collaboration diagram with the stereotype «passive output device interface» task.

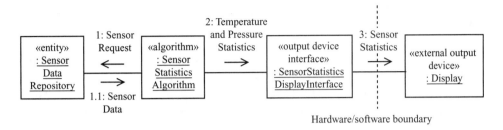

NB: The dashed line for the hardware/software boundary is for illustrative purposes only and does not conform to the UML notation.

Figure 14.3a *Analysis model: collaboration diagram*

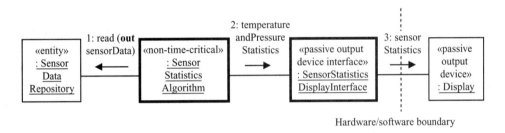

NB: The dashed line for the hardware/software boundary is for illustrative purposes only and does not conform to the UML notation.

Figure 14.3b *Design model: concurrent collaboration diagram*

Figure 14.3 *Example of a passive output device interface task and a non-time-critical, computationally intensive task*

14.3.5 Resource Monitor Tasks

A **resource monitor task** is a special case of the passive I/O task considered earlier. An input or output device that receives requests from multiple sources should have a resource monitor task to coordinate these requests, even if the device is passive. A resource monitor task has to sequence these requests so as to maintain data integrity and ensure that no data is corrupted or lost.

For example, if two or more tasks are allowed to write to a line printer simultaneously, output from the tasks will be randomly interleaved and a garbled report will be produced. To avoid this problem, it is necessary to design a line printer resource monitor task. This task receives output requests from multiple source tasks and has to deal with each request sequentially. Because the request from a second source task might arrive before the first task has finished, having a resource monitor task to handle the requests ensures that multiple requests are dealt with sequentially.

An example of a resource monitor task is given in Figure 14.4. `Floor Lamp Interface` is an output device interface object that receives requests from the multiple instances of `Elevator Control` to switch off floor lamps on a given floor (Figure 14.4a). The real-world floor lamp is a passive output device. Because this output device can receive requests from multiple sources, the `Floor Lamp`

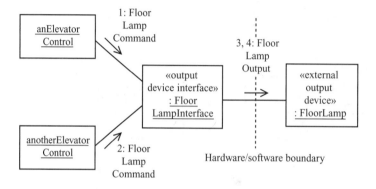

NB: The dashed line for the hardware/software boundary is for illustrative purposes only and does not conform to the UML notation.

Figure 14.4a *Analysis model: collaboration diagram*

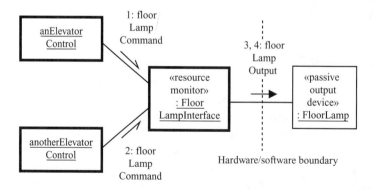

NB: The dashed line for the hardware/software boundary is for illustrative purposes only and does not conform to the UML notation.

Figure 14.4b *Design model: concurrent diagram*

Figure 14.4 *Example of a resource monitor task*

Interface object is structured as a resource monitor task—the Floor Lamp Interface task—that coordinates all floor lamp output requests for that floor (Figure 14.4b). The task is depicted on the concurrent collaboration diagram with the stereotype «resource monitor» task.

14.4 Internal Task Structuring Criteria

Whereas the I/O task structuring criteria are used to determine I/O tasks, the internal task structuring criteria are used to determine internal (i.e., non I/O) tasks.

14.4.1 Periodic Tasks

Many real-time and concurrent systems have activities that need to be executed on a periodic basis, for example, computing the distance traveled by the car or the current speed of the car. These periodic activities are typically handled by periodic tasks. Although periodic I/O activities are structured as periodic I/O tasks, periodic internal activities are structured as **periodic tasks**. In some cases, periodic activities are grouped into a temporally clustered task, as described in Section 14.6.1. Internal periodic tasks include *periodic algorithm tasks* and *periodic business logic* tasks.

An activity that needs to be executed periodically (i.e., at regular, equally spaced intervals of time) is structured as a separate periodic task. The task is activated by a timer event, performs the periodic activity, and then waits for the next timer event. The task's period is the time between successive activations.

As an example of a periodic task, consider the Distance Timer object shown in Figure 14.5a. The Distance Timer object is activated by a timer event. It then requests the Distance object to calculate the distance traveled by the car. The Distance object first reads the shaft rotation count and calibration constant, and then computes the cumulative distance traveled. The Distance Timer object is mapped to a periodic task (Figure 14.5b) that, when activated periodically, requests the Distance object to calculate the distance traveled by the car. The Distance Timer task is depicted on the concurrent collaboration diagram with the stereotype «periodic» task. Distance, Shaft Rotation Count, and Calibration Constant are all passive objects.

14.4.2 Asynchronous Tasks

Many real-time and concurrent systems have activities that need to be executed on demand. These demand-driven activities are typically handled by means of

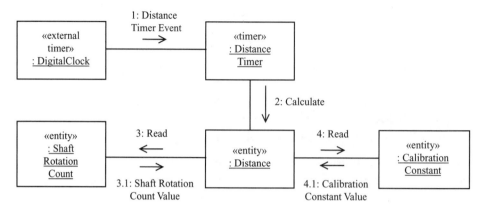

Figure 14.5a *Analysis model: collaboration diagram*

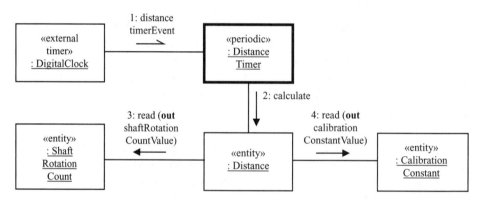

Figure 14.5b *Design model: concurrent collaboration diagram*

Figure 14.5 *Example of a periodic task*

asynchronous tasks. Whereas asynchronous I/O tasks are activated by the arrival of external interrupts, asynchronous internal tasks (also referred to as aperiodic tasks) are activated on demand by the arrival of internal messages or events.

An object that is activated on demand (i.e., when it receives an internal message or event sent by a different task) is structured as a separate **asynchronous task**. The task is activated on demand by the arrival of the message or event sent by the requesting task, performs the demanded request, and then waits for the next message or event. Internal asynchronous tasks include *asynchronous algorithm* and *asynchronous business logic* tasks.

An example of an asynchronous task is given in Figure 14.6. In the analysis model, the Cruiser object is activated on demand by the arrival of a Cruise

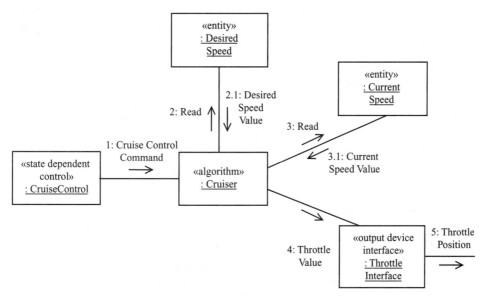

Figure 14.6a *Analysis model: collaboration diagram*

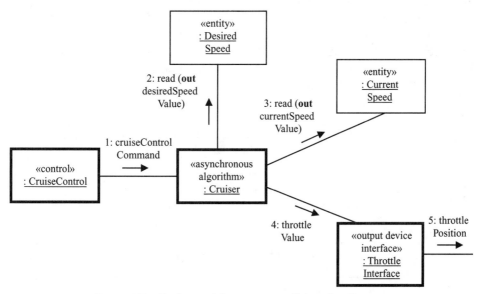

Figure 14.6b *Design model: concurrent collaboration diagram*

Figure 14.6 *Example of an asynchronous task*

Control Command message from the Cruise Control object, reads from the Current Speed and Desired Speed objects, calculates the adjustment to the throttle, and sends a Throttle Value message to the Throttle Interface object (Figure 14.6a). In the design model, the Cruiser object is structured as an asynchronous algorithm task called Cruiser, which is activated by the arrival of a cruise Control Command message. The Cruiser task is depicted on the concurrent collaboration diagram with the stereotype «asynchronous algorithm» task (Figure 14.6b). The Cruise Control and Throttle Interface objects are also structured as tasks. The Current Speed and Desired Speed objects are passive objects.

14.4.3 Control Tasks

In the analysis model, a state-dependent control object executes a statechart. Using the restricted form of statecharts whereby concurrency within an object is not permitted, it follows that the execution of a statechart is strictly sequential. Hence, a task, whose execution is also strictly sequential, can perform the control activity. A task that executes a sequential statechart (typically implemented as a state transition table) is referred to as a **control task**.

An example of a control task is shown in Figure 14.7. The state-dependent control object Cruise Control (Figure 14.7a), which executes the Cruise Control statechart, is structured as the Cruise Control task (Figure 14.7b) because execution of the statechart is strictly sequential. The task is depicted on the concurrent collaboration diagram with the stereotype «control» task.

Figure 14.7a *Analysis model: collaboration diagram*

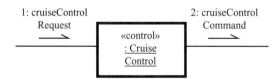

Figure 14.7b *Design model: concurrent collaboration diagram*

Figure 14.7 *Example of a control task*

Another example of a control task is the `Elevator Control` task, which executes the elevator statechart. There are multiple `Elevator Control` objects (depicted by using the multiple-instance notation in Figure 14.8a). Each `Elevator Control` instance is structured as a control task. Consequently, there is one `Elevator Control` task for each elevator, which is also depicted by using the multiple instance notation in Figure 14.8b.

In addition to state-dependent control objects, coordinator objects from the analysis model are mapped to *coordinator tasks*. In this case, the job of the task is to control other tasks, although it is not state-dependent.

14.4.4   User Interface Tasks

A user typically performs a set of sequential operations. Because the user's interaction with the system is a sequential activity, this can be handled by a **user interface task**. The speed of this task is frequently constrained by the speed of user interaction. As its name implies, a **user interface object** in the analysis model is mapped to a user interface task.

A user interface task usually interfaces with various standard I/O devices—such as the input keyboard, output display, and mouse—that are typically handled by the operating system. Because the operating system provides a standard interface to these devices, it is usually not necessary to develop special-purpose I/O device interface tasks to handle them.

The concept of one task per user is typical in many multiuser operating systems. For example, in the UNIX operating system, there is one task (process) per

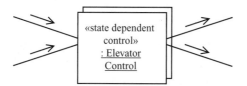

Figure 14.8a   *Analysis model: control object (multiple instances)*

Figure 14.8b   *Design model: one task for each elevator*

Figure 14.8   *Example of multiple control tasks of same type*

user. If, on the other hand, the user engages in several activities concurrently, one user interface task is allocated for each sequential activity. Thus, in the UNIX operating system, users can spawn background tasks. All the user interface tasks belonging to the same user execute concurrently.

The concept of one task per sequential activity is also used on modern workstations with multiple windows. Each window executes a sequential activity, so there is one task for each window. In the Windows operating system, it is possible for the user to have Word executing in one window and PowerPoint executing in another window. There is one user interface task for each window, and each of these tasks can spawn other tasks (for example, to overlap printing with editing).

An example of a user interface task is given in Figure 14.9. The object Opera- tor Interface accepts operator commands, reads from the Sensor Data Repository entity object, and displays data to the operator (Figure 14.9a). Because all operator interactions are sequential in this example, the Operator Interface object is structured as a user interface task (Figure 14.9b). The task is depicted on the concurrent collaboration diagram with the stereotype «user interface» task.

In a multiple-window workstation environment, a factory operator might view factory status in one window (supported by one user interface task) and acknowledge alarms in another window (supported by a different user interface task). An example of this is given in Figure 14.9c. There are two user interface tasks, Factory Status Window and Factory Alarm Window, which are active concurrently. The Factory Status Window task interacts with the passive Factory Status Repository object while the Factory Alarm Window task interacts with the passive Factory Alarm Repository object.

14.4.5 Multiple Tasks of Same Type

As pointed out earlier, it is possible to have many objects of the same type. Each object is mapped to a task, where all the tasks are instances of the same task type. In the case of a state-dependent control object, each object executes an instance of the same sequential statechart, although each object is likely to be in a different state. This is addressed by having one control task for each control object, where the control task executes the statechart.

It might be that, for a given application, there are too many objects of the same type to allow each to be mapped to a separate task. This issue is addressed by using task inversion, as described in Section 14.7.

An example of multiple control tasks of the same type comes from the Elevator Control System, as shown in Figure 14.8. The control aspects of a real-world elevator are modeled by means of a control object, Elevator Control, and

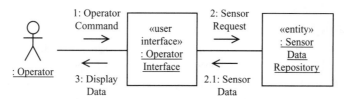

Figure 14.9a *Analysis model: collaboration diagram*

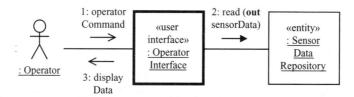

Figure 14.9b *Design model: concurrent collaboration diagram with one user interface task*

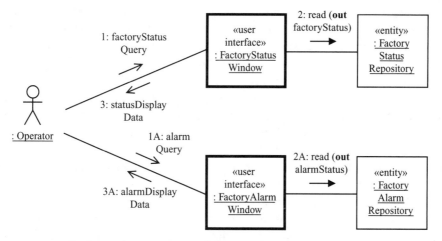

Figure 14.9c *Design model: concurrent collaboration diagram with two user interface tasks*

Figure 14.9 *Examples of user interface tasks*

defined by means of a sequential statechart. During task structuring, the Eleva-tor Control object is mapped to an Elevator Controller task. In a multiple-elevator system, there is one elevator task for each Elevator Control object. The tasks are identical, and each task executes an instance of the same statechart. However, each elevator is likely to be in a different state on its statechart.

14.5 Task Priority Criteria

Task priority criteria take into account priority considerations in task structuring; in particular, high- and low-priority tasks are considered. Task priority is often addressed late in the development cycle. The main reason for considering it during the task structuring phase is to identify any time-critical or non-time-critical computationally intensive objects that need to be treated as separate tasks. Priorities for most tasks are determined based on real-time scheduling considerations, as described in Chapter 17.

14.5.1 Time-Critical Tasks

A **time-critical task** is a task that needs to meet a hard deadline. Such a task needs to run at a high priority. High-priority time-critical tasks are needed in most real-time systems.

Consider the case where the execution of a time-critical object is followed by a non-time-critical object. One option is to group these objects together according to the sequential clustering criterion. However, to ensure that the time-critical object gets serviced rapidly, allocating it to its own high-priority task might be preferable. This is typically the case with an asynchronous interrupt-driven I/O task, where I/O interrupt handling is time critical.

As an example of a time-critical task, consider a Furnace Temperature Control object that monitors the temperature of a furnace. If the temperature is above 100 degrees Centigrade, the furnace must be switched off. Furnace Temperature Control is mapped to a high-priority task. It must execute within a predefined time; otherwise, the contents of the furnace could be damaged.

Other examples of time-critical tasks are control tasks and asynchronous I/O device interface tasks. A control task executes a statechart and needs to execute at a high priority because state transitions must be executed rapidly. An asynchronous I/O device interface task needs to have a high priority so it can service interrupts quickly; otherwise, there is a danger that it might miss interrupts. An example of a high-priority asynchronous input device interface task is the Cruise Control Lever Interface task in Figure 14.1.

14.5.2 Non-Time-Critical Computationally Intensive Tasks

A **non-time-critical computationally intensive task** may run as a low-priority task consuming spare CPU cycles. The concept of a low-priority computationally intensive task executing as a background task that is preempted by higher-priority foreground tasks has its origins in early multiprogramming systems and is typically supported by most modern operating systems.

An example of a non-time-critical computationally intensive task is given in Figure 14.3. The Sensor Statistics Algorithm object reads from the Sensor Data Repository, computes the mean and standard deviation of temperature and pressure, and then passes this data to the Sensor Statistics Display Interface object (Figure 14.3a). Because the Sensor Statistics Algorithm executes at a low priority, it is mapped to a low-priority background task (Figure 14.3a) that uses up spare CPU time. The statistics computed are for information purposes only, so it does not matter if the information displayed is slightly out of date. The Sensor Statistics Algorithm task is depicted on the concurrent collaboration diagram with the stereotype «non-time-critical» task.

A computationally intensive algorithm cannot always be mapped to a low-priority task. The priority of the algorithm is application-dependent. Hence, it is possible in some applications for a computationally intensive algorithm to be time-critical and thus need to be executed at a high priority.

14.6 Task Clustering Criteria

An analysis model can have a large number of objects, each of which is potentially concurrent and mapped to a candidate task. This high degree of concurrency in the analysis model provides considerable flexibility in the design. In fact, each object in the analysis model could be mapped to a task in the design model, as proposed by the actor model [Agha 1986, 1993]. However, if each object became a task, this would lead to a large number of small tasks, potentially resulting in increased system complexity and execution overhead.

The **task clustering criteria** are used to determine whether certain tasks, determined during the first stage of task structuring, could be consolidated further to reduce the overall number of tasks. The task clustering criteria were referred to elsewhere as *task cohesion criteria* [Gomaa 1993].

The tasks determined during the first phase of task structuring (by using the I/O, internal, and priority task structuring criteria described in the previous subsections) are referred to as candidate tasks. Candidate tasks can actually be combined into physical tasks, based on the task clustering criteria described in this subsection.

In COMET, the asynchronous nature of the tasks is analyzed. The clustering criteria provide a means of analyzing the concurrent nature of the candidate tasks, and hence provide a basis for determining whether two or more candidate tasks should be grouped into a single physical task and, if so, how. Thus, if two candidate tasks are constrained so they cannot execute concurrently and must instead execute sequentially, combining them into one physical task usually simplifies the design. There are exceptions to this general rule, as described later.

Although task clustering is shown as a second stage of task structuring, the experienced designer can combine the two stages.

This chapter describes task structuring by using the clustering criteria. However, the internal design of clustered tasks is described in Chapter 16.

14.6.1 Temporal Clustering

Certain candidate tasks may be activated by the same event, for example, a timer event. Each time the tasks are awakened, they execute some activity. If there is no sequential dependency between the candidate tasks—that is, no required sequential order in which the tasks must execute—the candidate tasks may be grouped into the same task, based on the **temporal clustering** criterion. When the task is activated, each of the clustered activities is executed in turn. Because there is no sequential dependency between these clustered activities, an arbitrary execution order needs to be selected by the designer.

Temporal clustering is usually applied to candidate tasks that are activated periodically. Thus, it is often the case that candidate tasks activated by the same periodic event and with the same frequency may be grouped into the same task, according to the temporal clustering criterion.

Example of Temporal Clustering

An example of temporal clustering is given in Figure 14.10. Consider two device interface objects, one of which receives inputs from a brake sensor while the other receives inputs from the engine sensor. If these were asynchronous input devices, each device would be handled by a separate asynchronous input device interface task, which would be activated by a device interrupt every time there was an input from the device. However, if the two sensors are passive, the only way for the system to be aware of a change in sensor status is for it to sample the sensors periodically. Figure 14.10a shows the two device interface objects structured as periodic input device interface tasks, depicted on the concurrent collaboration diagram with the stereotype «periodic input device interface» task.

In Figure 14.10a, the Engine Interface periodic device interface task periodically reads the current value of the engine sensor and sends changes in engine status by means of the engine On and engine Off messages. Similarly, the

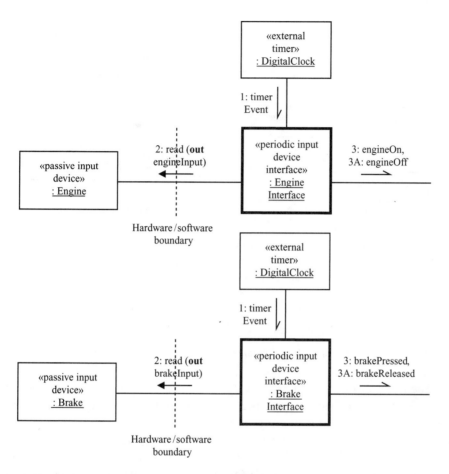

Figure 14.10a *Example of periodic I/O tasks*

Figure 14.10 *Example of temporal clustering*

Brake Interface periodic device interface task periodically reads the current value of the brake sensor and sends changes in brake status by means of the brake Pressed and brake Released messages.

Now, assume that the sensors are to be sampled with the same frequency, perhaps every 100 milliseconds. In this case, the Engine Interface and Brake Interface candidate tasks are grouped into a task called Auto Sensors, based on the temporal clustering criterion, as shown in Figure 14.10b. The Auto Sensors task is depicted on the concurrent collaboration diagram with the stereotype «temporal clustering» task.

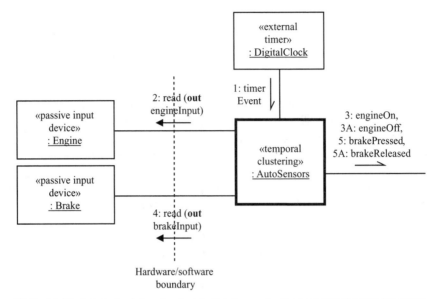

NB: The dashed line for the hardware/software boundary is for illustrative purposes only and does not conform to the UML notation.

Figure 14.10b   *Example of temporal clustering*

Figure 14.10   *Example of temporal clustering (continued)*

The Auto Sensors task is activated periodically by a timer event from the external timer and then samples the status of the brake and engine sensors. If there is a change in status in either of the sensors, it sends the appropriate message—for example, brake Pressed, if the brake is pressed. If coincidentally there is a change in both sensors, the task sends two messages, one for the brake and one for the engine. If there is no change in either sensor, no message is sent.

It should be noted that from the consumer task's perspective, it has no knowledge of whether a message it receives was sent by an asynchronous input device interface task, by a periodic input device interface task, or by a temporally clustered input task. Thus, any change to the characteristics of a producer input task is hidden from the consumer task.

Issues in Temporal Clustering

In deciding whether to combine candidate tasks into a temporally clustered task, some tradeoffs need to be considered:

- If one candidate task is more time-critical than a second candidate task, the tasks should not be combined; this gives the additional flexibility of allocating different priorities to the two tasks.

- If it is considered likely that two candidate tasks for temporal clustering could be executed on separate processors, they should be kept as separate tasks because each candidate task would execute on its own processor.

- Preference should be given in temporal clustering to tasks that are functionally related and likely to be of equal importance from a scheduling viewpoint.

- Period or sampling rate. Another issue is whether it is possible to group two periodic tasks that are functionally related to each other but have different periods into a temporally clustered task. This approach can be used if the periods are multiples of one another. However, this form of temporal clustering is weaker than if the periods are identical. For example, two periodic I/O device interface tasks may be grouped into one task if one task samples a sensor (A) every 50 msec and the second task samples another sensor (B) every 100 msec. The temporally clustered task has a period of 50 msec and samples sensor A every time it is activated and sensor B every second time it is activated.

An important issue to consider in combining periodic tasks into temporally clustered tasks is priority. One candidate task might be more time-critical than another task and therefore should be kept as a separate higher-priority task. This issue is illustrated by means of another example from the Cruise Control System. Maintenance Timer is a periodic temporally clustered task. However, grouping the Brake Interface and Maintenance Timer candidate tasks into one task based on temporal clustering is not desirable. It is very likely that monitoring the brake is more important than checking if auto maintenance is required. In fact, there is a difference of at least two orders of magnitude in the frequency with which these activities need to be performed. Thus the brake might need to be sampled every 100 msec, whereas checking for auto maintenance could be done every 10 sec.

The use of temporal clustering for related tasks is therefore recommended. Grouping periodic tasks that are not functionally related into one task is not considered desirable from a design viewpoint, although it might be done for optimization purposes if the tasking overhead is considered too high.

Taking temporal clustering to an extreme would result in one temporally clustered task executing all periodic operations. This approach is similar to the cyclic executive style of programming [Glass 1983], which is very difficult to maintain. With the cyclic executive approach, all periodic activities are grouped into one task, with different periodic events activating different operations. This approach requires a supervisory procedure that has to be activated with a period that is the highest common factor of the periods of all the activities handled by the task. Each time it is activated, the supervisory procedure has to decide which activity or activities to execute. For example, if there are three periodic activities with periods of 15, 20, and 25 msec, the combined temporally clustered task would need to have a period of 5 msec, resulting in a higher overhead than with three separate periodic tasks. One disadvantage is that the supervisory procedure duplicates the services provided by a multitasking kernel. Consequently, this approach is not considered desirable because it increases the complexity of the system and hence is likely to result in increased maintenance costs.

Merging periodic and temporal tasks to reduce task overhead is discussed further in Section 14.7.3 on design restructuring using **Temporal Task Inversion**.

14.6.2 Sequential Clustering

The execution of certain candidate tasks might be constrained by the needs of the application to be carried out in a sequential order. The first candidate task in the sequence is triggered by an asynchronous or periodic event. The other candidate tasks are then executed sequentially after it. These sequentially dependent candidate tasks may be grouped into a task based on the **sequential clustering** criterion.

Example of Sequential Clustering

As an example of sequential clustering, consider the two candidate tasks shown in Figure 14.11a. The Report Generator task is a periodic task, activated periodically to prepare a report. When activated, it reads information from various entity objects, prepares the report, and then sends the report to the Display Interface task, which outputs the report. The Display Interface task is a passive output device interface task, and the display is a passive output device dedicated to displaying this report. If the report is generated infrequently—perhaps once a minute—there is no advantage to overlapping the generation of the report with the display of the report. In this situation, the Report Generator and Display Interface candidate tasks can be combined into one sequentially clustered task (Figure 14.11b) instead of being structured as two separate tasks. The Report Generator & Display task is depicted on the concurrent collaboration diagram with the stereotype «sequential clustering» task.

Issues in Sequential Clustering

When combining successive tasks by using sequential clustering, the following guidelines apply:

- If the last candidate task in a sequence does not send an inter-task message, this terminates the group of tasks to be considered for sequential clustering. This happens with the Display Interface candidate task in Figure 14.11a, which ends a sequence of two sequentially connected candidate tasks by displaying the report.

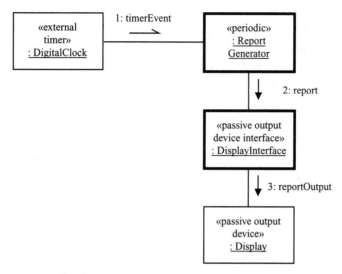

Figure 14.11a *Design model: concurrent collaboration diagram with two tasks*

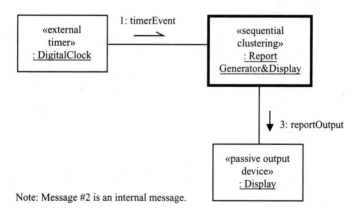

Figure 14.11b *Design model: concurrent collaboration diagram with one task*

Figure 14.11 *Example of sequential clustering*

- If the next candidate task in the sequence also receives inputs from another source and therefore can also be activated by receiving input from that source, this candidate task should be left as a separate task. This happens in the case of the Cruise Control task (Figure 14.1b), which can receive inputs from the Cruise Control Lever Interface task as well as from the Auto Sensors task (Figure 14.10b). The three candidate tasks are not combined.

If the next candidate task in the sequence is likely to hold up the preceding candidate task(s) such that they could miss either an input or a state change, the next candidate task should be structured as a separate, lower-priority task. This is what happens with the `Cruiser` task in Figure 14.6, which receives `cruise Control Command` messages from the `Cruise Control` task. The `Cruise Control` task must not miss any requests from other tasks that could cause a state change, so it is structured as a higher-priority control task separate from the `Cruiser` task.

- If the next candidate task in sequence is of a lower priority and follows a time-critical task, the two tasks should be kept as separate tasks. This is discussed in more detail in Task Priority Criteria in Section 14.5.

14.6.3   Control Clustering

A control object, which executes a sequential statechart, is mapped to a control task. In certain cases, the control task may be combined with other objects that execute actions triggered by or activities enabled by the statechart. This is referred to as **control clustering**.

In the analysis model, a state-dependent control object is defined by means of a sequential statechart. The control object should be structured as a separate control task (Section 14.4.3) because the execution of a statechart is defined to be strictly sequential. Furthermore, the control task may execute other state-dependent actions or activities within its thread of control. Consider the following cases:

- **State-dependent actions** that are triggered by the control object because of a state transition.

  Consider an action (designed as an operation provided by a separate object) that is triggered at the state transition and both starts and completes execution during the state transition. Such an action operation does not execute concurrently with the control object. When mapped to tasks, the operation is executed within the thread of control of the control task. If all the action operations of an object are executed within the thread of control of the control task, that object is combined with the control task, based on the **control clustering** task structuring criterion.

- **State-dependent activities** that are either enabled or disabled by the control object because of a state transition.

  Consider an activity (executed by a separate object) that is enabled at a state transition and then executes continuously until disabled at a subsequent state transition. This activity should be structured as a separate task, because both the control object and the activity will need to be active concurrently.

   This is particularly the case if the activity does not determine the event that causes the next change of state in the control object. In this case, the control object has to be in a separate concurrent task to receive the event from some other source so it can then disable the activity executing in a different task.

- **State-dependent activities** that are triggered by the control object because of a state transition and execute for the duration of the state.

   This case has to be analyzed carefully. If the activity (executed by a separate object) is deactivated by the control object, the activity should be structured as a separate task, because both the control object and activity will need to be active concurrently. However, if it is the activity itself that recognizes it is time for a state change, it will send an event to the control object to trigger the state change. Furthermore, if this is the *only* event that causes a state change (while the statechart is in this state), the activity may be grouped with the control object into one task according to the control clustering criterion, because only this activity can activate the control object and cause the state change. On the other hand, if the control object could also be activated by an event from another source, it must be structured as a separate task.

- A source object that sends messages to the control object, which causes it to change state. If these messages are the only events that cause the control object to change state, the source object may be grouped with the control object into one task according to the **sequential clustering** criterion.

Example of Control Clustering

An example of control clustering is given from the ATM Control problem. Figure 14.12a shows an analysis model collaboration diagram in which the state-dependent control object ATM Control executes the statechart. Actions resulting from different state transitions include the actions to Dispense Cash by sending a message to the output device interface object, Cash Dispenser Interface, and to Print Receipt by sending a message to the output device interface object, Receipt Printer Interface. Both these output devices are passive.

   The ATM statechart (Figure 14.12b) shows that, after sending the Dispense Cash message (event 2 on both Figures 14.12 a and 14.12b), ATM Control enters the Dispensing state and waits for the Cash Dispensed response

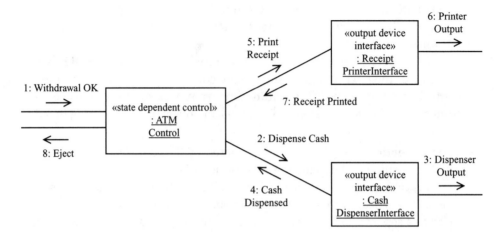

Figure 14.12a *Analysis model: collaboration diagram*

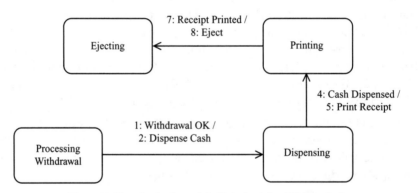

Figure 14.12b *Analysis model: Statechart for ATM control*

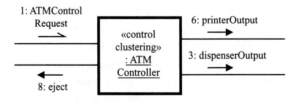

Figure 14.12c *Design model: concurrent collaboration diagram*

Figure 14.12 *Example of control clustering*

before continuing. The only way the statechart can leave Dispensing state is by receiving a Cash Dispensed response (event 4) from the Cash Dispenser Interface. The arrival of the Dispense Cash message awakens the Cash Dispenser Interface, which dispenses the cash (event 3), sends the Cash Dispensed response (event 4), and then loops back to wait for the next Dispense Cash message. As this example shows, no concurrent execution is possible between the ATM Control and Cash Dispenser Interface objects. The two objects may therefore be grouped into a control clustering task called the ATM Controller task. For the same reason, the Receipt Printer Interface object can also be grouped into the ATM Controller task.

Consequently, the state-dependent control object ATM Control and the output device interface objects Cash Dispenser and Receipt Printer are grouped into a control clustering task—the ATM Controller task—which is depicted with the stereotype «control clustering» task on the concurrent collaboration diagram shown in Figure 14.12c.

14.6.4 Mutually Exclusive Clustering

Mutually exclusive clustering occurs when there are a group of tasks where, because of the constraints of the application, only one of the tasks is eligible to be executed at any one time. These tasks may be grouped into one task according to the mutually exclusive clustering criterion.

Example of Mutually Exclusive Clustering

In the Cruise Control problem, there are three algorithm objects, which represent activities that are enabled on entry into a state and disabled on exit from the state, namely Acceleration, Cruiser, and Resumption (see Figure 14.13a). Each of these activities is a candidate for a separate asynchronous task. However, on further analysis, it is clear that these activities can never execute concurrently because each activity executes during a different Cruise Control state. Thus, the Acceleration activity executes throughout Accelerating state, the Cruiser activity executes throughout Cruising state, and the Resumption activity executes throughout Resuming state. Hence, the three activities are executed mutually exclusively and there is no advantage to structuring each activity as a separate task. Instead, they are combined into one task, called Speed Adjustment, based on the mutually exclusive clustering criterion, rather than three tasks, as depicted in Figures 14.13a and 14.13b.

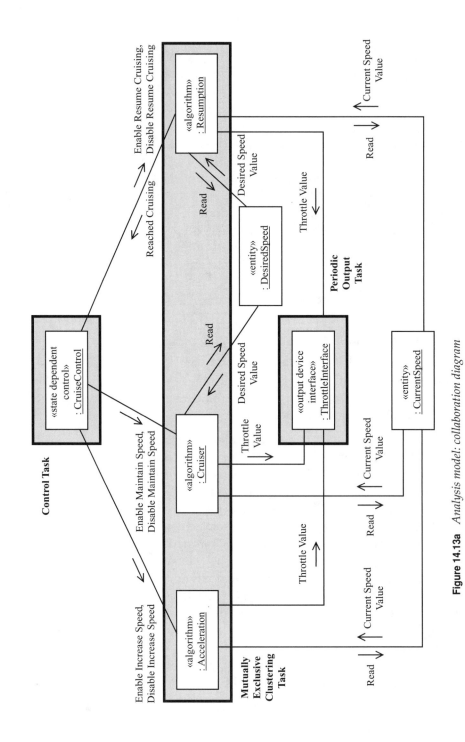

Figure 14.13a *Analysis model: collaboration diagram*

Figure 14.13 *Example of mutually exclusive clustering*

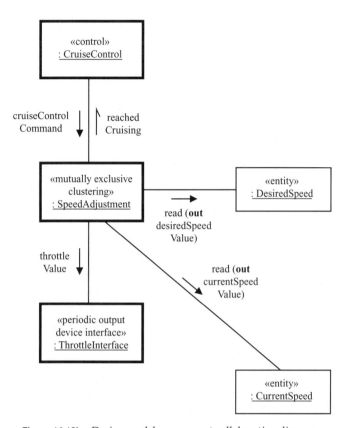

Figure 14.13b   *Design model: concurrent collaboration diagram*

Figure 14.13   *Example of mutually exclusive clustering (continued)*

14.7   Design Restructuring by Using Task Inversion

Task inversion is a concept that originated in Jackson Structured Programming and Jackson System Development [Jackson 1983], whereby the number of tasks in a system can be reduced in a systematic way. At one extreme, a concurrent solution can be mapped to a sequential solution.

The **task inversion** criteria are used for merging tasks to reduce task overhead. Task inversion may be used either during initial task structuring or during design restructuring. The task inversion criteria—and in particular multiple-instance task inversion—may be used during initial task structuring if high task overhead is anticipated. Alternatively, they may be used for design restructuring in situations where there are concerns about high tasking overhead. In particular, task inversion can be used if a performance analysis of the design indicates that the tasking overhead is too high.

Three forms of task inversion are described here: multiple instance task inversion, sequential task inversion, and temporal task inversion. The internal design of inverted tasks is described in Chapter 16.

14.7.1   Multiple-Instance Task Inversion

Handling multiple control tasks of the same type was described in Section 14.4.5. With this approach, several objects of the same type can be modeled by using one task instance for each object, where all the tasks are of the same type. The problem is that, for a given application, the system overhead for modeling each object by means of a separate task might be too high.

With **multiple-instance task inversion**, all identical tasks of the same type are replaced by one task that performs the same service. For example, instead of mapping each control object to a separate task, all control objects of the same type are mapped to the same task. Each object's state information is captured in a separate passive entity object.

As an example of multiple-instance task inversion, consider the Elevator Control System described in Section 14.4.5, where each Elevator Control object is mapped to a separate Elevator Control task. If the system overhead is too high to allow this, an alternative solution is to have only one Elevator Controller task for the whole system and to have a separate passive entity object for each elevator, Elevator State Information, which contains the state information for that elevator (see Figure 14.14). With task inversion, the main procedure of the task is a scheduling procedure, which reads all inputs to the task and decides for which elevator the data is intended, thereby ensuring that the appropriate elevator entity object is used.

14.7.2   Sequential Task Inversion

Sequential task inversion is used primarily in cases where there is tightly coupled communication between two or more tasks. The tasks are combined such that the producer task calls an operation provided by the consumer task rather than sending it a message. This is referred to as inversion of the consumer with respect to the producer. Each message type that can be sent from the producer to the consumer is replaced by a consumer operation that is called by the producer. The parameters of the message become the parameters of the call.

**Design model—one task
for each elevator**

**Design model—task inversion
one task for all elevators**

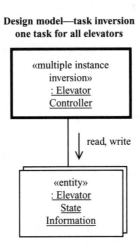

Figure 14.14 *Example of multiple instance task inversion*

As an example of sequential task inversion, consider the three-task sequence from the Cruise Control problem, where the Cruise Control task sends a cruise Control Command message to the Speed Adjustment task, which in turn sends throttle Value messages to the Throttle Interface task. All message communication is tightly coupled without reply. Sequential task inversion may be used to combine these three tasks into one task, the Inverted Cruise Control task, as shown in Figure 14.15.

14.7.3 Temporal Task Inversion

In **temporal task inversion**, which is similar to the weak forms of temporal clustering (see Section 14.6.1), two or more periodic tasks—periodic internal, periodic I/O, and/or temporally clustered—are combined into one task. The task has a timer-event-driven main scheduling procedure, which determines when it is time to call a particular operation to execute.

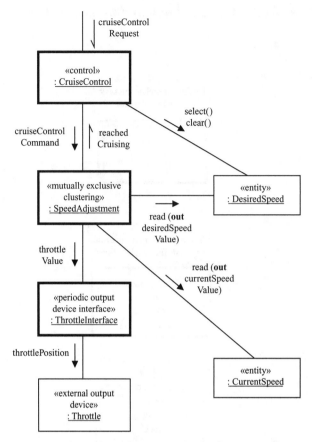

Figure 14.15a *Message communication between tasks*

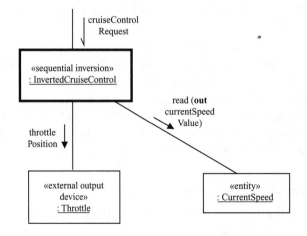

Figure 14.15b *Inverted task*

Figure 14.15 *Example of sequential task inversion*

Grouping temporal objects that are not functionally related into one task is not considered desirable from a design viewpoint. However, with temporal task inversion, this is done for optimization purposes in situations where the tasking overhead is considered too high.

Consider the following example of temporal task inversion. Two periodic tasks, both temporally clustered, `Auto Sensors` and `Calibration`, are combined into one task, the inverted `Periodic` task, for optimization reasons, as shown in Figure 14.16. This task is activated periodically by a timer event and monitors the auto sensor (brake and engine) inputs as well as the calibration inputs, although with different frequency. Each time the inverted `Periodic` task is activated by the timer event, it determines whether it is time to check the auto sensors or calibration inputs, or both. In the former case, it outputs `cruise Control Request` messages if there is a change in brake or engine status. In the latter case, it updates the `Calibration Constant` object.

14.8   Developing the Task Architecture

The task structuring criteria may be applied to the analysis model in the following order. In each case, a decision needs to be first made whether the analysis model object should be mapped to an active object (task) or passive object in the design model.

1. **Device interface tasks.** Start with the device interface objects that interact with the outside world. Determine whether the object should be structured as an asynchronous I/O device interface, a periodic I/O device interface, a passive I/O device interface, a resource monitor, or a temporally clustered periodic I/O task.

2. **Control tasks.** Analyze each state-dependent control object. Structure this object as a control task. Any object that executes an action (operation) triggered by the control task can potentially be combined with the control task based on the control clustering criterion. Any activity that the control task enables and subsequently disables should be structured as a separate task.

   Use the same approach for multiple state-dependent control objects of the same type. Check whether each object can be mapped to a separate task or whether it is necessary to use task inversion, particularly if there are a large number of tasks of the same type and task context-switching overhead is a concern.

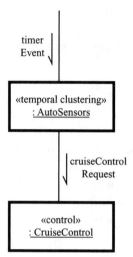

Figure 14.16a1 *Periodic task with temporal clustering*

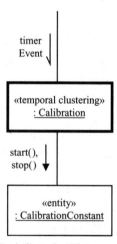

Figure 14.16a2 *Periodic task with temporal clustering*

Figure 14.16 *Example of temporal task inversion*

3. **Periodic tasks.** Analyze the internal periodic activities, which are structured as periodic tasks. Determine if any candidate periodic tasks are triggered by the same event. If they are, they may be grouped into the same task, based on the temporal clustering criterion. Other candidate tasks that execute in sequence may be structured into the same task, according to the sequential clustering criterion.

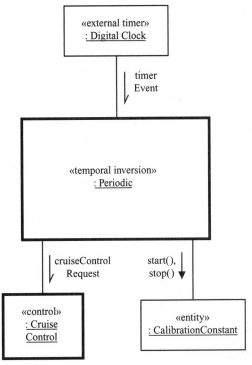

Figure 14.16b *Inverted periodic task*

Figure 14.17 *Example of temporal task inversion (continued)*

4. **Other internal tasks.** For each internal candidate task activated by an internal event, identify whether any adjacent candidate tasks on the concurrent collaboration diagram may be grouped into the same task according to the temporal, sequential, or mutually exclusive clustering criteria.

The guidelines for mapping analysis model objects to design model tasks are summarized in Table 14.1. In cases where the clustering criterion applies, this means that the analysis model object is designed as a passive object nested inside a clustered task, as described in more detail in Chapter 16.

Because a task might fall into more than one task structuring category, a task will be identified by the first criterion applied successfully to it. Subsequent criteria that apply to the task should either confirm the initial structuring decision or indicate that the decision should be revisited. For example, consider a device interface object that is initially structured as a passive output device interface task but is also activated by a control object. If it transpires that the output operation is

Table 14.1 *Mapping from Analysis Model Objects to Design Model Tasks*

Analysis Model (object)	Design Model (task)
User interface	User interface Sequential clustering Control clustering
Device interface (input, output, I/O)	Asynchronous device interface (input, output, I/O) Periodic device interface (input, output, I/O) Passive device interface (usually output device interface) Resource monitor (usually output device interface) Temporal clustering (usually input device interface) Sequential clustering Control clustering (usually output device interface)
System interface	Asynchronous system interface Any clustering criterion
Entity	Sequential server (Chapter 13) Concurrent server (Chapter 13) Any clustering criterion
Timer	Periodic Temporal clustering Sequential clustering
State dependent control	Control Control clustering
Coordinator	Coordinator Sequential clustering
Business logic	Asynchronous business logic Periodic business logic Any clustering criterion
Algorithm	Asynchronous algorithm Periodic algorithm Non-time-critical Any clustering criterion

always performed synchronously during a state transition, the initial task structuring decision should be questioned because the device interface object could be combined with the control object by using control clustering. Examples of considerations to be made in applying the task structuring criteria are given in the case studies described later.

14.8.1   Initial Concurrent Collaboration Diagram

After structuring the system into concurrent tasks, an initial concurrent collaboration diagram is drawn, showing all the tasks in the system. On this initial concurrent collaboration diagram, the interfaces between the tasks are still simple messages as depicted on the analysis model collaboration diagrams. An example of an initial concurrent collaboration diagram is given in Figure 14.17 for the ATM Client subsystem of the Banking System case study. Designing task interfaces is described next.

14.9   Task Communication and Synchronization

After structuring the system into concurrent tasks, the next step is to define the task interfaces. At this stage, the interfaces between tasks are still simple messages as depicted on the analysis model collaboration diagrams. It is necessary to map these interfaces to task interfaces in the form of message communication, event synchronization, or access to information hiding objects.

The UML notation for message communication is described in Chapter 2. In the collaboration diagrams developed for the analysis model and in the preliminary concurrent collaboration diagram for the design model, all communication is shown using simple messages. In this step of the design modeling, the task interfaces are defined and depicted on revised concurrent collaboration diagrams.

Message interfaces between tasks are either loosely coupled (asynchronous) or tightly coupled (synchronous), as introduced in Chapter 3. For tightly coupled message communication, two possibilities exist: tightly coupled message communication with reply and tightly coupled message communication without reply. The semantics of tightly coupled message communication are similar to those of the Ada rendezvous.

Various options for providing message communication services are described in Chapter 4. These include the operating system kernel, the constructs of a concurrent programming language, or a threads package. Alternatively, message communication connectors are used, as described in Chapter 16.

The various forms of inter-task communication are described next, with examples of their use. In each example, the initial concurrent collaboration diagram reflects task structuring decisions but not decisions on message communication and synchronization. In these diagrams, the simple message notation is carried over from the analysis model. The revised concurrent collaboration diagram depicts the task architecture after the decisions concerning inter-task communication and synchronization have been made.

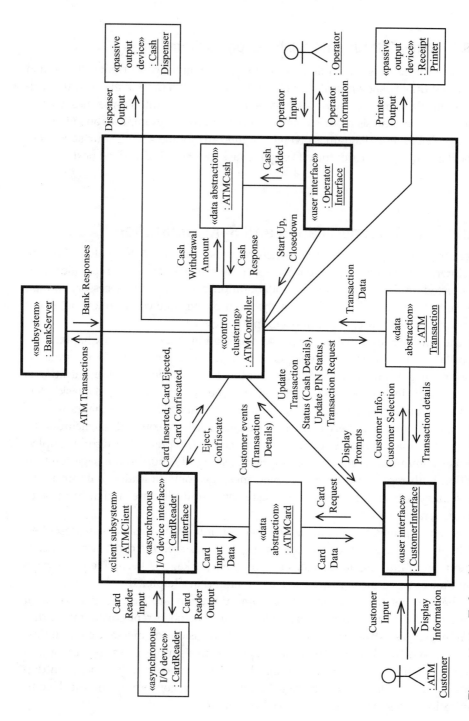

Figure 14.18 *Task architecture: Example of initial concurrent collaboration diagram for ATM Client subsystem*

14.9.1 Loosely Coupled (Asynchronous) Message Communication

With **loosely coupled message communication**, also referred to as **asynchronous message communication**, the producer sends a message to the consumer and continues without waiting for a response. Because the producer and consumer tasks proceed at different speeds, a first-in-first-out (FIFO) message queue can build up between producer and consumer. If no message is available when the consumer requests one, the consumer is suspended.

Consider the initial concurrent collaboration diagram (Figure 14.18a), which depicts the Cruise Control Lever Interface task sending a message to the Cruise Control task. It is desirable to map this message interface to loosely coupled (asynchronous) message communication, as depicted in the revised concurrent collaboration diagram (Figure 14.18b). The Cruise Control Lever Interface task sends the message and does not wait for it to be accepted by the Cruise Control task. This allows the Cruise Control Lever Interface task to quickly service any new external input that might arrive. Loosely coupled message communication also provides the greatest flexibility for the Cruise Control task, because it can wait on a queue of messages that arrive from multiple sources. It then accepts the first message that arrives, whatever the source.

An example of loosely coupled message communication in the Elevator Control System is given in Figure 14.4, which shows the Floor Lamp Interface

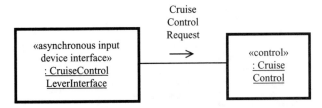

Figure 14.18a *Initial concurrent collaboration diagram with simple message*

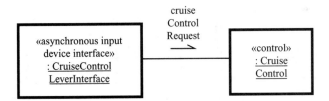

Figure 14.18b *Revised concurrent collaboration diagram with asynchronous message*

Figure 14.19 *Example of loosely coupled (asynchronous) message communication*

resource monitor task. This task receives requests from multiple elevators to switch off floor lamps. The requests are queued FIFO in a message queue. The Floor Lamp Interface task processes the requests in the order in which they arrive.

14.9.2   Tightly Coupled (Synchronous) Message Communication with Reply

In the case of **tightly coupled message communication with reply**, also referred to as **synchronous message communication with reply,** the producer sends a message to the consumer and then waits for a reply. When the message arrives, the consumer accepts the message, processes it, generates a reply, and sends the reply. The producer and consumer then both continue. The consumer is suspended if no message is available.

Tightly coupled message communication with reply can involve a single producer sending a message to a consumer and then waiting for a reply, in which case no message queue develops between the producer and the consumer. However, it can also involve multiple clients interacting with a single server, as illustrated by the following example.

An example of tightly coupled message communication with reply, involving multiple clients interacting with a single server, is given in Figure 14.19. The clients are ATM Client tasks, which send messages to the Bank Server task, as depicted on the initial concurrent collaboration diagram (Figure 14.19a). Each client needs to

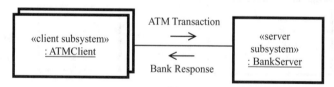

Figure 14.19a   *Initial concurrent collaboration diagram with simple messages*

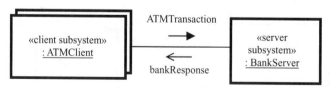

Figure 14.19b   *Revised concurrent collaboration diagram: synchronous message with reply*

Figure 14.20   *Example of tightly coupled (synchronous) message communication with reply*

be tightly coupled with the server, because it sends a message and then waits for a response. After receiving the message, the server processes the message, prepares a reply, and sends the reply to the client. The notation for tightly coupled message communication with reply on the concurrent collaboration diagram (Figure 14.19b) shows a synchronous message sent from the client to the server with a simple message, representing the response, sent by the server to the client.

14.9.3 Tightly Coupled (Synchronous) Message Communication without Reply

In the case of **tightly coupled message communication without reply**, also referred to as **synchronous message communication without reply**, the producer sends a message to the consumer and then waits for acceptance of the message by the consumer. When the message arrives, the consumer accepts the message, thereby releasing the producer. The producer and consumer then both continue. The consumer is suspended if no message is available.

An example of tightly coupled message communication without reply is shown in Figure 14.20. The `Sensor Statistics Display Interface` is a passive output device interface task. It accepts a message to display from the `Sensor`

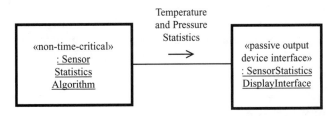

Figure 14.20a *Initial concurrent collaboration diagram with simple message*

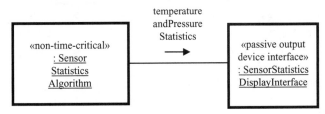

Figure 14.20b *Revised concurrent collaboration diagram: synchronous message without reply*

Figure 14.21 *Example of tightly coupled (synchronous) message communication without reply*

Statistics Algorithm task, as depicted on the initial concurrent collaboration diagram (Figure 14.20a). It displays the sensor statistics while the Sensor Statistics Algorithm task is computing the next set of values to display. Thus the computation is overlapped with the output.

The producer task, the Sensor Statistics Algorithm task, sends temperature and pressure statistics to the consumer task, the Sensor Statistics Display Interface, which then displays the information. In this example, the decision made is that there is no point in having the Sensor Statistics Algorithm task compute temperature and pressure statistics if the Sensor Statistics Display Interface cannot keep up with displaying them. Consequently, the interface between the two tasks is mapped to a tightly coupled message communication without reply interface, as depicted on the revised concurrent collaboration diagram (Figure 14.20b). The Sensor Statistics Algorithm computes the statistics, sends the message, and then waits for the acceptance of the message by the Sensor Statistics Display Interface before resuming execution. The Sensor Statistics Algorithm is held up until the Sensor Statistics Display Interface finishes displaying the previous message. As soon as the Sensor Statistics Display Interface accepts the new message, the Sensor Statistics Algorithm is released from its wait and computes the next set of statistics while the Sensor Statistics Display Interface displays the previous set. By this means, computation of the statistics (a compute-bound activity) can be overlapped with displaying of the statistics (an I/O bound activity), while preventing an unnecessary message queue build-up of statistics at the display task. Thus, the tightly coupled interface between the two tasks acts as a brake on the producer task.

14.9.4   Event Synchronization

Three types of event synchronization are possible: an external event, a timer event, and an internal event. An external event is an event from an external entity, typically an interrupt from an external I/O device. An internal event represents internal synchronization between a source task and a destination task. A timer event represents a periodic activation of a task. Events are depicted in UML, using the asynchronous message notation to depict an event signal.

An example of an external event, typically a hardware interrupt from an input device, is given in Figure 14.21. On the initial concurrent collaboration diagram, the simple message represents the input from the device (Figure 14.21a). The Cruise Control Lever «asynchronous input device» generates an interrupt when it has cruise Control Input. The interrupt activates the Cruise

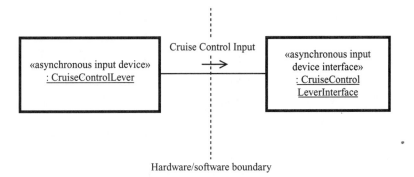

Hardware/software boundary

NB: The dashed line for the hardware/software boundary is for illustrative purposes only and does not conform to the UML notation.

Figure 14.21a *Initial concurrent collaboration diagram with simple message*

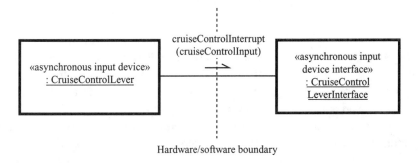

Hardware/software boundary

NB: The dashed line for the hardware/software boundary is for illustrative purposes only and does not conform to the UML notation.

Figure 14.21b *Revised concurrent collaboration diagram with external event*

Figure 14.22 *Example of external event*

Control Lever Interface «asynchronous input device interface» task, which then reads the cruise Control Input. This interaction could be depicted as an event signal input from the device, followed by a read by the task. However, it is more concise to depict the interaction as an asynchronous event signal sent by the device, with the input data as a parameter, as depicted on the revised concurrent collaboration diagram (Figure 14.21b).

An example of a timer event is given in Figure 14.22. The digital clock, which is an external timer device, generates a timer event to awaken the Distance

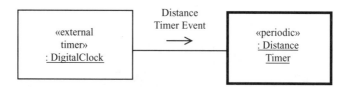

Figure 14.22a *Initial concurrent collaboration diagram with simple message*

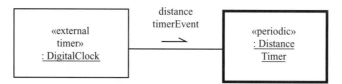

Figure 14.22b *Revised concurrent collaboration diagram with timer event*

Figure 14.23 *Example of timer event*

Timer «periodic» task. The Distance Timer task then performs a periodic activity—in this case, calculating the distance traveled by the car. The timer event is generated at fixed intervals of time. The simple message shown on the initial concurrent collaboration diagram (Figure 14.22a) is mapped to a timer event signal on the revised concurrent collaboration diagram (Figure 14.22b).

Internal event synchronization is used when two tasks need to synchronize their operations without communicating data between the tasks. The source task signals the event. The destination task waits for the event and is suspended until the event is signaled. It is not suspended if the event has previously been signaled. The event signal is depicted in UML by an asynchronous message that does not contain any data. An example of this is shown in Figure 14.23, in which the pick-and-place robot task signals the event part Ready. This awakens the drilling robot, which operates on the part and then signals the event part Completed, which the pick-and-place robot is waiting to receive.

14.9.5   Task Interaction via Information Hiding Object

It is also possible for tasks to exchange information by means of a passive information hiding object, as described in Sections 3.7 and 3.8. An example of task access to a passive information hiding object is given in Figure 14.24, in which the Sensor Statistics Algorithm task reads from the Sensor Data Repository entity object, and the Sensor Interface task updates the entity object. On the initial concurrent collaboration diagram, the Sensor Statistics Algo-

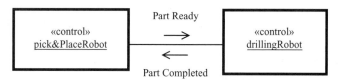

Figure 14.23a *Initial concurrent collaboration diagram with simple messages*

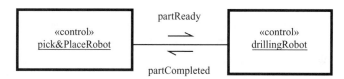

Figure 14.23b *Revised concurrent collaboration diagram with internal events*

Figure 14.24 *Example of internal events*

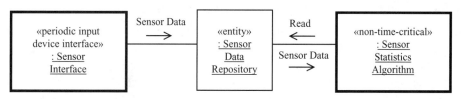

Figure 14.24a *Initial concurrent collaboration diagram with simple messages*

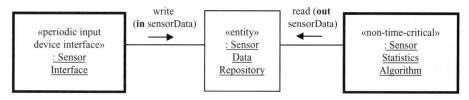

Figure 14.24b *Revised concurrent collaboration diagram with tasks invoking operations of passive object*

Figure 14.25 *Example of tasks invoking operations of passive object*

rithm task sends a simple message, Read, to the entity object and receives a Sensor Data response, which is also depicted as a simple message (Figure 14.24a). Because the task is reading from a passive information hiding object, this interface corresponds to an operation call. The entity object provides a read operation, which is called by the Sensor Statistics Algorithm task. The sensor

Data response is an output parameter of the call. The read operation is executed in the thread of control of the task. On the revised concurrent collaboration diagram (Figure 14.24b), the call to the read operation is depicted by using the synchronous message notation. The sensor Data response is depicted as the output parameter of the read synchronous message. The Sensor Interface task calls a write operation provided by the Sensor Data Repository entity object, with the sensor Data as an input parameter.

It is important to realize how the synchronous message notation used between two concurrent tasks differs from that used between a task and a passive object. The notation looks the same in the UML: an arrow with a filled-in arrowhead. The semantics are different, however. The synchronous message notation between two concurrent tasks represents tightly coupled message communication, as shown in Figures 14.19 and 14.20. The synchronous message notation between a task and a passive object represents an operation call, as shown in Figures 14.24.

14.9.6 Revised Concurrent Collaboration Diagram

After having determined the task interfaces, the initial concurrent collaboration diagram is revised to depict the various types of task interface. An example of the revised concurrent collaboration diagram is given for the ATM Client subsystem of the Banking System case study, as shown in Figure 14.25, in which the initial concurrent collaboration diagram of figure 14.17 is updated to show all the task interfaces.

14.10   Task Behavior Specifications

A **task behavior specification (TBS)** describes a concurrent task's interface, structure, timing characteristics, relative priority, event sequencing logic, and errors detected. The task's interface defines how it interfaces to other tasks. The task's structure describes how its structure is derived, using the task structuring criteria. The task's timing characteristics addresses frequency of activation and estimated execution time. This information is used for real-time scheduling purposes.

The TBS is introduced with the **task architecture** to specify the characteristics of each task. During task structuring, the TBS emphasizes the task inputs and outputs. One part of the TBS is defined later, during detailed software design (as described in Chapter 16)—namely the **task event sequencing logic**, which describes how the task responds to the input events it receives.

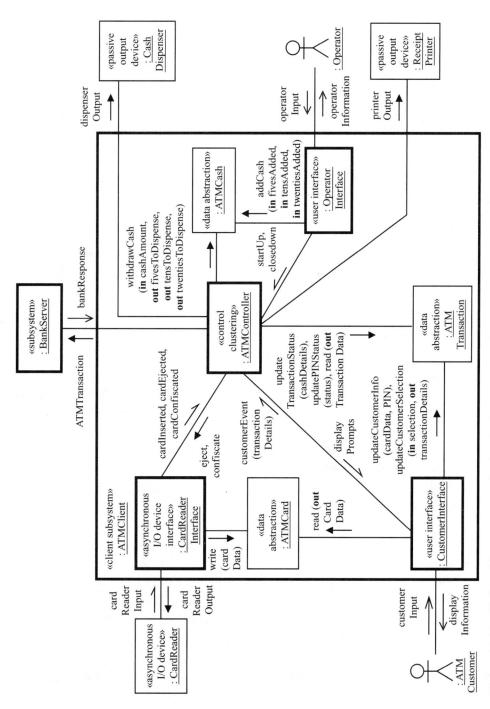

Figure 14.26 *Task architecture: example of revised concurrent collaboration diagram for ATM client subsystem*

The TBS is defined as follows:

1. **Task interface.** The task interface should include a definition of

   - **Messages inputs and outputs.** For each message interface (input or output) there should be a description of

     Type of interface. Loosely coupled, tightly coupled with reply, or tightly coupled without reply

     For each message type supported by this interface: message name and message parameters

   - **Events signaled (input and output).**

     Name of event

     Type of event: external, internal, timer

   - **External inputs or outputs.** Define the inputs from and outputs to the external environment.

   - **Passive objects referenced**

2. The **task structure information** includes the following:

   - Task structuring criterion used to design this task.
   - Analysis model objects mapped to this task.

3. **Timing characteristics.**

   - **Frequency of activation.** If periodic task: period T_i of task. If asynchronous task: estimated average and maximum frequency of activation by asynchronous events.

   - **Estimated execution time C_i for task.** If task has more than one path through it, estimated execution time for each of the major paths.

4. **Task's relative priority.** Allocate a priority to this task in relation to the other tasks in the system.

5. **Errors detected by this task.**

   This section describes the possible errors that could be detected during execution of this task.

6. The task's **event sequencing logic** describes how the task responds to each of its message or event inputs, in particular, what output is generated as a result of each input. The event sequencing logic is defined during the detailed software design step, as described in Chapter 16.

14.10.1   Example of Task Behavior Specification for Bank Server Task

The task behavior specification for the `Bank Server` task (described in Chapter 19 and illustrated in Figure 14.25) is described here:

TASK: Bank Server

1. TASK INTERFACE:

   Task inputs:

   Tightly Coupled Message Communication with Reply:

   Messages:

   - validatePIN
     Input Parameters: cardID, PIN

     Reply: PINValidationResponse

   - withdraw
     Input Parameters: cardID, account#, amount

     Reply: withdrawalResponse

   - query
     Input Parameters: cardID, account#

     Reply: queryResponse

   - transfer
     Input Parameters: cardID, fromAccount#, toAccount#, amount
     Reply: transferResponse

   Task outputs:

   Message replies as described previously.

2. TASK STRUCTURE:

   Criterion: Sequential Clustering

   Objects mapped to task:

   Bank Transaction Server, PIN Validation Transaction Manager,
   Withdrawal Transaction Manager, Query Transaction Manager,
   Transfer Transaction Manager, Checking Account,
   Savings Account, Debit Card, Card Account, Transaction Log.

3. TIMING CHARACTERISTICS:

   Activation: Asynchronous—message arrival from clients. Worst case inter-arrival time = 100 msec. Average inter-arrival time > 1 second.

   Execution time C_i: 10 ms per message

4. PRIORITY:

   High—Needs to be responsive to incoming messages.

5. ERRORS DETECTED:

   Unrecognized message.

6. TASK EVENT SEQUENCING LOGIC:

The event sequencing logic is defined during the detailed software design step, as described in Chapter 16.

14.10.2   Example of Task Behavior Specification for Card Reader Interface Task

The task behavior specification for the `Card Reader Interface` task (Chapter 19 and Figure 14.25) is described here:

TASK: `Card Reader Interface`

1. TASK INTERFACE:

   Task inputs:

   Event input: Card reader external interrupt to indicate that a card has been input.

   External Input: `cardReaderInput`

   Loosely Coupled Message Communication:

   - `eject`
   - `confiscate`

   Task outputs:

   External output: `cardReaderOutput`

   Loosely Coupled Message Communication:

   - `cardInserted`
   - `cardEjected`
   - `cardConfiscated`

   Passive objects accessed: `ATMCard`

2. TASK STRUCTURE:

   Criterion:
   Asynchronous Input Device Interface

   Objects mapped to task:
   `Card Reader Interface`

3. TIMING CHARACTERISTICS:

   Activation: Asynchronous—from external card reader. Worst case inter-arrival time = 500 msec. Average inter-arrival time > 5 minutes.

Execution time C_i: 5 ms per message

4. PRIORITY:

High—Needs to be responsive to incoming cards.

5. ERRORS DETECTED:

Unrecognized card. Card reader malfunction.

6. TASK EVENT SEQUENCING LOGIC:

The event sequencing logic is defined during the detailed software design step, as described in Chapter 16.

14.11 Summary

During the task structuring phase, the system is structured into concurrent tasks and the task interfaces are defined. To help determine the concurrent tasks, task structuring criteria are provided to assist in mapping an object-oriented analysis model of the system to a concurrent tasking architecture. The task communication and synchronization interfaces are also defined.

Each task, determined by using the task structuring criteria, executes a sequence of operations. However, the information hiding objects that provide the operations are not designed until the class design phase, which is described in Chapter 15. Following this, Chapter 16 describes the detailed software design, in which tasks that contain nested passive objects are designed, detailed task synchronization issues are addressed, connector classes are designed to encapsulate the details of inter-task communication, and each task's internal event sequencing logic is defined.

chapter

Class Design

I n the Class Design phase, the information hiding classes are designed, from which the passive objects are instantiated. These classes were originally determined during the object and class structuring phase of analysis modeling, as described in Chapter 9. A class uses **information hiding** to address *static structural concerns*, of which there are different kinds, such as hiding device information or data abstraction. In particular, this chapter describes the determining of the operations of each class and the design of the class interfaces. This chapter also describes the use of **inheritance** in software design. An introduction to information hiding, classes, and inheritance was given in Chapter 3. As pointed out in Chapter 3, the term "operation" refers to both the specification and the implementation of a function performed by an object.

The operations of a class can be determined from either the static model or the dynamic model. Although the static model is intended to show each class's operations, it is usually easier to determine operations from the dynamic model, in particular the collaboration diagrams or sequence diagrams. In this section, we show how a class's operations can be determined from the collaboration model, the finite state machine model, and the static model, although the primary emphasis is on the collaboration model.

15.1 Designing Information Hiding Classes

The information hiding classes designed in the Class Design phase are categorized by stereotype. The information hiding classes are documented by class interface specifications, as explained in Section 15.13.

Classes determined from the analysis model (Chapter 9)—that is, those determined from the problem domain—are categorized as entity classes, interface classes, control classes, and application logic classes. In addition, there are software decision classes, which relate to the solution domain and are developed later as required by the developers.

- **Entity classes.** Entity classes are the classes determined in the analysis model that encapsulate data. On class diagrams, they are depicted with the stereotype «entity». Entity objects, which are instances of entity classes, are usually long-lasting objects that store information. For database intensive applications, it is likely that, in some cases, the encapsulated data will need to be stored in a database. In this situation, the entity class will actually provide an interface to the database rather than encapsulating the data. Thus, during class design, entity classes are further categorized as **data abstraction classes,** which encapsulate data structures, or **wrapper classes.** A **wrapper class** hides the details of how to interface to an external system from which data needs to be retrieved; examples include a file management system or a database management system. A **database wrapper class** hides how data is accessed if it is stored in a database, usually a relational database. A **wrapper class** can also hide the details of how to interface to a legacy system, as described in Chapter 4.

- **Interface classes.** Interface to the external environment. Interface classes can be further categorized as

  - **Device interface classes.** Interface to a hardware I/O device

  - **User interface classes.** Provide an interface to a human user

  - **System interface classes.** Interface to an external system or subsystem

- **Control classes.** Provides the overall coordination for a collection of objects in a use case. Control classes may be **coordinator classes, state-dependent classes,** and **timer classes.** Coordinator classes and timer classes are assumed to be active classes (tasks) and so are not discussed in this section.

- **Application logic classes.** Encapsulates application specific logic and algorithms. Categorized as business logic classes or algorithm classes.

- **Software decision classes.** Hide decisions made by the software designers that are likely to change. Cannot usually be identified from the analysis model and instead are determined later in the design process.

15.2 Designing Class Operations

In this section, we describe how to determine the operations provided by each class. Although the static model is intended to show each class's operations, it is usually easier to determine operations from the dynamic model, in particular the collaboration model. This is because the dynamic model shows the message interaction between objects, and hence operations being invoked at the destination object receiving the message. Message passing between passive objects consists of an operation in one object invoking an operation provided by another object.

Several examples of class design are given in this chapter. In the collaboration diagrams, the passive object, whose operations are being designed, interacts with other objects. These objects, which invoke the operations of the passive object, could themselves be active or passive. Many of the examples given in this chapter show analysis model collaboration diagrams mapped to design model collaboration diagrams. The emphasis in these examples is on designing a particular class and its operations. Other design decisions that could be made, such as mapping the objects that invoke these operations to tasks, are deliberately not shown.

15.2.1 Designing Class Operations from the Interaction Model

In this section, we use the object interaction model to help determine each class's operations. Either sequence diagrams or collaboration diagrams may be used for this purpose. Thus a class's operations are determined by considering how an object instantiated from the class interacts with other objects. In particular, when two objects interact, one object provides an operation that is used by the other object. We will illustrate the design of class operations primarily from collaboration diagrams.

If two objects interact, it is necessary to know which of the two objects invokes an operation on the other object. This information cannot usually be determined from a class diagram in the static model because it only shows the static relationships between classes. On the other hand, the dynamic interaction model does show the direction in which one object sends a message to the other. If the objects are mapped to a sequential program, the sender object invokes an operation on the receiver object. In this situation, the message is mapped to an operation call. The name of the message is mapped to the name of the operation and the parameters of the message are mapped to the parameters of the operation.

An object's operations can be determined directly from the interaction diagrams on which it appears. In the analysis model, the emphasis is on capturing the information passed between objects and not on the precise syntax of the operation. Hence, the message shown on the collaboration diagram may be either a noun, reflecting the data that is passed, or a verb, reflecting an operation to be executed.

In the design model, the class's operations are specified. If the message is shown as a noun, it is now necessary to define the operation of the object that will receive this information. If the message is shown as a verb, the verb represents the name of the operation. It is important that the name given to the operation in the design model reflect a service provided by the class.

It is also necessary to consider whether the operation has any input and/or output parameters. In the analysis model, all messages on the collaboration diagrams are depicted as simple messages sent by sender objects to receiver objects. In some cases, a simple message represents a response to a previous message. All messages that invoke operations are depicted as synchronous messages on the design model collaboration diagrams. Simple messages depicted in the analysis model that actually represent responses—that is, data returned by an operation—are mapped to a return parameter of the operation.

For example, consider the ATM Card class (a data abstraction class as described in Section 5.3), which encapsulates the information read off an ATM card. Looking at the analysis model collaboration diagram in Figure 15.1a, it can be seen that the Card Reader Interface object sends the Card Input Data message to the ATM Card entity object. The Customer Interface object later sends a Card Request message to ATM Card, which returns Card Data. During design, the precise class interface is designed. In the design model (see Figure 15.1b), the simple message Card Input Data is mapped to a call to an operation, write (card Data), pro-

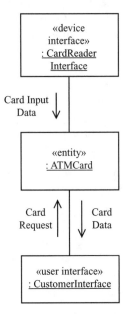

Figure 15.1a *Analysis model: collaboration diagram*

Figure 15.1 *Example of data abstraction class*

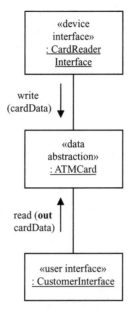

Figure 15.1b *Design model: collaboration diagram*

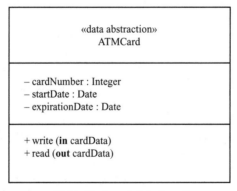

Figure 15.1c *Design model: class diagram*

Figure 15.1 *Example of data abstraction class (continued)*

vided by the ATM Card data abstraction object. The Card Request message sent by Customer Interface is mapped to a call to a read operation provided by ATM Card. The simple message Card Data is mapped to an output parameter of the read operation, as it represents the parameter returned by a call to the read operation. The operation calls are depicted, using the UML synchronous message notation. Figure 15.1c depicts the ATM Card data abstraction class. The attributes are depicted as well as the operations. The write operation has one input parameter card Data, the data to be written. The read operation has one output parameter, card Data, the data to be read.

After the object's operations have been determined from the collaboration diagram, the operation is specified in the static model, together with the class that provides the operation. Thus, proceeding in tandem with determining the class operations from the collaboration diagrams and depicting them on the class diagrams is beneficial. This approach is used throughout this chapter.

15.2.2   Designing Class Operations from the Finite State Machine Model

It is also possible to determine a class's operations from a statechart. A statechart has actions and activities that are initiated as a result of a state transition. These actions are typically mapped to operations provided by a class. All state-dependent actions and activities need to be depicted on the statecharts. If these actions are performed by passive classes, the operations can be defined from the statechart. Actions executed by concurrent tasks are addressed in Chapter 14.

An action or activity should also be depicted on a collaboration diagram or sequence diagram. However, because the use-case-based collaboration or sequence diagram usually shows scenarios (i.e., specific sequences of interaction among objects), it is possible that infrequently executed alternatives—for example, actions dealing with exceptions—might not be captured. In particular, a particular action might not be reflected on the use-case-based collaboration diagrams, although it should be shown on the consolidated collaboration diagrams, which are intended to depict all object interactions. All state-dependent actions and activities should be depicted on statecharts. An example of designing class operations from a statechart is given in Section 15.5.

15.2.3   Designing Class Operations from the Static Model

Determining a class's operations from the class diagrams of the static model is possible, in particular for the entity classes. Standard operations are create, read, update, delete. However, it is often possible to tailor operations to more specific needs of a particular data abstraction class by defining the services provided by the class. This will be illustrated by several examples in the following sections. Several examples are given in this chapter of the design of class operations. In these examples, the objects invoking the operations of the passive object are mostly depicted as passive, although they could also be active.

15.3   Data Abstraction Classes

Each entity class in the analysis model that encapsulates data is designed as a **data abstraction class**. An entity class stores some data and provides operations to access the data and to read or write to the data. The data abstraction class is used to encapsulate the data structure, thereby hiding the internal details of how the data structure is represented. The operations are designed as access procedures or functions whose internals, which define how the data structure is manipulated, are also hidden.

The information on the attributes encapsulated by the data abstraction class should be available from the static model of the problem domain (discussed in Chapter 8). The operations of the data abstraction class are determined by considering the services required by the client objects that use the data abstraction object in order to indirectly access the data structure. This can be determined by analyzing the usage pattern of the data abstraction object in the collaboration model. This is best illustrated by means of an example, as follows.

15.3.1   Example of Data Abstraction Class

As an example of a data abstraction class, consider the analysis model collaboration diagram shown in Figure 15.2a, which consists of two objects that need to access the ATM Cash data abstraction object. The attributes of ATM Cash are given in the static model. ATM Cash stores the amount of cash maintained by the ATM cash dispenser, in twenty, ten, and five dollar bills. It thus has internal variables to maintain the number of five dollar bills, the number of ten dollar bills, and the number of twenty dollar bills. Based on this, an ATM Cash class is designed that encapsulates four variables—cash Available, fives, tens, and twenties— whose initial values are all set to zero.

In addition to knowing what messages are sent to ATM Cash, it is also important to know the sequence in which the messages are sent. Thus, in the analysis model, when ATM Cash receives a Cash Withdrawal Amount message from the Cash Dispenser Interface object, containing the amount in dollars to be dispensed, it needs to compute how many bills of each denomination need to be dispensed to satisfy the request. In the analysis model, ATM Cash sends this information in a response message, Cash Response.

ATM Cash receives another kind of message from the Operator Interface object. The real-world ATM operator replenishes the ATM cash dispenser with new dollar bills of each denomination. This information needs to be conveyed to ATM Cash. After adding the cash to the dispenser, the operator confirms this to the Operator Interface object, which then sends a Cash Added message to the ATM Cash object, as shown in Figure 15.2a.

From the previous discussion, the operations of the ATM Cash class can be specified, as depicted in the Design Model collaboration diagram shown in Figure 15.2b. Two operations are needed to add Cash and withdraw Cash. The operation withdraw Cash has one input parameter, cash Amount, and three output parameters, fives To Dispense, tens To Dispense, and twenties To Dispense. The add Cash operation has three input parameters to indicate the number of bills of each denomination added: fives Added, tens Added, and twenties Added. The operation specifications are

```
withdrawCash (in cashAmount, out fivesToDispense, out tensToDispense,
out twentiesToDispense)
addCash (in fivesAdded, in tensAdded, in twentiesAdded)
```

The class diagram is depicted in Figure 15.2c.

An invariant maintained by objects of this class is that the total cash available for dispensing is equal to the sum of the value of the number of five dollar bills, the number of ten dollar bills, and the number of twenty dollar bills:

```
cashAvailable = 5 * fives + 10 * tens + 20 * twenties
```

Insufficient cash is an error case that needs to be detected. Such error situations are usually handled as exceptions.

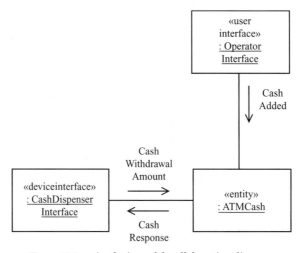

Figure 15.2a *Analysis model: collaboration diagram*

Figure 15.2 *Example of data abstraction class*

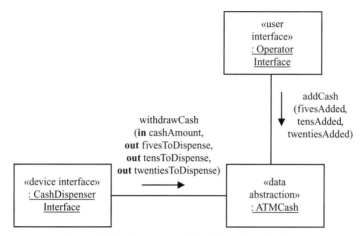

Figure 15.2b *Design model: collaboration diagram*

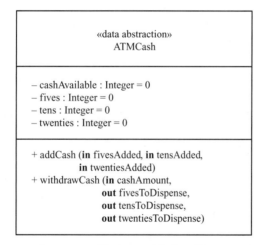

Figure 15.2c *Design model: class diagram*

Figure 15.2 *Example of data abstraction class (continued)*

15.4 Device Interface Classes

An important objective in developing a software system is to insulate users from changes to real-world I/O devices. A typical change to a real-world I/O device is to replace it with a different device that has the same overall functionality but implemented differently so it has a different hardware interface. For such a change to impact all users of the device is clearly undesirable, and the solution is to use a device interface class. A **device interface class** provides a virtual interface that hides the actual interface to the real-world I/O device.

With a device interface class, the information hiding concept is used to hide the design decision of how to interface to a specific I/O device. This is achieved by providing a virtual interface to the device and hiding the device-specific details inside the class. Thus, the device interface class hides the details of the actual interface to the real-world device.

Users access the device only by means of the virtual interface, which consists of a set of operations invoked by the users. When a change to the real-world device is made that impacts the real-world interface, this change is hidden from the device users by keeping the virtual interface—that is, the specification of the operations provided by the class—unchanged. The impact of the change is limited to the implementation of the operations. By this means, users of the class are insulated from changes to the real-world device.

During the Analysis Modeling Phase, device interface objects are determined by using the object structuring criteria described in Chapter 9. These software objects interface to the physical devices in the real world, which are external to the system. During the Class Design phase, each device interface class is designed. The device interface class hides the actual interface to the real-world device by providing a virtual interface to it.

15.4.1 Designing Operations of Device Interface Classes

Determining the operations provided by each device interface class is necessary. A device interface class interfaces to the real-world device and provides the operations that read from and/or write to the device.

A device interface class has an `initialize` operation. When an object is instantiated from the class, this operation is called at device initialization time to initialize the device and any internal variables used by the object. The other operations depend on the characteristics of the device. For example, an input device interface class is likely to have a `read` operation and an output device interface class is likely to have a `write` or `update` operation. A device interface class that provides both input and output is likely to have both `read` and `write` operations.

15.4.2 Input Device Interface Classes

An *input device interface class* needs an `initialize` operation to initialize the device and any internal variables used by the class. An input device interface class also typically needs a `read` operation. Of course, the implementation of these operations varies widely, depending on the characteristics of the input device. The implementation, which is necessarily highly I/O device-specific, is hidden from users of the device.

An example of an input device interface object is the `Gas Tank Interface` object, which has operations to `initialize` and `read`, as shown in Figure 15.3. In the analysis model (Figure 15.3a), the `Gas Tank Interface` object receives a request to `Read Fuel Amount` from the `Trip Fuel Consumption` object. The `Gas Tank Interface` object then requests the external `Gas Tank` object to read the fuel amount. In the design model (Figure 15.3b), the `read` operation is invoked on the external `Gas Tank` object and the response is the `fuel Input`. How this actually happens depends on the real-world interface (see Chapter 4 for a discussion on interfacing to I/O devices). The `Gas Tank Interface` object returns the `fuel Amount` to the requesting object.

The `Read Fuel Amount` message, which is received by the `Gas Tank Interface` in the analysis model, is depicted as a synchronous message in the design model, which represents a call to the `read` operation. The `Fuel Amount` message, which in the analysis model is the response to the `Read Fuel Amount` message, is mapped to a `fuel Amount` output parameter of the `read` operation.

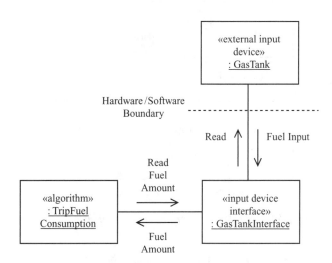

«external input device» : GasTank
Hardware / Software Boundary
Read
Fuel Input
Read Fuel Amount
«algorithm» : TripFuel Consumption
«input device interface» : GasTankInterface
Fuel Amount
NB: The dashed line for the hardware/software boundary is for illustrative purposes only and does not conform to the UML notation.

Figure 15.3a *Analysis model: collaboration diagram*

Figure 15.3 *Example of input device interface class*

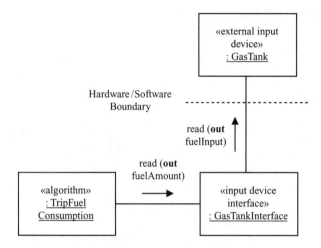

Hardware/Software Boundary

read (**out** fuelInput)

read (**out** fuelAmount)

NB: The dashed line for the hardware/software boundary is for illustrative purposes only and does not conform to the UML notation.

Figure 15.3b   *Design model: collaboration diagram*

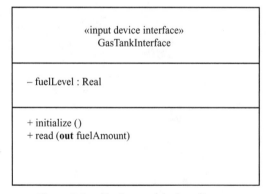

Figure 15.3c   *Design model: class diagram*

Figure 15.3   *Example of input device interface class (continued)*

The Gas Tank Interface device interface class is also depicted on a class diagram (see Figure 15.3c). It has two operations. The initialize operation is called at initialization time. The read operation is depicted with the fuel Amount as an output parameter. Thus, in the design model, the signature of the operation depicted on the class diagram is identical to that depicted on the collaboration diagram.

15.4.3   Output Device Interface Classes

An *output device interface class* also has an `initialize` operation. It may also have an `output` operation. For example, the `Throttle` device interface class has an `output` operation. However, if several different operations may be performed on the output device, the operations can be tailored to the usage of the device. Thus the `Cash Dispenser` class has an operation to `dispense Cash`, the `Receipt Printer` class has an operation to `print Receipt`, the `Elevator Door` Class has operations to `open` and `close`, and the `Elevator Motor` class has operations to move `up`, `down`, and `stop`.

As an example of an output device interface class, consider the analysis model collaboration diagram shown in Figure 15.4a. The «output device interface» object, `Trip Display Interface`, receives `Average Speed` and `Average`

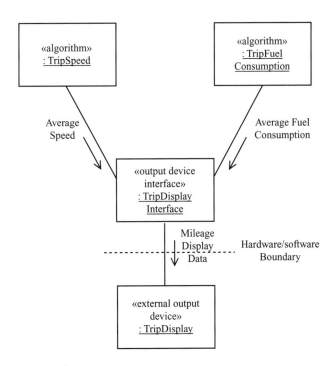

NB: The dashed line for the hardware/software boundary is for illustrative purposes only and does not conform to the UML notation.

Figure 15.4a   *Analysis model: collaboration diagram*

Figure 15.4   *Example of output device interface class*

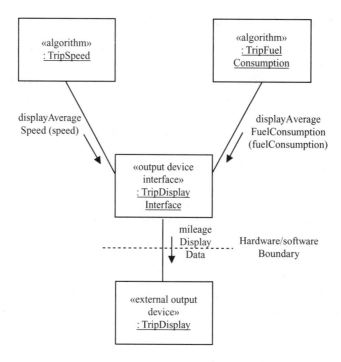

NB: The dashed line for the hardware/software boundary is for illustrative purposes only and does not conform to the UML notation.

Figure 15.4b *Design model: collaboration diagram*

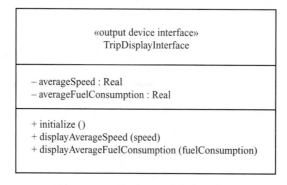

Figure 15.4c *Design model: class diagram*

Figure 15.4 *Example of output device interface class (continued)*

Fuel Consumption messages. It then outputs the contents of each message to the real-world Trip Display.

Consider the design of the Trip Display Interface class. This output device interface class (shown in Figure 15.4c) provides two operations, display Average Speed (speed) and display Average Fuel Consumption (fuel Consumption). In the example, the Trip Speed algorithm object calls the display Average Speed operation, passing to it the current value of the average speed. On the design model collaboration diagram, this is depicted as a synchronous message (operation call) with no return value (see Figure 15.4b). In the same way, the Trip Fuel Consumption algorithm object calls the display Average Fuel Consumption operation, passing to it the current value of fuel Consumption. The information hidden by the Trip Display Interface class is the details of how to format data for and interface to the real-world Trip Display.

15.5   State-Dependent Classes

A **state-dependent class** encapsulates the information contained on a statechart. During class design, the state-dependent class determined in the analysis model is designed. The statechart executed by the state-dependent object is mapped to a state transition table. Thus the state-dependent class hides the contents of the state transition table and maintains the current state of the object.

The state-dependent class provides the operations that access the state transition table and change the state of the object. In particular, one or more operations are designed to process the incoming events that cause state changes. One way of designing the operations of a state-dependent class is to have one operation for each incoming event. This means that each state-dependent class is designed explicitly for a particular statechart. However, it is desirable to make a state-dependent class more generic and hence more reusable.

A more generic state-dependent class would still hide the contents of the state transition table; however, it would support two generic operations, process Event and current State. The process Event operation is called when there is a new event to process, with the new event passed in as an input parameter. The current State operation is optional; it returns the ATM control state and is only needed in applications where the current state needs to be known by clients of the state-dependent class. The two operations are

```
processEvent (event)
currentState (): State
```

When called to process a new event, the process Event operation looks up the state transition table to determine the impact of this event, given the current state of the system and any specified conditions that must hold. The table indicates what the new state is (if any) and whether any actions are to be performed. The process Event operation then changes the state of the object and invokes the actions as operations on the appropriate objects.

An alternative and more reusable design is for the process Event to return the actions to be performed instead of invoking them directly, in which case the operation is

```
processEvent (in event, out action)
```

A state-dependent class is a generic class in that it can be used to encapsulate any state transition table. The contents of the table are application-dependent and are defined at the time the state-dependent class is instantiated and/or initialized.

An example of a state-dependent class from the Cruise Control System is the Calibration Control state-dependent class. The analysis model collaboration diagram in Figure 15.5a depicts the state-dependent control object Calibration Control, which executes the statechart shown in Figure 15.5b.

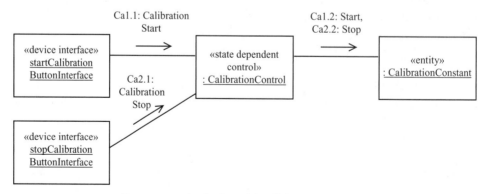

Figure 15.5a *Analysis model: collaboration diagram*

Figure 15.5 *Example of state-dependent control class*

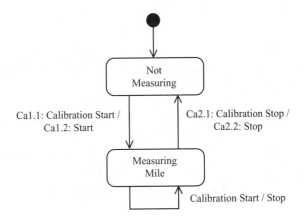

Figure 15.6b   *Analysis model: statechart*

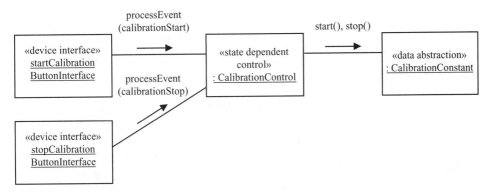

Figure 15.5c   *Design model: collaboration diagram*

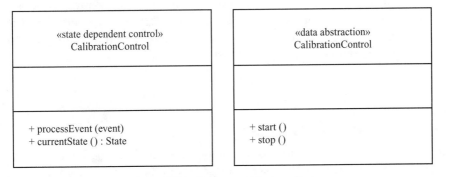

Figure 15.5d   *Design model: class diagram*

Figure 15.5   *Example of state-dependent control class (continued)*

The `Calibration Control` object receives the `Calibration Start` and `Calibration Stop` events from the two `Calibration Button Interface` objects. When the `Calibration Start` message is received (event Ca1.1), the statechart (Figure 15.5b) indicates that the `Start` action (Ca1.2) is to be performed. Consequently, the `Calibration Control` object sends the `Start` message to the `Calibration Constant` object, which executes the action. When the `Calibration Stop` message (event Ca2.1) is received, the statechart indicates that the `Stop` action (Ca2.2) is to be performed. Similarly, the `Calibration Control` object sends the `Stop` message to the `Calibration Constant` object, which executes the action.

In the design model (Figures 15.5c and 15.5d), the `Calibration Start` and `Calibration Stop` messages are mapped to calls to the `process Event` operation, which is provided by `Calibration Control`, with the `calibration Start` and `calibration Stop` events as input parameters. The actions `start` and `stop` are operations provided by the `Calibration Constant` data abstraction object and invoked by the `process Event` operation of the `Calibration Control` object.

15.6   Algorithm Hiding Classes

An **algorithm hiding class** hides an algorithm used in the application domain. Algorithm hiding classes are typically found in real-time systems, as well as in scientific and engineering applications. An algorithm hiding class typically hides both the algorithm as well as any local data used by the algorithm.

An example of an algorithm hiding class is the `Trip Speed` class shown in Figure 15.6, which hides the algorithm used in the Cruise Control and Monitoring System for calculating the average speed of the vehicle. It has operations to `reset` the calculation and to periodically `calculate` the average trip speed. Both the `reset` and `calculate` operations call the `display` operation of the `Trip Display Interface` object with the `average Speed` as parameter (see Figure 15.6b). The class diagram is depicted in Figure 15.6c.

15.7   User Interface Classes

A **user interface class** hides from other classes the details of the interface to the user. In a given application, the user interface might be a simple command line interface or might be a sophisticated graphical user interface (GUI). A command line interface is typically handled by one user interface class; however,

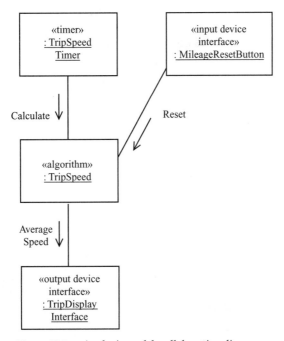

Figure 15.6a *Analysis model: collaboration diagram*

Figure 15.6 *Example of algorithm class*

several classes are typically used in the design of a GUI interface. Low-level user interface classes are widgets typically found in a user interface component library, such as windows, menus, buttons, and dialog boxes. Higher-level composite user interface classes are often created from these lower-level classes.

In the analysis model, the emphasis should be on identifying the composite user interface classes and capturing the information that needs to be entered by the user and the information that needs to be displayed to the user. Individual GUI screens can also be designed as part of the analysis model. In the design model for a GUI-based application, the GUI classes required for each of the individual screens are determined.

An example from a banking application is the Customer GUI class, which is a higher-level composite user interface class (see Figure 15.7a). Customer GUI is the main user interface to the ATM Customer. Customer GUI has operations for each of the windows displayed and used for interaction with the customer—display PIN Window, display Withdrawal Window, display Transfer Window, and display Query Window—as well as the main menu, display Menu. There is also an operation for a smaller window used to display prompts and information

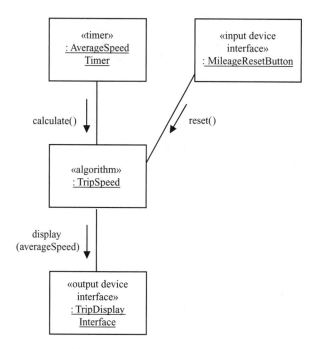

Figure 15.6b *Design model: collaboration diagram*

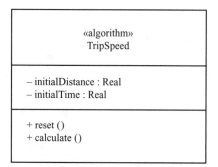

Figure 15.6c *Design model: class diagram*

Figure 15.6 *Example of algorithm class (continued)*

messages to the customer, where no customer input is expected. The parameter of this operation identifies the specific prompt or message that should be displayed. Each display window outputs information to the customer and then gets the customer input, which is returned as the output parameter(s) of the operation.

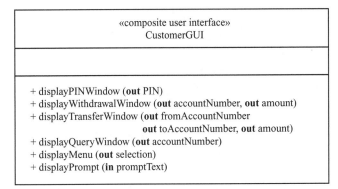

Figure 15.7a *User interface class with operations provided*

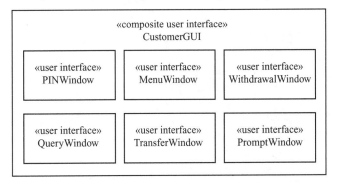

Figure 15.7b *Structure of composite user interface class*

Figure 15.7 *Example of user interface class*

The Customer GUI class is a composite user interface class that contains several lower-level GUI classes, as shown in Figure 15.7b. These include GUI classes for each of the windows used for interaction with the customer—the main Menu Window, the PIN Window, the Withdrawal Window, the Transfer Window, the Query Window, and the Prompt Window.

15.8 Business Logic Classes

A **business logic class** defines the decision-making, business-specific application logic for processing a client request. The goal is to encapsulate business rules that could change independently of each other into separate business logic classes. Usually a business logic object accesses various entity objects during its execution.

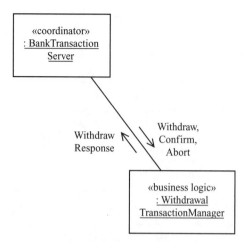

Figure 15.8a   *Analysis model: collaboration diagram*

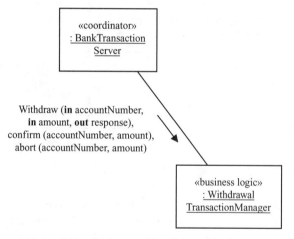

Figure 15.8b   *Design model: collaboration diagram*

Figure 15.8   *Example of business logic class*

An example of a business logic class is the `Withdrawal Transaction Man-ager` class (shown in Figure 15.8), which encapsulates the rules for processing an ATM withdrawal request. It has operations to `initialize`, `withdraw`, `confirm`, and `abort`. The operation `initialize` is called at initialization time; `withdraw` is called to withdraw funds from a customer account; `confirm` is called to confirm that the withdrawal transaction was successfully completed; and `abort` is called if the transaction was not successfully completed, for example, if the cash was not dis-

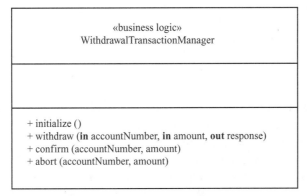

Figure 15.8c *Design model: class diagram*

Figure 15.8 *Example of business logic class (continued)*

pensed at the ATM. The operations are determined by careful study of the Bank Server analysis model collaboration diagram, as shown in Figure 15.8a, and the message sequence descriptions that identify the contents of the messages (see Chapter 19). From this, the design model collaboration diagram shown in Figure 15.8b and the class diagram shown in Figure 15.8c are determined.

15.9 Database Wrapper Classes

In the analysis model, an entity class is designed that encapsulates data. During design, a decision has to be made whether the encapsulated data is to be managed directly by the entity class or whether the data is actually to be stored in a database. The former case is handled by **data abstraction classes,** which encapsulate data structures (Section 15.3), and the latter is handled by **database wrapper classes**, which hide how the data is accessed if it is stored in a database.

Most databases in use today are relational databases, so the database wrapper class provides an object-oriented interface to the class. If a relational database is being used, any entity classes defined in the static model that are to be mapped to a relational database need to be determined.

The attributes of the analysis model entity class are mapped to a database relation, and the operations to access the attributes are mapped to a database wrapper class. A mapping approach is required to map entity classes to relations, because relations are flat files, whereas entity classes might not be. Primary keys need to be determined, and associations, which are shown explicitly on a class diagram, need to be mapped to foreign keys. Mapping a static model to a relational database is described in more detail in Rumbaugh et al. [1991], Blaha and Premerlani [1998].

The database wrapper class hides the details of how to access the data maintained in the relations, so it hides all the SQL statements. A database wrapper class usually hides the details of access to one relation. However, a database wrapper class might also hide a database view; that is, a SQL *join* of two or more relations [Korth and Silberschatz 1998].

An example of a database wrapper class is given in Figure 15.9. In the `Banking System` example, all persistent data is stored in a relational database. Hence, each entity class maintained at the `Bank Server` is mapped to both a database relation (flat file) and a database wrapper class. For example, consider the `Debit Card` entity class as depicted in the analysis model in Figure 15.9a. As the debit card data will actually be stored in a relational database, from a database perspective, the entity class is mapped to a relation. The attributes of the entity class are mapped to the attributes of the relation. In addition, a primary key needs to be determined; the attribute `card ID` is chosen because it uniquely locates a row in the `Debit Card` relation (Figure 15.9b). Furthermore, a foreign key is needed to represent the association `Customer` <u>owns</u> `Debit Card`. A foreign key is a primary key of one table that is embedded in another table. It represents the mapping of an association between classes into a table and hence allows navigation between tables. The primary key of the `Customer` relation is `Customer SSN`, so this is chosen as the foreign key in the `Debit Card` relation.

It is also necessary to design the `Debit Card` database wrapper class (Figure 15.9b), which has the following operations: `create`, `validate`, `check Daily Limit`, `clear Total`, `update`, `read`, and `delete`. These operations encapsulate the SQL statements for accessing the `Debit Card` relation. Note that because the class attributes can be updated separately, different `update` operations are provided for each of the attributes that are updated, such as `daily Limit` and `card Status`. A call to each of the operations results in execution of a SQL statement.

15.10   Software Decision Classes

A **software decision class** hides a design decision made by the software designer that is considered likely to change. Software decision classes are usually developed later in the design process. They are not determined from the analysis model, which relates to the problem domain.

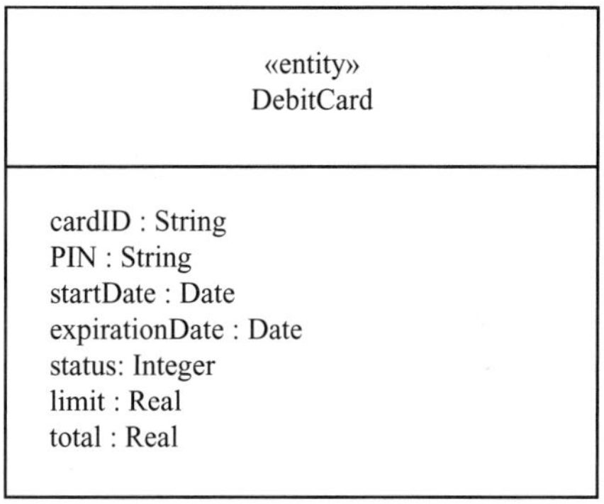

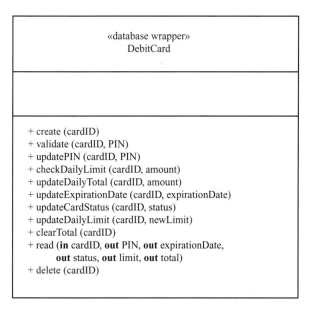

+-------------------------------------+
| «entity» |
| DebitCard |
+-------------------------------------+
| cardID : String |
| PIN : String |
| startDate : Date |
| expirationDate : Date |
| status: Integer |
| limit : Real |
| total : Real |
+-------------------------------------+

Figure 15.9a *Analysis model*

+---+
| «database wrapper» |
| DebitCard |
+---+
| |
+---+
| + create (cardID) |
| + validate (cardID, PIN) |
| + updatePIN (cardID, PIN) |
| + checkDailyLimit (cardID, amount) |
| + updateDailyTotal (cardID, amount) |
| + updateExpirationDate (cardID, expirationDate) |
| + updateCardStatus (cardID, status) |
| + updateDailyLimit (cardID, newLimit) |
| + clearTotal (cardID) |
| + read (**in** cardID, **out** PIN, **out** expirationDate, |
| **out** status, **out** limit, **out** total) |
| + delete (cardID) |
+---+

Relation in relational database :
DebitCard (<u>cardID</u>, PIN, startDate, expirationDate,
status, limit, total, *customerSSN*)

(underline = <u>primary key</u>, italic = *foreign key*)

Figure 15.9b *Design model*

Figure 15.9 *Example of database wrapper class*

Examples of software decision classes are encapsulated data structures, such as stacks, queues, and data tables chosen by the designer. Connector classes are also software decision classes, examples of which are given in Chapter 16.

15.11   Inheritance in Design

Inheritance can be used when designing two similar but not identical classes—in other words, classes that share many but not all characteristics. During architectural design, the classes need to be designed with inheritance in mind so that code sharing and adaptation can be exploited in detailed design and coding. Inheritance can also be used when adapting a design for either maintenance or reuse purposes. Used in this way, the biggest benefit is from using inheritance as an incremental modification mechanism [Wegner 1990].

15.11.1   Class Hierarchies

Class hierarchies (also referred to as generalization/specialization hierarchies and inheritance hierarchies) can be developed either top-down, bottom-up, or by some combination of the two approaches. Using a top-down approach, a class is designed that captures the overall characteristics of a set of classes. Specializing the class to form variant subclasses separates the differences among the classes. Alternatively, it can be recognized that an initial design contains classes that have some common properties (operations and/or attributes) as well as some variant properties. In this case, the common properties can be generalized into a superclass; these attributes and/or operations are inherited by the variant subclasses.

It should be noted that when designing with inheritance, the internals of the parent classes are visible to the subclasses. For this reason, design and reuse by subclasses is referred to as "white box reuse". Thus, inheritance breaks the encapsulation (information hiding) concept. The implementation of the child class is bound up with the implementation of the parent class, which can lead to problems with deep inheritance hierarchies. A change to a class high up in the inheritance hierarchy can have an impact on all its descendent classes. For this reason, it is best to limit the depth of class hierarchies.

15.11.2   Abstract Classes

An **abstract class** is a class with no instances. Because an abstract class has no instances, it is used as a template for creating subclasses instead of as a template for creating objects. Thus, it is used only as a superclass and defines a common interface for its subclasses. An **abstract operation** is an operation that is declared in an abstract class but not implemented. An abstract class must have at lease one abstract operation.

An abstract class defers all or some of its operation implementations to operations defined in subclasses. Given the interface provided by the abstract operation, a subclass can define the implementation of the operation. Different subclasses of the same abstract class can define different implementations of the same abstract operation. An abstract class can thus define an **interface** in the form of abstract operations. The subclasses define the implementation of the abstract operations and may extend the interface by adding other operations.

Some of the operations may be implemented in the abstract class, especially in cases where some or all of the subclasses need to use the same implementation. Alternatively, the abstract class may define a default implementation of an operation. A subclass may choose to override an operation defined by a parent class by providing a different implementation of the same abstract operation. This can be used when a particular subclass has to deal with a special case that requires a different implementation of the operation.

15.11.3 Polymorphism and Dynamic Binding

Polymorphism is Greek for "many forms." In object-oriented design, polymorphism is used to mean that different classes may have the same operation name. The specification of the operation is identical for each class; however, classes can implement the operation differently. This allows objects with identical interfaces to be substituted for each other at run-time.

Dynamic binding is used in conjunction with polymorphism and is the run-time association of a request to an object and one of its operations. With compile-time binding, the typical form of binding used with a procedural language, association of a request to an operation is done at compile time and cannot be changed at run-time. Dynamic binding means that the association of a request to an object's operation is done at run-time and can thus change from one invocation to the next. Looking at it from the requestor's point of view, a variable may reference objects of different classes at different times and invoke an operation of the same name on these different objects.

15.12 Examples of Inheritance

Three examples of inheritance in design are given next, illustrating the use of superclasses and subclasses, polymorphism and dynamic binding, and abstract classes.

15.12.1 Example of Superclasses and Subclasses

In a banking example, an Account class has two attributes, account Number and balance. Because it is necessary to be able to open and close accounts, read the account balance, and credit and debit the account, the following operations are specified for the Account class:

- open (accountNumber : Integer)
- close ()
- read Balance () : Real
- credit (amount : Real)
- debit (amount : Real)

The bank handles two types of accounts, checking accounts and savings accounts. This appears to be a good candidate for using inheritance, with a generalized account superclass and specialized subclasses for checking account and savings account. Questions we need to ask at this stage are what should be the generalized operations and attributes of the account superclass, what are the specialized operations and attributes of the checking account and savings account subclasses, and should the account class be an abstract class?

Before we can answer these questions, we need to understand in what ways checking and savings accounts are similar and in what ways they differ. First consider the attributes. It is clear that both checking and saving accounts need an account Number and a balance, so these attributes can be generalized and made attributes of the Account class, to be inherited by both the Checking Account and Savings Account subclasses. On the other hand, in this bank, savings accounts accrue interest but checking accounts do not. We need to know the accumulated interest on a savings account, so the attribute cumulative Interest is declared as an attribute of the Savings Account subclass. In addition, only three debits are allowed per month from savings accounts without a bank charge, so the attribute debit Count is also declared as an attribute of the Savings Account subclass. Two additional static class attributes are declared; these are attributes for which only one value exists for the whole class, which is accessible to all objects of the class. The static attributes are max Free Debits (maximum number of free debits, which is initialized to three) and bank Charge (the amount the bank charges for every debit over the maximum number of free debits, which is initialized to $1.50). A further requirement is that for checking accounts, it is desirable to know the last amount deposited in the account. Checking Account thus needs a specialized attribute called last Deposit Amount.

Both Checking Account and Savings Account will need the same operations as the Account class, namely open, close, read Balance, credit, and debit. The interface of these operations is defined in the Account superclass, so the two subclasses will inherit the same interface from Account. The open, close, and credit operations are done in the same way on checking and savings accounts, so the implementation of these operations can also be defined in Account and then be inherited. In the case of the Checking Account subclass, the implementation of the debit operation can also be inherited from Account. However, for Savings Account, the implementation of the debit operation is different. In addition to debiting the balance of the savings account, the debit operation must increment debit Count and deduct the bank Charge for every debit in excess of max Free Debits. There is also a need for an additional clear Debit Count operation, which reinitializes the debit Count to zero at the end of each month.

At first glance, it appears that the read operation is also identical for checking and savings accounts; however, a more careful examination reveals that this is not the case. When we read a checking account, we wish to read the balance and the last deposit amount. When we read a savings account, we wish to read the balance and the accumulated interest. The solution is to have more than one read operation. The generalized read operation is the read Balance operation, which is inherited by both checking account and savings account. A specialized read operation, read Cumulative Interest, is then added in the Savings Account subclass, and a specialized read operation, read Last Deposit Amount, is added to the checking account subclass.

The design of the Account generalization/specialization hierarchy is depicted in Figure 15.10 and described here.

Design of the Checking Account Subclass

1. Attributes of Checking Account subclass:

   Inherits the attributes account Number and balance. Both attributes are declared as protected in the Account superclass; hence, they are visible to the subclasses.

   Adds the attribute last Deposit Amount.

2. Operations of Checking Account subclass:

   Inherits the operations open, close, read Balance, credit, and debit.

   Adds the operation:

   read Last Deposit Amount () : Real

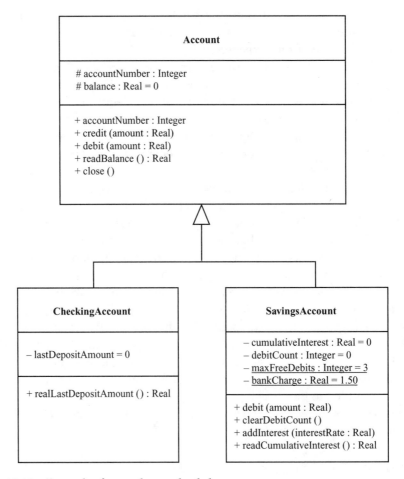

Figure 15.10 *Example of superclass and subclasses*

Design of the `Savings Account` Subclass

1. Attributes of `Savings Account` subclass:

   Inherits the attributes `account Number` and `balance`.

   Adds the attributes `cumulative Interest` and `debit Count`.

   Adds the static class attributes `max Free Debits` and `bank Charge`. Static attributes are depicted as underlined in UML, as shown in Figure 15.10.

2. Operations of `Savings Account` Subclass:

   Inherits both the specification and implementation of the operations `open`, `read Balance`, `credit`, and `close`.

Inherits the specification of the operation debit but redefines the implementation: debits account balance and deducts bank charge if maximum number of free debits has been exceeded.

Adds the operations:

- add Interest (interest Rate : Real). Add interest on a daily basis.
- read Cumulative Interest () : Real
- clear Debit Count () Reinitialize debit Count to zero at the end of each month.

15.12.2 Example of Polymorphism and Dynamic Binding

Now consider the instantiation of objects from these classes, as well as an example of the use of polymorphism and dynamic binding:

```
begin

private anAccount: Account;
Prompt customer for account type and withdrawal amount
if customer responds checking
   then -- assign customer's checking account to an Account
      . . .
      anAccount := customerCheckingAccount;
      . . .
 elseif customer responds savings
     then -- assign customer's savings account to an Account

      . . .
      anAccount := customerSavingsAccount;
      . . .
endif;
. . .
-- debit an Account, which is a checking or savings account
anAccount.debit (amount);
. . .
end;
```

In this example, if the account type is a checking account, an Account is assigned a Checking Account object. Executing anAccount.debit will invoke the debit operation of the Checking Account object. If, on the other hand, the account is a savings account, executing anAccount.debit will invoke the debit operation of a Savings Account object. A different variant of the debit operation is executed for savings accounts than for checking accounts, because the specialized variant for savings accounts has an additional bank charge if the maximum number of free debits has been exceeded.

It should be noted that an object of type Checking Account or type Savings Account may be assigned to an object of type Account but not vice versa. This is because every Checking Account subclass **is a**(n) Account superclass and every Savings Account subclass **is a**(n) Account superclass. However, the reverse is not possible because not every account is a checking account—it might be a savings account!

15.12.3 Example of Inheritance with Abstract Class

As an example of inheritance with an abstract class, consider the automobile Maintenance class from the Cruise Control and Monitoring System. Although Oil Change Maintenance, Air Filter Maintenance, and Major Service Maintenance could all be designed as separate classes, greater code sharing can be obtained by designing them as subclasses of the Maintenance superclass. The generalization/specialization hierarchy for the Maintenance class is given in Figure 15.11.

The superclass Maintenance is designed as an abstract class; it specifies two operations, reset and check. An encapsulated data type is shared by both operations—namely, initial Mileage, which is the cumulative distance traveled when the previous maintenance service was carried out. When called, the reset operation calls the read operation provided by the Distance object, which returns the cumulative Distance traveled; reset assigns the current cumulative distance to initial Mileage. The check maintenance operation is an abstract operation; thus the operation is specified in the Maintenance class but its implementation is deferred to the subclasses.

A maintenance subclass—for example, Oil Change Maintenance—inherits the overall structure from the Maintenance class, including the type definition of initial Mileage and the full definition (specification and implementation) of the reset operation, as well as the specification of the abstract check maintenance operation. The Oil Change Maintenance subclass now needs to add the implementation of the check operation. This operation needs to define the mileage at which an oil change is needed—possibly 5,000 miles—and the oil change message that needs to be output when this mileage is exceeded. It also needs to identify the operation display Oil Change Message to call from the Maintenance Display Interface class. The check operation also calls the read operation of the Distance object to determine the current cumulative distance traveled. It subtracts from this value the initial Mileage to determine whether 5,000 miles have elapsed and hence whether it is time for oil filter maintenance to be carried out on the vehicle.

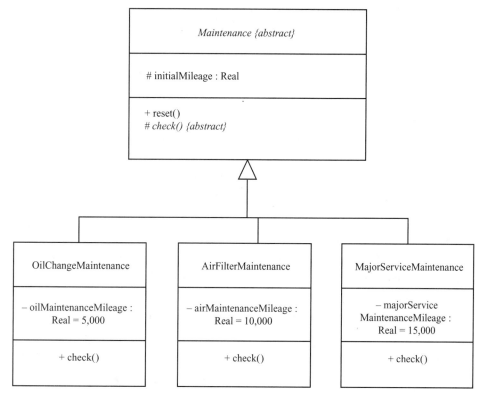

Figure 15.11   *Example of abstract superclass and subclasses*

15.13   Class Interface Specifications

A **class interface specification** defines the interface of the information hiding class, including the specification of the operations provided by the class. It defines the following:

- Information hidden by information hiding class: for example, data structure(s) encapsulated in the case of a data abstraction class or device interfaced to in the case of a device interface class.

- Class structuring criterion used to design this class.

- Assumptions made in specifying the class: for example, whether the operations of an object instantiated from the class can be concurrently accessed by more than one task or whether one operation needs to be called before another.

- Anticipated changes. This is to encourage consideration of design for change.
- Superclass (if applicable).
- Inherited operations (if applicable).
- Operations provided by the class. For each operation, define
  - Function performed
  - Precondition (a condition that must be true when the operation is invoked)
  - Postcondition (a condition that must be true at the completion of the operation)
  - Invariant (a condition that must be true at all times)
  - Input parameters
  - Output parameters
  - Operations used from other classes

The information in the class interface specification may be documented in narrative or tabular form. An example of the narrative documentation is given next.

15.13.1   Example of Class Interface Specification

An example of a class interface specification for an information hiding class is now given for the sensor/actuator data abstraction class depicted in Figure 15.12.

Information Hiding Class: Sensor Actuator Repository

Information Hidden: Encapsulates sensor/actuator data structure. Stores current values of sensors and actuators.

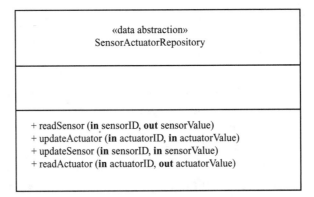

Figure 15.12 *Example of class defined by class interface specification*

Class structuring criterion: Data abstraction class.

Assumptions: Operations may be concurrently accessed by more than one task.

Anticipated changes: Currently supports Boolean sensors and actuators only. Possible extension to support analog sensors and actuators.

Superclass: None

Inherited operations: None

Operations provided:

1. `readSensor` (**in** `sensorID,` **out** `sensorValue`)

   Function: Given the sensor ID, returns the current value of the sensor

   Precondition: Sensor value has previously been updated.

   Invariant: Sensor value remains unchanged.

   Postcondition: Sensor value has been read.

   Input parameters: `sensorID`

   Output parameters: `sensorValue`

   Operations used: None

2. `updateActuator` (**in** `actuatorID,` **in** `actuatorValue`)

   Function: Used to update the value of the actuator in preparation for output

   Precondition: Actuator exists.

   Postcondition: Actuator value has been updated.

   Input parameters: `actuatorID, actuatorValue`

   Output parameters: None

   Operations used: None

3. `updateSensor` (**in** `sensorID,` **in** `sensorValue`)

   Function: Used to update sensor value with new reading from the external environment

   Precondition: Sensor exists.

   Postcondition: Sensor value has been updated.

   Input parameters: `sensorID, sensorValue`

   Output parameters: None

   Operations used: None

4. readActuator (**in** actuatorID, **out** actuatorValue)

Function: Used to read the new value of the actuator to output to the external environment

Precondition: Actuator value has previously been updated.

Invariant: Actuator value remains unchanged.

Postcondition: Actuator value has been read.

Input parameters: actuatorID

Output parameters: actuatorValue

Operations used: None

15.14 Summary

In the Class Design phase, the information hiding classes are designed, from which the passive objects are instantiated. These classes were originally determined during the object and class structuring step in analysis modeling, as described in Chapter 9. A class uses **information hiding** to address *static structural concerns,* of which there are different kinds, such as hiding device information or data abstraction. In particular, this chapter has described the determining of the operations of each class and the design of the class interfaces. This chapter also described the use of **inheritance** in software design. For more information on the design of classes and inheritance and on the use of preconditions, postconditions, and invariants in software construction, an excellent reference is Meyer [1997]. Another informative reference that describes these topics from a UML perspective is Page-Jones [1999].

Detailed Software Design

A fter structuring the system into tasks (in Chapter 14) and designing the information hiding classes (in Chapter 15), this chapter describes the detailed software design. In this step, the internals of composite tasks that contain nested objects are designed, detailed task synchronization issues are addressed, connector classes are designed that encapsulate the details of inter-task communication, and each task's internal event sequencing logic is defined. Several examples are given in Pseudocode of the detailed design of task synchronization mechanisms, connector classes for inter-task communication, and task event sequencing logic.

The detailed subsystem software design is depicted on a detailed concurrent collaboration diagram, which adds more detail to the concurrent collaboration diagram developed during task structuring. It depicts the internal design of clustered tasks and the design of connector objects.

16.1 Design of Composite Tasks

This section describes the detailed design of composite tasks, which contain nested objects. This includes tasks that were structured by using the task clustering and inversion criteria. Such tasks are usually designed as composite active classes that contain nested passive classes.

After considering the relationship between tasks and classes, this section describes situations where it is useful to divide the responsibility between tasks and classes. Next, the design of two composite tasks is described in detail: a temporal clustering task and a control clustering task.

16.1.1   Relationship between Tasks and Classes

The relationship between tasks and classes is handled as follows. The active object, the task, is activated by an external, internal, or timer event. It then calls an operation provided by the passive object. The passive object may be nested inside the task or may be outside the task. These two cases are designed differently.

A class whose operations are used exclusively by a task can be nested inside the task. A class whose operations are used by more than one task must reside outside the tasks. If a class is accessed by more than one task, the class's operations must synchronize access to the data it encapsulates, as described in Section 16.2.

Because the internals of a class's operations are designed differently depending on how the class is accessed, it is important to clearly define the context in which the class is to be used. Document this information as an assumption in the class specification.

For reasons of code modularity and reuse, it might be undesirable to physically nest classes inside the task when they are accessed by only one task. However, it must be clearly stated in the class assumptions that these classes are designed without any internal synchronization such that only one task can access them.

16.1.2   Division of Responsibility between Tasks and Classes

At times it is useful to divide responsibility between a task and a nested class. This is an example of separation of concerns, where control, sequencing, and communication responsibilities are given to the task and structural details are given to the nested information hiding class. This division of responsibility is illustrated by means of the following examples.

When interfacing to an input/output device, you can use an asynchronous or periodic device interface task (see Chapter 14) with a *nested* device interface object (see Chapter 15). The object addresses the details of how to read from or write to the real-world device, and the task addresses issues of when and how the task is activated and communication with other active or passive objects. Consider how this works in the case of an input device. The task is activated by an external or timer event, calls an operation provided by the passive object to read the input, and then either sends the data in a message to a consumer task or invokes the operation of a data abstraction object.

A device interface object accessed by only one task does not need to provide any synchronization of access to the device. However, if the device is to be accessed by more than one task, the internals of the device interface object have to be redesigned to allow this. Alternatively, you can ensure sequential access to the device interface object by designing a resource monitor task (see Chapter 14) to

receive all I/O requests. This task then invokes the operations of the device interface object.

Another example of division of responsibility occurs between a control task
and a nested state-dependent object. The object encapsulates the state transition
table and maintains the current state of the object, as described in Chapter 15. The
control task (see Chapter 14) receives messages containing events from several
producer tasks, extracts the event from the message, and calls the state-dependent
object with the event as an input parameter. The object returns the action to be
performed, and the task initiates the action by sending a message or invoking an
operation on another object.

In cases like these, where the responsibility is divided between a task and a
nested object, it is not usually necessary to depict the task's internal structure on a
diagram. Instead, the structure is described in the task's event sequencing logic,
examples of which are given in Section 16.4. However, in more complex situations, where the task is a composite task with several nested objects, depicting the
internal structure of the task is useful.

A **composite task** is a task that encapsulates the nested objects it contains. A
composite task with several nested objects can be depicted on a detailed **concurrent
collaboration diagram**. All functionality provided by the task is provided by the
objects it contains. Each composite task has a coordinator object, which receives the
task's incoming messages and can then invoke operations provided by other nested
objects. Detailed examples of such composite tasks are described next.

16.1.3   Temporal Clustering Task and Device Interface Objects

Consider the case of polled I/O from both the task structuring and class structuring perspectives. With polled I/O, structure the task according to either periodic
I/O (for one I/O device) or temporal clustering (for two or more I/O devices)
task structuring criteria. Each passive I/O device is encapsulated in a device
interface class. Define the operations provided by the device interface class. Place
the device interface class inside the task.

Consider the dynamic behavior. The task is activated by a timer event. It then
calls the operations provided by each device interface object to obtain the latest
status of each device.

An example of polled I/O is given in Figure 16.1. The collaboration diagram
from the analysis model shows the two device interface objects, Brake Interface and Engine Interface (Figure 16.1a), which monitor the brake and
engine sensors respectively. The brake and engine sensors are sampled periodically and with the same frequency.

From a task structuring perspective, the `Engine Interface` and `Brake Interface` device interface objects are grouped into a task called `Auto Sensors` based on the temporal clustering criterion. The `Auto Sensors` task (Figure 16.1b) is activated periodically by a timer event, at which time it reads the current values of the sensors. If there is a change in the engine and/or brake sensor status, it sends a message(s) to the `Cruise Control` task.

From a class structuring perspective, two separate device interface classes are created for the engine and brake sensors (Figure 16.1c). Each device interface class supports two operations: for the engine sensor, the operations are read (**out** engine Status) and initialize. For the brake sensor, they are read (**out** brake Status) and initialize.

From a combined task and class perspective, the `Auto Sensors` task is structured as a composite task. It contains three objects, a coordinator object, the `Auto Sensors Monitor`, and the `Brake Interface` and `Engine Interface` input device interface objects.

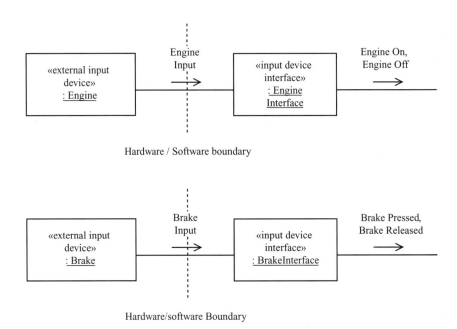

NB: The dashed line for the hardware/software boundary is for illustrative purposes only and does not conform to the UML notation.

Figure 16.1a *Analysis model: device interface objects*

Figure 16.1 *Example of temporal clustering and device interface objects*

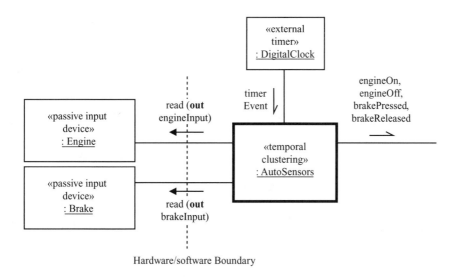

Figure 16.1b *Design model: temporal clustering task*

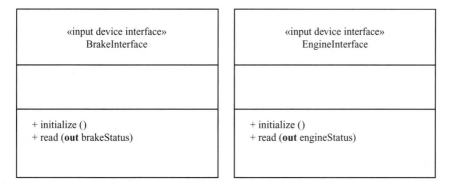

Figure 16.1c *Design model: device interface classes*

Figure 16.1 *Example of temporal clustering and device interface objects (continued)*

Consider the dynamic behavior as depicted in Figure 16.1d. The Auto Sensors task is activated periodically by a timer event. At this time, the Auto Sensors Monitor coordinator object reads the current values of the sensors by calling each of the operations, Engine Interface.read (**out** engine Status)

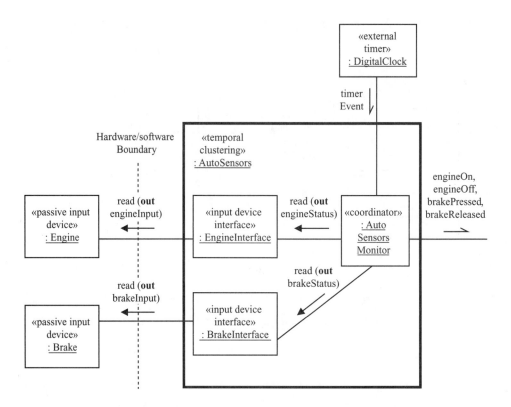

NB: The dashed line for the hardware/software boundary is for illustrative purposes only and does not conform to the UML notation.

Figure 16.1d   *Temporal clustering task with nested device interface objects*

Figure 16.1   *Example of temporal clustering and device interface objects (continued)*

and `Brake Interface.read (`**`out`** `brake Status)`. If there is a change in the engine and/or brake sensor status, it sends a message(s) containing the new value(s) to the `Cruise Control` task.

By separating the concerns of **how** a device is accessed into the device interface class from the concerns of **when** the device is accessed into the task, greater flexibility and potential reuse is achieved. Thus, for example, the brake device interface class could be used in different applications by an asynchronous input device interface task, a periodic input device interface task, or a temporally clustered periodic I/O task. Furthermore, the characteristics of different brake sensors could be hidden inside the device interface class, while preserving the same virtual device interface.

16.1.4   Control Clustering Task and Information Hiding Objects

The next case to be considered is that of task control clustering and information hiding objects. The control task is activated asynchronously. It calls operations provided by one or more passive objects.

Figure 16.2 gives an example of a control task and the objects to which it inter-faces. The collaboration diagram from the analysis model (Figure 16.2a) shows that the control object ATM Control sends messages that invoke operations (at different state transitions) on two objects, namely the Receipt Printer Inter-face and Cash Dispenser Interface objects.

From a task structuring perspective, the state-dependent control object ATM Control is structured as a control task because the execution of its statechart is strictly sequential. Furthermore, the control task executes other operations (state-dependent actions) in its thread of control, based on the control clustering crite-rion, as described in Section 14.6.3. Figure 16.2b depicts the control clustering task, the ATM Controller.

From a class structuring perspective (Figure 16.2c), there are three passive classes: a state-dependent class ATM Control, which hides the structure and content of the ATM Control state transition table, and two output device inter-face classes, the Receipt Printer Interface and Cash Dispenser

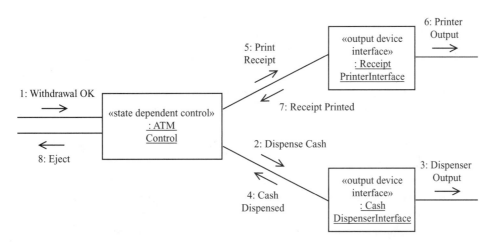

Figure 16.2a   *Analysis model: collaboration diagram*

Figure 16.2   *Example of a control clustering task with passive objects*

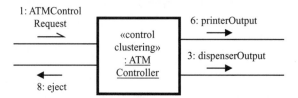

Figure 16.2b   *Control clustering task*

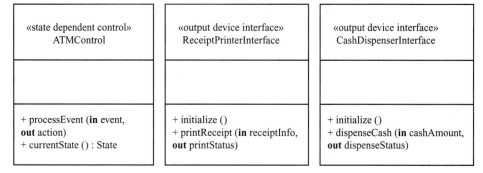

Figure 16.2c   *Information hiding classes*

Figure 16.2   *Example of a control clustering task with passive objects (continued)*

`Interface` objects. `ATM Control` provides an operation `process Event`, which is called to process a new event and returns the action to be performed. The `Receipt Printer Interface` provides an operation `print Receipt`. The `Cash Dispenser Interface` object provides an operation `dispense Cash`.

From a combined task and class structuring perspective (Figure 16.2d), there is one task, the `ATM Controller` task, which is structured as a composite task. It contains one coordinator object called the `ATM Coordinator`, which provides the overall coordination. When a new `ATM Control Request` arrives at the `ATM Controller`, it is received by the `ATM Coordinator`, which extracts the event from the request and calls `ATM Control.process Event` (**in** event, **out** action). `ATM Control` looks up the state transition table, given the current state and the new event. The entry in the table contains the new state

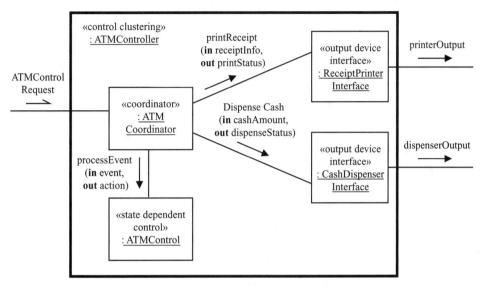

Figure 16.2d *Control clustering task with nested passive objects*

Figure 16.2 *Example of a control clustering task with passive objects (continued)*

and the action(s) to be performed. ATM Control returns the action to be performed. The ATM Coordinator then initiates the action. If the action is to dispense cash, it invokes the dispense Cash operation of the cash Dispenser Interface object, with the cash Amount as the input parameter and the dispense Status as the output parameter. If the action is to print the receipt, it invokes the print Receipt operation of the Receipt Printer Interface object, with the receipt Info as the input parameter and the print Status as the output parameter.

16.2 Synchronization of Access to Classes

If a class is accessed by more than one task, the class's operations must synchronize the access to the data it encapsulates. This section describes mechanisms for providing this synchronization. Synchronization using the mutual exclusion algorithm and the multiple readers and writers algorithm are described.

16.2.1   Example of Synchronization of Access to Class

As an example of synchronization of access to a class, consider a data abstraction class—the Analog Sensor Repository class, which encapsulates a sensor data repository. In designing this class, one design decision relates to whether the sensor data structure is to be designed as an array or a linked list. Another design decision relates to the nature of the synchronization required, whether an object of this class is to be accessed by more than one task concurrently, and—if so—whether mutual exclusion or the multiple readers & writers algorithm is required. These design decisions relate to the design of the class and need not concern users of the class.

By separating the concerns of **what** the class does—namely the specification of the operations—from **how** it does it—namely the internal design of the class—any changes to the internals of the class have no impact on users of the class. Possible changes are

- Changes to the internal data structure, for example, from array to linked list
- Changes to the internal synchronization of access to the data, for example, from mutual exclusion to multiple readers and writers

The impact of these changes is only on the internals of the class, namely, the internal data structure and the internals of the operations that access the data structure.

16.2.2   Operations Provided by Data Abstraction Class

For the same external interface of the Analog Sensor Repository data abstraction class, consider two different internal designs for the synchronization of access to the sensor data repository: mutual exclusion and multiple readers and writers.

In the sensor repository example, the Analog Sensor Repository data abstraction class provides the following two operations (see Figure 16.3).

```
readAnalogSensor (in sensorID, out sensorValue, out upperLimit,
out lowerLimit, out alarmCondition)
```

This operation is called by reader tasks that wish to read from the sensor data repository. Given the sensor ID, this operation returns the current sensor value, upper limit, lower limit, and alarm condition to users who might wish to manipulate or display the data. The range between the lower limit and upper limit is the

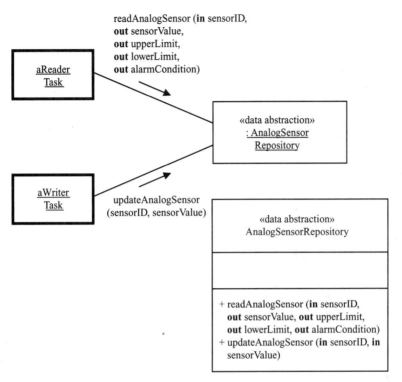

Figure 16.3 *Example of concurrent access to data abstraction object*

normal range within which the sensor value can vary without causing an alarm. If the value of the sensor is below the lower limit or above the upper limit, the alarm Condition is equal to low or high, respectively.

```
updateAnalogSensor (in sensorID, in sensorValue)
```

This operation is called by writer tasks that wish to write to the sensor data repository. It is used to update the value of the sensor in the data repository with the latest reading obtained by monitoring the external environment. It checks whether the value of the sensor is below the lower limit or above the upper limit, and sets the value of the alarm Condition to low or high, respectively. If the sensor value is within the normal range, the alarm Condition is set to normal.

16.2.3 Synchronization Using Mutual Exclusion

Consider first the mutual exclusion solution using a binary semaphore in which the acquire and release operations on the semaphore are provided by the operating system. To ensure mutual exclusion in the sensor repository example, each task must execute an **acquire** operation on the semaphore `read Write Semaphore` (initially set to 1) before it starts accessing the data repository. It must also execute a **release** operation on the semaphore after it has finished accessing the data repository. The Pseudocode for the `read` and `update` operations is as follows:

```
class AnalogSensorRepository
private readWriteSemaphore : Semaphore := 1
public readAnalogSensor (in sensorID, out sensorValue, out
upperLimit, out lowerLimit, out alarmCondition)
 -- Critical section for read operation.
 acquire (readWriteSemaphore);
 sensorValue := sensorDataRepository (sensorID, value);
 upperLimit := sensorDataRepository (sensorID, upLim);
 lowerLimit := sensorDataRepository (sensorID, loLim);
 alarmCondition := sensorDataRepository (sensorID, alarm);
 release(readWriteSemaphore);
end readAnalogSensor;
```

In the case of the `update` operation, in addition to updating the value of the sensor in the data repository, it is also necessary to determine whether the sensor's alarm condition is high, low, or normal.

```
public updateAnalogSensor (in sensorID, in sensorValue)
 -- Critical section for write operation.
 acquire (readWriteSemaphore);
 sensorDataRepository (sensorID, value) := sensorValue;
 if sensorValue ≥ sensorDataRepository (sensorID, upLim)
   then sensorDataRepository (sensorID, alarm) := high;
 elseif sensorValue ≤ sensorDataRepository (sensorID, loLim)
   then sensorDataRepository (sensorID, alarm) := low;
   else sensorDataRepository (sensorID, alarm) := normal;
 end if;
 release(readWriteSemaphore);
end updateAnalogSensor;
```

16.2.4 Synchronization of Multiple Readers and Writers

With the multiple readers and writers solution, multiple reader tasks may access the data repository concurrently, and writer tasks have mutually exclusive access to it. Two binary semaphores are used, `reader Semaphore` and `read Write`

Semaphore, which are both initially set to 1. A count of the number of readers, number Of Readers, is also maintained, initially set to 0. The reader Sema-phore is used by readers to ensure mutually exclusive updating of the reader count. Writers use the read Write Semaphore to ensure mutually exclusive access to the sensor data repository. This semaphore is also accessed by readers. It is acquired by the first reader prior to reading from the data repository and released by the last reader after having finished reading from the data repository. The Pseudocode for the read and update operations is as follows:

```
class AnalogSensorRepository
private numberOfReaders : Integer := 0;
 readerSemaphore: Semaphore := 1;
 readWriteSemaphore: Semaphore := 1;
public readAnalogSensor (in sensorID, out sensorValue, out
upperLimit, out lowerLimit, out alarmCondition)
 -- Read operation called by reader tasks. Several readers are
 -- allowed to access the data repository providing there is no
 -- writer accessing it.
 acquire (readerSemaphore);
 Increment numberOfReaders;
 if numberOfReaders = 1 then acquire (readWriteSemaphore);
 release (readerSemaphore);
 sensorValue := sensorDataRepository (sensorID, value);
 upperLimit := sensorDataRepository (sensorID, upLim);
 lowerLimit := sensorDataRepository (sensorID, loLim);
 alarmCondition := sensorDataRepository (sensorID, alarm);
 acquire (readerSemaphore);
 Decrement numberOfReaders;
 if numberOfReaders = 0 then release (readWriteSemaphore);
 release (readerSemaphore);
end readAnalogSensor;
```

The Pseudocode for the update operation is similar to that for the mutual exclusion example because it is necessary to ensure that writer tasks that call the update operation have mutually exclusive access to the sensor data repository.

```
public updateAnalogSensor (in sensorID, in sensorValue)
 -- Critical section for write operation.
 acquire (readWriteSemaphore);
 sensorDataRepository (sensorID, value) := sensorValue;
 if sensorValue ≥ sensorDataRepository (sensorID, upLim)
   then sensorDataRepository (sensorID, alarm) := high;
 elseif sensorValue ≤ sensorDataRepository (sensorID, loLim)
   then sensorDataRepository (sensorID, alarm) := low;
   else sensorDataRepository (sensorID, alarm) := normal;
```

```
  end if;
  release (readWriteSemaphore);
end updateAnalogSensor;
end AnalogSensorRepository;
```

This solution solves the problem; however, it intertwines the synchronization solution with the access to the data repository. It is possible to separate these two concerns, as described next.

16.2.5 Synchronization of Multiple Readers and Writers by Using a Monitor

This section describes a monitor solution to the multiple readers and writers problem. The characteristics of monitors are described in Chapter 3. Recall that the operations of a monitor are executed mutually exclusively; hence, a mutual exclusion solution to the Analog Sensor Repository problem can easily be achieved by using monitors, as illustrated in Chapter 3. However, a multiple readers and writers solution cannot use a monitor solution for the design of the Analog Sensor Repository class, because the read Analog Sensor operation needs to be executed by several readers concurrently. Instead, the synchronization aspects of the multiple readers and writers algorithm are encapsulated in a monitor, which is then used by the redesigned Analog Sensor Repository class. Two solutions to this problem are presented, the first providing the same functionality as the previous section. The second solution provides an added capability, that of preventing writer starvation.

A Read Write monitor is declared that uses two semaphore monitors and provides four mutually exclusive operations. The semaphores are the reader Semaphore and the read Write Semaphore (initialization of a semaphore is done by the monitor, as described in Chapter 3). The four mutually exclusive operations are the start Read, end Read, start Write, and end Write operations. A reader task calls the start Read operation before it starts reading and the end Read operation after it has finished reading. A writer task calls the start Write operation before it starts writing and the end Write operation after it has finished writing. The design of the semaphore monitor is described in Section 3.8.2. A semaphore monitor provides an acquire operation—which is called to first get hold of the resource and involves a possible delay if the resource is initially busy—and a release operation to signal the release of the resource.

The start Read operation has to first acquire the reader Semaphore, increment the number of readers, and then release the semaphore. If the reader count was zero, then start Read also has to acquire the read Write Semaphore, which is acquired by the first reader and released by the last reader. Although monitor operations are executed mutually exclusively, the reader Semaphore is still needed. This is because it is possible for the reader to be suspended, waiting for the read Write Semaphore semaphore, and hence release the Read Write monitor lock. If another reader now acquires the monitor lock by calling start Read or end Read, it would be suspended, waiting for the reader Semaphore.

The design of the Read Write monitor is described next:

```
monitor ReadWrite
 -- Design for multiple readers/single writer access to resource
 -- Declare an integer counter for the number of readers.
 -- Declare semaphore for accessing count of number of readers
 -- Declare a semaphore for mutually exclusive access to buffer
private numberOfReaders : Integer = 0;
readerSemaphore: Semaphore;
readWriteSemaphore: Semaphore;

public startRead ()
 -- A reader calls this operation before it starts to read
 readerSemaphore.acquire;
 if numberOfReaders = 0 then readWriteSemaphore.acquire ();
 Increment numberOfReaders;
 readerSemaphore.release;
end startRead;

public endRead ()
 -- A reader calls this operation after it has finished reading
 readerSemaphore.acquire;
 Decrement numberOfReaders;
 if numberOfReaders = 0 then readWriteSemaphore.release ();
 readerSemaphore.release;
end endRead;

public startWrite ()
 -- A writer calls this operation before it starts to write
 readWriteSemaphore.acquire ();
end startRead;

public endWrite ()
 -- A writer calls this operation after it has finished writing
 readWriteSemaphore.release ();
end endWrite;
end ReadWrite;
```

To take advantage of the Read Write monitor, the Analog Sensor Repository is now redesigned to declare its own private instance of the Read Write monitor. The read analog Sensor operation now calls the start Read operation of the monitor before reading from the repository and calls the end Read operation after finishing reading. The update Analog Sensor operation calls the start Write operation of the monitor before updating the repository and calls the end Write operation after completing the update.

```
class AnalogSensorRepository
private multiReadSingleWrite : ReadWrite
public readAnalogSensor (in sensorID, out sensorValue, out
upperLimit, out lowerLimit, out alarmCondition)
 multiReadSingleWrite.startRead();
 sensorValue := sensorDataRepository (sensorID, value);
 upperLimit := sensorDataRepository (sensorID, upLim);
 lowerLimit := sensorDataRepository (sensorID, loLim);
 alarmCondition := sensorDataRepository (sensorID, alarm);
 multiReadSingleWrite.endRead();
end readAnalogSensor;

public updateAnalogSensor (in sensorID, in sensorValue)
 -- Critical section for write operation.
 multiReadSingleWrite.startWrite();
 sensorDataRepository (sensorID, value) := sensorValue;
 if sensorValue ≥ sensorDataRepository (sensorID, upLim)
   then sensorDataRepository (sensorID, alarm) := high;
 elseif sensorValue ≤ sensorDataRepository (sensorID, loLim)
   then sensorDataRepository (sensorID, alarm) := low;
   else sensorDataRepository (sensorID, alarm) := normal;
 end if;
 multiReadSingleWrite.endWrite();
end updateAnalogSensor;
end AnalogSensorRepository;
```

16.2.6   Synchronization of Multiple Readers and Writers without Writer Starvation

The previous solution to this problem has a limitation in that a busy reader population could indefinitely prevent a writer from accessing the buffer, a problem referred to as "writer starvation." The following monitor solution prevents this problem by adding a writer Waiting semaphore. The start Write operation now acquires the writer Waiting semaphore before acquiring the read Write semaphore. The start Read operation acquires (and then releases) the writer Waiting semaphore before acquiring the reader Semaphore.

The reason for these changes is explained in the following scenario. Assume that several readers are reading and a writer now attempts to write. It successfully acquires the writer Waiting semaphore but is then suspended while trying to acquire the read Write semaphore, which is held by the readers. If a new reader tries to read from the buffer, it calls start Read and is then suspended, waiting to acquire the writer Waiting semaphore. Gradually, the current readers will finish reading until the last reader reduces the reader count to zero and releases the read Write semaphore. The semaphore is now acquired by the waiting writer, which releases the writer Waiting semaphore, thereby allowing a reader or writer to acquire the semaphore. The monitor solution is given next—compared with the previous solution, the start Read and start Write operations have changed.

```
monitor ReadWrite
  -- Prevent writer starvation by adding new semaphore.
  -- Design for multiple readers/single writer access to resource.
  -- Declare an integer counter for the number of readers.
  -- Declare semaphore for accessing count of number of readers
  -- Declare a semaphore for mutually exclusive access to buffer
  -- Declare a semaphore for writer waiting
private numberOfReaders : Integer = 0
  readerSemaphore: Semaphore
  readWriteSemaphore: Semaphore
  writerWaitingSemaphore: Semaphore

public startRead ()
  -- A reader calls this operation before it starts to read
  writerWaitingSemaphore.acquire
  writerWaitingSemaphore.release
  readerSemaphore.acquire;
  if numberOfReaders = 0 then readWriteSemaphore.acquire ();
  Increment numberOfReaders;
  readerSemaphore.release;
end startRead;

public endRead ()
  -- A reader calls this operation after it has finished reading
  readerSemaphore.acquire;
  Decrement numberOfReaders;
  if numberOfReaders = 0 then readWriteSemaphore.release ();
  readerSemaphore.release;
end endRead;

public startWrite ()
  -- A writer calls this operation before it starts to write
  writerWaitingSemaphore.acquire();
```

```
    readWriteSemaphore.acquire ();
    writerWaitingSemaphore.release();
    end startRead;

    public endWrite ()
    -- A writer calls this operation after it has finished writing
    readWriteSemaphore.release ();
    end endWrite;
    end ReadWrite;
```

No change is required in the design of the Analog Sensor Repository class to take advantage of this variant.

16.3   Designing Connectors for Inter-Task Communication

Connector classes encapsulate the details of inter-task communication, such as loosely and tightly coupled message communication. A multi-tasking kernel can provide services for inter-task communication and synchronization. Some concurrent programming languages such as Ada and Java provide mechanisms for inter-task communication and synchronization. Neither of these languages supports loosely coupled message communication. To provide this capability, it is necessary to design a Message Queue information hiding class, which encapsulates a message queue and provides operations to access the queue. This kind of information hiding class is categorized as a **connector** class.

This section describes the design of three connectors to handle loosely coupled message communication, tightly coupled message communication without reply, and tightly coupled message communication with reply. Each connector is designed as a monitor, which combines the concepts of information hiding and task synchronization as described in Chapter 3. The connectors also use *condition synchronization*, as described in Section 3.8.2. These monitors are used in a single processor or multiprocessor system with shared memory.

16.3.1   Design of Message Queue Connector

A message queue connector is used to encapsulate the communication mechanism for **loosely coupled message communication**. The connector is designed as a monitor that encapsulates a message queue, usually implemented as a linked list. The connector provides synchronized operations to send a message, which is called by a producer task, and receive a message, which is called by a consumer task (see Figure 16.4). The producer is suspended if the queue is full (messageCount

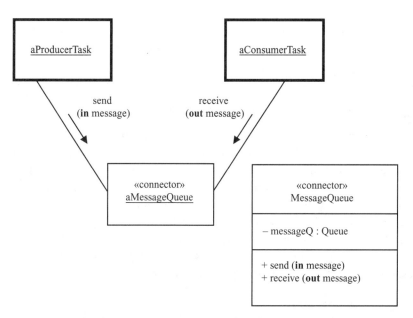

Figure 16.4   *Example of message queue connector*

= maxCount). The producer is reactivated when a slot becomes available to accept the message. After adding the message to the queue, the producer continues executing and might send additional messages. The consumer is suspended if the message queue is empty (messageCount = 0). When a new message arrives, the consumer is activated and given the message. The consumer is not suspended if there is a message on the queue. It is assumed that there can be several producers and one consumer.

```
monitor MessageQueue
  -- Encapsulate message queue that holds max of maxCount messages
  -- Monitor operations are executed mutually exclusively;
private maxCount : Integer;
private messageCount : Integer := 0;
public send (in message)
 while messageCount = maxCount do wait;
 place message in buffer;
 Increment messageCount;
 if messageCount = 1 then signal;
end send;

public receive (out message)
 while messageCount = 0 do wait;
```

```
remove message from buffer;
Decrement messageCount;
if messageCount = maxCount-1 then signal;
end receive;
end MessageQueue;
```

16.3.2   Design of Message Buffer Connector

A message buffer connector is used to encapsulate the communication mechanism for **tightly coupled message communication without reply**. The connector is designed as a monitor that encapsulates a single message buffer and provides synchronized operations to send a message and receive a message (see Figure 16.5). The producer task calls the send operation and the consumer task calls the receive operation. The producer is suspended if the buffer is full. After it has written the message into the buffer, the producer is suspended until the consumer receives the message. The consumer is suspended if the message buffer is empty. It is assumed that there is only one producer and one consumer.

```
monitor MessageBuffer
  -- Encapsulate a message buffer that holds at most one message.
  -- Monitor operations are executed mutually exclusively
```

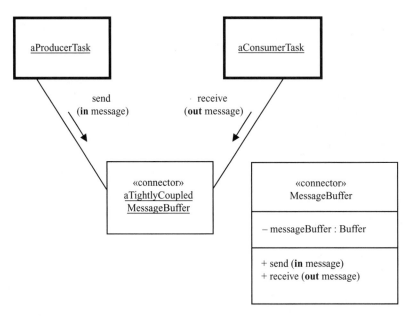

Figure 16.5   *Example of message buffer connector*

```
private messageBufferFull : Boolean := false;
public send (in message)
 place message in buffer;
 messageBufferFull := true;
 signal;
 while messageBufferFull = true do wait;
end send;

public receive (out message)
 while messageBufferFull = false do wait;
 remove message from buffer;
 messageBufferFull := false;
 signal;
end receive;
end MessageBuffer;
```

16.3.3 Design of Message Buffer & Response Connector

A message buffer and response connector is used to encapsulate the communication mechanism for **tightly coupled message communication with reply**. The connector is designed as a monitor that encapsulates a single message buffer and a single response buffer. It provides synchronized operations to send a message, receive a message, and send a reply (see Figure 16.6). The producer calls the send message operation, and the consumer calls the receive message and send reply operations. After it has written the message into the buffer, the producer is suspended until the response is received from the consumer. The consumer is suspended if the message buffer is empty. It is assumed that there is only one producer and one consumer.

```
monitor MessageBuffer&Response
  -- Encapsulates a message buffer that holds at most one message
  -- and a response buffer that holds at most one response.
  -- Monitor operations are executed mutually exclusively.
private messageBufferFull : Boolean = false;
private responseBufferFull : Boolean = false;
public send (in message, out response)
 place message in buffer;
 messageBufferFull := true;
 signal;
 while responseBufferFull = false do wait;
 remove response from response buffer;
 responseBufferFull := false;
end send;
```

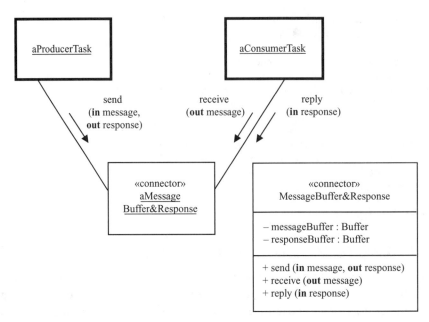

Figure 16.6 *Example of message buffer and response connector*

```
public receive (out message)
 while messageBufferFull = false do wait;
 remove message from buffer;
 messageBufferFull := false;
end receive;

public reply (in response)
 Place response in response buffer;
 responseBufferFull := true;
 signal;
end reply;
end MessageBuffer&Response;
```

16.3.4 Design of Cooperating Tasks Using Connectors

Next, consider the design of a group of cooperating tasks that communicate by means of connector objects. This is illustrated by means of an example taken from the ATM Client subsystem of the Banking System case study. The connectors for the ATM Client subsystem are depicted on Figure 16.7; there are two message queue connectors and one message buffer connector.

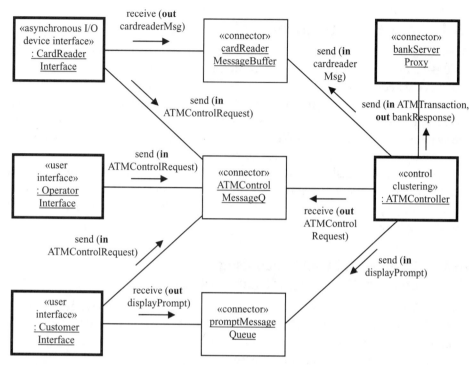

Figure 16.7 *Example of cooperating tasks using connectors*

The ATM Control Message Q encapsulates the queue of input messages to the ATM Controller task, for which there are several producers. The prompt Message Queue encapsulates the queue of messages sent by the ATM Controller to the Customer Interface task. In each case, a producer calls the send operation of the message queue connector object, and the consumer calls the receive operation. There is also a card Reader Message Buffer connector object to encapsulate the synchronous communication without reply between the ATM Controller and the Card Reader Interface task.

Finally, there is a bank Server Proxy connector object, which acts as a proxy for the Bank Server. This connector hides the details of how to communicate with the remote Bank Server by using synchronous communication with reply. For example, in Java, the proxy would use a remote method invocation interface, as described in Chapter 4.

16.4 Task Event Sequencing Logic

During the detailed software design, the task event sequencing logic section of the Task Behavior Specification, originally defined in Chapter 14, is specified. The task's **event sequencing logic** describes how the task responds to each of its message or event inputs—in particular, what output is generated as a result of each input. The event sequencing logic is described informally in Pseudocode or in Precise English and may be supplemented by a diagram—for example, to define a state transition diagram for a control task.

For a composite task with several nested objects, a nested coordinator object receives the task's incoming messages and then invokes operations provided by other nested objects. In such cases, the coordinator object executes the task's event sequencing logic.

16.4.1 Example of Event Sequencing Logic for Sender and Receiver Tasks

The event sequencing logic for a sender task, which sends messages to other tasks, is given next. The exact form of the send (message) will depend on whether this is a service provided by the operating system or whether it uses a connector, as described in the previous section.

```
loop
  Prepare message containing message name (type) and optional
  message parameters;
  send (message) to receiver;
endloop;
```

The event sequencing logic for a receiver task, which receives incoming messages from other tasks, is

```
loop
  receive (message) from sender;
  Extract message name and any message parameters from message
  case message of
   message type 1:
     objectA.operationX (optional parameters);
     ....
   message type 2:
     objectB.operationY (optional parameters);
  .....
   endcase;
endloop;
```

If a connector called a `Connector` is used, the send message becomes

```
aConnector.send (message)
```

and the receive message becomes

```
aConnector.receive (message)
```

Several examples of task event sequencing logic are given for tasks in the Banking System case study described in Chapter 19. The event sequencing logic for the `Bank Server`, `Card Reader Interface`, and `ATM Controller` tasks are described.

16.5   Summary

After structuring the system into tasks (in Chapter 14) and designing the information hiding classes (in Chapter 15), this chapter has described the detailed software design. In this step, the internals of composite tasks that contain nested objects are designed, detailed task synchronization issues are addressed, connector classes are designed that encapsulate the details of inter-task communication, and each task's internal event sequencing logic is defined. Several examples were given in Pseudocode of the detailed design of task synchronization mechanisms, connector classes for inter-task communication, and task event sequencing logic.

Performance Analysis of Concurrent Real-Time Software Designs

P erformance analysis of software designs is particularly important for real-time systems. The consequences of a real-time system failing to meet a deadline can be catastrophic.

Quantitative analysis of a real-time system design allows the early detection of potential performance problems. The analysis is for the software design conceptually executing on a given hardware configuration with a given external workload applied to it. Early detection of potential performance problems allows alternative software designs and hardware configurations to be investigated.

This chapter describes performance analysis of software designs by applying real-time scheduling theory. Real-time scheduling is a particularly appropriate approach for hard real-time systems that have deadlines that must be met [Sha and Goodenough 1990]. With this approach, the real-time design is analyzed to determine whether it can meet its deadlines.

This chapter describes two approaches for analyzing the performance of a design. The first approach uses **real-time scheduling theory**, and the second uses **event sequence analysis**. The two approaches are then combined. Both real-time scheduling theory and event sequence analysis are applied to a design consisting of a set of concurrent tasks. Consequently, the performance analysis can start as soon as the task architecture has been designed, as described in Chapter 14.

17.1 Real-Time Scheduling Theory

Real-time scheduling theory addresses the issues of priority-based scheduling of concurrent tasks with hard deadlines. The theory addresses how to determine whether a group of tasks, whose individual CPU utilization is known, will meet their deadlines. The theory assumes a priority preemption scheduling algorithm, as described in Chapter 4. This section is based on the reports and book on real-time scheduling produced at the Software Engineering Institute [Sha and Goodenough 1990, SEI 1993], which should be referenced for more information on this topic.

As real-time scheduling theory has evolved, it has gradually been applied to more complicated scheduling problems. Problems that have been addressed include scheduling independent periodic tasks, scheduling in situations where there are both periodic and aperiodic (asynchronous) tasks, and scheduling in cases where task synchronization is required.

17.1.1 Scheduling Periodic Tasks

Initially, real-time scheduling algorithms were developed for independent periodic tasks—that is, periodic tasks that do not communicate or synchronize with each other [Liu 1973]. Since then, the theory has been developed considerably so it can now be applied to practical problems, as will be illustrated in the examples. In this chapter, it is necessary to start with the basic rate monotonic theory for independent periodic tasks to understand how it has been extended to address more complex situations.

A periodic task has a period T (the frequency with which it executes) and an execution time C (the CPU time required during the period). Its CPU utilization U is the ratio C/T. A task is schedulable if all its deadlines are met, that is, if the task completes its execution before its period elapses. A group of tasks is considered schedulable if each task can meet its deadlines.

For a set of independent periodic tasks, the **rate monotonic algorithm** assigns each task a fixed priority based on its period, such that the shorter the period of a task, the higher its priority. Consider three tasks t_a, t_b, and t_c, with periods 10, 20, 30, respectively. The highest priority is given to t_a, the task with the shortest period; the medium priority is given to task t_b; and the lowest priority is given to t_c, the task with the longest period.

17.1.2 Utilization Bound Theorem

According to the rate monotonic scheduling theory, a group of n independent periodic tasks can be shown to always meet their deadlines, providing the sum of the ratios C/T for each task is below an upper bound of overall CPU utilization.

The **Utilization Bound Theorem** [Liu 1973] states that:

Utilization Bound Theorem (Theorem 1):
A set of n independent periodic tasks scheduled by the rate monotonic algorithm will always meet its deadlines for all task phasings, if:

$$\frac{C_1}{T_1} + \ldots + \frac{C_n}{T_n} \le n(2^{1/n} - 1) = U(n)$$

where C_i and T_i are the execution time and period of task t_i, respectively.

The upper bound $U(n)$ converges to 69 percent (ln 2) as the number of tasks approaches infinity. The utilization bounds for up to nine tasks, according to the Utilization Bound Theorem, are given in Table 17.1. This is a worst-case approximation, and for a randomly chosen group of tasks, Lehoczky, Sha, and Ding [1989] showed that the likely upper bound is 88 percent. For tasks with harmonic periods—that is, with periods that are multiples of each other—the upper bound is even higher.

The rate monotonic algorithm has the advantage of being stable in conditions where there is a transient overload. In other words, a subset of the total number of tasks—namely, those with the highest priorities (and hence, shortest periods)—will still meet their deadlines if the system is overloaded for a relatively short time. The lower priority tasks, namely those with longer periods, might occasionally miss their deadlines as the processor load increases.

As an example of applying the Utilization Bound Theorem, consider three tasks with the following characteristics, where all times are in milliseconds and the utilization $U_i = C_i/T_i$:

Task t_1: $C_1 = 20$; $T_1 = 100$; $U_1 = 0.2$

Task t_2: $C_2 = 30$; $T_2 = 150$; $U_2 = 0.2$

Task t_3: $C_3 = 60$; $T_3 = 200$; $U_3 = 0.3$

Table 17.1   *Utilization Bound Theorem*

Number of Tasks n	Utilization Bound U(n)
1	1.000
2	0.828
3	0.779
4	0.756
5	0.743
6	0.734
7	0.728
8	0.724
9	0.720
Infinity	0.690

It is assumed that the context switching overhead, once at the start of the task's execution and once at the end of its execution, is included in the CPU times.

The total utilization of the three tasks is 0.7, which is below 0.779, the Utilization Bound Theorem's upper bound for three tasks. Thus, the three tasks can meet their deadlines in all cases.

However, consider that the task t_3's characteristics are instead as follows:

Task t_3: $C_3 = 90$; $T_3 = 200$; $U_3 = 0.45$

In this case, the total utilization of the three tasks is 0.85, which is higher than 0.779, the Utilization Bound Theorem's upper bound for three tasks. Thus, the Utilization Bound Theorem indicates that the tasks do not meet their deadlines. Next, a check is made to determine whether the first two tasks can meet their deadlines.

Given that the rate monotonic algorithm is stable, the first two tasks can be checked by using the Utilization Bound Theorem. The utilization of these two tasks is 0.4, well below the Utilization Bound Theorem's upper bound for two tasks of 0.828. Thus, the first two tasks always meet their deadlines. Given that the Utilization Bound Theorem is a pessimistic theorem, a further check can be made to determine whether Task t_3 can meet its deadlines by applying the more exact Completion Time Theorem.

17.1.3   Completion Time Theorem

If a set of tasks have a utilization greater than the Utilization Bound Theorem's upper bound, the Completion Time Theorem, which gives a more exact schedulability criterion [Lehoczky, Sha, and Ding 1989], can be checked. For a set of independent periodic tasks, the Completion Time Theorem provides an exact determination of whether the tasks are schedulable. The theorem assumes a worst case of all the periodic tasks ready to execute at the same time. It has been shown that in this worst case, if a task completes execution before the end of its first period, it will never miss a deadline [Liu and Layland 1973; Lehoczky, Sha, and Ding 1989]. The Completion Time Theorem therefore checks whether each task can complete execution before the end of its first period.

> **Completion Time Theorem (Theorem 2):**
> **For a set of independent periodic tasks, if each task meets its first deadline when all tasks are started at the same time, the deadlines will be met for any combination of start times.**

To do this, it is necessary to check the end of the first period of a given task t_i, as well as the end of all periods of higher priority tasks. Following the rate monotonic theory, these tasks will have shorter periods than t_i. These periods are referred to as scheduling points. Task t_i will execute once for a CPU amount of C_i during its period T_i. However, higher priority tasks will execute more often and can preempt t_i at least once. It is therefore necessary to consider the CPU time used up by the higher priority tasks as well.

The Completion Time Theorem can be illustrated graphically with a **timing diagram**, a diagram that shows the time-ordered execution sequence of a group of tasks. Consider the example given earlier of the three tasks with the following characteristics:

Task t_1: $C_1 = 20$; $T_1 = 100$; $U_1 = 0.2$

Task t_2: $C_2 = 30$; $T_2 = 150$; $U_2 = 0.2$

Task t_3: $C_3 = 90$; $T_3 = 200$; $U_3 = 0.45$

The execution of the three tasks is illustrated by the timing diagram shown in Figure 17.1. In COMET, the timing diagram is a time-annotated **sequence diagram**, based on the UML sequence diagram. The tasks are shown as active throughout, with the shaded portions identifying when tasks are executing. Because there is one CPU in this example, only one task can execute at any one time.

Given the worst case of the three tasks being ready to execute at the same time, t_1 executes first because it has the shortest period and hence the highest priority. It completes after 20 msec, after which the task t_2 executes for 30 msec. On completion of t_2, t_3 executes. At the end of the first scheduling point, $T_1 = 100$, which corresponds to t_1's deadline; t_1 has already completed execution and thus met its deadline. Task t_2 has also completed execution and easily met its deadline, and t_3 has executed for 50 msec out of the necessary 90.

At the start of task t_1's second period, t_3 is preempted by task t_1. After executing for 20 msec, t_1 completes and relinquishes the CPU to task t_3 again. Task t_3 executes until the end of period T_2 (150 msec), which represents the second scheduling point due to t_2's deadline. Because t_2 completed before T_1 (which is less than T_2) elapsed, it easily met its deadline. At this time, t_3 has used up 80 msec out of the necessary 90.

Task t_3 is preempted by task t_2 at the start of t_2's second period. After executing for 30 msec, t_2 completes, relinquishing the CPU to task t_3 again. Task t_3 executes for another 10 msec, at which time it has used up all its CPU time of 90 msec, thereby completing before its deadline. Figure 17.1 shows the third scheduling point, which is both the end of t_1's second period ($2T_1 = 200$) and the end of t_3's first period ($T_3 = 200$). Figure 17.1 also shows that each of the three tasks

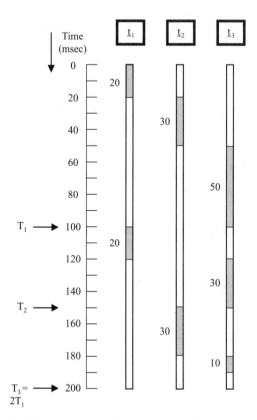

NB: UML notation for sequence diagram has been extended for this figure.

Figure 17.1 *Timing diagram (time-annotated sequence diagram)*

completes execution before the end of its first period, thus they successfully meet their deadline.

Figure 17.1 shows that the CPU is idle for 10 msec before the start of t_1's third period (also the start of t_3's second period). It should be noted that a total CPU time of 190 msec was used up over the 200 msec period, giving a CPU utilization for this 200 msec period of 0.95, although the overall utilization is 0.85. After an elapsed time equal to the least common multiple of the three periods (600 msec in this example) the utilization averages out to 0.85.

17.1.4 Mathematical Formulation of Completion Time Theorem

The Completion Time Theorem can be expressed mathematically in Theorem 3 [Sha and Goodenough 1990] as follows:

Mathematical Formulation of Completion Time Theorem (Theorem 3):
A set of n independent periodic tasks scheduled by the rate monotonic algorithm will always meet its deadlines for all task phasings, if and only if:

$$\forall i, 1 \leq i \leq n, \min \sum_{j=1}^{i} C_j \frac{1}{pT_k} \left\lceil \frac{pT_k}{T_j} \right\rceil \leq 1$$
$$(k, p) \in R_i$$

where C_j and T_j are the execution time and period of task t_j respectively and $R_i = \{(k, p) | 1 \leq k \leq i, p = 1, \ldots, \lfloor T_i/T_k \rfloor \}$.

In the formula, t_i denotes the task to be checked and t_k denotes each of the higher priority tasks that impact the completion time of task t_i. For a given task t_i and a given task t_k, each value of p represents a scheduling point of task t_k. At each scheduling point, it is necessary to consider task t_i's CPU time C_i once, as well as the CPU time used by the higher priority tasks. Hence, you can determine whether t_i can complete its execution by that scheduling point.

Consider Theorem 3 applied to the three tasks, which were illustrated with the timing diagram in Figure 17.1. The timing diagram is a graphical representation of what Theorem 3 computes. Again, the worst case is considered of the three tasks being ready to execute at the same time. The inequality for the first scheduling point, $T_1 = 100$, is given from Theorem 3:

$C_1 + C_2 + C_3 \leq T_1$ $20 + 30 + 90 > 100$ $p = 1, k = 1$

For this inequality to be satisfied, all three tasks would need to complete execution within the first task t_1's period T_1. This is not the case, because before t_3 completes, it is preempted by t_1 at the start of t_1's second period.

The inequality for the second scheduling point, $T_2 = 150$, is given from Theorem 3:

$2C_1 + C_2 + C_3 \leq T_2$ $40 + 30 + 90 > 150$ $p = 1, k = 2$

For this inequality to be satisfied, task t_1 would need to complete execution twice and tasks t_2 and t3 would each need to complete execution once within the second task t_2's period T_2. This is not the case, because t_3 is preempted by task t_2 at the start of t_2's second period.

The inequality for the third scheduling point, which is both the end of t_1's second period ($2T_1 = 200$) and the end of t_3's first period ($T_3 = 200$), is given from Theorem 3:

$2C_1 + 2C_2 + C_3 \leq 2T_1 = T_3$ $40 + 60 + 90 < 200$ $p = 2, k = 1$ or $p = 1, k = 3$

This time the inequality is satisfied and all three tasks meet their deadlines. As long as all three tasks meet at least one of the scheduling point deadlines, the tasks are schedulable.

17.1.5   Scheduling Periodic and Aperiodic Tasks

When dealing with aperiodic (asynchronous) tasks as well as periodic tasks, the rate monotonic theory needs to be extended. An **aperiodic task** is assumed to arrive randomly and execute once within some period T_a, which represents the minimum inter-arrival time of the event that activates the task. The CPU time C_a used by the aperiodic task to process the event is reserved as a ticket of value C_a for each period T_a. When the event arrives, the aperiodic task is activated, claims its ticket, and consumes up to C_a units of CPU time. If the task is not activated during the period T_a, the ticket is discarded. Thus, based on these assumptions, the CPU utilization of the aperiodic task is C_a/T_a. However, this represents the worst-case CPU utilization because, in general, reserved tickets are not always claimed.

If there are many aperiodic tasks in the application, the *sporadic server algorithm* [Sprunt, Lehoczy, and Sha 1989] can be used. From a schedulability analysis viewpoint, an aperiodic task (referred to as the sporadic server) is equivalent to a periodic task whose period is equal to the minimum inter-arrival time of the events that activate the aperiodic task. Hence T_a, the minimum inter-arrival time for an aperiodic task t_a can be considered the period of an equivalent periodic task. Each aperiodic task is also allocated a budget of C_a units of CPU time, which can be used up at any time during its equivalent period T_a. In this way, aperiodic tasks can be placed at different priority levels according to their equivalent periods and treated as periodic tasks.

17.1.6   Scheduling with Task Synchronization

Real-time scheduling theory has also been extended to address task synchronization. The problem here is that a task that enters a critical section can block other, higher priority tasks that wish to enter the critical section. The term **priority inversion** is used to refer to the case where a low priority task prevents a higher priority task from executing, typically by acquiring a resource needed by the latter.

Unbounded priority inversion can occur because the lower priority task, while in its critical section, could itself be blocked by other higher priority tasks. One solution to this problem is to prevent preemption of tasks while in their critical sections. This is acceptable only if tasks have very short critical sections. For long critical sections, lower priority tasks could block higher priority tasks that do need to access the shared resource.

The **priority ceiling protocol** [Sha and Goodenough 1990] avoids mutual deadlock and provides bounded priority inversion; that is one lower priority task, at most, can block a higher priority task. Only the simplest case of one critical section is considered here.

Adjustable priorities are used to prevent lower priority tasks from holding up higher priority tasks for an arbitrarily long time. While a low priority task t_l is in its critical section, higher priority tasks can become blocked by it because they wish to acquire the same resource. If that happens, t_l's priority is increased to the highest priority of all the tasks blocked by it. The goal is to speed up the execution of the lower priority task so blocking time for higher priority tasks is reduced.

The priority ceiling P of a **binary semaphore** S is the highest priority of all tasks that may acquire the semaphore. Thus, a low priority task that acquires S can have its priority increased up to P, depending on what higher priority tasks it blocks.

Another case that could occur is **deadlock**, where two tasks each need to acquire two resources before they can complete. If each task acquires one resource, neither will be able to complete, because each one is waiting for the other to release its resource—a deadlock situation. The priority ceiling protocol overcomes this problem [Sha and Goodenough 1990].

The rate monotonic scheduling theorems need to be extended to address the priority inversion problem, as described in the next section.

17.2   Advanced Real-Time Scheduling Theory

In real-world problems, situations often arise where the rate monotonic assumptions do not hold. There are many practical cases where tasks have to execute at actual priorities different from their rate monotonic priorities. It is therefore necessary to extend the basic rate monotonic scheduling theory to address these cases. One case is given in the previous section concerning lower priority tasks blocking higher priority tasks from entering critical sections.

A second case often happens when there are aperiodic tasks. As discussed in Section 17.1.5, aperiodic tasks can be treated as periodic tasks, with the worst-case inter-arrival time considered the equivalent periodic task's period. Following the rate monotonic scheduling algorithm, if the aperiodic task has a longer period than a periodic task, it should execute at a lower priority than the periodic task. However, if the aperiodic task is interrupt-driven, it will need to execute as soon as the interrupt arrives, even if its worst-case interarrival time, and hence equivalent period, is longer than that of the periodic task.

17.2.1 Priority Inversion

The term **priority inversion** is given to any case where a task cannot execute because it is blocked by a lower priority task. In the case of rate monotonic priority inversion, the term "priority" refers to the *rate monotonic priority*; that is, the priority assigned a task based entirely on the length of its period and not on its relative importance. A task may be assigned an actual priority that is different from the rate monotonic priority. *Rate monotonic priority inversion* refers to a task A preempted by a higher priority task B, when in fact task B's rate monotonic priority is lower than A's (i.e., B's period is longer than A's).

This is illustrated by the following example of rate monotonic priority inversion, in which there is a periodic task with a period of 25 msec and an interrupt-driven task with a worst-case interarrival time of 50 msec. The periodic task has the higher rate monotonic priority because it has the shorter period; however, in practice, giving the interrupt-driven task the higher actual priority is preferable so it can service the interrupt as soon as it arrives. Whenever the interrupt-driven task preempts the periodic task, this is considered a case of priority inversion relative to the rate monotonic priority assignment, because if the interrupt-driven task had been given its rate monotonic priority, it would not have preempted the periodic task.

It is necessary to extend the basic rate monotonic scheduling theory to address these practical cases of rate monotonic priority inversion. This has been achieved by extending the basic algorithms to take into account the blocking effect from lower priority tasks as well as preemption by higher priority tasks that do not observe rate monotonic priorities [SEI 1993]. Because rate monotonic scheduling theory assumes rate monotonic priorities, preemption by higher priority tasks that do not observe the rate monotonic priorities is treated in a similar way to blocking by lower priority tasks.

Consider a task t_i with a period T_i during which it consumes C_i units of CPU time. The extensions to Theorems 1–3 mean it is necessary to consider explicitly each task t_i to determine whether it can meet its first deadline. In particular, four factors need to be considered for each task:

a. **Preemption time by higher priority tasks with periods less than t_i.** These tasks can preempt t_i many times. Call this set H_n and let there be j tasks in this set. Let C_j be the CPU time for task j and T_j the period of task j, where $T_j < T_i$, the period of task t_i. The utilization of a task j in the H_n set is given by C_j/T_j.

b. **Execution time for the task t_i.** Task t_i executes once during its period T_i and consumes C_i units of CPU time.

c. **Preemption by higher priority tasks with longer periods.** These are tasks with non-rate monotonic priorities. They can only preempt t_i once, because they have longer periods than t_i. Call this set H_1 and let there be k tasks in this set. Let the CPU time used by a task in this set be C_k. The worst-case utilization of a task k in the H_1 set is given by C_k/T_i, because this means k preempts t_i and uses up all its CPU time C_k during the period T_i.

d. **Blocking time by lower priority tasks, as described in the previous section.** These tasks can also execute only once, because they have longer periods. Blocking delays have to be analyzed on an individual basis for each task to determine its worst-case blocking situation as given by the priority ceiling protocol. If B_i is the worst case blocking time for a given task t_i, the worst case blocking utilization for the period T_i is B_i/T_i.

17.2.2 Generalized Utilization Bound Theorem

Because for any given task t_i, factors a and b of the preceding paragraph are taken care of by Theorems 1–3, the generalization of these theorems is necessary to take into account factors c and d. Theorem 1, the **Utilization Bound Theorem**, is extended to address all four factors described in the preceding paragraph as follows:

Generalized Utilization Bound Theorem (Theorem 4):

$$U_i = \left(\sum_{j \in H_n} \frac{C_j}{T_j} \right) + \frac{1}{T_i} \left(C_i + B_i + \sum_{k \in H_1} C_k \right)$$

U_i is the utilization bound during a period T_i for task t_i. The first term in the Generalized Utilization Bound Theorem is the total preemption utilization by higher priority tasks with periods of less than t_i. The second term is the CPU utilization by task t_i. The third term is the worst-case blocking utilization experienced by t_i. The fourth term is the total preemption utilization by higher priority tasks with longer periods than t_i.

By substituting the values in the equation for Theorem 4, the utilization U_i can be determined for a given task. If U_i is less than the worst-case upper bound, this means the task t_i will meet its deadline. It is important to realize that the utilization bound test needs to be applied to each task, because in this generalized theory, where rate monotonic priorities are not necessarily observed, the fact that a given task meets its deadline is no guarantee that a higher priority task will meet its deadline.

17.2.3 Generalized Completion Time Theorem

As before, if the Generalized Utilization Bound Theorem fails, a more precise test is available that verifies whether each task can complete execution during its period. This is a generalization of the **Completion Time Theorem**. The **Generalized**

Completion Time Theorem determines whether t_i can complete execution by the end of its period, given preemption by higher priority tasks and blocking by lower priority tasks. The theorem assumes the worst case that all tasks are ready for execution at the start of the task t_i's period. Pictorially, the **Generalized Completion Time Theorem** can be illustrated by drawing a timing diagram for all the tasks up to the end of task t_i's period T_i.

17.2.4   Real-Time Scheduling and Design

Real-time scheduling theory can be applied to a set of concurrent tasks at the design stage or after the tasks have been implemented. In this book, the emphasis is on applying real-time scheduling theory at the design stage. During design, because all CPU times are estimates, it is best to err on the side of caution. For real-time tasks with hard deadlines, it is therefore safer to rely only on the more pessimistic **Utilization Bound Theorem**. This theorem has a worst-case upper bound utilization of 0.69, although the real-time scheduling theory frequently predicts upper bounds higher than this. If this worst-case upper bound cannot be satisfied, alternative solutions should be investigated. From a pessimistic designer's perspective, a predicted upper bound utilization of higher than 0.69 is acceptable, providing the utilization above 0.69 is entirely due to lower priority soft real-time or non-real-time tasks. For these tasks to miss their deadlines occasionally is not serious.

It is also the case at design time that the designer has the freedom to choose the priorities to be assigned to the tasks. In general, wherever possible, priorities should be assigned according to the rate monotonic theory. This is most easily applied to the periodic tasks. Estimate the worst-case inter-arrival times for the aperiodic tasks, and attempt to assign the rate monotonic priorities to these tasks. Interrupt-driven tasks will often need to be given the highest priorities to allow them to quickly service interrupts. This means that an interrupt-driven task may need to be allocated a priority that is higher than its rate monotonic priority. If two tasks have the same period and hence the same rate monotonic priority, it is up to the designer to resolve the tie. In general, assign the higher priority to the task that is more important from an application perspective.

17.2.5   Example of Applying Generalized Real-Time Scheduling Theory

As an example of applying the generalized real-time scheduling theory, consider the following case. There are four tasks, of which two are periodic and two are aperiodic. One of the aperiodic tasks, t_a, is interrupt-driven and must execute within 200 msec of the arrival of its interrupt or data will be lost. The other aperiodic task, t_2, has a worst-case interarrival time of T_2, which is taken to be the period of the equivalent periodic task. The detailed characteristics are as follows, where all times are in msec and the utilization $U_i = C_i/T_i$:

Periodic task t_1: $C_1 = 20$; $T_1 = 100$; $U_1 = 0.2$

Aperiodic task t_2: $C_2 = 15$; $T_2 = 150$; $U_2 = 0.1$

Interrupt-driven aperiodic task t_a: $C_a = 4$; $T_a = 200$, $U_a = 0.02$

Periodic task t_3: $C_3 = 30$; $T_3 = 300$; $U_3 = 0.1$

In addition, t_1, t_2, and t_3 all access the same data repository, which is protected by a semaphore s. It is assumed that the context switching overhead, once at the start of a task's execution and once at the end of its execution, is included in the CPU times.

If tasks were allocated priorities strictly according to their rate monotonic priorities, t_1 would have the highest priority, followed respectively by t_2, t_a, and t_3. However, because of t_a's stringent response time need, it is given the highest priority. The priority assignment is therefore t_a highest, followed respectively by t_1, t_2, and t_3.

The overall CPU utilization is 0.42, which is below the worst-case utilization bound of 0.69. However, it is necessary to investigate each task individually because rate monotonic priorities have not been assigned.

First consider the interrupt driven task t_a. Task t_a is the highest priority task, which always gets the CPU when it needs it. Its utilization is 0.02 and so it will have no difficulty meeting its deadline.

Next consider the task t_1, which executes for 20 msec during its period T_1 of duration 100 msec. Applying the **Generalized Utilization Bound Theorem**, it is necessary to consider the following four factors:

a. **Preemption time by higher priority tasks with periods less than T_1.** There are no tasks with periods less than T_1.

b. **Execution time C_1 for the task $t_1 = 20$.** Execution utilization = $U_1 = 0.2$.

c. **Preemption by higher priority tasks with longer periods.** The task t_a falls into this category. Preemption utilization during the period $T_1 = C_a/T_1 = 4/100 = 0.04$.

d. **Blocking time by lower priority tasks.** Both t_2 and t_3 can potentially block t_1. Based on the priority ceiling algorithm, at most one lower priority task can actually block t_1. The worst case is t_3, because it has a longer CPU time of 30 msec. Blocking utilization during the period $T_1 = B_3/T_1 = 30/100 = 0.3$.

Worst-case utilization = preemption utilization + execution utilization + blocking utilization = $0.04 + 0.2 + 0.3 = 0.54$ < worst-case upper bound of 0.69. Consequently, t_1 will meet its deadline.

Next consider task t_2, which executes for 15 msec during its period T_2 of duration 150 msec. Again, applying the **Generalized Utilization Bound Theorem**, it is necessary to consider the following four factors:

a. **Preemption time by higher priority tasks with periods less than T_2.** Only one task, t_1, has a period less than T_2. Its preemption utilization = $U_1 = 0.2$.

b. **Execution time C_2 for the task t_2 = 15.** Execution utilization = $U_2 = 0.1$.

c. **Preemption by higher priority tasks with longer periods.** The interrupt-driven task t_a falls into this category. Preemption utilization during the period $T_2 = C_a / T_2 = 4/150 = 0.03$. Total preemption utilization by t_1 and t_a = $0.2 + 0.03 = 0.23$.

d. **Blocking time by lower priority tasks.** The task t_3 can block t_2. In the worst case, it blocks t_2 for its total CPU time of 30 msec. Blocking utilization during the period $T_2 = B_3/T_2 = 30/150 = 0.2$.

Worst-case utilization = preemption utilization + execution utilization + blocking utilization = $0.23 + 0.1 + 0.2 = 0.53$ < worst-case upper bound of 0.69. Consequently, t_2 will meet its deadline.

Finally, consider task t_3, which executes for 30 msec during its period T_3 of duration 300 msec. Once again applying the **Generalized Utilization Bound Theorem**, it is necessary to consider the following four factors:

a. **Preemption time by higher priority tasks with periods less than t_3.** All three higher priority tasks fall into this category, so total preemption utilization = $U_1 + U_2 + U_a = 0.2 + 0.1 + 0.02 = 0.32$.

b. **Execution time C_3 for the task t_3.** Execution utilization = $U_3 = 0.1$

c. **Preemption by higher priority tasks with longer periods.** No tasks fall into this category.

d. **Blocking time by lower priority tasks.** No tasks fall into this category.

Worst-case utilization = preemption utilization + execution utilization = $0.32 + 0.1 = 0.42$ < worst case upper bound of 0.69. Consequently, t_3 will meet its deadline. In conclusion, all four tasks will meet their deadlines.

17.3   Performance Analysis Using Event Sequence Analysis

During the requirements phase of the project, the system's required response times to external events are specified. After task structuring, a first attempt at allocating time budgets to the concurrent tasks in the system can be made. Event sequence analysis is used to determine the tasks that need to be executed to service a given external event. An **event sequence diagram**, which is based on a **concurrent collaboration diagram**, is used to show the sequence of internal events and tasks activated after the arrival of the external event. The approach is described next.

Consider an external event. Determine which I/O task is activated by this event and then determine the sequence of internal events that follow. This necessitates identifying the tasks that are activated and the I/O tasks that generate the system response to the external event. Estimate the CPU time for each task. Estimate the CPU overhead, which consists of context switching overhead, interrupt handling overhead, and inter-task communication and synchronization overhead. It is also necessary to consider any other tasks that execute during this period. The sum of the CPU times for the tasks that participate in the event sequence, plus any additional tasks that execute, plus CPU overhead, must be less than or equal to the specified system response time. If there is some uncertainty over the CPU time for each task, allocate a worst-case upper bound.

To estimate overall CPU utilization, it is necessary to estimate, for a given time interval, the CPU time for each task. If there is more than one path through the task, estimate the CPU time for each path. Next, estimate the frequency of activation of tasks. This is easily computed for periodic tasks. For asynchronous tasks, consider the average and maximum activation rates. Multiply each task's CPU time by its activation rate. Sum all the task CPU times and then compute CPU utilization.

An example of applying the event sequence analysis approach is given in Section 17.5.

17.4   Performance Analysis Using Real-Time Scheduling Theory and Event Sequence Analysis

This section describes how the real-time scheduling theory can be combined with the event sequence analysis approach. Instead of considering individual tasks, it is necessary to consider all the tasks in an event sequence. The task activated by the external event executes first and then initiates a series of internal events, resulting in activation and execution of other internal tasks. It is necessary to determine whether all the tasks in the event sequence can be executed before the deadline.

Initially attempt to allocate all the tasks in the event sequence the same priority. These tasks can then collectively be considered one equivalent task from a real-time scheduling viewpoint. This equivalent task has a CPU time equal to the sum of the CPU times of the tasks in the event sequence, plus context switching overhead, plus message communication or event synchronization overhead. The worst-case inter-arrival time of the external event that initiates the event sequence is then made the period of this equivalent task.

To determine whether the equivalent task can meet its deadline, it is necessary to apply the real-time scheduling theorems. In particular, it is necessary to consider preemption by higher priority tasks, blocking by lower priority tasks, and execution time of this equivalent task. An example of combining event sequence analysis with real-time scheduling using the equivalent task approach is given in the next section, for the cruise control problem.

In some cases, you cannot assume that all the tasks in the event sequence can be replaced by an equivalent task. This happens if one of the tasks is used in more than one event sequence or if executing the equivalent task at that priority would prevent other tasks from meeting their deadlines. In such cases, the tasks in the event sequence need to be analyzed separately and assigned different priorities. In determining whether the tasks in the event sequence will meet their deadlines, it is necessary to consider preemption and blocking on a per task basis; however, it is still necessary to determine whether all tasks in the event sequence will complete before the deadline.

17.5 Example of Performance Analysis Using Event Sequence Analysis

As an example of event sequence analysis, consider the Cruise Control subsystem of the Cruise Control and Monitoring System. The event sequence diagram in Figure 17.2, which is based on the task architecture diagram for the Cruise Control subsystem, is used to assist in this analysis. Assume that all the tasks in the Monitoring subsystem, as well as the Calibration task in the Cruise Control subsystem, have lower priorities and can therefore be ignored initially.

Assume that the first case to be analyzed is that of the driver engaging the cruise control lever in the ACCEL position, resulting in controlled acceleration of the car. A performance requirement is that the system must respond to the driver's action within 250 msec. The sequence of internal events following the driver's action is shown by the event sequence on the concurrent collaboration diagram in Figure 17.2.

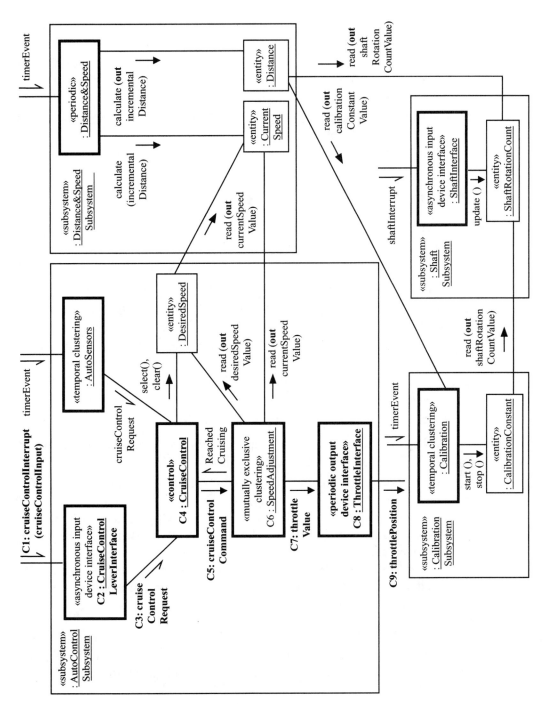

Figure 17.2 *Event sequence for Cruise Control input*

Assume that the Cruise Control subsystem is in Initial state. Consider the case of the ACCEL cruise control input. The event sequence is as follows, with the CPU time to process each event given in parentheses (where C_i is the CPU time required to process event i). Some events are internal to a given task to explicitly account for all the CPU time used.

C1: The cruise Control Interrupt arrives from the external Cruise Control Lever.

C2: The Cruise Control Lever Interface reads the ACCEL input from the Cruise Control Lever.

C3: The Cruise Control Lever Interface sends a cruise control request message to Cruise Control.

C4: Cruise Control receives the message, executes its state transition diagram, and changes state from Initial to Accelerating.

C5: Cruise Control sends an increase speed command message to Speed Adjustment.

C6: Speed Adjustment executes the command and computes the throttle value.

C7: Speed Adjustment sends a throttle value message to the Throttle Interface task.

C8: The Throttle Interface computes the new throttle position.

C9: The Throttle Interface outputs the throttle position to the real-world throttle. (C9 is an output operation and uses no CPU time).

The event sequence diagram (Figure 17.2) shows that four tasks (Cruise Control Lever Interface, Cruise Control, Speed Adjustment, and Throttle Interface) are required to support the ACCEL external event. There is also a minimum of four context switches required, $4*C_x$, where C_x is the context switching overhead.

The total CPU time for the tasks in the event sequence (C_e) is the sum of CPU time for all the tasks in the event sequence, plus CPU time for message communication and context switching overhead:

$$C_e = C_1 + C_2 + C_3 + C_4 + C_5 + C_6 + C_7 + C_8 + 4*C_x$$

Assume that message communication overhead C_m is the same in all cases. The times C_3, C_5, and C_7 should therefore be equal to C_m, and the execution time C_e is equal to

$$C_e = C_1 + C_2 + C_4 + C_6 + C_8 + 3*C_m + 4*C_x \qquad \text{(equation 1)}$$

To determine the system response time, it is also necessary to consider other tasks that could execute during the time when the system must respond to the external event. Consider the other tasks in Figure 17.2. Assume that Auto Sensors (C_{10}) is periodically activated every 100 milliseconds; it could therefore execute three times before the 250 millisecond deadline. Shaft Interface (C_{11}) is activated once every shaft rotation and therefore could execute up to 25 times, or once every 10 msec, during this time, assuming a maximum shaft rotation rate of 6000 rpm. Finally, Distance & Speed (C_{12}) is activated periodically once every quarter of a second and therefore executes once. Every time another task intervenes, there could be two context switches, assuming that the executing task is preempted and then resumes execution after completion of the intervening task. These three tasks could therefore impose an additional 58 context switches.

The total CPU time for these three tasks C_a, including system overhead, is given by

$$C_a = 3 * (C_{10} + 2*C_x) + 25 * (C_{11} + 2*C_x) + (C_{12} + 2*C_x) \qquad \text{(equation 2)}$$

The estimated response time to the external event has to be greater than or equal to the total CPU time. This total is the sum of the tasks in the event sequence, plus the CPU time for other tasks that execute during this period, including all system overhead.

The total CPU time C_t is given by:

$$C_t = C_e + C_a \qquad \text{(equation 3)}$$

Estimates need to be made for each of the above timing parameters before the equations can be solved. The estimates are given in Table 17.2. Because the CPU is intended for real-time processing, it is assumed that context switching is carried out in 0.5 msec.

Substituting for the estimated timing parameters from Table 17.2 in equation (1) results in an estimated value for C_e of 35 msec. Substituting for the estimated timing parameters in equation (2) gives an estimated value for C_a of 79 msec. From equation (3), the estimated total CPU time C_t is 114 msec. This is well below the specified response time of 250 msec.

It is possible to experiment with different values of the parameters to see how susceptible the estimated response time is to error. For example, if the context switching time were 1 msec instead of 0.5 msec, C_e would increase to 37 msec and Ca would increase to 108 msec. This would give a total CPU time C_t of 145 msec, which is an increase of 31 msec over the first estimate. This is still well below the specified response time of 250 msec.

Table 17.2 *Cruise Control CPU Times*

Task	C_i (msec)	Periodic tasks $(C_i + 2 \cdot C_x)$ (msec)	Event sequence tasks $(C_i + C_x + C_m)$ (msec)
Cruise Control Interrupt (C_1)	1		
Cruise Control Lever Interface (C_2)	4		
Total Cruise Control Input ($C_1 + C_2$)	5		6
Cruise Control (C_4)	6		7
Speed Adjustment (C_6)	14	15	16
Throttle Interface (C_8)	5	6	6
Message communication overhead (C_m)	1		
Context switching overhead (C_x)	0.5		
Auto Sensors (C_{10})	5	6	
Shaft Interface (C_{11})	1	2	
Distance & Speed (C_{12})	10	11	

Total CPU time used by tasks in event sequence = 35 msec

17.6 Example of Performance Analysis Using Real-Time Scheduling Theory

This section applies the real-time scheduling theory to the Cruise Control & Monitoring System. In applying the theory, consider first a steady state involving only the periodic tasks. After that, the driver-imposed aperiodic demands on the system are considered.

Consider the worst steady state case, namely the case of maximum CPU demand, with the car operating under automated control at the maximum rate of shaft revolutions. For the periodic tasks, consider the period of each task T_i, the CPU time required by the task C_i, and each task's CPU utilization, which is the ratio $U_i = C_i / T_i$. The CPU time for each periodic task includes the CPU time for two context switches. The steady state periodic tasks are described next, with the estimated timing parameters given in Table 17.3.

Table 17.3 *Cruise Control and Monitoring System Real-Time Scheduling: Periodic Task Parameters*

Task	CPU time C_i	Period T_i	Utilization U_i	Priority
Shaft Interface	2	10	0.20	1
Auto Sensors	6	100	0.06	2
Distance & Speed	11	250	0.04	4
Calibration	5	500	0.01	6
Speed Adjustment	15	250	0.06	5
Throttle Interface	6	100	0.06	3
Trip Reset Button Interface	4	500	0.01	7
Trip Averages Timer	20	1,000	0.02	9
Maintenance Reset Button Interface	6	1,000	0.01	8
Maintenance Timer	15	2,000	0.01	10

Total utilization $U_n = 0.48$

- **Shaft Interface.** It is assumed that Shaft Interface is a periodic task. It is actually aperiodic, because it is activated by a shaft interrupt. However, the interrupt arrives on a regular basis, every shaft rotation, so the task is assumed to behave as a periodic task. Assume a worst case of 6000 rpm, meaning there will be an interrupt every 10 msec, which therefore represents the minimum period of the equivalent periodic task. Because this task has the shortest period, it is assigned the highest priority. Its CPU time is 2 msec, including two context switches of 0.5 msec each.

- **Auto Sensors.** This task has a period of 100 msec and a CPU time of 6 msec, including two context switches of 0.5 msec each.

- **Distance & Speed.** This task has a period of 250 msec and a CPU time of 11 msec, including two context switches of 0.5 msec each.

- **Calibration.** This task has a period of 500 msec and a CPU time of 5 msec.

- **Speed Adjustment.** When activated under automated control, this task executes periodically every 250 msec to compute the throttle value and has a CPU time of 15 msec.

- **Throttle Interface.** When activated under automated control, this task executes periodically every 100 msec to output the throttle position and has a CPU time of 6 msec.

- **Trip Reset Buttons Interface.** This task has a period of 500 msec and a CPU time of 4 msec.

- **Trip Averages Timer.** This task executes relatively infrequently, with a period of 1 sec and a CPU time of 20 msec. It is not time-critical.

- **Maintenance Reset Button Interface.** This task has a period of 1 sec and a CPU time of 6 msec.

- **Maintenance Timer.** This task executes even less frequently, with a period of 2 sec and a CPU time of 15 msec. It is also not time-critical.

The rate monotonic priorities of the tasks are assigned such that higher priorities are allocated to tasks with shorter periods. Thus, the highest priority task is Shaft Interface, which has a period of 10 msec. Two tasks have a period of 100 msec: Throttle Interface and Auto Sensors. Auto Sensors is always active, but Throttle Interface is only active under automated vehicle control. Auto Sensors is given the higher priority because an input it receives (such as brake pressed) might impact the throttle. Two tasks have a period of 250 msec: the higher priority is given to Speed & Distance because it computes current speed that is then used by Speed Adjustment if it is active. The lowest priority task is Maintenance Timer, which has the longest period.

From Table 17.3, the total utilization of the ten periodic tasks is 0.48, well below the theoretical worst-case upper bound of 0.69 given by the **Utilization Bound Theorem**. Therefore, according to the rate monotonic algorithm, all the tasks are able to meet their deadlines.

It should be pointed out that the access time to the shared data stores consists of just one read instruction or one write instruction. This is so small that the potential delay time due to blocking of one task by another is considered negligible. Cases where significant priority inversion delays can occur due to a lower priority task blocking higher priority tasks by accessing a shared data repository are described in the real-time scheduling of the Elevator Control System in Chapter 18.

17.7 Example of Performance Analysis Using Real-Time Scheduling Theory and Event Sequence Analysis

Next, consider the case when the driver initiates an external event, either by using the cruise control lever or by pressing the brake. This requires considering the tasks in the event sequence, as well as the periodic tasks. The first solution uses an equivalent aperiodic task to replace the four tasks in the event sequence.

17.7.1   Equivalent Aperiodic Task

It is necessary to consider the impact of the additional load imposed by the driver-initiated external event on the steady state load of the periodic tasks. This is done by considering the impact of the tasks in the event sequence on the steady state analysis described previously for the periodic tasks. The worst case is when the vehicle is already under automated control. If the car were not under automated control, the `Speed Adjustment` and `Throttle Interface` tasks would not be executing and thus the load on the CPU would be lighter.

Consider an input from the cruise control lever. As described in the event sequence analysis and shown in the event sequence diagram, the tasks required to process this input are `Cruise Control Lever Interface`, `Cruise Control`, `Speed Adjustment`, and `Throttle Interface`. The CPU time to process this input is given by equation 1 (see Section 17.5). Although four tasks are involved in the event sequence, they have to execute in strict sequence because each task is activated by a message sent by its predecessor in the sequence. We can therefore assume, to a first approximation, that the four tasks are equivalent to one aperiodic task whose CPU time is C_e. C_e is the sum of the CPU times of the four individual tasks plus message communication overhead and context switching overhead. The equivalent aperiodic task is referred to as the "event sequence task."

From the real-time scheduling theory, an aperiodic task can be treated as a periodic task whose period is given by the minimum inter-arrival time of the aperiodic requests. Let the period for the equivalent periodic event sequence task be T_e. Assume that T_e is also the necessary response time to the driver's input. For example, if T_e is 250 msec, the desired response to the driver's input of pressing the brake or requesting to deactivate cruise control is 250 msec. For the equivalent periodic event sequence task, it is assumed that the driver can initiate external events at the rate of four per second, a truly worst and highly unlikely case. Nevertheless, if it can be shown that the system can support this worst-case situation, confidence in the system's performance will be high.

When assigning a priority to the event sequence task, the task is initially assigned its rate monotonic priority. Because the aperiodic event sequence task has the same period as two other periodic tasks, `Speed Adjustment` and `Distance & Speed`, it is given the highest priority of the three. However, `Shaft Interface`, `Throttle Interface`, and `Auto Sensors` all have shorter periods and hence higher rate monotonic priorities than the event sequence task. The real-time scheduling parameters for this case, as well as the assigned task priorities, are given in Table 17.4 (Case 1).

Table 17.4 *Cruise Control and Monitoring System Real-Time Scheduling: Periodic & Event Sequence Task Parameters*

Task	CPU time C_i	Period T_i	Utilization U_i	Priority (Case 1)	Priority (Case 2)
Shaft Interface	2	10	0.20	1	1
Auto Sensors	6	100	0.06	2	3
Distance & Speed	11	250	0.04	5	5
Calibration	5	500	0.01	7	7
Speed Adjustment	15	250	0.06	6	6
Throttle Interface	6	100	0.06	3	4
Trip Reset Button Interface	4	500	0.01	8	8
Trip Averages Timer	20	1,000	0.02	10	10
Maintenance Reset Button Interface	6	1,000	0.01	9	9
Maintenance Timer	15	2,000	0.01	11	11
Event Sequence Task	35	250	0.14	4	2

Total utilization = 0.62
Priorities: Case 1 Rate monotonic priorities assigned
             Case 2 Non-rate monotonic priorities assigned

Substituting the CPU estimates from Table 17.2 into equation 1 (see Section 17.5), the CPU time C_e of the equivalent event sequence task is 35 msec. Given the equivalent period T_e of 250 sec, the task CPU utilization is 0.14. Because the total CPU utilization of the periodic tasks is 0.48, the total periodic and event sequence task CPU utilization is 0.62, which is below the worst-case upper bound of 0.69 given by the **Utilization Bound Theorem**. Consequently, the event sequence task can meet its deadline, as can all the periodic tasks.

It should be noted that we can treat the pressing of the brake by the driver in the same way as an input from the cruise control lever. In the brake pressed case, the tasks in the event sequence are Auto Sensors, Cruise Control, Speed Adjustment, and Throttle Interface, with the last three identical to those for a cruise control lever input. From Table 17.2, the estimated CPU time for Auto Sensors of 5 msec is the same as for Cruise Control Lever Interface. Therefore, the CPU time to process a brake press is similar to that for a cruise control input. Although the period for Auto Sensors is 100 msec, we assume that successive inputs from the real world occur at a maximum rate of four per second, and these inputs may be either brake inputs or cruise control lever inputs. The high sampling rate for Auto Sensors is to ensure that the brake or engine inputs are not missed.

We can therefore assume that the brake pressed case is similar to the cruise control lever input case, and treat both in the same way. Thus, the same event sequence analysis holds for an external event resulting from either a cruise control lever input or a brake input.

17.7.2   Assigning Non-Rate Monotonic Priorities

One assumption and one approximation were made in the first solution. Consider first the assumption that all tasks can be allocated their rate monotonic priorities. A problem with giving the event sequence task its rate monotonic priority is that the task could potentially miss the cruise control interrupt if it has to wait for Shaft Interface, Throttle Interface, and Auto Sensors to execute. On the other hand, giving the event sequence task the highest priority means that Shaft Interface would miss its deadlines because the CPU time for the event sequence task is 35 msec and the period of Shaft Interface is 10 msec.

To avoid this, the event sequence task is given a lower priority than the Shaft Interface task but a higher priority than the Throttle Interface and Auto Sensors tasks. This means the event sequence task is given a higher priority than its rate monotonic priority, as shown in Table 17.4 (Case 2). Because of this, it is necessary to check each task explicitly to determine whether it meets its deadline.

The two highest priority tasks, Shaft Interface and the event sequence task, have a combined utilization of 0.34, so they will have no difficulty meeting their deadlines. However, the next highest priority tasks, Throttle Interface and Auto Sensors, could both potentially get delayed by the event sequence task. A worst-case analysis is required to show that they would not miss their deadlines, given that they each have a period of 100 msec.

Consider a worst-case CPU burst of duration 100 msec with Shaft Interface active ten times, the four tasks in the event sequence active once, and Throttle Interface and Auto Sensors each active once. Shaft Interface consumes 10*2 msec = 20 msec. The four tasks in the event sequence consume 35 msec. The Throttle Interface and Auto Sensors tasks consume a further 6 msec each. The total CPU time consumed is 67 msec, which is less than the 100 msec period of Throttle Interface and Auto Sensors. Thus, all the tasks meet their deadlines.

It should be noted that although the overall CPU utilization is 62 percent, bursts of activity can lead to transient loads that are much higher. For example, in the 100 msec worst-case CPU burst described above, the total utilization of the three steady state tasks and the one event sequence task is 67 percent, thereby still allowing lower-priority tasks to execute. For example if the next highest priority task, Distance & Speed, were to also execute in this busy 100 msec, the CPU utilization would increase to 78 percent. Thus the real-time scheduling algorithm guarantees that all tasks can meet their deadlines, no matter what sudden bursts of activity occur.

17.7.3 Detailed Analysis of Aperiodic Tasks

A more comprehensive analysis of the cruise control problem is obtained by treating each of the four tasks in the event sequence separately. The CPU parameters for each of the four tasks are shown in Tables 17.2 and 17.5, where each task has its context switching and message communication overhead added to its CPU time.

Table 17.5 *Cruise Control and Monitoring System Real-Time Scheduling: Periodic and Aperiodic Task Parameters*

Task	CPU time C_i	Period T_i	Utilization U_i	Priority
Shaft Interface	2	10	0.20	1
Auto Sensors	6	100	0.06	3
Distance & Speed	11	250	0.04	7
Calibration	5	500	0.01	8
Speed Adjustment *	16	250	0.06	6
Throttle Interface *	6	100	0.06	4
Trip Reset Button Interface	4	500	0.01	9
Trip Averages Timer	20	1,000	0.02	11
Maintenance Reset Button Interface	6	1,000	0.01	10
Maintenance Timer	15	2,000	0.01	12
Cruise Control Lever Interface*	6	250	0.02	2
Cruise Control*	7	250	0.03	5

*Tasks in event sequence

In addition, the CPU time for the `Cruise Control Lever Interface` task is the sum of C_1 and C_2. All the tasks in the event sequence are treated as periodic tasks with a period equal to the minimum interarrival time of 250 msec. The only exception is `Throttle Interface`, which, in addition to being in the event sequence, also executes periodically with a period of 100 msec.

To ensure that tasks in the event sequence get a timely response, they are assigned high priorities where possible. In particular, to respond to external interrupts quickly, the first task in the event sequence, `Cruise Control Lever Interface`, is assigned the second highest priority after `Shaft Interface`. Because its priority is higher than two tasks with a shorter period, `Throttle Interface` and `Auto Sensors`, the assigned priority of `Cruise Control Lever Interface` is above the rate monotonic priority; however, the three other tasks in the event sequence are assigned their rate monotonic priorities. `Throttle Interface`, which has a period of 100 msec, is allocated the fourth highest priority, just below `Auto Sensors`, which has the same period. The other two tasks in the event sequence, `Cruise Control` and `Speed Adjustment`, both with the same period of 250 msec, are assigned the next two highest priorities.

To carry out a full analysis, it is necessary to apply the *Generalized Real-Time Scheduling Theory*, where each task must be checked explicitly against its upper bound. The timing diagram shown in Figure 17.3 illustrates this analysis.

Shaft Interface is the highest priority task, with a period of 10 msec. Whenever it needs to execute, it preempts all other tasks to execute for 2 msec, so it easily meets its deadline. Cruise Control Lever Interface is considered with the other tasks in the event sequence because it is important to determine that all four tasks complete before the 250 msec deadline.

Consider the four tasks in the event sequence over the period T_e of 250 msec. As before, the objective is to determine that the four tasks will complete execution before the 250 msec deadline. It is necessary to apply the **Generalized Utilization Bound Theorem** and consider the following four factors

a. **Execution time for the tasks in the event sequence.** The total execution time for the four tasks in the event sequence, $C_e = 35$ msec and $T_e = 250$ msec. Execution utilization = 0.14.

b. **Preemption time by higher priority tasks with periods less than 250 msec, the period of the tasks in the event sequence.** There are three tasks in this set. `Shaft Interface`, with a period of 10 msec, can preempt any of the four tasks a maximum of 25 times for a total of 25*2 = 50 msec. `Throttle Interface` and `Auto Sensors`, with periods of 100 msec, can each preempt the three lower priority tasks in the event sequence up to three times for a total of 3 * (6+6) = 36 msec.

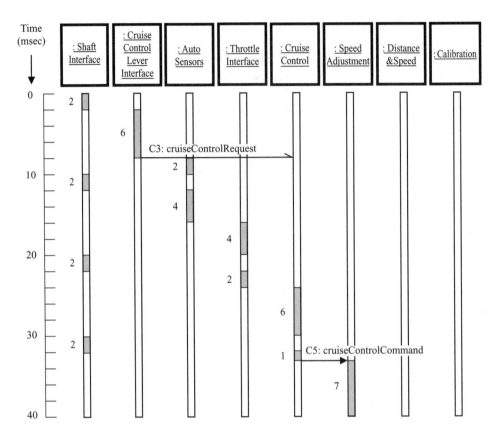

NB: UML notation for sequence diagram has been extended for this figure.

Figure 17.3a *Time-annotated sequence diagram*

Figure 17.3 *Cruise Control & Monitoring System*

- Total preemption time = 50 + 36 = 86
- Total preemption utilization = 0.2 + 0.06 + 0.06 = 0.32

c. **Preemption by higher priority tasks with longer periods.** There are no such tasks.

d. **Blocking time by lower priority tasks.** There are no such tasks.

After considering these four factors, we now determine the total elapsed time and total utilization:

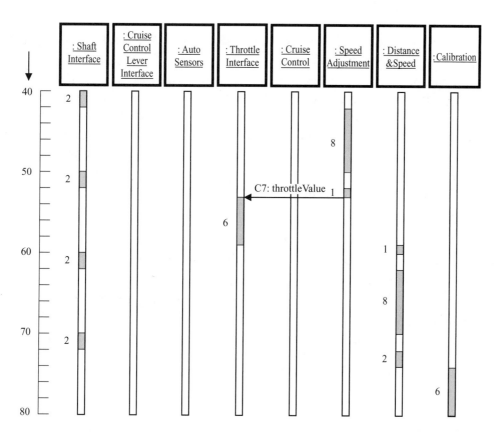

NB: UML notation for sequence diagram has been extended for this figure.

Figure 17.3b *Time-annotated sequence diagram*

Figure 17.3 *Cruise Control & Monitoring System (continued)*

Total elapsed time = Total preemption time + total execution time = 86 + 35 = 121 < 250

Total utilization = preemption utilization + execution utilization = 0.32 + 0.14 = 0.46 < 0.69

The total utilization of 0.46 is less than the **Generalized Utilization Bound Theorem's** upper bound of 0.69, so the four tasks in the event sequence all meet their deadlines.

To determine whether the two tasks with the shorter period of 100 msec meet their deadlines, it is necessary to check preemption and execution times during the 100 msec period.

a. **Execution time for the two tasks.** These are considered together because they have the same period. Total execution time = 6 + 6 = 12 msec. Execution utilization = 0.06 + 0.06 = 0.12.

b. **Preemption time by higher priority tasks with periods less than 100 msec.** The only task in this set, Shaft Interface, can preempt 10 times during the 100 msec for a total preemption time of 10*2 = 20 msec. Preemption utilization = 0.2

c. **Preemption by higher priority tasks with longer periods.** The only task in this set is Cruise Control Lever Interface, which can preempt once and execute for 6 msec. Preemption utilization = 0.06.

d. **Blocking time by lower priority tasks.** There are no such tasks.

After considering these four factors, we now determine the total utilization:

Total preemption utilization = 0.2 + 0.06 = 0.26

Total utilization = preemption utilization + execution utilization = 0.26 + 0.12 = 0.38 < 0.69

The total utilization of 0.38 is less than the **Generalized Utilization Bound Theorem's** upper bound of 0.69, so the two periodic tasks with shorter periods both meet their deadlines. A similar analysis for each of the lower priority periodic tasks shows that each of these tasks meets its deadline. The timing diagram shows two of these, Distance & Speed and Calibration.

17.8 Design Restructuring

If the proposed design does not meet the performance goals, the design needs to be restructured. This is achieved by applying the **task clustering criteria** and **task inversion criteria**. In particular, the weaker forms of **task clustering** (also referred to as **temporal task inversion**) and the other forms of task inversion, **multiple instance task inversion** and **sequential task inversion**, can be applied.

If there is a performance problem in the cruise control example, one attempt at design restructuring is to apply sequential task inversion. Consider the case where the Cruise Control task sends a speed command message to the Speed Adjustment task, which in turn sends throttle messages to the Throttle Interface task. These three tasks may be combined into one task using sequential task inversion, the inverted Cruise Control task with passive objects for Speed Adjustment and Throttle Interface (as described in Chapter 14 and shown in Figure 14.15). This eliminates the message communication overhead between these tasks, as well as the context switching overhead. Let the CPU time for the inverted task be C_v. Then, referring to Table 17.2:

$$C_v = C_4 + C_6 + C_8 \qquad\qquad\qquad\qquad \text{(equation 4)}$$

The CPU time for the two tasks in the new event sequence C_{ee} is now given by

$$C_{ee} = C_1 + C_2 + C_v + C_m + 2{}^*C_x \qquad\qquad\qquad \text{(equation 5)}$$

It is interesting to compare equation 5 (with two tasks in the event sequence) with equation 1 in Section 17.5 (with four tasks in the event sequence): the message communication overhead is reduced from $3{}^*C_m$ to C_m, and the context switching overhead is reduced from $4{}^*C_x$ to $2{}^*C_x$. Given the estimated timing parameters times in Table 17.2 and substituting for them in equations (4) and (5) results in a reduction of total CPU time from 35 msec to 32 msec. If the message communication and context switching overhead times were larger, the savings would be more substantial. For example, if C_m is 3 msec and C_x is 2 msec, the total aperiodic CPU time would decrease from 47 msec to 37 msec.

17.9 Estimation and Measurement of Performance Parameters

The following performance input parameters need to be determined through estimation or measurement before the performance analysis is carried out. These are independent variables whose values are inputs to the performance analysis. Dependent variables are variables whose values are estimated by the real-time scheduling theory.

A major assumption made for the real-time scheduling is that all tasks are locked in main memory so there is no paging overhead. Paging overhead adds another degree of uncertainty and delay that cannot be tolerated in hard real-time systems.

The following are individual task parameters that need to be estimated for each task involved in the performance analysis:

a. **The task's period T_i, which is the frequency with which it executes.** For a periodic task, the period is fixed (refer to Chapter 14 for more details on periodic tasks). For an aperiodic task, use the worst case (i.e., minimum) external event interarrival time for an input task, and then extrapolate from this for downstream internal tasks that participate in the same event sequence.

b. **The execution time C_i, which is the CPU time required for the period.** At design time, this figure is an estimate. Estimate the number of source lines of code for the task, and then estimate the number of compiled lines of code. Use benchmarks of programs developed in the selected source language executing on the selected hardware with the selected operating system. Compare benchmark results with size of the task to estimate compiled code execution time. When the task has been implemented, substitute performance measurements of the task executing on the hardware for the task estimates.

The following three system CPU overheads need to be determined by performance measurements of benchmark programs developed in the selected source language executing on the selected hardware with the selected operating system:

a. **Context switching overhead.** The CPU time for the operating system to switch the CPU allocation from one task to another (see Chapter 4).

b. **Interrupt handling overhead.** The CPU time required to handle an interrupt.

c. **Inter-task communication and synchronization overhead.** The CPU time to send a message or signal an event from a source task to a destination task. This will depend on the communication and synchronization primitives used by the tasks in the real-time application.

These overhead parameters need to be factored into the computation of task CPU time, as illustrated in the previous examples.

17.10 Summary

This chapter has described the performance analysis of software designs by applying real-time scheduling theory. This approach is particularly appropriate for hard real-time systems with deadlines that must be met. This chapter has described two approaches for analyzing the performance of a design: **real-time scheduling theory** and **event sequence analysis**. The two approaches were then combined. Both approaches are applied to a design consisting of a set of concurrent tasks. Consequently, the performance analysis can start as soon as the task architecture has been designed, as described in Chapter 14. It can then be refined as the real-time application development progresses through detailed software design and implementation.

A detailed performance analysis case study was presented of the Cruise Control and Monitoring System, showing a progressively more detailed analysis. The analysis and design of this application is given in Chapter 20. The cruise control example was shown for a real-time system executing on a single CPU. A second case study, the Elevator Control System, is described in Chapter 20. Two solutions are presented: a centralized design and a distributed design. The performance of both designs is analyzed, using a combination of real-time scheduling theory and event sequence analysis.

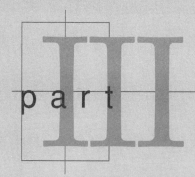

part III

Case Studies in Concurrent, Distributed, and Real-Time Application Design

chapter 18

Elevator Control System Case Study

This case study consists of an Elevator Control System that controls one or more elevators. The system has to schedule elevators to respond to requests from users at various floors and control the motion of the elevators between floors.

First an analysis model is developed. Then the same analysis model is mapped, in one case, to a non-distributed design and, in a second case, to a distributed design.

The Elevator Control System has been the subject of several studies, including Jackson [1983], Gomaa [1993], Sanden [1994], and Douglass [1999b].

18.1 Problem Description

For each elevator, there are

- **A set of elevator buttons.** A user presses a button to select a destination.
- **A corresponding set of elevator lamps.** Indicate the floors to be visited by the elevator.
- **An elevator motor.** Controlled by commands to move up, move down, and stop.
- **An elevator door.** Controlled by commands to open and close the door.

For each floor, there are

- **Up and down floor buttons.** A user presses a button to request an elevator.
- **A corresponding pair of floor lamps.** Indicate the directions that have been requested.

At each floor, and for each elevator, there is a pair of direction lamps to indicate whether an arriving elevator is heading in the up or down direction. For the top and bottom floors, there is only one floor button, one floor lamp, and (for each elevator) one direction lamp. There is also an arrival sensor at each floor in each elevator shaft to detect the arrival of an elevator at the floor.

The hardware characteristics of the I/O devices are that the elevator buttons, floor buttons, and arrival sensors are asynchronous; that is, an interrupt is generated when there is an input from one of these devices. The other I/O devices are all passive. The elevator and floor lamps are switched on by the hardware, but must be switched off by the software. The direction lamps are switched on and off by the software.

18.2   Use Case Model

The Elevator Control System has two actors: one representing the Elevator User who wishes to use the elevator and the second representing the Arrival Sensor. The Elevator User interacts with the system via the elevator buttons and the floor buttons.

The Elevator User actor initiates two use cases, as shown in Figure 18.1. From the problem definition, the following use cases are identified:

Select Destination. The user in the elevator presses an up or down elevator button to select a destination floor to which to move.

Request Elevator. The user at a floor presses an up or down floor button to request an elevator.

The use case descriptions are given next.

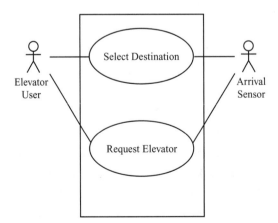

Figure 18.1   *Elevator Control System actors and use cases*

18.2.1 Select Destination Use Case

Actors: Elevator User (primary), Arrival Sensor
Precondition: User is in the elevator.
Description:

1. User presses an up elevator button. The elevator button sensor sends the elevator button request to the system, identifying the destination floor the user wishes to visit.

2. The new request is added to the list of floors to visit. If the elevator is stationary, the system determines in which direction the system should move in order to service the next request. The system commands the elevator door to close. When the door has closed, the system commands the motor to start moving the elevator, either up or down.

3. As the elevator moves between floors, the arrival sensor detects that the elevator is approaching a floor and notifies the system. The system checks whether the elevator should stop at this floor. If so, the system commands the motor to stop. When the elevator has stopped, the system commands the elevator door to open.

4. If there are other outstanding requests, the elevator visits these floors on the way to the floor requested by the user. Eventually, the elevator arrives at the destination floor selected by the user.

Alternatives:

- User presses down elevator button to move down. System response is the same as for the main sequence.
- If the elevator is at a floor and there is no new floor to move to, the elevator stays at the current floor, with the door open.

Postcondition: Elevator has arrived at the destination floor selected by the user.

18.2.2 Request Elevator Use Case

Actors: Elevator User (primary), Arrival Sensor
Precondition: User is at a floor and wants an elevator.
Description:

1. User presses an up floor button. The floor button sensor sends the user request to the system, identifying the floor number.

2. The system selects an elevator to visit this floor. The new request is added to the list of floors to visit. If the elevator is stationary, the system determines in which direction the system should move in order to service the next request.

The system commands the elevator door to close. After the door has closed, the system commands the motor to start moving the elevator, either up or down.

3. As the elevator moves between floors, the arrival sensor detects that the elevator is approaching a floor and notifies the system. The system checks whether the elevator should stop at this floor. If so, the system commands the motor to stop. When the elevator has stopped, the system commands the elevator door to open.

4. If there are other outstanding requests, the elevator visits these floors on the way to the floor requested by the user. Eventually, the elevator arrives at the floor in response to the user request.

Alternative:

- User presses down floor button to move down. System response is the same as for the main sequence.

- If the elevator is at a floor and there is no new floor to move to, the elevator stays at the current floor, with the door open.

Postcondition: Elevator has arrived at the floor in response to user request.

18.2.3 Abstract Use Cases

Analysis of the two use cases indicates two common sequences that can be factored out into abstract use cases, which can then be included in the revised and simplified versions of the original use cases. The first abstract use case is the situation where the elevator is dispatched in response to a user request. This common part of the two use cases can be factored out into an abstract use case called Dispatch Elevator. The common sequence dealing with the stopping of the elevator can also be factored out into an abstract use case called Stop Elevator at Floor. The relationship among the use cases is shown in Figure 18.2. Both the Select Destination and Request Elevator use cases include the two abstract use cases, which are described next.

18.2.4 Stop Elevator at Floor Abstract Use Case

Actor: Arrival Sensor

Precondition: Elevator is moving.

Description:

As the elevator moves between floors, the arrival sensor detects that the elevator is approaching a floor and notifies the system. The system checks whether the ele-

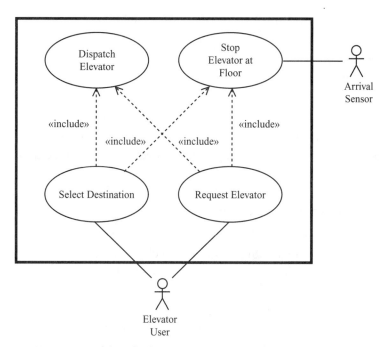

Figure 18.2 *Use case model with abstract use cases*

vator should stop at this floor. If so, the system commands the motor to stop. When the elevator has stopped, the system commands the elevator door to open.

Alternative: The elevator is not required to stop at this floor and so continues past the floor.

Postcondition: Elevator has stopped at floor, with door open.

18.2.5 Dispatch Elevator Abstract Use Case

Precondition: Elevator has at least one floor to visit.

Description:

The system determines in which direction the system should move in order to service the next request. The system commands the elevator door to close. When the door has closed, the system commands the motor to start moving the elevator, either up or down.

Postcondition: Elevator is moving in the commanded direction.

Alternative: If the elevator is at a floor and there is no new floor to move to, the elevator stays at the current floor, with the door open.

18.2.6   Select Destination Concrete Use Case

The `Select Destination` concrete use case is rewritten to take advantage of the abstract use cases, as follows:

Actor: Elevator User

Precondition: User is in the elevator.

Description:

1. User presses an up (or down) elevator button. The elevator button sensor sends the elevator button request to the system, identifying the destination floor the user wishes to visit.

2. The new request is added to the list of floors to visit. If the elevator is stationary, include `Dispatch Elevator` abstract use case.

3. Include `Stop Elevator at Floor` abstract use case.

4. If there are other outstanding requests, the elevator visits these floors on the way to the floor requested by the user, following the above sequence of dispatching and stopping. Eventually, the elevator arrives at the destination floor selected by the user.

Alternative: User presses down elevator button to move down. System response is the same as in the main sequence.

Postcondition: Elevator has arrived at the destination floor selected by the user.

18.2.7   Request Elevator Concrete Use Case

The `Request Elevator` concrete use case is rewritten to take advantage of the abstract use cases as follows:

Actor: Elevator User

Precondition: User is at a floor and wants an elevator.

Description:

1. User presses an up floor button. The floor button sensor sends the user request to the system, identifying the floor number.

2. The system selects an elevator to visit this floor. The new request is added to the list of floors to visit. If the elevator is stationary, then include `Dispatch Elevator` abstract use case.

3. Include `Stop Elevator at Floor` abstract use case.

4. If there are other outstanding requests, the elevator visits these floors on the way to the floor requested by the user, following the above sequence of dispatching and stopping. Eventually, the elevator arrives at the floor in response to the user request.

Alternative: User presses down floor button to move down. System response is the same as for the main sequence.

Postcondition: Elevator has arrived at the floor in response to user request.

18.3 Static Model of the Problem Domain

The static model captures the static relationships in the Elevator Control System. Initially, consider the real-world classes in the problem domain, for which the class diagram is shown in Figure 18.3. The `Elevator` is a composite class composed of one `Motor`, one `Door`, n `Elevator Buttons`, and n `Elevator Lamps`. `Floor` is also a composite class, composed of `Floor Button` and `Floor Lamp`. There are usually two instances of each (one up and one down); however, the top and bottom floors have only one instance of each.

The `Elevator` class also has associations with the `Arrival Sensor` class, which notifies it of imminent arrival at a floor, and the `Direction Lamp` class, which it switches on and off. The `Direction Lamp` class has an association with the `Floor` class. There are one or two direction lamps at each floor for each elevator—usually two, but only one at the top and bottom floors.

When considering the system context class diagram, it is apparent that, apart from the composite classes, all the real-world classes in Figure 18.3 are in fact

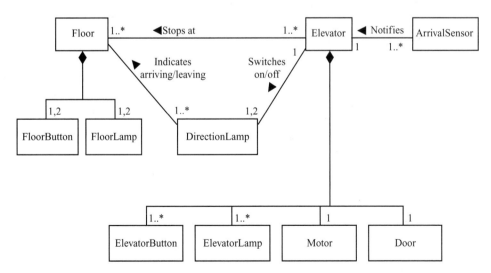

Figure 18.3 *Conceptual static model for Elevator Control System*

external devices to the Elevator Control System, either sensors or actuators. Thus, they are depicted on a system context class diagram as external input or output device classes that interface to the Elevator Control System (see Figure 18.4).

18.4 Object Structuring

Now consider the software objects in the Elevator Control System in preparation for dynamic modeling. The Elevator object is a composite object composed of several other objects. Because it receives inputs from external objects and controls external objects, several of its constituent objects are device interface objects that interface to external I/O devices, namely, the elevator sensors and actuators.

For every external device object, there is a corresponding software device interface object. Thus, a given elevator receives elevator requests via Elevator Button Interface objects, of which there is one per floor. An elevator also has a Door Interface object to interface to the real-world door and a Motor Interface object that interfaces to the real-world motor. An elevator also outputs lamp commands to the Elevator Lamp Interface objects, of which there is one per

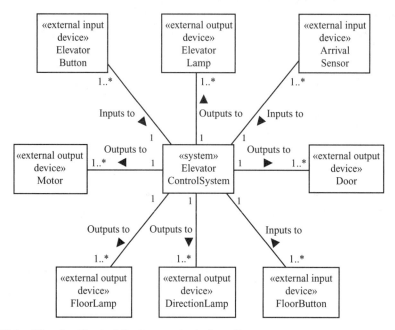

Figure 18.4 *Elevator Control System context class diagram*

floor. The Floor composite class is composed of the Floor Button Interface and Floor Lamp Interface device interface classes. Two instances of each class are at every floor except the top and bottom floors, where there is one instance of each class. There is also an Arrival Sensor Interface object, which sends messages to the Elevator Control object as it approaches a floor, and a Direction Lamp Interface object to interface to the real-world direction lamp.

In addition to these device interface objects determined from the context class diagram, there is a need for entity objects and control objects. An entity object is needed for each elevator, which we call Elevator Status & Plan. The elevator status has information on whether the elevator is moving up, moving down, or idle, as well as the current floor if it is at a floor or the last floor if it is moving between floors. It also includes an elevator plan, which is a list of all the floors the elevator is committed to visit.

Each elevator has a state-dependent control object called Elevator Control, which controls the elevator motor and door. This object controls the door's opening and closing and controls the motor's starting to move up, starting to move down, or stopping. The states of the Elevator Control object are depicted on an elevator statechart. Because requests for the elevator can come at any time, a decision is made to have a separate coordinator object, called the Elevator Manager, to receive all incoming requests for the elevator and to update the elevator plan. An additional problem is that when an elevator request comes from a floor button, an elevator needs to be selected to service the request. For this reason, a decision is made to have a coordinator object, the Scheduler, which selects the appropriate elevator to service a floor request.

18.5 Dynamic Model

The next step is to define the object interactions that correspond to each use case. In this case study, we use collaboration diagrams. A collaboration diagram is developed for each use case to depict the objects that participate in the use case and the sequence of object interactions. In addition, if the collaboration involves the Elevator Control state-dependent control object, which executes a statechart, the event sequence is depicted on the Elevator Control statechart. The message descriptions for each use case are given next.

18.5.1 Collaboration Diagram for Select Destination Use Case

The collaboration diagram for the Select Destination use case is depicted in Figure 18.5. Because the Elevator Button Request could arrive while the

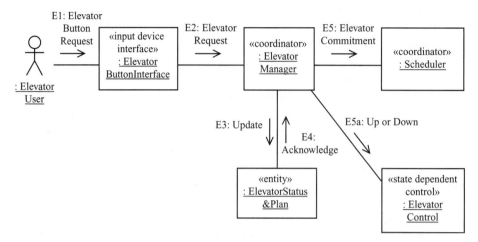

Figure 18.5 *Collaboration diagram for Select Destination use case*

elevator (in particular Elevator Control) is busy servicing a previous request, the Elevator Manager object is given the responsibility of handling the request. The message sequence description is as follows:

E1: The Elevator Button Request arrives at the Elevator Button Interface object.

E2: The Elevator Button Interface object sends the Elevator Request to the Elevator Manager object.

E3: The Elevator Manager sends the request to Elevator Status & Plan, which adds the request to the list of floors to be visited.

E4: The elevator plan is updated. An acknowledgement is returned to the Elevator Manager object, which identifies whether the elevator is idle.

E5: The Elevator Manager sends an Elevator Commitment message to the Scheduler, to inform it that this elevator is committed to visit the given floor.

E5a: If the elevator is idle, the Elevator Manager sends an Up (or Down) message to the Elevator Control object, directing it to move in the desired direction. This case is handled by the Dispatch Elevator use case.

18.5.2 Collaboration Diagram for Request Elevator Use Case

The collaboration diagram for the Request Elevator use case is depicted on Figure 18.6. Because the request comes from a floor button, a decision has to be

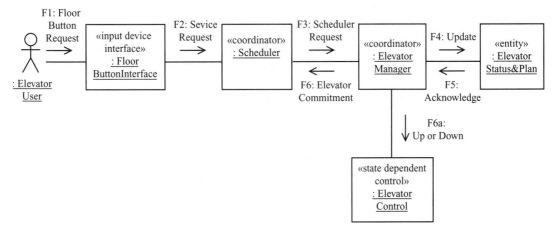

Figure 18.6 *Collaboration diagram for Request Elevator use case*

made about which elevator should service the request. This decision is made by the Scheduler, which has information about the status (location and direction of each elevator) and plan (list of floors each elevator is committed to visit). The message sequence description is as follows:

F1: The Floor Button Request arrives at the Floor Button Interface object.

F2: The Floor Button Interface object sends a Service Request to the Scheduler object.

F3: The Scheduler object selects an elevator and sends a Scheduler Request to the Elevator Manager object in the selected Elevator composite object.

F4: The Elevator Manager object sends an Update message to the Elevator Status & Plan to add the new request to the elevator plan of which floor it is to visit.

F5: An acknowledgement is returned to the Elevator Manager object, which identifies whether the elevator is idle.

F6: The Elevator Manager object sends an Elevator Commitment message to the Scheduler.

F6a: If the elevator is idle, the Elevator Manager sends an Up (or Down) message to the Elevator Control object, directing it to move in the desired direction. This case is handled by the Dispatch Elevator use case.

18.5.3   Collaboration Diagram for Stop Elevator at Floor Use Case

Because the Stop Elevator at Floor use case is state-dependent, it is depicted on both a collaboration diagram (see Figure 18.7) and a statechart (see Figure 18.8). The sequence of states entered is given in the message sequence description, as follows. The precondition is that the elevator is in Elevator Moving state on the statechart. The message sequence description is as follows:

A1: The Arrival Sensor Interface object receives an input from the arrival sensor external entity.

A2: The Arrival Sensor Interface object sends the floor number in the Approaching Floor message to the Elevator Control object.

A3: The Elevator Control object sends a Check This Floor message to the Elevator Status & Plan object, which checks whether the floor at which the elevator is arriving is one where it should stop.

A 4: As the elevator is arriving at a requested floor, the Elevator Status & Plan object sends the Approaching Requested Floor message to the Elevator Control object. The message contains the floor number and the future direction. On receiving this message, Elevator Control transitions from Elevator Moving state to Elevator Stopping state.

A5: As a result of the transition to Elevator Stopping state, the Elevator Control object commands the Motor Interface object to Stop.

A5a (parallel sequence): Elevator Control sends an On Direction Lamp (with up or down as a parameter) to the Direction Lamp Interface object, which switches on the real-world direction lamp (A5a.1).

A6: The Motor Interface object sends the Stop Motor Command to the real-world motor.

A7: The Motor Interface object receives the Motor Response.

A8: Motor Interface object sends an Elevator Stopped message to the Elevator Control object, which then transitions to Elevator Door Opening state.

A9: On transitioning to Elevator Door Opening state, the Elevator Control object sends the Door Interface object a command to Open Door.

A9a (parallel sequence because there are four actions associated with the state transition): The Elevator Control object sends an Off Elevator Lamp message to the Elevator Lamp Interface object, which then sends an Elevator Lamp Output to the external lamp to switch it off (A9a.1).

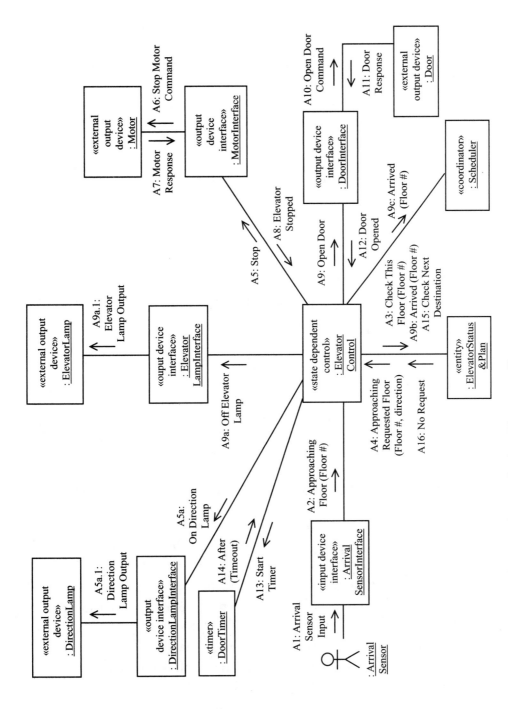

Figure 18.7 *Collaboration diagram for Stop Elevator at Floor use case*

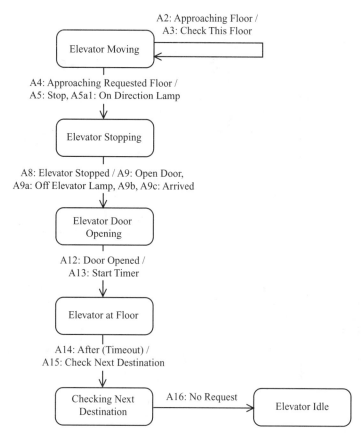

Figure 18.8 *Stop Elevator at Floor use case: statechart for Elevator Control*

The Elevator Control object sends the Arrived message to both the Elevator Status & Plan object (A9b, third parallel sequence) and the Scheduler object (A9c, fourth parallel sequence).

A10: The Door Interface object sends the Open Door Command to the real-world door.

A11: The Door Interface object receives the Door Response.

A12: The Door Interface object sends a Door Opened message to the Elevator Control object, which then transitions to Elevator at Floor state.

A 13: The Elevator Control object starts a timer.

A14: A timer event is generated after a period of time equal to timeout, causing the Elevator Control object to transition to Checking Next Destination state.

A15: As a result of the transition, Elevator Control sends a Check Next Destination message to the Elevator Status & Plan object. The objective is to determine the next destination just prior to departure, in case there has been a recent update to the plan. If the elevator does not have any outstanding requests, it transitions to Elevator Idle state (event A16). Otherwise, use the Dispatch Elevator use case.

Note that A9, A9a, A9b, and A9c are parallel sequences resulting from four output events of the same transition. The events in these parallel sequences are non-deterministic. Thus event A9a.1 (which follows A9a) could occur before or after event A10 (which follows A9). Note that the main sequence does not receive a suffix (such as A9d), because this would make the subsequent event sequence numbering more complicated.

18.5.4 Collaboration Diagram for Dispatch Elevator Abstract Use Case

In the collaboration diagram for the Dispatch Elevator abstract use case, the starting preconditions are different, depending on which use case is including the abstract use case. Consider first how this use case is executed by the Stop Elevator at Floor use case. On entering Checking Next Destination state, Elevator Control sends a Check Next Destination message to Elevator Status & Plan (event A15 on Figure 18.8). Elevator Status & Plan sends an Up Request (or Down Request) message to Elevator Control, informing it of the direction in which to move, which is the first event of the Dispatch Elevator abstract use case (Figure 18.9).

In the second case, the Elevator Control object is in Elevator Idle state. Elevator Manager receives a message from either the Scheduler (Figure 18.6) or the Elevator Button Interface (Figure 18.5) with a request for the elevator to visit a floor. Elevator Manager sends a message to Elevator Status & Plan to update the plan. If the elevator is busy servicing a request, Elevator Status & Plan returns an Acknowledge message with a null parameter. On the other hand, if the elevator is idle, Elevator Status & Plan returns an Acknowledge message with an up (or down) parameter. In this case, the Elevator Manager sends an Up Request (or Down Request) message to Elevator Control.

Because the Up or Down message arrives at Elevator Control from a different source in these two cases, the message sequence description that follows refers to a source object sending the message. This can be considered an input parameter to the collaboration model. In the scenario depicted on the collaboration diagram, the Elevator Status & Plan object sends the Up Request (Figure 18.9).

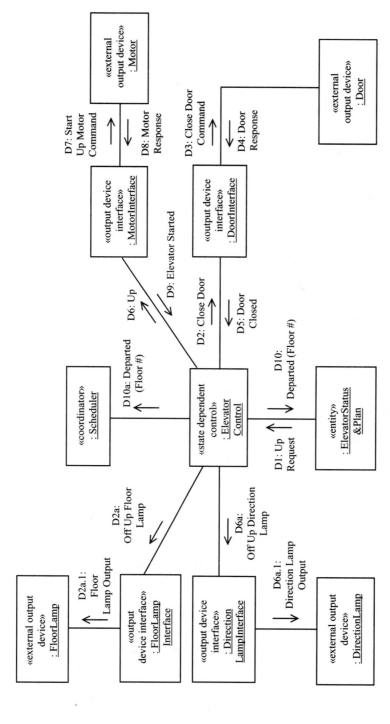

Figure 18.9 *Collaboration diagram for Dispatch Elevator use case*

Because this use case is state-dependent, it is also depicted on a statechart (see Figure 18.10). The message sequence description is as follows:

Precondition: Elevator is in either `Elevator Idle` state or `Checking Next Destination` state.

D1: {`Source object`} sends `Elevator Control` an `Up Request` message. `Elevator Control` transitions to `Door Closing to Move Up` state.

D2: As a result of this state transition, there are two concurrent output events. `Elevator Control` sends a `Close Door` command to `Door Interface`. On the statechart, the `Close Door` event (as well as one other output event) is shown as an entry action, because the `Up Request` event can arrive from either the `Elevator Idle` state or the `Checking Next Destination` state. It is more concise to depict one entry action on the statechart instead of two actions, one on each of the incoming state transitions.

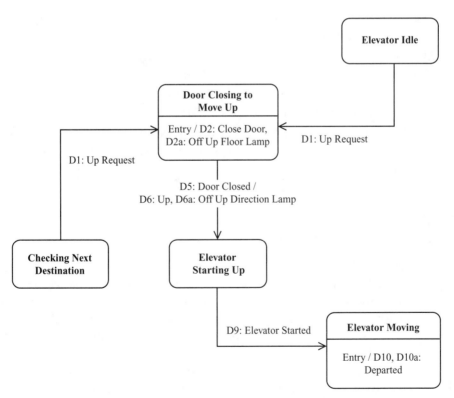

Figure 18.10 *Dispatch Elevator use case: statechart for Elevator Control*

D2a (parallel sequence): `Elevator Control` sends an `Off Up Floor Lamp` to the `Floor Lamp Interface` object, which switches off the real-world floor lamp (D2a.1).

D3: `Door Interface` sends a `Close Door Command` to the real-world door.

D4: The real-world door sends a `Door Response` when the door is closed.

D5: The `Door Interface` sends a `Door Closed` message to `Elevator Control`, which transitions to `Elevator Starting Up` state.

D6: `Elevator Control` sends an `Up` command to the `Motor Interface` object.

D6a: `Elevator Control` sends an `Off Up Direction Lamp` request to the `Direction Lamp Interface` object, which switches off the direction lamp (D6a.1).

D7: The `Motor Interface` object sends the `Start Up Motor Command` to the real-world motor.

D8: The real-world motor sends a `Motor Response` when the elevator has started moving upward.

D9: The `Motor Interface` object sends an `Elevator Started` message to `Elevator Control`, which transitions to `Elevator Moving` state.

D10: `Elevator Control` sends a `Departed` message to both the `Elevator Status & Plan` (D10) and `Scheduler` (D10a) objects.

The sequence of steps is the same if the elevator receives a `Down Request` message and departs to move down. `Up` is replaced by `Down` in the message sequence description.

18.6 Statechart Model

Because the statechart modeling involves two state-dependent use cases, it is necessary to consolidate the two partial statecharts and consider alternative branches to create a complete statechart. The complete statechart, showing both the `Stop Elevator at Floor` and `Dispatch Elevator` event sequences, is depicted in Figure 18.11. Additional states have been added to show the alternative when the door is closing to move down.

This is a flat statechart; hence, there is an opportunity for making it a hierarchical statechart by defining superstates to represent the major states of the elevator. The superstates and substates of the elevator are shown on a hierarchical statechart and described next. The top-level statechart (showing events but not

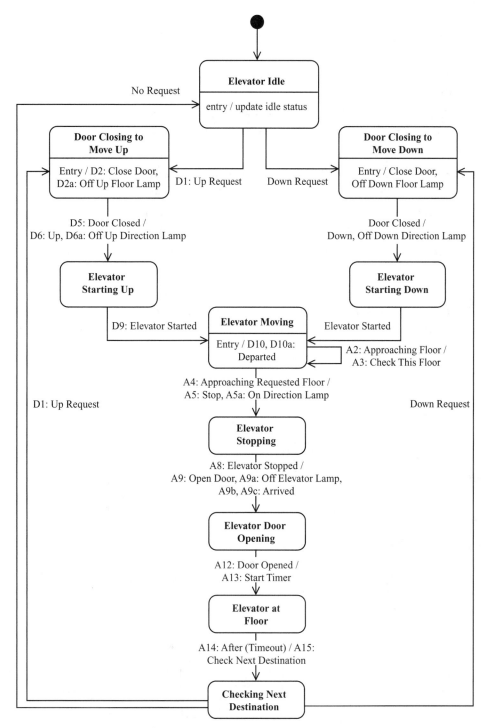

Figure 18.11 *Statechart for Elevator Control*

actions) is depicted in Figure 18.12, and the complete statechart is depicted in Figure 18.13:

1. `Elevator Idle`. The elevator is stationary at a floor and there is no outstanding request for it. Elevators are idle with the door open.

2. `Preparing to Move Up`. This superstate consists of the following substates:
   - `Door Closing to Move Up`. An elevator enters this state when it starts closing the door to satisfy a request for it to visit another floor farther up.
   - `Elevator Starting Up`. An elevator enters this state when the door has closed and it is waiting for the motor to start moving the elevator up.

3. `Preparing to Move Down`. This superstate consists of the following substates:
   - `Door Closing to Move Down`. An elevator enters this state when it starts closing the door in order to satisfy a request for it to visit another floor farther down.
   - `Elevator Starting Down`. An elevator enters this state when the door has closed and it is waiting for the motor to start moving the elevator down.

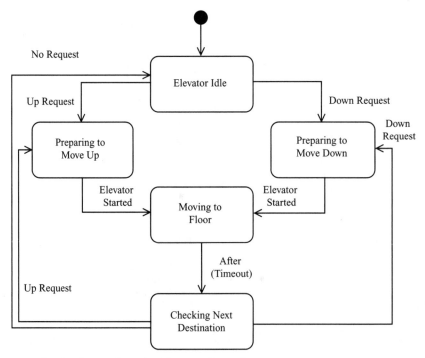

Figure 18.12 *Top-level statechart for Elevator Control*

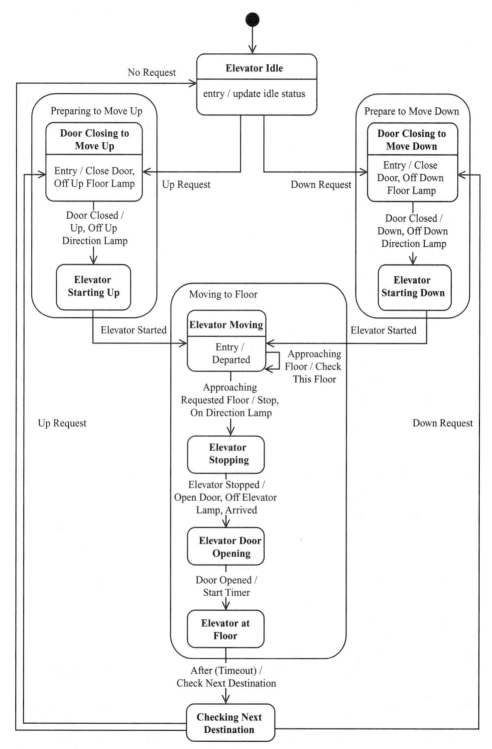

Figure 18.13 *Hierarchical statechart for Elevator Control*

The Door Closing to Move Up and the Door Closing to Move Down states are different because the input events Up Request and Down Request that cause the transitions into these states are different (see Figure 18.13). More importantly, the output events when leaving the states, Up and Down, are also different.

4. Moving to Floor. This superstate consists of the following substates:

- Elevator Moving. An elevator enters this state when it has started its journey up or down.
- Elevator Stopping. This state is entered when the elevator is approaching a floor at which it has to stop.
- Elevator Door Opening. This state is entered when the elevator has stopped at a floor and the door is opening.
- Elevator at Floor. This state is entered when the elevator door has completed opening.

5. Checking Next Destination. In this state, the elevator is checking which floor to visit next and hence in which direction to move, Up or Down, or whether to enter Elevator Idle state. This state is entered when a timer event expires while in Elevator at Floor state.

18.7 Consolidation of Collaboration Diagrams

The consolidation of the four collaboration diagrams respectively supporting the four use cases is shown in Figure 18.14, which shows all the objects that participate in the use cases and all the interactions between these objects. Some objects participate in more than one use case. For example, the Door Interface, Motor Interface, and Elevator Control objects participate in both the Stop Elevator at Floor and Dispatch Elevator use cases. Other objects—for example, Floor Button Interface and Arrival Sensor Interface—participate in only one use case.

For objects that participate in only one use case, all their message interactions are depicted on the collaboration diagram for that use case. However, for objects that participate in more than one use case, their message interactions are a consolidation of interactions from various collaboration diagrams. Thus, the Open Door and Door Opened messages to and from the Door Interface object originate from the Stop Elevator at Floor use case (see Figure 18.7). However, the Close Door and Door Closed messages originate from the Dispatch Elevator use case (see Figure 18.9).

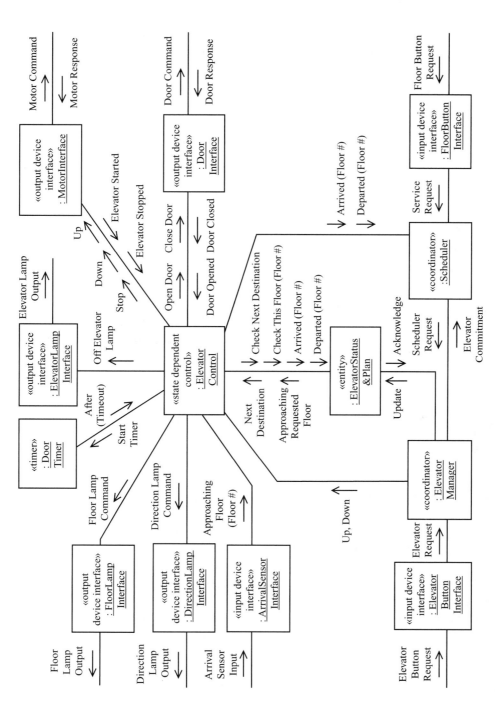

Figure 18.14 *Elevator Control System: consolidated collaboration diagram*

481

All object interactions must be shown on the consolidated collaboration diagram. This includes alternatives that usually do not appear on collaboration diagrams, which typically depict the main sequence through each use case. Thus, Figure 18.14 shows all the down messages as well as the up messages. In addition, message names can be aggregated. Thus Direction Lamp Command is an aggregation of four possible messages, On Up Direction Lamp, Off Up Direction Lamp, On Down Direction Lamp, and Off Down Direction Lamp. The composition of aggregate message names needs to be defined in a message dictionary.

18.8   Subsystem Structuring

Next, the system is structured into subsystems. Because this is a potentially distributed application, the geographical location and aggregation/composition guidelines take precedence. Thus, all elevator objects are part of an Elevator Subsystem composite object, of which there are n. In particular, Door Interface, Motor Interface, Elevator Button Interface (m instances, one per floor), and Elevator Lamp Interface (also m instances, one per floor), are all constituents of one elevator. In addition, each elevator needs an Elevator Control object, an Elevator Manager object, and an Elevator Status & Plan object. There also m floors in the system, and there is a Floor Subsystem composite object that consists of Floor Lamp Interface and Floor Button Interface objects. Some other objects have m x n instances, and so could be in a Floor Subsystem, an Elevator Subsystem, or a completely separate subsystem. The Arrival Sensor Interface (one per floor in each elevator shaft) is one such example. This object is placed in the Elevator Subsystem because it is more tightly coupled with this subsystem, as indicated by its participation in the Stop Elevator at Floor use case. Direction Lamp Interface, on the other hand, is allocated to the Floor Subsystem, because its primary affiliation is with each floor. Finally, the Scheduler coordinator object is allocated to its own subsystem, because it is independent of the number of floors and elevators.

The overall subsystem structure, consisting of the Elevator Subsystem, Floor Subsystem, and Scheduler, is shown in Figure 18.15. The Elevator Subsystem is a control subsystem, the Floor Subsystem is a data collection subsystem, and the Scheduler is a coordinator subsystem. The structure of the Elevator Subsystem is shown in Figure 18.16, and the structure of the Floor Subsystem is shown in Figure 18.17.

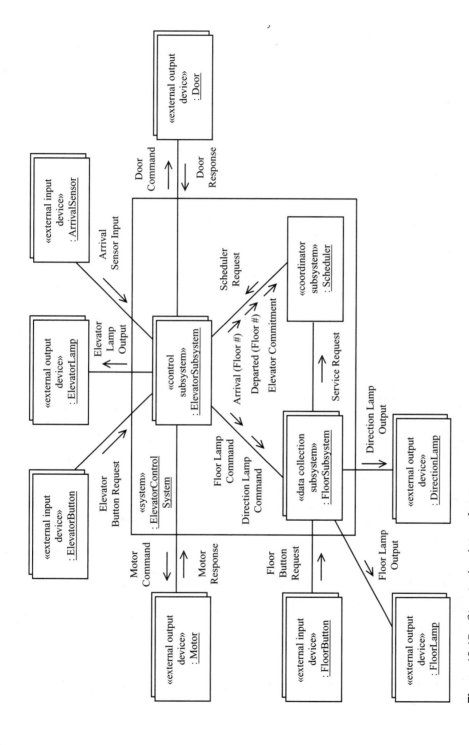

Figure 18.15 *Structuring into subsystems*

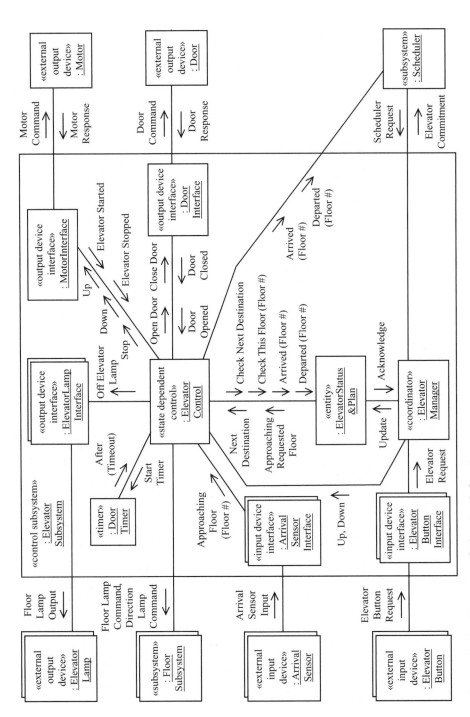

Figure 18.16 *Structure of Elevator Subsystem*

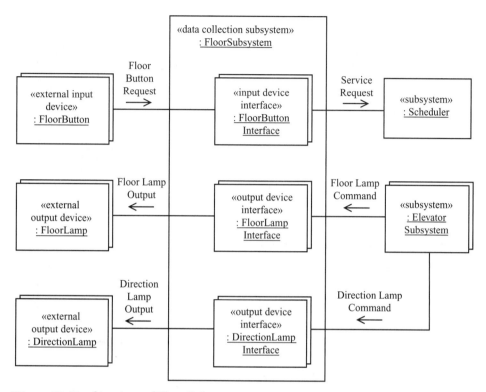

Figure 18.17 *Structure of Floor Subsystem*

In addition, a refined static model is now developed, which is depicted on a class diagram. This class diagram is derived from the overall subsystem architecture and the structure of each subsystem. The class diagram shows all the classes from which the objects in the collaboration diagrams are instantiated, as well as the relationships between these classes, which represent collaborations. Figure 18.18 shows the refined static model, in which each subsystem is shown as a composite class composed of several classes. There are software counterparts to the static model of the problem domain developed earlier (see Figure 18.3). The Elevator Subsystem composite class has several more constituent classes. These include the device interface classes—for example, Motor Interface—which interface to the external classes—for example, Motor—shown on the earlier static model. However, the Elevator Subsystem is also composed of several other classes, including three control classes (state-dependent control, coordinator, and timer) and one entity class. Similar observations can be made about the Floor Subsystem composite class and its constituent classes. The operations of each class are defined in the sections 18.9.5 and 18.11 on Class Design.

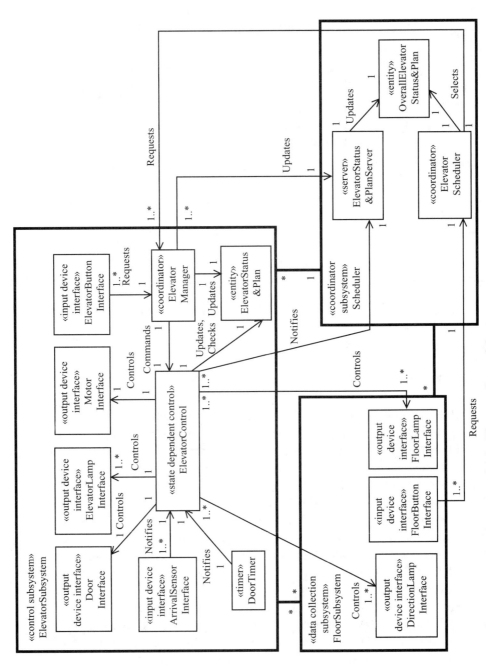

Figure 18.18 *Refined static model for Elevator Control System*

18.9   Structuring System into Tasks

Next, task structuring is considered. To structure the system into tasks, it is necessary to analyze all the objects on the collaboration diagrams and apply the task structuring criteria. We will perform this by analyzing each of the collaboration diagrams in turn.

In the distributed Elevator Control System, there is one instance of the `Elevator Subsystem` for each elevator and one instance of the `Floor Subsystem` for each floor, as depicted in Figure 18.15. However, for a non-distributed Elevator Control System, some simplifications can be made. In this case, the Elevator Control System is mapped to a single CPU or tightly coupled multiprocessor configuration (i.e., with shared memory).

An important aspect of the non-distributed solution is that the `Elevator Status & Plan` entity object is accessible to all elevators as well as to the `Scheduler`, so that one centralized repository of data can be used. This solution does not work in a loosely coupled distributed system, where there is no shared memory. The distributed Elevator Control System solution is described in Section 18.10.

18.9.1   Determine Elevator Subsystem Tasks

Consider the task architecture of the `Elevator Subsystem` in the non-distributed case.

Consider the `Select Destination` collaboration diagram in Figure 18.5. Start with the device interface object that receives input from the actor and then consider the sequence of interactions. The object `Elevator Button Interface` is structured as a separate task, `Elevator Buttons Interface`, based on the asynchronous input device interface task structuring criterion. Using task inversion, one task is designed to handle all elevator buttons rather than one task per button. The `Elevator Buttons Interface` task is activated by the arrival of an interrupt when any of the elevator buttons is pressed. It then reads the elevator button input and sends the elevator request to the `Elevator Manager` so it can be ready to service the next interrupt. The `Elevator Manager`, which is a coordinator object, receives messages from `Elevator Buttons Interface` in this use case and also the `Scheduler` in the `Request Elevator` use case in Figure 18.6. It is structured as a coordinator task, activated by the arrival of a `Scheduler` or `Elevator Request` message. `Elevator Status & Plan` is a passive data abstraction object that does not have a separate thread of control.

Now consider the `Stop Elevator at Floor` use case in Figure 18.7. The `Arrival Sensor Interface` object is structured as an asynchronous input device interface task, Arrival Sensors Interface, for the same reason as the Elevator Buttons Interface, and sends the floor number to the Elevator Control object, which is considered next.

Consider the Elevator Control statechart shown in Figure 18.13. This is a case of a state-dependent control object that executes a statechart. During the analysis phase, the control aspects of a real-world elevator object are mapped to a control object, Elevator Control (see Figures 18.7 and 18.9). In the case of multiple elevators, the control of each elevator is independent, and this is modeled by having one Elevator Control object for each elevator. During task structuring, each Elevator Control object is mapped to a separate Elevator Controller task. Each task executes the statechart for that elevator, as shown in Figure 18.13.

The Elevator Controller task interacts with several output device interface objects, which interact directly with the external environment, namely, the motor, door, and elevator lamps. It is given that all these devices are passive (i.e. they do not generate I/O interrupts), so asynchronous output tasks are not required. Each output request is executed on demand, so a periodic output task is not required. Furthermore, the calling task always has to wait for the output request to complete, so a passive output task is not required. In this case, the device output object does not need to be structured as a separate task; it is combined with the Elevator Controller task according to the control clustering criterion. For example, if the Elevator Controller initiates the Close Door action, it waits for the Door Closed response because the elevator cannot start until the door has been closed.

Consider the execution of the Elevator Controller in more detail. The Elevator Controller receives the Approaching Floor message when it is in the Elevator Moving state (see Figure 18.8). It forwards the message to Elevator Status & Plan, requesting it to Check This Floor. A state change takes place only if the elevator plan indicates that the elevator should stop at this floor, in which case the Elevator Status & Plan object sends the Approaching Requested Floor message. This in turn causes the Elevator Controller to transition to Elevator Stopping state and output the Stop action. The Stop message is sent to the elevator Motor Interface object (see Figure 18.7). Elevator Controller transitions out of this state only when it receives an Elevator Stopped response from the Motor Interface object. Thus the Elevator Controller and Motor Interface objects cannot execute concurrently. A similar analysis shows that the Elevator Controller and Door Interface objects cannot execute concurrently. Consequently, the Elevator Controller task is combined with the Motor Interface and Door Interface objects, based on the control clustering criterion.

The `Elevator Manager` (one instance in the non-distributed solution) executes asynchronously with the `Elevator Controller` task because a request for the elevator could come at any time while the `Elevator Controller` is executing. Consequently, the `Elevator Manager` is structured as a separate coordinator task. It is activated asynchronously by either an `Elevator Request` or a `Scheduler Request` and usually executes independent of the `Elevator Controller` task. The only interaction between the two tasks is when the elevator is in `Idle` state and a new request arrives. In that case, the `Elevator Manager` awakens the `Elevator Controller` task.

In summary, for the non-distributed `Elevator Control System`, the `Elevator` subsystem is structured into four tasks: the `Elevator Buttons Interface`, the `Arrival Sensors Interface`, the `Elevator Manager`, and the `Elevator Controller`. There is one instance of each of the first three tasks and one instance per elevator of the `Elevator Controller` task. Each instance of the `Elevator Controller` task is identical and executes its own copy of the `Elevator Control` statechart. The preliminary task architecture is shown on the initial concurrent collaboration diagram in Figure 18.19.

18.9.2   Determine Floor Subsystem Tasks

Consider the task architecture of the `Floor` subsystem. The `Floor` subsystem, shown in Figure 18.17, is structured as follows. The `Floor Button Interface` object is structured as a separate task, `Floor Buttons Interface`, based on the asynchronous input device interface and task inversion task structuring criteria. In the non-distributed solution, the `Floor Buttons Interface` task handles the inputs for all the floor buttons, one or two per floor. It is activated by an interrupt, handles the interrupt, and then sends the `Service Request` to the `Scheduler` so it can be ready to handle the next interrupt.

The floor lamps and direction lamps are passive output devices. The device output objects are the `Floor Lamp Interface` and `Direction Lamp Interface` objects. It is possible for the multiple instances of the `Elevator Controller` task to send requests concurrently to the floor lamps and direction lamps. In this case, it is necessary to have a resource monitor task for each device to ensure that output requests are handled sequentially. Thus, a `Floor Lamps Monitor` task and a `Direction Lamps Monitor` task are needed. The `Floor Lamp Interface` device interface objects for all elevators are mapped to the `Floor Lamps Monitor` task. The `Direction Lamp` device interface objects for all elevators are mapped to the `Direction Lamps Monitor` task. The tasks determined for the `Floor Subsystem` for the non-distributed Elevator Control System are

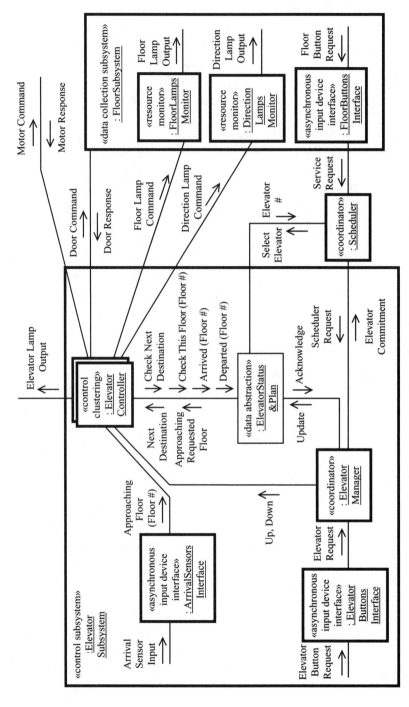

Figure 18.19 *Non-distributed Elevator Control System: task architecture*

shown in Figure 18.19. An alternative design is to have one resource monitor task for both direction and floor lamps; however, on balance, it is considered more flexible to have two resource monitor tasks.

18.9.3   Determine Scheduler Subsystem Tasks

In the non-distributed solution, the Scheduler is a subsystem consisting of one coordinator object, which is structured as a coordinator task. The Scheduler task is activated on demand—in particular, when it receives a Service Request—and selects the most appropriate elevator to handle a floor request.

Because this is a non-distributed solution, the Scheduler can read directly from the Elevator Status & Plan. Consequently, there is no need for the multiple instances of the Elevator Controller task to send Arrived and Departed status messages to the Scheduler. The task architecture for the non-distributed solution is depicted in Figure 18.19.

18.9.4   Define Task Interfaces

Consider how the task interfaces are determined. First consider the message interfaces between concurrent tasks. These are mapped to either loosely coupled or tightly coupled message communication. It is only necessary to consider the interfaces between objects that are mapped to separate tasks. It is also necessary to define the messages precisely, with the name and parameters of each message specified.

The message interface between the Elevator Buttons Interface and Elevator Manager tasks, shown in Figure 18.19, is mapped to a loosely coupled message communication interface (see Figure 18.20). This ensures that the Elevator Buttons Interface is not held up after it has sent a message to the Elevator Manager. The Scheduler also sends scheduler Request messages to the same queue. Because the Scheduler will often be busy when a message is sent to it, the message interface between the Floor Buttons Interface and the Scheduler, shown in Figure 18.19, is also mapped to a loosely coupled message communication interface (see Figure 18.20).

The message interface between the Arrival Sensors Interface and the Elevator Controller, shown in Figure 18.19, is mapped to a tightly coupled message communication interface (see Figure 18.20). The reason for this is that when the Arrival Sensors Interface sends the approaching Floor message, the Elevator Controller is always inactive, as it is in Elevator Moving state. Hence, the Arrival Sensors Interface task should not be held up for a significant period.

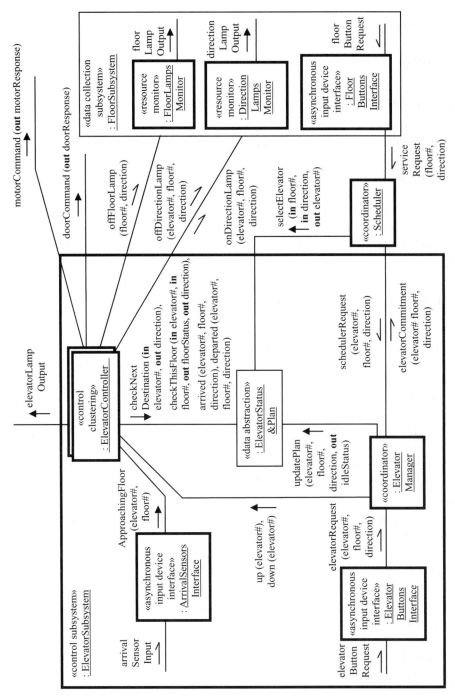

Figure 18.20 *Non-distributed Elevator Control System: task interfaces*

The message interface between the Elevator Manager and Elevator Controller, shown in Figure 18.19, is mapped to a tightly coupled message communication interface between the Elevator Manager and Elevator Controller tasks (see Figure 18.20). The Elevator Manager can send up or down messages. The interface is tightly coupled because the Elevator Manager only sends messages to the Elevator Controller if the latter is idle and needs to be awakened.

Consider the interface between the Elevator Controller task and the two resource monitor tasks, Floor Lamps Monitor and Direction Lamps Monitor. The Elevator Controller sends floor lamp command messages to the Floor Lamps Monitor task and direction lamp command messages to the Direction Lamps Monitor task (see Figure 18.19). This is mapped to a loosely coupled message interface between the Elevator Controller and the Floor Lamps Monitor. The interface is loosely coupled to allow multiple instances of Elevator Controller to send messages to the Floor Lamps Monitor (see Figure 18.20) without being held up. For the same reason, the interface between the Elevator Controller and Direction Lamps Monitor tasks is also handled by loosely coupled message communication.

Consider the passive entity objects that are accessed by more than one task. The entity object, Elevator Plan & Status, is a data abstraction object that encapsulates the elevator status and plan. The non-distributed solution has one instance of this object, allowing for a centralized repository. The object is accessed by the multiple instances of the Elevator Controller task, the Elevator Manager task, and the Scheduler (see Figure 18.20). Task access to the passive object must be synchronized so that its operations are executed mutually exclusively.

18.9.5 Design of Data Abstraction Class

There is one data abstraction class in the centralized non-distributed solution, the Elevator Status & Plan class. The status of the elevator is the current location (floor number) and direction (up, down, or idle) of the elevator. The plan is the floors it is committed to visit. The non-distributed solution has one instance of this class, allowing for a centralized repository, as depicted in Figure 18.21a.

To determine the operations of the data abstraction class, it is necessary to determine how the data abstraction object is accessed. Figure 18.19 shows three different tasks that access the data abstraction object, namely, the Scheduler and the Elevator Manager and Elevator Controller tasks (multiple instances of the latter task, one for each elevator). The Scheduler reads the plan and status of each elevator to select an elevator to service an outstanding floor request. This

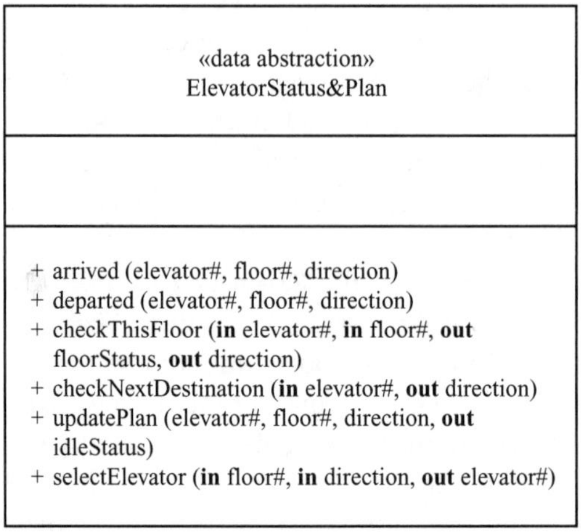

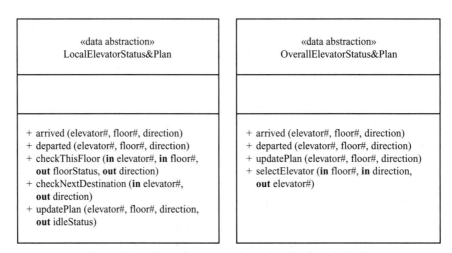

Figure 18.21a *Data abstraction class for centralized solution*

Figure 18.21b *Data abstraction classes for distributed solution*

Figure 18.21 *Data abstraction classes*

function is handled by an operation called `select Elevator`. The `Elevator Manager` updates the elevator plan and checks to see if the elevator is idle. This function is handled by an operation `update Plan`. The `Elevator Controller` task accesses the `Elevator Status & Plan` in four different ways via four separate messages sent at different times, to update status by indicating the elevator `arrived` or `departed`, to check `This Floor`, and to check `Next Destina-`

tion. Each of these messages is mapped to a call to an operation of the data abstraction class (see Figure 18.21).

The operation check This Floor is called with a floor # and elevator # as input parameters, determines whether the elevator should stop at this floor or not, and updates the status and plan for that elevator accordingly. This operation returns the floor Status, which is either stop if the elevator should stop or pass if the elevator should not, and direction, which is a preliminary indication of the direction in which the elevator should next travel. The operation check Next Destination (which is called later) checks in which direction the elevator should travel next. The operation sets the elevator status to up, down, or idle, if there are no outstanding requests, and returns direction, respectively one of three possible responses, up Request, down Request, or no Request.

18.9.6   Discussion of Alternative Task Architectures

An alternative task architecture to the one just described is to have, for each elevator, one instance each of the Elevator Buttons Interface, Arrival Sensors Interface, and Elevator Manager tasks in addition to the Elevator Controller task. In a single-CPU environment, this solution is avoided because of the additional system overhead.

In a multiprocessor situation, however, there could be one CPU for each elevator, which would have one instance each of the Elevator Buttons Interface, Arrival Sensors Interface, Elevator Manager, and Elevator Controller tasks. The Scheduler, Floor Buttons Interface, Floor Lamps Monitor, and Direction Lamps Monitor tasks would execute on a separate CPU. In the case of multiple CPUs with shared memory, the Elevator Plan & Status data abstraction object would reside, as before, in the shared memory.

If there is no shared memory between the processors, the Elevator Plan & Status data abstraction object cannot be accessed directly by the tasks. The design of the distributed Elevator Control System is described next.

18.10   Design of Distributed Elevator Control System

In the distributed Elevator Control System, the physical configuration consists of multiple nodes interconnected by a local area network. In a distributed configuration, it is necessary to enforce the rule that all communication between distributed subsystems is only by means of messages. The overall distributed software architecture is shown in Figure 18.22, which shows multiple instances of the Elevator

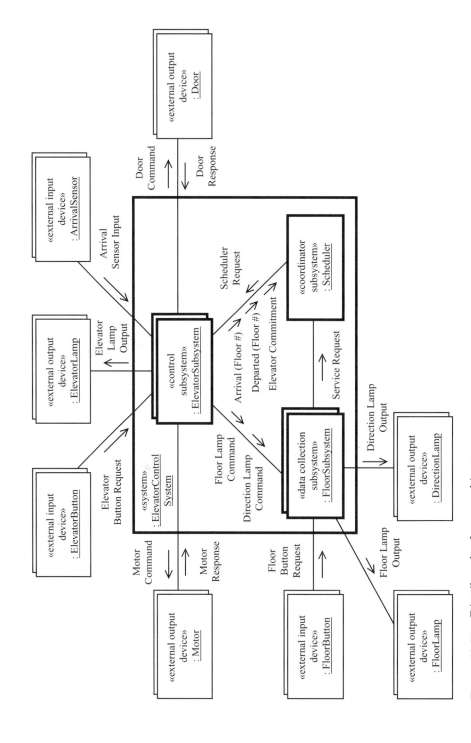

Figure 18.22 *Distributed software architecture*

Subsystem (one instance per elevator), multiple instances of the Floor Subsystem (one instance per floor), and one instance of the Scheduler subsystem. All communication between the subsystems is via loosely coupled message communication.

There is no shared memory in a distributed configuration; thus, the Scheduler and the multiple instances of the Elevator Subsystem cannot directly access the Elevator Status & Plan data abstraction object as in the nondistributed solution. One solution to this problem is to embed the Elevator Status & Plan data abstraction object in a server task. Instead of calling an operation of the data abstraction object, a client task would send a synchronous message with reply to the Elevator Status & Plan Server task. However, this solution presents the potential danger of creating a bottleneck at this server because it has several clients, namely the Scheduler and the multiple instances of the Elevator Manager and Elevator Controller tasks.

Instead, an alternative solution is to use replicated data. Each instance of the Elevator Subsystem maintains its own local instance of the Elevator Status & Plan data abstraction object, called Local Elevator Status & Plan, that holds the status and plan of its own elevator. The Scheduler also maintains a copy of the Elevator Status & Plan data abstraction object. However, the Scheduler's copy maintains the status and plan of all the elevators and is called the Overall Elevator Status & Plan. These data abstraction classes are depicted in Figure 18.21b.

18.10.1   Structure of Elevator Subsystem

In the distributed design, there is one instance of the Elevator Subsystem for each elevator. Each instance of the Elevator Subsystem is composed of one instance each of the Elevator Controller, Elevator Buttons Interface, Arrival Sensors Interface, and Elevator Manager tasks. In addition, each instance of the Elevator Subsystem also maintains its own local instance of the Elevator Status & Plan data abstraction object.

The task architecture for the Elevator Subsystem is shown in Figure 18.23. The Elevator Manager task receives Elevator Request messages from the Elevator Buttons Interface task, receives Scheduler Request messages from the Scheduler, and sends Elevator Commitment messages to the Scheduler. The Elevator Controller sends elevator status messages to both the Floor Subsystem and Scheduler.

The revised task architecture, shown in Figure 18.24, depicts the task interfaces, including how tasks access the information hiding objects. The design of the

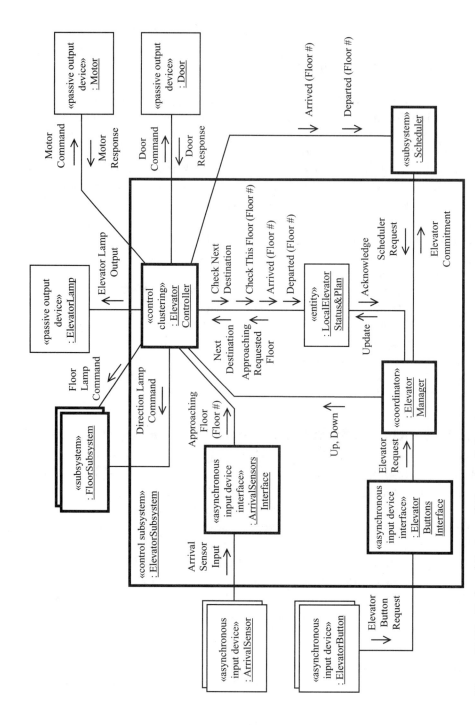

Figure 18.23 *Task architecture of Elevator Subsystem*

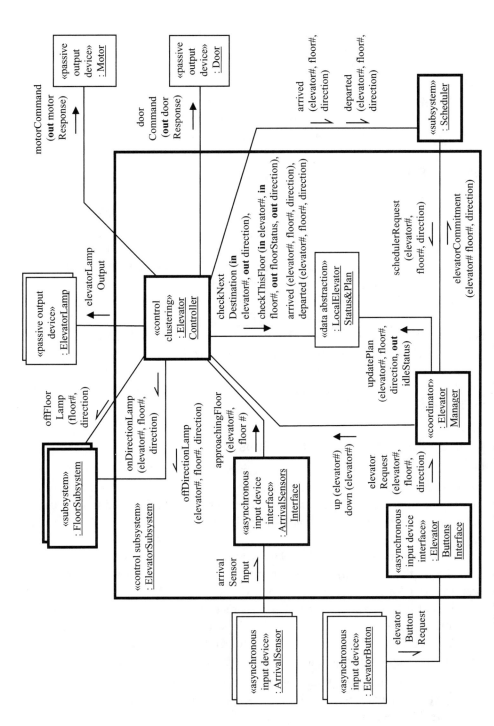

Figure 18.24 *Task Architecture of Elevator Subsystem: task interfaces*

Local Elevator Status & Plan data abstraction object is simpler than the centralized solution shown in Figure 18.21a because it supports only one elevator and does not need a select Elevator operation (see Figure 18.21b).

During target system configuration (as described in Section 18.13), each instance of the Elevator Subsystem is typically mapped to an elevator node. Thus, each elevator node can execute independent of the other nodes.

18.10.2 Structure of Floor Subsystem

In the distributed solution to this problem, there is one instance of the Floor subsystem for each floor. Each instance of the Floor Subsystem has one instance each of the Floor Buttons Interface, Floor Lamps Monitor, and Direction Lamps Monitor tasks. Thus, there is one task for each kind of I/O device.

The task architecture for the Floor Subsystem is shown in Figure 18.25. The tasks in this subsystem are similar to the non-distributed solution shown in Figure 18.19, except that there are multiple instances of them, one per floor.

The Floor Buttons Interface task sends Service Requests for this floor to the Scheduler. Both the Floor Lamps Monitor and Direction Lamps Monitor receive elevator status messages for this floor in the form of lamp command messages from the multiple instances of the Elevator Controller task. The revised task architecture depicting the task interfaces is shown in Figure 18.26.

18.10.3 Structure of Scheduler Subsystem

There is one instance of the Scheduler subsystem, which consists of two tasks and one information hiding object. The information hiding object is the Overall Elevator Status & Plan data abstraction object, which contains the current status of each elevator and the plan for each elevator of what floors it is committed to visit (see Figure 18.21b).

At any given node, both the Elevator Controller and Elevator Manager access the Local Elevator Status & Plan data abstraction object. However, in order for the Scheduler to know each elevator's status and plan, each instance of the Elevator Controller sends status messages to the Scheduler to report on the elevator's arrival at and departure from each floor. In addition, the Elevator Manager sends the Scheduler the following two kinds of commitment messages, which identify the floors the elevator is planning to visit:

1. Notification messages, which originate because a passenger in the elevator presses an elevator button; these messages inform the Scheduler of the floors this elevator will visit for this reason.

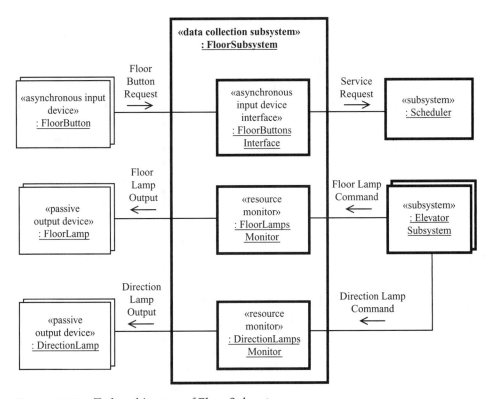

Figure 18.25 *Task architecture of Floor Subsystem*

2. Acknowledgment messages, which are responses from the Elevator Sub-system to the Scheduler Request messages sent by the Scheduler requesting the elevator to move to certain floors to pick up passengers.

The Scheduler Subsystem is structured into two tasks: the Elevator Status & Plan Server task (a server task) and the Elevator Scheduler task (a coordinator task). The former task receives the status and commitment messages and updates the Overall Elevator Status & Plan data abstraction object. The Elevator Scheduler task receives the Service Request messages from the multiple instances of the Floor Buttons Interface tasks. Every time it receives a Service Request message, the Elevator Scheduler task checks to see if an elevator is due to visit the floor in question. If not, it selects an elevator and sends a Scheduler Request message to the Elevator Manager task for that elevator. The task architecture for the Scheduler Subsystem is shown in Figure 18.27. The revised task architecture depicting the task interfaces is shown in Figure 18.28.

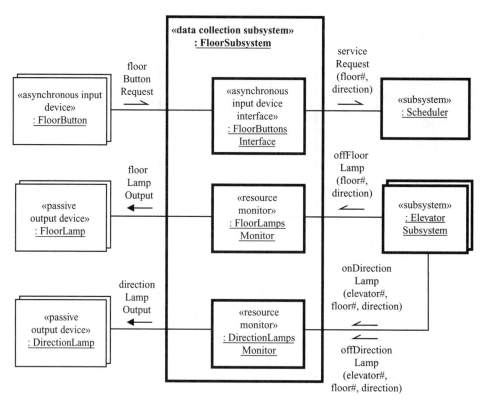

Figure 18.26 *Task architecture of Floor Subsystem: task interfaces*

The Overall Elevator Status & Plan data abstraction object provides the arrived, departed, update Plan, and select Elevator operations (see Figures 18.21b and 18.28). The Elevator Status & Plan Server task calls the arrived or departed operations when it receives a status message. It calls update Plan when it receives a commitment message.

18.10.4 Subsystem Interfaces

After the task interfaces in the three subsystems are defined, the distributed software architecture can be updated to show the subsystem interfaces, as shown in Figure 18.29. All the interfaces are actually handled by the tasks in the subsystems, as shown in the earlier figures.

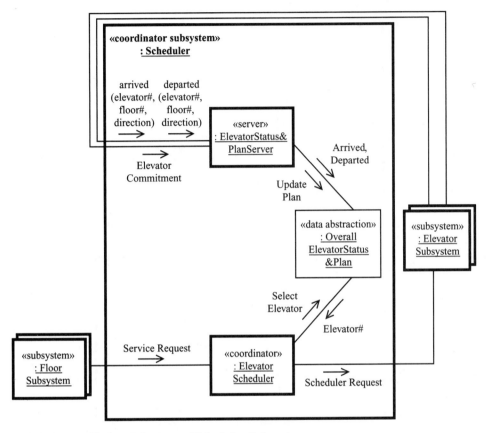

Figure 18.27 *Task architecture of Scheduler Subsystem*

18.11 Design of Information Hiding Classes

The classes were determined during the object structuring step. In this step, the operations of each class are designed. The data abstraction classes were described earlier. This section describes the design of the other information hiding classes.

18.11.1 Design of Device Interface Classes

A device interface class hides the actual interface to the real-world device by providing a virtual interface to it. There is one device interface class for each I/O device type. The operations provided by a device interface class are determined

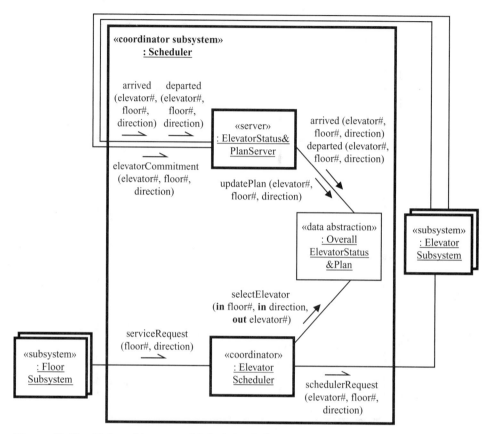

Figure 18.28 *Task architecture of Scheduler Subsystem: task interfaces*

by considering the functions each object needs to support. The device interface classes are depicted in Figure 18.30a and described as follows:

- Elevator Button Interface. Provides two operations: read, which reads the value of an elevator button sensor, and initialize.

- Floor Button Interface. Provides two operations: read, which reads the value of a floor button sensor, and initialize.

- Arrival Sensor Interface. Provides two operations: read, which reads the value of an Arrival sensor, and initialize.

- Motor Interface. Provides up, down, and stop operations, as determined by the Up, Down, and Stop messages the Motor Interface object receives (see Figure 18.14).

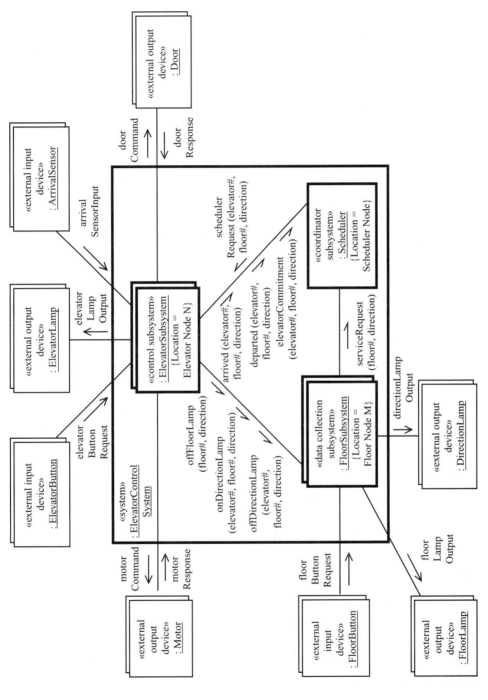

Figure 18.29   *Distributed software architecture: subsystem interfaces*

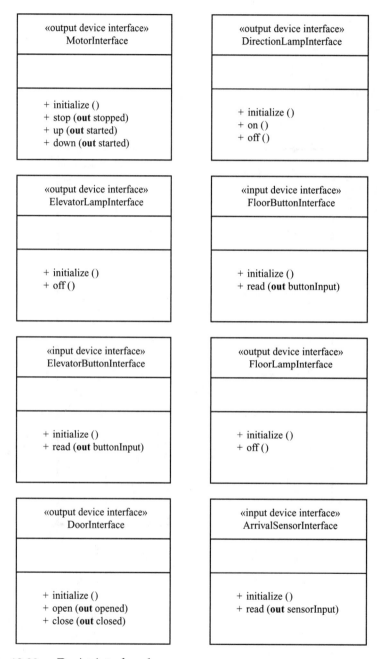

Figure 18.30a *Device interface classes*

- `Door Interface`. Provides operations to `open` and `close`, as determined by the `Open Door` and `Close Door` messages the `Door Interface` object receives (see Figure 18.14).

- `Elevator Lamp Interface`. Provides an operation to switch `off` an elevator lamp. It is given that the hardware switches the elevator lamp on, so providing a switch on elevator lamp operation is not required in software. The `off` operation is determined by the `Off Elevator Lamp` message the `Elevator Lamp Interface` object receives (see Figure 18.14).

- `Floor Lamp Interface`. Provides an operation to switch `off` a floor lamp. It is given that the hardware switches the floor lamp on, so providing a switch on elevator lamp operation is not required in software. The `off` operation is determined by the `Off Floor Lamp` message the `Floor Lamp Interface` object receives (Figure 18.14).

- `Direction Lamp Interface`. Provides operations to switch `on` a direction lamp and to switch `off` a direction lamp. The `on` and `off` operations are respectively determined by the `On` and `Off Direction Lamp` messages the `Direction Lamp Interface` object receives (see Figure 18.14).

18.11.2 Design of State-Dependent Class

There is one state-dependent class, the `Elevator Control` class, which encapsulates the statechart (implemented as a state transition table) shown in Figure 18.13. It supports two operations, `process Event` and `current State`. The `Elevator Control` state-dependent class is nested within the `Elevator Controller` task. Because there are multiple instances of this task, there will also be multiple instances of the state-dependent class, one for each elevator. The state-dependent class is depicted in Figure 18.30b.

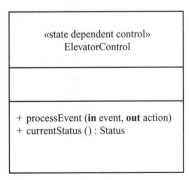

Figure 18.30b *State-dependent control class*

18.12   Developing Detailed Software Design

Now that the tasks and information hiding classes have been defined, the next step is to perform the detailed software design. This includes the design of the connector objects and the design of the composite tasks to show the nested information hiding objects.

18.12.1   Design of Elevator Connector Objects

The task interfaces in the distributed `Elevator Subsystem` depicted in Figure 18.24 are conceptual; they represent loosely coupled or tightly coupled message communication. During detailed software design, the precise interfaces are designed by using connector objects, as depicted in Figure 18.31. Thus, incoming messages to the `Elevator Controller` are tightly coupled without reply. This interface is mapped to a connector object called the `elevator Controller Message Buffer`. Usually, such a connector is between one producer and one consumer; however, in this case the producer tasks—the `Arrival Sensors Interface` and the `Elevator Manager`—always send their messages in differ-

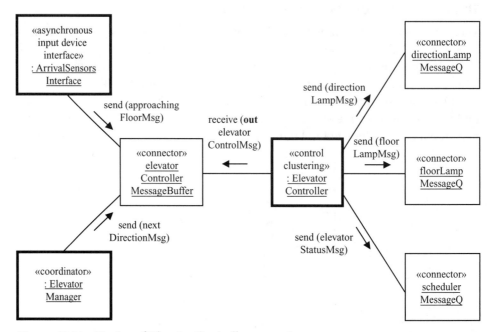

Figure 18.31 *Design of Elevator Controller connectors*

ent states of the Elevator Controller. Thus, the Arrival Sensors Interface sends the approaching Floor Message to the Elevator Controller in Elevator Moving state, and the Elevator Manager sends the next Direction Message in Elevator Idle state. Consequently, the messages to the Elevator Controller never overlap, and one message buffer connector can be used instead of two.

The Elevator Controller has three loosely coupled message communication interfaces for which it is the producer. In all three cases, the consumers are in different distributed subsystems. Consequently, three message queue connectors are used for this purpose (see Figure 18.31), which hide the details of the asynchronous message communication to potentially remote tasks over the local area network. The scheduler Message Q encapsulates the details of message communication to the Scheduler. The direction Lamp Message Q and the floor Lamp Message Q both encapsulate the details of message communication to tasks in the Floor Subsystem.

For a distributed application, the connectors need to be designed so they can determine at run time whether the destination task is on the same node or on a remote node, as described in Chapter 4. The sender tasks should be unaware of the location of the receiver tasks. This location transparency allows for a much more flexible distributed software configuration policy in which distributed subsystems are designed as distributed components. Component instances are mapped to physical nodes at system configuration time.

18.12.2 Design of Composite Tasks

Now consider the detailed software design of the composite clustered Elevator Controller task to show the information hiding objects it contains. The information hiding objects for each elevator are placed inside the Elevator Controller task for that elevator. These are the Elevator Control state-dependent control object and the device interface objects for the passive I/O devices supporting each elevator: the Door Interface, the Motor Interface, and multiple instances of the Elevator Lamp Interface. There is also a Door Timer object and an Elevator Coordinator object to provide the overall coordination for the task. Figure 18.32 shows the detailed software design of the Elevator Controller task.

Each resource monitor task is also designed as a composite task. The device interface objects for passive I/O devices supporting multiple elevators (the Direction Lamp Interface and the Floor Lamp Interface) are placed inside the resource monitor task for the device, namely, the Direction Lamps

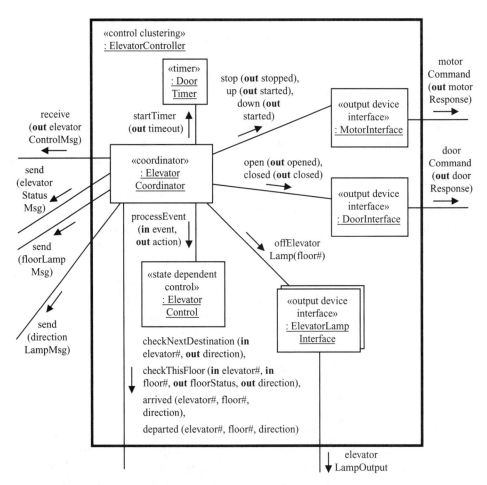

Figure 18.32   *Detailed software design of Elevator Controller*

Monitor and the Floor Lamps Monitor. The tasks receive messages from multiple elevators and ensure sequential access to the Direction Lamp Interface and Floor Lamp Interface device interface objects (see Figure 18.26). Thus the Direction Lamps Monitor receives Direction Lamp messages from the Elevator Controller tasks, requesting it to set or clear a given direction lamp. It calls the on or off operation of the appropriate Direction Lamp Interface device interface object, given the elevator and floor numbers (which it receives in the message) as parameters. The Floor Lamps Monitor has a similar design.

Each device interface object for an asynchronous I/O device is placed inside the asynchronous device interface task supporting that device. For example, the multiple instances of the `Elevator Button Interface` device interface object are placed inside the `Elevator Buttons Interface` task.

18.13 Target System Configuration

During target system configuration, the subsystems are mapped to physical nodes. One possible physical configuration is one node for each instance of the `Elevator Subsystem` (one node per physical elevator), one node for each instance of the `Floor Subsystem` (one node per physical floor), and one node for the `Scheduler`. Thus, if there are n elevators and m floors, this physical configuration would require n + m + 1 physical nodes. This example is shown on the deployment diagram in Figure 18.33, which shows each of the physical nodes.

Another possible configuration is for all instances of the `Floor Subsystem` to be mapped to one node. In that case, a possible optimization is for each of the `Floor Subsystem` tasks to handle the I/O devices for all floors instead of just one floor. Thus, the `Floor Buttons Interface` would monitor the buttons for all floors instead of one floor. Similarly, the `Floor Lamps Monitor` would handle the floor lamps for all floors and the `Direction Lamps Monitor` would handle the direction lamps for all floors. This configuration would not require a change in the task architecture of the `Floor Subsystem`, which would still be structured as shown in Figure 18.26.

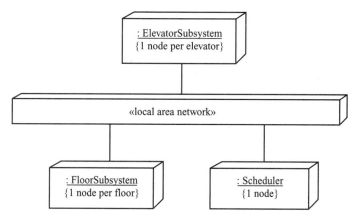

Figure 18.33 *Distributed Elevator Control System deployment diagram*

The `Scheduler` could continue to be mapped to a separate node, or it could be mapped to the same physical node as the `Floor Subsystem`. In the latter case, this physical configuration would require n + 1 physical nodes.

18.14   Performance Analysis of Non-Distributed Elevator Control System

This section describes applying real-time scheduling theory to analyze the performance of the non-distributed version of the Elevator Control System, prior to considering the distributed version in the next section.

18.14.1   Performance Analysis Scenario

It is necessary to consider one specific configuration of the Elevator Control System and then analyze the worst-case situation for it by applying the real-time scheduling theory. Consider a building with ten floors and three elevators. Hence, there are three instances of the `Elevator Controller` task. Assume the following worst-case scenario:

- Elevator button interrupts arrive with a maximum frequency of 10 times a second, which represents a minimum inter-arrival time of 100 msec. It is assumed that this is a busy period, with several passengers on each elevator going to different floors. Because there are 10 floors and three elevators, a total of 30 buttons could be pressed. This worst-case scenario assumes that all 30 buttons are pressed within three seconds!

- Floor button interrupts arrive with a maximum frequency of 5 times a second, which represents a minimum inter-arrival time of 200 msec. Because each floor has an Up and a Down button (except the top and bottom floors, which have only one button), there are a total of 18 floor buttons. This means that in the worst case, all 18 buttons could be pressed within 3.6 seconds.

- All three elevators are in motion and arrive at floors simultaneously. This is interpreted to mean that the three floor-arrival interrupts arrive within 50 msec of each other. This is actually the most time-critical aspect of the problem, because when a floor arrival interrupt is received, the `Elevator Controller` has to determine whether the elevator should stop at this floor or not. If it does need to stop, the controller must stop the elevator before the floor has been passed.

This scenario is addressed by the following three event sequences, which correspond to three of the four use cases: `Select Destination`, `Request Eleva-`

tor, and Stop Elevator at Floor. Because this worst-case scenario has all the elevators arriving at floors, it is mutually exclusive with the fourth use case, the Dispatch Elevator use case, in which elevators leave floors. The Dispatch Elevator use case is less time-critical because it is heavily I/O bound, involving the door closing, which is relatively slow, and the motor starting.

18.14.2   Event Sequences

Consider first the following event sequences for the non-distributed system, which correspond to the use cases, as shown in Figure 18.34:

Stop Elevator at Floor event sequence (Period = T_a):

A1: The Arrival Sensors Interface receives and processes the interrupt.

A2: The Arrival Sensors Interface sends approaching Floor message to the Elevator Controller.

A3: The Elevator Controller receives message and checks the Elevator Status & Plan object to determine whether the elevator should stop or not.

A4: The Elevator Controller invokes stop Motor operation if it should stop.

Select Destination event sequence (Period = T_b):

E1: The Elevator Buttons Interface receives and processes the interrupt.

E2: The Elevator Buttons Interface sends elevator Request message to the Elevator Manager.

E3: The Elevator Manager receives message and records destination in Elevator Status & Plan object.

Request Elevator event sequence (Period = T_c):

F1: The Floor Buttons Interface receives and processes the interrupt.

F2: The Floor Buttons Interface sends service Request message to the Scheduler.

F3: The Scheduler receives message and interrogates Elevator Status & Plan object to determine whether an elevator is on its way to this floor. Assume not, so that the Scheduler selects an elevator.

F4: The Scheduler sends a scheduler Request message identifying the selected elevator to the Elevator Manager.

F5: The Elevator Manager receives message and records destination in Elevator Status & Plan object.

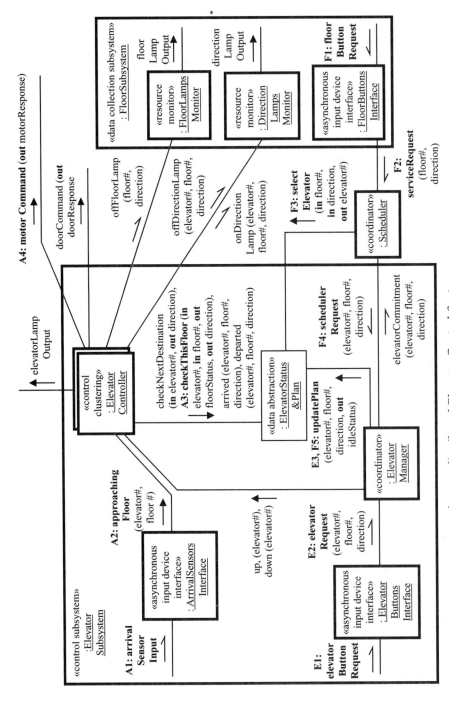

Figure 18.34 *Event sequences for non-distributed Elevator Control System*

Although none of the tasks in the Elevator Control System are periodic, the aperiodic tasks are treated as periodic tasks with a period equal to the minimum event interarrival time.

18.14.3 Priority Assignments

The task parameters for the non-distributed Elevator Control System are shown in Table 18.1. Every task's CPU time includes the context switching time, a maximum of two context switches per task. Message handling overhead has been divided equally between the sender and receiver tasks. The periods of all the tasks in a given event sequence are the same, because it is the arrival of the external event that initiates the event sequence. The Elevator Manager task is treated as if it were two separate tasks because it appears in two different event sequences. Its period is 100 msec in the first case, the activation frequency of the Elevator Buttons Interface, and 200 msec in the second case, the activation frequency of the Floor Buttons Interface.

It is also observed that the periods of the three asynchronous input device interface tasks (all interrupt-driven) are multiples of each other; therefore, these three tasks can be ready to be activated at virtually the same time. Because interrupts must be handled quickly so as not to be missed, the three interrupt-handling tasks need to be processed ahead of all other tasks and are therefore assigned the highest priorities. Doing this violates the rate monotonic priority assignments because, for example, the Floor Buttons Interface has a longer period than the Elevator Controller but is assigned a higher priority.

The interrupt-driven tasks execute at a higher priority than the other tasks in the event sequence. Because of this, the tasks in the event sequence cannot be treated as one equivalent task of the same period but consuming a greater CPU time, as was done with the Cruise Control example in Chapter 17. Instead, they are treated as separate tasks having the same period.

Consider the priorities that should be assigned to the tasks by the designer (see Table 18.1). Apart from the three interrupt-driven input device interface tasks, tasks are allocated their rate monotonic priorities. The interrupt-driven Arrival Sensors Interface task is allocated the highest priority, which is also its rate monotonic priority. However, the interrupt-driven Elevator Buttons Interface and Floor Buttons Interface tasks are given the second and third highest priorities, thereby violating the rate monotonic assumptions. The Elevator Controller is given the next highest priority according to the rate monotonic assignment because it has the shortest period. Although Elevator Manager is in two event sequences, it is given a priority according to its shorter period.

Table 18.1 *Elevator Control System Real-Time Scheduling Task Parameters*

Task	CPU time C_i	Period T_i	Utilization U_i	Assigned Priority
Stop Elevator at Floor event sequence				
Arrival Sensors Interface	2	50	0.04	1
Elevator Controller	5	50	0.10	4
Total elapsed time = 34 msec			Total utilization = 0.68	
Select Destination event sequence				
Elevator Buttons Interface	3	100	0.03	2
Elevator Manager (Case b)	6	100	0.06	5
Total elapsed time = 47 msec			Total utilization = 0.47	
Request Elevator event sequence				
Floor Buttons Interface	4	200	0.02	3
Scheduler	20	200	0.10	6
Elevator Manager (Case c)	6	200	0.03	
Total elapsed time = 76 msec			Total utilization = 0.38	
Other Tasks				
Floor Lamps Monitor	5	500	0.01	7
Direction Lamps Monitor	5	500	0.01	8

18.14.4   Real-Time Scheduling for Non-Distributed Environment

Adding up the task utilizations from Table 18.1 gives a total utilization of 0.4, well below the worst-case utilization bound of 0.69 given by the **utilization bound theorem**. However, because the rate monotonic priorities are violated, a more detailed real-time analysis is needed.

The analysis is done for each event sequence, because the elapsed time to complete each event sequence is critical, rather than the elapsed time of each individual task. In the analysis, it is necessary to consider preemption by tasks with a higher priority as well as blocking by tasks with a lower priority (see Chapter 17).

Preemption comes from tasks in other event sequences, which have both a shorter period and a higher priority. These tasks are liable to preempt more than once. Preemption can also come from higher priority tasks with longer periods—

for example, higher priority, interrupt-driven tasks from event sequences with longer periods. These tasks can preempt only once. Lower priority task blocking time comes from lower priority tasks acquiring resources required by higher priority tasks—in this case, the Elevator Status & Plan object.

The real-time scheduling analysis for each of the event sequences is given next. The analysis is also illustrated by the timing diagram (a time-annotated sequence diagram) in Figure 18.35, in which the worst case is assumed of all three external interrupts arriving simultaneously. This figure only depicts the tasks and message communication between tasks. Access to passive objects is not depicted because it occurs within the task's thread of control.

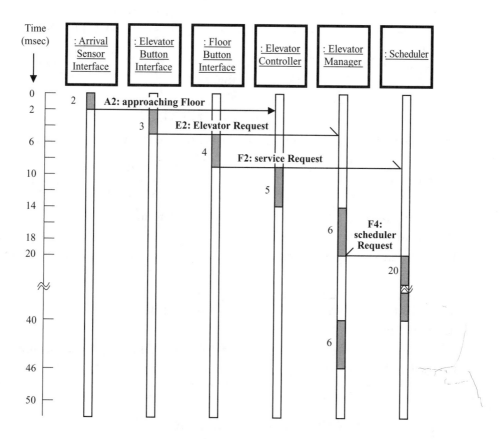

NB: UML notation for sequence diagram has been extended for this figure.

Figure 18.35   *Elevator Control System: time-annotated sequence diagram*

18.14.5 Stop Elevator at Floor Event Sequence

Tasks in event sequence: Arrival Sensors Interface and Elevator Controller. From Table 18.1, it is given that the period of this event sequence = T_a = 50 msec.

Consider the four factors from the generalized real-time scheduling theory (see Chapter 17):

a. **Execution time for tasks in event sequence:** 2 msec for Arrival Sensors Interface, followed by 5 msec for Elevator Controller, giving a total execution time C_a of 7 msec. Execution utilization $U_e = C_a/T_a = 7/50 = 0.14$.

b. **Preemption by higher priority tasks with shorter periods:** Because this event sequence has the shortest period, there are no such tasks.

c. **Preemption by higher priority tasks with longer periods:** Both Elevator Buttons Interface and Floor Buttons Interface can preempt Elevator Controller. Possible 3 msec from Elevator Buttons Interface to handle elevator button interrupt plus 4 msec from Floor Buttons Interface to handle floor button interrupt.

Total preemption time $P_a = 3 + 4 = 7$ msec.
Preemption utilization $U_p = P_a/T_a = 7/50 = 0.14$.

d. **Blocking time from lower priority task:** Possible 20 msec from Scheduler in critical section accessing object can block Elevator Controller.

Total worst-case blocking time $B_a = 20$ msec.
Worst-case blocking utilization $U_b = B_a/T_a = 20/50 = 0.40$.

After considering these four factors, we now determine the total elapsed time and total utilization:

Total elapsed time = execution time + preemption time + worst-case blocking time = $C_a + P_a + B_a = 7 + 7 + 20 = 34$ msec < period of 50 msec.

Total utilization = execution utilization + preemption utilization + worst-case blocking utilization = $U_e + U_p + U_b = 0.14 + 0.14 + 0.40 = 0.68$ < worst-case upper bound of 0.69.

According to both the **Generalized Utilization Bound Theorem** and the **Generalized Completion Time Theorem**, the tasks in the Stop Elevator at Floor event sequence can always meet their deadlines.

18.14.6 Select Destination Event Sequence

Tasks in event sequence: Elevator Buttons Interface and Elevator Manager. From Table 18.1, it is given that the period of this event sequence = T_b = 100 msec.

Consider the four factors from the generalized real-time scheduling theory (see Chapter 17):

a. **Execution time for tasks in event sequence:** Elevator Buttons Interface for 3 msec followed by Elevator Manager for 6 msec, giving a total execution time $C_b = 3+6 = 9$ msec. Execution utilization $U_e = C_b/T_b = 0.09$.

b. **Preemption by higher priority tasks with shorter periods:** Arrival Sensors Interface and Elevator Controller (preempts Elevator Manager) can each execute twice during the 100 msec period, giving a preemption time of 14 msec.

c. **Preemption by higher priority task with longer period:** Possible 4 msec from Floor Buttons Interface to handle floor button interrupt (preempts Elevator Manager).

Total preemption time by higher priority tasks with both shorter and longer periods $C_p = 14 + 4 = 18$. Total preemption utilization $U_p = C_p/T_b = 18/100 = 0.18$.

d. **Blocking time from lower priority task:** Possible 20 msec from Scheduler in critical section accessing object (blocks Elevator Manager). Total worst-case blocking time $B_b = 20$ msec. Worst-case blocking utilization $U_b = B_b/T_b = 0.20$.

After considering these four factors, we now determine the total elapsed time and total utilization:

Total elapsed time = execution time + total preemption time + worst-case blocking time = $9 + 18 + 20 = 47$ msec < period of 100 msec.

Total utilization = $U_p + U_e + U_b = 0.09 + 0.18 + 0.20 = 0.47 <$ worst-case upper bound of 0.69.

According to both the **Generalized Utilization Bound Theorem** and the **Generalized Completion Time Theorem**, the tasks in the Select Destination event sequence can always meet their deadlines.

18.14.7 Request Elevator Event Sequence

Tasks in event sequence: Floor Buttons Interface, Scheduler, and Elevator Manager (appears in two event sequences). From Table 18.1, it is given that the period of this event sequence = $T_c = 200$ msec.

Consider the four factors from the generalized real-time scheduling theory (see Chapter 17):

a. **Execution time for tasks in event sequence:** Floor Buttons Interface executes once for 4 msec, followed by Scheduler, which executes once for 20 msec. This is followed by Elevator Manager, which executes once for

6 msec, giving a total execution time $C_c = 4 + 20 + 6 = 30$ msec. Execution utilization $U_c = C_c/T_c = 0.15$.

b. **Preemption by higher priority tasks with shorter periods:** `Arrival Sensors Interface` and `Elevator Controller` (preempts `Elevator Manager` and `Scheduler`) can each execute four times for a total of 28 msec.

`Elevator Buttons Interface` and `Elevator Manager` (preempts `Scheduler`) can execute twice for a total of 18 msec.

Total preemption time $C_p = 28 + 18 = 46$ msec. Preemption utilization $U_p = C_p/T_c = 0.23$.

c. **Preemption by higher priority tasks with longer periods:** Because this event sequence has the longest period, there are no such tasks.

d. **Blocking time:** Blocking due to access of the object by other tasks has already been taken into account, so there is no additional blocking time.

After considering these four factors, we now determine the total elapsed time and total utilization:

Total elapsed time = execution time + total preemption time + worst-case blocking time = $30 + 46 + 0 = 76$ msec < period of 200 msec.

Total utilization = $U_e + U_p = 0.15 + 0.23 = 0.38$ < worst-case upper bound of 0.69.

According to both the **Generalized Utilization Bound Theorem** and the **Generalized Completion Time Theorem**, the tasks in the `Request Elevator` event sequence can always meet their deadlines.

18.15 Performance Analysis of Distributed Elevator Control System

The previous example shows that the single processor system can handle the 3-elevator, 10-floor case satisfactorily. However, it is clear that as the number of elevators and floors increases, the CPU load will grow and the system will eventually get overloaded. For example, to handle 6 elevators and 20 floors, it can be assumed that to a first approximation the utilization would double to 0.8. Repeating the analysis for the worst-case floor arrival event sequence shows that deadlines would sometimes be missed. With 12 elevators and 40 floors, the required utilization is 1.2, which is obviously impossible to achieve with this configuration.

18.15.1 Performance Analysis Scenario

Consider instead the distributed design shown in Figure 18.29, where there is one node per elevator, one node per floor, and one scheduler node. Assume that the same processors are used so that task execution times do not change and that, in addition, there is a deterministic local area network whose capacity is 100 MBaud.

Consider the 12-elevator and 40-floor scenario. The load on each individual elevator node and each individual floor node should be less than that on the single CPU of the centralized scenario. However, assume that the arrival rates do not change—an extremely unlikely worst case. The task parameters for the Distributed Elevator Control System are given in Table 18.2. The CPU utilization for the Elevator Subsystem is 0.23, and the CPU utilization for the Floor Subsystem is 0.04, suggesting that one floor node could easily handle more than one floor.

The node that needs to be analyzed in more detail is the Scheduler node, because this represents a potential bottleneck. With four times as many floors, it is assumed that the Elevator Scheduler task's period is shortened by a factor of 4, from 200 msec to 50 msec. Assume that the Elevator Status & Plan Server, which receives messages from the multiple instances of the Elevator Subsystem, has a period of 10 msec and an execution time of 2 msec to update the Overall Elevator Status & Plan object. From Table 18.2, the Elevator Scheduler node utilization is 0.6, which is below the upper utilization bound of 0.69 given by the **Utilization Bound Theorem**.

Table 18.2 *Distributed Elevator Control System Real-Time Scheduling Task Parameters*

Task	CPU time C_i	Period T_i	Utilization U_i	Assigned Priority
Elevator Subsystem:				
Arrival Sensors Interface	2	50	0.04	1
Elevator Controller	5	50	0.10	3
Elevator Buttons Interface	3	100	0.03	2
Elevator Manager	6	100	0.06	4
Floor Subsystem:				
Floor Buttons Interface	4	200	0.02	1
Floor Lamps Monitor	5	500	0.01	2
Direction Lamps Monitor	5	500	0.01	3
Scheduler Subsystem:				
Elevator Status and Plan Server	2	10	0.20	1
Elevator Scheduler	20	50	0.40	2

Network transmission delay = 2 msec
Elapsed time for Stop Elevator at Floor event sequence = 41 msec < 50 msec
Elapsed time for Select Destination event sequence = 48 msec < 100 msec
Elapsed time for Request Elevator event sequence = 82 msec < 200 msec

18.15.2 Real-Time Scheduling for Distributed Environment

Consider the three critical event sequences for the distributed configuration, which are described in the next section and illustrated in Figures 18.36–18.38.

Stop Elevator at Floor event sequence (Period = T_a):

A1: The Arrival Sensors Interface receives and processes interrupt.

A2: The Arrival Sensors Interface sends approaching Floor message to the Elevator Controller.

A3: The Elevator Controller receives message and checks the Local Elevator Status & Plan object to determine whether the elevator should stop or not.

A4: The Elevator Controller invokes stop Motor operation if it should stop.

A5: The Elevator Controller sends arrived message over the LAN to the Scheduler subsystem, where it is received by the Elevator Status & Plan Server.

A6: The Elevator Status & Plan Server calls the arrived operation of the Overall Elevator Status & Plan data abstraction object.

Select Destination event sequence (Period = T_b):

E1: The Elevator Buttons Interface receives and processes interrupt.

E2: The Elevator Buttons Interface sends elevator Request message to the Elevator Manager.

E3: The Elevator Manager receives message and records destination in the Local Elevator Status & Plan object.

E4: The Elevator Manager sends an elevator Commitment message over the LAN to the Scheduler subsystem, where it is received by the Elevator Status & Plan Server.

E5: The Elevator Status & Plan Server calls the update Plan operation of the Overall Elevator Status & Plan data abstraction object.

Request Elevator event sequence (Period = T_c):

F1: The Floor Buttons Interface receives and processes interrupt.

F2: The Floor Buttons Interface sends service Request message over the LAN to the Elevator Scheduler task in the Scheduler subsystem.

F3: The Elevator Scheduler receives message and interrogates Overall Elevator Status & Plan object to determine whether an elevator is on its way to this floor. Assume not, so that the Elevator Scheduler selects an elevator.

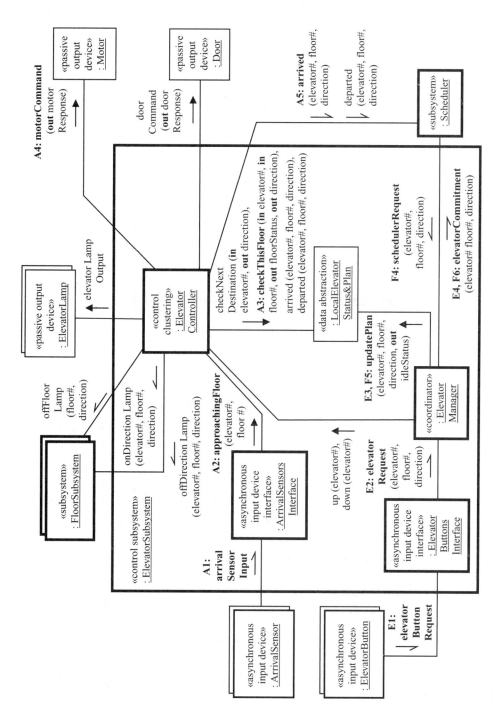

Figure 18.36 *Event sequence for Distributed Elevator Subsystem*

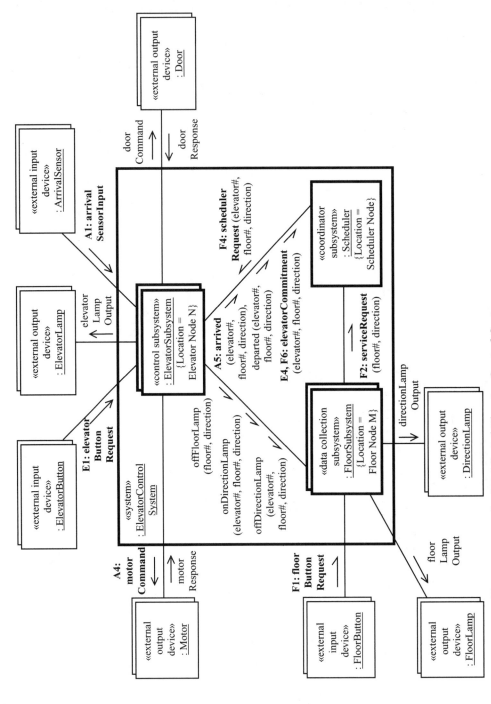

Figure 18.37 *Event sequence for Distributed Elevator Control System*

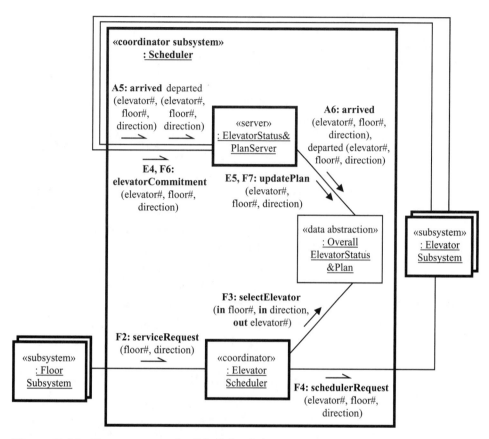

Figure 18.38 *Event sequence for Scheduler Subsystem*

F4: The `Elevator Scheduler` sends a `scheduler Request` message identifying the selected elevator over the LAN to the `Elevator Manager` task in the selected elevator's instance of the `Elevator Subsystem`.

F5: The `Elevator Manager` receives message and records destination in the `Local Elevator Status & Plan` object.

F6: The `Elevator Manager` sends an `elevator Commitment` message over the LAN to the `Scheduler` subsystem, where it is received by the `Elevator Status & Plan Server`.

F7: The `Elevator Status & Plan Server` calls the `update Plan` operation of the `Overall Elevator Status & Plan` data abstraction object.

18.15.3 Stop Elevator at Floor Event Sequence

This Stop Elevator at Floor event sequence is handled entirely by tasks in the Elevator Subsystem and the Scheduler Subsystem, as shown in Figures 18.36–18.38. First, consider the Elevator Subsystem.

Tasks in event sequence: Arrival Sensors Interface and Elevator Controller. Period of event sequence = T_a = 50 msec.

Consider the four factors from the generalized real-time scheduling theory (see Chapter 17):

a. **Execution time for tasks in event sequence:** 2 msec for Arrival Sensors Interface followed by 5 msec for Elevator Controller, giving a total execution time C_a of 7 msec. $U_e = C_a/T_a = 7/50 = 0.14$.

b. **Preemption by higher priority tasks with shorter periods:** Because this event sequence has the shortest period, there are no such tasks.

c. **Preemption by higher priority tasks with longer periods:** Possible 3 msec from Elevator Buttons Interface to handle elevator button interrupt. Preemption time C_p = 3. Preemption utilization $Up = 3/50 = 0.06$.

d. **Blocking time from lower priority task:** Possible blocking of 6 msec from Elevator Manager. Total worst-case blocking time B_a = 6 msec. Worst-case blocking utilization $U_b = B_a/T_a = 6/50 = 0.12$.

After considering these four factors, we now determine the total elapsed time and total utilization:

Total elapsed time = execution time + preemption time + worst-case blocking time = 7 + 3 + 6 = 16 msec < period of 50 msec.

Total Utilization = $U_e + U_p + U_b$ = 0.14 + 0.06 + 0.12 = 0.32 < worst-case upper bound of 0.69.

According to both the **Generalized Utilization Bound Theorem** and the **Generalized Completion Time Theorem**, the Elevator Subsystem tasks in the Stop Elevator at Floor event sequence can always meet their deadlines. This is a hard deadline, which if missed could mean the elevator would fail to stop at the floor. The utilization is less than in the non-distributed case, because there are fewer tasks in the Elevator Subsystem.

Now consider the time for processing the arrived message (A5), which is sent over the network. Consider the network transmission delay:

A5: Elevator Controller sends the arrived message over the network to the Scheduler subsystem. Assume the size of the message, including all header information required by the communication protocol, is 25 bytes or

200 bits. Given the network capacity of 100 MBaud, the transmission delay D_t is $200/100,000 = 2$ msec.

Consider next the Scheduler subsystem (see Figure 18.38):

A5.1: Elevator Status & Plan Server task receives message. Assume 1 msec delay for receiving and processing message sent over network, $C_m = 1$ msec.

A6: Elevator Status & Plan Server calls the arrived operation of Overall Elevator Status & Plan object, $C_s = 2$ msec.

Possible blocking time for access to object by Elevator Scheduler $B_s = 20$ msec.

Worst-case elapsed time in Scheduler subsystem $E_u = C_m + C_s + B_s = 1 + 2 + 20 = 23$ msec.

Having considered the two subsystems as well as network transmission delay, the worst-case elapsed time to process the Stop Elevator at Floor event sequence, E_a, is computed as follows:

E_a = Elevator Subsystem elapsed time E_e + Transmission Delay D_t + Scheduler subsystem elapsed time for updating the Overall Elevator Status & Plan E_u.

Substituting for these values,

$E_t = 16 + 2 + 23 = 41$ msec

the total worst-case elapsed time to service the Stop Elevator at Floor event sequence is thus estimated to be 41 msec, which is below the required response time of 50 msec. In fact, it is not essential for the arrived status message to be processed within the deadline. What is critical is stopping the motor, which is easily handled.

18.15.4   Select Destination Event Sequence

The Select Destination event sequence is also handled entirely by tasks in the Elevator Subsystem and the Scheduler Subsystem, as shown in Figures 18.36–18.38. First, consider the Elevator Subsystem.

Tasks in event sequence: Elevator Buttons Interface and Elevator Manager. Period of event sequence = $T_b = 100$ msec.

Consider the four factors from the generalized real-time scheduling theory (see Chapter 17):

a. **Execution time for tasks in event sequence:** Elevator Buttons Interface for 3 msec, followed by Elevator Manager for 6 msec, giving a total execution time of 9 msec, $U_e = 0.09$.

b. **Preemption by higher priority tasks with shorter periods:** Arrival Sensors Interface and Elevator Controller (preempts Elevator Manager) can each execute twice during the 100 msec period, giving a total preemption time of 14 msec, $U_p = 0.14$.

c. **Preemption by higher priority tasks with longer periods:** There are no such tasks.

d. **Blocking time from lower priority task.** There is no blocking time because all the tasks in the Elevator Subsystem have already been accounted for in considering the preemption time and execution time.

After considering these four factors, we now determine the total elapsed time and total utilization:

Total elapsed time = execution time + preemption time = 9 + 14 = 23 msec < period of 100 msec.

Total utilization = $U_e + U_p$ = 0.09 + 0.14 = 0.23 < worst-case upper bound of 0.69.

According to both the **Generalized Utilization Bound Theorem** and the **Generalized Completion Time Theorem**, the Elevator Subsystem tasks in the Select Destination event sequence can always meet their deadlines. Once again, the utilization is less than in the centralized case.

In this event sequence, the Elevator Manager sends an elevator Commitment message over the LAN to the Scheduler subsystem. This is handled in a similar way to the arrived message in the previous message. Thus, there is an additional 2-msec network transmission delay (event E4) and worst-case Eu = 23 msec to update the Overall Elevator Status & Plan object by the Elevator Status and Plan Server (event E5).

Having considered the two subsystems as well as the network transmission delay, the worst-case elapsed time to process the Select Destination event sequence, E_b, is computed as follows:

E_b = Elevator Subsystem elapsed time E_e + transmission delay D_t + Scheduler subsystem elapsed time E_u (for updating the Overall Elevator Status & Plan).

Substituting for these values,

$E_t = 23 + 2 + 23 = 48$ msec

the total worst-case elapsed time to service the Select Destination event sequence is thus estimated to be 48 msec, which is below the required response time of 100 msec.

18.15.5   Request Elevator Event Sequence

The Request Elevator event sequence spans more than one distributed subsystem because it requires tasks from all three subsystems to participate in processing it (see Figures 18.36–18.38). Although the overall CPU utilization of each node has been shown to be adequate, the overall elapsed time is still a concern. It is necessary to apply the **real-time scheduling theory** to each of the nodes in turn, given the task parameters of Table 18.2. The period of this event sequence = T_c = 200 msec.

Consider first the Floor Subsystem (see Figure 18.37):

F1: Floor Buttons Interface receives and processes interrupt. Floor Buttons Interface is the highest priority task in this subsystem, so there is no possibility of preemption. There is also no possibility of blocking. Execution time = C_f = 4 msec.

F2: Floor Buttons Interface sends message. Message processing overhead for preparing message to be sent over network, C_m = 1 msec.

Total elapsed time in Floor Subsystem $E_f = C_f + C_m = 4 + 1 = 5$ msec
Consider next the network transmission delay:

F2.1: The service Request message is sent over the network to the Scheduler subsystem. Assume the size of the message, including all header information required by the communication protocol, is 25 bytes or 200 bits. Given the network capacity of 100 MBaud, the transmission delay D_t is 200/100,000 = 2 msec.

Consider next the Scheduler subsystem (see Figure 18.38):

F2.2: Elevator Scheduler task receives message. Assume 1 msec delay for receiving and processing message sent over network, Cm = 1 msec.

F3: Elevator Scheduler interrogates Overall Elevator Status & Plan object to determine whether an elevator is on its way to this floor. Assume not, so that the Elevator Scheduler selects an elevator and sends a scheduler Request message to the Elevator Manager, C_s = 20 msec. Assume 1 msec delay for preparing message to be sent over network, C_m = 1 msec.

Possible blocking time for access to object by Elevator Status & Plan Sérver Bs = 2 msec
Worst-case elapsed time in Scheduler subsystem $E_s = C_m + C_s + C_m + B_s = 1 + 20 + 1 + 2 = 24$ msec

Consider next the network transmission delay:

F3.1: The scheduler Request message is sent over the network to the Elevator Subsystem. As before, transmission delay D_t = 2 msec.

Consider next the Elevator Subsystem (see Figure 18.36):

F4: Elevator Manager receives and processes scheduler Request message, $C_m = 1$ msec.

F5: Elevator Manager records destination in Local Elevator Status & Plan object. CPU time for F4 and F5 is $C_e = 6$ msec.

F6: Elevator Manager sends elevator Commitment message to the Scheduler subsystem. Message preparation time $C_m = 1$ msec.

Execution time: Elevator Manager executes once for $C_m + C_e + C_m = 1 + 6 + 1 = 8$ msec.

There are several possible delays in the Elevator Subsystem:

a. Preemption time: Arrival Sensors Interface and Elevator Controller can each execute once for a total of 7 msec.

   Elevator Buttons Interface and Elevator Manager (handling elevator button message) can execute once for a total of 9 msec.
   Total preemption time = 7 + 9 = 16 msec.

b. Blocking time: Note that blocking due to access of the object by other tasks has already been taken into account, so there is no additional blocking time.

Worst-case elapsed time in Elevator Subsystem E_e = execution time + total preemption time = 16 + 8 = 24 msec.

There is an additional 2 msec network transmission delay (event F6.1). As before, there is a worst-case elapsed time, $E_u = 23$ msec, to update the Overall Elevator Status & Plan object by the Elevator Status and Plan Server (event F7).

Having considered each of the three subsystems as well as network transmission delays, the worst-case elapsed time to process the Request Elevator event sequence, E_t, is computed as follows:

E_t = Floor Subsystem elapsed time E_f + transmission delay D_t + Scheduler subsystem elapsed time E_s (for elevator scheduling) + transmission delay D_t + Elevator Subsystem elapsed time E_e + transmission delay D_t + Scheduler subsystem elapsed time E_u (for updating the Overall Elevator Status & Plan).

Substituting for these values,

$$E_t = 5 + 2 + 24 + 2 + 24 + 2 + 23 = 82 \text{ msec}$$

the total worst-case elapsed time to service the Request Elevator event sequence is thus estimated to be 82 msec. It should be noted that this is well below the required response time of 200 msec. Even if the network transmission delay were 10 msec instead of 2 msec for each message, the overall elapsed time would only increase to 106 msec.

chapter

19

Banking System
Case Study

T his chapter describes a banking case study that is a client/server case study. This is a popular example; various other treatments of it are given in Rumbaugh et al. [1991]; Jacobson [1992]; Jacobson, Booch, and Rumbaugh [1999]; and Wirfs-Brock, Wilkerson, and Wiener [1990]. This case study has been used to illustrate several aspects of the COMET method in previous chapters. This chapter describes the full case study.

19.1 Problem Description

A bank has several automated teller machines (ATMs), which are geographically distributed and connected via a wide area network to a central server. Each ATM machine has a card reader, a cash dispenser, a keyboard/display, and a receipt printer. By using the ATM machine, a customer can withdraw cash from either a checking or savings account, query the balance of an account, or transfer funds from one account to another. A transaction is initiated when a customer inserts an ATM card into the card reader. Encoded on the magnetic strip on the back of the ATM card are the card number, the start date, and the expiration date. Assuming the card is recognized, the system validates the ATM card to determine that the expiration date has not passed, that the user-entered PIN (personal identification number) matches the PIN maintained by the system, and that the card is not lost or stolen. The customer is allowed three attempts to enter the correct PIN; the card is confiscated if the third attempt fails. Cards that have been reported lost or stolen are also confiscated.

If the PIN is validated satisfactorily, the customer is prompted for a withdrawal, query, or transfer transaction. Before a withdrawal transaction can be approved, the system determines that sufficient funds exist in the requested account, that the maximum daily limit will not be exceeded, and that there are sufficient funds at the local cash dispenser. If the transaction is approved, the requested amount of cash is dispensed, a receipt is printed containing information about the transaction, and the card is ejected. Before a transfer transaction can be approved, the system determines that the customer has at least two accounts and that there are sufficient funds in the account to be debited. For approved query and transfer requests, a receipt is printed and the card ejected. A customer may cancel a transaction at any time; the transaction is terminated and the card is ejected. Customer records, account records, and debit card records are all maintained at the server.

An ATM operator may start up and close down the ATM to replenish the ATM cash dispenser and for routine maintenance. It is assumed that functionality to open and close accounts and to create, update, and delete customer and debit card records is provided by an existing system and is not part of this problem.

19.2 Use Case Model

The use cases are described in the **Use Case Model**. There are two actors, namely the ATM Customer and the Operator, who are the users of the system. The customer can withdraw funds from a checking or savings account, query the balance of the account, and transfer funds from one account to another. The customer interacts with the system via the ATM card reader, keyboard/display, cash dispenser, and receipt printer. The ATM operator can shutdown the ATM, replenish the ATM cash dispenser, and start the ATM. Because an actor represents a role played by a user, there can be multiple customers and operators.

Consider the ATM operator use cases. There are use cases for Add Cash (in order to replenish the ATM cash locally), Startup, and Shutdown, as shown in Figure 19.1.

Consider the use cases initiated by the ATM Customer. Because there are three transaction types initiated by a customer, we start by considering three use cases: Withdraw Funds, Query Account, and Transfer Funds, one for each transaction type, as described in Chapter 7. Comparing the three use cases, it can be seen that the first part of each use case—namely, the PIN validation—is common to all three use cases. This common part of the three use cases is factored out as an abstract inclusion use case called Validate PIN.

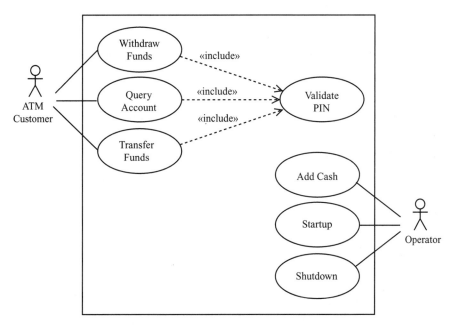

Figure 19.1 *Banking System use case model*

The Withdraw Funds, Query Account, and Transfer Funds use cases can then each be rewritten more concisely as concrete use cases that include the Validate PIN abstract use case. The relationship between the use cases is shown in Figure 19.1. The concrete Withdraw Funds use case starts by including the description of the Validate PIN abstract use case and then continues with the Withdraw Funds description. The concrete Transfer Funds use case also starts with the description of the Validate PIN abstract use case, but then continues with the Transfer Funds description. The revised concrete Query Account use case is similarly organized. The abstract use case and concrete use cases are described next.

19.2.1 Validate PIN Abstract Use Case

Use Case Name: Validate PIN

Summary: System validates customer PIN.

Actor: ATM Customer

Precondition: ATM is idle, displaying a Welcome message.

Description:

1. Customer inserts the ATM Card into the Card Reader.
2. If the system recognizes the card, it reads the card number.
3. System prompts customer for PIN number.
4. Customer enters PIN.
5. System checks the expiration date and whether the card is lost or stolen.
6. If card is valid, the system then checks whether the user-entered PIN matches the card PIN maintained by the system.
7. If PIN numbers match, the system checks what accounts are accessible with the ATM Card.
8. System displays customer accounts and prompts customer for transaction type: Withdrawal, Query, or Transfer.

Alternatives:

- If the system does not recognize the card, the card is ejected.
- If the system determines that the card date has expired, the card is confiscated.
- If the system determines that the card has been reported lost or stolen, the card is confiscated.
- If the customer-entered PIN does not match the PIN number for this card, the system re-prompts for the PIN.
- If the customer enters the incorrect PIN three times, the system confiscates the card.
- If the customer enters Cancel, the system cancels the transaction and ejects the card.

Postcondition: Customer PIN has been validated.

19.2.2 Withdraw Funds Concrete Use Case

Use Case Name: Withdraw Funds

Summary: Customer withdraws a specific amount of funds from a valid bank account.

Actor: ATM Customer

Dependency: Include `Validate PIN` abstract use case.

Precondition: ATM is idle, displaying a Welcome message.

Description:

1. Include `Validate PIN` abstract use case.
2. Customer selects Withdrawal, enters the amount, and selects the account number.

3. System checks whether customer has enough funds in the account and whether the daily limit will not be exceeded.

4. If all checks are successful, system authorizes dispensing of cash.

5. System dispenses the cash amount.

6. System prints a receipt showing transaction number, transaction type, amount withdrawn, and account balance.

7. System ejects card.

8. System displays Welcome message.

Alternatives:

- If the system determines that the account number is invalid, it displays an error message and ejects the card.

- If the system determines that there are insufficient funds in the customer's account, it displays an apology and ejects the card.

- If the system determines that the maximum allowable daily withdrawal amount has been exceeded, it displays an apology and ejects the card.

- If the ATM is out of funds, the system displays an apology, ejects the card, and shuts down the ATM.

Postcondition: Customer funds have been withdrawn.

19.2.3   Query Account Concrete Use Case

Use Case Name: Query Account

Summary: Customer receives the balance of a valid bank account.

Actor: ATM Customer

Dependency: Include `Validate PIN` abstract use case.

Precondition: ATM is idle, displaying a Welcome message.

Description:

1. Include `Validate PIN` abstract use case.

2. Customer selects Query, enters account number.

3. System reads account balance.

4. System prints a receipt showing transaction number, transaction type, and account balance.

5. System ejects card.

6. System displays Welcome message.

Alternative: If the system determines that the account number is invalid, it displays an error message and ejects the card.

Postcondition: Customer account has been queried.

19.2.4 Transfer Funds Concrete Use Case

Use Case Name: Transfer Funds

Summary: Customer transfers funds from one valid bank account to another.

Actor: ATM Customer

Dependency: Include `Validate PIN` abstract use case.

Precondition: ATM is idle, displaying a Welcome message.

Description:

1. Include `Validate PIN` abstract use case.
2. Customer selects Transfer and enters `amount`, `from account`, and `to account`.
3. If the system determines the customer has enough funds in the `from account`, it performs the transfer.
4. System prints a receipt showing transaction number, transaction type, amount transferred and account balance.
5. System ejects card.
6. System displays Welcome message.

Alternatives:

- If the system determines that the `from account` number is invalid, it displays an error message and ejects the card.
- If the system determines that the `to account` number is invalid, it displays an error message and ejects the card.
- If the system determines that there are insufficient funds in the customer's `from account`, it displays an apology and ejects the card.

Postcondition: Customer funds have been transferred.

19.3 Static Modeling

We start the static modeling by considering the problem domain and the system context, and then continue with static modeling of the entity classes.

19.3.1   Static Modeling of the Problem Domain

The conceptual static model of the problem domain is given in the class diagram depicted in Figure 19.2. A bank has several ATMs. Each ATM is a composite class consisting of a `Card Reader`, a `Cash Dispenser`, a `Receipt Printer`, and a user, the `ATM Customer`, who interacts with the system by using a keyboard/display. The `Card Reader` reads an `ATM Card`, which is a plastic card and hence a physical entity. The `Cash Dispenser` dispenses `ATM Cash`, which is also a physical entity in terms of paper money of given denominations. The `Receipt Printer` prints a `Receipt`, which is a paper physical entity. The physical entities represent classes in the problem domain and are usually modeled by software entity classes, as described later in this section. In addition, the `Operator` is also an external user, whose job is to maintain the ATM. As with the `ATM Customer`, the `Operator` interacts with the system via a keyboard/display.

19.3.2   Static Modeling of the System Context

The system context class diagram, which uses the static modeling notation, is developed to show the external classes to which the Banking System, shown as one aggregate class, has to interface. We develop the context class diagram by considering the physical classes determined during static modeling of the problem domain.

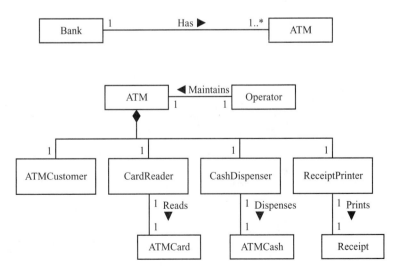

Figure 19.2 *Conceptual static model for problem domain: physical classes*

The external classes correspond to the users and I/O devices depicted in Figure 19.2. Thus, they are the Card Reader, the Cash Dispenser, the Receipt Printer, the ATM Customer who interacts with the system via a keyboard/display, and the Operator who also interacts with the system via a keyboard/display. There is one instance of each of these external classes for each ATM. The system context class diagram for the Banking System (see Figure 19.3) depicts the system as one aggregate class that receives input from and provides output to the external classes.

19.3.3   Static Modeling of the Entity Classes

The static model of the entity classes is shown in Figure 19.4. The attributes of each entity class are given in Figures 19.5–19.7.

Figure 19.4 shows the Bank entity class, which has a one-to-many relationship with the Customer class and the Debit Card class. The Bank class is unusual in that it will only have one instance; its attributes are the bank Name and bank Address. The Customer has a many-to-many relationship with Account. As there are both checking accounts and savings accounts, which have some common attributes, the Account class is specialized to be either a Checking Account or a Savings Account. Thus, some attributes are common to all accounts, namely the account Number and balance. Other attributes are

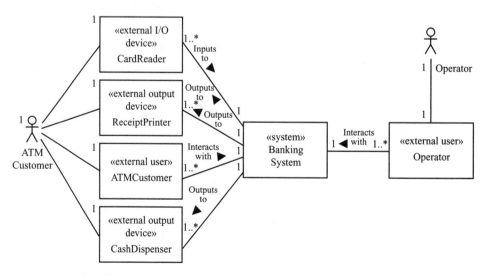

Figure 19.3   *Banking System context class diagram*

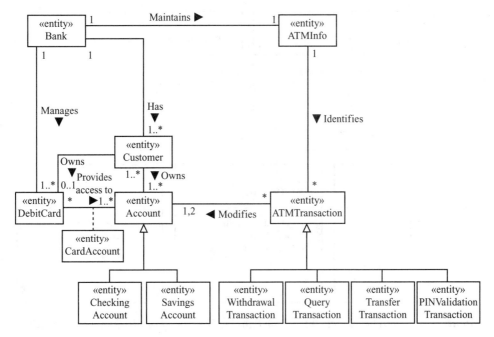

Figure 19.4 *Conceptual static model for problem domain: entity classes*

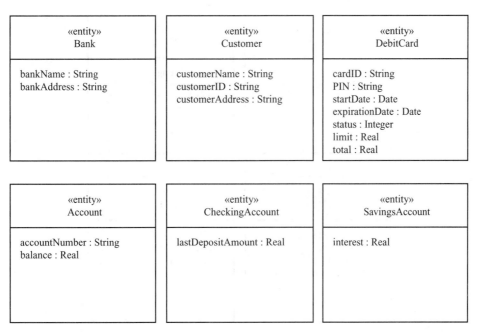

Figure 19.5 *Conceptual static model for Banking System: class attributes*

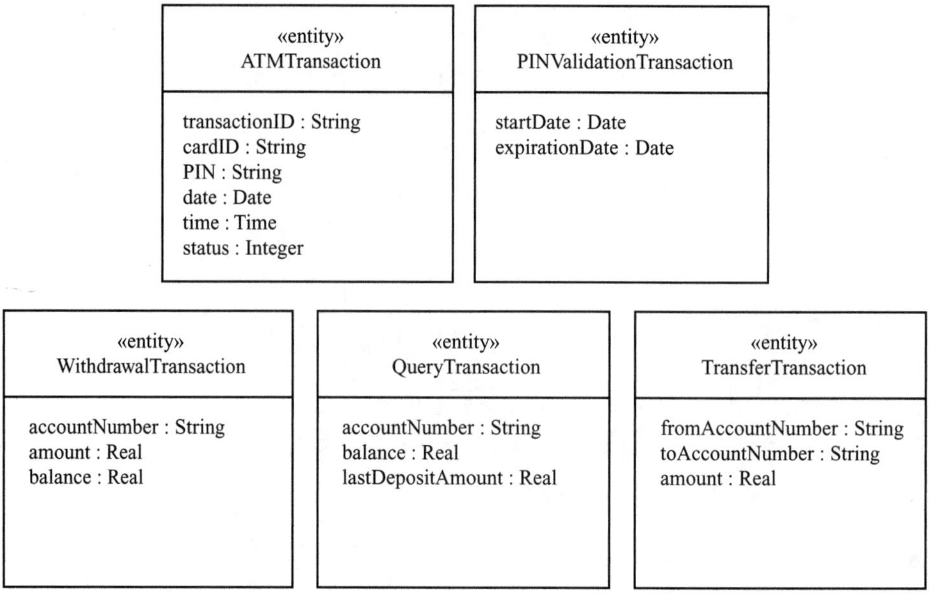

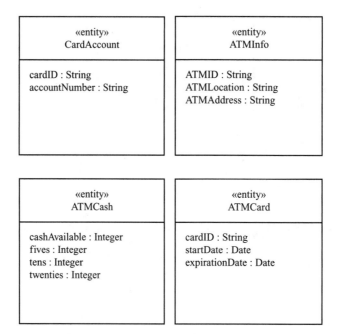

Figure 19.6 *Conceptual static model for Banking System: class attributes (continued)*

Figure 19.7 *Conceptual static model for Banking System: class attributes (continued)*

specific to Checking Account (namely last Deposit Amount) and Savings Account (namely the accumulated interest).

An Account is modified by an ATM Transaction, which is specialized to depict the different types of transactions as a Withdrawal Transaction, Query Transaction, Transfer Transaction, or PIN Validation Transaction. The common attributes of a transaction are in the superclass ATM Transaction and consist of transaction ID, card ID, PIN, date, time, and status. Other attributes are specific to the particular type of transaction. Thus for the Withdrawal Transaction, the specific attributes maintained by the subclass are account Number, amount, and balance. For a Transfer Transaction, the attributes maintained by the subclass are from Account Number (checking or savings), to Account Number (savings or checking), and amount.

There is also a Card Account association class. Association classes are needed in cases where the attributes are of the association, rather than of the classes connected by the association. Thus, in the many-to-many association between Debit Card and Account, the individual accounts that can be accessed by a given debit card are attributes of the Card Account association class and not of either Debit Card or Account.

Entity classes are also required to model the physical classes described in Section 19.3.1 and depicted in Figure 19.2. These include ATM Card, representing the information read off the magnetic strip on the plastic card. ATM Cash holds the amount of cash maintained at an ATM, in five-, ten-, and twenty-dollar bills. The Receipt holds information about a transaction, and because it holds similar information to the Transaction class described earlier, a separate entity class is unnecessary.

19.4   Object Structuring

We next consider structuring the system into objects in preparation for defining the dynamic model. The object structuring criteria help determine the objects in the system. After the objects and classes have been determined, a collaboration diagram or sequence diagram is developed for each use case to show the objects that participate in the use case and the dynamic sequence of interactions between them.

19.4.1   Client/Server Subsystem Structuring

Because the Banking System is a client/server application, some of the objects reside at the ATM client and some reside at the bank server, so we start by identifying subsystems, which are aggregate or composite objects. In client/server systems, the subsystems are often easily identifiable. Thus in the Banking System, there is a client subsystem called ATM Client Subsystem, of which one instance is located at each ATM machine. There is also a central server subsystem, the Bank Server Subsystem, of which there is one subsystem (see Figure 19.8). This is an example of geographical subsystem structuring, where the geographical distribution of the system is given in the problem description. Both subsystems are depicted as aggregate classes, with a one-to-many association between the Bank Server Subsystem and the ATM Client Subsystem. All the external classes interface to the ATM Client Subsystem.

The four use cases initiated by the ATM Customer (shown in Figure 19.1) are all client/server use cases, in that part of each use case executes on the ATM Client and part on the Bank Server. However, the operator-initiated use cases execute entirely at the client. Before we determine the objects that participate in each use case, it is advantageous to structure each of the client/server use cases into a client use case and a server use case, as shown in Figure 19.9. For example, the

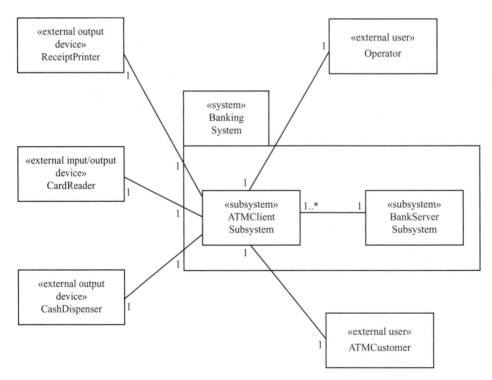

Figure 19.8 *Banking System: major subsystems*

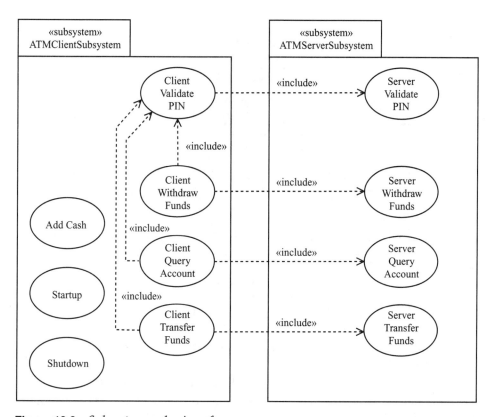

Figure 19.9 *Subsystem packaging of use cases*

abstract use case for `Validate PIN` is structured into two further abstract use cases, `Client Validate PIN` and `Server Validate PIN`. This allows the objects that participate in the server use case to be used with other client use cases—for example, from a human teller instead of an automated teller. It also allows the objects that participate in the client use case to be used with other server user cases, a less likely situation but still possible in an electronic commerce federation.

19.4.2   ATM Client Object Structuring: Interface Objects

Next the software objects at the `ATM Client` are determined. First, consider the interface objects. The interface classes are determined from the system context diagram, as shown in Figure 19.10, which shows the Banking System as a package.

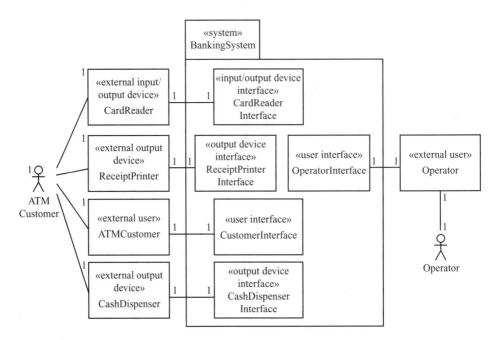

Figure 19.10 *Banking System external classes and interface classes*

We design one interface class for each external class. The device interface classes are the `Card Reader Interface`, through which ATM cards are read, the `Cash Dispenser Interface`, which dispenses cash, and the `Receipt Printer Interface`, which prints receipts. There is also the `Customer Interface`, which is the user interface class that interacts with the customer via the keyboard/display, displaying textual messages, prompting the customer, and receiving the customer's inputs. The `Operator Interface` class provides the user interface to the ATM operator, who replenishes the ATM machine with cash. There is one instance of each of these interface classes for each ATM.

19.4.3 ATM Client Object Structuring: Objects in Use Cases

Next, consider the individual use cases and determine the objects that participate in them. First, consider the `Validate PIN` abstract use case, which describes the customer inserting the ATM Card into the card reader, the system prompting for the PIN, and the system checking whether the customer-entered PIN matches the PIN maintained by the system for that ATM card number. From this use case, we first determine the need for the `Card Reader Interface` object to read the ATM card. The information read off the ATM card needs to be stored, so we identify the need for an entity object to store the ATM Card information. The Customer Interface object is used for interacting with the customer via the keyboard/display, in this case to prompt for the PIN. The information to be sent to the Bank Server Subsystem for PIN validation is stored in an ATM Transaction. For PIN validation, the transaction information needs to contain the PIN number and the ATM Card number. To control the sequence in which actions take place, we identify the need for a control object, ATM Control.

Next consider the objects in the Withdraw Funds use case, which is entered if the PIN is valid and the customer selects withdrawal. In this use case, the customer enters the amount to be withdrawn and the account to be debited, the system checks whether the withdrawal should be authorized, and if positive, dispenses the cash, prints the receipt, and ejects the card. For this use case, additional objects are needed as follows. The information about the customer withdrawal, including the account number and withdrawal amount, needs to be stored in the ATM Transaction object. To dispense the cash, a Cash Dispenser Interface object is needed. We also need to maintain the amount of cash in the ATM, so we identify the need for an entity object called ATM Cash, which is decremented every time there is a cash withdrawal. Finally, we need a Receipt Printer Interface object to print the receipt. As before, the ATM Control object controls the sequencing of the use case.

Inspecting the other use cases reveals that one additional object is needed, namely, the Operator Interface object, which participates in all use cases initiated by the Operator actor. The Operator Interface object needs to send startup and shutdown events to ATM Control because operator maintenance and ATM customer activities are mutually exclusive.

Given the above analysis, Figure 19.11 shows the classes in the ATM Client Subsystem, which is depicted as a package. In addition to the device interface classes and user interface classes depicted in Figure 19.10, there are also three entity classes and one state-dependent control class.

19.4.4   Object Structuring in Server Subsystem

Several entity objects are bank-wide and need to be accessible from any ATM. Consequently, these objects must be stored at the server. These objects include Customer objects that hold information about bank customers, Account objects (both checking and saving) that hold information about individual bank accounts, and Debit Card objects that hold information about all the debit cards maintained at the bank. The classes from which these objects are instantiated all appear on the static model of the entity classes depicted in Figure 19.4.

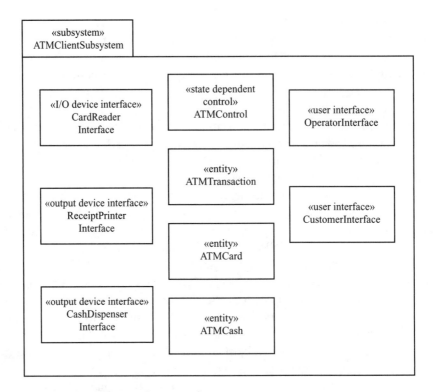

Figure 19.11 *ATM Client subsystem classes*

In the Bank Server Subsystem, the entity classes are Customer, the Account superclass, Checking Account and Savings Account subclasses, and Debit Card. There is also the ATM Transaction object, which migrates from the client to the server. The client sends the transaction request to the server, which sends a response to the client. The transaction is also stored at the server as an entity object in the form of a Transaction Log, so that a transaction history is maintained. The transient data sent as part of the ATM Transaction message might differ from the persistent transaction data; for example, transaction status is known at the end of the transaction but not during it.

Business logic objects are also needed at the server to define the business-specific application logic for processing client requests. In particular, each ATM transaction type needs a transaction manager to specify the business rules for handling the transaction. The business logic objects are the PIN Validation Transaction Manager, the Withdrawal Transaction Manager, the Query Transaction Manager, and the Transfer Transaction Manager.

19.5 Dynamic Modeling

The dynamic model depicts the interaction among the objects that participate in each use case. The starting point for developing the dynamic model is the use cases and the objects determined during object structuring. The sequence of inter-object message communication to satisfy the needs of a use case is depicted on either a sequence diagram or a collaboration diagram. Usually one or the other of the diagrams suffices. In this example, both diagrams are developed for the client subsystem to allow a comparison of the two approaches.

Because the Banking System is a client/server system, the decision was made earlier to structure the system into client and server subsystems, as shown in Figure 19.8. The use cases were also divided into abstract client and server use cases, and the collaboration diagrams are structured for client and server subsystems.

The collaboration diagrams depicted in Figures 19.12 and 19.16 are for the Client Validate PIN and Client Withdraw Funds use cases. Collaboration diagrams are also needed for the Transfer Funds and Query Account use cases, as well as for the use cases initiated by the operator.

The Client Validate PIN and Client Withdraw Funds client use cases are state-dependent use cases. The state-dependent aspects of the use case are defined by the ATM Control object, which executes the ATM statechart. The state-dependent dynamic analysis approach is used to determine how the objects interact with each other. Statecharts are shown for the two use cases in Figures 19.14 and 19.18, respectively. The dynamic analysis for these two client use cases is described in Sections 19.5.1 and 19.5.2, respectively.

The Bank Server processes transactions from multiple ATMs in the order it receives them. The processing of each transaction is self-contained; thus the server part of the use cases is not state-dependent. Consequently, a non-state-dependent dynamic analysis is needed for these use cases. The collaboration diagrams for the Server Validate PIN and Server Withdraw Funds use cases are given in Figures 19.15 and 19.19. The dynamic analysis for these two server use cases is given in Sections 19.5.2 and 19.5.4, respectively.

Consider how the objects interact with each other. A detailed example is given for the Validate PIN and Withdraw Funds use cases. On the client side, both collaboration diagram and sequence diagrams are shown. The same message sequence numbering and message sequence description applies to both the sequence diagram and the collaboration diagram.

19.5.1   Message Sequence Description for Client Validate PIN Use Case

The `Client Validate PIN` use case starts with the customer inserting the ATM card into the card reader. The message sequence number starts at 1, which is the first external event initiated by the actor. Subsequent numbering in sequence, representing the objects in the system reacting to the actor, is 1.1, 1.2, 1.3 and ends with 1.4, the system's response displayed to the actor. The next input from the actor is the external event numbered 2, followed by the internal events 2.1, 2.2, and so on. The following message sequence description corresponds to the collaboration diagram shown in Figure 19.12 and the sequence diagram in Figure 19.13.

Because the `Validate PIN` use case is state-dependent, it is also necessary to consider the ATM statechart, which is executed by the `ATM Control` object. In particular, the interaction between the statechart (shown in Figure 19.14) and `ATM Control` (depicted on the collaboration diagram) needs to be considered. The following message sequence description also addresses the states and transitions on the statechart that correspond to the events on the collaboration diagram in

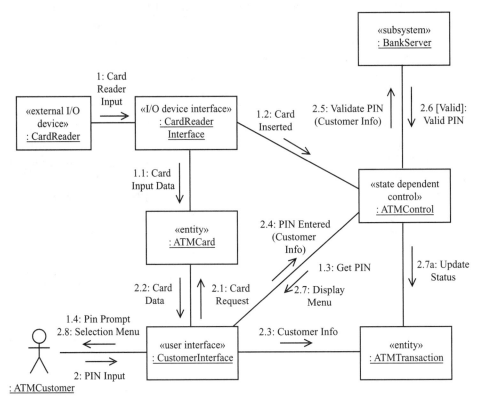

Figure 19.12   *Collaboration diagram: ATM Client Validate PIN use case*

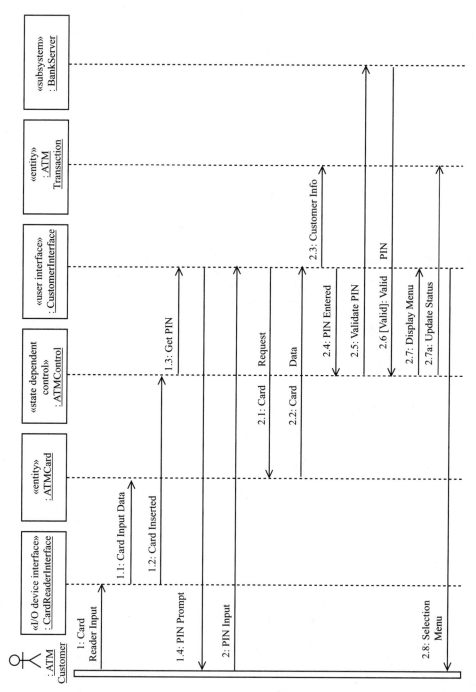

Figure 19.13 *Sequence diagram: ATM Client Validate PIN use case*

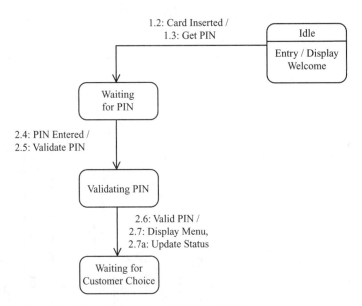

Figure 19.14 *Statechart for ATM Control: Validate PIN use case*

Figure 19.12 and the events on the sequence diagram in Figure 19.13. The message sequence description is as follows:

1: The ATM Customer actor inserts the ATM card into the Card Reader. The Card Reader Interface object reads the card input.

1.1: The Card Reader Interface object sends the Card Input Data, containing card ID, start Date, and expiration Date, to the entity object ATM Card.

1.2: Card Reader Interface sends the Card Inserted event to ATM Control. As a result, the ATM Control statechart transitions from Idle state (the initial state) to Waiting for PIN state. The output event associated with this transition is Get PIN.

1.3: ATM Control sends the Get PIN event to Customer Interface.

1.4: Customer Interface displays the Pin Prompt to the ATM Customer actor.

2: ATM Customer inputs the PIN number to the Customer Interface object.

2.1: Customer Interface requests Card Data from ATM Card.

2.2: ATM Card provides the Card Data to the Customer Interface.

2.3: Customer Interface sends the Customer Info, containing card ID, PIN, start Date, and expiration Date, to the ATM Transaction entity object.

2.4: Customer Interface sends the PIN Entered (Customer Info) event to ATM Control. This causes ATM Control to transition from Waiting for PIN state to Validating PIN state. The output event associated with this transition is Validate PIN.

2.5: ATM control sends a Validate PIN (Customer Info) request to the Bank Server.

2.6: Bank Server validates the PIN and sends a Valid PIN response to ATM Control. As a result of this event, ATM Control transitions to Waiting for Customer Choice state. The output events for this transition are Display Menu and Update Status.

2.7: ATM Control sends the Display Menu event to the Customer Interface.

2.7a: ATM Control sends an Update Status message to the ATM Transaction.

2.8: Customer Interface displays a menu showing the Withdraw, Query, and Transfer options to the ATM Customer actor.

Chapter 11 also describes the alternative paths through the use cases and shows these on the collaboration diagrams and statecharts.

19.5.2 Message Sequence Description for Server Validate PIN Use Case

Consider the Server Validate PIN abstract use case. To validate the PIN at the server, the Debit card entity object, which contains all the information pertinent to all debit cards that belong to the bank, needs to be accessed. If PIN validation is successful, the Card Account entity object needs to be accessed to retrieve the account numbers of the accounts that can be accessed by this debit card.

In addition, each transaction has a **business logic object** that encapsulates the business application logic to manage the execution of the transaction. The business logic object receives the transaction request from the ATM Control object at the client and then interacts with the entity objects to determine what response to return to ATM Control. For example, the business logic object for the PIN Validation transaction is the PIN Validation Transaction Manager.

The following message sequence description for the Server Validate PIN use case corresponds to the collaboration diagram shown in Figure 19.15.

V1: ATM Client sends the PIN Validation Request to the PIN Validation Transaction Manager. The PIN Validation Transaction Manager contains the business logic to determine whether the customer entered PIN matches the PIN stored in the bank server database.

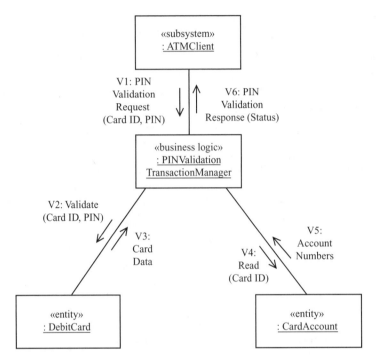

Figure 19.15 *Collaboration diagram: Bank Server Validate PIN use case*

V2: `PIN Validation Transaction Manager` sends a Validate (Card ID, PIN) message to the `Debit Card` entity object, requesting it to validate this customer's debit card, given the card ID and customer-entered PIN.

V3: `Debit Card` checks that customer-entered PIN matches the `Debit Card` record PIN, that card status is okay (not reported missing or stolen), and that the expiration date has not passed. If the card passes all checks, `Debit Card` sends `PIN Validation Transaction Manager` a positive response.

V4: If validation is positive, `PIN Validation Transaction Manager` sends a message to the `Card Account` entity object requesting it to return the account numbers that may be accessed for this card ID.

V5: `Card Account` responds with the valid account numbers.

V6: `PIN Validation Transaction Manager` sends a `PIN Validation Response` to the `ATM Client`. If the PIN validation checks are satisfactory, the account numbers are also sent.

Alternatives:

- If customer PIN does not match `Debit Card` record PIN, send Invalid PIN response.
- If customer PIN does not match `Debit Card` record PIN for the third time, send Third Invalid response.
- If the Card Status is Lost or Stolen, send Confiscate response.
- If the expiration date has expired, send Confiscate response.

19.5.3 Message Sequence Description for Client Withdraw Funds Use Case

The message sequence description for the `Client Withdraw Funds` use case addresses the messages on the collaboration diagram (see Figure 19.16) and the sequence diagram (see Figure 19.17). It also describes the relevant states and transitions on the ATM statechart (see Figure 19.18). The message numbering is a continuation of that described for the `Client Validate PIN` use case in Section 19.5.1.

3: ATM Customer actor inputs withdrawal selection to `Customer Interface`, together with the account number for checking or savings account and withdrawal amount.

3.1: `Customer Interface` sends the customer selection to `ATM Transaction`.

3.2: `ATM Transaction` responds to `Customer Interface` with the `Transaction Details`. `Transaction Details` contains `transaction ID`, `card ID`, `PIN`, `date`, `time`, `account Number`, and `amount`.

3.3: `Customer Interface` sends the `Withdrawal Selected (Transaction Details)` request to `ATM Control`. `ATM Control` transitions to `Processing Withdrawal` state. Two output events are associated with this transition, `Request Withdrawal` and `Display Wait`.

3.4: `ATM Control` sends a `Request Withdrawal` transaction containing the `Transaction Details` to the `Bank Server`.

3.4a: `ATM Control` sends a `Display Wait` message to `Customer Interface`.

3.4a.1: `Customer Interface` displays the `Wait Prompt` to the `ATM Customer`.

3.5: `Bank Server` sends a `Withdrawal OK (Cash Details)` response to `ATM Control`. `Cash Details` contains the amount to be dispensed and the account balance. This event causes `ATM Control` to transition to `Dispensing` state. The output events are `Dispense Cash` and `Update Status`.

3.6: `ATM Control` sends a `Dispense Cash (Cash Details)` message to `Cash Dispenser Interface`.

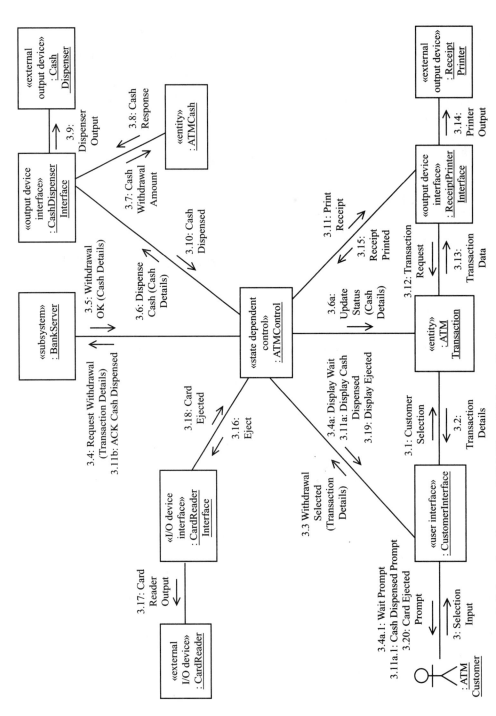

Figure 19.16 *Collaboration diagram: ATM Client Withdraw Funds use case*

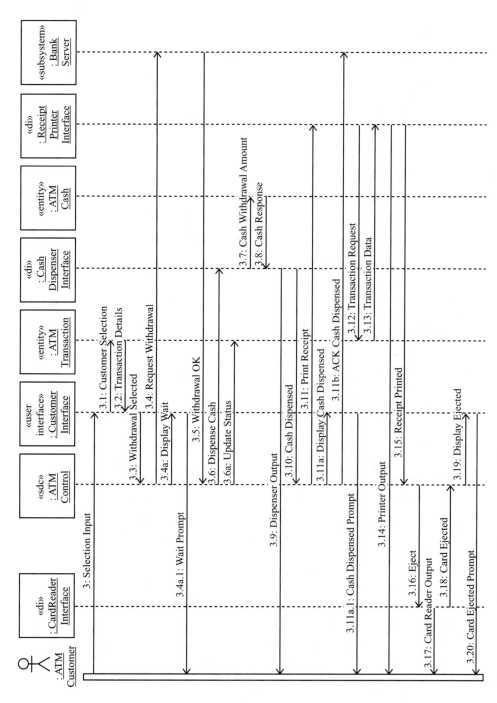

Figure 19.17 *Sequence diagram: ATM Client Withdraw Funds use case*

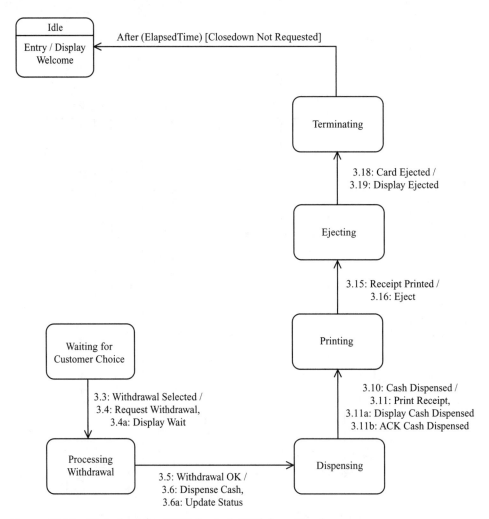

Figure 19.18   *Statechart for ATM Control: Withdraw Funds use case*

3.6a: ATM Control sends an Update Status (Cash Details) message to ATM Transaction.

3.7: Cash Dispenser Interface sends the Cash Withdrawal Amount to ATM Cash.

3.8: ATM Cash sends a positive Cash Response to the Cash Dispenser Interface.

3.9: Cash Dispenser Interface sends the Dispenser Output command to the Cash Dispenser external output device to dispense cash to the customer.

3.10: Cash Dispenser Interface sends the Cash Dispensed event to ATM Control. As a result, ATM Control transitions to Printing state. The three output events associated with this transition are Print Receipt, Display Cash Dispensed, and ACK Cash Dispensed.

3.11: ATM Control sends Print Receipt event to Receipt Printer Interface.

3.11a: ATM Control requests Customer Interface to Display Cash Dispensed message.

3.11a.1: Customer Interface displays Cash Dispensed prompt to ATM Customer.

3.11b: ATM Control sends an Acknowledge Cash Dispensed message to the Bank Server.

3.12: Receipt Printer Interface requests Transaction Data from ATM Transaction.

3.13: ATM Transaction sends the Transaction Data to the Receipt Printer Interface.

3.14: Receipt Printer Interface sends the Printer Output to the Receipt Printer external output device.

3.15: Receipt Printer Interface sends the Receipt Printed event to ATM Control. As a result, ATM Control transitions to Ejecting state. The output event is Eject.

3.16: ATM Control sends the Eject event to Card Reader Interface.

3.17: Card Reader Interface sends the Card Reader Output to the Card Reader external I/O device.

3.18: Card Reader Interface sends the Card Ejected event to ATM Control. ATM Control transitions to Terminated state. The output event is Display Ejected.

3.19: ATM Control sends the Display Ejected event to the Customer Interface.

3.20: Customer Interface displays the Card Ejected prompt to the ATM Customer.

19.5.4 Message Sequence Description for Server Withdraw Funds Use Case

The **business logic object** that participates in the Server Withdraw Funds use case is the Withdrawal Transaction Manager, which encapsulates the logic for determining whether the customer is allowed to withdraw funds from the selected account. The other business logic objects that participate in the server use cases are the Transfer Transaction Manager, which encapsulates the logic for determining whether the customer can transfer funds from one account to another, and the Query Transaction Manager. The latter is sufficiently simple that a separate business logic object is not strictly necessary; the functionality can be handled by the read operation of the Account object. However, to be consistent with the other business logic objects, it is kept as a separate object.

A detailed analysis is given for the Server Withdraw Funds use case. A similar approach is needed for the Server Transfer Funds and Server Query Account use cases. The following message sequence description corresponds to the collaboration diagram shown in Figure 19.19 for the Server Withdraw Funds use case.

W1: ATM Client sends the Withdrawal Request to the Withdrawal Transaction Manager, which contains the business logic for determining whether a withdrawal can be allowed. The incoming withdrawal transaction consists of transaction ID, card ID, PIN, date, time, account Number, and amount.

W2: Withdrawal Transaction Manager sends a Check Daily Limit (Card ID, Amount) message to Debit Card, with the card ID and amount requested. Debit Card checks whether the daily limit for cash withdrawal has been exceeded for this card ID. Debit Card determines if

Total Withdrawn Today + Amount Requested ≤ Daily Limit

W3: Debit Card responds to Withdrawal Transaction Manager with a positive or negative Daily Limit Response.

W4: If the response is positive, Withdrawal Transaction Manager sends a message to Account (which is an instance of either Checking Account or Savings Account) requesting it to debit the customer's account if there are sufficient funds in the account. Account determines whether there are sufficient funds in the account:

Account Balance – Amount Requested ≥ 0

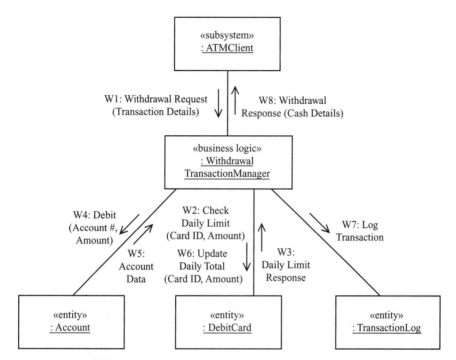

Figure 19.19 *Collaboration diagram: Bank Server Withdraw Funds use case*

If there are sufficient funds, Account decrements the balance by the Amount Requested.

W5: Account responds to Withdrawal Transaction Manager with Account Data consisting of withdrawal status (positive or negative) and balance.

W6: If the account was debited satisfactorily, the Withdrawal Transaction Manager sends an Update Daily Total (Card ID, Amount) to Debit Card so it increments the total withdrawn today by the amount requested in the Debit Card record.

W7: Withdrawal Transaction Manager logs the transaction with the Transaction Log.

W8: Withdrawal Transaction Manager returns Withdrawal Response to the ATM Client. The response consists of transaction ID, card ID, PIN, date, time, status (in this case Withdrawal OK), account Number, amount, and balance.

Alternatives:

- If the account number is invalid, send Invalid Account Number response to ATM Client.
- If there are insufficient funds in customer account, send Insufficient Funds response to ATM Client.
- If the daily limit has been exceeded, send Daily Limit Exceeded response to ATM Client.

19.6   ATM Statechart

Because there is one control object, ATM Control, a statechart needs to be defined for it. Partial statecharts are shown corresponding to the Validate PIN and Withdraw Funds use cases in Figures 19.14 and 19.18, respectively. It is necessary to develop similar statecharts for the other use cases, and develop states and transitions for the alternative paths of the use cases, which in this application address error situations. Flat statecharts are used initially for the use cases. Consolidating the statecharts for all the use cases leads to an ungainly flat statechart, as shown in Figure 10.2. Developing a hierarchical statechart for the class ATM Control can show more structure. The integrated hierarchical statechart, showing all the states and input events, is shown in Figure 10.14. It would be too cluttered to also show the output events on this figure. One of the advantages of a hierarchical statechart is that it can be presented in stages, as is shown for the ATM statechart with output events added in Figures 19.20–19.23. The event sequence numbers shown on these figures correspond to the object interactions previously described.

Five states are shown on the top-level statechart in Figure 19.20: Closed Down (which is the initial state), Idle, and three superstates, Processing Customer Input, Processing Transaction, and Terminating Transaction. Each superstate is decomposed into its own statechart, as shown on Figures 19.21–19.23, respectively.

At system initialization time, given by the event Startup, the ATM transitions from the initial Closed Down state to Idle state. The event Display Welcome is triggered on entry into Idle state. In Idle state, the ATM is waiting for a customer-initiated event.

The Processing Customer Input superstate (see Figure 19.21) is decomposed into three substates, Waiting for PIN, Validating PIN, and Waiting for Customer Choice:

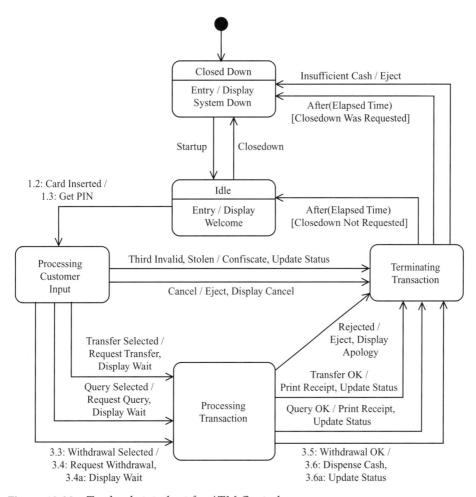

Figure 19.20 *Top-level statechart for ATM Control*

1. Waiting for PIN. This substate is entered from Idle state when the customer inserts the card in the ATM, resulting in the Card Inserted event. In this state, the ATM waits for the customer to enter the PIN.

2. Validating PIN. This substate is entered when the customer enters the PIN. In this substate, the Bank Server validates the PIN.

3. Waiting for Customer Choice. This substate is entered as a result of a Valid PIN event, indicating a valid PIN was entered. In this state, the customer enters a selection: Withdraw, Transfer, or Query.

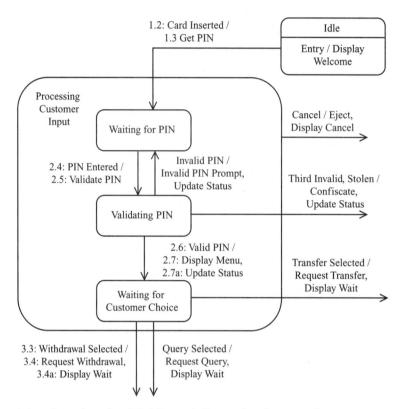

Figure 19.21 *Statechart for ATM Control: Processing Customer Input superstate*

The Processing Transaction superstate (see Figure 19.22) is also decomposed into three substates, one for each transaction: Processing Withdrawal, Processing Transfer, and Processing Query. Depending on the customer's selection—for example, withdrawal—the appropriate substate within Processing Transaction—for example, Processing Withdrawal—is entered, during which the customer's request is processed.

The Terminating Transaction superstate (see Figure 19.23) has substates for Dispensing, Printing, Ejecting, Confiscating, and Terminating.

The statechart is developed by considering the different states of the ATM as the customer actor proceeds through each of the use cases, starting with the Validate PIN use case. When a customer inserts an ATM card, the event Card Inserted causes the ATM to transition to the Waiting for PIN substate of the Processing Customer Input superstate (see Figure 19.21). During this time, the ATM is waiting for the customer to input the PIN. The output event, Get PIN,

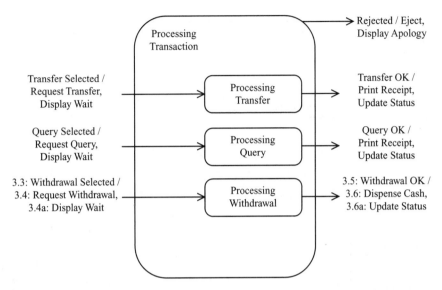

Figure 19.22 *Statechart for ATM Control: Processing Transaction superstate*

results in a display prompt to the customer. When the customer enters the PIN number, the PIN Entered event causes a transition to the Validating PIN substate, during which the Bank Server determines whether the customer-entered PIN matches the PIN stored by the Banking System for this particular card. There are four possible state transitions out of the Validating PIN state. If the two PIN numbers match, the Valid PIN transition is taken to the Waiting for Customer Choice state. If the PIN numbers do not match, the Invalid PIN transition is taken to re-enter the Waiting for PIN state and allow the customer to enter a different PIN number. If the customer-entered PIN is still invalid after the third attempt, the Third Invalid transition is taken to the Confiscating substate of the Terminating Transaction superstate.

The customer can also press the Cancel button on the ATM machine in any of the three Processing Customer Input substates. The Cancel event transitions the ATM to the Ejecting substate of the Terminating Transaction superstate. Because the Cancel event can occur in any of the three substates of the Processing Customer Input superstate, it is more concise to show the Cancel transition leaving the superstate.

From Waiting for Customer Choice state, the customer may select Withdraw, Query, or Transfer and enter the appropriate substate within the Processing Transaction superstate (see Figure 19.22); for example, Processing Withdrawal. When a Withdrawal transaction is completed, the event Withdrawal OK is

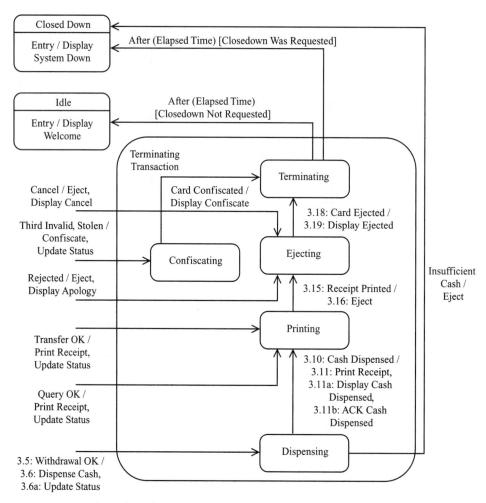

Figure 19.23 *Statechart for ATM Control: Terminating Transaction superstate*

issued if the customer has enough funds, and the Dispensing substate of the Ter-minating Transaction superstate is entered (see Figure 19.23). Alternatively, if the customer has insufficient funds or has exceeded the daily withdrawal limit, a Rejected event is issued. The actions associated with the transition to Dispensing state are to Dispense Cash and Update Status. After the Cash Dispensed event has taken place, the ATM transitions to Printing state to print the receipt. The action Print Receipt is initiated at the transition. When the receipt is printed, the state Ejecting is entered and the Eject action is initiated. When the card has been ejected (event Card Ejected), the Terminating state is entered.

For the `Query` and `Transfer` transactions, the sequence of states following approval of the transaction is similar except that no cash is dispensed, as can be seen on the ATM statecharts.

19.7   Design of Banking System

Next, the analysis model of the Banking System is mapped to a design model. The steps in this process are

1. Consolidate the collaboration model. Develop a consolidated collaboration diagram.
2. Structure the Banking System into subsystems. Define the interfaces of the subsystems.
3. For each subsystem, structure the system into concurrent tasks.
4. For each subsystem, design the information hiding classes.
5. Develop the detailed software design.

19.8   Consolidating the Collaboration Model

Because the Banking System is a client/server system (Section 19.4), a decision was made earlier to structure the system into client and server subsystems, as shown in Figure 19.8. The collaboration diagrams are also structured for client and server subsystems.

The collaboration diagrams for the `Client Validate PIN` and `Client Withdraw Funds` use cases are depicted in Figures 19.12 and 19.16. Collaboration diagrams are also needed for the `Client Transfer Funds` and `Client Query Account` use cases, as well as for the use cases initiated by the operator. The consolidated collaboration diagram for the `ATM Client Subsystem` (see Figure 19.24) is the result of the merger of all these use case-based collaboration diagrams.

Some objects participate in all the client-side collaborations, such as `ATM Control`, but others participate in as few as one, such as the `Cash Dispenser Interface`. Some of the messages depicted on the consolidated collaboration diagram are aggregate messages, such as `Customer Events` and `Display Prompts`. The consolidated diagram must also include messages from all the alternative sequences, as described in Chapter 11. Thus the `Confiscate` and `Card Confiscated` messages originate from alternative sequences in which the

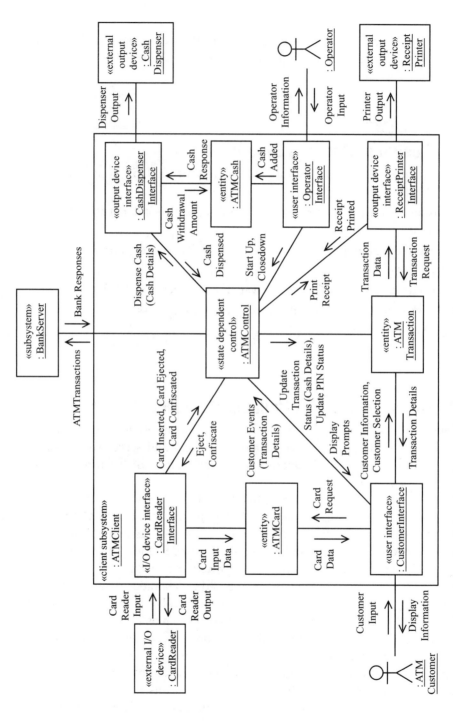

Figure 19.24 *Consolidated collaboration diagram for ATM Client subsystem*

customer transaction is unsuccessful. Similarly, the aggregate Display Prompts messages include messages dealing with incorrect PIN entry, insufficient cash in the customer account, and so on.

Based on the consolidated collaboration diagram for the ATM Client Subsystem, the static model can also be revised. Whereas the static model developed earlier reflected the problem domain, this static model reflects the software classes in the ATM Client Subsystem, as depicted on the class diagram on Figure 19.25. We develop the revised static model by considering the objects on the consolidated collaboration diagram for this subsystem (see Figure 19.24) and designing the classes from which these objects are instantiated. The direction of navigability on the class diagram reflects the direction in which the objects communicate with each other on the consolidated collaboration diagram.

Now consider the Bank Server Subsystem. Figures 19.15 and 19.19 are the collaboration diagrams for the Server Validate PIN and Server Withdraw

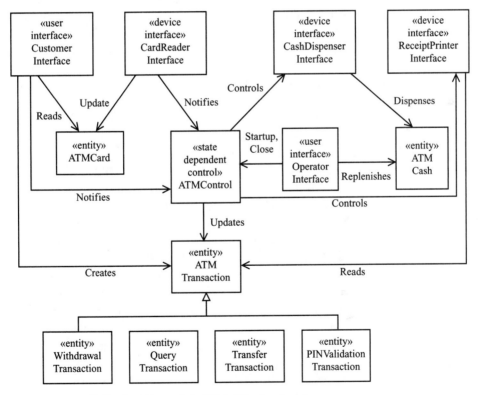

Figure 19.25 *Refined static model: ATM Client subsystem*

Funds use cases. Additional collaboration diagrams are needed for the `Server Transfer Funds` and `Server Query Account` use cases. The consolidated collaboration diagram for the `Bank Server Subsystem` is shown in Figure 19.26. For each transaction, there is a transaction manager object that encapsulates the business logic for the transaction. These are the `PIN Validation Transaction Manager`, `Withdrawal Transaction Manager`, `Query Transaction Manager`, and `Transfer Transaction Manager` objects. In addition, there is a need for a coordinator object, the `Bank Transaction Server`, that receives client requests and delegates them to the appropriate transaction manager. The revised static model for the `Bank Server Subsystem` is described in Section 19.11.

19.9   Structuring the System into Subsystems

In the case of the Banking System, the step of structuring the system into subsystems is straightforward. There are two subsystems, the `ATM Client Subsystem` and the `Bank Server Subsystem`, as initially depicted in Figure 19.8. The two subsystems might also be depicted on a high-level collaboration diagram, as shown in Figure 19.27.

Figure 19.27 is an analysis level collaboration diagram showing the two subsystems and simple messages passed between them. The `ATM Client Subsystem` sends `ATM Transactions` to the `Bank Server Subsystem`, which responds with `Bank Responses`. `ATM Transactions` is an aggregate message consisting of the PIN Validation, Withdraw, Query, Transfer, Confirm, and Abort messages. The `Bank Responses` are responses to these messages.

The next step is to consider the distributed nature of the application and define the distributed message interfaces. Because this is a client/server subsystem, there are multiple instances of the client subsystem and one instance of the server subsystem. Each subsystem instance executes on its own node. In the design model, each of these subsystems is an active subsystem, consisting of at least one task. The message interface is **tightly coupled message communication with reply**. Each client sends a message to the server and then waits for a response. Because the server can receive messages from several clients, a message queue can build up at the server. The server processes incoming messages on a FIFO basis. The design model collaboration diagram is depicted in Figure 19.28.

The next step is to structure each subsystem into concurrent tasks. In the following sections, first the design of the `ATM Client Subsystem` is considered and then the design of the `Bank Server Subsystem`.

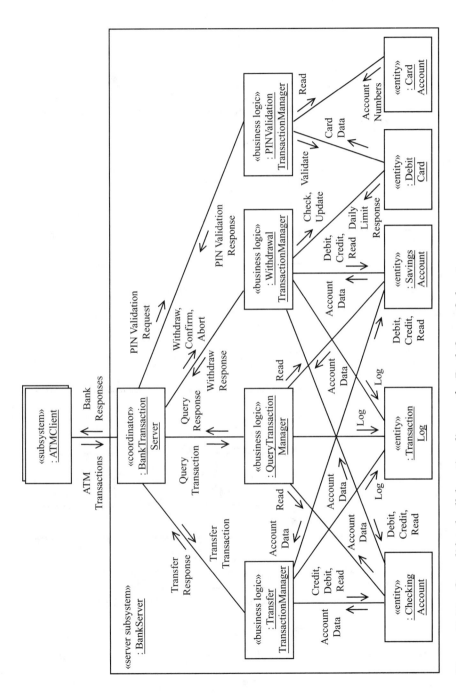

Figure 19.26 *Consolidated collaboration diagram for Bank Server Subsystem*

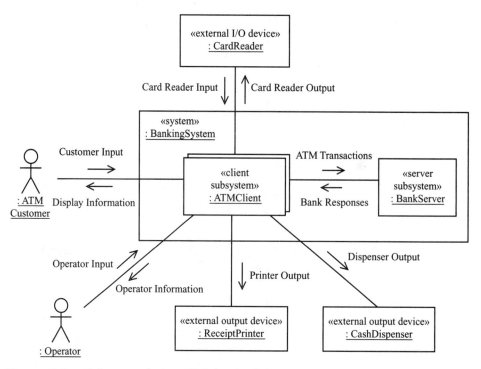

Figure 19.27 *Subsystem design: High-level collaboration diagram for Banking System*

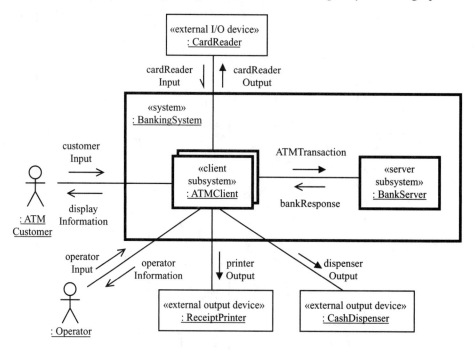

Figure 19.28 *Subsystem interfaces: high-level concurrent collaboration diagram for Banking System*

19.10 Design of ATM Client Subsystem

To determine the tasks in a system, it is necessary to understand how the objects in the application interact with each other. This is best depicted on the analysis model collaboration diagram, which shows the sequence of messages passed between objects in support of a given use case. For the ATM Client Subsystem, consider the collaboration diagrams for the Client Validate PIN and Client Withdraw Funds use cases in addition to the consolidated collaboration diagram for this subsystem. The task design described in this section leads to the concurrent collaboration diagram shown in Figure 19.29.

19.10.1 Design the ATM Subsystem Concurrent Task Architecture

Consider the collaboration diagram supporting the Validate PIN use case (see Figure 19.12). The first object to participate in the collaboration is the Card Reader Interface object, which is a device interface object that interfaces to the real-world card reader. The characteristics of the Card Reader external I/O device are that it is an asynchronous I/O device that generates an interrupt when some input is available. The Card Reader Interface object is structured as an asynchronous I/O device interface task, as shown in Figure 19.29. Initially the task is dormant. It is activated by an interrupt, reads the card reader input, and converts it into some internal form. It then writes the contents of the card to the ATM Card entity object. ATM Card is a passive object and thus does not need a separate thread of control. It is further categorized as a data abstraction object.

The Card Reader Interface task then sends a Card Inserted message to ATM Control, which is a state-dependent control object that executes the ATM Control statechart. ATM Control is structured as a control task because it needs to have a separate thread of control to allow it to react to incoming asynchronous events from a variety of sources. On receiving the Card Inserted message, ATM Control executes the statechart (see Figure 19.21). The action associated with the state transition is to send a Get PIN message to Customer Interface, which is a user interface object that interacts with the user, providing outputs to the display and receiving inputs from the keypad. Customer Interface is structured as a user interface task with its own separate thread of control. It prompts the customer for the PIN, receives the PIN, reads the card information from ATM Card, and then writes the card and PIN information to ATM Transaction, which is also a passive data abstraction object. Because the ATM Card and ATM Transaction data abstraction objects are each accessed by more than one task, they are both placed outside any task.

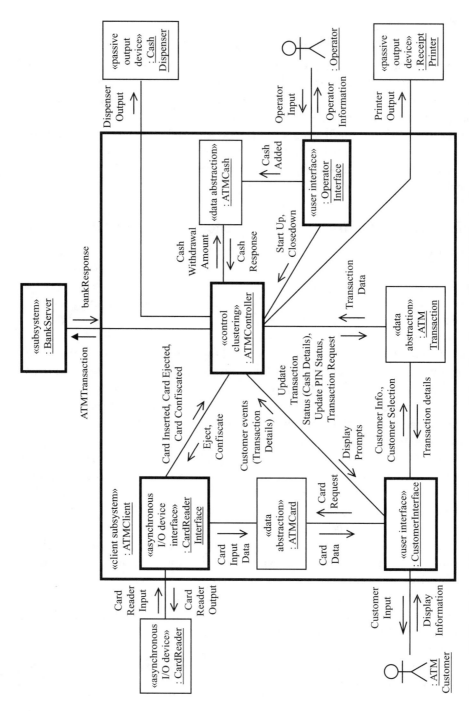

Figure 19.29 *Task architecture: initial concurrent collaboration diagram for ATM Client subsystem*

Next, consider the collaboration diagram supporting the Withdraw Funds use case, which has many of the same objects as the Validate PIN collaboration diagram. The additional objects are Receipt Printer Interface, Cash Dispenser Interface, and ATM Cash. To understand how ATM Control interacts with the Receipt Printer Interface and Cash Dispenser Interface objects, it is necessary to analyze the ATM Control statechart, as explained in Chapter 14.

After sending the Request Withdrawal transaction to the server, ATM Control is in Processing Withdrawal state (see Figure 19.22). On receiving the Withdrawal OK response from the server, it transitions to Dispensing state (see Figure 19.23). The output event associated with this transition is Dispense Cash, which is sent as a message to the Cash Dispenser Interface object. The external Cash Dispenser is a passive output device, so it does not need a separate asynchronous I/O task. The only way for ATM Control to leave the Dispensing state is by receiving either a Cash Dispensed message or an Insufficient Cash message (see Figure 19.23), both from the Cash Dispenser Interface object. Thus it is not possible for ATM Control and Cash Dispenser Interface to execute concurrently, so ATM Control and Cash Dispenser Interface can be combined into one task, the ATM Controller, based on the **control clustering** task structuring criterion. By conducting a similar analysis, we determine that it is not possible for ATM Control and the Receipt Printer Interface object to execute concurrently, so Receipt Printer Interface can also be combined with the ATM Controller task, based on **control clustering**. The ATM Controller task, which has one thread of control, is depicted on the concurrent collaboration diagram (see Figure 19.29). The design of this composite task is considered later.

The Operator Interface user interface object (see Figure 19.24), which participates in the three operator-initiated use cases, is also mapped to a user interface task (see Figure 19.29). The ATM Cash entity object is a passive data abstraction object that is accessed by both the ATM Controller and Operator Interface tasks. Consequently, ATM Cash cannot be placed inside the ATM Controller or the Operator Interface and must be placed outside any task.

To summarize, there is one asynchronous I/O device interface task, Card Reader Interface, one control clustered task, ATM Controller, and two user interface tasks, Customer Interface and Operator Interface. There are three passive entity objects, ATM Card, ATM Transaction, and ATM Cash, which are all categorized further as data abstraction objects.

19.10.2 Define the ATM Subsystem Task Interfaces

To determine the task interfaces, it is necessary to analyze the way the objects (active or passive) interact with each other. First, consider the interaction of the tasks just determined with the passive data abstraction objects. In each case, the task calls an operation provided by the passive object. This has to be a synchronous call, because the operation executes in the thread of control of the task. Similarly, all other operations of the data abstraction objects are invoked as synchronous calls. Because each of these passive objects is invoked by more than one task, it is necessary for the operations to synchronize the access to the data. The operations provided by these passive objects are described in the next section.

Next consider the message interaction between the tasks. Consider the interface between the Card Reader Interface and ATM Controller tasks. It is desirable for this to be loosely coupled, so an asynchronous message interface is used, as shown in Figure 19.30. This means the Card Reader Interface task can send a message to ATM Controller and not have to wait for it to be accepted. There is also a message interface in the opposite direction because the ATM Controller sends Eject and Confiscate messages to the Card Reader Interface task. This is designed as a tightly coupled message interface because, after sending a message to ATM Controller, the Card Reader Interface waits for an Eject or Confiscate return message. The Card Reader Interface task's responses are loosely coupled, providing the greatest flexibility in the interface between the Card Reader Interface and ATM Controller tasks.

Consider the interface between Customer Interface and ATM Controller. Should it be loosely coupled or tightly coupled? First, consider a tightly coupled with response scenario. Customer Interface sends a Withdrawal request to ATM Controller, which then sends the transaction to the Bank Server. After receiving the Server's response, ATM Controller sends a display prompt to Customer Interface. In the meantime, it is not possible for Customer Interface to have any interaction with the customer, because it is suspended, waiting for the response from the ATM Controller. This is undesirable from the customer's viewpoint. Consider, instead, a loosely coupled interface, as shown in Figure 19.30. With this approach, Customer Interface sends the Withdrawal request to ATM Controller and does not wait for a response. In this case, Customer Interface can respond to customer inputs such as a Cancel request before a response is received from the server. Customer Interface receives responses from ATM Controller as a separate loosely coupled message interface. Customer Interface is designed to be capable of receiving inputs from either the customer or the ATM Controller. It processes whichever input comes first.

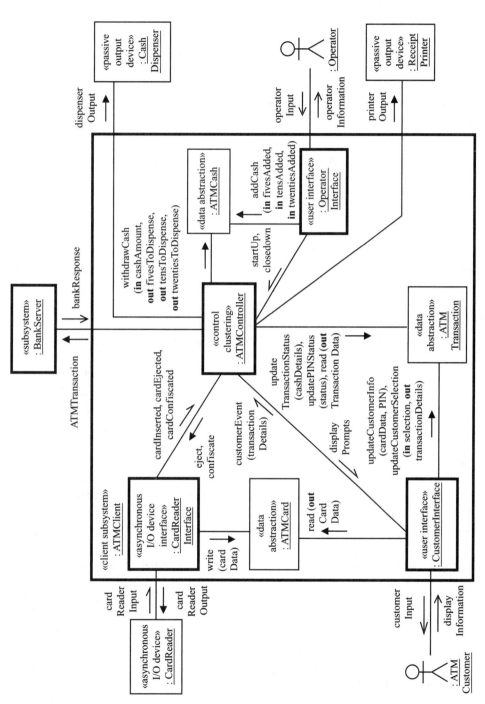

Figure 19.30 *Task architecture: revised concurrent collaboration diagram for ATM Client subsystem*

The `Operator Interface` task's interface is also loosely coupled. The operator actor's requests are independent of the customer's requests, so messages from the customer and the operator could arrive in any order at the `ATM Controller`. To allow for this, the `ATM Controller` receives all incoming messages on a message queue and processes them on a FIFO basis. In Figure 19.30, the concurrent collaboration diagram is updated to show the task interfaces.

19.10.3   Design the ATM Client Information Hiding Classes

The objects and classes for the `Banking System` are initially determined in the analysis model. Active classes are determined during task design. In this phase, the passive classes are designed. Further categorization of passive classes is also possible during design; for example, entity classes are categorized further as data abstraction classes or database wrapper classes. During class design, the class interfaces are designed. To determine the class interfaces, it is necessary to consider how the objects on the collaboration diagrams interact with each other.

First, consider the design of the entity classes in the `ATM Client Subsystem`. Because there is no database in the `ATM Client Subsystem`, all the entity classes encapsulate their own data and are therefore categorized further as data abstraction classes. The `ATM Client Subsystem` has three data abstraction classes: `ATM Card`, `ATM Transaction`, and `ATM Cash`. The attributes of data abstraction classes are determined during the conceptual static modeling of the entity classes, as described in Section 19.3. The operations of these classes are determined by analyzing the way they are used on the collaboration diagrams.

The design of the `ATM Cash` class is described in Chapter 15. Consider the design of the `ATM Card` object. As given by the `Validate PIN` collaboration diagram, two objects use `ATM Card`: `Card Reader Interface` and `Customer Interface` (see Figure 19.12). `ATM Card` encapsulates the information read off an ATM card. From the static model, its attributes are `card ID`, `start Date`, and `expiration date`. From the collaboration diagram for `Validate PIN`, the `Card Reader Interface` object reads the physical ATM card and then writes the information it has read (the values of the three attributes) to the `ATM Card` object. Thus, the `ATM Card` object needs to provide a `write` operation. The `Customer Interface` object later reads the `ATM Card` data in order to create an ATM `Transaction`—thus a `read` operation is also needed.

For the `ATM Transaction` class, the attributes are also determined from the static model, but its operations are determined from the way it is accessed by other objects, as given on the collaboration diagrams. The operations are `update Customer Information`, `update Customer Selection`, `update PIN Sta-`

tus, update Transaction Status, and read. The first two operations are invoked by the Customer Interface task. The other three operations are invoked by the ATM Controller task. There is one state-dependent control class, namely ATM Control. The operations are process Event and current State, which are standard operations for a state-dependent class.

Next, consider the design of the device interface classes. The Card Reader Device Interface is a passive class that hides the details of how to access the real-world card reader. Its operations are initialize and read. From the analysis model, the following passive output device interface classes are depicted: Receipt Printer Interface and Cash Dispenser Interface. To determine the operations, we examine the analysis model collaboration diagrams. Because the Receipt Printer Interface and Cash Dispenser Interface are both output device interface classes, they have similar interfaces. They each need an initialize operation. They also each need an output operation. In the case of the Receipt Printer Interface class, the output operation is print, but in the case of the Cash Dispenser Interface class, the output operation is dispense. There are also two user interface classes, namely, Customer Interface and Operator Interface. Both of these are active and were considered during task design. The design of the classes is shown in more detail in Figure 19.31, which shows the attributes and operations of the classes.

19.10.4   Develop the ATM Client Subsystem Detailed Software Design

In this phase, the detailed software design is developed, which depicts the design of the connector classes and the internal design of the composite active objects (tasks) that have passive objects (class instances) nested inside them.

First consider the design of the ATM Controller. It has a loosely coupled message communication interface through which it receives messages. The actual kind of communication mechanism can be encapsulated in a connector object, the ATM Control Message Q, as shown in Figure 19.32. The Card Reader Interface, Customer Interface, and Operator Interface are all producer tasks that call the send operation of the connector to send ATM Control Request messages to the ATM Controller. The messages are queued FIFO in a message queue maintained by the connector. The ATM Controller calls the receive operation of the connector to receive the ATM Control Request messages. Another message queue connector, the prompt Message Queue, is used by the ATM Controller to send display prompt messages to the Customer Interface task. There is also a tightly coupled message buffer connector, the card Reader Message Buffer, used by the ATM controller to send eject and

«data abstraction» ATMTransaction	«state dependent control» ATMControl
− transactionID : String − cardID : String − PIN : String = null − selection : TransactionType − transactionData : TransactionRecord	
+ updateCustomerInfo (cardData, PIN) + updateCustomerSelection (**in** selection, **out** transactionDetails) + updatePINStatus (status) + updateTransactionStatus (cashDetails) + reat (**out** transaction Data)	+ processEvent (**in** event, **out** action) + currentState () : State

«data abstraction» ATMCash	«output device interface» ReceiptPrinterInterface
− cashAvailable : Integer = 0 − fives : Integer = 0 − tens : Integer = 0 − twenties : Integer = 0	

+ addCash (**in** fivesAdded, **in** tensAdded,
  in twentiesAdded)
+ withdrawCash (**in** cashAmount,
  out fivesToDispense,
  out tensToDispense,
  out twentiesToDispense)
	+ initialize ()
	+ printReceipt (**in** receiptInfo,
	  out printerStatus)

«data abstraction» ATMCard	«output device interface» CashDispenserInterface
− cardNumber : String − startDate : Date − expirationDate : Date	
+ write (**in** cardData) + read (**out** cardData)	+ initialize () + dispenseCash (**in** cashAmount, **out** dispenseStatus)

Figure 19.31 *ATM client information hiding classes*

confiscate messages to the Card Reader Interface task. Finally, a bank Server Proxy connector object acts as a proxy for tightly coupled message (synchronous) communication with response to the Bank Server. This connector needs to be active to hide the details of how to communicate with the remote Bank Server. For example, in Java, this would use a remote method invocation interface. When the ATM Controller sends a message to the Bank Server, it waits for the response.

Next, consider the internal design of the ATM Controller, which is a composite task designed as a control clustering task. The design is described in Chapter 16, Section 16.4, and depicted in Figure 19.33. It consists of a coordinator object, ATM Coordinator, which receives incoming messages and coordinates the execution of the three other objects. The state-dependent control object, ATM Control, encapsulates the ATM statechart, which is implemented as a state transition table. The other two objects are the Cash Dispenser Interface and the Receipt Printer Interface output device interface objects.

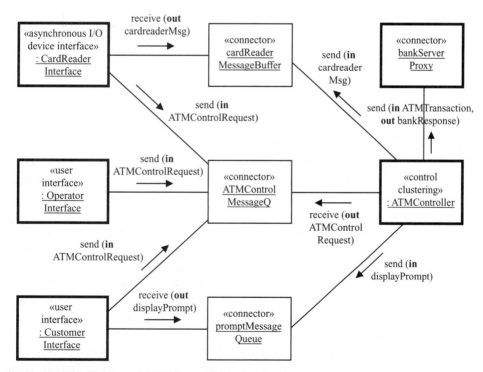

Figure 19.32   *Design of ATM Controller connectors*

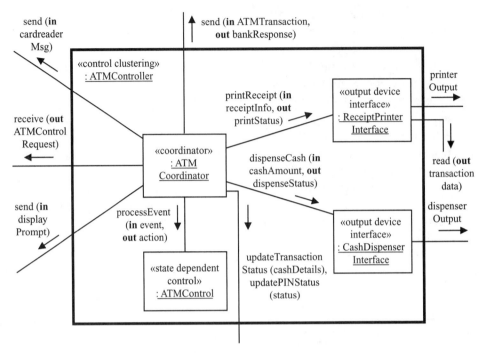

Figure 19.33 *Detailed software design of ATM Controller*

19.11   Design of Bank Server Subsystem

Because the bank server holds the centralized database for the Banking System, we start the design of the Bank Server Subsystem by considering some important design decisions concerning the static model. The conceptual static model of the entity classes (see Figures 19.4–19.7) contains several entity classes that actually reside at the Bank Server. After structuring the system into subsystems and developing the consolidated collaboration model, we can develop a revised static model of the Bank Server. This refined static model is developed from the original static model of the entity classes (see Figure 19.4) as well as the objects in the Bank Server consolidated collaboration diagram (see Figure 19.26), as described in Chapter 12. The revised static model for the Bank Server Subsystem is depicted on the class diagram in Figure 19.34.

Furthermore, a business decision is made that the entity classes at the server, which were originally depicted in the static model of the problem domain (see

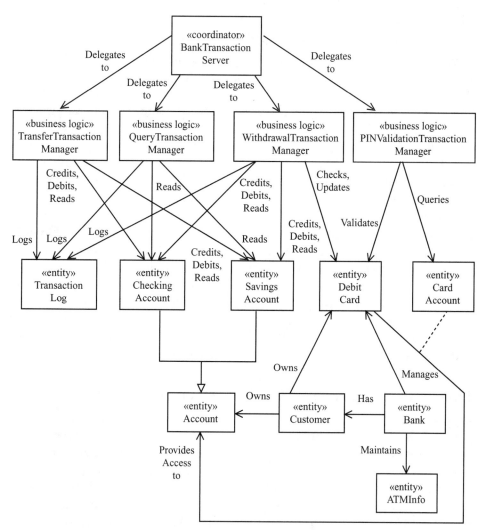

Figure 19.34   *Refined static model: Bank Server Subsystem*

Figure 19.4), are to be stored as relations (flat files) in a relational database. Thus, during design we determine that the entity classes at the server do not actually encapsulate any data but rather encapsulate the interface to the relational database and are actually database wrapper classes. The design of these classes is described later in this section.

19.11.1 Design the Bank Server Subsystem Concurrent Task Architecture

Now consider the Bank Server Subsystem design. A decision is made to use a sequential server. As long as the throughput of the server is fast enough, this is not a problem. In a sequential server, the whole server is designed as one task; thus, it is designed as one program with one thread of control. Each transaction is received on a FIFO message queue and is processed to completion before the next transaction is started.

The Bank Server Subsystem is designed as one task according to the **sequential clustering** criterion for task structuring. Inside the task are the coordinator object (the Bank Transaction Server), the business logic objects (PIN Validation Transaction Manager, Withdrawal Transaction Manager, Query Transaction Manager, and Transfer Transaction Manager), and the entity classes, now categorized further as database wrapper classes. The initial task design for the server subsystem, consisting of one task, is shown in Figure 19.35.

The Bank Transaction Server task receives the incoming transaction messages and replies with the bank responses. It delegates the transaction processing to the transaction managers, which in turn access the database wrapper objects. All communication internal to the Bank Server Subsystem is synchronous, corresponding to operation calls, as described next.

19.11.2 Design the Bank Server Information Hiding Classes

Chapter 15 describes the design of database wrapper classes as well as the mapping of analysis model entity classes to design model database wrapper classes and relations (flat files) for a relational database. At the Bank Server, the database wrapper classes are Account, Checking Account, Savings Account, Debit Card, Card Account, and Transaction Log. Each of these classes encapsulates an interface to a database relation. Because a relational database consists of flat files and does not support class hierarchies, from a database perspective, the Account generalization/specialization hierarchy is flattened so that the attributes of the Account superclass are assigned to the Checking Account and Savings Account relations [Rumbaugh et al. 1991, Blaha and Premerlani 1998]. However, in the Bank Server class design of the database wrappers, the Account generalization/specialization hierarchy is preserved so that the Checking Account and Savings Account database wrapper classes inherit generalized operations from the Account superclass. The design of the database wrapper classes is shown in Figure 19.36.

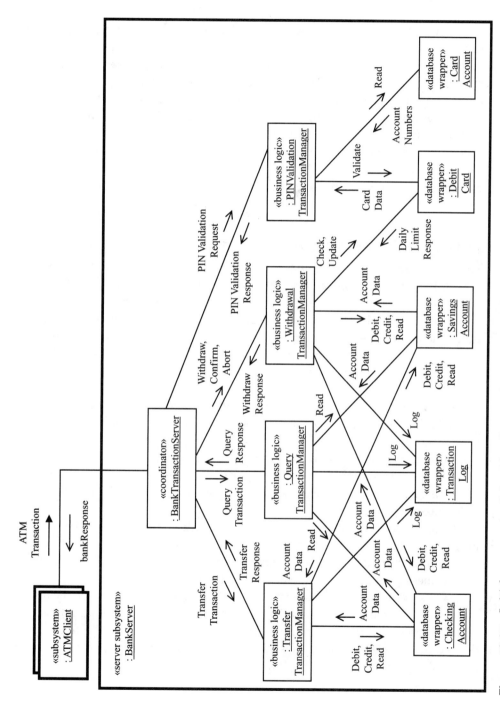

Figure 19.35 *Initial concurrent collaboration diagram for Bank Server Subsystem*

There are also four business logic classes whose interfaces need to be designed. These are the PIN Validation Transaction Manager, the Withdrawal Transaction Manager, the Query Transaction Manager, and the Transfer Transaction Manager. Each transaction manager handles an atomic transaction. For example, the Withdrawal Transaction Manager provides a withdraw operation, which is called to handle a customer request to withdraw funds, as well as two other operations. The confirm operation is called when an ATM Client confirms that the cash was dispensed to the client. The abort operation is called when an ATM Client aborts the transaction, for example, because the cash dispenser failed to dispense the cash or the customer cancelled the transaction.

19.11.3 Design the Bank Server Interfaces

The Bank Server is a sequential server subsystem. In particular, the design of the Bank Server task, which is structured according to the **sequential clustering** criterion, needs to be considered at this stage. The task is a composite task composed of passive objects. The Bank Transaction Server receives incoming transactions and delegates them to the business logic objects, namely, the PIN Validation Transaction Manager, the Withdrawal Transaction Manager, the Query Transaction Manager, and the Transfer Transaction Manager.

The Bank Transaction Server actually receives the messages FIFO from the ATM Clients. For each message, it determines the type of the transaction and then delegates the transaction processing to the appropriate transaction manager. Each transaction is processed to completion, with the response returned to the Bank Transaction Server, which in turn sends the response to the appropriate ATM Client. The Bank Transaction Server then processes the next transaction message.

Figure 19.35 shows the initial design of the Bank Server Subsystem, including the Bank Transaction Server task, which contains all the passive objects. In the initial concurrent collaboration diagram for the Bank Server, all interfaces are simple messages. Figure 19.37 shows the final version of the Bank Server Subsystem concurrent collaboration diagram. Communication between the multiple clients and the server is tightly coupled with reply. All internal interaction within the server is between passive objects, and hence all internal interfaces are defined in terms of operation calls (depicted by using the synchronous message notation).

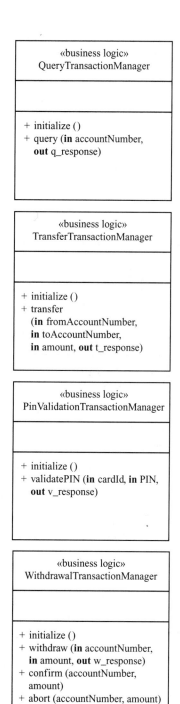

Figure 19.36a *Bank Server business logic classes*

Figure 19.36 *Bank Server information hiding classes*

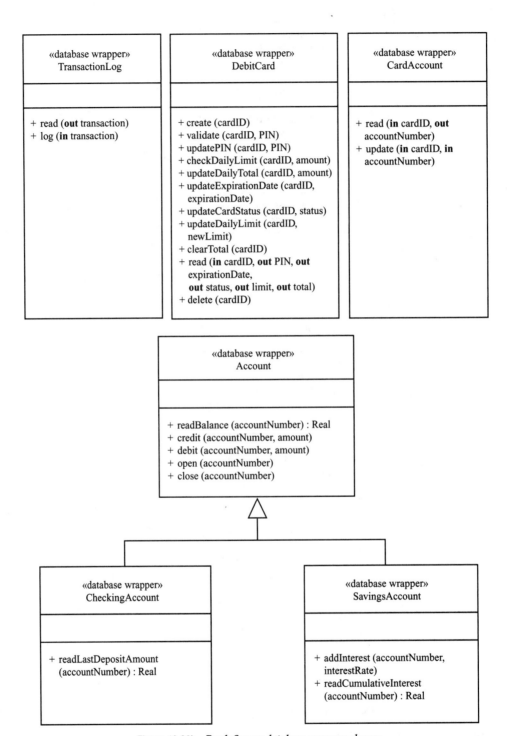

Figure 19.36b *Bank Server database wrapper classes*

19.12   Configuration of Banking System

Because this is a client/server subsystem, there are multiple instances of the client subsystem and one instance of the server subsystem. Each subsystem instance executes on its own node, as depicted in the deployment diagram in Figure 19.38.

19.13   Alternative Design Considerations

An alternative design decision is to use a concurrent server, in which the Bank Transaction Server and each of the business logic objects are designed as separate tasks. With this concurrent server design, the Bank Transaction Server would delegate a transaction to a business logic object and then immediately accept the next transaction. Thus multiple transactions would be processed concurrently at the server. This solution should be adopted if the sequential server design is inadequate for handling the transaction load. For more information on the design of concurrent servers, refer to Chapter 13.

19.14   Task Behavior Specifications

Examples of the task behavior specifications, in particular for the Card Reader Interface and ATM Controller tasks in the ATM Client Subsystem and for the Bank Server task in the Bank Server Subsystem, are given in Chapter 14. This section describes the event sequencing logic for these tasks.

19.14.1   Example of Event Sequencing Logic for Card Reader Interface Task

The Card Reader Interface task (see Figure 19.30) is awakened by a card reader external event, reads the card input, writes to the ATM Card object, sends a card Inserted message to the ATM Controller, and then waits for a message. If the message sent by the ATM Controller is eject, the card is ejected, and if it is confiscate, the card is confiscated.

The Card Reader Interface task here uses a nested card Reader DI device interface object to encapsulate the details of how to read, eject, or confiscate a card. This passive object provides operations to initialize, read, eject, and confiscate a card. There is also a passive data abstraction object, ATM Card, that is outside the task and is used to store the contents of the card.

Either the message queue between the Card Reader Interface task (producer) and the ATM Controller (consumer) is provided by the operating system

588

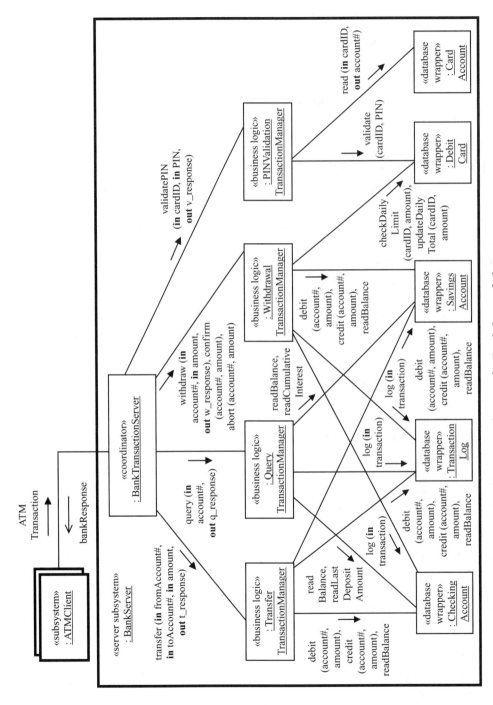

Figure 19.37 *Revised concurrent collaboration diagram for Bank Server Subsystem*

Figure 19.38 *Deployment diagram for Banking System*

or a message queue connector is used, as described in the previous section. This example uses a connector called the ATM Control Message Q (see Figure 19.32). The synchronous communication between the ATM Controller and the Card Reader Interface task can be provided as a service of the operating system or by a message buffer connector. This example uses a connector called card Reader Message Buffer (see Figure 19.32).

```
-- Initialize Card Reader;
cardReaderDI.initialize();
loop
-- Wait for external interrupt from card reader
wait (cardReaderEvent);
-- Read card data held on card's magnetic strip
cardReaderDI.read (cardInput);
if card recognized
then -- Write card data to ATM Card object;
  ATMCard.write (cardData);
  -- send card Inserted message to ATM Controller
  ATMControlMessageQ.send (cardInserted);
  -- Wait for message from ATM Controller
  cardReaderMessageBuffer.receive (message);
  if message = eject
  then -- Eject card
     cardReaderDI.eject ();
     -- Send card Ejected message to ATM Controller
     ATMControlMessageQ.send (cardEjected);
  elseif message = confiscate
     then -- confiscate card
       cardReaderDI.confiscate ();
       -- Send card Confiscated message to ATM Controller;
       ATMControlMessageQ.send (cardConfiscated);
     else error condition;
  end if;
else -- card was not recognized so eject;
   cardReaderDI.eject ();
end if;
end loop;
```

19.14.2   Example of Event Sequencing Logic for ATM Controller Task

The ATM Controller is at the heart of the ATM Client subsystem (see Figure 19.30) and interacts with several tasks. In this example, connectors are used to interconnect the tasks, as illustrated in Figure 19.32. The ATM Controller has an input message queue connector, the ATM Control Message Q, from which it receives messages from all its producers. The ATM Controller sends messages to several tasks. It sends synchronous messages without reply to the Card Reader Interface task, using a message buffer connector called card Reader Message Buffer. It sends asynchronous messages to the Customer Interface task via the prompt Message Queue connector. It sends synchronous messages with response to the Bank Server via a bank Server Proxy, which is a connector task that handles the details of sending messages to and receiving responses from the remote Bank Server.

Because it is state-dependent, the ATM Controller task does not process incoming events but instead processes the state-dependent actions as given by the statechart. The implementation of the statechart is encapsulated in the ATM Control state-dependent object. Given the new event, the process Event operation returns the action(s) to be performed. Most events are received on the ATM Controller Message Q, although there are three exceptions to this. Because the communication with the Bank Server is synchronous, the response is received as the output parameter of the send operation. Because of the decision to group the Cash Dispenser Interface and the Receipt Printer Interface objects into the same task as the ATM Controller by using control clustering, the dispense Cash and print Receipt actions are operation calls that return whether the dispensing and printing was successful. The following Pseudocode assumes that the actions are successful. When an event is generated internally, the variable new Event is set to the value of this event and the Boolean variable outstanding Event is set to true. Examples of such internal events are withdrawal Response (several synchronous bank responses are possible as described in the next section in the event sequencing logic for the Bank Server) or cash Dispensed.

```
loop
   -- Messages from all senders are received on Message Queue
   ATMControlMessageQ.receive (message);
   -- Extract the event name and any message parameters
   -- Given the incoming event, lookup state transition table;
   -- change state if required; return action to be performed;
   newEvent = message.event
   outstandingEvent = true;
while outstandingEvent do
   ATMControl.processEvent (in newEvent, out action);
   outstandingEvent = false;
   -- Execute action(s) as given on ATM Control statechart
   case action of
```

```
Get PIN: -- Prompt for PIN;
  promptMessageQueue.send (displayPINPrompt);
Validate PIN: --Validate customer entered PIN at bank server;
  bankServerProxy.send (in validatePIN, out validationResponse);
  newEvent = validationResponse;
  outstandingEvent = true;
Display Menu: -- Display selection menu to customer;
  promptMessageQueue.send (displayMenu);
  ATMTransaction.updatePINStatus (valid);
Invalid PIN Action: -- Display Invalid PIN prompt;
  promptMessageQueue.send (displayInvalidPINPrompt);
  ATMTransaction.updatePINStatus (invalid);
Request Withdrawal: -- Send withdraw request to bank server;
  promptMessageQueue.send (displayWait);
  bankServerProxy.send
      (withdrawalRequest, out withdrawalResponse);
  newEvent = withdrawalResponse;
  outstandingEvent = true;
Request Query: -- Send query request to bank server;
  promptMessageQueue.send (displayWait);
  bankServerProxy.send (in queryRequest, out queryResponse);
  newEvent = queryResponse;
  outstandingEvent = true;
Request Transfer: -- Send transfer request to bank server;
  promptMessageQueue.send (displayWait);
  bankServerProxy.send (transferRequest, out transferResponse);
  newEvent = transferResponse; outstandingEvent = true;
Dispense: -- Dispense cash and update transaction status;
  ATMTransaction.updateTransactionStatus (withdrawalOK);
  cashDispenserInterface.dispenseCash
    (in cashAmount, out dispenseStatus);
  newEvent = cashDispensed; outstandingEvent = true;
Print: -- Print receipt and send confirmation to bank server;
  promptMessageQueue.send (displayCashDispensed);
  bankServerProxy.send (in confirmRequest);
  receiptPrinterInterface.printReceipt
    (in receiptInfo, out printStatus);
  newEvent = receiptPrinted;
  outstandingEvent = true;
Eject: -- Eject ATM card;
  cardReaderMessageBuffer.send (eject);
Confiscate: -- Confiscate ATM card;
  cardReaderMessageBuffer.send (confiscate);
  ATMTransaction.updatePINStatus (thirdInvalid);
Display Ejected: -- Display Card Ejected prompt;
  promptMessageQueue.send (displayEjected);
Display Confiscated: -- Display Card Confiscated prompt;
  promptMessageQueue.send (displayConfiscated);
  ...
  end case;
 end while;
end loop;
```

19.14.3 Example of Event Sequencing Logic for Bank Server Task

The Bank Server receives messages from all the ATM Clients (see Figure 19.37). Although the communication is synchronous with reply, a message queue can build up at the Bank Server as it receives messages from multiple clients. In this sequential solution, the Bank Server is a composite task structured according to the sequential clustering criterion. The server processes each request to completion before starting the next.

```
loop
receive (Client, Message) from Bank Server Message Queue;
Extract message name and message parameters from message;
case Message of
 Validate PIN:
    -- Check that ATM Card is valid and that PIN entered by
    -- customer matches PIN maintained by Server;
    PINValidationTransactionManager.ValidatePIN
       (in CardId, in PIN, out validationResponse);
    -- If successful, validation Response is valid and return
    -- Account Numbers accessible by this debit card;
    -- otherwise validation Response is invalid,
    -- third Invalid, or stolen;
    reply (Client, validationResponse);
 Withdrawal:
    -- Check that daily limit has not been exceeded and that
    -- customer has enough funds in account to satisfy request
    -- If all checks are successful, then debit account.
    WithdrawalTransactionManager.withdraw
       (in AccountNumber, in Amount, out withdrawalResponse);
    -- If approved, then withdrawal Response is
    -- {successful, currentBalance};
    -- otherwise withdrawalResponse is {unsuccessful};
    reply (client, withdrawalResponse);
 Query:
    -- Read account balance.
    queryTransactionManager.query
       (in accountNumber, out queryresponse);
    -- Query Response = Current Balance and either Last Deposit
    -- Amount (checking account) or Interest (savings acount);
    reply (client, queryResponse);
 Transfer:
    -- Check that customer has enough funds in From Account to
    -- satisfy request. If approved, then debit From Account
    -- and credit To Account;
    transferTransactionManager.transfer (in fromAccount#,
       in toAccount#, in amount, out transferResponse);
    -- If approved, then transfer Response is
```

```
      -- {successful, Current Balance of From Account};
      -- otherwise Transfer Response is {unsuccessful};
      reply (client, transferResponse);
   Confirm:
      -- Confirm withdrawal transaction was completed successfully
      withdrawalTransactionManager.confirm (in accountNumber);
   Abort:
      -- Abort withdrawal transaction
      withdrawalTransactionManager.abort (in accountNumber);
   end case;
   end loop;
```

chapter

Cruise Control and Monitoring System Case Study

T his chapter describes an automobile Cruise Control and Monitoring System case study, which is a real-time embedded system case study. This is a popular example; various other treatments of it are given in Booch [1986], Ward [1986], Hatley and Pirbhai [1988], Gomaa [1993], and Shaw [1995]. This case study has been used to illustrate several aspects of the COMET method in previous chapters. This chapter describes the full case study.

20.1 Problem Description

This section presents the problem description for the Cruise Control and Monitoring System case study.

The informal problem description, in the form of a memo from the Marketing Division to the Engineering Division, is the starting point for the analysis and design of the Cruise Control and Monitoring System:

To: Vehicle Systems Engineering Division
From: GMU Product Line Marketing Group
Subject: Cruise Control and Monitoring System

As you might already know, we have decided to incorporate a combined cruise control and monitoring system in next year's GMU (Grand Motoring Unit) model. None of our subcompact models have previously offered such features as standard equipment, but we believe that making this system standard equipment on the sports version of next year's model will increase its perceived value far more than the incremental cost to build it. The system will be an option on the economy model. This memo summarizes the key features that Marketing wants the system to have. However, we are leaving the specification of the detailed requirements to Vehicle Systems, subject to our review. Engineering continues to insist that the design, of both the hardware and the microcomputer software, is its domain.

Automatic Cruise Control Functions:

The automatic cruise control system is activated and controlled by a cruise control lever at the right hand side of the steering wheel column. The cruise control lever has three switch positions: ACCEL, RESUME, and OFF. The required cruise control functions are

ACCEL

With the cruise control lever held in this position, the car accelerates without using the accelerator pedal. After releasing the lever, the achieved speed is maintained (referred to as the cruising speed) and also "memorized."

OFF

By moving the control lever to the OFF position, the cruise control can be switched off in any driving and operating condition.

The cruise control is automatically switched off in any operation when the foot brake is pressed.

RESUME

By moving the lever to RESUME, the last "memorized" speed can be resumed. The "memorized" speed is cancelled by switching off the ignition.

Calibration Functions:

The driver may reset the calibration constant, which is the number of shaft rotations per mile, as follows:

- Press the Calibration Start button at the start of the measured mile to initiate the Calibration process.
- Press the Calibration Stop button at the end of the measured mile to terminate the Calibration process.

Monitoring Functions:

The required vehicle monitoring functions are

1. Display of average speed from the start of a trip on a trip display screen. The driver may reset the start of the trip.
2. Display of average fuel consumption from the start of a trip on a trip display screen. The driver may reset the start of the trip.

3. Driver notification of required vehicle maintenance, as follows:
   - 5,000 miles for oil change
   - 10,000 miles for air filter change and oil change
   - 15,000 miles for major service

Three reset buttons are to be available for the maintenance technician to reinitialize the maintenance indicators after a service has been carried out.

The maintenance messages are to be displayed on a maintenance display screen. When the car is within 250 miles of a maintenance threshold, there should be an intermittent message given. When the car is within 50 miles of the maintenance threshold, the message should be on constantly. Multiple messages can be on at the same time if the car has not been properly serviced.

There should be no unpredictable interaction between the use of the cruise control system and the use of the monitoring functions. Next year, we might decide to include just the cruise control function as standard equipment on some models. We might also decide to offer the trip average speed and average fuel consumption functions as a separate option from the maintenance functions in future.

20.1.1   Cruise Control as a Process Control Problem

The cruise control function of the Cruise Control and Monitoring System can be viewed as a process control problem [Shaw 1995], as shown in Figure 20.1. The speed control algorithm is enabled and disabled as a result of inputs received from the driver via the automobile sensors. Speed Control has a set point, the desired cruising speed, and a controlled variable, the current speed of the car. The speed control algorithm compares the set point with the controlled variable with the goal of increasing or decreasing the current speed as necessary to make it equal to the desired speed, plus or minus some delta value. It achieves this by making positive or negative adjustments to the throttle, which are input to the engine. The engine increases or decreases the speed of the car by increasing or decreasing the shaft (wheel) rotation. The shaft triggers a pulse every time it completes a full rotation. The system determines the current speed of the car—the controlled variable—from the shaft rotation count.

20.2   Use Case Model

Starting with the problem description, the use case model is developed as a description of the software requirements. When there are a large number of use cases, it is useful to group related use cases into a package. This grouping may be

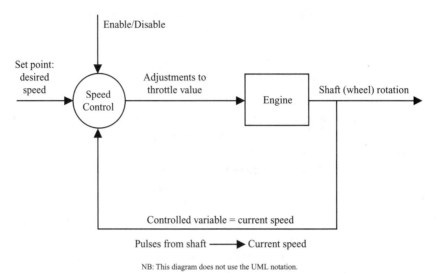

Figure 20.1 *Speed Control algorithm for Cruise Control*

based around the actor who initiates the use case or around the functionally related use cases, which may not be initiated by the same actor. Because the system consists of two major sets of functional requirements, the cruise control requirements and the monitoring requirements, the use cases are organized into two use case packages, the Cruise Control Use Case Package and the Monitoring Use Case Package.

There are four actors, two human actors, one input device, and the timer. The two humans are the Driver, who initiates several of the use cases, and the Technician. Most of the input devices are not separate actors because the human actors initiate their usage; however, the Shaft is an actor in its own right because its inputs are independent of the Driver. Many of the use cases are initiated periodically, so the Timer is an actor.

20.2.1 Cruise Control Use Cases

The use cases in the Cruise Control Use Case Package shown in Figure 20.2 are as follows:

- The Driver-initiated use cases:
  - Control Speed. In this use case, the driver selects cruise control and the system automatically controls the speed of the vehicle, using the algorithm depicted in Figure 20.1.

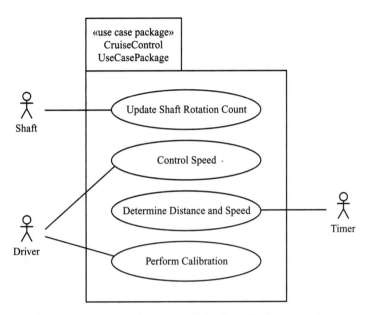

Figure 20.2 *Use case model: Cruise Control Use Case Package*

- Perform Calibration. In this use case, the driver presses the Start and Stop Calibration buttons to recompute the calibration constant.

- The Shaft-initiated use case:

  - Update Shaft Rotation Count. The shaft generates an interrupt at the conclusion of each shaft revolution. A count of the number of shaft rotations is maintained, from which the Cumulative Distance traveled by the car and the Current Speed of the car are calculated.

The Current Speed is needed by the Control Speed use case. Several use cases need the cumulative distance for calculating the trip speed, calculating the trip fuel consumption, and checking on maintenance. Instead of making these all part of the same use case, they are split off into separate use cases. Furthermore, the calculation of the distance traveled and current speed are split off into a separate use case from Update Shaft Rotation Count, because the computation of distance and speed is a separate periodic activity.

- The Timer-initiated use case:

  - Determine Distance and Speed. Periodically, the system calculates the Cumulative Distance traveled by the car and the Current Speed of the car.

20.2.2 Monitoring Use Cases

The use cases in the `Monitoring Use Case Package` shown in Figure 20.3 are as follows:

- The `Driver`-initiated use cases:
  - `Reset Trip Speed`. In this use case, the driver presses the Trip Speed Reset button to reinitialize the calculation of the average trip speed.
  - `Reset Trip Fuel Consumption`. In this use case, the driver presses the Trip Fuel Consumption Reset button to reinitialize the calculation of the average trip fuel consumption.
- The `Timer`-initiated use cases:
  - `Calculate Trip Speed`. Periodically, the system calculates the average trip speed of the car.
  - `Calculate Trip Fuel Consumption`. Periodically, the system calculates the average trip fuel consumption of the car.
  - `Check Oil Maintenance`. Periodically, the system checks whether an oil change is required.
  - `Check Air Filter Maintenance`. Periodically, the system checks whether an air filter service and oil change is required.
  - `Check Major Service Maintenance`. Periodically, the system checks whether a major service is required.
- The `Technician`-initiated use cases:
  - `Reset Oil Maintenance`. After performing an oil change, the maintenance technician presses the Oil Change Reset button to reinitialize the oil change distance counter.
  - `Reset Air Filter Maintenance`. After performing an air filter service, the maintenance technician presses the Air Filter Service Reset button to reinitialize the air filter service distance counter.
  - `Reset Major Service Maintenance`. After performing a major service, the maintenance technician presses the Major Service Reset button to reinitialize the major service distance counter.

20.3 Use Case Descriptions

Descriptions of each use case in terms of the sequence of actor inputs and system responses are given next.

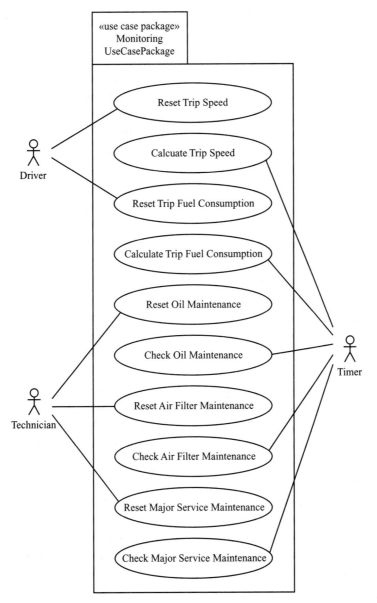

Figure 20.3 *Use case model: Monitoring Use Case Package*

20.3.1   Driver-Initiated Use Cases

Use Case Name: Update Shaft Rotation Count

Actor: Shaft

Summary: This use case describes the activation of the shaft at the conclusion of each shaft revolution.

Precondition: The car is in motion.

Description:

An interrupt is generated at each shaft revolution. This is used to keep track of the number of shaft revolutions, which is used for calculating the Cumulative Distance traveled by the car and the Current Speed of the car.

Alternatives: Error condition—Shaft Interrupt is not received.

Postcondition: Shaft rotation count has been updated.

Use Case Name: Control Speed

This use case is described in Chapter 10.

Use Case Name: Perform Calibration

Actor: Driver

Summary: The driver presses the Start and Stop Calibration buttons to recompute the calibration constant.

Precondition: A previous value for the calibration constant exists. A nominal initial value is set in the factory.

Description:

There are two calibration buttons, the Calibration Start and Calibration Stop buttons. The `Driver` actor presses the Calibration Start button at the start of the measured mile to initiate the calibration process. At the end of the measured mile, the driver presses the Calibration Stop button. The system computes the calibration constant, which is the number of shaft rotations per mile.

Alternatives:

- If the driver presses the Calibration Start button twice in succession, the system restarts the calibration process.
- If the newly computed value of the calibration constant is more than ten percent different from the nominal value, the system will not update the calibration constant.

Postcondition: Calibration constant has been updated.

Use Case Name: Reset Trip Speed

Actor: Driver

Summary: Driver requests the system to reinitialize the calculation of the average trip speed.

Precondition: The trip averages display is operational.

Description:

The driver presses the Trip Speed Reset button. The system reinitializes the calculation of the average trip speed and clears the trip average speed value on the trip averages display.

Postcondition: The trip average speed has been reinitialized.

Use Case Name: Reset Trip Fuel Consumption.

Actor: Driver

Summary: Driver requests the system to reinitialize the calculation of the average trip fuel consumption.

Precondition: The trip averages display is operational.

Description:

The driver presses the Trip Fuel Consumption Reset button. The system reinitializes the calculation of the average trip fuel consumption and clears the trip average fuel consumption value on the trip averages display.

Postcondition: The trip average fuel consumption has been reinitialized.

20.3.2   Timer-Initiated Use Cases

Use Case Name: Determine Distance and Speed

Actor: Timer

Summary: This use case periodically calculates the Cumulative Distance traveled by the car and the Current Speed of the car.

Precondition: The car is in motion and the shaft rotation count has been updated.

Description:

The Cumulative Distance is updated by adding the incremental distance to it. First, the incremental shaft rotation count (current shaft rotation count minus previous shaft rotation count) is calculated, and then this count is converted to the incremental distance by dividing it by the calibration constant (number of shaft rotations per mile). The Current Speed is calculated by dividing the incremental distance by the incremental time (current time minus previous time).

Alternatives: None.

Postcondition: Cumulative Distance and Current Speed have been updated.

Use Case Name: Calculate Trip Speed

Actor: Timer

Summary: Periodically, the system calculates the average trip speed of the car.

Precondition: The initial trip distance and time are stored.

Description:

The timer activates the use case. The system determines the distance traveled by the car and the current time. It compares these values with the initial trip distance and time to compute the trip average speed of the car, which is output to the trip averages display.

Postcondition: The trip average speed has been computed and displayed.

Use Case Name: Calculate Trip Fuel Consumption

Actor: Timer

Summary: Periodically, the system calculates the average trip fuel consumption of the car.

Precondition: The initial trip distance and fuel level are stored.

Description:

The timer activates the use case. The system determines the distance traveled by the car and the current fuel level. It compares these values with the initial trip distance and fuel level to compute the trip average fuel consumption, which is output to the trip averages display.

Alternative: If the fuel level reading indicates that fuel has been added to the car, then the calculation compensates for this.

Postcondition: The trip average fuel consumption has been computed and displayed.

Use Case Name: Check Maintenance

Actor: Timer

Summary: Periodically, the system checks whether the next service is required.

Precondition: The distance at which the last service was performed is stored (for a brand new car, this value is initially equal to zero).

Description:

The timer activates the use case. The system determines the distance traveled by the car and compares this value with the distance at which the last service was performed. It then compares the difference with the distance at which the next scheduled service is due. If it is within 250 miles of a maintenance threshold, an intermittent message should be displayed. When the car is within 50 miles of the maintenance threshold, the message should be displayed constantly.

Postcondition: The maintenance check has been completed. A message has been output if maintenance is required.

There are three versions of the above use case, for oil maintenance, air maintenance, and major service maintenance.

20.3.3 Technician-Initiated Use Cases

Use Case Name: Reset Maintenance

Actor: Technician

Summary: The maintenance technician presses the Service Reset button to indicate that the service has been completed.

Precondition: Technician has completed the service.

Description:

The maintenance technician presses the Service Reset button. The system stores the distance at which the service was performed.

Postcondition: The distance at which the service was performed is stored.

There are three versions of the above use case, for oil maintenance, air maintenance, and major service maintenance.

20.4   Problem Domain Static Modeling

During the initial static modeling of the problem domain, the real-world classes are determined. In a real-time embedded system, the real-world classes are primarily physical I/O devices—in particular, sensors and actuators—which the actor uses to interact with the system. After these have been determined, the I/O devices are depicted as external classes on the system context model, as shown on a class diagram.

The various sensors and actuators are depicted in the static model of the problem domain, as depicted in Figure 20.4. The sensors are the Cruise Control Lever to enter cruise control requests, the Engine sensor to switch the engine on and off, the Brake sensor to press and release the brake, and the Shaft sensor to detect shaft rotations. There is one actuator, the Throttle actuator, to automatically control the speed of the vehicle. The sensors and actuator used for cruise

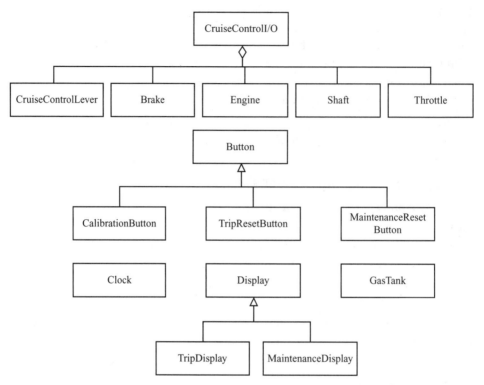

Figure 20.4 *Static model of problem domain*

control can be considered part of the Cruise Control I/O aggregate class. Various buttons are used in the system, the Calibration Button, Trip Reset Button, and Maintenance Reset Button classes, which are generalized into a Button class. Two other output devices, the Trip Display and the Maintenance Display classes, are generalized into a Display class. Two other real-world classes are the Gas Tank and the Clock.

The system context model is then derived from the static model of the problem domain. The system context class diagram defines the interface between the system and the external environment. It is depicted on a class diagram and shows the multiplicity of the associations between the external classes and the system, which is depicted as one aggregate class.

In the cruise control problem, the driver initiates many of the inputs. One option would be to make the driver an external class in the system context model. However, the driver is not a good choice for an external class, because the driver actually interacts with the system via several I/O devices that should be explicitly depicted as external classes. These are the cruise control lever, the engine sensor, the brake sensor, the calibration buttons, and the trip reset buttons. Consequently, each of these I/O devices should be modeled as a separate external class. Thus there should be external classes for `Cruise Control Lever`, `Brake sensor`, `Engine sensor`, `Calibration Button`, and `Trip Reset Button`, as depicted in Figure 20.5.

The `Shaft` actor interacts with the system via the `Shaft` external I/O device class. The `Timer` actor needs an external timer class called `Clock`. The maintenance `Technician` actor interacts with the system by means of `Maintenance Reset Buttons`. All the external classes (excluding the aggregate and generalized classes) are shown as interfacing to the system. The external classes are either external input devices or external output devices, except the `Clock`, which is an external timer. The actors who use these I/O devices are also depicted. The complete system context class diagram for the Cruise Control and Monitoring System is given in Figure 20.5.

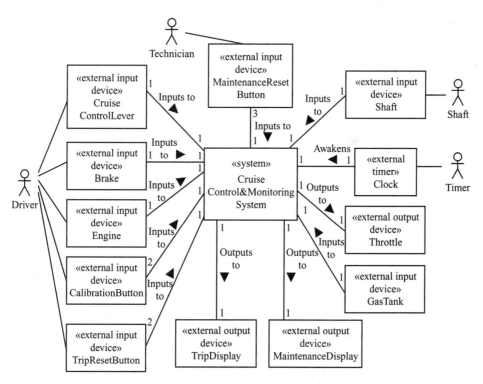

Figure 20.5 *Cruise Control and Monitoring System: system context class diagram*

20.5 Dynamic Modeling

After the use cases have been specified, the next step depends on the kind of system being developed, in particular, whether a better understanding of the system can be obtained by analyzing its structural properties or its dynamic properties. Because the Cruise Control and Monitoring System is a real-time system, a better understanding of the system can be obtained by studying the dynamic properties before the structural properties.

From the use cases, the objects participating in each use case can be determined by using the object structuring criteria. For a state-dependent use case, a statechart can be developed to show the different states of the use case. Later, the statechart is encapsulated inside a state-dependent control object, which provides the overall control and sequencing for the use case. The dynamic characteristics are determined by analyzing the interactions between the objects.

For each use case, the objects participating in the use case are determined. For a state-dependent use case, the statechart is developed first and then the interactions between the objects that participate in the use case are analyzed.

20.5.1 Initial Subsystem Structuring

In the Cruise Control and Monitoring System, it is clear from the problem description that there are two subsystems: the Cruise Control Subsystem and the Monitoring Subsystem. Because the cumulative distance traveled by the car is computed in the Determine Distance and Speed use case, and used by the use cases in the Monitoring Subsystem, we determine that the Monitoring Subsystem (and each of the subsystems within it) depends on the Cruise Control Subsystem. Each subsystem can be depicted as a package, as shown in Figure 20.6, which explicitly depicts the dependency relationship.

A more detailed analysis indicates that the Monitoring Subsystem could be split further into a Trip Averages Subsystem and a Maintenance Subsystem. The interdependencies between the use cases in the Cruise Control Subsystem need further analysis before any further subsystem packaging can be done. It is also possible to show the allocation of external devices to subsystems. The goal is to have an external device interface to only one subsystem apart from the external timer. This is depicted on a class diagram (see Figure 20.7), which is a refinement of the system context class diagram.

20.5.2 Non-State-Dependent Dynamic Modeling of the Cruise Control Subsystem

The dynamic modeling is applied to each subsystem in turn, first the Cruise Control Subsystem and then the Monitoring Subsystem.

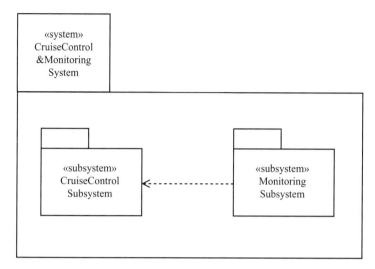

Figure 20.6 *Cruise Control & Monitoring System: initial determination of major subsystems*

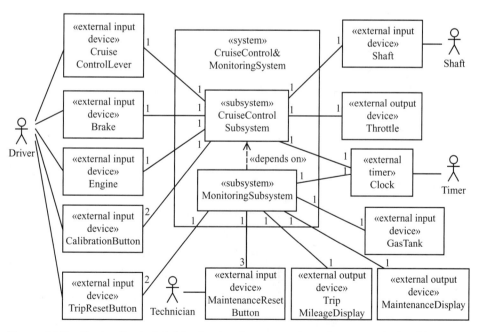

Figure 20.7 *Cruise Control & Monitoring System: major subsystem relationships*

Of the four use cases in the Cruise Control Subsystem, two are non-state-dependent and two are state-dependent. The non-state-dependent use cases are the Update Shaft Rotation Count and Determine Distance and Speed use cases. The collaboration diagram for the Update Shaft Rotation Count use case is shown in Figure 20.8, and the message descriptions follow.

In this use case, the Shaft actor is an external input device that generates the Shaft Input that activates the Shaft Interface device interface object (Event Sh1 on the collaboration diagram shown in Figure 20.8). The Shaft Interface object updates the Shaft Rotation Count entity object (Event Sh1.1). This simple use case does not need a control object. Because there is no control decision to be made, the device interface object can update the entity object directly.

The collaboration diagram for the Determine Distance and Speed use case is shown in Figure 20.9, and the message descriptions follow:

For this use case, the Clock external timer periodically wakes up the distance Timer software object (event D1 on Figure 20.9) to initiate the event sequence. The distance Timer activates the Distance object to calculate the

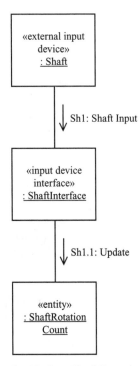

Figure 20.8 *Collaboration diagram for Update Shaft Rotation Count use case*

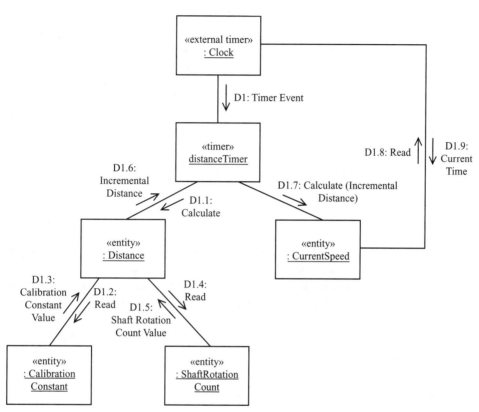

Figure 20.9 *Collaboration diagram for Determine Distance and Speed use case*

cumulative distance (event D1.1). The `Distance` object has both an algorithm aspect because it has to calculate the cumulative distance traveled by the car and an entity aspect because it stores the cumulative distance, which is read by other objects. The main reason for this object's existence is to maintain the cumulative distance, so it is classified as an entity object.

When activated by the `distance Timer`, the `Distance` object reads the `Calibration Constant` (Events D1.2 and D1.3) and the `Shaft Rotation Count` (Events D1.4 and D1.5). The `Distance` object then calculates the incremental distance as described in the use case and adds this to the cumulative distance, which is maintained by the object. Finally, the `Distance` object sends the incremental distance to the `distance Timer` object (Event D1.6), and the timer object sends the incremental distance as a parameter of the `Calculate` message to the `Current Speed` object (D1.7), which calculates the current speed. The `Current Speed` object first has to read the `Clock` to get the current time (D1.8, D1.9), from which the previous time is subtracted to get the incremental time. To derive the current speed, the incremental distance is divided by the incremental time.

It should be noted that the `distance Timer` object is a control object that first invokes the calculation of the incremental distance and then the calculation of the current speed. There is no interface object, because this computation is internal and the results are not output. The `Shaft Interface` object is involved in the previous use case by updating the `Shaft Rotation Count`.

20.5.3 State-Dependent Dynamic Modeling: Cruise Control

Next, consider the state-dependent dynamic modeling for the `Cruise Control` subsystem. There are two state-dependent use cases to be considered: `Control Speed` and `Perform Calibration`.

For the `Control Speed` use case, the derivation of the statechart from the use case is described in Chapter 10. The derivation of the collaboration diagram and the description of the interdependence between the collaboration diagram and the statechart are described in Chapter 11. The `Control Speed` collaboration diagram is shown in Figure 20.10.

The `Cruise Control` state-dependent control object is defined by the `Cruise Control` statechart, which is depicted in Figure 20.11. The `Cruise Control` states and transitions are as follows:

- `Idle`. In this state, the engine is switched off.

- `Engine Running`. This is a superstate, which consists of the following three substates:

    1. `Initial`. When the driver turns the engine on, the car enters `Initial` state. The car stays in this state as long as no attempt is made to engage cruise control. In `Initial` state, unlike `Cruising Off` state, there is no previously stored cruising speed.

    2. `Cruising Off`. When the driver either engages the lever in the OFF position (Off event) or presses the brake, cruise control is deactivated and the car returns to manual operation.

    3. `Automatic Control`. This substate is itself a superstate, which consists of the following three substates:

        a. `Accelerating`. When the driver engages the cruise control lever in the ACCEL position (event `Accel`), the car enters `Accelerating` state and accelerates automatically, providing the brake is not pressed (condition Brake = Off).

        b. `Cruising`. When the driver releases the lever (event `Cruise`), the current speed is saved as the cruising speed and the car enters `Cruising`

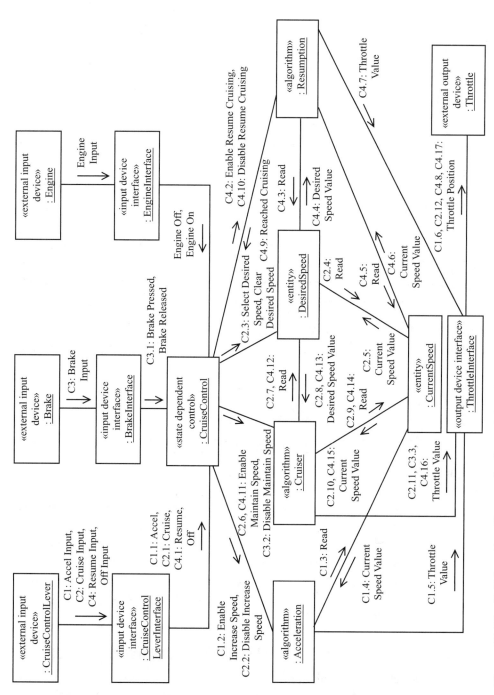

Figure 20.10 *Collaboration diagram for Control Speed use case*

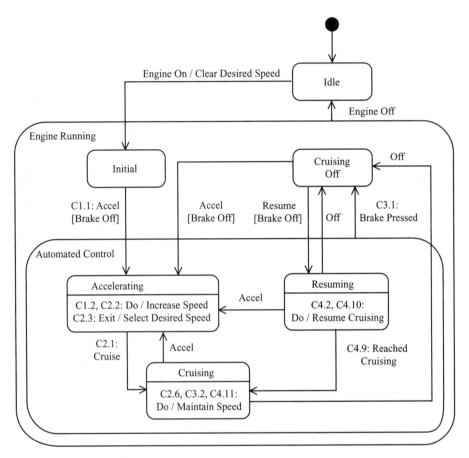

Figure 20.11   *Cruise Control statechart*

state. In this state, the car speed is automatically maintained at the cruising speed.

c. Resuming. When the driver engages the lever in the RESUME position (event Resume), and providing the brake is not pressed, the car automatically accelerates or decelerates to the most recent cruising speed. When the car reaches the desired speed, it enters Cruising state (transition Reached Cruising).

20.5.4   State-Dependent Dynamic Modeling: Calibration Control

Next, consider the dynamic analysis of the Perform Calibration use case, which is also state-dependent. Consider the use case as described earlier. The

Perform Calibration collaboration diagram is depicted in Figure 20.12 and the statechart for the Calibration Control object is depicted in Figure 20.13.

A device interface object is needed for each calibration button, the start Calibration Button Interface and the stop Calibration Button Interface. A state-dependent object, Calibration Control, is needed to execute the Calibration Control statechart. An entity object, Calibration Constant, is needed to store the value of the constant. The main purpose of this use case is to compute the value of this constant.

The Calibration Control statechart (see Figure 20.13) has two states: the initial Not Measuring state, which is the normal state, and the Measuring Mile state, in which the calibration process is performed.

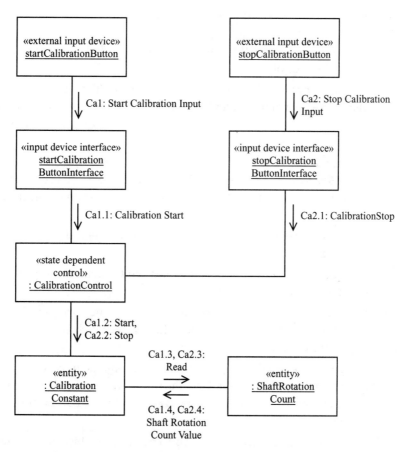

Figure 20.12 *Collaboration diagram for Perform Calibration use case*

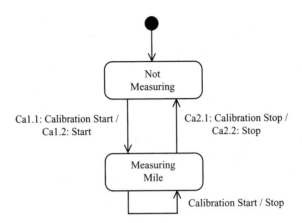

Figure 20.13 *Statechart for Calibration Control object*

Consider a scenario where the Start Calibration button is pressed, followed by the Stop Calibration button:

Ca1: The driver presses the Start Calibration button. The `start Calibration Button` external input device detects that the button has been pressed and sends the `Start Calibration Input` to the `start Calibration Button Interface` object.

Ca1.1: The `start Calibration Button Interface` object sends the `Calibration Start` event to the `Calibration Control` object. `Calibration Control` transitions to `Measuring Mile` state from the initial `Not Measuring` state.

Ca1.2: The action associated with the transition is to send the `Start` message to the `Calibration Constant` object.

Ca1.3: The `Calibration Constant` object sends a read message to the `Shaft Rotation Count` object.

Ca1.4: The `Shaft Rotation Count` object returns the current value of the count. `Calibration Constant` stores this value, which is the shaft rotation count at the start of the measured mile.

Ca2: The driver presses the Stop Calibration button. The `stop Calibration Button` external input device detects the button has been pressed and sends the `Stop Calibration Input` to the `stop Calibration Button Interface` object.

Ca2.1: The `stop Calibration Button Interface` object sends the `Calibration Stop` event to the `Calibration Control` object. `Calibration Control` transitions to `Not Measuring` state.

Ca2.2: The action associated with the transition is to send the `Stop` message to the `Calibration Constant` object.

Ca2.3: The `Calibration Constant` object sends a `Read` message to the `Shaft Rotation Count` object.

Ca2.4: The `Shaft Rotation Count` object returns the current value of the count, which is the shaft rotation count at the end of the measured mile. `Calibration Constant` computes and stores the value of the calibration constant by subtracting the shaft rotation count at the start of the measured mile value from the shaft rotation count at the end of the measured mile.

20.5.5 Dynamic Modeling of the Monitoring Subsystem: Trip Speed Use Cases

The `Monitoring Subsystem` is not state-dependent, so none of the use cases allocated to it are state-dependent. Consider the trip use cases first. The trip average speed and trip average fuel consumption use cases are similar. These are followed by the description of maintenance use cases.

In the `Reset Trip Speed` use case, when the `Driver` actor presses the Trip Speed Reset button, the trip start distance and strip start time are initialized. In the `Calculate Trip Speed` use case, the system periodically computes the trip average speed and displays the value on the trip averages display. The `Reset Trip Fuel Consumption` and `Calculate Fuel Consumption` use cases behave in a similar way, except that the system displays the trip average fuel consumption.

Consider the collaboration diagram we develop for the `Reset Trip Speed` use case. The driver initiates this use case by pressing the Trip Speed Reset button (event S1). Then consider the `Calculate Trip Speed` use case, which is started by the clock (event S2). The same collaboration diagram is used for the two use cases (see Figure 20.14) because they are interdependent.

S1: The driver presses the Trip Speed Reset button. The `trip Speed Reset Button` external device detects that the button has been pressed and sends a `Trip Speed Reset Input` message to the `trip Speed Reset Button Interface` object.

S1.1: The `trip Speed Reset Button Interface` object sends a `Trip Speed Reset` message to the `Trip Speed` algorithm object.

S1.2, S1.3: `Trip Speed` reads the current value of the `Cumulative Distance`, held in the `Distance` object, and stores this value as the initial distance.

S1.4, S1.5: `Trip Speed` reads the `Current Time` and stores this value as the initial time.

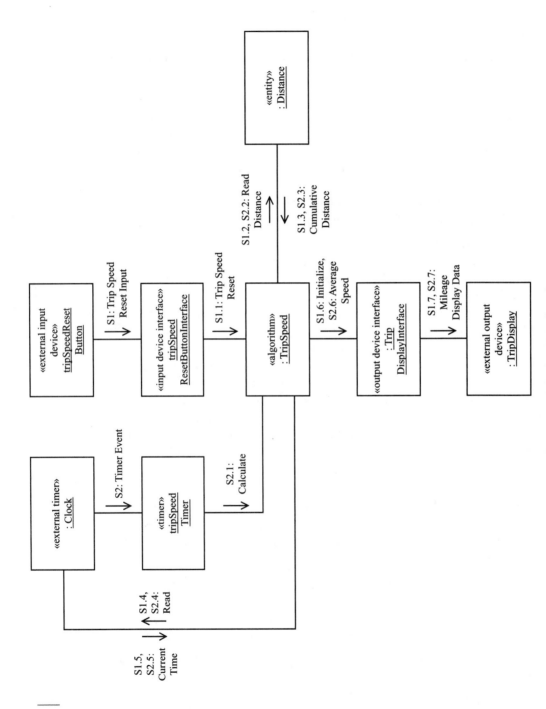

Figure 20.14 *Collaboration diagram for Reset and Calculate Trip Speed use cases*

S1.6, S1.7: `Trip Speed` sends a message to the `Trip Display Interface` object to clear the display.

S2: The external `Clock` sends a timer event to the `trip Speed Timer` object.

S2.1: The `trip Speed Timer` object sends the `Calculate` message to the `Trip Speed` algorithm object.

S2.2, S2.3: `Trip Speed` reads the current value of the `Cumulative Distance` and stores this value as the current distance.

S2.4, S2.5: `Trip Speed` reads the current time and stores this value. `Trip Speed` computes the trip average speed = (current distance minus initial distance) / (current time minus initial time).

S2.6, S2.7: `Trip Speed` sends the trip `Average Speed` to the `Trip Display Interface` object, which displays this information to the driver.

20.5.6 Dynamic Modeling of the Monitoring Subsystem: Trip Fuel Consumption Use Cases

The collaboration diagram for the `Reset Trip Fuel Consumption` and `Calculate Fuel Consumption` use cases is similar to the `Trip Speed` collaboration diagram, except that the fuel level in the gas tank is read instead of the clock time (see Figure 20.15). The details are as follows:

F1: The driver presses the Fuel Consumption Reset button. The `fuel Consumption Reset Button` detects that the button has been pressed and sends a `Fuel Consumption Reset Input` message to the `fuel Consumption Reset Button Interface` object.

F1.1: The `fuel Consumption Reset Button Interface` object sends a `Fuel Consumption reset` message to the `Trip Fuel Consumption` algorithm object.

F1.2: `Trip Fuel Consumption` requests the `Gas Tank Interface` object to read the fuel level.

F1.3, F1.4: The `Gas Tank Interface` object reads the `Fuel Input`, which is the fuel level in the `Gas Tank` external input device (sensor).

F1.5: `Gas Tank Interface` returns the `Fuel Amount` to the `Trip Fuel Consumption` object, which stores this value as the initial fuel level.

F1.6, F1.7: `Trip Fuel Consumption` reads the current value of the `Cumulative Distance`, held in the `Distance` object, and stores this value as the initial distance.

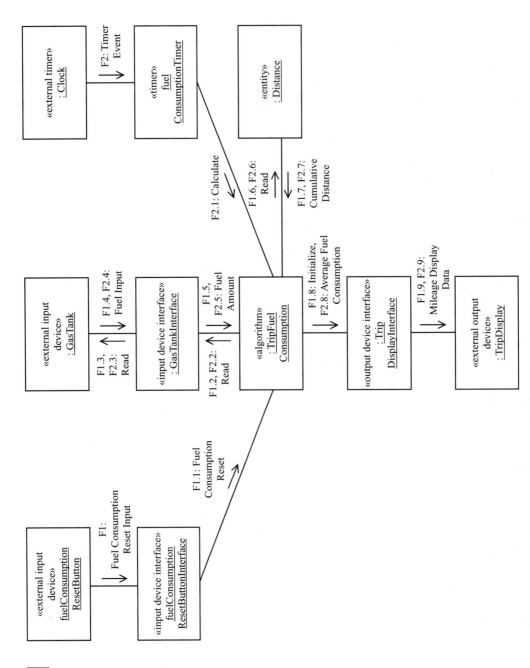

Figure 20.15 *Collaboration diagram for Reset and Calculate Trip Fuel Consumption use cases*

F1.8, F1.9: `Trip Fuel Consumption` sends a message to the `Trip Display Interface` object to clear the display.

F2: The external `Clock` sends a timer event to the `fuel Consumption Timer` object.

F2.1: The `fuel Consumption Timer` object sends the `Calculate` message to the `Fuel Consumption` algorithm object.

F2.2: `Trip Fuel Consumption` requests the `Gas Tank Interface` object to read the fuel level.

F2.3, F2.4: The `Gas Tank Interface` object reads the `Fuel Input` from the `Gas Tank` external input device (sensor).

F2.5: `Gas Tank Interface` returns the `Fuel Amount` to the `Trip Fuel Consumption` object, which stores this value as the current fuel level.

F2.6, F2.7: `Trip Fuel Consumption` reads the current value of the `Cumulative Distance` and stores this value as the current distance. `Trip Fuel Consumption` computes the trip average fuel consumption = (current distance minus initial distance) / (current fuel level minus initial fuel level). The algorithm has to check for and compensate for the case of filling the gas tank between two successive readings.

F2.8, F2.9: `Trip Fuel Consumption` sends the trip `Average Fuel Consumption` to the `Trip Display Interface` object, which displays the information to the driver.

20.5.7 Dynamic Modeling of the Maintenance Use Cases

Next, consider the maintenance use cases. There are three pairs of maintenance use cases, one for each type of service. The three pairs of maintenance use cases are very similar, so only one of them is described here. The `Reset Maintenance` use case is executed when a service has been completed and the maintenance technician presses the appropriate Maintenance Reset button; the current distance is then stored as the initial distance. In the `Calculate Maintenance` use case, the system periodically determines the distance elapsed since the previous service and compares this value with the distance at which a service is required. If a service is required, the appropriate message is output to the maintenance display. Within 250 miles of the service, an intermittent message is displayed to the driver. Within 50 miles of the service, the message is displayed constantly.

Consider the collaboration diagram for the Reset Oil Maintenance and Calculate Oil Maintenance use cases, as shown in Figure 20.16. The message sequence description is shown for the oil maintenance case, as follows:

M1: After completing an oil change, the mechanic presses the Oil Change Reset button. The oil Change Reset Button detects that the button has

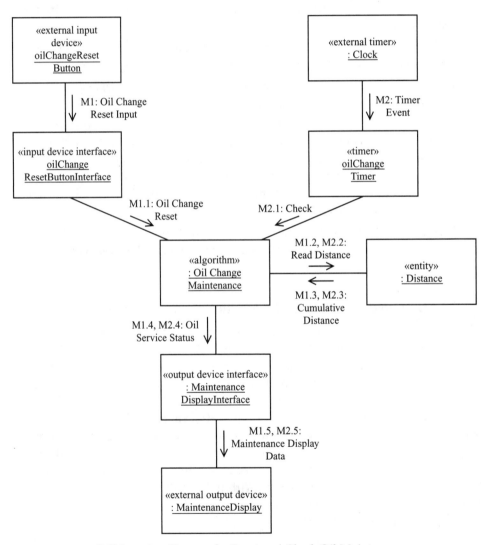

Figure 20.16 *Collaboration diagram for Reset and Check Oil Maintenance use cases*

been pressed and sends an `Oil Change Reset Input` message to the `oil Change Reset Button Interface` object.

M1.1: The `oil Change Reset Button Interface` object sends an `Oil Change Reset` message to the `Oil Change Maintenance` algorithm object.

M1.2, M1.3: `Oil Change Maintenance` reads the current value of the `Cumulative Distance`, held in the `Distance` object, and stores this value as the initial distance.

M1.4, M1.5: `Oil Change Maintenance` sends a message to the `Maintenance Display Interface` object to clear the display.

M2: The external `Clock` sends a timer event to the `oil Change Timer` object.

M2.1: The `oil Change Timer` object sends the `Check` message to the `Oil Change Maintenance` algorithm object.

M2.2, M2.3: `Oil Change Maintenance` reads the current value of the `Cumulative Distance`, held in the `Distance` object, and stores this value as the current distance. `Oil Change Maintenance` subtracts the initial distance from the current distance and checks whether it is time for an oil change.

M2.4, M2.5: Within 250 miles of the next scheduled service, `Oil Change Maintenance` sends a warning message to the `Maintenance Display Interface` object, which displays the message intermittently to the driver. Within 50 miles of the next scheduled service, `Oil Change Maintenance` sends a warning message to the `Maintenance Display Interface` object, which displays it constantly.

20.6 Subsystem Structuring

A subsystem provides a larger-grained information hiding solution than an object. To structure the system into subsystems, we start with the collaboration model. Because of the large number of objects in this system, we will not attempt to develop one consolidated collaboration diagram for the whole system. Instead, we will start with each use-case-based collaboration diagram and initially make it the basis of a subsystem. In some cases, we will allocate the objects in highly coupled use cases to the same subsystem because they are functionally related. We will then consider how the subsystems relate to each other and, where necessary, combine smaller subsystems into larger ones.

Each collaboration diagram forms the basis of a subsystem because the objects in it are related to each other. The objects have higher coupling because they communicate with each other and have lower (or no) coupling with objects in other collaboration diagrams. If an object participates in more than one collaboration diagram, it needs to be allocated to a single subsystem—usually the subsystem with which it is most highly coupled. In some cases, a subsystem may incorporate the objects from more than one collaboration diagram if the diagrams and the use cases on which they are based are functionally related and share common objects.

20.6.1 Subsystem Structuring within Cruise Control Subsystem

We initially consider the `Cruise Control Subsystem`, which is a major subsystem that can be decomposed further into smaller subsystems.

First consider the `Update Shaft Rotation Count` use case. The two objects in the use case, the `Shaft Interface` and `Shaft Rotation Count` objects, form the basis of the `Shaft Subsystem`, which is a data collection subsystem (see Figure 20.17).

Next, consider the `Determine Distance and Speed` use case. The `Distance Timer`, `Distance`, and `Current Speed` objects are all allocated to the

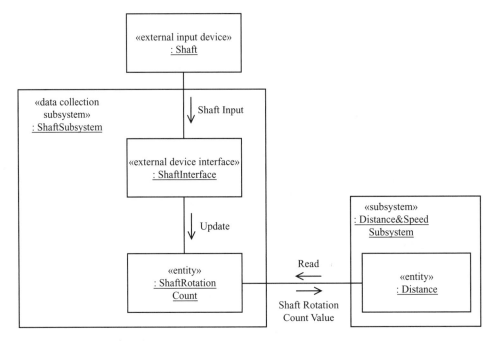

Figure 20.17 *Shaft Subsystem*

same subsystem (see Figure 20.18), Distance & Speed. This is a data analysis subsystem, because it computes results used by other subsystems. Two other objects that are part of the use case are not allocated to this subsystem. The Shaft Rotation Count object has already been allocated to the Shaft Subsystem, and an object cannot be in two subsystems. The Calibration Constant object is not allocated to this subsystem because it has a stronger affiliation with the Calibration use case, where its value is computed, than with this use case, where its value is only read.

All the objects participating in the Calibration use case are allocated to the Calibration Subsystem (see Figure 20.19), except for the Shaft Rotation Count object. The Calibration Subsystem is a combined data collection (because it receives external inputs), data analysis subsystem (because it computes the value of a constant), and control subsystem (because it executes a statechart). However, it is categorized as a data analysis subsystem because that is its predominant function.

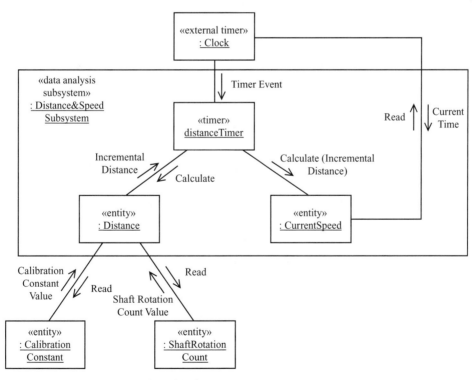

Figure 20.18 *Distance & Speed Subsystem*

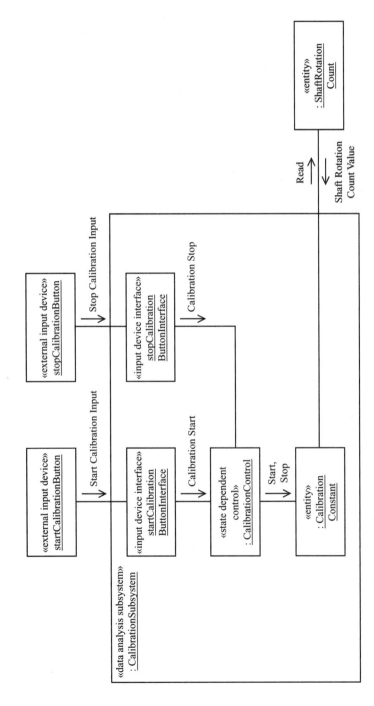

Figure 20.19 *Calibration Subsystem*

The objects in the Control Speed use case form the basis for the Auto Control Subsystem. Only one of the objects in this use case, Current Speed, also participates in another use case. Because the Current Speed object has a stronger affiliation with the Determine Distance and Speed use case (and hence subsystem) where it is updated, it is not made part of the Cruise Control Subsystem. Auto Control is a control subsystem and is depicted in Figure 20.20.

20.6.2 Subsystem Structuring within Monitoring Subsystem

Next, we consider the subsystems within the Monitoring Subsystem, which is also a major subsystem that can be decomposed further.

We start by considering the monitoring use cases. All the objects in the Trip Speed use cases are allocated to the same subsystem except Distance, which is part of the Distance & Speed Subsystem. The objects in the Trip Fuel Consumption use cases could be allocated to a different subsystem; however, it is more useful to place them in the same Trip Averages Subsystem (see Figure 20.21) because the functionality is similar, they share the Trip Display Interface object, and the two reset button interface objects are instances of the same class.

For similar reasons, it is convenient to group the objects from the six Maintenance use cases into a Maintenance Subsystem (see Figure 20.22). Both subsystems are combined data collection and data analysis subsystems. However, they are categorized as data analysis subsystems, as that is their predominant function.

20.6.3 Subsystem Dependencies

The subsystems and their dependencies on each other are depicted in Figure 20.23, where each subsystem is depicted as a package. The subsystems are shown as a hierarchy, such that each subsystem requires the presence of the subsystem below it but not the subsystem above it.

The reason for these dependencies is shown in Figure 20.24, which shows the subsystems and only those objects that are used by other subsystems. Thus both the Calibration and Distance & Speed Subsystems need the value of Shaft Rotation Count, which is computed by the Shaft Subsystem. The Distance & Speed Subsystem also needs the value of the Calibration Constant, which is computed by the Calibration Subsystem. The Auto Control Subsystem needs the value of the Current Speed, which is computed and maintained by the Distance & Speed Subsystem. In the Monitoring Subsystem, the Trip Averages and Maintenance Subsystem both need the value of the Cumulative Distance, which is also computed and maintained by the Distance & Speed Subsystem.

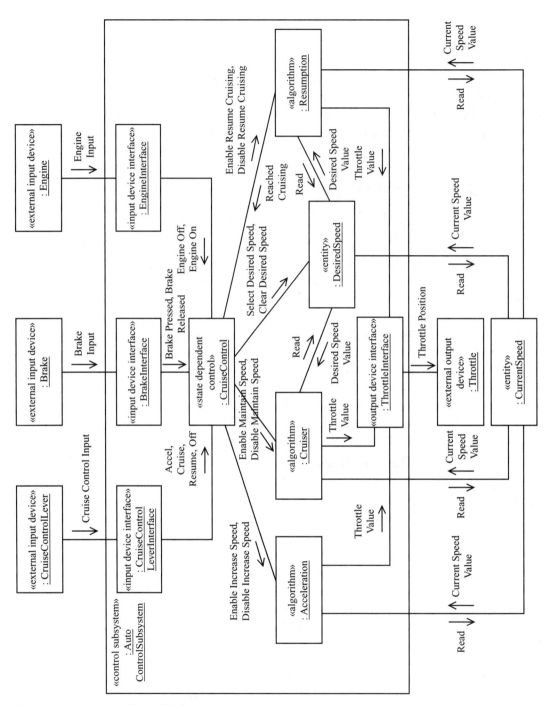

Figure 20.20 *Auto Control Subsystem*

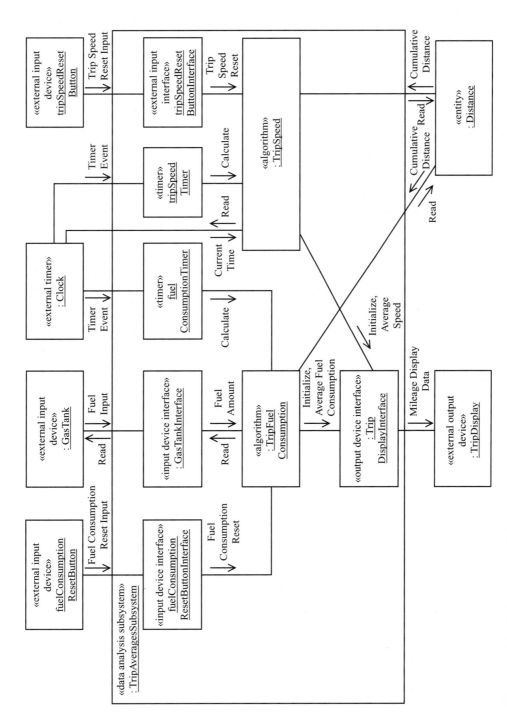

Figure 20.21 *Trip Averages Subsystem*

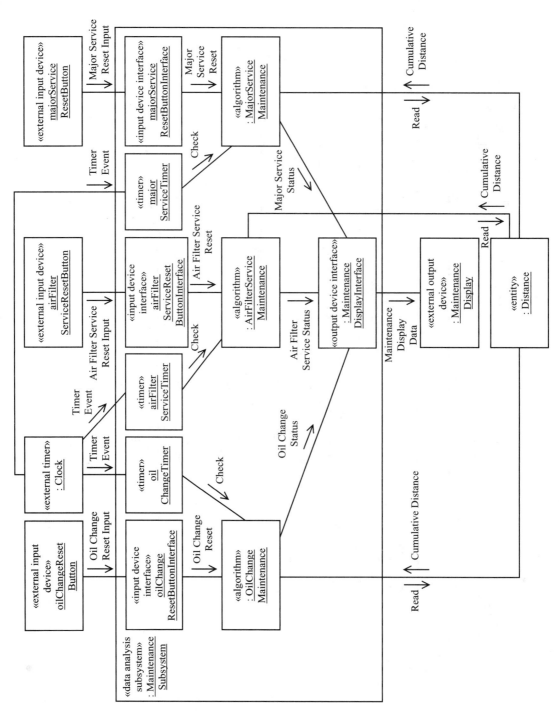

Figure 20.22 *Maintenance Subsystem*

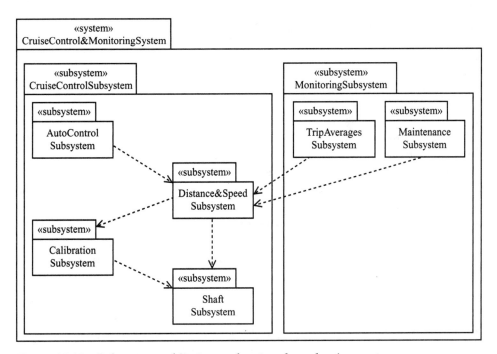

Figure 20.23 *Subsystem architecture: subsystem dependencies*

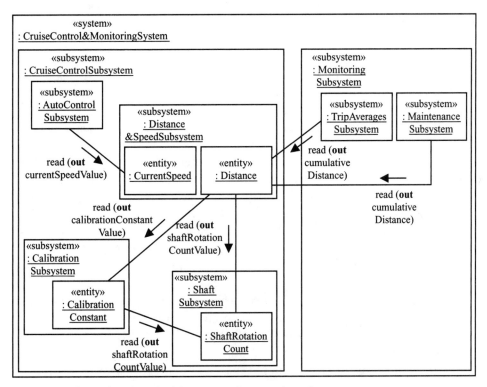

Figure 20.24 *Subsystem Architecture: subsystem interfaces*

With this system structure, no subsystems depend on the `Trip Averages` and `Maintenance Subsystems`. Consequently, the system could be configured to exclude either or both of these subsystems, as requested in the problem description given in Section 20.1.

As an alternative, it is also possible to consider combining the `Shaft`, `Calibration`, and `Distance & Speed Subsystems` into one subsystem. Combining the `Shaft` and `Distance & Speed Subsystems` into one subsystem is not feasible, because doing so would introduce a circular dependency between this alternative `Shaft, Distance & Speed Subsystem` and the `Calibration Subsystem`. On balance, the subsystem structure shown in Figure 20.23 is considered the most flexible.

20.7 Refined Static Modeling

The static model for the whole system is now developed. The initial problem domain static model (shown in Figure 20.4) is quite high level, so the static model is developed primarily from the collaboration model. The static model is developed for the two major subsystems, the `Cruise Control` and `Monitoring Subsystems` (Figure 20.6). The class diagram for the `Cruise Control Subsystem` is shown in Figure 20.25. Most relationships among classes are associations. Generalizations are made in cases where classes share some common properties; thus, the `State Machine` class is a generalization of the two state machine classes, `Cruise Control State Machine` and `Calibration Control`. The `Cruise Control Algorithm` superclass is a generalization of the three algorithm classes, `Acceleration`, `Cruiser`, and `Resumption`.

The class diagram for the `Monitoring Subsystem` is shown in Figure 20.26. In this subsystem, the `Maintenance` class is a generalization of the algorithm classes, `Oil Change Maintenance`, `Air Filter Maintenance`, and `Major Service Maintenance`. The `Display Interface` class is a generalization of the `Trip Display Interface` and `Maintenance Display Interface` classes. There is a superclass for all `Button Input Device Interface` classes, which is specialized into `Calibration Button Interface`, `Trip Reset Button Interface`, and `Maintenance Reset Button Interface`. In this case, the classes are in different subsystems.

In some cases, the objects shown on the collaboration diagrams are instances of the same class. Thus, the `start Calibration Button Interface` and the `stop Calibration Button Interface` are instances of the `Calibration Button Interface` class. There are also multiple instances of the `Trip Reset Button Interface` and `Maintenance Reset Button Interface` classes.

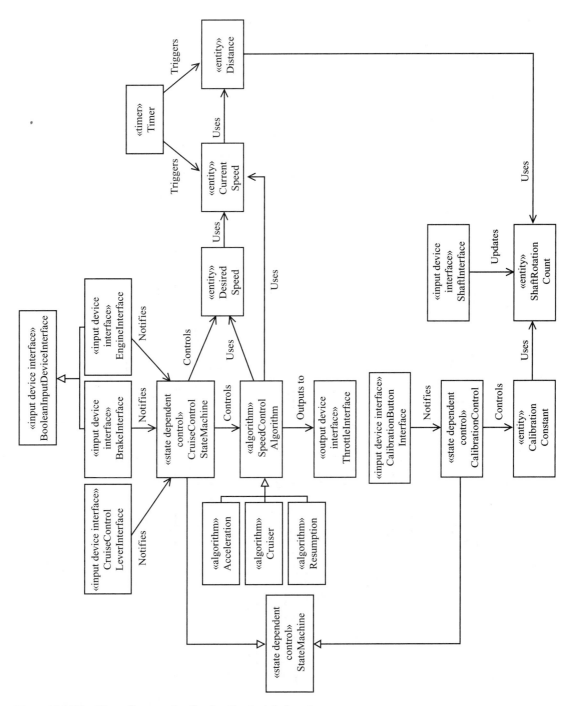

Figure 20.25 *Class diagram for Cruise Control Subsystem*

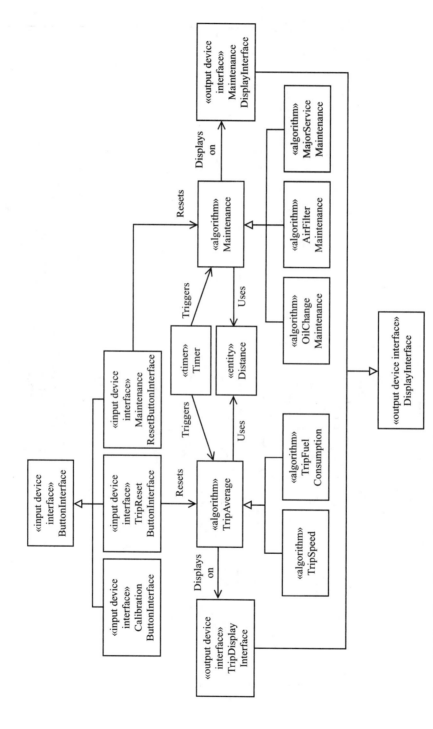

Figure 20.26 *Class diagram for Monitoring Subsystem*

20.8   Structuring the System into Tasks

After developing the analysis model and structuring the system into subsystems, the next step is to structure the system into concurrent tasks. Each major subsystem is considered in turn, first the `Cruise Control Subsystem` and then the `Monitoring Subsystem`.

This section describes applying the task structuring criteria to the collaboration diagrams for each subsystem to determine the concurrent tasks. Each subsystem collaboration diagram is considered in turn, starting with those that receive inputs from the external environment via device interface objects. In each case, two figures are shown, the first depicting the task structuring decisions made on the collaboration diagram. The second depicts the resulting task architecture shown on a concurrent collaboration diagram.

20.8.1   Defining I/O Device Characteristics

Before proceeding further with the task structuring step, certain information needs to be obtained relating to the I/O devices—in particular, whether the devices are asynchronous or passive. For a passive I/O device, it is necessary to determine the frequency with which the device is polled.

Assume that the I/O devices for the Cruise Control and Monitoring System have the following characteristics. (Passive input devices that need to be polled have their polling frequency in parentheses, and passive output devices that need to be updated have their update frequency in parentheses.)

- **Asynchronous input devices.** Cruise control lever and drive shaft.

- **Passive input devices.** Brake sensor (100 msec), engine sensor (100 msec), gas tank sensor (on demand), calibration buttons (500 msec), mileage reset buttons (500 msec), maintenance reset buttons (every second).

- **Passive output devices.** Throttle (updated every 100 msec), mileage display (updated every second), maintenance display (updated every two seconds).

20.8.2   Determining Shaft Subsystem Tasks

Consider the `Update Shaft Rotation Count` collaboration diagram in Figure 20.8, in which there is one device interface object, `Shaft Interface`. The drive shaft is an asynchronous input device. Consequently, the `Shaft Interface` object is structured as an asynchronous input device interface task that increments the shaft rotation count every time it is activated, as shown in Figures 20.27 and 20.28. This task must also be a high priority task because it is essential for it

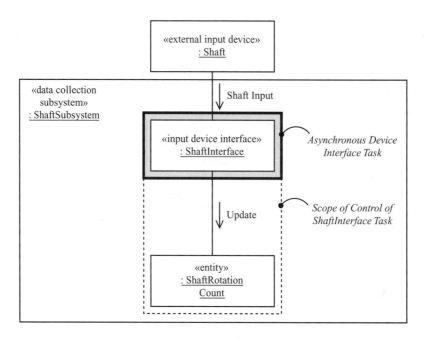

NB: The shaded box, dashed box, italic text, and curved lines are used to illustrate task structuring and are not part of the UML notation.

Figure 20.27 *Shaft Subsystem: task structuring*

not to miss any rotations; otherwise, errors would be made in the computations for incremental distance and current speed.

The Shaft Rotation Count is a passive entity object that is accessed by more than one task and so is kept outside the Shaft task.

20.8.3 Determining Calibration Subsystem Tasks

Consider the Perform Calibration collaboration diagram (see Figure 20.12), in which there are two device interface objects, the start Calibration Button Interface and stop Calibration Button Interface. The calibration buttons are passive and need to be polled every 500 milliseconds; consequently, a temporally clustered task is designed. Consider further the other objects with which this task interacts.

Calibration Control is a control object and therefore forms the basis of a control task. However, Calibration Control can only be activated by an input from either one of the Calibration Button Interface objects and cannot be active concur-

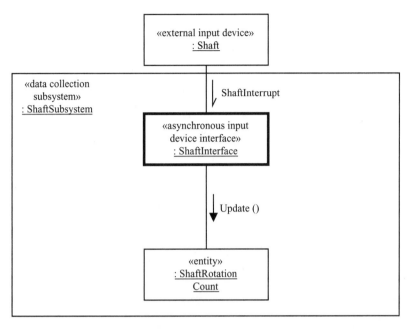

Figure 20.28   *Shaft Subsystem: task architecture*

rently with them. Consequently, the Calibration Control object can be combined with the Calibration Button Interface objects into one task, based on the **sequential clustering** criterion. Entity objects, such as Calibration Constant, that are updated in one use case but read in a different use case cannot usually be combined into the same task. They need to be outside the tasks because they are typically updated by a writer task and read by a reader task(s). However, the operations of the data abstraction object are executed within the thread of control of the task. Figure 20.29 shows the three objects that form the basis of the task. Figure 20.30 shows the Calibration task, which is periodically activated by a timer event, at which time it polls the calibration buttons. Note that in this example, the Calibration task is structured by using a combination of several **task clustering criteria**. In this situation, the criterion shown in the stereotype is the first task clustering criterion used, namely, **temporal clustering**.

20.8.4   Determining Distance and Speed Subsystem Tasks

Next, consider the `Determine Distance and Speed` collaboration diagram. Consider the `Distance Timer` object, shown in Figure 20.9. This object is

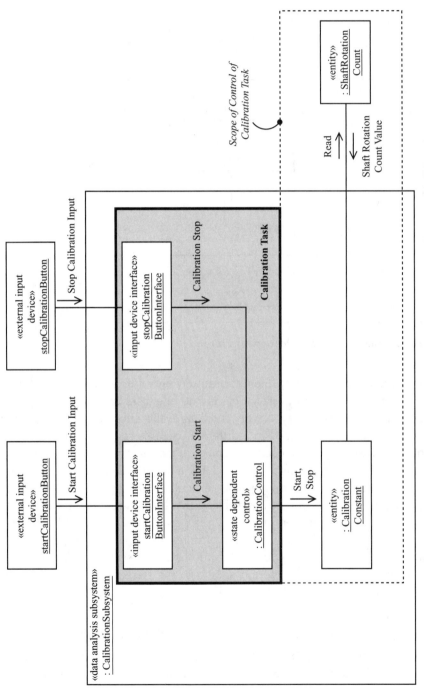

Figure 20.29 *Calibration Subsystem: task structuring*

NB: The shaded box, dashed box, italic text, and curved lines are used to illustrate task structuring and are not part of the UML notation.

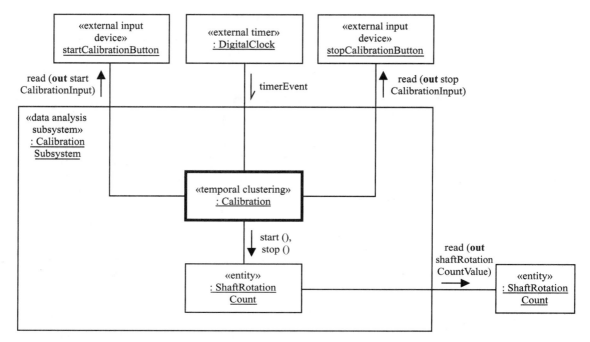

Figure 20.30 *Calibration Subsystem: task architecture*

activated periodically by the external clock and is therefore structured as a periodic task called Distance & Speed, as shown in Figure 20.31. This task (see Figure 20.32) is a periodic task because it is activated at regular intervals by the timer event to compute the cumulative distance traveled and the current speed.

The Distance & Speed task invokes the calculate operation of the Distance object to calculate the distance traveled by the car (see Figure 20.32). The calculate operation executes in the thread of control of the Distance & Speed task. The Distance object also has a read operation, which is called by tasks in the Monitoring Subsystem that need to know the cumulative distance traveled by the car (not shown in Figure 20.32). The calculate operation is called periodically and independent of the read operation. Because the Distance object is accessed by more than one task, it must reside outside the Distance & Speed task. When invoked, the Distance.calculate operation invokes the read operation of the Shaft Rotation Count object (which returns the shaft Rotation Count Value) and the read operation of the Calibration Constant object (which returns the calibration Constant Value) and then computes the cumulative distance traveled. Both the Shaft Rotation Count.read and the Calibration Constant.read operations also execute in

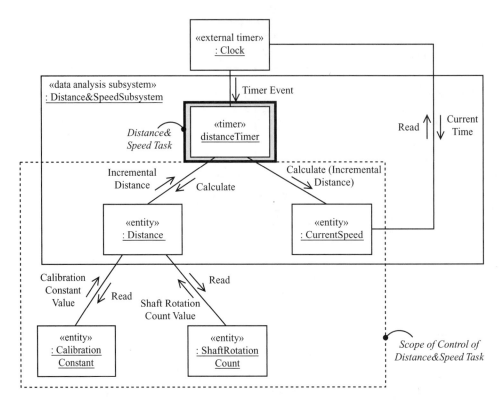

NB: The shaded box, dashed box, italic text, and curved lines are used to illustrate task structuring and are not part of the UML notation.

Figure 20.31 *Distance & Speed Subsystem: task structuring*

the thread of control of the Distance & Speed task. However, the Calibration Constant and Shaft Rotation Count objects must also reside outside the Distance & Speed task because they are updated by other tasks.

The Distance.calculate operation returns the incremental Distance to the Distance & Speed task, which then invokes the calculate operation of the Current Speed object to compute the speed of the car. This object's read operation is invoked by tasks in the Auto Control Subsystem, as described in the next section. Consequently, the Current Speed object also remains outside the Distance & Speed task.

20.8.5 Determining Auto Control Subsystem Tasks

Next, consider the Auto Control Subsystem, in particular, the Control Speed collaboration diagram shown in Figure 20.10. Start with the input device interface

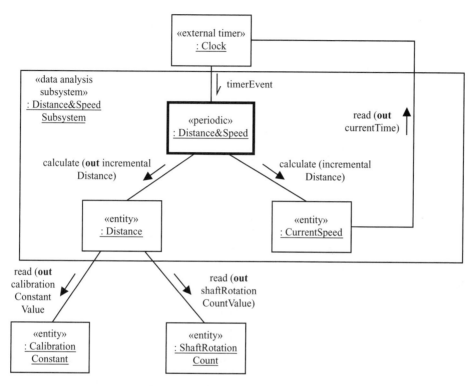

Figure 20.32   *Distance & Speed Subsystem: task architecture*

objects, which receive inputs from external input devices, and then follow the sequence of internal messages that result from the arrival of the external message. The task structuring decisions are shown in two figures, 20.33a and 20.33b, for clarity. The resulting concurrent collaboration diagram is shown in Figure 20.34.

The `Cruise Control Lever Interface` device interface object reads inputs from the cruise control lever. Because the lever is an asynchronous input device, `Cruise Control Lever Interface` is structured as an asynchronous input device interface task, as shown in Figures 20.33a and 20.34. This task is activated by a cruise control interrupt when there is new cruise control input, as shown in the concurrent collaboration diagram in Figure 20.34.

The brake and engine sensors are both passive input devices. Furthermore, they both need to be polled every 100 milliseconds. The `Brake Interface` and `Engine Interface` input device interface objects are therefore combined into a temporally clustered periodic input task called `Auto Sensors`, as shown in Figure 20.33a. This task is activated by a timer event every 100 msec, as shown

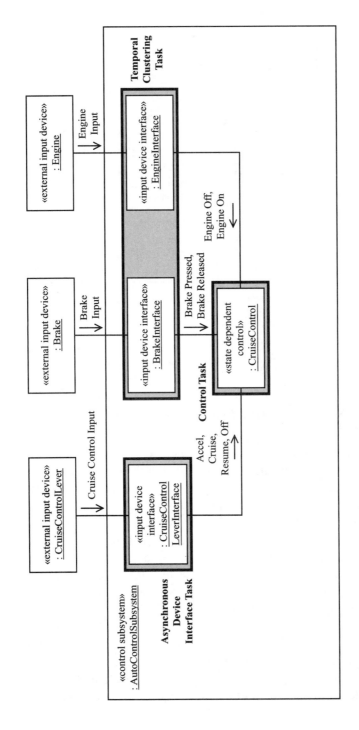

NB: Shaded boxes are used to illustrate task structuring and are not part of the UML notation.

Figure 20.33a *Auto Control Subsystem: task structuring*

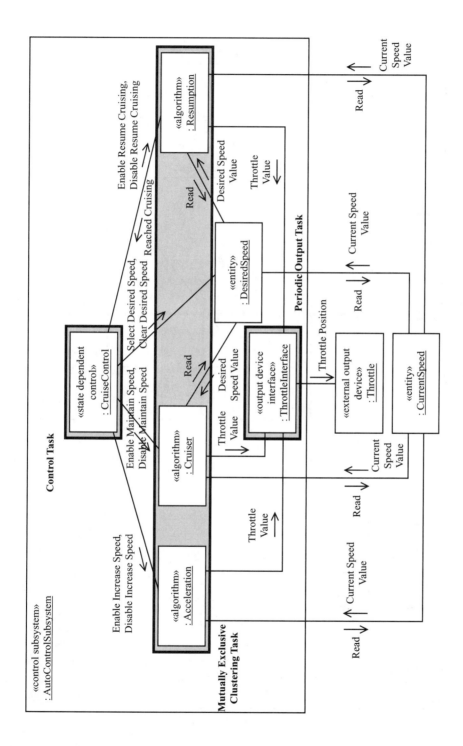

Figure 20.33b *Auto Control Subsystem: task structuring (continued)*

NB: Shaded boxes are used to illustrate task structuring and are not part of the UML notation.

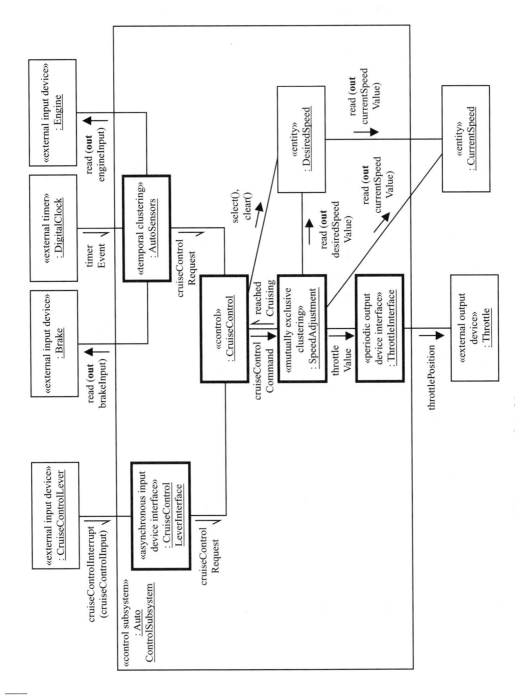

Figure 20.34 *Auto Control Subsystem: task architecture*

in Figure 20.34, at which time the `Auto Sensors` task polls the brake and engine external devices.

After considering the device interface objects, the control objects are considered next. In particular, consider the `Cruise Control` object, which is part of the `Control Speed` collaboration diagram shown in Figure 20.10. The control object `Cruise Control`, which executes the cruise control statechart, needs to be decoupled from the two device interface tasks because it receives inputs from more than one source and the order of events is not known. It is therefore structured separately as a high priority control task so state transitions appear to be instantaneous, as shown in Figures 20.33a and 20.34.

Next, consider the algorithm objects that are activated by `Cruise Control`. If an algorithm object is enabled and then runs continuously until subsequently disabled, it should be structured as a separate task because both the control object and controlled (algorithm) object need to be active concurrently. The three algorithm objects depicted in Figure 20.10, `Acceleration`, `Cruiser`, and `Resumption`, are all enabled and disabled at state transitions. Because they execute concurrently with the `Cruise Control` task, they need to be in separate tasks; however, the execution of these three algorithm objects is mutually exclusive, because each object executes its algorithm in a different state on the `Cruise Control` statechart (see Figure 20.11). Thus the `Acceleration` object is active throughout the `Accelerating` state, the `Cruiser` object is active throughout the `Cruising` state, and the `Resumption` object is active throughout the `Resuming` state. These three algorithm objects can therefore be grouped into one task, `Speed Adjustment`, based on the **mutually exclusive clustering** criterion, as shown in Figures 20.33b and 20.34. The `Speed Adjustment` task executes the speed control algorithm described in Section 20.1.1, of which there are three variants as described later.

Because the throttle is a passive output device, the `Throttle Interface` object is structured as a periodic output device interface task, also called `Throttle Interface`, that outputs the throttle position to the real-world throttle actuator (see Figures 20.33b and 20.34). It is a periodic output task and not a passive output task because it periodically outputs small adjustments to the throttle to provide smooth vehicle motion.

20.8.6 Defining Cruise Control Subsystem Task Interfaces

After the objects have been structured into tasks, the next stage is to analyze and define the task interfaces. Task interfaces are analyzed from the viewpoint of whether they are loosely or tightly coupled.

The Shaft, Calibration, and Distance & Speed Subsystems all consist of tasks that do not interact directly with other tasks. All interactions in these subsystems are between tasks (active objects) and passive objects; in each case, the task invokes one or more operations of the passive object. The design of the interfaces to the passive objects is addressed in more detail during the next step, Class Design.

Consider the task architecture for the Auto Control Subsystem shown in Figure 20.34. The Cruise Control task receives messages from the Cruise Control Lever Interface, Auto Sensors, and Speed Adjustment tasks. Because more than one message might arrive in quick succession at the receiver and it is important for the sender tasks not to wait for their messages to be accepted, this interface should be loosely coupled. Furthermore, because it is important to maintain the sequence of these messages, the task interface chosen is a FIFO message queue, as shown in Figure 20.34 and described in more detail in Section 20.10.2.

On the other hand, consider the interface between Cruise Control and Speed Adjustment. Because the enabling or disabling of a speed command takes place at the state transition, it is desirable for the Speed Adjustment task to accept the command from Cruise Control without delay. The interface between these two tasks should therefore be tightly coupled. There is no response from Speed Adjustment to Cruise Control, so the interface is tightly coupled without reply, as shown in Figure 20.34.

However, there is one situation where Speed Adjustment needs to send a message to Cruise Control. In Resuming state, when Speed Adjustment detects that the cruising speed has been reached, it sends an asynchronous reached Cruising message to Cruise Control. The two tasks must be loosely coupled in this situation, because it is possible for Cruise Control to receive a message, for example brake Pressed, from another source while in Resuming state.

The interface between Speed Adjustment and Throttle Interface is also tightly coupled without reply, because as soon as Speed Adjustment has computed a new throttle value, it should be accepted by the Throttle Interface task.

20.8.7 Designing Data Abstraction Classes

The design of the task interfaces also includes the design of entity objects accessed directly by the tasks. In the cruise control problem, all the entity objects are data abstraction objects. This is a real-time system that does not use a database. A data abstraction class encapsulates data that needs to be stored. The data is accessed indirectly via the operations.

The data abstraction classes are all in the Cruise Control Subsystem, as depicted on the class diagram in Figure 20.25. The operations are determined by considering how the objects are accessed on the collaboration diagrams. The design of these data abstraction classes is described next and depicted in Figure 20.35:

- Shaft Rotation Count. This data abstraction class hides how the shaft rotation count is updated. It has operations to update and read the shaft rotation count. These operations are determined by examining the collaboration diagram for the Shaft Subsystem in Figure 20.17 to determine how the Shaft Rotation Count object is accessed.

- Calibration Constant. This data abstraction class hides how the calibration constant is computed. It provides three operations in the form of access procedures: start, which is called to store the shaft rotation count at the start of the measured mile; stop, which is called to compute the calibration constant at the end of the measured mile; and read. The operations are determined by inspecting the collaboration diagram for the Calibration Subsystem (see Figure 20.19).

- Current Speed. This data abstraction class hides how the current speed of the vehicle is computed. It supports two operations: update, for computing

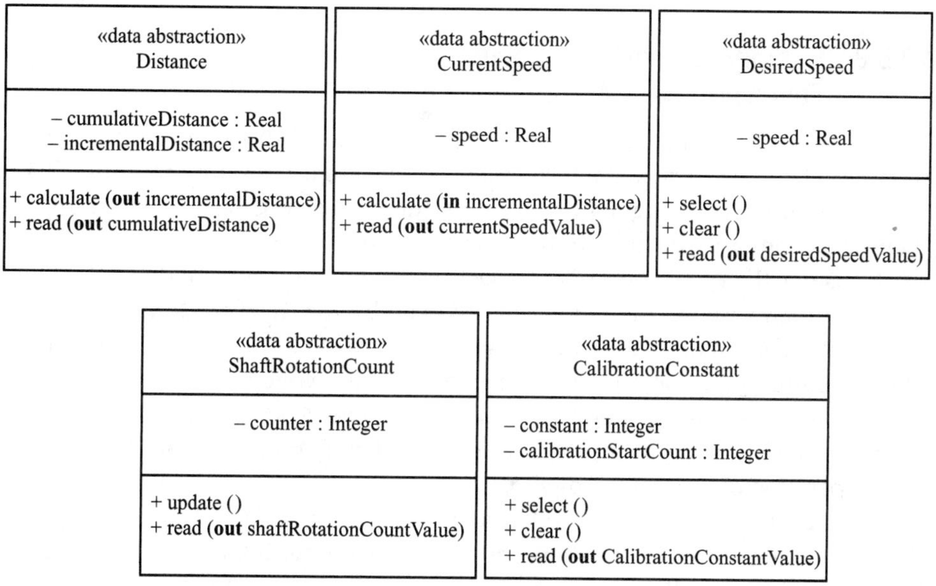

«data abstraction» Distance	«data abstraction» CurrentSpeed	«data abstraction» DesiredSpeed
– cumulativeDistance : Real – incrementalDistance : Real	– speed : Real	– speed : Real
+ calculate (**out** incrementalDistance) + read (**out** cumulativeDistance)	+ calculate (**in** incrementalDistance) + read (**out** currentSpeedValue)	+ select () + clear () + read (**out** desiredSpeedValue)

«data abstraction» ShaftRotationCount	«data abstraction» CalibrationConstant
– counter : Integer	– constant : Integer – calibrationStartCount : Integer
+ update () + read (**out** shaftRotationCountValue)	+ select () + clear () + read (**out** CalibrationConstantValue)

Figure 20.35 *Data abstraction classes*

the value of the current speed, and read. The update operation is determined from the collaboration diagram for Determine Distance and Speed (see Figure 20.9), and the read operation is determined from the Control Speed collaboration diagram (see Figure 20.10), because the algorithm objects need to read the current speed.

- Desired Speed. This data abstraction class hides how the desired speed of the car (i.e., the cruising speed) is maintained. It provides three operations in the form of access procedures: select, which reads the current speed and stores it as the desired speed; clear, which is called at initialization time; and read. The select and clear operations can be determined from both the Control Speed collaboration diagram in Figure 20.10 and the Cruise Control statechart in Figure 20.11, where they appear as actions that take place at specific state transitions.

- Distance. This data abstraction class hides how distance is computed. It maintains both the cumulative and incremental distance traveled. It supports two operations, calculate and read. The calculate operation, which is derived from the Determine Distance and Speed collaboration diagram in Figure 20.9, computes the incremental distance traveled since it was last called. The read operation provides the cumulative distance traveled by the vehicle and is called by the algorithm objects in the Monitoring Subsystem, as shown in Figures 20.21, 20.22, and 20.24.

20.8.8 Designing Interfaces between Tasks and Data Abstraction Objects

The interfaces between the tasks and the passive data abstraction objects are now designed. Because these data abstraction objects are accessed by multiple tasks, the objects must be designed as monitors (described in Chapters 3 and 16), so their operations are executed mutually exclusively.

Consider the Desired Speed object whose operations were defined earlier. Its select and clear operations are invoked by the Cruise Control task in Figure 20.34, and its read operation is invoked by the Speed Adjustment task. The Current Speed object has its read operation invoked by the Cruise Control (via the select operation of the Desired Speed object) and Speed Adjustment tasks. The Distance & Speed task in Figure 20.32 calls the calculate operation of Current Speed.

The task interfaces for all the tasks in the Cruise Control Subsystem are shown in Figure 20.36, which shows how the subsystems interact with each other. In this application, all interactions between the lower-level subsystems are by means of calls to operations provided by data abstraction objects.

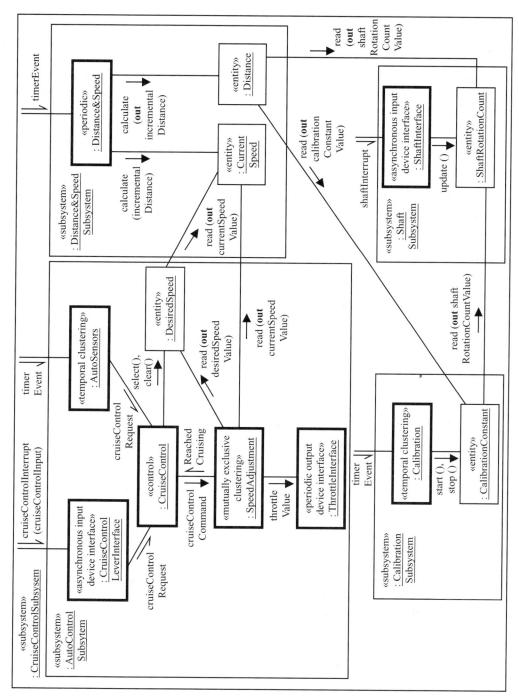

Figure 20.36 *Cruise Control Subsystem: subsystem and task architecture*

20.8.9 Determining Monitoring Subsystem Tasks

Now consider the tasks in the Monitoring Subsystem. As before, first consider the I/O tasks. Both the mileage reset buttons and the maintenance reset buttons are passive devices. Furthermore, the mileage reset buttons are polled with a frequency of every half second (500 msec), and the maintenance reset buttons need to be polled with a frequency of once per second. One option is to combine all the button input device interface objects into one task, based on **temporal clustering**. However, as requested in the problem definition, it is desirable to have a system that can be configured to have only the Trip Averages Subsystem and not the Maintenance Subsystem, or vice versa. Consequently, from a software configuration and reuse perspective, the decision is made to design two temporal clustering tasks for polling the reset buttons, one for each subsystem.

First consider the Trip Averages Subsystem. The task structuring decisions are shown in Figure 20.37 and the resulting task architecture is shown in Figure 20.38. As described in the previous paragraph, there is a separate temporally clustered task, Trip Reset Button Interface, as initially shown in Figure 20.37a and then in Figure 20.38.

Next, consider the timer objects. They initiate the periodic execution of the algorithm objects. The timer objects in the Trip Averages Subsystem are trip Speed Timer and fuel Consumption Timer. The average trip speed and the average fuel consumption need to be calculated with the same frequency; consequently, the two objects are combined into one temporally clustered task called Trip Averages Timer, as shown in Figures 20.37b and 20.38.

The algorithms to calculate the averages are encapsulated in the Trip Speed and Trip Fuel Consumption algorithm objects, respectively. Both the Trip Reset Button Interface and the Trip Averages Timer tasks access these algorithm objects. Consequently, these passive objects are placed outside the two tasks, as shown in Figure 20.38.

The Trip Display Interface object interfaces to a passive output device, which is only accessed on demand. Furthermore, overlapping computation with I/O gives no advantage because the computation is performed infrequently. Thus, there is no reason to structure this object as a task. It is accessed by both the Trip Reset Button Interface and the Trip Averages Timer tasks, so it is placed outside the two tasks, as shown in Figure 20.38.

For similar reasons, the Maintenance Subsystem is structured into two temporally clustered tasks, the Maintenance Reset Button Interface and the Maintenance Timer tasks, as shown in Figures 20.39 (a and b) and 20.40.

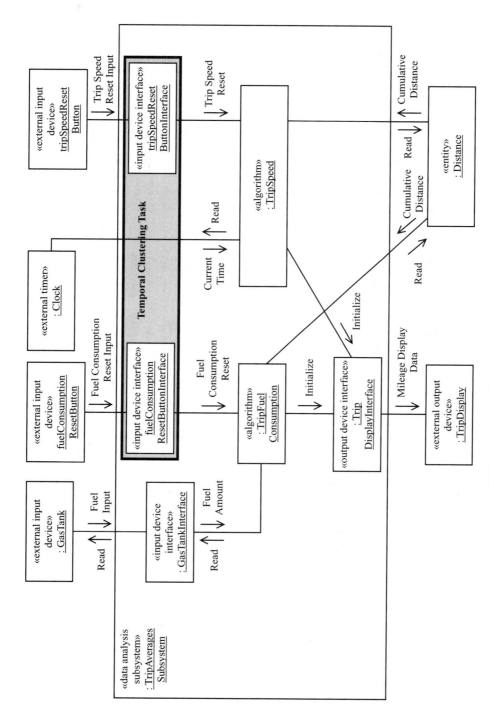

NB: Shaded boxes are used to illustrate task structuring and are not part of the UML notation.

Figure 20.37a *Trip Averages Subsystem: task structuring*

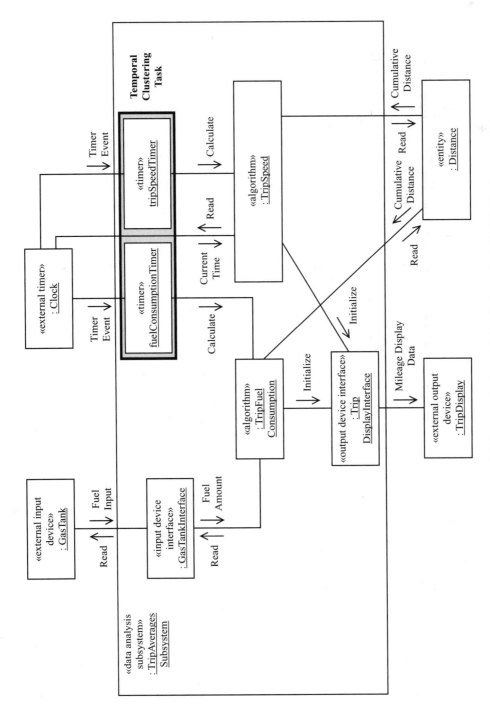

NB: Shaded boxes are used to illustrate task structuring and are not part of the UML notation.

Figure 20.37b *Trip Averages Subsystem: task structuring (continued)*

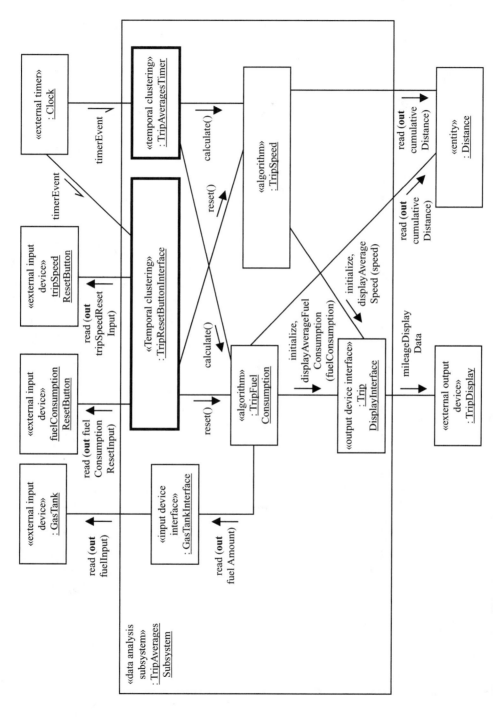

Figure 20.38 *Trip Averages Subsystem: task architecture*

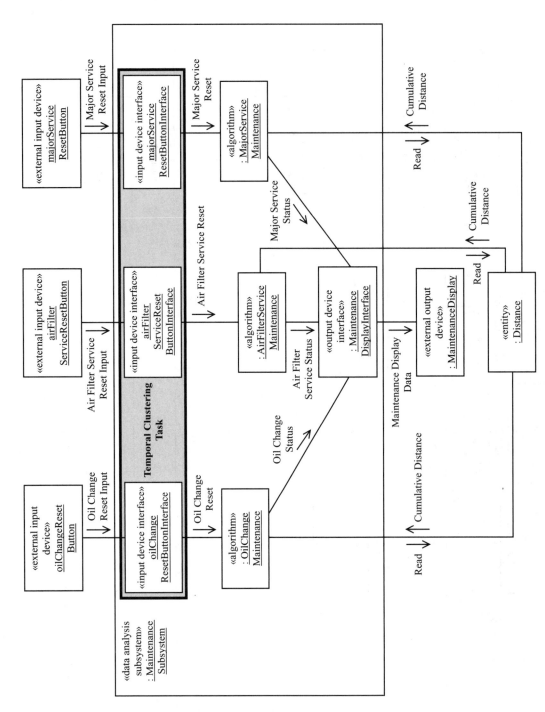

NB: Shaded boxes are used to illustrate task structuring and are not part of the UML notation.

Figure 20.39a *Maintenance Subsystem: task structuring*

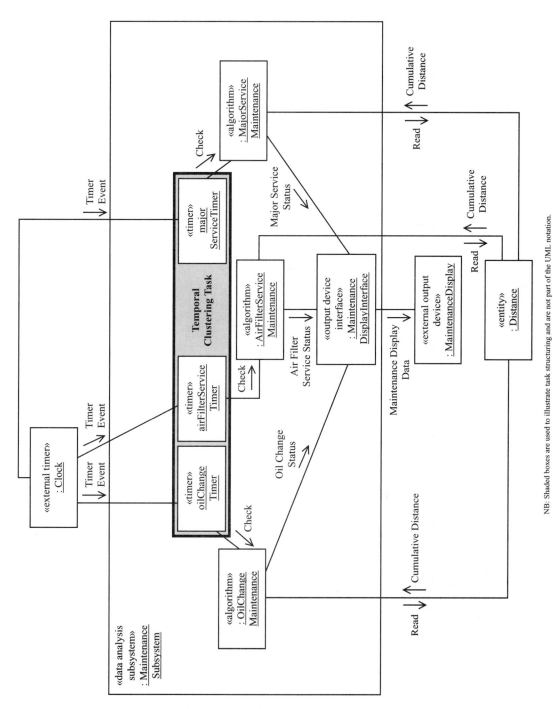

Figure 20.39b *Maintenance Subsystem: task structuring (continued)*

NB: Shaded boxes are used to illustrate task structuring and are not part of the UML notation.

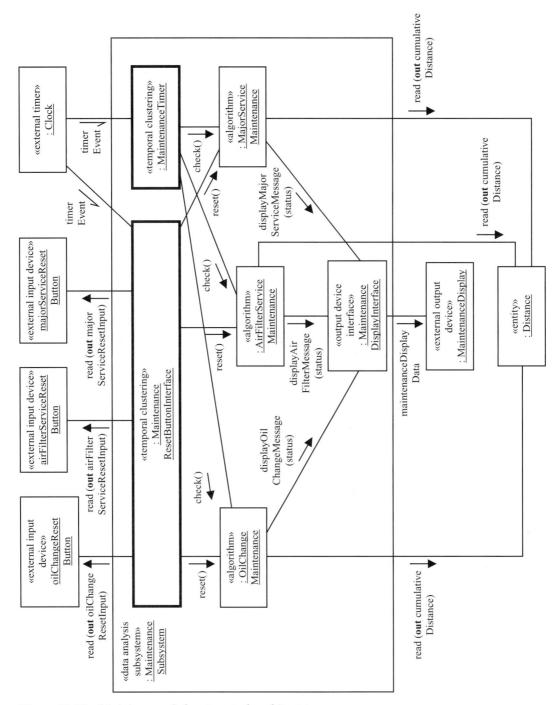

Figure 20.40 *Maintenance Subsystem: task architecture*

20.8.10   Developing Monitoring Subsystem Task Architecture and Interfaces

The task architecture for the two Monitoring Subsystems, the Trip Averages Subsystem and the Maintenance Subsystem, is shown in Figures 20.38 and 20.40, respectively, from which it can be seen that all four tasks in this subsystem are periodic.

The tasks in these subsystems do not interact directly with other tasks. All interactions are between tasks (active objects) and passive objects; thus the task interaction in these subsystems is indirect, via the algorithm objects. In each case, the task invokes operations in various passive algorithm objects. The operations of the algorithm objects and the Display Interface object execute in the thread of control of the invoking task. Task access to these operations needs to be synchronized so the operations of any given object are executed mutually exclusively.

The design of the interfaces for the passive objects is addressed in more detail during the next step, Class Design.

20.9   Information Hiding Class Design

During the Class Design phase, the information hiding classes are designed. In particular, the operations of each class are determined and the external interface of each class is specified. The classes are depicted on the class diagrams for the static model, as depicted in Figures 20.25 and 20.26 and described in Section 20.7. Where appropriate, classification hierarchies are designed. For this case study, the categories of information hiding classes are device interface classes (input and output), entity classes, state-dependent control classes, and algorithm classes. The entity classes are all data abstraction classes, as described previously in Section 20.8.7. This section describes the design of the other classes.

20.9.1   Defining Device Interface Classes

A device interface class hides the actual interface to the real-world device by providing a virtual interface to it. There is one device interface class for each type of I/O device and one device interface object for each instance of an I/O device. During the analysis and modeling phase, the external devices and device interface objects are determined. During design, the device interface classes are designed. In particular, it is now necessary to determine the operations provided by each device interface class.

The device interface classes are nested inside device interface tasks or tasks structured by using the clustering criteria. The input device interface classes are shown in Figure 20.41 (a and b) and consist of the following:

- `Engine Interface`. The `Engine Interface` input device interface class in Figure 20.41a hides how to interface to the engine sensor. It provides two operations: `read`, which reads the engine sensor, and `initialize`, which initializes the device interface class's internal data structures and performs any necessary device initialization.

- `Brake Interface`. The `Brake Interface` input device interface class in Figure 20.41a hides how to interface to the brake sensor. It provides two operations: `read`, which reads the brake sensor, and `initialize`.

- `Cruise Control Interface`. The `Cruise Control Interface` input device interface class in Figure 20.41a hides how to interface to the cruise control lever. It provides two operations: `read`, which reads the cruise control lever input, and `initialize`, which initializes the device interface class's internal data structures and performs any necessary device initialization.

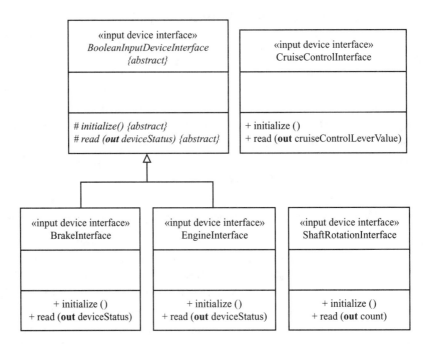

Figure 20.41a *Input device interface classes*

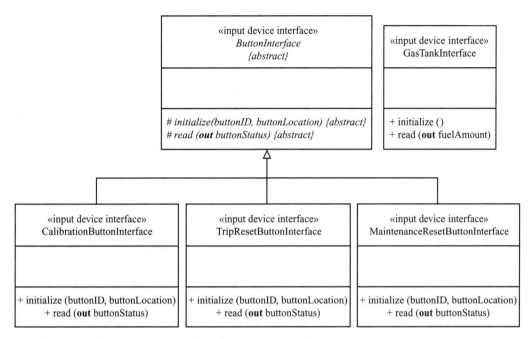

Figure 20.41b *Input device interface classes (continued)*

- `Shaft Rotation Interface`. The `Shaft Rotation Interface` input device interface class in Figure 20.41a hides how to handle shaft rotation inputs. It provides two operations: `read`, which reads the shaft input, and `initialize`.

- `Calibration Button Interface`. The `Calibration Button Interface` input device interface class in Figure 20.41b hides how to read inputs from the calibration buttons. It provides two operations: `read`, which reads the calibration input, and `initialize`.

- `Gas Tank Interface`. The `Gas Tank Interface` input device interface class in Figure 20.41b hides how to interface to the gas tank sensor. It provides two operations: `read`, to read the gas tank fuel level (converted to gallons), and `initialize`.

- `Trip Reset Button Interface`. The Trip Reset Button Interface input device interface class in Figure 20.41b hides how to interface to the mileage reset buttons. It provides two operations: `read`, to read the inputs from the mileage reset buttons, and `initialize`.

- Maintenance Reset Button Interface. The Maintenance Reset Button Interface input device interface class in Figure 20.41b hides how to read inputs from the maintenance reset buttons. It provides two operations: read, to read the inputs from the maintenance reset buttons, and initialize.

Further examination of the above classes reveals the potential for defining abstract superclasses that provide a common class interface for their subclasses:

- The abstract superclass Boolean Input Device Interface in Figure 20.41a provides a common class interface for input devices that provide Boolean inputs, such as the Brake Interface device, which provides Brake Pressed and Brake Released inputs. In particular, it provides a common class interface for the Brake Interface and Engine Interface subclasses. It is assumed that although the operation specifications are the same for the two subclasses, the operation implementations vary because they deal with the specifics of the individual device types.

- The abstract superclass Button Interface in Figure 20.41b provides a common class interface for all button input devices that need to be pressed to indicate a driver choice. In this case study, there are three types of buttons: calibration buttons, trip reset buttons, and maintenance reset buttons. The same abstract class can be used, which defines a common set of attributes and operation specifications, but the operation implementations vary, allowing the flexibility of having different types of buttons. It should be noted, however, that this is a design decision. If, alternatively, it is considered that all the buttons are identical, only one button class is required, with one instance of this class for each button object.

The output device interface classes in the Cruise Control and Monitoring System are shown in Figure 20.42 and consist of the following:

- Throttle Output Interface. The Throttle Output Interface output device interface class hides how to interface to the throttle. It provides two operations: output, which outputs to the real-world throttle, and initialize, which initializes the device interface class's internal data structures and performs any necessary device initialization.

- Trip Display Interface. The Trip Display Interface output device interface class hides how to interface to the trip display. It provides operations to display Average Speed and display Average Fuel Consumption, as well as to initialize.

- Maintenance Display Interface. The Maintenance Display Interface output device interface class hides how to interface to the

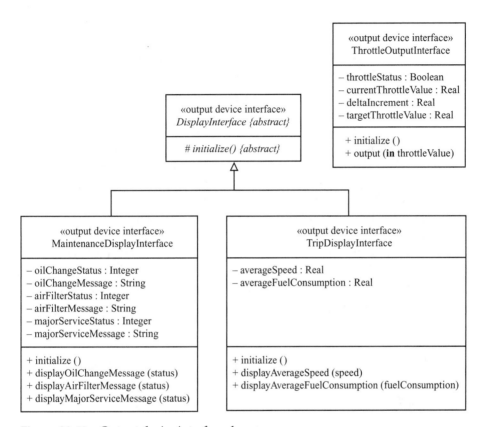

Figure 20.42 *Output device interface classes*

maintenance display. It provides operations to `display Oil Change Message`, `display Air Filter Message`, and `display Major Service Message`, as well as to `initialize`.

The abstract superclass `Display Interface` in Figure 20.42 provides a common class interface for `Trip Display Interface` and `Maintenance Display Interface`. Each subclass extends the interface by adding the appropriate display device specific operations.

20.9.2 Defining State-Dependent Classes

For this case study, the state-dependent classes are `Cruise Control` and `Calibration Control`, both in the `Cruise Control Subsystem`. The state-dependent classes are specified by statecharts in the analysis model, which are implemented as state transition tables. Because the Monitoring Subsystem is not state-dependent, it does not have any state-dependent classes. The abstract superclass State Machine provides a template for all state-dependent classes, consisting of attributes and abstract operations, as shown in Figure 20.43.

- Cruise Control State Machine. This state-dependent class encapsulates the Cruise Control statechart (see Figure 20.11). It provides two operations, process Event and current State, standard operations for state-dependent classes. The specification of these operations is provided in the abstract superclass, as shown in Figure 20.43. The operation process Event has the event that causes a state transition as an input parameter and returns the action, which results from a state transition, to be performed. Each action is performed by an operation of a different information hiding class, namely Desired Speed (see Figures 20.34 and 20.35) or Speed Control Algorithm, as described in the next section. (It should be noted that the Cruise Control State Machine class is nested insider the Cruise Control task and so needs a different name. The tasks deals with communication and sequencing; the class encapsulates the statechart).

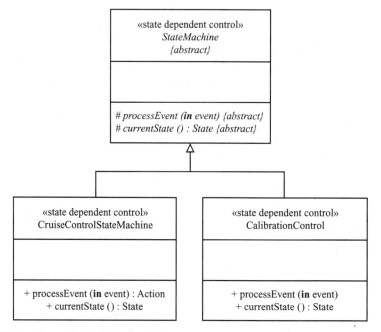

Figure 20.43 *State-dependent classes*

- `Calibration Control`. This state-dependent class encapsulates the `Calibration Control` statechart (see Figure 20.13). It provides the same two operations, `process Event` and `current State`, as shown in Figure 20.43.

20.9.3   Defining Algorithm Classes

Algorithm classes encapsulate the various algorithms used in this case study, which are considered liable to change independently of each other. They are depicted in Figures 20.44a–20.44c and consist of the following:

- `Speed Control Algorithm`. The abstract superclass `Speed Control Algorithm` provides a common class interface for its three algorithm subclasses (see Figure 20.44a), which all deal with automatic speed control and compute the `throttle` value, which is then passed to the throttle device interface object. The superclass encapsulates the speed control algorithm described in Section 20.1.1, which has three variants encapsulated in each of the subclasses. The three subclasses are `Acceleration`, `Cruise`, and `Resumption`. Each subclass has an `enable` operation to initiate the execution of the algorithm and a

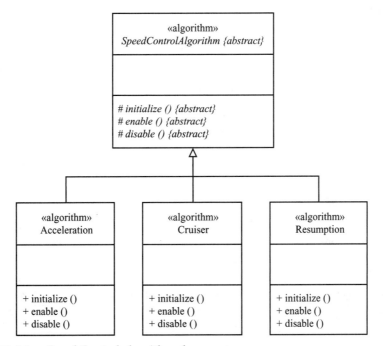

Figure 20.44a   *Speed Control algorithm classes*

`disable` operation to terminate the algorithm. These operations can be determined from both the `Control Speed` collaboration diagram (see Figure 20.10) and the `Cruise Control` statechart (see Figure 20.11), where they appear as activities that are enabled on entry into a specific state and disabled on exit from that state.

- `Maintenance`. The abstract superclass `Maintenance` provides a common class interface for its three subclasses, `Oil Change Maintenance`, `Air Filter Maintenance`, and `Major Service Maintenance`, as described in Chapter 15 and depicted in Figure 20.44b. Each subclass hides how its maintenance checking is provided, including at what distance to output a maintenance message and which maintenance display operation to invoke. Two abstract operations are provided in the abstract superclass, `reset` and `check`.

- `Trip Average`. The abstract superclass `Trip Average` provides a common class interface for its two subclasses (see Figure 20.44c), `Trip Speed` and `Trip Fuel Consumption`. Two abstract operations are provided, `reset` and `calculate`. The `Trip Speed` subclass hides how the average speed is computed, which is then output to the mileage display. The `Trip Fuel Consumption` subclass hides how the average fuel consumption is computed, which is then output to the mileage display.

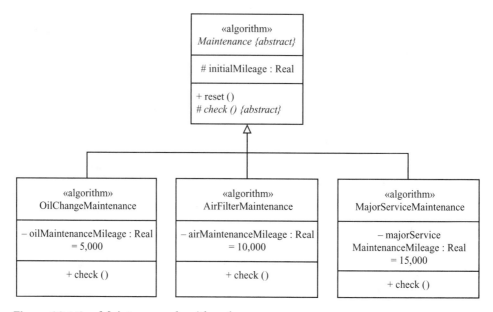

Figure 20.44b   *Maintenance algorithm classes*

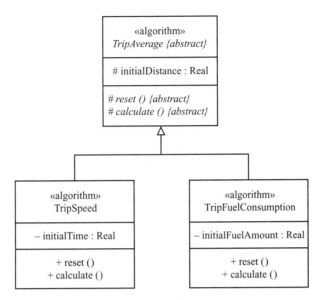

Figure 20.44c   *Trip Average algorithm classes*

20.10   Developing Detailed Software Design

After designing the information hiding classes, the next step is to develop the detailed software design that depicts the internal structure of clustered tasks, the detailed design of data abstraction objects accessed by more than one task, and the design of connector classes. The detailed software design is shown on more detailed concurrent collaboration diagrams, which depict the structure of composite tasks. In particular, detailed concurrent collaboration diagrams are used to show the structure of composite tasks that contain more than one object, typically tasks structured by using one of the **task clustering** criteria.

20.10.1   Designing Clustered Tasks

Consider first the clustered tasks in the Cruise Control Subsystem and its constituent subsystems. The Auto Control Subsystem has two such tasks, the Auto Sensors task and the Speed Adjustment task, as shown in Figure 20.34. The Auto Sensors task (see Figure 20.45) is structured according to the **temporal clustering** criterion and is periodically activated by a timer event. Described in more detail in Chapter 16, it has a coordinator object, the Auto Sensors Monitor,

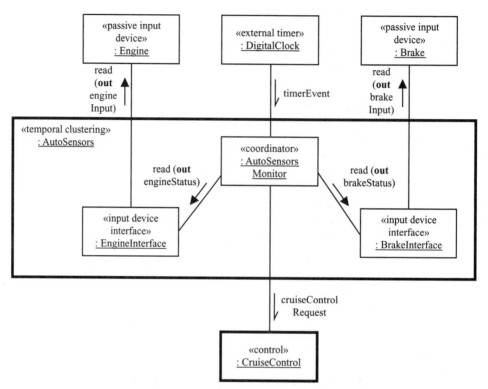

Figure 20.45 *Detailed software design of Auto Sensors task*

which is activated by the timer event and then requests the Engine Interface and Brake Interface objects to respectively sample the passive input devices. For each new input, the Auto Sensors task sends a loosely coupled cruise Control Request message to the Cruise Control task. If there is no new input, no message is sent.

The Speed Adjustment task in Figure 20.46 is structured according to the **mutually exclusive clustering** criterion. It has a coordinator object, the Speed Adjustment Coordinator, which receives cruise Control Commands from the Cruise Control task. Depending on the command, the coordinator object will enable or disable one of the algorithm objects, Acceleration, Cruiser, or Resumption.

The Speed Adjustment task has an interesting problem: how to keep the algorithm activity running while at the same time responding to commands from the Cruise Control task that could disable the activity. When Speed Adjustment Coordinator receives an enable command, it will invoke the enable oper-

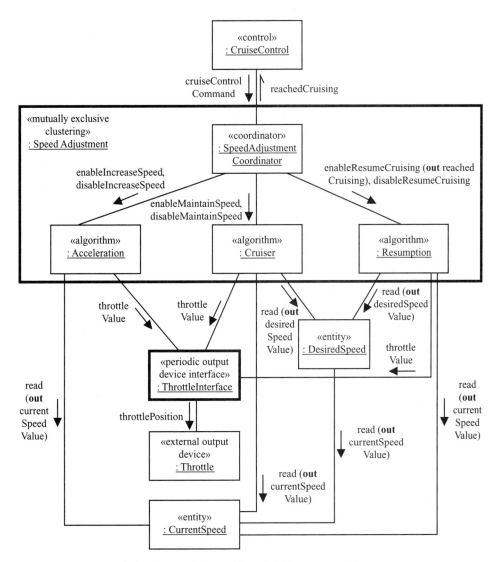

Figure 20.46 *Detailed software design of Speed Adjustment task*

ation of the appropriate algorithm object—for example, the enable Increase Speed operation of the Acceleration object—which will compute the throttle value and send it to the Throttle Interface task. If control remains within this operation, however, how can the Speed Adjustment Coordinator react to a disable command? The solution is as follows: First, the enable operation returns control to the Speed Adjustment Coordinator as soon as it has output the throttle value. The Speed Adjustment Coordinator then waits for the next cruise control command with a timeout corresponding to the frequency with which throttle values need to be computed and sent to the Throttle Interface task. If the timer expires without having received a command, Speed Adjustment Coordinator invokes the same operation it invoked previously, which can then resume its desired activity (in this example, increasing speed). If on the other hand, the Speed Adjustment Coordinator receives a disable command from Cruise Control, it will call the disable Increase Speed operation, which will then send a negative throttle value to the Throttle Interface task to inform it to stop controlling the real-world throttle. If instead, the Speed Adjustment Coordinator receives an enable Maintain Speed command, it will invoke the enable Maintain Speed operation of the Cruise algorithm object. Thus the appropriate disable operation is invoked only if automated control is being deactivated. If there is to be a state change from one of the Automated Control substates (see Figure 20.11) to another (for example, Accelerating to Cruising), there is no need to invoke a disable followed by an enable, so the call to the disable operation is omitted.

Consider next the Calibration Subsystem, where there is one task, the Calibration task, which is also structured according to the **temporal clustering** criterion (see Figure 20.47). This task consists of a coordinator object, the Calibration Monitor, as well as two device interface objects and one state-dependent control object. The Calibration Monitor is activated by a timer event and then calls the read operations of the two Calibration Button Interface objects, which sample the external calibration buttons to determine if there are any inputs. Assume the driver has pressed the Start button. This will be detected by the start Calibration Button Interface object, which then calls the process event (calibration Start) operation of the Calibration Control state-dependent object. As the Calibration Control statechart indicates (see Figure 20.13), the calibration Start results in a state transition and invoking of the start action.

The Monitoring Subsystem has four tasks, structured according to the **temporal clustering** criterion. Consider the Trip Reset Button Interface task in Figure 20.48. It has a coordinator object, Trip Reset Button Monitor, that is activated by a timer event and then calls the read operations of the button interface objects. If a button has been pressed (for example, the Trip Speed Reset button), the trip Speed Reset Button Interface object will call the reset operation of the Trip Speed algorithm object. The Maintenance Reset Button Interface task operates in a similar way.

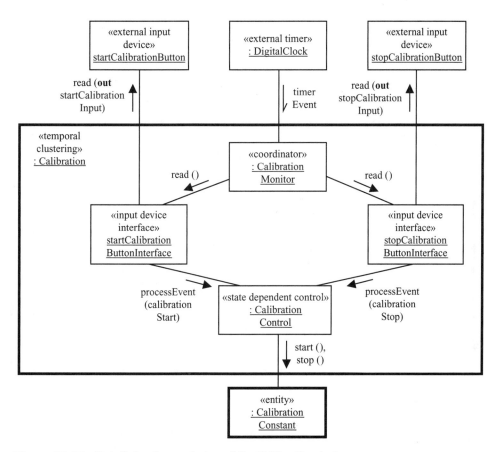

Figure 20.47 *Detailed software design of the Calibration task*

20.10.2 Designing Connector Objects

Now consider the design of the connector objects, which are used to encapsulate the details of inter-task message communication. Figures 20.34 and 20.36 show the only case of loosely coupled (asynchronous) message communication in the system. If this design is being mapped to a language that does not support this form of communication, such as Java or Ada, a message buffering connector object is required, as described in Chapter 16.

The Cruise Control Lever Interface, Auto Sensors, and Speed Adjustment tasks all send asynchronous cruise Control Request messages to Cruise Control. A cruise Control Message Queue connector object is

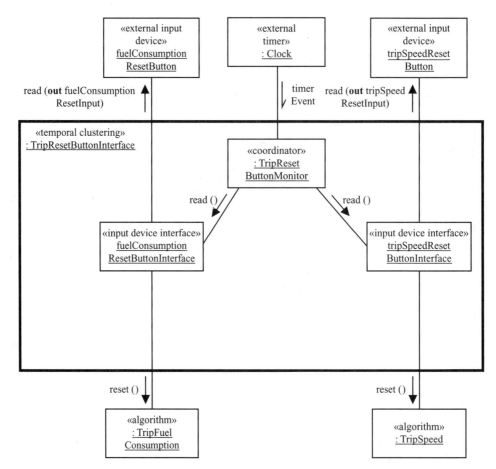

Figure 20.48 *Detailed software design of Trip Reset Button Interface task*

designed to encapsulate the message queue, as shown in Figure 20.49. The send operation is invoked by the three producer tasks, and the receive operation is invoked by the Cruise Control consumer task. As with all connectors, the operations are executed mutually exclusively.

Furthermore, as Figure 20.34 indicates, the interface between the producer Cruise Control and consumer Speed Adjustment tasks has a tightly coupled (synchronous) message interface without reply. This is handled by a speed Adjustment Message Buffer connector object, which buffers at most one message between the two tasks and holds up the producer until the consumer has accepted the message.

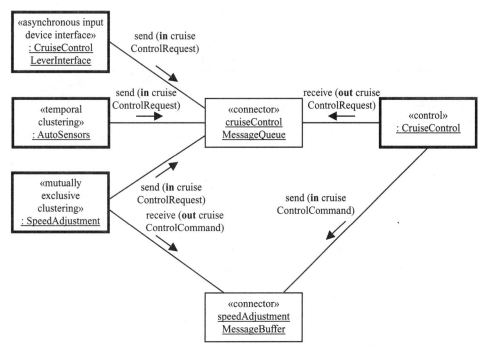

Figure 20.49   *Design of Cruise Control connector objects*

20.11   Software Architecture of Distributed Automobile System

Now, consider the evolution of the automobile Cruise Control and Monitoring System into a Distributed Automobile System. The Shaft, Calibration, and Distance & Speed Subsystems are required to compute the Cumulative Distance traveled by the car and the Current Speed, as shown in Figure 20.24. The Auto Control, Trip Averages, and Maintenance Subsystems read the Cumulative Distance and Current Speed on a regular basis.

This suggests a software architecture for a Distributed Automobile System, which is depicted in Figure 20.50. The Shaft, Calibration, and Distance & Speed Subsystems are allocated to an Auto Measurement component that executes on the Auto Measurement node. Other nodes are clients of this node. The Auto Control, Trip Averages, and Maintenance Subsystems are designed as distributed components that are allocated to their own nodes. Each

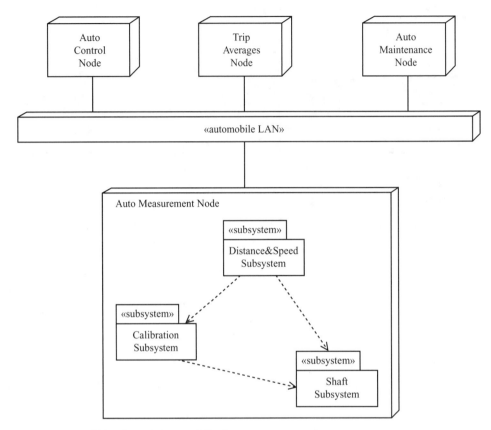

Figure 20.50   *Distributed Automobile System*

component subscribes to receive notification of updates to the variable it uses. Thus, the Auto Control component subscribes to receive notification of Current Speed updates, and the Trip Averages and Maintenance components subscribe to receive notification of Cumulative Distance updates.

This distributed software architecture can evolve further because other components could be added that use current speed and cumulative distance, such as components to display the current speed and cumulative distance traveled. Furthermore, additional sensor data collection, control, and data analysis components could be added to the distributed software architecture.

c h a p t e r

Distributed Factory Automation System Case Study

A s an example of the design of a distributed application, a Factory Automation System is considered. This is a highly distributed application, with several clients and servers, a real-time control component, and examples of client/server communication as well as peer-to-peer communication.

21.1 Problem Description

In a high-volume, low-flexibility assembly plant, manufacturing workstations are physically laid out in an assembly line (see Figure 21.1). Parts are moved between workstations on a conveyor belt. A part is processed at each workstation in sequence. Because workstations are programmable, variations on a given product can be handled. Typically, a number of parts of the same type are produced, followed by a number of parts of a different type.

Each manufacturing workstation has an assembly robot for assembling the product and a pick-and-place robot for picking parts off and placing parts on the conveyor. Each robot is equipped with sensors and actuators. Sensors are used for monitoring operating conditions (for example, detecting part arrival), and actuators are used for switching automation equipment on and off (for example, switching the conveyor on and off). The first workstation is the receiving workstation and the last workstation is the shipping workstation. These workstations have only a pick-and-place robot. All other workstations are referred to as line workstations—they have the assembly robot in addition to the pick-and-place robot. Factory operators view workstation status and alarms.

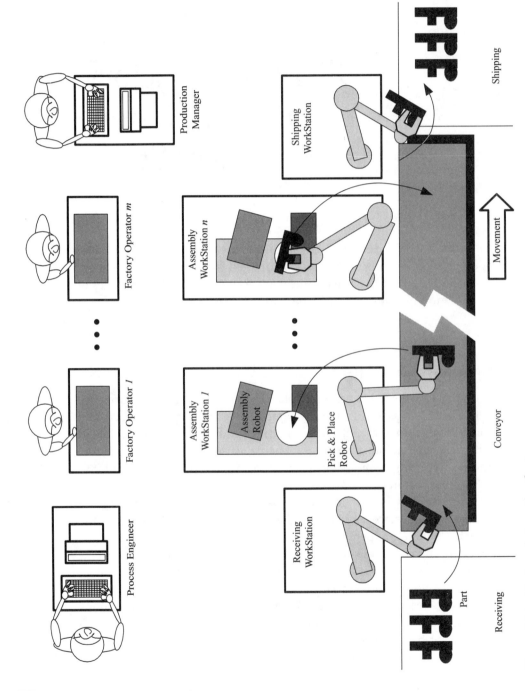

Figure 21.1 *Factory Automation System*

The manufacturing steps required to manufacture a given part in the factory, from raw material to finished product, are defined in a process plan. The process plan defines the part type and the sequence of manufacturing operations. Each operation is carried out at a workstation. Process engineers create process plans and their constituent operations.

The processing of new parts in the factory is initiated by the creation of a work order by a human production manager. The work order defines the quantity of parts required for a given part type.

21.2   Use Case Model

The human actors are the Production Manager, Factory Operator, and Process Engineer. In addition, there are actors that correspond to external systems. These are the Assembly Robot and Pick & Place Robot actors. As described in Chapter 7, use cases can be grouped into packages based on the major actors who initiate and participate in related use cases. Use case packages can be defined for each of the major actors in the Factory Automation System, namely, the Process Engineer Use Case Package, the Factory Operator Use Case Package, and the Production Manager Use Case Package. The use cases are briefly described next and illustrated in Figures 21.2–21.4.

For each actor, the use cases they initiate are defined. Several use cases are initiated by the Factory Operator, as depicted in the Factory Operator Use Case Package in Figure 21.2 and described here.

- View Alarms. The factory operator views outstanding alarms and acknowledges that the cause of an alarm is being attended to. The operator may also subscribe to receive notification of alarms of a given type.

- View Workstation Status. The factory operator requests to view the current status of one or more workstations. The operator may also subscribe to receive notification of changes in workstation status.

- Generate Workstation Status and Notify. Workstation status is generated on an ongoing basis, for example, when a part starts or completes processing at a workstation. Operators are notified of workstation status events they have subscribed to.

- Generate Alarm and Notify. If an alarm condition is detected during part processing, an alarm is generated. Operators are notified of alarms they have subscribed to.

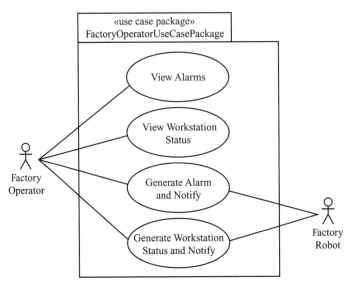

Figure 21.2 *Factory Operator use cases*

A process engineer defines several manufacturing operations and then creates a process plan to define a sequence of operations to manufacture a part. Two related use cases are developed for this purpose and grouped into the Process Engineer Use Case Package (see Figure 21.3). The process engineer uses a Create/Update Operation use case to create, update, and modify manufacturing operations. Create/Update Operation is a base use case, which is executed once for each operation created. The process engineer can then use a Create/Update Process Plan use case to create, update, and modify a process plan that defines the sequence of operations to manufacture a part. The Create/Update Process Plan use case extends the Create/Update Operation use case. Thus, an optional alternative in the Create/Update Operation is to create a process plan.

The Production Manager initiates the Create/Modify Work Order use case to create and modify work orders. The Production Manager also initiates a complex use case, called Manufacture Part, which involves processing parts in the factory. These use cases are grouped into a Production Manager Use Case Package (see Figure 21.4). In Manufacture Part, the production manager releases a work order to be processed in the factory. Each part starts processing at the receiving workstation, where a raw part is loaded onto the conveyor belt. At the next workstation, it is picked off the conveyor belt by the pick-and-place robot, has a manufacturing operation performed on it by the assembly robot, and is then placed back on the conveyor belt by the pick-and-place robot and transported to the

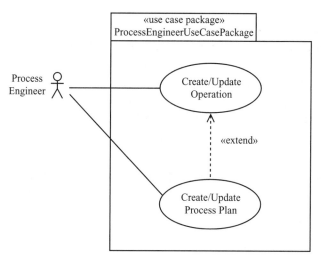

Figure 21.3   *Process Engineer use cases*

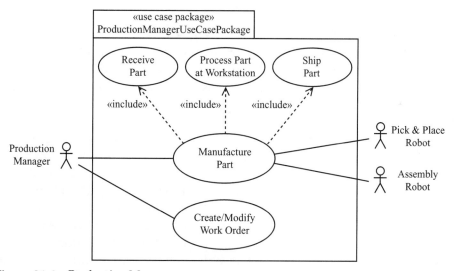

Figure 21.4   *Production Manager use cases*

next workstation. This process continues until the finished part reaches the shipping workstation, where it is picked off the conveyor in preparation for shipping to the customer. A just-in-time algorithm is used in the factory. This means a workstation only receives a part when it is ready to process a part, so parts do not pile up at each workstation.

By examining the Manufacture Part use case, it can be determined that the use case is made more general by breaking it up into the following three abstract use cases, which are included by the Manufacture Part concrete use case.

A. Receive Part. The receiving workstation receives the request from the production manager to manufacture a new part and sends the part to the first line manufacturing workstation in sequence.

B. Process Part at Workstation. The line manufacturing workstation receives the part from the previous workstation (referred to as the predecessor workstation), performs the assembly operation on the part, and sends the part to the next line manufacturing workstation in sequence (referred to as the successor workstation). This use case is repeated several times.

C. Ship Part. The last line manufacturing workstation sends the finished part to the shipping workstation, which sends an acknowledgement of part completion to the production manager.

21.3   Conceptual Static Model of the Problem Domain

Because this application is more information-intensive than the Elevator Control System or the Cruise Control and Monitoring System, the static modeling of the problem domain is particularly important, as it was in the Banking System. Static models are developed of both the overall problem domain and the system context, and are depicted on class diagrams.

The static model for the Factory Automation System is shown in Figure 21.5. Because a factory consists of workstations, the Factory is modeled as an aggregate class composed of Factory Workstation classes. There are three types of manufacturing workstations: line workstations, receiving workstations, and shipping workstations—this is modeled as a generalization/specialization hierarchy. The Factory Workstation class is specialized to be a Receiving Workstation subclass, a Shipping Workstation subclass, or a Line Workstation subclass. Because a workstation can generate multiple alarms, there is a one-to-many relationship between the Factory Workstation class and the Alarm class. The Factory Workstation also generates Workstation Status, which is viewed by the Factory Operator.

A process plan defines the steps for manufacturing a part of a given type; it contains several operations, where an operation defines a single manufacturing step carried out at a workstation. Consequently, there is a one-to-many associa-

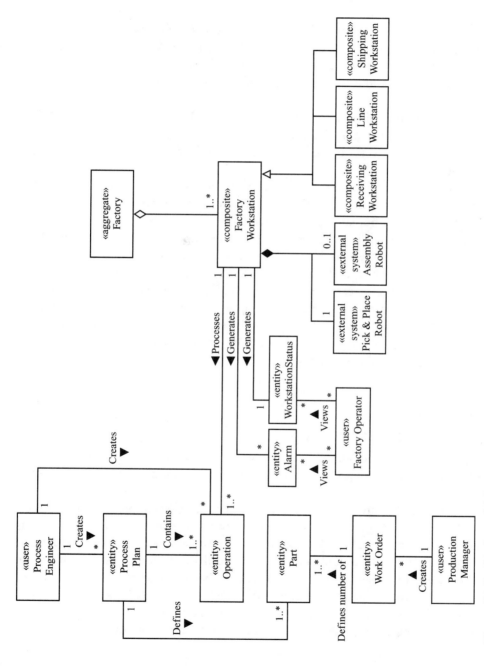

Figure 21.5 *Static model for Factory Automation System*

tion between the `Process Plan` class and the `Operation` class. Because several different operations are processed at a given factory workstation, there is also a one-to-many association between the `Factory Workstation` class and the `Operation` class. A work order defines the number of parts to be manufactured of a given part type. Thus a `Work Order` class has a one-to-many association with the `Part` class. Because a process plan defines how all parts of a given part type are manufactured, the `Process Plan` class also has a one-to-many association with the `Part` class.

The attributes of the classes in the static model are depicted in Figure 21.6. It is necessary to determine the attributes before developing the collaboration diagrams, because several of the collaborations read or update the values of these attributes.

The system context diagram in Figure 21.7 shows the external classes that interface to the system and is depicted by a class diagram. Three of the external classes represent types of human users who interface to the system, namely the `Process Engineer`, `Production Manager`, and `Factory Operator`. The factory workstations are part of the system and so do not appear on the context diagram. However, the `Assembly Robot` and the `Pick & Place Robot` are external systems, and hence are modeled as external classes. Each of the robots is controlled by a robot controller, and its manufacturing operations—namely, the information about the robot programs to be executed—are downloaded from the Factory Automation System. Comparing the external classes with the actors, it can be seen that in this case study, the external classes correspond to the actors.

21.4   Object Structuring

During dynamic modeling, we analyze how the objects participate in the use cases. In this step, we analyze how the Factory Automation System is structured into objects.

Entity objects are long-living objects that store information. The entity objects for this system are `Process Plan`, `Operation`, `Work Order`, and `Part`. There is also a `Workstation Status` object and an `Alarm` object. The entity objects are depicted in the static model in Figure 21.5 and their attributes are given in Figure 21.6. The entity objects are all server objects that are accessed by various client objects. Hence, on the collaboration diagrams, the entity objects are depicted as server objects: `Process Plan Server`, `Operation Server`, `Work Order Server`, `Part Server`, `Workstation Status Server`, and `Alarm Server`.

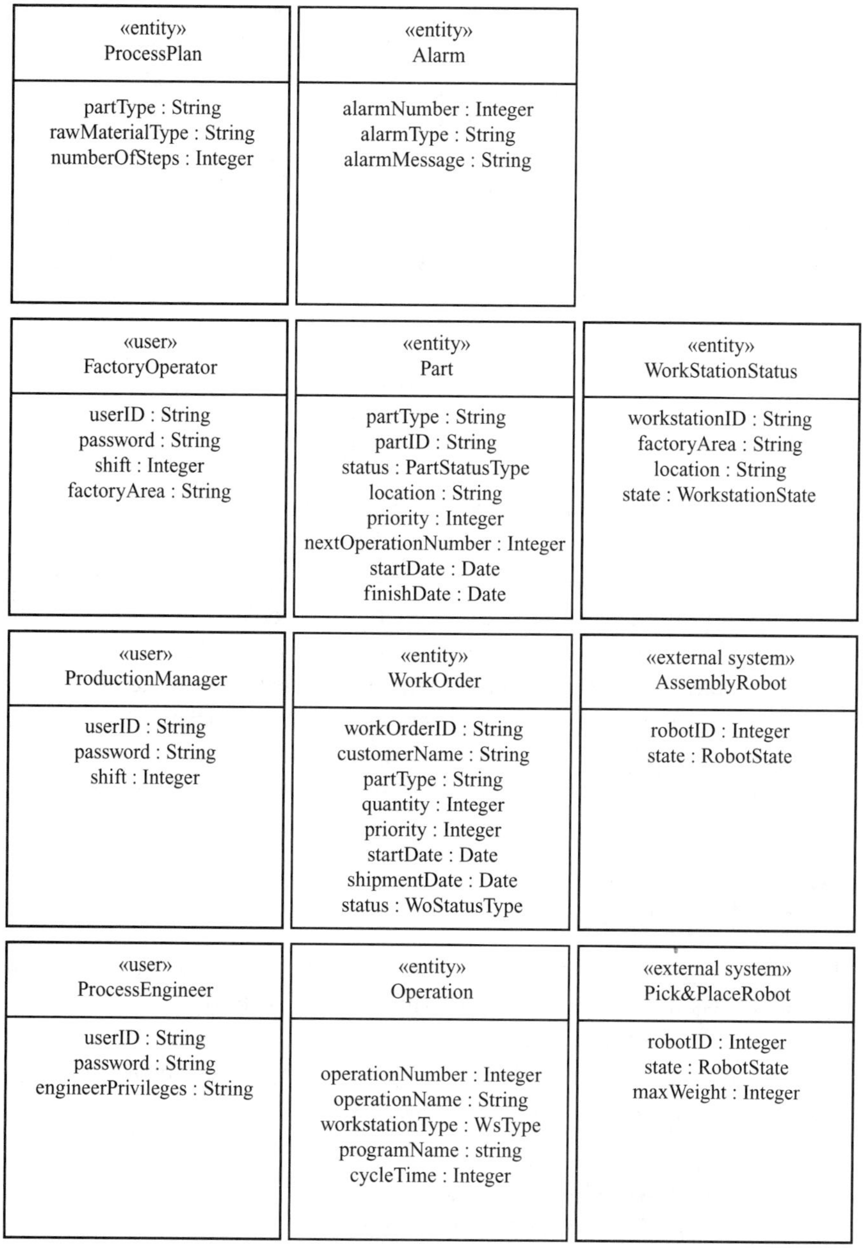

Figure 21.6 *Classes and attributes for Factory Automation System*

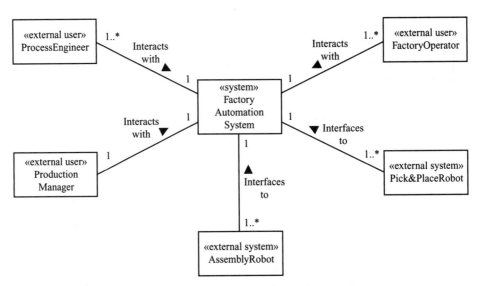

Figure 21.7 *Factory Automation System context class diagram*

For each of the human actors, there needs to be a user interface object. These are `Process Engineer Interface` user interface object, `Production Manager Interface` user interface object, and `Factory Operator Interface` user interface object. To control a manufacturing workstation, there needs to be a `Workstation Controller` object. There is one `Receiving Workstation Controller`, one `Shipping Workstation Controller`, and several instances of the `Line Workstation Controller`, one for each line workstation.

21.5   Dynamic Model

The dynamic dependencies are shown in the dynamic model, consisting of collaboration diagrams and statecharts, as described in this section.

Collaboration diagrams are developed corresponding to the use cases described in Section 21.2. These depict the objects determined in Section 21.4, the use cases they participate in, and the messages passed among them.

21.5.1   Collaboration Diagrams for Factory Operator Client/Server Use Cases

Consider first the `Factory Operator` use cases. Two of these are client/server use cases, in which a client—in this case, a user interface client—interacts with a server. First consider the `View Alarms` client/server use case, depicted in Figure 21.8:

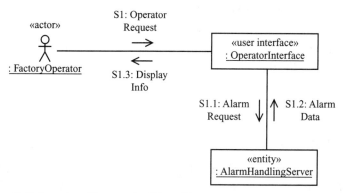

Figure 21.8 *Collaboration diagram for View Alarms use case*

S1: The operator requests an alarm handling service, for example, to view alarms or to subscribe to receive alarm messages of a specific type.

S1.1: The `Operator Interface` object sends the alarm request to the `Alarm Handler Server`.

S1.2: The `Alarm Handler Server` performs the request—for example, reads the list of current alarms or adds the name of this client to the subscription list—and sends a response to the `Operator Interface` object.

S1.3: The `Operator Interface` object displays the response—for example, alarm information—to the operator.

The use case for `View Workstation Status` is also a client/server use case and is very similar (Figure 21.9):

V1: The operator requests a workstation status service—for example, to view current status of workstation.

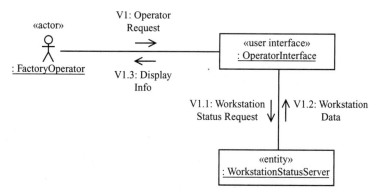

Figure 21.9 *Collaboration diagram for View Workstation Status use case*

V1.1: The Operator Interface object sends a workstation status request to the Workstation Status Server.

V1.2: The Workstation Status Server responds—for example, with the requested workstation status data.

V1.3: The Operator Interface object displays the workstation status information to the operator.

21.5.2   Collaboration Diagrams for Subscriber Notification Use Cases

Two other use cases are subscriber notification use cases, in which a client is notified of new events previously subscribed to in a client/server use case. Consider the Generate Alarm and Notify subscriber notification use case, shown in Figure 21.10:

M1: The Workstation Controller object receives workstation input from the external robot, indicating a problem condition.

M2: The Workstation Controller object sends an alarm to the Alarm Handling Server.

M3: The Alarm Handling Server sends a multicast message containing the alarm to all subscribers registered to receive messages of this type.

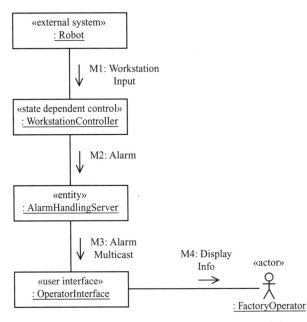

Figure 21.10   *Collaboration diagram for Generate Alarm and Notify use case*

M4: The `Operator Interface` object receives the alarm notification and displays the information to the operator.

The `Generate Workstation Status and Notify` use case is also a subscriber notification use case and is shown in Figure 21.11:

N1: The `Workstation Controller` object receives workstation input from the external robot, indicating a change in workstation status, for example, part completed.

N2: The `Workstation Controller` object sends a workstation status message to the `Workstation Status Server`.

N3: The `Workstation Status Server` sends a multicast message containing the new workstation status to all subscribers registered to receive messages of this type.

N4: The `Operator Interface` object receives the workstation status message and displays the information to the operator.

21.5.3   Collaboration Diagrams for Production Management Client/Server Use Cases

Now consider the `Process Planning` use cases initiated by the `Process Engineer`. A process engineer has to create manufacturing operations and then

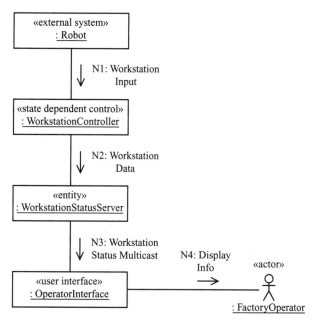

Figure 21.11   *Collaboration diagram for Generate Workstation Status and Notify use case*

create a process plan that consists of a sequence of operations. We can use two use cases for this purpose, `Create/Update Operation` and `Create/Update Process Plan`, where `Create/Update Process Plan` extends `Create/Update Operation` (see Figure 21.3). First, consider the `Create/Update Operation` use case (see Figure 21.12):

O1: The `Process Engineer` inputs information for creating an operation to the `Process Engineer Interface` object. This includes the operation name, workstation type, and robot programs to be used.

O1.1: The `Process Engineer Interface` object sends `Create Operation` request to the `Operation Server`.

O1.2: The `Operation Server` responds with `Operation Information`.

O1.3: The `Process Engineer Interface` object displays the `Operation Information` to the `Process Engineer`. The engineer may iterate creating more operations.

Now consider the `Create/Update Process Plan` use case (also shown in Figure 21.12), which extends `Create/Update Operation` because it creates the process plan from operations created in the `Create/Update Operation` use case.

P2: The `Process Engineer` inputs information for creating a process plan to the `Process Engineer Interface` object. This includes the plan name and part type, raw material, and operation information for the first manufacturing operation.

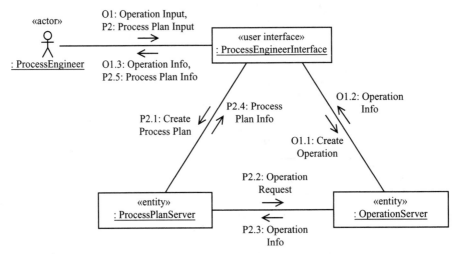

Figure 21.12 *Collaboration diagram for Create/Update Operation and Create/Update Process Plan use cases*

P2.1: The `Process Engineer Interface` object sends `Create Process Plan` request to `Process Plan Server`.

P2.2: The `Process Plan Server` sends operation request to `Operation Server`.

P2.3: The `Operation Server` responds with information about the requested operation.

P2.4: The `Process Plan Server` sends `Process Plan Info` to `Process Engineer Interface` object.

P2.5: The `Process Engineer Interface` object displays the process plan information to the `Process Engineer` actor. The engineer adds other operations to the process plan.

Next consider the `Create/Modify Work Order` use case initiated by the `Production Manager`, which involves accessing of three entity objects—namely `Work Order Server`, `Part Server`, and `Process Plan Server`— by the production manager (see Figure 21.13).

R1: The `Production Manager` inputs `Production Input` to the `Production Manager Interface` object. This includes the type of part to be manufactured.

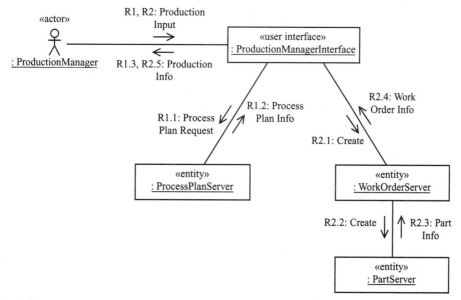

Figure 21.13 *Collaboration diagram for Create/Modify Work Order use case*

R1.1: The Production Manager Interface object sends a Process Plan Request to the Process Plan Server, which retrieves process plan information given the part type.

R1.2: The Process Plan Server sends Process Plan information to the Production Manager Interface object.

R1.3: The Production Manager Interface object displays Process Plan information to the Production Manager.

R2: The Production Manager inputs work order information to the Production Manager Interface object. This includes work order name, part type, and number of parts to be manufactured of this type.

R2.1: The Production Manager Interface object sends a Create message to the Work Order Server.

R2.2: Work Order Server sends a Create request to the Part Server for each part to be manufactured.

R2.3: The Part Server acknowledges part creation.

R2.4: The Work Order Server responds with work order information to the Production Manager Interface object.

R2.5: The production information is displayed to the user.

21.5.4 Distributed Control Use Cases

The next use case is a complex use case initiated by the Production Manager and called Manufacture Part, which involves processing a part through the factory. This use case involves three different types of Workstation Controller, a Receiving Workstation Controller object, several Line Workstation Controller objects, and a Shipping Workstation Controller object. There is one instance of the Line Workstation Controller class for each manufacturing workstation, and the instances are connected in series. When a work order is released to the factory by the production manager, a Start Part message identifying the part ID and number of parts required is sent to the Receiving Workstation Controller. This ensures that for each part to be manufactured, a piece of raw material of the appropriate type is obtained and loaded onto the conveyor. At the shipping workstation, the Shipping Workstation Controller object removes finished parts from the conveyor and places them in a shipping area.

With a just-in-time algorithm, a workstation requests a part only when it is ready to process a part, so parts do not pile up at a workstation. When a workstation completes a part, it waits for a message from its successor workstation requesting the part. When the message is received, the Workstation Controller sends the Place command to the Pick & Place Robot to place the part on the conveyor. Next, the Workstation Controller sends a Part Coming message to the successor workstation and a Part Request message to the predecessor workstation. The Receiving Workstation Controller maintains a count of the remaining number of parts for a given work order. The Shipping Workstation Controller controls the removal of each finished part from the conveyor in preparation for shipping, after which it sends a Part Complete message to Production Manager Interface.

The three abstract use cases for part manufacturing (shown in Figure 21.4) are as follows:

A. **Receive Part.** Receiving Workstation Controller sends part to first Line Workstation Controller in sequence.

B. **Process Part at Workstation.** Line Workstation Controller N sends part to Line Workstation Controller N+1. This use case is repeated several times.

C. **Ship Part.** Last Line Workstation Controller sends part to Shipping Workstation Controller.

A concrete use case for a part that has to visit w line workstations consists of one execution of use case A, w-1 (where w is the number of line workstation controllers) executions of use case B, and one execution of use case C. The three part manufacturing abstract use cases are shown on collaboration diagrams, on which events are labeled A, B, and C, corresponding to the three use cases shown above.

In general, we refer to a workstation controller receiving a part from a predecessor workstation controller (which could be a receiving or line workstation controller) and sending a part to a successor workstation controller (which could be a line or shipping workstation controller).

As the Workstation Controller is a state-dependent control object, it is defined by means of a statechart, which is described next, prior to the detailed description of the three use cases.

21.5.5 Line Workstation Controller Statechart

The statechart for a Line Workstation Controller (LWC) consists of two orthogonal statecharts, the Part Processing statechart and the Part Requesting statechart. The two orthogonal statecharts are depicted as superstates on a high-level statechart, with a dashed line separating them (see Figure 21.14). At any one time, a workstation controller is in one of the substates of the Part Processing superstate (see Figure 21.15), reflecting the current situation in processing the part at this workstation, and in one of the substates of the Part

Requesting superstate (see Figure 21.16), reflecting whether or not a part has been requested by the successor workstation. This does not imply that there is any concurrency within a Line Workstation Controller object, merely that it is simpler to model these relatively independent event occurrences in this way.

The Part Processing superstate contains the following substates. The transitions between the substates are described in the context of the collaboration diagrams:

- Awaiting Part from Predecessor Workstation. This is the initial state, in which the workstation is idle waiting for the arrival of a part.

- Part Arriving. LWC enters this state when it receives a message from the Predecessor Workstation indicating that the next part is on the way.

- Robot Picking. LWC enters this state when the part has arrived at the workstation. The Pick & Place Robot is picking the part off the conveyor belt and bringing it to the workstation.

- Assembling Part. LWC enters this state when it receives a message indicating that the part is ready at the workstation. The assembly robot is assembling the part.

- Robot Placing. The Pick & Place Robot is placing the part on the conveyor belt to send to the successor workstation. This state is entered when robot assembly has been completed and a part request has been received from the successor workstation.

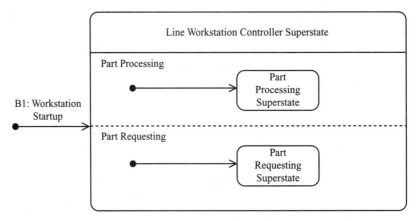

Figure 21.14 *Line Workstation Controller statechart: Superstates for Line Workstation Controller*

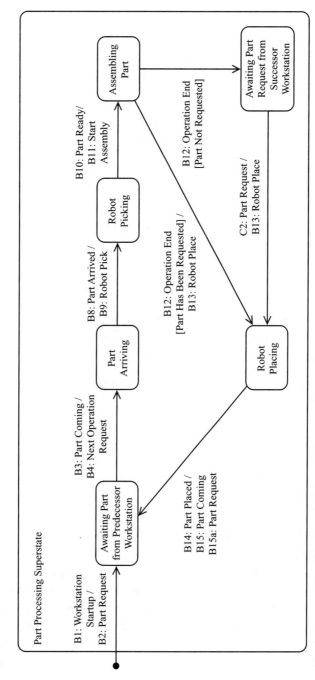

Figure 21.15 *Line Workstation Controller statechart: Statechart for Part Processing superstate*

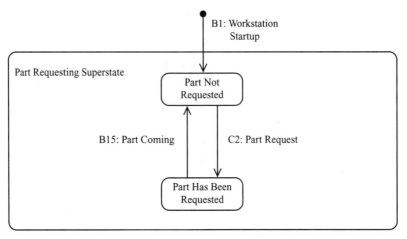

Figure 21.16 *Line Workstation Controller statechart: Statechart for Part Requesting superstate*

- `Awaiting Part Request from Successor Workstation`. This state is entered when robot assembly has been completed but a part request has not yet been received from the successor workstation.

The `Part Requesting` superstate has the following substates:

- `Part Not Requested`. A part has not been requested by the successor workstation.
- `Part Has Been Requested`. A part has been requested by the successor workstation.

These two substates are used as conditions to be checked in the `Part Processing` statechart for determining what state to enter when robot assembly has completed.

21.5.6   Manufacture Part Use Cases

The details of the three part manufacturing use cases are given next (see Figures 21.14–21.19). Each `Line` and `Shipping Workstation Controller` sends a `Part Request` message to its predecessor workstation at initialization. This is shown by the B2 and C2 messages, which are also shown on the statechart in Figure 21.15. The production manager actor initiates the main event sequence by creating a work order (A1). To make an abstract use case more reusable, we allow an object in one use case to send a message to an object in another use case. Although the message numbers in the two use cases are usually different, we say that the message numbers are equivalent. The event sequences are as follows.

At system initialization, the following events occur:

B1, C1: Workstation Startup. When this internal event occurs, the `Workstation Controller` transitions to the `Awaiting Part from Predecessor Workstation` state, as shown in the statechart in Figure 21.15.

B2, C2: As a result of the state transition, the `Workstation Controller` object sends a `Part Request` message to the predecessor `Workstation Controller` object. `Part Request` is an output event on the `Part Processing` statechart that is propagated to the `Part Requesting` statechart, where it appears as an input event that causes a transition from `Part Not Requested` state to `Part Has Been Requested` state.

In the collaboration diagram for the `Receive Part` abstract use case (see Figure 21.17), the `Receiving Workstation Controller` sends a part to the first `Line Workstation Controller`. The message sequence description is as follows:

A1: The actor, the human production manager, initiates processing of a work order, which necessitates starting the manufacturing of each part in the work order.

A2: The `Production Manager Interface` sends a `Start Part` message to the `Receiving Workstation Controller`, containing the part type and number of parts to be manufactured.

A3: The `Receiving Workstation Controller` sends a command to the `Pick & Place Robot` to place on the conveyor the raw material from which the part is to be manufactured.

A4: The `Pick & Place Robot` places the material on the conveyor and notifies `Receiving Workstation Controller`.

A5 = B3: The `Receiving Workstation Controller` sends a `Part Coming` message to `Line Workstation Controller`. This message constitutes the end of the `Receiving Workstation Controller` use case and the next event in the event sequence of the `Line Workstation Controller` use case.

In the collaboration diagram for the `Process Part at Workstation` abstract use case (see Figure 21.18), the predecessor `Line Workstation Controller` sends a part to this `Line Workstation Controller`. The following event sequence is shown on both the collaboration diagram and the statechart for the `Line Workstation Controller`:

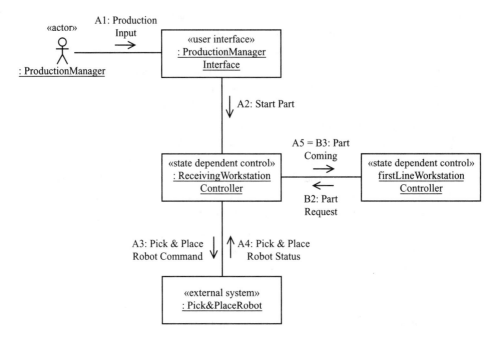

Figure 21.17 *Collaboration diagram for Receive Part use case*

B3: On receiving the `Part Coming` message from the predecessor workstation, `Line Workstation Controller` transitions into `Part Arriving` state (see Figure 21.15).

B4: The action associated with the state transition is `Line Workstation Controller` issues a `Next Operation Request` to the `Process Plan Server` containing the part type and current process step number (initially 1).

B5: The `Process Planning Server` increments the process step number for this part's process plan, determines the operation ID for this process step, and issues an operation request to the `Operation Server` for the next operation in sequence.

B6: The `Operation Server` retrieves the operation information and sends it back.

B7: The `Process Plan Server` sends the operation information to the `Line Workstation Controller`.

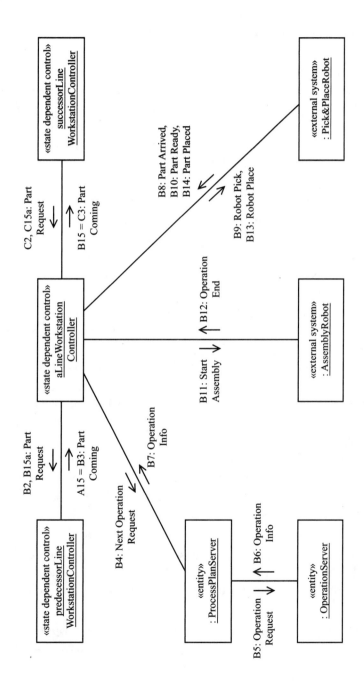

NB: The labels A15 = B3 and B15 = C3 are used to emphasize that these two pairs of message sequence numbers each refer to the same message and are not part of the UML notation.

Figure 21.18 *Collaboration diagram for Processing Part at Workstation use case*

B8: A sensor at the `Pick & Place Robot` detects part arrival at the workstation and sends a `Part Arrived` message to `Line Workstation Controller`. This causes `Line Workstation Controller` to transition to `Robot Picking` state.

B9: As a result of the state transition, `Line Workstation Controller` sends a command to the `Pick & Place Robot` to pick the part off the conveyor.

B10: The `Pick & Place Robot` picks the part off the conveyor and places it in the workstation. On completion, the `Pick & Place Robot` notifies the `Line Workstation Controller`. The `Line Workstation Controller` transitions to `Assembling Part` state.

B11: The `Line Workstation Controller` sends the `Start Assembly` command to the `Assembly Robot`, which assembles the part.

B12: On completion of the assembly operation, the `Assembly Robot` sends an `Operation End` status message. If a part has been requested (C2), the `Line Workstation Controller` transitions to `Robot Placing` state. If part has not been requested, the `Line Workstation Controller` transitions to `Awaiting Part Request from Successor Workstation`.

B13: As a result of the transition, the `Line Workstation Controller` sends a command to the `Pick & Place Robot` to place the part on the conveyor.

B14: On completion, `Pick & Place Robot` notifies `Line Workstation Controller` of `Part Placed`. The `Line Workstation Controller` transitions to `Awaiting Part from Predecessor Workstation`. As a result of the transition, two concurrent actions take place, B15 and B15a.

B15 = C3: The `Line Workstation Controller` sends a `Part Coming` message to the successor workstation. `Part Coming` is an output event on the `Part Processing` statechart that is propagated to the `Part Requesting` statechart, where it appears as an input event that causes a transition from `Part Has Been Requested` state to `Part Not Requested` state.

B15a (parallel sequence): The `Line Workstation Controller` sends a `Part Request` message to the predecessor workstation.

The collaboration diagram for the `Ship Part` abstract use case (see Figure 21.19), in which the last `Line Workstation Controller` sends a part to the `Shipping Workstation Controller`, consists of the following event sequence:

C4: At the `Shipping Workstation Controller`, a sensor detects part arrival and the `Pick & Place Robot` sends the `Part Arrived` message.

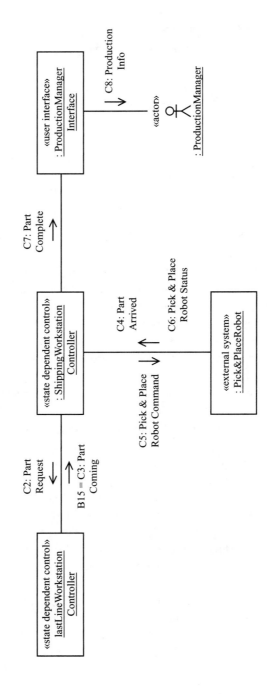

NB: The label B15 = C3 is used to emphasize that these two message sequence
numbers refer to the same message and is not part of the UML notation.

Figure 21.19 *Collaboration diagram for Ship Part use case*

C5, C6: The Pick & Place Robot picks the part off the conveyor and notifies the Shipping Workstation Controller.

C7: The Shipping Workstation Controller stores the part in the finished parts inventory and sends a Part Complete message to Production Manager Interface.

C8: Production Manager Interface displays the part completion information to the human production manager.

21.6 Subsystem Structuring

Because of the size of the system, it is not practical to show one consolidated collaboration diagram for the Factory Automation System. Instead, let us consider how the system can be structured into subsystems and then develop the subsystem collaboration diagram.

Some subsystems can be determined relatively easily because of geographical distribution or server responsibility. One of the most common forms of geographical distribution involves clients and servers, which are always allocated to different subsystems: a client subsystem and a server subsystem.

For other subsystems, it is helpful to consider the use-case-based collaboration diagrams, because they show the objects that communicate frequently with each other. This is generally a good basis for subsystem structuring, because objects that communicate frequently with each other should be in the same subsystem, providing they are not geographically distributed.

Furthermore, we differentiate between aggregate subsystems and composite subsystems. A composite subsystem is structured according to the subsystem structuring criteria and, in this distributed application, adheres to the principle of geographical distribution, namely, objects in different geographical locations are never in the same composite subsystem. Each composite subsystem is a distributed component type, which can be instantiated and configured to execute on its own node. An aggregate subsystem is a subsystem grouped by functional similarity—that is, the objects it contains (which may be composite objects) are grouped together because they are functionally similar or interact with each other in the same collaborations.

The subsystem collaboration diagram for the Factory Automation System (see Figure 21.20) shows the subsystems in the Factory Automation System and the interfaces between them. Subsystem collaboration diagrams are shown for the Process Planning and Production Management subsystems in Figures 21.21

and 21.22, respectively. A further subsystem collaboration diagram is shown for the Part Processing subsystem in Figure 21.23. Now consider how the subsystem structuring decisions are made.

First, consider the client/server collaborations. From the View Alarms collaboration diagram, we determine that the Alarm Handler Server is a server subsystem and the Operator Interface client object is actually a composite object that forms the Operator Interface user interface subsystem (see Figure 21.20). Although there is one instance of the Alarm Handler Server, there are many instances of the Operator Interface subsystem, one for each operator. Similarly, from the View Workstation Status use case, we determine that the Workstation Status Server is a server subsystem; there is one instance of this subsystem for each workstation.

Next, consider the process planning (Create/Update Operation and Create/Update Process Plan) collaboration diagrams. As before, the Process Engineer Interface object is a user interface object and forms the basis of a client user interface subsystem. Because the Process Plan Server and the Operation Server, two entity objects, are used together, these objects are composed into a composite server subsystem, the Process Planning Server subsystem. An aggregate Process Planning subsystem consists of the Process Planning Server and the Process Engineer Interface composite subsystems (see Figure 21.21).

In the Create/Modify Work Order use case, the Production Manager Interface (a user interface object) and the Part Server and Work Order Server entity objects are allocated to a Production Management aggregate subsystem. As before, the Production Manager Interface object is a user interface object and forms the basis of a client user interface subsystem. Because the Part Server and Work Order Server (two entity objects) are used together, these objects are composed into a composite server subsystem, the Production Management Server subsystem (see Figure 21.22). The Process Plan Server, which also participates in the Work Order Management use case, is not part of the Production Management subsystem because it has already been allocated to the Process Planning subsystem.

The objects of the Manufacture Part use cases form three control subsystems, a Line Workstation Controller, of which there are several instances; a Receiving Workstation Controller, of which there is one instance; and a Shipping Workstation Controller, of which there is also one instance. A Part Processing aggregate subsystem consists of four composite subsystems, the three control subsystems, and one server subsystem, the Workstation Status Server (see Figure 21.23).

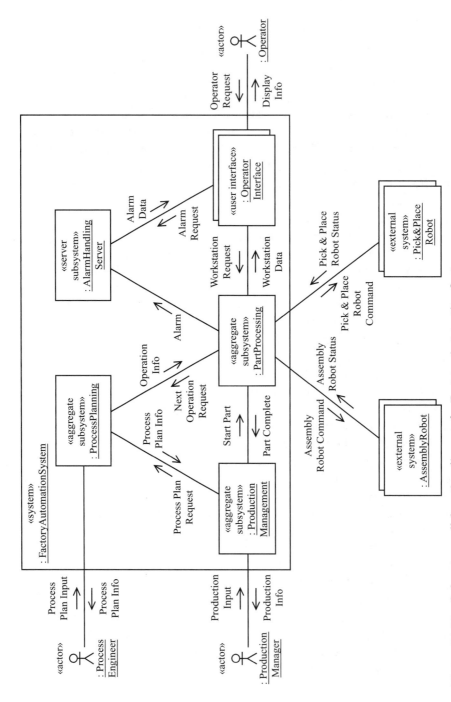

Figure 21.20 *Subsystem collaboration diagram for Factory Automation System*

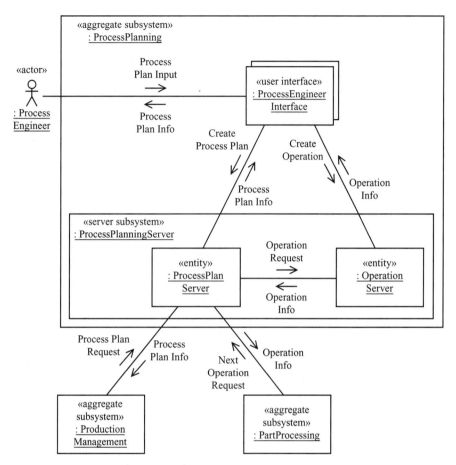

Figure 21.21 *Process Planning subsystem*

The objects in the subscriber notification use cases are already allocated to various subsystems.

A static model of all the composite classes of the Factory Automation System is shown in Figure 21.24. It shows each composite class, which is a component type that can be instantiated and allocated to execute on its own node at system configuration time. The associations between the composite classes are also depicted. This static model is determined from the subsystem collaboration diagrams. The associations correspond to the connections between components on the collaboration diagrams. The direction of navigation corresponds to the primary direction in which messages are sent from a source component to a destination component, for example, from a client to a server.

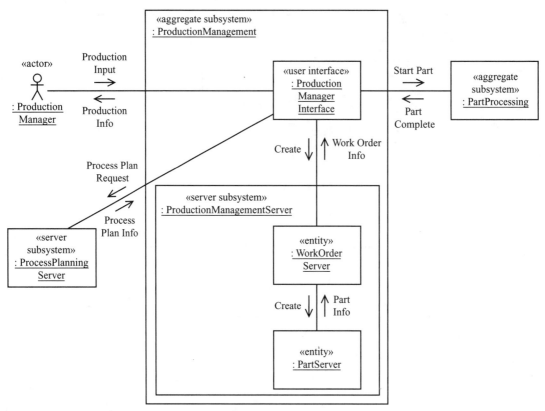

Figure 21.22 *Production Management subsystem*

21.7 Distributed Software Architecture

In mapping the analysis model to a distributed software architecture, it is necessary to ensure that the distributed subsystems are configurable. To ensure that the subsystems are designed as components capable of effectively operating in a distributed environment, it is necessary to apply the distributed component configuration criteria described in Chapter 13. The actual decisions for a given application of allocating component instances to physical nodes are made later, at system configuration time. In a distributed environment, each component potentially executes on its own physical node and all communication between components is by means of messages.

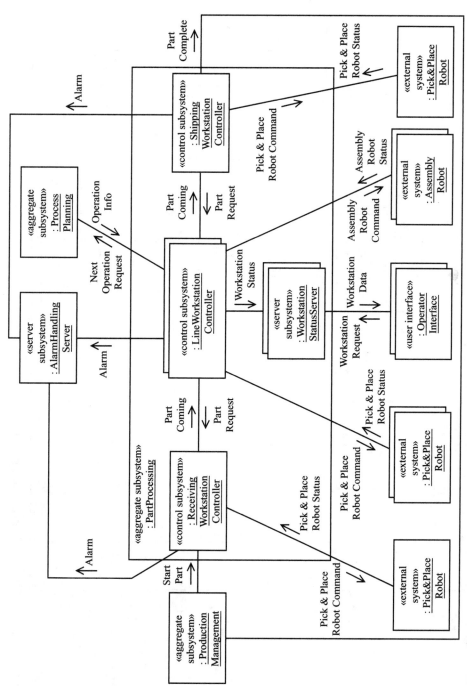

Figure 21.23 *Subsystem collaboration diagram for Part Processing subsystem*

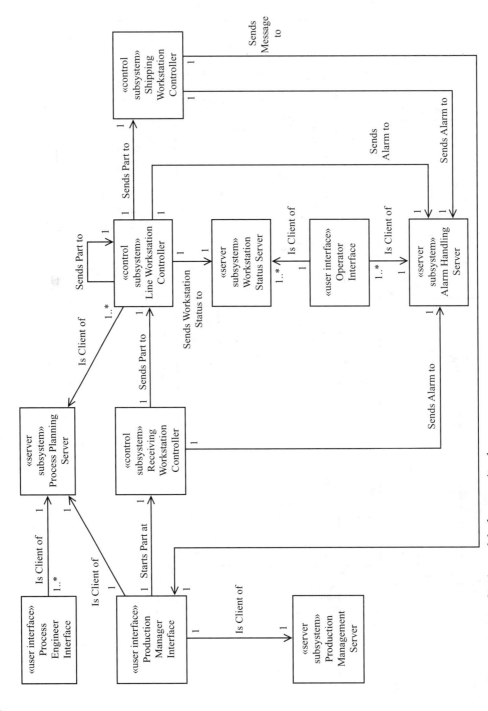

Figure 21.24 *Static model of composite classes*

21.7.1 Applying Component Configuration Criteria

In Figure 21.23, there is one instance of each of the Receiving Workstation Controller and Shipping Workstation Controller subsystems and several instances of the Line Workstation Controller subsystem. Each of these subsystems is an autonomous component that performs a specific site related service. Each component is able to operate independently for a significant period of time, so it can be operational even if other nodes are temporarily unavailable. Because these are control components, having them on separate nodes ensures that predictable performance can be achieved. Furthermore, special-purpose hardware, such as sensors and actuators, is often likely to be associated with a workstation controller.

There are several server subsystems, each of which is a component that can potentially operate on a separate node. There is one instance each of the Process Planning Server, Production Management Server, and Alarm Handling Server. Best performance is likely to be achieved by allocating each server component its own node so it can respond promptly to client requests.

For the Workstation Status Server subsystem, one option is to have one server component for the whole system. Another, more decentralized option is to have one instance of this component per workstation, in which case each component instance of the Workstation Status Server could be assigned to the same node as the corresponding Line Workstation Controller. There are two reasons for this: the relatively high message traffic between the Line Workstation Controller and Workstation Status Server components and the likelihood of enough capacity on each workstation node to support both components.

Finally, there are several user interface subsystems, each of which is a client component that could potentially be allocated its own node. These are Production Manager Interface (one instance), Process Engineer Interface (one instance per process engineer), and Operator Interface (one instance per operator). These client components would interact with one or more server components.

21.7.2 Message Communication between Component Subsystems

Consider the message communication interfaces between component subsystems, as initially shown in Figures 21.20–21.23. On these figures, all messages are depicted as simple messages. It is now necessary to design the precise message communication interfaces, as shown in Figures 21.25–21.28.

Loosely coupled (asynchronous) message communication is frequently used in distributed applications. An example of this kind of message communication is between Part Processing and the Alarm Handling Server (see Figure 21.25).

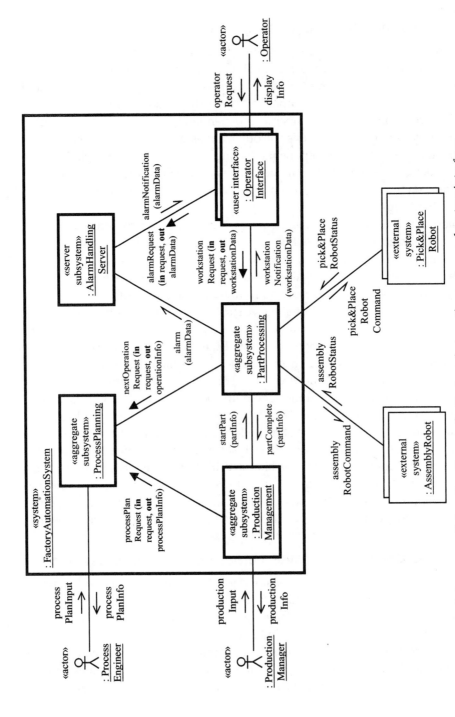

Figure 21.25 *Subsystem collaboration diagram for Factory Automation system: subsystem interfaces*

Alarms are sent from the individual workstations to the Alarm Handling Server. When a new alarm message is received by the Alarm Handling Server, it multicasts the alarm to all instances of the Operator Interface component that have subscribed to receive alarms of this type.

Multiple client/single server (synchronous) message communication is also frequently used in distributed applications. An example of this kind of message communication is shown in Figure 21.26, where the server component is the Process Plan Server, which responds to service requests from multiple clients. The Process Engineer Interface component, of which there are typically multiple instances, sends new and updated process plans and operations to

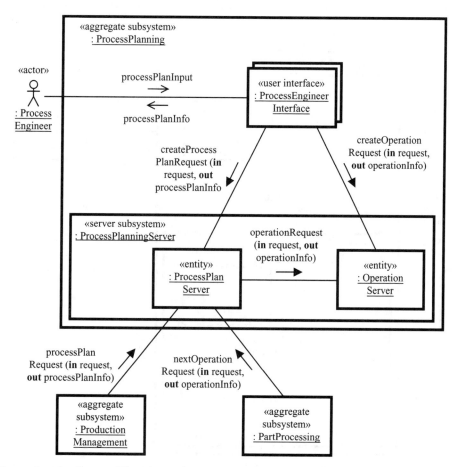

Figure 21.26 *Process Planning subsystem: subsystem interfaces*

the server. The server responds to requests for operation information from the multiple instances of the `Line Workstation Controller` component and to requests for process plan information from the `Production Manager Interface` component (see Figure 21.27).

Next, consider the message communication interfaces in the Part Processing subsystem shown in Figure 21.28. For greatest flexibility, communication among the various `Workstation Controller` components is loosely coupled, as is the communication between these components and the `Production Manager Interface`, the `Alarm Handling Server`, and the external robot systems.

In some distributed applications with multiple servers of the same type, it is useful to provide multiple-client/multiple-server message communication. Consider an example of this kind of message communication. At each workstation,

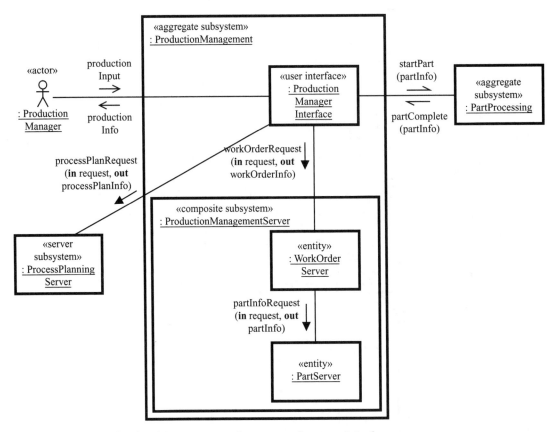

Figure 21.27 *Production Management subsystem: subsystem interfaces*

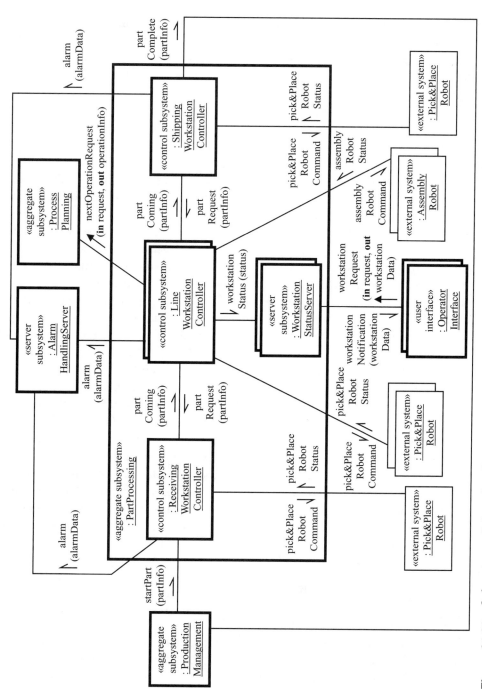

Figure 21.28 *Subsystem collaboration diagram for Part Processing subsystem: subsystem interfaces*

there is a Workstation Status Server component, which encapsulates the workstation status data repository (see Figure 21.28). The data maintained by the Workstation Status Server component is updated via messages sent by the local Line Workstation Controller component. The clients of the Workstation Status Server component are the multiple instances of the Operator Interface component.

With simple client/server message communication, the Operator Interface client requests to receive some data it can display to the user. However, it is also desirable for a factory display to be updated either periodically or whenever a change in status occurs, without the Operator Interface component having to explicitly send a message request each time. This is addressed by multicast message communication. The Operator Interface component sends a message to the Workstation Status Server, requesting to subscribe to that workstation's client group, which consists of all instances of the Operator Interface component that wish to receive this workstation's status. The Workstation Status Server sends workstation status in the form of workstation Notification multicast messages on an ongoing basis to each member of its client group. An Operator Interface component has to explicitly inform the Workstation Status Server when it no longer wishes to receive status messages by sending it an unsubscribe message.

In this type of environment, it is also desirable for an Operator Interface client to receive data from several workstations concurrently; for example, a factory status display needs status information from each workstation in the factory. An Operator Interface component makes a request for a given workstation's status by sending a subscription message to the appropriate Workstation Status Server component, which responds with notification messages containing that workstation's data whenever the status is updated. Because Operator Interface sends subscription requests to several Workstation Status Servers, receiving loosely coupled messages means it can receive workstation Notification messages from different servers in any order and update the display accordingly.

21.8 System Configuration

Further decisions need to be made to configure individual target systems. The number of workstations needs to be defined. Parameters of parameterized component subsystems need to be defined, such as workstation ID and alarm

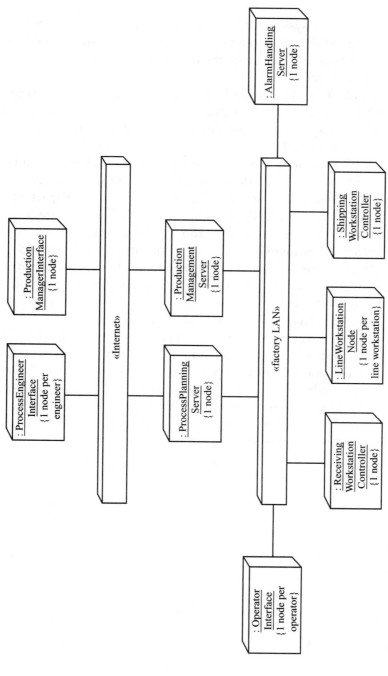

Figure 21.29 *Deployment diagram for Factory Automation System*

names. Component instances need to be connected together and allocated to physical nodes.

Consider the system configuration of the Factory Automation System. The distributed design can be mapped to different target system configurations dictated by the size of the factory, the number of users, expected throughput, and hardware availability.

Consider first a highly distributed configuration. The Receiving Workstation Controller and Shipping Workstation Controller components are each allocated to a separate node. Each instance of the Line Workstation Controller component, together with its companion Workstation Status Server component, is allocated to a separate physical node—the Line Workstation Node—to achieve localized autonomy and adequate performance. Thus the failure of one workstation node does not immediately impact other workstation nodes, although part throughput is delayed. Each instance of the Process Engineer Interface, Production Manager Interface, and Operator Interface components is allocated to a separate user interface node. The Alarm Handling Server, Production Management Server, and Process Planning Server components are each mapped to a separate server node. A deployment diagram for this particular target system configuration (one of the many possible configurations) in shown in Figure 21.29.

An alternative, less distributed configuration is to allocate the Process Planning Server, Production Management Server, and Alarm Handling Server components to a larger server node. Even greater centralization could be achieved by adding the Process Engineer Interface and Production Manager Interface to this node, making it a multiuser interactive node. In this scenario, only the Workstation Controller and Operator Interface components would have their own nodes.

chapter

Electronic Commerce System Case Study

The Electronic Commerce System case study is a highly distributed World Wide Web-based application. The solution uses software agents as intermediaries between user interface clients and servers. In addition, object brokers provide a standardized interface to several heterogeneous legacy databases.

22.1 Electronic Commerce Problem

In the electronic commerce problem, there are customers and suppliers. Each customer has a contract with a supplier for purchases from that supplier, as well as one or more bank accounts through which payments to suppliers can be made. Each supplier provides a catalog of items, accepts customer orders, and maintains accounts with each customer for receiving payment.

A customer is able to browse through several World Wide Web-based catalogs provided by the suppliers and make selections of items that need to be purchased. The customer's order needs to be checked against the available contracts to determine if there is a valid customer contract with the supplier, which will be used for charging the purchase. Each contract has operations funds committed to it. It is necessary to determine that sufficient funds are available for the customer order. Assuming that the contract and funds are in place, a delivery order is created and sent to the catalog supplier. The supplier confirms the order and enters a planned shipping date. As time passes, the shipping order is monitored and both supplier and customer are notified if there is a shipping delay. When the order is shipped, the customer is notified. The customer acknowledges when the shipment is received, and the delivery order is updated. After receipt of shipment, authorization for payment of the invoice is made. The invoice is checked against the contract, available funds, and delivery order status, after which the invoice is sent to accounts payable, which authorizes payment of funds. Payment is made through electronic funds transfer from the customer bank to the supplier bank. The application uses several legacy databases, so an object broker technology, such as CORBA, is required.

22.2   Use Case Model

The use case model for the Electronic Commerce System is depicted in Figure 22.1. There are three actors, the Customer, the Supplier, and the Bank. The customer initiates three use cases: Browse Catalog, Place Requisition, and Confirm Delivery. The supplier initiates three use cases: Process Delivery Order, Confirm Shipment, and Send Invoice. These are the main use cases in the application; other, less important use cases for querying the servers and monitoring progress have been omitted for brevity.

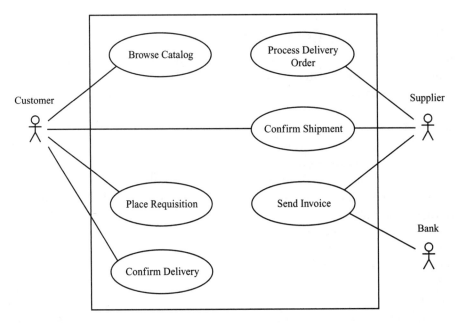

Figure 22.1   *Electronic Commerce System: use cases*

The use cases are briefly described next. In the `Browse Catalog` use case, the customer browses the various WWW catalogs and views various catalog items from a given supplier's catalog. In the `Place Requisition` use case, the customer selects items from the catalog and then makes a requisition request. The system has to find a customer contract with the catalog supplier for which there are sufficient operations funds. If a valid contract is found, the system authorizes the requisition and sends a purchase request to the supplier. In the `Process Delivery Order` use case, the system retrieves a delivery order, determines that the inventory is available to fulfill the order, and displays the order to the supplier.

In the `Confirm Shipment` use case, the supplier prepares the shipment manually and then confirms the shipment. In the `Confirm Delivery` use case, when the shipment arrives at the customer, the customer confirms the delivery. The operations funds are committed for payment. In the `Send Invoice` use case, the supplier sends an invoice to the customer organization. After receiving confirmation of delivery, the invoice is approved by the customer organization's Accounts Payable, and an electronic payment request is sent to the customer's bank.

22.3   Agent Support for Electronic Commerce System

An approach to addressing the Electronic Commerce System by using software agents is outlined in this section and described in more detail in the next section. In this example, there are client agents and server agents, where each agent defines the business rules for some aspect of the electronic commerce domain. In this application, the client agents are user agents that act on behalf of users and assist users in performing their jobs. To achieve this, the client agents interact with server agents. The server agents receive requests from client agents. To satisfy a client agent request, a server agent typically interacts with server objects and with other agents.

The use of software agents is illustrated conceptually in Figure 22.2. In the Electronic Commerce problem, there are two types of client agents: the `Customer Agent` and the `Supplier Agent`. There is one instance of the `Customer Agent` for each customer and one instance of the `Supplier Agent` for each supplier. There are three server agents, with many instances of each. The server agents are

- `Requisition Agent`, one instance for each requisition
- `Delivery Order Agent`, one instance for each delivery order
- `Invoice Agent`, one instance for each invoice

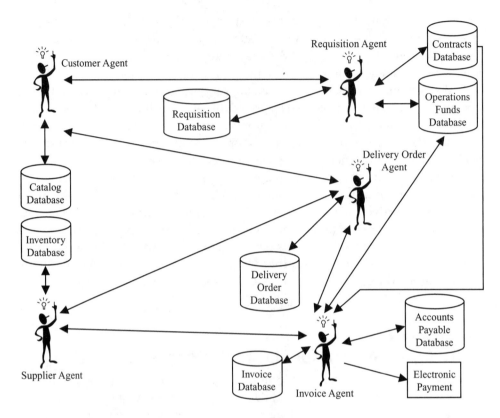

Figure 22.2 *Agent-based Electronic Commerce System: conceptual view*

The Customer Agent is a client agent that acts on behalf of the human customer. The Customer Agent (see Figure 22.2) assists the customer who wishes to
order one or more items from a catalog. It takes the customer's request and interacts with the server agents to further the processing of the customer's selection
and to track the status. The customer may select several items from a catalog.
When a customer completes catalog selection, the Customer Agent acts on
behalf of the customer and initiates certain actions. In particular, when the customer makes a catalog selection, the Customer Agent sends a requisition request
to a Requisition Agent.

The Requisition Agent is a server agent that queries various databases
and communicates with various agents to ensure the processing of a customer-
initiated requisition. It queries the Requisition Database, Contracts Database, and

Operations Funds Database, as well as communicating with the `Customer Agent`. It sends a contract query to the Contracts Database to determine if a contract is in place. It sends a funds query to the Operation Funds Database to determine if the funds are in place. If the response to both queries is positive, the `Requisition Agent` authorizes the requisition and sends the requisition status to the `Customer Agent`. The `Customer Agent` sends a purchase request to a `Delivery Order Agent`.

The `Supplier Agent` is a client agent that is instantiated to work with the supplier. It retrieves a delivery order from the `Delivery Order Agent` and helps the supplier fulfill the order. The `Supplier Agent` updates the inventory database, and the order status is sent to the `Delivery Order Agent` and `Customer Agent`. The customer eventually acknowledges receipt of the goods, and the delivery order is updated to reflect the receipt date.

The `Supplier Agent` sends the invoice to an `Invoice Agent` at the customer organization. When notified by the `Delivery Order Agent` that the goods have been received, the `Invoice Agent` (see Figure 22.2) queries the Contracts Database and Operations Funds Database. If both responses are positive, the `Invoice Agent` authorizes payment and sends the invoice to the Accounts Payable Database, which updates the account. The `Invoice Agent` then sends the electronic payment to the customer's bank.

22.4   Object Broker Support
for Electronic Commerce System

Several legacy databases are used in this application. Each of these is a standalone database residing on a mainframe. There is a need for integrating these databases into the electronic commerce application, using an object broker such as provided by CORBA (see Chapters 4 and 13 for more information on object brokers).

The legacy databases in the customer organizations are the contracts database, the operations funds database, the requisition database, the invoice database, and the accounts payable database. The legacy databases in the supplier organizations are the catalog database, the inventory database, and the delivery order database.

To integrate these databases into the electronic commerce application, the server objects that access the databases need to be database wrapper objects that encapsulate the details of how to read and update the individual databases. Thus the `Requisition Server`, `Contracts Server`, `Operations Funds Server`,

`Accounts Payable Server`, `Invoice Server`, `Catalog Server`, `Delivery Order Server`, and the `Inventory Server` are all database wrapper objects.

In addition, to maintain low coupling between clients, agents, and servers, an object broker name service is used to maintain the location of the specific services. Servers and agents register their services and locations with the object broker. When a service is required, the location of the service is determined by sending a message to the object broker. An example is given in Figure 22.3 in which a client agent, the `Customer Agent`, determines from the `Broker` the location of a server agent, the `Delivery Order Agent`. The `Customer Agent` then communicates directly with the `Delivery Order Agent`.

22.5 Static Modeling of the Problem Domain

A static model of the problem domain is developed and depicted on a class diagram (see Figure 22.4). Because this is a data-intensive application, the emphasis is on the entity classes, many of which represent the data stored in the legacy databases. The database wrapper objects will map between the conceptual objects and the actual databases. Because each customer and supplier organization is liable to have its own specific legacy database, many individual solutions to the wrapper problem are likely to exist. However, by using object broker and wrapper technology, it is possible to have a systematic way of integrating the disparate legacy databases into a general solution.

Figure 22.4 shows the entity classes for all the important problem domain entities and the relationships among these classes. The classes include the `Requisition`,

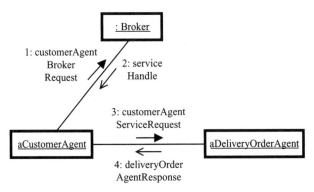

Figure 22.3 *Object broker in Agent-based Electronic Commerce System*

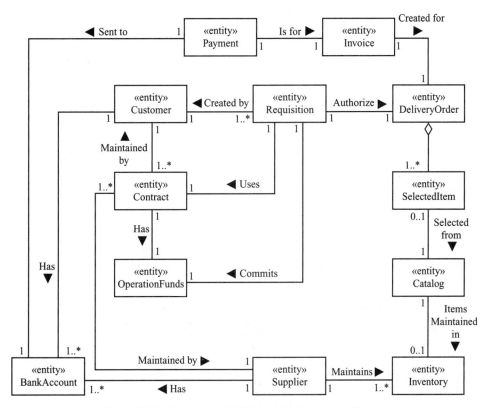

Figure 22.4 *Static model for Agent-based Electronic Commerce System*

`Contract`, `Operations Funds`, `Payment`, `Invoice`, `Catalog`, `Delivery Order`, and `Inventory` classes. The attributes for each class are shown in Figure 22.5.

22.6 Collaboration Model

For each use case, a collaboration diagram is developed, depicting the objects that participate in the use case and the sequence of messages passed between them.

22.6.1 Collaboration Model for Browse Catalog

The collaboration diagram for the first use case, `Browse Catalog`, is shown in Figure 22.6. The message descriptions are as follows:

«entity» Customer	«entity» Inventory	«entity» BankAccount
customerID : Integer address : String telephoneNumber : String faxNumber : String	itemID : Integer itemDescription : String quantity : Integer price : Real reorderTime : Date	bankID : Integer locationOfBank : String bankAccountNumber : String accountType : String

«entity» DeliveryOrder	«entity» Contract	«entity» Supplier
orderID : Integer plannedShipDate : Date actualShipDate : Date creationDate : Date orderStatus : OrderStatusType amountDue : Real receivedDate : Date	contractID : Integer maxPurchase : Real	supplierID : Integer address : String telephoneNumber : String faxNumber : String

«entity» Invoice	«entity» SelectedItem	«entity» Catalog
invoiceID : Integer amountDue : Real invoiceDate : Date	itemID : Integer unitCost : Real quantity : Integer	itemID : Integer itemDescription : String unitCost : Real

«entity» Payment	«entity» Requisition	«entity» OperationFunds
paymentID : String amount : Real date : Date status : PaymentStatusType	requistionID : Integer amount : Real status : RequisitionStatusType	operationFundsID : Integer totalFunds : Real committedFunds : Real reservedFunds : Real

Figure 22.5   *Classes in Agent-based Electronic Commerce System*

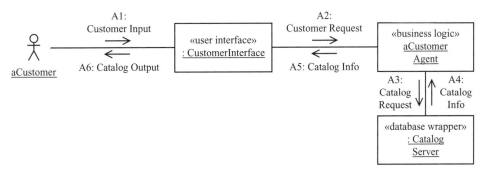

Figure 22.6 *Collaboration diagram for Browse Catalog use case*

A1: The customer makes a catalog request via the `Customer Interface`.

A2: The `Customer Agent` is instantiated to assist the customer. Based on the customer's request, the `Customer Agent` selects one or more catalogs for the customer to browse.

A3: The `Customer Agent` requests information from `Catalog Server`.

A4: The `Catalog Server` sends catalog information to the `Customer Agent`.

A5: The `Customer Agent` forwards the information to the `Customer Interface`.

A6: The `Customer Interface` displays the catalog to the customer.

22.6.2 Collaboration Model for Place Requisition

In the collaboration diagram for the `Place Requisition` use case (see Figure 22.7), the `Requisition Agent` sends a contract query to the `Contracts Server` to determine if a contract is in place. It sends a funds query to the `Operation Funds Server` to determine if the funds are in place. If the response to both queries is positive, the `Requisition Agent` authorizes the requisition and sends the requisition status to the `Customer Agent`. The `Customer Agent` sends a purchase request to a `Delivery Order Agent`. The message descriptions are as follows:

B1: The customer selects items from catalog and requests creation of a requisition.

B2: The `Customer Interface` forwards the request to the `Customer Agent`.

B3: The `Customer Agent` instantiates the `Requisition Agent`, passing to it the customer's requisition request.

B4: The `Requisition Agent` sends a contract query to the `Contracts Server`.

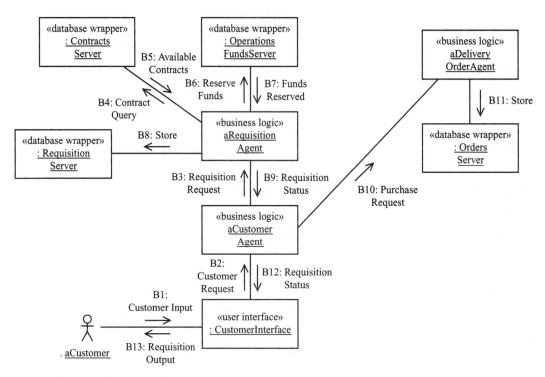

Figure 22.7 *Collaboration diagram for Place Requisition use case*

B5: The Contracts Server returns the contracts available between the customer and the supplier.

B6: The Requisition Agent sends a reserve funds request to the Operations Funds Server, to hold the funds from a given contract for this requisition.

B7: The Operations Funds Server confirms that the funds have been reserved.

B8: The Requisition Agent approves the requisition and sends it to be stored at the Requisition Server.

B9: The Requisition Agent sends the requisition status to the Customer Agent.

B10: The Customer Agent instantiates a Delivery Order Agent and sends the purchase request to it.

B11: The Delivery Order Agent creates a new delivery order and stores it with the Orders Server.

B12: The Customer Agent sends the requisition status to the Customer Interface.

B13: The Customer Interface displays the requisition status to the customer.

22.6.3 Collaboration Model for Process Delivery Order

In the collaboration diagram for the next use case, Process Delivery Order (see Figure 22.8), the Supplier Agent queries the Delivery Order Agent for a new delivery order, and the Delivery Order Agent selects a delivery order. The Supplier Agent checks the inventory and displays the order and inventory information to the supplier via the user interface. The steps are as follows:

C1: The supplier requests a new delivery order.

C2: The Supplier Interface forwards the request to the Supplier Agent.

C3: The Supplier Agent sends the order request to the Delivery Order Agent.

C4, C5: The Delivery Order Agent selects a delivery order by querying the Orders Server.

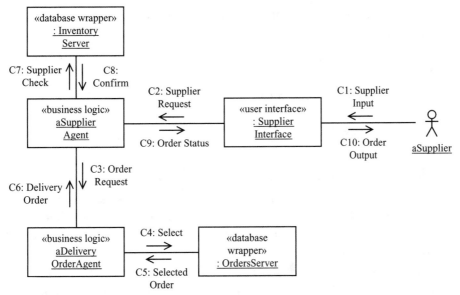

Figure 22.8 *Collaboration diagram for Process Delivery Order use case*

C6: The `Delivery Order Agent` sends the delivery order to the `Supplier Agent`.

C7, C8: The `Supplier Agent` checks that the items are available in inventory.

C9: The `Supplier Agent` sends the order status to the `Supplier Interface`.

C10: The `Supplier Interface` displays the delivery order and inventory information to the supplier.

22.6.4   Collaboration Model for Confirm Shipment

In the collaboration diagram for the `Confirm Shipment` use case (see Figure 22.9), the supplier prepares the shipment manually. The supplier then confirms the shipment by entering the shipping information, including the shipping date. The `Supplier Agent` updates the inventory and the order status is sent to the `Delivery Order Agent` and to the `Customer Agent`, which displays the order status to the customer.

S1: The supplier inputs the shipping information.

S2: The `Supplier Interface` sends the supplier request to the `Supplier Agent`.

S3: The `Supplier Agent` updates the inventory stored at the `Inventory Server`.

S4: The `Supplier Agent` sends the order status to the `Delivery Order Agent`.

S5: The `Delivery Order Agent` updates the `Orders Server`.

S6: The `Delivery Order Agent` sends the order status to the `Customer Agent`.

S7: The `Customer Agent` forwards the order status to the `Customer Interface`.

S8: The `Customer Interface` displays the order status to the customer.

22.6.5   Collaboration Model for Confirm Delivery

In the collaboration diagram for the `Confirm Delivery` use case (see Figure 22.10), when the shipment arrives at the customer, the customer acknowledges receipt of the goods, and the delivery order is updated to reflect the receipt date. The `Requisition Agent` is also notified:

R1: The customer acknowledges the receipt of shipment.

R2: The `Customer Interface` sends the customer confirmation to the `Customer Agent`.

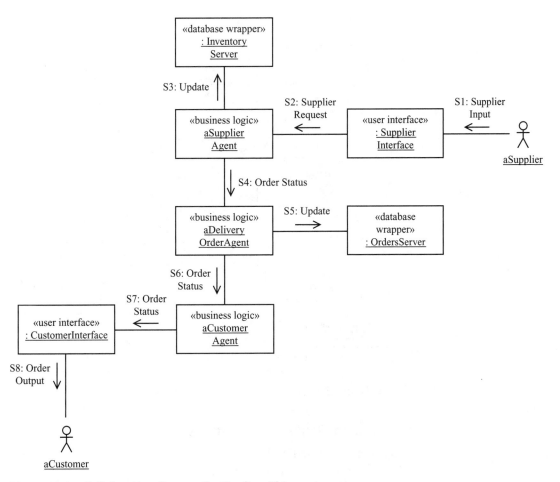

Figure 22.9 *Collaboration diagram for Confirm Shipment use case*

R3: The Customer Agent sends a Shipment Received message to the Delivery Order Agent.

R4: The Delivery Order Agent updates the status at the Orders Server.

R5: The Customer Agent sends a Shipment Received message to the Requisition Agent.

R6: The Requisition Agent updates the status of the requisition stored at the Requisition Server.

R7, R8: The Requisition Agent commits the funds for this requisition with the Operations Funds Server.

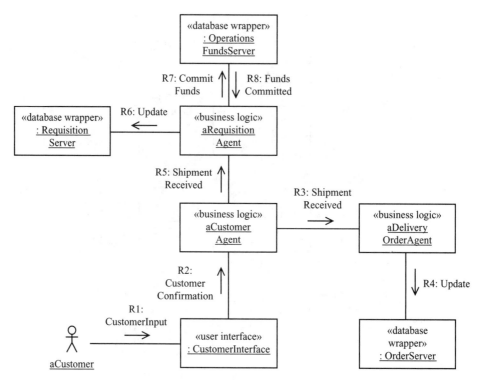

Figure 22.10   *Collaboration diagram for Confirm Delivery use case*

22.6.6   Collaboration Model for Send Invoice

Because the supplier confirmed earlier that the goods were sent to the customer in the Confirm Shipment use case, the Supplier Agent sends the invoice automatically, as shown in the collaboration diagram for the Send Invoice use case (see Figure 22.11). The arrival of the invoice at the customer organization causes the instantiation of an Invoice Agent to follow through on the invoice. The Invoice Agent subscribes to the Delivery Order Agent to be notified when the goods have been received. When notified of receipt of the goods, the Invoice Agent queries the Contracts Server and Operations Funds Server. If both responses are positive, the Invoice Agent authorizes payment and sends the invoice to the Accounts Payable Server, which updates the account. The Invoice Agent then sends the electronic payment to the customer's Bank Server and the invoice status to the supplier. The steps are as follows:

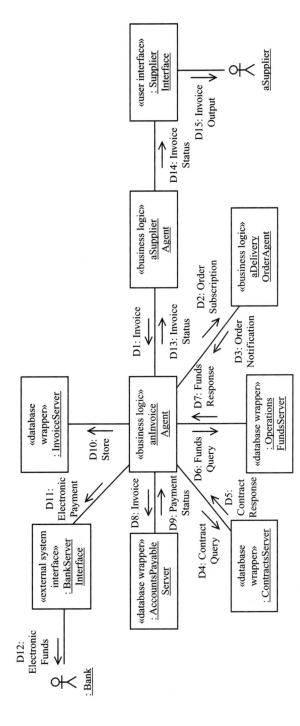

Figure 22.11 *Collaboration diagram for Send Invoice use case*

D1: The Supplier Agent sends the invoice information to the Invoice Agent.

D2: The Invoice Agent subscribes to the Delivery Order Agent.

D3: The Delivery Order Agent notifies the Invoice Agent that the goods have been received.

D4: The Invoice Agent sends a contract query to the Contracts Server.

D5: The Contracts Server confirms the contract.

D6: The Invoice Agent sends a funds query to the Operations Funds Server.

D7: The Operations Funds Server confirms that the funds are available and committed.

D8: The Invoice Agent sends the invoice to the Accounts Payable Server.

D9: The Accounts Payable Server sends the payment status to the Invoice Agent.

D10: The Invoice Agent stores the invoice at the Invoice Server.

D11: The Invoice Agent sends the electronic payment to the customer's bank via the Bank Server Interface.

D12: Bank Server Interface sends the electronic funds to the customer's bank for payment to the supplier.

D13: The Invoice Agent sends the invoice status to the Supplier Agent.

D14: The Supplier Agent sends the invoice status to the Supplier Interface.

D15: The Supplier Interface displays the invoice status to the Supplier.

22.7 Distributed Software Architecture

The collaboration diagrams are now merged to create the initial software architecture for the Agent-based Electronic Commerce System, which is depicted as a consolidated collaboration diagram in Figure 22.12. This diagram depicts the client, agent, and server objects from the individual use-case-based collaboration diagrams, as well as all their interactions.

Next, the distributed software architecture is developed and depicted on a concurrent collaboration diagram, as shown in Figure 22.13. In this highly distributed application, all the objects are active and all communication is by messages.

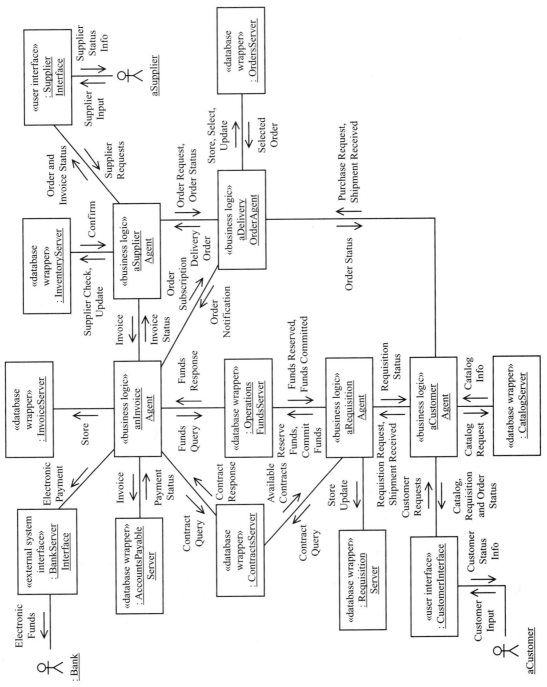

Figure 22.12 *Consolidated collaboration diagram in Agent-based Electronic Commerce System*

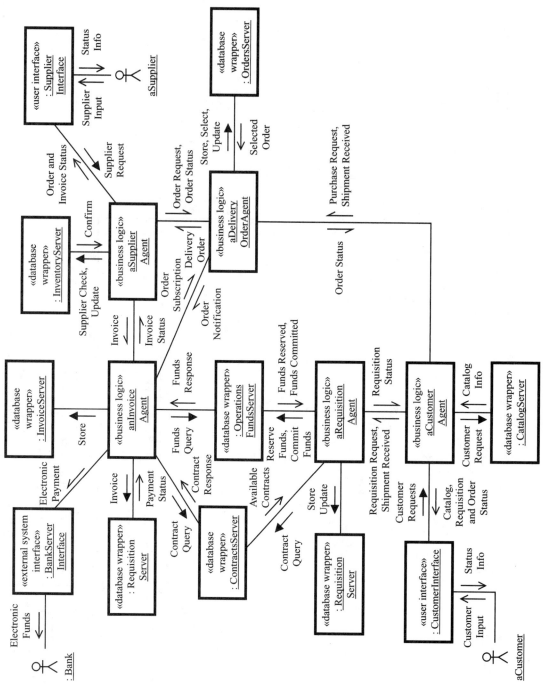

Figure 22.13 *Concurrent collaboration diagram in Agent-based Electronic Commerce System*

Message communication between user interface objects and agents is synchronous with reply, as are messages between the agents and servers. For greater flexibility, all message communication between cooperating agents is asynchronous.

Figure 22.14 shows the subsystem collaboration diagram, where the objects from the previous figure have been allocated to subsystems. There are three major subsystems. There is one instance of the Customer Organization Subsystem per customer organization, one instance of the Supplier Organization Subsystem per supplier organization, and one instance of the Bank Subsystem per bank. The banks are actually outside the scope of the Electronic Commerce System, although they play an important role because all electronic funds transfers between customers and supplier are through the banks. The message communication shown on Figure 22.14 is between objects in different subsystems, but corresponds to the message communication shown in Figure 22.13.

Figure 22.14 shows that the Customer Organization Subsystem is composed of several subsystems. There is the Payment Subsystem, which is an aggregate subsystem consisting of the Invoice Server, the Accounts Payable Server, the Bank Server Interface, and the Invoice Agent. The Contract Subsystem is also an aggregate subsystem consisting of the Contracts Server, the Operations Funds Server, the Requisition Server, and the Requisition Agent. The Customer Agent Subsystem is a coordinator subsystem consisting of the Customer Agent only. The Customer Interface Subsystem is a user interface subsystem and consists of the Customer Interface only. The message communication between the subsystems is also shown. All asynchronous communication is between agents in different subsystems.

The Supplier Organization Subsystem is also composed of several subsystems. There are three server subsystems, including the Catalog Subsystem, which consists of the Catalog Server only, and the Inventory Subsystem, which consists of the Inventory Server only. The Order Subsystem consists of the Orders Server and the Delivery Order Agent. There is also a Supplier Agent Subsystem, which consists of the Supplier Agent only, and the Supplier Interface Subsystem, which consists of the Supplier Interface only.

The subsystems may also be depicted on a subsystem class diagram, as shown in Figure 22.15, which shows the multiplicity of associations between the subsystems. Thus, each Customer Organization Subsystem has one instance each of the Payment and Contract Subsystems and multiple instances of the Customer Agent and Customer Interface Subsystems, with a one-to-one association between the Customer Agent and Customer Interface Subsystems. Each Supplier Organization Subsystem has one instance each of the Inventory,

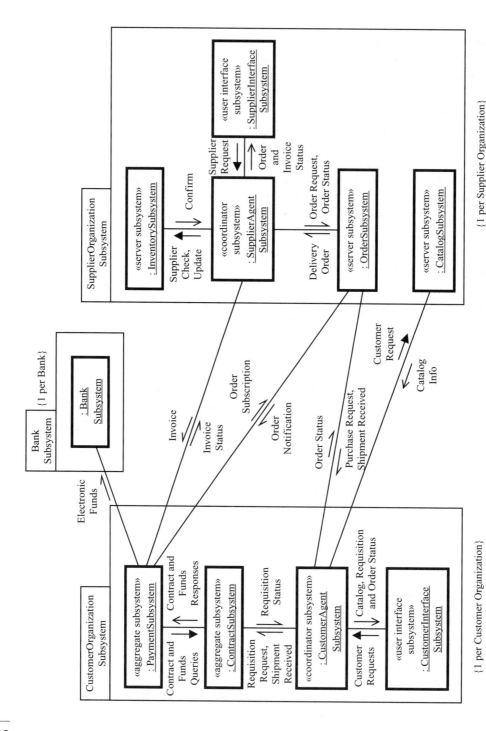

Figure 22.14 *Subsystem Collaboration diagram in Agent-based Electronic Commerce System*

{1 per Supplier Organization}

{1 per Bank}

{1 per Customer Organization}

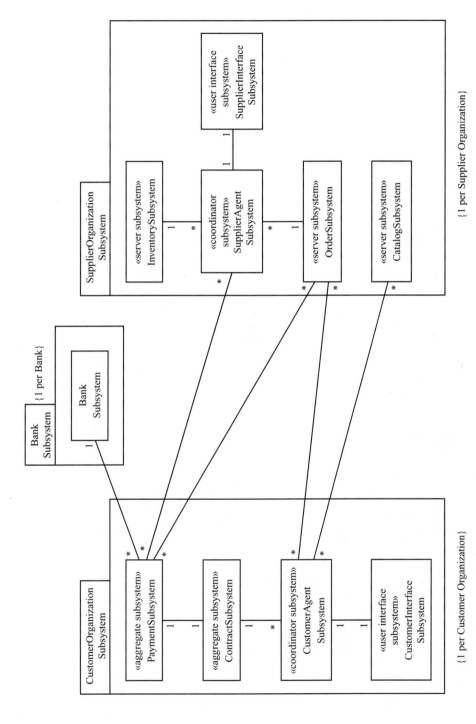

{1 per Supplier Organization}

{1 per Customer Organization}

Figure 22.15 *Subsystem Class diagram in Agent-based Electronic Commerce System*

733

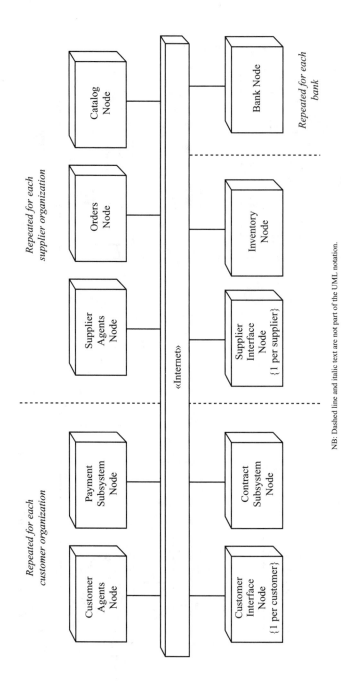

NB: Dashed line and italic text are not part of the UML notation.

Figure 22.16 *Deployment diagram for Agent-based Electronic Commerce System*

Catalog, and Order Subsystems and multiple instances of the Supplier Agent and Supplier Interface Subsystems, with a one-to-one association between the Supplier Agent and Supplier Interface Subsystems.

The Agent-based Electronic Commerce System is highly distributed, as shown in the deployment diagram in Figure 22.16, which shows multiple nodes at each customer and supplier organization, as well as a bank node for each bank. For each Customer Organization Subsystem and Supplier Organization Subsystem, there are nodes corresponding to the subsystems depicted in Figure 22.15. One instance of the Customer Interface and Supplier Interface subsystems exists for each individual customer and supplier, respectively.

The Customer Interface and Supplier Interface user interface objects could be implemented as Java applets that are downloaded from Web servers to run on client nodes in the distributed configuration. There is one Customer Agent for each customer client and one Supplier Agent for each supplier client. The agent objects execute on the same node as the Web servers from which the applets are downloaded. The agents can then communicate with other servers and agents executing on other nodes.

Conventions and Alternative Notations

T his appendix describes the conventions used in this book. It also describes alternative UML notations for stereotypes and active objects.

A.1 Conventions Used in This Book

For improved readability, the conventions used for names of classes, objects, and so on, as depicted on the figures are sometimes different from the descriptions of the same names in the text. In the figures, examples are shown in Times Roman font. However, in the body of the text, examples are shown in `Courier` font to distinguish them from the regular font. The conventions used in the book vary, depending on the phase of the project. The conventions for capitalization are different in the analysis model (which is less formal) than in the design model (which is more formal).

A.1.1 Requirements Modeling

Use cases are shown in `Courier` with initial uppercase and spaces in multi-word names, e.g., `Withdraw Funds`.

A.1.2 Analysis Modeling

The naming conventions for the analysis model are as follows.

Classes

Classes are shown in `Courier` with initial letter uppercase. In the figures, there are no spaces in multi-word names, such as `CheckingAccount`. However, in the text, spacing is introduced to improve the readability: `Checking Account`.

Attributes are shown as initial letter lowercase, e.g., `balance`. For multi-word attributes, there are no spaces between the words in the figure, although spaces are introduced in the text. The first word of the multi-word name is initial letter lowercase; subsequent words are initial letter uppercase, e.g., `account Number`.

The type of the attribute is initial letter uppercase, such as `Boolean`, `Integer`, or `Real`.

Objects

Objects may be depicted in various ways. They are always underlined in the figures but they are not underlined in the text. Furthermore, an object may be depicted as

- **An individual named object.** In this case, the first letter of the first word is lowercase and subsequent words are first letter uppercase. In the figures, the objects appear as <u>aCheckingAccount</u> and <u>anotherCheckingAccount</u>. In the text, these objects would appear as `a Checking Account` and `another Checking Account`.

- **An individual unnamed object.** Some objects are shown in the figures as class instances without a given object name, such as <u>:CheckingAccount</u>. In the text, this object is referred to as `Checking Account`. For improved readability, the colon is removed and a space is introduced between the individual words of a multi-word name.

This means that, depending on how the object is depicted in the figures, an object will sometimes appear in the text with a first word initial letter uppercase and sometimes with a first word initial letter lowercase.

Messages

In the analysis model, messages are always depicted as simple messages (see Figure 2.11) because no decision has yet been made about the message type. Messages are depicted with initial letter uppercase. Multi-word messages are shown with spaces, such as `Simple Message Name`.

Statechart Notation

States, events, conditions, actions, and activities are all shown with initial letter uppercase and spaces in multi-word names, for example, the state `Waiting for PIN`, the event `Cash Dispensed`, and the action `Dispense Cash`.

A.1.3   Design Modeling

The naming conventions for the design model are as follows:

Active and Passive Classes

The naming conventions for active classes (task types) and passive classes are the same as for classes in the analysis model.

Active and Passive Objects

The naming conventions for active objects (tasks) and passive objects are the same as for objects in the analysis model.

Messages

In the design model, the first letter of the first word of the message is lowercase and subsequent words are first letter uppercase. In the figures, there is no space between words, as in `alarmMessage`. However, in the text, a space is introduced for improved readability, as in `alarm Message`.

Message parameters are shown as initial letter lowercase, for example, the message parameter `speed`. For multi-word attributes, there are no spaces between the words in the figure, although spaces are introduced in the text. The first word of the multi-word name is initial letter lowercase and subsequent words are initial letter uppercase, for example, the message parameter `cumulativeDistance` in the figure and `cumulative Distance` in the text.

A.2   Alternative Notation for Stereotypes

The UML **stereotype** notation allows a modeler to tailor a UML modeling element to a specific problem. In UML, stereotypes are depicted in guillemets usually within the modeling element (e.g., class or object), as depicted in Figure A.1 (alternative a). However, the UML also allows stereotypes to be depicted as symbols. One of the most common such representations was introduced by Jacobson [1992] and is used in the Unified Software Development Process [Jacobson, Booch,

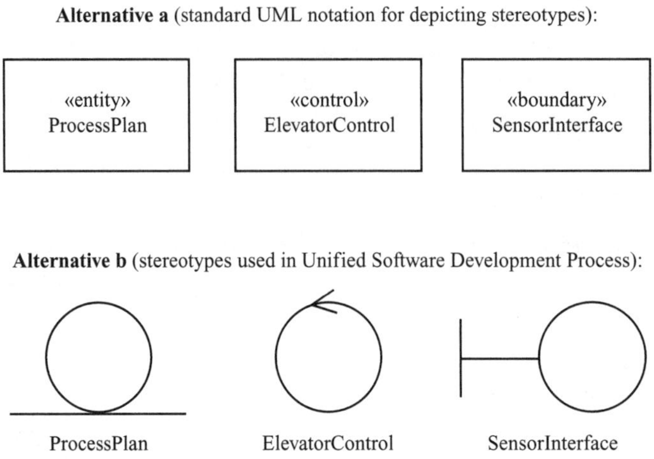

Alternative a (standard UML notation for depicting stereotypes):

| «entity»
ProcessPlan | «control»
ElevatorControl | «boundary»
SensorInterface |

Alternative b (stereotypes used in Unified Software Development Process):

ProcessPlan   ElevatorControl   SensorInterface

Figure A.1   *Alternative notations for UML stereotypes*

and Rumbaugh 1999] during analysis modeling. Stereotypes are used to represent «entity» classes, «boundary» classes (which are equivalent to «interface» classes in COMET) and «control» classes. Figure A.1 (alternative b) depicts the Process Plan «entity» class, the Elevator Control «control» class, and the Sensor Interface «boundary» class, using Jacobson's stereotype symbols.

A.3   Alternative Notation for Active Objects

This book has used the standard UML notation for **active objects** (referred to as **tasks** in COMET) and **passive objects**. In UML, an active object is depicted as a box with a thick border, and a passive object is depicted as a box with a thin border (see Chapter 2). However, some CASE tools do not support the standard UML notation for active objects, in which case no visual distinction is made between active and passive objects. In COMET, the term **task** is not usually part of the stereotype name for an active object. As depicted in Figure A.2 (alternative a), the thick border of the Report Generator «periodic» object visually identifies this to be a periodic task. If such visual distinction is not supported, the alternative is to insert "task" into the stereotype name. The object in Figure A.2 (alternative b) has a thin border; however, the stereotype «periodic task» identifies Report Generator to be an active object.

Alternative a (standard UML notation for depicting active objects):

«periodic»
: Report
Generator

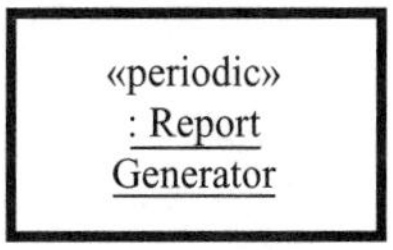

Alternative b (may be used to depict active objects if standard UML not supported):

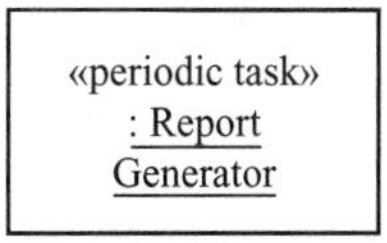
«periodic task»
: Report
Generator

Figure A.2 *Alternative notations for UML active objects (tasks)*

Glossary

Abstract class: A class that cannot be directly instantiated [Booch, Rumbaugh, and Jacobson 1998].

Abstract data type: A data type defined by the operations that manipulate it, thus hiding its representation details.

Abstract interface specification: A specification that defines the external view of the information hiding class, that is, all the information required by the user of the class.

Abstract operation: An operation that is declared in an *abstract class* but not implemented.

Action: A computation that executes as a result of a *state transition*.

Active object: An autonomous object that has its own thread of control; a concurrent task. See *Task*.

Activity: A computation that executes for the duration of a *state*.

Actor: An outside user or related set of users who interact with the system [Rumbaugh, Booch, and Jacobson 1999].

Aggregate class: A class that represents the "whole" in an aggregation relationship [Booch, Rumbaugh, and Jacobson 1998].

Aggregate subsystem: A logical grouping of lower-level subsystems and/or objects.

Aggregation: A whole/part relationship.

Algorithm object: An object that encapsulates an algorithm used in the problem domain.

Analog data: Continuous data that can in principle have an infinite number of values.

Analysis modeling: A phase of the COMET object-oriented software life cycle in which static and dynamic modeling are performed. See also *Static modeling, Dynamic modeling*.

Aperiodic task: A task that is activated on demand. Same as *Asynchronous task*.

Application logic object: An object that hides the details of the application logic separately from the data being manipulated.

Association: A relationship between two or more classes.

Asynchronous I/O device interface task: A task that interfaces to an I/O device and is activated by interrupts from that device.

Asynchronous I/O device: An I/O device that generates an interrupt when it has produced some input or when it has finished processing an output operation.

Asynchronous message communication: A form of communication in which a producer task sends a message to a consumer task and does not wait for a response; a message queue could potentially build up between the tasks. Also referred to as *loosely coupled message communication*.

Asynchronous task: A task that is activated on demand.

Behavioral analysis: A strategy to help determine how the objects that participate in a use case interact with each other. Also referred to as *dynamic analysis*.

Behavioral model: Model that describes the responses of the system to the inputs it receives from the external environment. Also referred to as *dynamic model*.

Binary semaphore: A Boolean variable used to enforce mutual exclusion.

Black box specification method: A specification that describes the externally visible characteristics of the system.

Broadcast communication: A form of group communication in which unsolicited messages are sent to all recipients.

Brokered communication: Message communication in a distributed object environment in which clients and servers interact via an object broker. See *Object broker*.

Boundary object: Same as *interface object*.

Business logic object: An object that encapsulates the business rules (business specific application logic) for processing a client request.

Callback: An operation handle sent by a *client* in an asynchronous request to a *server* and used by the server to respond to the client request.

Class: An object type; hence, a template for objects. An implementation of an abstract data type.

Class diagram: A UML diagram that depicts the static view of a system in terms of classes and the relationships between classes.

Class interface specification: A specification that defines the externally visible view of a class, including the specification of the operations provided by the class.

Class structuring criteria: See *Object structuring criteria*.

Client: A requester of services in a *client/server* system.

Client/server system: A system that consists of clients that request services and one or more servers that provide services.

Collaboration diagram: A UML *interaction diagram* that depicts a dynamic view of a system in which objects interact with each other by using messages.

COM (Component Object Model): A Microsoft component technology that provides a framework for application interoperation in a Windows environment.

COMET (Concurrent Object Modeling and architectural design mEThod): A software design method for concurrent, distributed and real-time applications.

Completion time theorem: A real-time scheduling theorem: For a set of independent periodic tasks, if each task meets its first deadline when all tasks are started at the same time, the deadlines will be met for any combination of start times.

Component: An active self-contained object with a well-defined interface, capable of being used in different applications from that for which it was originally designed.

Component based system: A system in which an infrastructure is provided that is specifically intended to accommodate preexisting components.

Composite subsystem: A *component* subsystem that encapsulates the objects it contains.

Composite task: A task that contains nested objects.

Composition: A stronger form of whole/part relationship than an aggregation; the part objects are created, live, and die together with the composite (whole) object.

Computer Assisted Software Engineering (CASE) tool: A software tool supporting a software engineering method or notation.

Concrete class: A class that can be directly instantiated [Booch, Rumbaugh, and Jacobson 1998].

Concurrent (as in problem, processing, system, or application): Many activities happening in parallel, where the order of incoming events is not usually predictable and is often overlapping; a system or application with many threads of control.

Concurrent collaboration diagram: A *collaboration diagram* that depicts a network of concurrent tasks and their interfaces in the form of loosely coupled and tightly coupled message communication, event synchronization, and access to passive information hiding objects.

Concurrent process: Same as *Concurrent task, Task.*

Concurrent server: A *server* that services multiple *client* requests in parallel.

Concurrent task: See *Task.*

Condition: The value of a Boolean variable that represents some aspect of the system that can be true or false over some finite interval of time.

Connector: An object that encapsulates the interconnection protocol between two or more components.

Consolidated collaboration diagram: A synthesis of several *collaboration diagrams* depicting all the objects and interactions shown on the individual diagrams.

Control clustering: A task structuring criterion by which a control object is combined into a task with the objects it controls.

Control object: An object that provides overall coordination for the objects that participate in a use case.

Control task: A task that makes decisions that control the execution of other tasks; the task conceptually executes a sequential *statechart*.

Coordinator object: An overall decision-making object that determines the overall sequencing for a collection of related objects and is not state-dependent.

CORBA (Common Object Request Broker Architecture): An open systems standard developed by the Object Management Group for *middleware* technology; the standard allows communication between distributed objects on heterogeneous platforms.

Critical section: The section of an object's internal logic that is mutually exclusive.

Data abstraction: An approach for defining a data structure or data type by the set of operations that manipulate it, thus separating and hiding the representation details.

Data abstraction class: A class that encapsulates a data structure or data type, thereby hiding the representation details; operations provided by the class manipulate the hidden data.

Data replication: The same data is duplicated in more than one location in a distributed application to speed up access to the data.

Database wrapper class: A class that hides how to access data stored in a database.

Deadlock: A situation in which two or more tasks are suspended indefinitely because each task is waiting for a resource acquired by another task.

Deployment diagram: A UML diagram that shows the physical configuration of the system in terms of physical nodes and physical connections between the nodes, such as network connections.

Design concept: A fundamental idea that can be applied to designing a system.

Design method: A systematic approach for creating a design. It helps identify the design decisions to be made, the order in which to make them, and the criteria used in making them.

Design modeling: A phase of the COMET object-oriented software life cycle in which the software architecture of the system is designed.

Design notation: A graphical, symbolic, or textual means of describing a design.

Design pattern: A description of a recurring design problem to be solved, a solution to the problem, and the context in which that solution works.

Design strategy: An overall plan and direction for performing a design.

Device interface object: An information hiding object that hides the characteristics of an I/O device and presents a virtual device interface to its users.

Discrete data: Data that arrives at specific time intervals.

Distributed: A system or application that is concurrent in nature and executes in an environment consisting of multiple nodes, which are in geographically different locations.

Distributed kernel: A nucleus of an operating system that supports distributed applications.

Distributed processing environment: A system configuration where several geographically dispersed nodes are interconnected by means of a local area or wide area network.

Distributed server: A *server* whose functionality is spread over several nodes.

Dynamic analysis: A strategy to help determine how the objects that participate in a use case interact with each other. Also referred to as *behavioral analysis*.

Dynamic modeling: A view of a problem or system in which control and sequencing is considered, either within an object, by means of a finite state machine, or by considering the sequence of interaction among objects.

Encapsulation: Same as *Information hiding*.

Entity object: A long-living object, in many cases persistent, that encapsulates data.

Entry action: An *action* that is performed on entry into a *state*.

Environment simulator: A tool that models the inputs arriving from the external entities that interface to the system and feeds them to the systems being tested.

Event (in *concurrent processing*): An external or internal stimulus used for synchronization purposes. It can be an external interrupt, a timer expiration, an internal signal, or an internal message.

Event (on *interaction diagram*): A stimulus that arrives at an object at a point in time.

Event (on *statechart*): The occurrence of a stimulus that can cause a state transition on a statechart.

Event sequence analysis: Performance analysis of the sequence of tasks that need to be executed to service a given external event.

Event sequence diagram: A diagram that identifies the sequence of tasks required to process an external event; may be depicted on a *collaboration diagram* or *sequence diagram*.

Event sequencing logic: Same as *task event sequencing logic*.

Event synchronization: Control of task activation by means of signals. Three types of event synchronization are possible: external interrupts, timer expiration, and internal signals from other tasks.

Event trace: A time-ordered description of each external input and the time at which it occurred.

Exit action: An *action* that is performed on exit from a *state.*

External class: A class that is outside the system and part of the external environment.

External event: An event from an external object, typically an interrupt from an external I/O device.

Finite state machine: A conceptual machine with a finite number of states and transitions that are caused by input events. The notation used to represent a finite state machine is a *state transition diagram, statechart,* or *state transition table.*

Formal method: A software engineering method that uses a formal specification language, that is, a language with mathematically defined syntax and semantics.

Generalization/specialization: A relationship in which common attributes and operations are abstracted into a superclass (generalized class) and are then inherited by subclasses (specialized classes).

I/O task structuring criteria: A category of the *task structuring criteria* that addresses how device interface objects are mapped to I/O tasks and when an I/O task is activated.

Incremental software development: An iterative approach to developing software in stages.

Information hiding: The concept of encapsulating software design decisions in objects in such a way that the object's interface reveals only what its users need to know.

Information hiding class: A class that is structured according to the information hiding concept. The class hides some aspect of the system and is accessed by means of operations.

Information hiding class specification: A specification of the external view of the information hiding class, including its operations.

Inheritance: A mechanism for sharing and reusing code between classes.

Interaction diagram: The name given to a UML diagram that depicts a dynamic view of a system in terms of objects and the sequence of messages passed between them; actually depicted on a UML *collaboration diagram* or UML *sequence diagram.*

Interface object: An object that is part of the application, which interfaces to the external environment. Also referred to as a *boundary object.*

Interface: The external specification of a *class, task,* or *component.*

Internal event: A means of synchronization between two tasks.

Internal task structuring criteria: A category of the *task structuring criteria* that addresses how internal objects are mapped to internal tasks and when an internal task is activated.

JavaBeans: A Java-based component technology.

Jini (Java Intelligent Network Infrastructure): A connection technology used in embedded systems and network-based computing applications for interconnecting computers and devices.

Loosely coupled message communication: A form of communication in which a producer task sends a message to a consumer task and does not wait for a response; a message queue could potentially build up between the tasks. Also referred to as *asynchronous message communication*.

Mathematical model: A mathematical representation of a system.

Message buffer and response connector: A connector object that encapsulates the communication mechanism for *tightly coupled (synchronous) message communication with reply*. See *Connector*.

Message buffer connector: A connector object that encapsulates the communication mechanism for *tightly coupled (synchronous) message communication without reply*. See *Connector*.

Message dictionary: Used to define all aggregate messages (depicted on interaction diagrams) that consist of several individual messages.

Message queue connector: A connector object that encapsulates the communication mechanism for *loosely coupled (asynchronous) message communication*. See *Connector*.

Message sequence description: A narrative description of the sequence of messages sent from source objects to destination objects, as depicted on a collaboration diagram or sequence diagram, describing what happens when each message arrives at a destination object.

Middleware: A layer of software that sits above the heterogeneous operating system to provide a uniform platform above which distributed applications can run [Bacon 1997].

Monitor: A data object that encapsulates data and has operations that are executed mutually exclusively.

Multicast communication A form of group communication in which subscribers receive event notifications. See *subscription/notification*.

Multiple instance task inversion: An optimization technique where all identical tasks of the same type are replaced by one task that performs the same service.

Multiple readers and writers: An algorithm that allows multiple readers to access a shared data repository concurrently; however, writers must have mutually exclusive access to update the data repository.

Mutual exclusion: Only allowing one task to have access to shared data at a time, which can be enforced by means of binary semaphores or through the use of monitors.

Mutually exclusive clustering: A task structuring criterion in which a group of objects are combined into a task because only one object is eligible to be executed at any one time.

Negotiated communication: A communication approach used in multi-agent systems to allow software agents to negotiate with each other so they can cooperatively make decisions.

Node: In a distributed environment, each node consists of one or more processors with shared memory.

Non-time-critical computationally intensive task: A low-priority compute-bound task that consumes spare CPU cycles.

Object: An instance of a class that contains both hidden data and operations on that data.

Object broker, object request broker: An intermediary in interactions between clients and servers.

Object structuring criteria: A set of heuristics for assisting a designer in structuring a system into objects.

Object-based design: A software design method based on the concept of *information hiding*.

Object-oriented analysis: An analysis method that emphasizes identifying real-world objects in the problem domain and mapping them to software objects.

Object-oriented design: A software design method based on the concept of objects, classes, and inheritance.

Operation: A specification of a function performed by a class. An access procedure or function provided by a class.

Package: A UML grouping of model elements.

Passive I/O device: A device that does not generate an interrupt on completion of an input or output operation. The input from a passive input device needs to be read either on a polled basis or on demand.

Passive I/O device interface task: A task that interfaces to a passive I/O device and either reads from it or writes to it on demand.

Passive object: An object that has no thread of control; an object with operations that are invoked directly or indirectly by *active objects*.

Performance analysis: A quantitative analysis of a real-time software design conceptually executing on a given hardware configuration with a given external workload applied to it.

Performance model: An abstraction of the real computer system behavior, developed for the purpose of gaining greater insight into the performance of the system, whether or not the system actually exists.

Periodic I/O device interface task: A task that interfaces to a passive I/O device and polls the device on a regular basis.

Periodic task: A task that is activated periodically (i.e., at regular, equally spaced intervals of time) by a timer event.

Petri net: A dynamic mathematical model with a graphical notation consisting of places and transitions, used for modeling concurrent systems.

Priority ceiling protocol: An algorithm that provides bounded priority inversion; that is, at most one lower priority task can block a higher priority task. See *Priority inversion*.

Priority inversion: A case where a task cannot execute, because it is blocked by a lower priority task.

Priority message queue: A queue where each message has an associated priority. The consumer always accepts higher priority messages before lower priority messages.

Process: (as in concurrent processing): See *Task*.

Pseudocode: A form of structured English used to describe the algorithmic details of an object.

Queuing model: A mathematical representation of a computer system that analyzes contention for limited resources.

Rate monotonic algorithm: A real-time scheduling algorithm that assigns higher priorities to tasks with shorter periods.

Real-time: A problem, system, or application that is concurrent in nature and has timing constraints whereby incoming events must be processed within a given timeframe.

Real-time scheduling theory: A theory for priority-based scheduling of concurrent tasks with hard deadlines. It addresses how to determine whether a group of tasks, whose individual CPU utilization is known, will meet their deadlines.

Remote method invocation (RMI): A *middleware* technology that allows distributed Java objects to communicate with each other.

Requirements modeling: A phase of the COMET object-oriented software life cycle in which the functional requirements of the system are defined in terms of actors and use cases.

Resource monitor task: A task that ensures sequential access to a resource.

RMI: See *Remote method invocation*.

Scenario: A specific path through a use case.

Semaphore: See *Binary semaphore*.

Sequence diagram: A UML *interaction diagram* that depicts a dynamic view of a system in which the objects participating in the interaction are depicted horizontally, the vertical dimension represents time, and the sequence of message interactions is depicted from top to bottom.

Sequential (as in problem, system, or application): A case where activities happen in strict sequence; a system or application with only one thread of control.

Sequential clustering: A task structuring criterion in which objects that are constrained to execute sequentially are mapped to a task.

Sequential server: A *server* that completes one *client* request before it starts servicing the next.

Sequential task inversion: An optimization technique where tasks are combined such that the producer task calls an operation provided by the consumer rather than sending it a message.

Server: A provider of services that are requested by *clients*.

Simulation model: An algorithmic representation of a system, reflecting system structure and behavior, that explicitly recognizes the passage of time, hence providing a means of analyzing the behavior of the system over time.

Software architecture: A high-level design that describes the overall structure of a system in terms of components and their interconnections, separate from the internal details of the individual components.

Software decision class: A class that hides a software design decision that is considered likely to change.

State: A recognizable situation that exists over an interval of time.

State transition: A change in state that is caused by an input event.

State transition diagram: A graphical representation of a finite state machine in which the nodes represent states and the arcs represent transitions between states.

State transition table: A tabular representation of a finite state machine.

Statechart, statechart diagram: A UML hierarchical state transition diagram in which the nodes represent states and the arcs represent transitions between states.

State-dependent control object: An information hiding object that hides the details of a finite state machine; that is, the object encapsulates a statechart, a state transition diagram, or the contents of a state transition table.

Static modeling: A static, structural view of a problem or system.

Stereotype: A stereotype defines a new building block that is derived from an existing UML modeling element but is tailored to the modeler's problem [Booch, Rumbaugh, and Jacobson 1998].

Subscription/notification: A form of group communication in which subscribers receive event notifications. See *Multicast communication*.

Substate: A *state* that is part of a superstate.

Subsystem: A significant part of the whole system; provides a subset of the overall system functionality.

Subsystem collaboration diagram: A high-level *collaboration diagram* depicting the subsystems and their interactions.

Subsystem structuring criteria: A set of heuristics for assisting a designer in structuring a system into subsystems.

Superstate: A composite state.

Synchronous message communication: A form of communication in which a producer task sends a message to a consumer task and then immediately waits for an acknowledgment. Also referred to as *tightly coupled message communication*.

Synchronous message communication with reply: A form of communication in which a producer task sends a message to a consumer task and then waits for a reply. Also referred to as *tightly coupled message communication with reply*.

Synchronous message communication without reply: A form of communication in which a producer task sends a message to a consumer task and then waits for acceptance of the message by the consumer. Also referred to as *tightly coupled message communication without reply*.

System context class diagram: A *class diagram* that depicts the relationships between the system (depicted as one aggregate class) and the external classes outside the system.

System interface object: An object that hides the interface to an external system or subsystem.

Task (also *concurrent task, thread, process*): An active object that has its own thread of control. A task represents the execution of a sequential program or a sequential component of a concurrent program. Each task deals with a sequential thread of execution; there is no concurrency within a task.

Task architecture: A description of the concurrent tasks in a system or subsystem in terms of their interfaces and interconnections.

Task behavior specification (TBS): A specification that describes a concurrent task's interface, structure, timing characteristics, relative priority, errors detected, and *task event sequencing logic*.

Task clustering criteria: A category of the *task structuring criteria* that addresses whether and how objects should be grouped into concurrent tasks.

Task event sequencing logic: A description of how a task responds to each of its message or event inputs, and, in particular, the output generated as a result of each input.

Task interface: A message, event, or access to a passive information hiding object.

Task inversion: An optimization concept that originated in Jackson Structured Programming and Jackson System Development, whereby the tasks in a system can be merged in a systematic way.

Task inversion criteria: A category of the *task structuring criteria* that is based on the concept of *task inversion*.

Task priority criteria: A category of the *task structuring criteria* that addresses the importance of executing a given task relative to others.

Task structuring: A stage in software design where the objective is to structure a concurrent application into concurrent tasks and define the task interfaces.

Task structuring criteria: A set of heuristics for assisting a designer in structuring a system into concurrent tasks.

TBS: See *Task behavior specification*.

Temporal clustering: A task structuring criterion by which activities that are not sequentially dependent but are activated by the same event are grouped into a task.

Temporal task inversion: The case where two or more periodic tasks—periodic internal, periodic I/O, and/or temporally clustered—are combined into one task for optimization purposes.

Thread: Same as *Task*.

Tightly coupled message communication: A form of communication in which a producer task sends a message to a consumer task and then immediately waits for an acknowledgment. Also referred to as *synchronous message communication*.

Tightly coupled message communication with reply: A form of communication in which a producer task sends a message to a consumer task and then waits for a reply. Also referred to as *synchronous message communication with reply*.

Tightly coupled message communication without reply: A form of communication in which a producer task sends a message to a consumer task and then waits for acceptance of the message by the consumer. Also referred to as *synchronous message communication without reply*.

Time-critical task: A task that needs to meet a hard deadline.

Timed Petri net: A *Petri net* that allows finite times to be associated with the firing of transitions.

Timer event: A stimulus used for the periodic activation of an active object, for example, a task.

Timer object: A control object that is activated by an external timer.

Timing diagram: A diagram that shows the time-ordered execution sequence of a group of tasks.

Transaction: A request from a *client* to a *server* that must be completed in its entirety or not at all.

Two-phase commit protocol: An algorithm used in distributed applications to synchronize updates to ensure that an atomic transaction is either committed or aborted.

UML (The Unified Modeling Language): A language for visualizing, specifying, constructing, and documenting the artifacts of a software-intensive system [Booch, Rumbaugh, and Jacobson 1998].

Use case: A description of a sequence of interactions between one or more *actors* and the system.

Use case diagram: A UML diagram that shows a set of *use cases* and *actors* and their relationships [Booch, Rumbaugh, and Jacobson 1998].

Use case model: A description of the functional requirements of the system in terms of *actors* and *use cases*.

Use case package: A group of related *use cases*.

User interface object: An object that hides the details of the interface to a human user.

User interface task: A task that interacts sequentially with a user.

Utilization bound theorem: A real-time scheduling theorem that states the conditions under which a set of n independent periodic tasks scheduled by the *rate monotonic algorithm* will always meet their deadlines.

Visibility: Defines whether an element of a class (attribute or operation) is visible from outside the class.

Wrapper object: A distributed application object that handles the communication and management of client requests to legacy applications [Mowbray and Ruh 1997].

Bibliography

Agha, G. *Actors: A Model of Concurrent Computation in Distributed Systems.* Cambridge, Mass.: MIT Press, 1986.

Agha, G. "Abstraction and Modularity Mechanisms for Concurrent Computing." *Research Directions in Concurrent Object-Oriented Programming.* Edited by G. Agha, P. Wegner, and A. Yonezawa. Cambridge, Mass.: MIT Press, 1993.

Agresti, W. W. *New Paradigms for Software Development.* Los Alamitos, Calif.: IEEE Computer Society Press, 1986.

Awad, M., J. Kuusela, and J. Ziegler. *Object-Oriented Technology for Real-Time Systems.* Englewood Cliffs, N.J.: Prentice Hall, 1996.

Bacon, J. *Concurrent Systems.* 2d ed. Reading, Mass.: Addison-Wesley, 1997.

Barnes, J. *Programming in Ada 95.* Reading, Mass.: Addison-Wesley, 1995.

Basili, B. R., and A. J. Turner. "Iterative Enhancement: A Practical Technique for Software Development." *IEEE Trans. Software Eng.* SE-1, no. 4 (December 1975): 390–396.

Bass, L., P. Clements, and R. Kazman. *Software Architecture in Practice.* Reading, Mass.: Addison-Wesley, 1998.

Beizer, B. *Software System Testing and Quality Assurance.* 2d ed. New York: Van Nostrand Reinhold, 1990.

Beizer, B. *Black-Box Testing: Techniques for Functional Testing of Software and Systems.* New York: John Wiley & Sons, 1995.

Berners-Lee, T., R. Cailliau, A. Loutonen, H. F. Nielsen, and A. Secret. "The World-Wide Web." *Communications of the ACM* 37 (1994): 76–82.

Bic, L., and A. C. Shaw. *The Logical Design of Operating Systems.* Englewood Cliffs, N.J.: Prentice Hall, 1988.

Blaha, J. M., and W. Premerlani. *Object-Oriented Modeling and Design for Database Applications.* Englewood Cliffs, N.J.: Prentice Hall, 1998.

Boehm, B. W. "Software Engineering." *IEEE Transactions on Computers* 25, no. 12 (December 1976): 1226–1241.

Boehm, B. W. *Software Engineering Economics.* Englewood Cliffs, N.J.: Prentice Hall, 1981.

Boehm, B. W. "A Spiral Model of Software Development and Enhancement." *IEEE Computer* 21, no. 5 (May 1988): 61–72.

Boehm, B. W., and F. Belz. *Experiences with the Spiral Model as a Process Model Generator.* Proceedings 5th International Software Process Workshop. N.p., 1989.

Booch, G. "Object Oriented Development." *IEEE Transactions on Software Engineering* 12, no. 2 (February 1986): 211–221.

Booch, G. *Object-Oriented Design with Applications.* Reading, Mass.: Addison-Wesley, 1991.

Booch, G. *Object-Oriented Design with Applications.* 2d ed. Reading, Mass.: Addison-Wesley, 1994.

Booch, G., J. Rumbaugh, and I. Jacobson. *The Unified Modeling Language User Guide.* Reading, Mass.: Addison-Wesley, 1998.

Box, D. *Essential COM.* Reading, Mass.: Addison-Wesley, 1998.

Brinch Hansen, P. *Operating System Principles.* Englewood Cliffs, N.J.: Prentice Hall, 1973.

Brooks, F. *The Mythical Man-Month.* Anniversary ed. Reading, Mass.: Addison-Wesley, 1995.

Budgen, D. *Software Design.* Reading, Mass.: Addison-Wesley International Computer Science Series, 1994.

Buhr, R. J. A., and R. S. Casselman. *Use Case Maps for Object-Oriented Systems.* Englewood Cliffs, N.J.: Prentice Hall, 1996.

Burns, A., and A. J. Wellings. *Real-Time Systems and their Programming Languages.* 2d ed. Reading, Mass.: Addison-Wesley, 1996.

Buschmann, F., R. Meunier, H. Rohnert, and P. Sommerlad. *Pattern Oriented Software Architecture: A System of Patterns.* New York: John Wiley & Sons, 1996.

Cameron, J. "An Overview of JSD." *IEEE Transactions on Software Engineering* 12, no. 2 (February 1986): 222–240.

Cameron, J. *JSP & JSD: The Jackson Approach to Software Development.* 2d ed. Los Alamitos, Calif.: IEEE Computer Society Press, 1989.

Chen, P. "The Entity Relationship Model—Towards a Unified View of Data." *ACM Transactions on Database Systems* 1, no. 1 (1976): 9–36.

Coad, P., and E. Yourdon. *Object-Oriented Analysis.* Englewood Cliffs, N.J.: Prentice Hall, 1991.

Coad, P., and E. Yourdon. *Object-Oriented Design*. Englewood Cliffs, N.J.: Prentice Hall, 1992.

Cobb, R. H., and H. D. Mills. "Engineering Software under Statistical Quality Control." *IEEE Software* 7, no. 6 (November 1990): 44–54.

Cobryn, C. "UML 2001: A Standardization Odyssey." *Communications ACM* 42, no. 10 (October 1999): 29–37.

Coleman, D., P. Arnold, S. Bodoff, C. Dollin, H. Gilchrist, F. Hayes, and P. Jeremaes. *Object Oriented Development,—The Fusion Method*. Englewood Cliffs, N.J.: Prentice Hall, 1993.

Comer, D. *Computer Networks and Internets*. Englewood Cliffs, N.J.: Prentice Hall, 1999.

Coolahan, J., and N. Roussopoulos. "Timing Requirements for Time-Driven Systems Using Augmented Petri Nets." *IEEE Transactions on Software Engineering* 26, no. 9 (September 1983): 603–616.

Cooling, J. E. *Software Design for Real-Time Systems*. London: Chapman and Hall, 1991.

Cooling, J. E. *Real-Time Software Systems, An Introduction to Structured and Object-Oriented Design*. N.p.: International Thompson Computer Press, 1997.

Coulouris, G., J. Dollimore, and T. Kindberg. *Distributed Systems: Concepts and Design*. Reading, Mass.: Addison-Wesley International Computer Science Series, 1994.

Courtois, P. J., F. Heymans, and D. L. Parnas. "Concurrent Control with Readers and Writers." *Communications ACM* 10 (October 1971): 667–668.

Dahl, O., and C. A. R. Hoare. "Hierarchical Progam Structures." *Structured Programming*. Edited by O. Dahl, E. W. Dijkstra, and C. A. R. Hoare. London: Academic Press, 1972: 175–220.

David, R., and H. Alla. "Petri Nets for Modeling of Dynamic Systems—A Survey." *Automatica* 30, no. 2 (1994): 175–202.

Davis, A. *Software Requirements: Objects, Functions, and States*. Englewood Cliffs, N.J.: Prentice Hall, 1993.

Davis, A. *201 Principles of Software Development*. New York: McGraw Hill, 1995.

DeMarco, T. *Structured Analysis and System Specification*. Englewood Cliffs, N.J.: Prentice Hall, 1978.

Dijkstra, E. W. "Co-operating Sequential Processes." *Programming Languages*. Edited by F. Genuys. London: Academic Press, 1968: 43–112.

Dijkstra, E. W. "Notes on Structured Programming." *Structured Programming*. Edited by O. Dahl, E. W. Dijkstra, and C. A. R. Hoare. London: Academic Press, 1972: 1–72.

Douglass, B. P. *Doing Hard Time: UML, Objects, Frameworks, and Patterns in Real-Time Software Development*. Reading, Mass.: Addison-Wesley, 1999a.

Douglass, B. P. *Real-Time UML*. 2d ed. Reading, Mass.: Addison-Wesley, 1999b.

Elmstrom, R., R. Lintulampi, and M. Pezze. "Giving Semantics to SA/RT by Means of High-Level Timed Petri Nets." *Real-Time Systems* 5 (Netherlands), no.2–3 (May 1993): 249–271.

Eriksson, H. E., and M. Penker. *UML Toolkit*. New York: John Wiley & Sons, 1998.

Fagan, M. "Design and Code Inspections to Reduce Errors in Program Development." *IBM Systems Journal* 15, no. 3 (1976).

Fairley, R. *Software Engineering Concepts*. New York: McGraw Hill, 1985.

Faulk, S. R., and D. L. Parnas. "On Synchronization in Hard Real Time Systems." *Communications ACM* (March 1988).

Fowler, M., and K. Scott. *UML Distilled*. 2d ed. Reading, Mass.: Addison-Wesley, 1999.

Freeman, P. "The Context of Design." *Software Design Techniques*. 4th ed. Edited by P. Freeman and A. I. Wasserman. Silver Spring, Md.: IEEE Computer Society Press, 1983a.

Freeman, P. "The Nature of Design." *Software Design Techniques*. 4th ed. Edited by P. Freeman and A. I. Wasserman. Silver Spring, Md.: IEEE Computer Society Press, 1983b.

Freeman, P., and A. I. Wasserman, eds. *Software Design Techniques*. 4th ed. Silver Spring, Md.: IEEE Computer Society Press, 1983.

Gamma, E., R. Helm, R. Johnson, and J. Vlissides. *Design Patterns: Elements of Reusable Object-Oriented Software*. Reading, Mass.: Addison-Wesley, 1995.

Gane, C., and T. Sarson. *Structured Systems Analysis: Tools and Techniques*. Englewood Cliffs, N.J.: Prentice Hall, 1979.

Genesereth, M., and S. P. Ketchpel. "Software Agents." *CACM* 37 (1994): 48–53.

Glass, R. L., ed. *Real-Time Software*. Englewood Cliffs, N.J.: Prentice Hall, 1983.

Goldberg, A., and D. Robson. *Smalltalk-80: The Language and Its Implementation*. Reading, Mass.: Addison-Wesley, 1983.

Gomaa, H. "A Hybrid Simulation/Regression Model of a Virtual Storage Computer System." *The Computer Journal* (November 1981a).

Gomaa, H. *Prototyping as a Tool in the Specification of User Requirements*. Proceedings 5th International Conference on Software Engineering. Los Alamitos, Calif.: IEEE Computer Society Press, 1981b.

Gomaa, H. *The Impact of Rapid Prototyping on Specifying User Requirements*. Proceedings ACM Workshop on Rapid Prototyping. Columbia, Md.: April 1982a.

Gomaa, H. *A Partially Automated Method for Testing Interactive Systems*. Proceedings IEEE Conference on Computer Software and Applications (Compsac) Conference. Chicago, Ill.: November 1982b.

Gomaa, H. "A Software Design Method for Real Time Systems." *Communications ACM* 27, no. 9 (September 1984): 938–949.

Gomaa, H. "Prototypes—Keep Them or Throw Them Away?" *State of the Art Report on Prototyping*. Maidenhead, UK: Pergamon Infotech Ltd., 1986a, 41–54.

Gomaa, H. "Software Development of Real Time Systems." *Communications ACM* 29, no. 7 (July 1986b): 657–668.

Gomaa, H. "A Software Design Method for Distributed Real Time Applications." *Journal of Systems and Software* (February 1989a).

Gomaa, H. *Structuring Criteria for Real Time System Design*. Proceedings 11th International Conference on Software Engineering. Los Alamitos, Calif.: IEEE Computer Society Press, May 1989b.

Gomaa, H. *Software Design Methods for Concurrent and Real-Time Systems*. Reading, Mass.: Addison-Wesley, 1993.

Gomaa, H. "Concurrent Systems Design." *Encyclopedia of Software Engineering*. Edited by J. Marciniak. New York: John Wiley & Sons, 1994, 172–179.

Gomaa, H. "Reusable Software Requirements and Architectures for Families of Systems." *Journal of Systems and Software* (April 1995).

Gomaa, H. "Use Cases for Distributed Real-Time Software Architectures." *Journal of Parallel and Distributed Computing Practices* 1, no. 2 (1998): 1–14.

Gomaa, H. *Inter-Agent Communication in Cooperative Information Agent-Based Systems*. Proceedings Cooperative Information Agent Workshop. Berlin: Springer Verlag, 1999.

Gomaa, H., and G. Farrukh. *Automated Configuration of Distributed Applications from Reusable Software Architectures*. Proceedings IEEE International Conference on Automated Software Engineering. Lake Tahoe, Calif.: November 1997.

Gomaa, H., D. Menasce, and L. Kerschberg. "A Software Architectural Design Method for Large-Scale Distributed Information Systems." *Journal of Distributed Systems Engineering* (September 1996): 162–172.

Harel, D. "On Visual Formalisms." *CACM* 31, no. 5 (May 1988): 514–530.

Harel, D., and E. Gary. *Executable Object Modeling with Statecharts*. Proceedings 18th International Conference on Software Engineering. Berlin: March 1996.

Harel, D., and M. Politi. *Modeling Reactive Systems with Statecharts*. New York: McGraw Hill, 1998.

Hatley, D., and I. Pirbhai. *Strategies for Real Time System Specification*. New York: Dorset House, 1988.

Heninger, K. "Specifying Software Requirements for Complex Systems: New Techniques and Their Applications." *IEEE Transactions on Software Engineering* SE-6 no. 1 (January 1980): 2–13.

Hoare, C. A. R. "Monitors: An Operating System Structuring Concept." *Communications ACM* 17, no. 10 (October 1974): 549–557.

Hoare, C. A. R. *Communicating Sequential Processes*. Englewood Cliffs, N.J.: Prentice Hall, 1985.

Hofmeister, C., R. Nord, and D. Soni. *Applied Software Architecture*. Reading, Mass.: Addison-Wesley, 1999.

IEEE Standard Glossary of Software Engineering Terminology. IEEE/STD610.12–1990, Institute of Electrical and Electronic Engineers, 1990.

Jackson, M. *Principles of Program Design*. London: Academic Press, 1975.

Jackson, M. *System Development*. Englewood Cliffs, N.J.: Prentice Hall, 1983.

Jacobson, I. *Object-Oriented Software Engineering*. Reading, Mass.: Addison-Wesley, 1992.

Jacobson, I., G. Booch, and J. Rumbaugh. *The Unified Software Development Process*. Reading, Mass.: Addison-Wesley, 1999.

Jacobson, I., M. Griss, and P. Jonsson. *Software Reuse—Architecture, Process and Organization for Business Success*. Reading, Mass.: Addison-Wesley, 1997.

Jensen, K. "Coloured Petri Nets. Basic Concepts, Analysis Methods and Practical Use." Volume 1, *Basic Concepts. Monographs in Theoretical Computer Science*. Berlin: Springer-Verlag, Second corrected printing, 1997.

Kleinrock, L. *Queueing Systems*. Volume 1. New York: John Wiley & Sons, 1975.

Korth, H., and A. Silberschatz. *Database System Concepts*. 3d ed. New York: McGraw Hill, 1998.

Kramer, J., and J. Magee. "Dynamic Configuration for Distributed Systems." *IEEE Transactions on Software Engineering* 11, no. 4 (April 1985): 424–436.

Lamb, D. A. *Software Engineering: Planning for Change*. Englewood Cliffs, N.J.: Prentice Hall, 1988.

Larman, C. *Applying UML and Patterns*. Englewood Cliffs, N.J.: Prentice Hall, 1998.

Lea, D. *Concurrent Programming in Java: Design Principles and Patterns*. 2d ed. Reading, Mass.: Addison-Wesley, 1999.

Lehoczy, J. P., L. Sha, and Y. Ding. *The Rate Monotonic Scheduling Algorithm: Exact Characterization and Average Case Behavior*. Proceedings IEEE Real-Time Systems Symposium. San Jose, Calif.: December 1987.

Liu, C. L., and J. W. Layland. "Scheduling Algorithms for Multiprogramming in Hard Real-Time Environments." *Journal ACM* 20, no. 1 (January 1973). Also in Stankovic, J. A. and K. Ramamritham. *Hard Real-Time Systems* (1988).

Magee, J., and J. Kramer. *Concurrency: State Models & Java Programs*. New York: John Wiley & Sons, 1999.

Magee, J., N. Dulay, and J. Kramer. "Regis: A Constructive Development Environment for Parallel and Distributed Programs." *Journal of Distributed Systems Engineering* (1994): 304–312.

Magee, J., J. Kramer, and M. Sloman. "Constructing Distributed Systems in Conic." *IEEE Transactions on Software Engineering* 15, no. 6 (June 1989): 663–675.

McCracken, D., and M. Jackson. "Life Cycle Concept Considered Harmful." *ACM Software Engineering Notes* 7, no. 2 (1982): 28–32.

Menascé, D. A., and V. A. F. Almeida. *Capacity Planning for Web Performance: Metrics, Models, and Methods.* Upper Saddle River, N.J.: Prentice Hall, 1998.

Menascé, D. A., V. A. F. Almeida, and L. Dowdy. *Capacity Planning and Performance Modeling: From Mainframes to Client-Server Systems.* Upper Saddle River, N.J.: Prentice Hall, 1994.

Menascé, D. A., and H. Gomaa. *On a Language Based Method for Software Performance Engineering of Client/Server Systems.* First International Workshop on Software Performance Engineering. Santa Fe, N.Mex.: October 12–16, 1998.

Menascé, D. A., and H. Gomaa. "A Method for Design and Performance Modeling of Client/Server Systems." Forthcoming in *IEEE Transactions on Software Engineering* (2000).

Menascé, D. A., H. Gomaa, and L. Kerschberg. *A Performance-Oriented Design Methodology for Large-Scale Distributed Data Intensive Information Systems.* Proceedings First IEEE International Conference on Engineering of Complex Computer Systems. Southern Florida: November 6–10, 1995.

Meyer, B. "Reusability: The Case for Object-Oriented Design." *IEEE Software* 4, no. 2 (March 1987): 50–64.

Meyer, B. *Object-Oriented Software Construction.* 2d ed. Englewood Cliffs, N.J.: Prentice Hall, 1997.

Mills, K., and H. Gomaa. *A Knowledge-Based Approach for Automating a Design Method for Concurrent and Real-Time Systems.* Proceedings Eighth International Conference on Software Engineering and Knowledge Engineering. Lake Tahoe, Calif.: June 1996.

Mowbray, T., and W. Ruh. *Inside CORBA—Distributed Object Standards and Applications.* Reading Mass.: Addison-Wesley, 1997.

Myers, G. *The Art of Software Testing.* New York: John Wiley & Sons, 1979.

Nielsen, K., and K. Shumate. *Designing Large Real Time Systems with Ada.* New York: McGraw Hill, 1988.

Nutt, G. *Centralized and Distributed Operating Systems.* Englewood Cliffs, N.J.: Prentice Hall, 1992.

Orfali, R., and D. Harkey. *Client/Server Programming with Java and CORBA.* 2d ed. New York: John Wiley & Sons, 1998.

Orfali, R., D. Harkey, and J. Edwards. *Essential Distributed Objects Survival Guide.* New York: John Wiley & Sons, 1996.

Orfali, R., D. Harkey, and J. Edwards. *Essential Client/Server Survival Guide*. 3d ed. New York: John Wiley & Sons, 1999.

Orr, K. *Structured Systems Development*. New York: Yourdon Press, 1977.

Page-Jones, M. *The Practical Guide to Structured Systems Design*. 2d ed. Englewood Cliffs, N.J.: Prentice Hall, 1988.

Page-Jones, M. *What Every Programmer Should Know about Object-Oriented Design*. Englewood Cliffs, N.J.: Prentice Hall, 1995.

Page-Jones, M. *Fundamentals of Object-Oriented Design in UML*. Reading, Mass.: Addison-Wesley, 1999.

Parnas, D. "On the Criteria for Decomposing a System into Modules." *Communications ACM* 15, no. 12 (December 1972).

Parnas, D. *On a "Buzzword": Hierarchical Structure*. Proceedings IFIP Congress 1974. N.p.: North Holland Publishing Company, 1974, 336–339.

Parnas, D. "Designing Software for Ease of Extension and Contraction." *IEEE Transactions on Software Engineering* 5, no. 3 (March 1979).

Parnas, D., and P. Clements. "A Rational Design Process: How and Why to Fake It." *IEEE Transactions on Software Engineering* SE-12, no. 2, (February 1986): 251–257.

Parnas, D., P. Clements and D. Weiss. *The Modular Structure of Complex Systems*. Proceedings Seventh IEEE International Conference on Software Engineering. Orlando, Fla.: March 1984.

Parnas, D., and D. Weiss. *Active Design Reviews: Principles and Practices*. Proceedings Eighth IEEE International Conference on Software Engineering. London: September 1985.

Peckham, J., and F. Maryanski. "Semantic Data Models." *ACM Computing Surveys* 20, no. 3 (September 1988): 153–190.

Peterson, J. *Petri Net Theory and the Modeling of Systems*. Englewood Cliffs, N.J.: Prentice Hall, 1981.

Pettit, R., and H. Gomaa. *A Software Design Method for Ada 95 Based Concurrent and Real-Time Systems*. Proceedings ACM Tri-Ada 95. Anaheim, Calif.: November 1995.

Pettit, R., and H. Gomaa. *Integrating Petri Nets with Design Methods for Concurrent and Real-Time Systems*. Proceedings IEEE Workshop on Real-Time Applications. Montreal: October 1996.

Pitt, J., M. Anderton, and R. J. Cunningham. "Normalized Interactions between Autonomous Agents: A Case Study in Inter-Organizational Project Management." *Computer Supported Cooperative Work: The Journal of Collaborative Computing* no. 5 (1996): 201–222.

Pooley, R., and P. Stevens. *Using UML*. Reading Mass.: Addison-Wesley, 1999.

Pressman, R. *Software Engineering: A Practioner's Approach*. 4th ed. New York: McGraw Hill, 1996.

Quatrani, T. *Visual Modeling with Rational Rose and UML*. Reading, Mass.: Addison-Wesley, 1998.

Rosenberg, D., and K. Scott. *Use Case Driven Object Modeling with UML*. Reading, Mass.: Addison-Wesley, 1999.

Rumbaugh, J., J. M. Blaha, W. Premerlani, F. Eddy, and W. Lorenson. *Object-Oriented Modeling and Design*. Englewood Cliffs, N.J.: Prentice Hall, 1991.

Rumbaugh, J., G. Booch, and I. Jacobson. *The Unified Modeling Language Reference Manual*. Reading, Mass.: Addison-Wesley, 1999.

Sanden, B. *Software Systems Construction*. Englewood Cliffs, N.J.: Prentice Hall, 1994.

Schneider, G., and J. P. Winters. *Applying Use Cases: A Practical Guide*. Reading, Mass.: Addison-Wesley, 1998.

Selic, B. "Turning Clockwise: Using UML in the Real-Time Domain." *Communications ACM* 42, no. 10 (October 1999): 46–54.

Selic, B., G. Gullekson, and P. Ward. *Real-Time Object-Oriented Modeling*. New York: John Wiley & Sons, 1994.

Sha, L., and J. B. Goodenough. "Real-Time Scheduling Theory and Ada." *IEEE Computer* 23, no. 4 (April 1990). Also *CMU/SEI-89-TR-14*, Software Engineering Institute, Pittsburgh, Pa., 1989.

Shan, Y. P., and R. H. Earle. *Enterprise Computing with Objects*. Reading, Mass.: Addison-Wesley, 1998.

Shaw, M. "Beyond Objects: A Software Design Paradigm Based on Process Control." *ACM Software Engineering Notes* 20, no.1 (January 1995).

Shaw, M., and D. Garlan. *Software Architecture: Perspectives on an Emerging Discipline*. Englewood Cliffs, N.J.: Prentice Hall, 1996.

Silberschatz, A., and P. Galvin. *Operating System Concepts*. 5th ed. Reading Mass.: Addison-Wesley, 1998.

Simpson, H. "The MASCOT Method." *IEE/BCS Software Engineering Journal* 1, no. 3 (1986): 103–120.

Simpson, H., and K. Jackson. "Process Synchronization in MASCOT." *The Computer Journal* 17, no. 4 (1979).

Shlaer, S., and S. Mellor. *Object Oriented Systems Analysis*. Englewood Cliffs, N.J.: Prentice Hall, 1988.

Shlaer, S., and S. Mellor. *Object Lifecycles—Modeling the World in States*. Englewood Cliffs, N.J.: Prentice Hall, 1992.

Smith, C. U. *Performance Engineering of Software Systems*. Reading Mass.: Addison-Wesley, 1990.

Software Engineering Institute, Carnegie Mellon University. *A Practioner's Handbook for Real-Time Analysis—Guide to Rate Monotonic Analysis for Real-Time Systems*. Boston: Kluwer Academic Publishers, 1993.

Sommerville, I. *Software Engineering.* 6th ed. Reading, Mass.: Addison-Wesley, 2000.

Sprunt, B., J. P. Lehoczy, and L. Sha. "Aperiodic Task Scheduling for Hard Real-Time Systems." *The Journal of Real-Time Systems* 1 (1989): 27–60.

Stankovic, J. A., and K. Ramamritham. *Hard Real-Time Systems.* Washington, D.C.: IEEE Computer Society Press, 1988.

Stansifer, R., M. Beaven, and D. Marinescu. "Modeling Concurrent Programs with Colored Petri Nets." *J. Syst. Soft.* Vol. 26 (1994): 129–148.

Stroustrup, B. *The C++ Programming Language.* Reading Mass.: Addison-Wesley, 1986.

Szyperski, C. *Component Software.* Reading Mass.: Addison-Wesley, 1997.

Tai, K. C., R. H. Carver, and E. E. Obaid. "Debugging Concurrent Ada Programs by Deterministic Execution." *IEEE Transactions on Software Engineering* 17, no. 1 (January 1991): 45–63.

Tanenbaum, A. S. *Modern Operating Systems.* Englewood Cliffs, N.J.: Prentice Hall, 1992.

Tanenbaum, A. S. *Distributed Operating Systems.* Englewood Cliffs, N.J.: Prentice Hall, 1994.

Tanenbaum, A. S. *Computer Networks.* 3d ed. Englewood Cliffs, N.J.: Prentice Hall, 1996.

Texel, P., and C. Williams. *Use Cases Combined With Booch/OMT/UML: Process and Products.* Englewood Cliffs, N.J.: Prentice Hall, 1997.

Timmerman, M. "Is Windows CE 2.0 a Real Threat to the RTOS World?" *Real-Time Magazine* (Third Quarter 1998a): 20–24.

Timmerman, M. "Windows NT Real-Time Extensions: Better or Worse?" *Real-Time Magazine* (Third Quarter 1998b): 11–19.

Ward, P. "The Transformation Schema: An Extension of the Data Flow Diagram to Represent Control and Timing." *IEEE Transactions of Software Engineering* SE-12, no. 2 (February 1986): 198–210.

Ward, P., and S. Mellor. *Structured Development for Real-Time Systems.* Vols. 1, 2, and 3. New York: Yourdon Press, 1985.

Warmer, J., and A. Kleppe. *The Object Constraint Language: Precise Modeling with UML.* Reading, Mass.: Addison-Wesley, 1999.

Wegner, P. "Concepts and Paradigms of Object-Oriented Programming." *OOPS Messenger, ACM Press* 1, no. 1 (August 1990).

Wirfs-Brock, R., B. Wilkerson, and L. Wiener. *Designing Object-Oriented Software.* Englewood Cliffs, N.J.: Prentice Hall, 1990.

Yourdon, E. *Modern Structured Analysis.* Englewood Cliffs, N.J.: Prentice Hall, 1989.

Yourdon, E., and L. Constantine. *Structured Design.* 2d ed. Englewood Cliffs, N.J.: Prentice Hall, 1979.

Zave, P. "The Operational Versus the Conventional Approach to Software Development." *Communications ACM* 27, no. 2 (February 1984): 104–118.

Index

Doing Hard Time

Developing Real-Time Systems with UML, Objects, Frameworks, and Patterns
By Bruce Powel Douglass
Addison-Wesley Object Technology Series

Doing Hard Time is written to facilitate the daunting process of developing real-time systems. The author presents an embedded systems programming methodology that has been proven successful in practice. The process outlined in this book allows application developers to apply practical techniques—garnered from the mainstream areas of object-oriented software development—to meet the demanding qualifications of real-time programming.

0-201-49837-5 • Hardcover • 800 pages • ©1999

Real-Time UML, Second Edition

Developing Efficient Objects for Embedded Systems
By Bruce Powel Douglass
Addison-Wesley Object Technology Series

The Unified Modeling Language is particularly suited to modeling real-time and embedded systems. *Real-Time UML, Second Edition* is the introduction that developers of real-time systems need to make the transition to object-oriented analysis and design with UML. The book covers the important features of the UML, and shows how to effectively use these features to model real-time systems. Special in-depth discussions of finite state machines, object identification strategies, and real-time design patterns are also included to help beginning and experienced developers alike.

0-201-65784-8 • Paperback • 368 pages • ©2000

Real-Time Programming

A Guide to 32-bit Embedded Development
By Rick Grehan, Robert Moote, and Ingo Cyliax

This book teaches you how to write software for real-time embedded systems—software that meets unforgiving objectives under numerous constraints. The authors present the key topics that are relevant to all forms of real-time embedded development and offer complete coverage of the embedded development cycle, from design through implementation. A practical, hands-on approach is emphasized, allowing you to start building real-time embedded systems immediately using commercial, off-the-shelf hardware and software.

0-201-48540-0 • Paperback with CD-ROM • 720 pages • ©1999

An Embedded Software Primer

By David E. Simon

This book is written as an easy, accessible introduction for any programmer who wants to make the transition from more traditional software development to embedded systems. David Simon introduces the broad range of applications for embedded software and then reviews each major issue facing developers. *An Embedded Software Primer* teaches you the implications of limited memory and processor resources and how embedded software handles external events without human intervention. It also explores the role of real-time operating systems and how developers seek to reduce time-to-market without compromising quality.

0-201-61569-X • Paperback • 448 pages • ©1999